臨濟錄
The *Record of Linji*

臨濟錄
The *Record* of *Linji*

A New Translation of the Linjilu *in the Light of Ten Japanese Zen Commentaries*

JEFFREY L. BROUGHTON

WITH ELISE YOKO WATANABE

OXFORD
UNIVERSITY PRESS

OXFORD
UNIVERSITY PRESS

Oxford University Press is a department of the University of Oxford.
It furthers the University's objective of excellence in research,
scholarship, and education by publishing worldwide.

Oxford   New York

Auckland   Cape Town   Dar es Salaam   Hong Kong   Karachi
Kuala Lumpur   Madrid   Melbourne   Mexico City   Nairobi
New Delhi   Shanghai   Taipei   Toronto

With offices in

Argentina   Austria   Brazil   Chile   Czech Republic   France Greece
Guatemala   Hungary   Italy   Japan   Poland   Portugal   Singapore
South Korea   Switzerland   Thailand   Turkey   Ukraine   Vietnam

Oxford is a registered trade mark of Oxford University Press in the UK and certain other countries.

Published in the United States of America by
Oxford University Press
198 Madison Avenue, New York, NY 10016

Library of Congress Cataloging-in-Publication Data
Yixuan, d. 867.
[Linji lu. English]
The record of Linji: a new translation of the Linjilu in the light of ten Japanese
Zen commentaries / Jeffrey L. Broughton with Elise Yoko Watanabe.
pages cm
Includes bibliographical references and index.
ISBN 978-0-19-993643-4—ISBN 978-0-19-993641-0
1. Linji (Sect)—Early works to 1800.
2. Zen Buddhism—Early works to 1800. 3. Yixuan, d. 867. Linji lu.
4. Zen literature—Japan. I. Broughton, Jeffrey L., 1944– II. Title.
BQ9399.I554L5513   2013
294.3'85—dc23   2012018346

1 3 5 7 9 8 6 4 2

Printed in the United States of America
on acid-free paper

For Philip B. Yampolsky (1920–1996)

拄杖

三 尺 烏 藤 本 現 成
箇 中 毫 髮 不 容 情
佛 魔 凡 聖 俱 搥 殺
方 顯 金 剛 正 眼 睛

The Staff

Three feet of black rattan—always ready to go;
Here, not one bit of conceptualization is tolerated.
"Buddha/Māra," "worldling/ārya" killed with a whack;
Only then—the thunderbolt eye manifests.

—quatrain by the Song dynasty Chan Master Chichan
Yuanmiao (癡禪元妙; 1111–1164)

—CBETA, X86, no. 1611, p. 703, a17–18 //Z 2B:21, p. 44,
b15–16 //R148, p. 87, b15–16. See Record of Linji, 12.2.

Contents

Acknowledgments   ix

Abbreviations   xi

Introduction   3

Record of the Sayings of Chan Master Linji Huizhao of Zhenzhou

Part I: *Dharma-Hall Convocations*   30

Part II: *Sangha Instruction*   37

Part III: *Calibrating and Adjudicating [Appraising
    the Level of Understanding and Rendering a Judgment]*   78

Part IV: *Record of the Karman [of the Master's Career]*   88

Part V: *Stupa Record of Chan Master Linji Huizhao*   101

Yuanjue Zongyan's Xuanhe 2 (1120) Linjilu *Edition (LJL)*   103

Appendix 1: *Pre-Song Linji and Puhua Sayings and Episodes
    Preserved in the* Collection of the Patriarchal Hall (Zutangji)   119

Appendix 2: *Pre-Song Linji Sayings Preserved in the*
    Mind-Mirror Record (Zongjinglu/Xinjinglu)   127

Notes   129

Bibliography   289

Index   293

Acknowledgments

ELISE YOKO WATANABE has worked with me on this translation of the *Linjilu*. Her literary acumen has been invaluable. I thank her.

Abbreviations

Anonymous
: *Notes on Linji* (*Rinzai shō* 臨濟鈔) in six fascicles
Woodblock print in Chinese by an anonymous Japanese author published in 1630

CBETA
: Chinese Buddhist Electronic Text Association: http://www.cbeta.org

Chitetsu
: *Zuigan's Notes on the Record of Linji* (*Rinzairoku Zuigan shō* 臨濟錄瑞巖鈔) in eight fascicles
Woodblock print in Chinese by Kensō Chitetsu (見叟智徹; ?-1687) of Zuigan Monastery (Tanba in the Kyoto area) published in 1671

Daitoku-ji
: Kirchner, Thomas Yūhō, ed. *The Record of Linji.* Honolulu: University of Hawai'i Press, 2009

Demiéville
: Demiéville, Paul, trans. *Entretiens de Lin-tsi.* Paris: Fayard, 1972

Dōchū
: *Washing the Mind in the Sayings Record of Chan Master Linji Huizhao* (Rinzai Eshō zenji goroku *soyaku* 臨濟慧照禪師語錄疏瀹) in five fascicles
Manuscript (1726) in Chinese by Mujaku Dōchū (無著道忠; 1653–1744)

Dōkū
: *Extracting the Essential Points of the Record of Linji* (Rinzairoku *satsuyō* 臨濟錄撮要) in five fascicles
Woodblock print in Chinese by Tetsugai Dōkū (鉄崖道空; 1626–1703) published in 1691

Eishu
: *Notes on the Record of Linji* (Rinzairoku *shō* 臨濟錄鈔) in four fascicles (also known as the *Kana Notes* [*Kana shō* カナ鈔])
Woodblock print by Bannan Eishu (萬安英種; 1591–1654) published in 1632; in a mixed style of Japanese and Chinese

Iriya   Iriya Yoshitaka, trans. *Rinzairoku*. Tokyo: Iwanami
                        shoten, 1989

Kassan   *Kassan's Notes on the Record of Linji* (Rinzairoku
                        Kassan shō 臨濟錄夾山鈔) in ten fascicles
                        Woodblock print in Chinese published in 1654 by
                        an otherwise unknown Kassan (夾山)

Komazawa   Komazawa daigaku toshokan, ed. *Shinsan zenseki
                        mokuroku*. Tokyo: Komazawa daigaku toshokan,
                        1962

Kōunshi   *Plucking Leaves from the Sayings Record of Linji*
                        (Rinzai goroku *tekiyō* 臨濟語錄摘葉) in eight
                        fascicles
                        Woodblock print in Chinese by an otherwise
                        unknown Kōunshi (耕雲子) published in 1698

LJL   The "standard" 1120 edition of the *Zhenzhou Linji
                        Huizhao chanshi yulu* 鎮州臨濟慧照禪師語錄
                        or *Linjilu* 臨濟錄 reprinted (and likely edited)
                        by the Chan master Yuanjue Zongyan
                        圓覺宗演 (translation based on this edition as
                        found in Yanagida below)

Mujaku Dictionaries   Yanagida Seizan, ed. *Zenrin shōki sen Kattōgo sen
                        Zenrin kushū benbyō. Zengaku sōsho, 9.* 2 vols.
                        Kyoto: Chūbun shuppansha, 1979. Mujaku
                        Dōchū's encyclopedic *Notes on Images and Im-
                        plements of the Zen Forest* (completed 1741) and
                        his dictionary of words in Chan texts, *Notes on
                        Kudzu Words* (1739).

Myōō   *Direct Account of the Record of Linji* (Rinzairoku
                        chokki 臨濟錄直記) in three fascicles (date
                        unknown)
                        Manuscript in Japanese by Kūkoku Myōō
                        (空谷明應; 1328–1407)

Nakamura   Nakamura Bunbō. *Gendaigo yaku* Rinzairoku.
                        Tokyo: Daitō shuppan, 1990

Shukitsu   *Takudō's Comments on Old Cases of the Record of Linji*
                        (Rinzairoku *Takudō nenko* 林際录晫同拈古) in
                        six fascicles
                        Woodblock print in Chinese by Takudō Shukitsu
                        (晫同守佶) published in 1680

Shūshin

Kohan's Record of Secret-Consultation Instructions on the Record of Linji (Rinzairoku *Kohan missan seieki roku* 臨濟錄古帆密参請益錄) in one fascicle (date unknown)

Manuscript in Japanese by Kohan Shūshin (古帆周信; 1570–1641)

T

Takakusu Junjirō and Watanabe Kaigyoku, eds. *Taishō shinshū daizōkyō*. 100 vols. Tokyo: Taishō issaikyō kankōkai, 1924–1934

Tiansheng *Linjilu*

The earliest complete version of the *Linjilu*, found as the Linji entry in the *Tiansheng guangdenglu* 天聖廣燈錄 (*Extended Lamp Record of the Tiansheng Era*), which was compiled in 1029 and issued in 1036 (this version virtually identical to the LJL except in the order of the contents)

Watson

Watson, Burton, trans. *The Zen Teachings of Master Lin-chi*. New York: Columbia University Press, 1999

Yanagida

Yanagida Seizan, trans. *Rinzairoku. Butten kōza* 30. Tokyo: Daizō shuppan, 1972 (the following translation and Chinese text have incorporated Yanagida's section numbers, allowing ready access to his annotations)

Zengo

Iriya Yoshitaka and Koga Hidehiko. *Zengo jiten*. Kyoto: Shibunkaku shuppan, 1991

臨濟錄
The *Record of Linji*

Introduction

> *The Head Seat said [to Linji], "Have you had an audience yet [with the Abbot Preceptor Huangbo]?" The Master said, "No, no audience. I wouldn't know what on earth to ask." The Head Seat said, "Why don't you go ask the Abbot Preceptor what is the real meaning of the buddha-dharma?" The Master right away went to ask. Before he had even finished his question, Huangbo instantly gave him a whack.*
>
> —Record of Linji

> *The* person *of Silla eats the chilled noodles.* [新羅人喫冷淘]
> —*A gloss on the above from the Japanese Zen Monk*
> Kōunshi's Record of Linji *commentary* Plucking Leaves from the Sayings Record of Linji *(1698)*[1]

THE CHINESE CHAN text entitled *Linjilu* 臨濟錄 (*Record of Linji*) is the most prominent work in all of Chan literature, attracting readers with its memorably earthy and iconoclastic style of discourse. In recent decades there have been a number of translations of the *Linjilu* into Japanese and European languages,[2] but none have taken full advantage of the riches found in pre-modern Japanese Zen commentaries *on the Linjilu* that have come down to us in manuscript and woodblock-print format. Thanks to a facsimile edition of ten such commentaries (three in Japanese and seven in Chinese) published in a 1980 Japanese compendium,[3] the translation of the *Linjilu* that follows can attempt something different from previous translations: *to embrace the traditional Japanese Zen commentarial tradition and to embed many of its exegeses directly into the translation.*

Most of the notes to this new translation consist of excerpts from these ten Japanese Zen commentaries on the *Linjilu*. The reader is warned that these notes, with some small exceptions, will not address some of the usual concerns of modern Chan scholarship: birth and death dates for each master mentioned, questions of lineage, details of the late Tang dynasty context of Linji the historical figure (d. 866/867), geographical information, the tracing of intertextualities with other works of Chan literature, and so forth. Such matters have been addressed comprehensively in previous translations, and there is no need to duplicate their work.[4] Instead, the emphasis here is on how this text has been understood and explicated within the walls of Japanese Zen from about the late 1300s, when Five-Mountains (Gozan) Zen flourished in Kyoto and Kamakura, down through the mid-Edo period of the early 1700s.

The primary goal of this translation is to present a glimpse into the in-house "traditional Zen" reading of the *Linjilu* as laid down during these centuries. Wherever possible, the interpretations of the Zen commentators have been inserted directly into the text, using brackets. (In instances where the commentators are at odds with modern scholarship and lexicography, this translation has preferred modern research. These instances are duly noted.)

Two subsidiary goals are:

1. To capture the vernacular *(baihua)* flavor of the *Linjilu*; in particular, this translation has employed English idioms freely in order to emphasize the *baihua* register.
2. To give the reader access, wherever possible, to the multiple meanings in a line or word, when they are the crucial pivot upon which the sense of the passage rests. To this end, the translation has used slashes (/ = "or") or italics to indicate the possible meanings at play. Such wordplay is intrinsic to the Chan records as a genre: it is important not to attribute to "Zen inscrutability" what should be credited to linguistic genius. (Note that slashes within brackets usually indicate alternate glosses by the Zen commentators.)

The Linjilu *as a "Literary Portrait"*

The compelling figure of Linji that we know today is not an exact replica of the one that surfaces in the earliest extant fragments of Linji sayings and episodes. These fragments appear in the *Zutangji* 祖堂集 *(Collection of the Patriarchal Hall)*, which dates Linji's death to 866. The *Zutangji*, dated 952 of the Southern Tang, contains an entry for Linji presumably excerpted from the *Separate Record* (*bielu* 別錄) it mentions. In other words, a freestanding *Separate Record* [*of Linji*] therefore must have been in circulation before 952.[5] Regrettably, the *Separate Record* itself has been lost to us. The *Zutangji* also contains an independent entry for the crazy trickster Puhua that presents him as a Master in his own right, though strongly associated with Linji. (See Appendix 1 for a translation of both entries.) We can go no further back than these snippets preserved in the *Zutangji*.[6]

The two *Zutangji* entries have some passages that are quite parallel to those in the freestanding "standard" version of the *Linjilu* (hereafter LJL) reissued (and probably even edited by) the Chan master Yuanjue Zongyan (圓覺宗演) in Xuanhe 宣和 2 (1120), which is the version used for this translation and also used by the Zen commentators.[7] However, the two *Zutangji* entries also present significant differences from the LJL, including entire episodes that do not appear in the LJL.

Unfortunately, there is no way to track "the evolution of the *Linjilu*" from the fragments in the *Zutangji* down to the "finished" product, Yuanjue Zongyan's LJL. All we can say is that there are divergences, some of them significant. On the whole, compared to the tone of the *Zutangji* fragments, the LJL noticeably bears the trappings of the ideology of Song dynasty Linji Chan, the ideology of a "separate transmission outside the teachings" (*jiaowai biechuan* 教外別傳), including a distinctly anti-scholastic tone.[8] For instance, the *Zutangji* includes an episode in which Linji, already a Chan monk who is in training under Huangbo, lectures to Huangbo's colleague Dayu on the one-hundred-fascicle *Yoga Treatise* (*Yuqie lun* 瑜伽論, i.e., the *Yogacārabhūmi-śāstra*), discussing the teachings of consciousness-only (*weishi* 唯識) in an overnight hours-long session (to Dayu's scathing disapproval).[9] This enormous and complex *Yoga Treatise*, the definitive text of the Yogācāra school, exhaustively delineates the practices and fruits of the seventeen stages leading to "nirvana with no remainder" (buddhahood). But in section 59.1 of the LJL, Linji only studies *vinaya*, sutras, and treatises as a very young monk, prior to his converting to Chan and then studying with Huangbo. In his ensuing dialogue with Dayu (section 38.2 of the LJL), Linji has no investment in any scholastic treatise, and the *Yoga Treatise*—the very epitome of what Chan derides as the verbal entanglement of "kudzu"—does not figure at all. The *Zutangji* materials, while not amounting to anywhere near an adequate sample, do not have Linji evincing nearly as strident an anti-scholastic tone. "Linji" has clearly undergone manipulation to take the consistent tone he has now in the LJL.

The LJL, with its editorial interventions, is much closer to what we might consider "based on a true story," rather than a literal "record of the words and actions of the ninth-century Chan master Linji compiled by his disciples."[10] To accept the LJL at face value, as a more or less "authentic," purely nonfictional transcript, is to ignore and to underestimate the cumulative artistry that intervened in the process leading eventually to the LJL. In fact, as the following examples show, "Linji" is a compelling literary character molded, to a significant extent, by editors who must be credited with enhancing "Linji" through their sheer verbal élan. For example, "five-*skandhas* body field" in the *Zutangji* is "red-meatball" in the LJL, and the euphemism "thing of impurity" is "piece of dried shit." Elements found in the LJL that are missing in the *Zutangji* are: "a 'buddha' is like a fellow in a cangue with a lock"; "'arhats' and 'independent buddhas' are like toilet excrement," and "'*bodhi*' and 'nirvana' are like posts to which you hitch a donkey."[11] Literary ingenuity and an ear for effect were vital to the process that shaped the LJL.[12] Indeed, the LJL qualifies as a superb work of *baihua* (vernacular) Chinese literature, above and beyond its customary valuation as a Buddhist religious classic. The "Linji" of the LJL, as depicted in a series of strategically framed vignettes and discourses, endures as an indelible character in our imagination precisely because he has transcended any literal biography; much as, in Western literature, the Samuel Johnson of the *Life of Johnson* has done, thanks to the framing of his chronicler James Boswell: "Boswell 'delineates' Johnson and causes us to 'see him live' not only by pictorializing but by dramatizing—by setting his protagonist in motion within a sequence of *carefully scripted playlets* [italics added]."[13]

The LJL in Japan Through the Edo Period

An early reference to the LJL in Japan involves the eminent Zen monk and literary figure Gidō Shūshin 義堂周信 (1325–1388), who was born and raised in Tosa on the island of Shikoku. In an autobiographical work, Gidō's entry for Genkō 2 (1332), when he was eight years old, reads: "One day, among various books in the family library, I found a one-volume *Record of Linji*. I was delighted and read it. It was as if I had learned it in a past birth. My parents considered this astonishing and came to think I had some innate genius."[14] This precocious eight-year-old grew up to become one of the most famous monks of Five-Mountains (Gozan) Zen.

As an adult, however, Gidō Shūshin apparently focused on the works of Dahui Zonggao (大慧宗杲; 1089–1163) and the case collection *Blue Cliff Collection* (*Biyanji* 碧巖集), not the LJL.[15] He was not unique—during the period of Five-Mountains Zen (roughly 1300–1500), case collections like the *Blue Cliff Collection* and *Gateless Gate* (*Wumenguan* 無門關) generally overshadowed the LJL.

The Five-Mountains period was a great era of printing Chinese books in Japan, and from that period six printed editions of the LJL (plus one manuscript) are listed in the standard reference work, *Newly Edited Catalogue of Zen Books* (*Shinsan zenseki mokuroku*; hereafter Komazawa).[16] The LJL was but one of a total of 273 works printed by the Five-Mountains monasteries during the Muromachi period (1392–1573), 78 of them purely secular Chinese works.[17] In content, the Five-Mountains editions consisted mainly of Chinese Chan books plus Tang and Song poetry and prose collections, Chinese rhyme books, Chinese classics and histories, and so forth. This, of course, was not a mass publishing industry; these books were printed in small numbers for use by Zen monks and the cultured elite. A commercial publishing industry really began around 1600—the Tokugawa peace, in fact, ushered in a printing boom.[18] We see this transformation in the case of the LJL: Komazawa lists an astonishing twenty-eight printed editions (plus one manuscript) during the Edo period (ca. 1603–1867).[19] Interest in the LJL during the Edo was extremely high, and perhaps this had something to do with the spark ignited within Rinzai Zen by the arrival in Nagasaki, in 1654, of the Linji Chan master Yinyuan Longqi/Ingen Ryūki 隱元隆琦, who brought Ming dynasty Chan.[20]

Japanese Zen Commentaries on the LJL Through the Mid-Edo Period

In both Japan and China, there appear to be no extant commentaries on the *Linjilu* by Chinese authors. In their absence, it is important not to give the Japanese Zen commentarial tradition sole credit for its overall reading of the *Linjilu*. We have no way of telling how much of the Zen reading is uniquely Japanese, rather than a more or less faithful perpetuation of Chinese Chan sources now lost to us. As an example, one possible Chinese informant on the *Linjilu* could have been the Linji Chan master Yishan Yining/Issan Ichinei (一山一寧; 1247–1317), who arrived in Japan in 1299.[21] The erudite Yining, who is cited by a number of our ten Japanese commentators on the *Linjilu*,[22] may have brought with him oral traditions and/or written commentaries on the *Linjilu* that are no longer extant. The same could hold true for other Chinese Chan monks who came to Japan, as well as for Japanese Zen monks returning from pilgrimage to Chan monasteries in China. If this was so, such Chinese works have been lost as far as we know; but they may well continue to echo down to us through the Zen commentarial tradition.

The earliest known LJL "commentary" done on Japanese soil, or brought to Japan from China, is a lost Kamakura-period work attributed to a Chinese Chan master: *Record of Expositions of the Record of Linji* (Rinzairoku *teishō ki* 臨濟錄提唱記) by Lanxi Daolong/Rankei Dōryū 蘭溪道隆 (1213–1278).[23] Daolong arrived in Japan in 1246 and ended up in Kamakura in eastern Japan. Hōjō Tokiyori, the fifth shogunal regent, and the master Daolong conceived a plan to erect a monastery that would strictly follow the Chinese Chan model, and in 1253 Kenchō-ji began operation with Daolong as its founding abbot. We know of the existence of one other lost Kamakura-period work, the *Old Commentary of [National Teacher] Daitō on the Record of Linji* (Rinzairoku *Daitō koshō*; 臨濟錄大燈古抄) by Shūhō Myōchō (宗峰妙超; 1282–1337), the founder of Daitoku-ji in Kyoto.[24] In the subsequent Muromachi period, and particularly during the early Edo period (1600s) and the mid-Edo period (first half of the 1700s), there was an explosion of commentaries on the LJL. Komazawa lists thirty-seven, of which six are no longer extant.[25] Of the extant thirty-one, seven are woodblock prints and the rest manuscripts. These are held in collections and libraries throughout Japan, and some remain difficult to access.

The Ten Commentaries

The Japanese Zen scholar Yanagida Seizan selected ten commentaries from this extensive corpus of thirty-one and published them in a facsimile edition in 1980.[26] Yanagida apparently concentrated on woodblock prints from the early Edo period (seven printed texts and one manuscript), but he also included one Muromachi-period manuscript and one mid-Edo period manuscript (1726). Yanagida's focus clearly was on printed texts; a time frame from early to mid-Edo period; and those commentators who stand out as relatively well-known figures in the history of Japanese Zen. In other words, he appears to have chosen those commentaries that, in his judgment, had the most significant influence in the long run on Japanese Zen's understanding of the LJL. The following translation has relied heavily on these ten commentaries.

Before going into the details, what can we say about these ten as a set? Two observations come to mind. The first is that, for the most part, they belong to a "commentarial tradition" much like that of the Indian commentaries on Nāgārjuna's *Root Verses on the Middle Way* (*Mūlamadhyamakakārikā*): that is, they show "a subtle—at first glance unnoticeable—process of continuous perpetuation of the preexisting commentaries, where every new author was bound by the authority of his predecessors, recycled their words without concern for plagiarism, and only sporadically diverged through modification, improvement, or outright critical assessment."[27] For this reason, there is a lot of overlap among these commentaries: they are drawing from an inherited common pool of assumptions of what is important in the LJL. At the most fundamental level, the commentaries seem to presume that the following are the quintessential Zen themes embodied in the LJL:

1. The "Zen personal-realization-of-the-meaning-beyond-words" (referred to variously as *gashū* 我宗, *konoshū* 此宗, *shūkō* 宗綱, and so on);
2. Realization of "that one person" (*na* [= *ano*] *ichinin* 那一人 = the person who has no characteristics or form = the true person) and "the original portion" (*honbun* 本分 = *tathatā*/reality);
3. A strong imperative not to engage in "intellectual understanding, emotional assessments, calculations, and plans" (*chige jōryō keikaku anbai* 知解情量計較按排); "mental reflection and conjecture" (*shiryō bokudo* 思量卜度); "mental reflection and calculation" (*shiryō keido* 思量計度); "calculation and conjecture" (*keikaku bokudo* 計較卜度), and so on;
4. The practice of cross-legged sitting (*zazen* 坐禪) or "smooth-and-steady sitting" (*onza* 穩坐).

The second observation is that the ten commentaries fall into two genres. One early-Edo commentary (no. 1, below) is a "secret-consultation record" (*missanroku* 密参録), that is, an "answer paper" or "script" for *kōan* training. (In some Zen lineages, *kōan* training had become a mere shell, an empty formality, and these scripts were transmitted in secret, in the manner of esoteric Buddhism.) The remaining nine commentaries are much more in the conventional exegetical mold—we could call them "explanation" or "gloss" style commentaries. Let us first look at the secret-consultation record:

1. *Kohan's Record of Secret-Consultation Instructions on the Record of Linji* (Rinzairoku *Kohan missan seieki roku* 臨濟錄古帆密参請益錄) in one fascicle (1633):

Manuscript in Japanese with the look of scribbled notes (does not give full LJL text but only numbered *kōan*-style "cases" with their immediate context) by Kohan Shūshin (古帆周信; 1570–1641).[28]

This commentary consists of "sixty-one cases" (*rokujūichi soku* 六十一則) from the LJL with attached "comments" (*agyo* 下吾 = 下語) and "discriminations" (*ben* 弁). Most of the cases are three to four characters in length. Examples are: "the true man who can't be ranked" (case no. 4: *mui shinjin* 無位真人), "the open-air pillar" (case no. 24: *rochū* 露柱), and "the Chan block and cushion" (case no. 36: *zenpan futon* 禅板蒲團).

The remaining explanation-style commentaries focus on providing explications or glosses. They concentrate, to a great extent, on dealing directly with the words and phrases of the LJL, on elucidating its ideas and themes (sometimes in a poetic fashion), and on tracing sources in the Buddhist canon. They are thus considerably closer to our conception of notes in an annotated translation of a Chan text. The nine explanation-style commentaries are:

2. *Direct Account of the Record of Linji* (Rinzairoku *chokki* 臨濟錄直記) in three fascicles (c. 1400):

Neatly written manuscript in Japanese (LJL text and commentary in same size characters) by Kūkoku Myōō (空谷明應; 1328–1407).[29]

In selected sections of the text, Myōō attaches "comments" (*agyo* 下吾 = 下語); he provides "discriminations" (*ben* 弁), that is, more or less straightforward exegeses, in all sections. This commentary specializes in explicating the LJL in terms of the technical terminology of Buddhism: *vāsanā* ("habit energy from past births"), *prapañca* ("joke discourse"), *antarā-bhava* ("intermediate state between death and rebirth"), *māyopama-samādhi* ("the like-an-illusion *samādhi*"), and so forth.

3. *Notes on Linji* (*Rinzai shō* 臨濟鈔) in six fascicles:

Woodblock print in Chinese (LJL text in large characters) by an anonymous Japanese author, published in 1630.

This commentary is oriented to the texts of "within-the-teachings Chan" such as Zongmi's *Chan Prolegomenon*, Yanshou's *Mind-Mirror Record* (*Zongjinglu* 宗鏡錄), and the *Glossary of the Patriarchal Courtyard* (*Zuting shiyuan* 祖庭事苑); accordingly, it cites quite a few sutras and treatises.

4. *Notes on the Record of Linji* (Rinzairoku *shō* 臨濟錄鈔) in four fascicles (also known as the *Kana Notes* [*Kana shō* カナ鈔]):

Woodblock print (LJL text in large characters) by Bannan Eishu (萬安英種; 1591–1654),[30] published in 1632; in a mixed style of Japanese and Chinese.

It is noteworthy that this very useful commentary, which contains many concise glosses, and quotes many earlier commentaries, was authored by an erudite Sōtō monk. We might say that its specialization is philology—at a level comparable to that of Mujaku Dōchū's commentary (see no. 10 below).

5. *Kassan's Notes on the Record of Linji* (Rinzairoku *Kassan shō* 臨濟錄夾山鈔) in ten fascicles:

Woodblock print in Chinese (LJL text in large characters), published in 1654 by an otherwise unknown Kassan 夾山.

This commentary often cites Mahāyāna sutras—especially a set of three: the *Śūraṃgama*, *Perfect Awakening*, and *Huayan*. It also brings in Zongmi's *Chan Prolegomenon*.

6. *Zuigan's Notes on the Record of Linji* (Rinzairoku *Zuigan shō* 臨濟錄瑞巖鈔) in eight fascicles:

Woodblock print in Chinese (LJL text and commentary in same size characters) by Kensō Chitetsu (見叟智徹; ?–1687) of Zuigan Monastery,[31] published in 1671.

This commentary arranges the LJL under the three rubrics of "old cases" (*kosoku* 古則), "host-and-guest discriminations" (*shuhin ben* 主賓弁), and "speaking Chan" (*setsuzen* 說禪; according to Chitetsu, Zen masters of the "separate transmission outside the teachings" do, in fact, maintain the teachings principle [*deśanā-naya*] by "speaking Zen"). The specialization of this commentary is the *Laṅkāvatāra Sūtra*. Chitetsu uses Yogācāra terminology and assumes that "Zen is the *siddhānta-naya* [i.e., personal-realization-of-the-meaning-beyond-words] of the buddhas." [禪是如來之自宗通]

7. *Takudō's Comments on Old Cases of the Record of Linji* (Rinzairoku *Takudō nenko* 林際録皐同拈古) in six fascicles:

Woodblock print in Chinese (LJL text and commentary in same size characters) by Takudō Shukitsu (皐同守佶),[32] published in 1680.

This commentary often utilizes sutras and treatises in its exegesis.

8. *Extracting the Essential Points of the Record of Linji* (Rinzairoku *satsuyō* 臨濟錄撮要) in five fascicles:

Woodblock print in Chinese (LJL text in large characters) by Tetsugai Dōkū (鉄崖道空; 1626–1703),[33] published in 1691.

Dōkū quotes a number of sutras and old commentaries, but focuses to a great extent on the *Śūraṃgama Sūtra*, implicitly suggesting its centrality to the LJL. Since other commentaries also frequently cite this sutra, it is probably fair to conclude that the consensus of the commentaries is that the *Śūraṃgama* is the most important sutra for the LJL.

9. *Plucking Leaves from the Sayings Record of Linji* (Rinzai goroku *tekiyō* 臨濟語錄摘葉)[34] in eight fascicles:

Woodblock print in Chinese (LJL text in large characters) by an otherwise unknown Kōunshi 耕雲子, published in 1698.

This very useful commentary, perhaps the most poetic and metaphorical of the ten, cites an extremely wide range of sutras, treatises, and commentaries on sutras and treatises. The *Śūraṃgama, Huayan, Vimalakīrti,* and *Perfect Awakening* are prominent in the exegesis.

10. *Washing the Mind in the Sayings Record of Chan Master Linji Huizhao* (Rinzai Eshō zenji goroku *soyaku* 臨濟慧照禪師語錄疏瀹)[35] in five fascicles:

Manuscript (1726) in Chinese (gives only those portions of the LJL text commented upon; text and commentary in same size characters, with text marked by triangles) by Mujaku Dōchū (無著道忠; 1653–1744).[36]

This commentary has a dual specialization: philology; and explanations of the functions, daily life, conventions, material culture, personnel, and so on, of Chan/Zen monastic life. Although Dōchū's commentary, the most philologically rigorous of the Edo commentaries, is almost objective and scientific in a modern sense and a direct forerunner of the modern scholarly annotation of Chan texts, it still belongs to the traditional Zen fabric.

All ten commentaries, taken as a whole, furnish us with an Edo-period sample of what might be considered "the traditional Zen reading of the LJL": what the Edo-period Zen commentators presumed remains valid even today. Because the commentarial tradition is inherently conservative, Edo-period views on the LJL have been perpetuated and are still current in Rinzai Zen establishments, influencing the way we in the West have "read" the LJL—and even "read" Zen itself[37]—although we may not be aware of it. This conservatism may have a bonus: if some of the assumptions of lost Chinese commentaries on the LJL were also perpetuated, these Edo commentaries are probably now the closest we can ever get to the Chinese Chan world that gave us "Linji" and the LJL.

Selecting Excerpts from the Commentaries

Given that the total volume of available commentarial material in Yanagida's compendium is staggeringly large (over 1,400 dense pages), it was necessary to adhere to a restrictive set of criteria in deciding which excerpts were to be given in the notes (and, to a lesser extent, embedded into the translation itself).[38] Excerpts have been worked directly into the translation, using brackets, wherever the excerpt enhanced the reading of the text and did not unduly disrupt its flow. Also, slashes have been used within brackets on occasion to show alternate commentarial readings. From the ten commentaries, the following sorts of material have been selected:

1. Glosses of words and phrases;
2. Equivalencies between LJL terms and classical Buddhist terms;
3. Equivalencies between everyday words and Zen terms;
4. Establishment of linkages between themes in the LJL and sutra teachings;
5. Contradictory interpretations in two or more commentaries;
6. Two interpretations in one commentary;
7. Highly metaphorical glosses;
8. Glosses consisting of a line or couplet of Chinese poetry;
9. References to secular works such as the Chinese classics;
10. Asides on the part of the commentator;
11. Rhetorical questions posed by the commentator;
12. Explanations of the functions, daily life, conventions, material culture, personnel, and so forth, of Chan/Zen monastic life;
13. Paraphrases in Japanese;
14. Japanese analogues;
15. Editorial emendations.

Detailed examples of each follow. (Topics addressed by the ten commentaries that have not been much used in this translation are listed separately at the end of this section.)

1. Glosses of Words and Phrases

LJL 1.3: "Question: 'Whose house tune does the Master sing? Whose Chan style does his succeed?' The Master [Linji] said, 'I was at Huangbo's place—three times I raised a question, and three times I got whacked.' The monk *dithered* [*niyi* 擬議]. The Master [Linji] gave a shout and immediately followed it with a hit: 'Don't go around driving nails into the sky!'"

The term *niyi* 擬議 appears nine times in the LJL, with the above as the first mention; usually it describes the behavior of a monk who is on the losing end in a dialogue with the Master. The following is a composite of glosses at various appearances of the term:

- Dōchū, 1269: "*niyi* 擬議 is a word from the *Changes* much used in Zen records. It has the meaning 'was about to answer but not yet capable of doing so.'"
- Kassan, 457, Chitetsu, 623, and Kōunshi, 1118: "[*niyi* 擬議] is like comparing several [options for a response]."
- Kassan, 449: "[The response on the part of the monk was] insipid and did not arrive at the wellspring."
- Anonymous, 215: "This monk has lost the rut of the wheel in the road."
- Chitetsu, 615: "It's just that this monk comes up one phrase short."
- Myōō, 5: "[This monk] gulped down his breath-energy, swallowed any audible, and was confused."
- Shūshin, 128: "[*niyi* 擬議 means the response was] too slow."
- Kōunshi, 1113: "*niyi* 擬議 is the same as 'sunk in thought.'"
- Dōkū, 996: "*niyi* 擬議 has the meaning 'about to speak' or 'about to move.'"

The term *niyi* 擬議 is always pejorative. In each episode the character who evinces *niyi* comes off badly. This marks a repeated and persistent ideal of a spontaneous reaction over premeditation of any sort. Previous studies and translations of LJL have not sufficiently emphasized the central role of this term—it is the theme of many LJL sections.

> LJL 3: "The monk dithered. The Master, thrusting him back, said, '[This] "true person who can't be ranked"—what a magnificent *piece of dried shit [ganshijue* 乾屎橛]!'"

- Eishu, 341, and Anonymous 218: "The meaning [of *ganshijue* 乾屎橛] is 'dried shit *resembling* a stub/peg/cylinder.'"
- Kōunshi, 1118: "*ganshijue* 乾屎橛 is dried shit *like* a stub/peg/cylinder."

> LJL 13.24: "[Linji said,] 'Even when you are approaching fifty, you are [still] intently schlepping *corpses [sishi* 死屍] down byways, running around all-under-heaven, shouldering your *baggage [danzi* 擔子].'"

- Eishu, 390: "'Corpses' are the dead words of heterodox masters. . . . 'Baggage' refers to the written word, the injunctions of the ancients."
- Kassan, 539: "'Baggage' refers to understanding [based on] *avidyā*, the *kleśas*, the written word, verbal phrases, etc."
- Dōkū, 1047: "'Corpses' refers to the physical body of five feet."
- Kōunshi, 1190: "'Corpses' refers to terms and phrases—it is like saying 'the dead phrase.' 'Baggage' refers to perplexity arising from terms and phrases."
- Dōchū, 1335: "It is just [ordinary] traveling baggage."

> LJL **13**.26: "[Linji said,] 'If a person comes with a level of beholding that is off the charts, here I instantly [employ] *unreserved functioning* [*quanti zuoyong* 全體作用] and do not put him through [any ranking according to] configuration of sense faculties.'"

- Myōō, 56: "*quanti zuoyong* 全體作用 means that Linji's whole body directly is the buddha nature."
- Eishu, 391: "*quanti zuoyong* 全體作用 means that there is nothing left behind/kept back."
- Kassan, 541: "*quanti zuoyong* 全體作用 is the type in which [the Master] wordlessly bows his head and returns to the *fangzhang*. Or it is Vimalakīrti's single silence, etc. The student just looks on."
- Dōkū, 1048: "*quanti zuoyong* 全體作用 is the type in which [the Master] wordlessly bows his head and returns to the *fangzhang*. It is the approach used with Advanced Seat Ding [in section **31** of the LJL]."
- Kōunshi, 1191: "'Level of beholding that is off the charts' is vision that surpasses the buddhas and patriarchs. *quanti zuoyong* 全體作用 is wordlessly bowing the head, returning to the *fangzhang*, turning to take a look, correcting one's sitting posture, etc. It is a strategy of not falling into words and phrases."

A major LJL theme is *quanti zuoyong* 全體作用, which refers, in a teaching situation, to the master's non-verbal, unconstrained embodiment of the spontaneity of the buddha nature, encompassing all potentialities. Guifeng Zongmi, who closely investigated the teachings of the Chan houses of middle and late Tang dynasty China, considered this a defining characteristic of the Hongzhou house of Chan,[39] and Song dynasty Linji Chan traced itself to Hongzhou.

2. Equivalencies Between LJL Terms and Classical Buddhist Terms

LJL 10.3: "If you don't have enough confidence in yourself, right away in a fluster you will submit to being spun around by '*all the vishayas*' [*yiqie jing* 一切境]. You will be turned around by the *myriad vishayas* [*wanjing* 萬境], and you will not be able to be free."

- Chitetsu, 673: "*yiqie jing* 一切境 means the eye, ear, nose, tongue, body, and mind plus forms, audibles, smellables, tastables, touchables, and dharmas [*liu jing* 六境 = six vishayas], as well as the fifty-one mentals [i.e., the number of *caitasa* or 'mentals' in the Yogācāra system]."

This translation uses the Sanskrit term "vishaya," an approximation of the correct form *ṣaḍ-viṣayāḥ* ("the five sensory fields and the thought-field"), to render the Chinese term *jing* 境. The term *jing* is ubiquitous in the LJL.[40] A central theme of the LJL is that one must not "be rotated" or "be turned" passively by vishayas—one must actively "ride" or "operate" or "manipulate" vishayas. LJL always privileges an active stance over a passive one. This active/passive dichotomy is built directly into the grammar and phrasing of the text. The passive is expressed by such wording as *bei* 被 (passive signifier); *shou* 受 (passive signifier); *sui* 隨 ("follow/accord with"); *xun* 徇 ("submit to/give in to"), while the active is expressed by such wording as *cheng* 乘 ("ride/operate"); *neng* 能 ("can/be able to/be capable of"); *yong* 用 ("use"); *ziyou* 自由 ("freedom"); *zuo* 作 ("do/make"), and so on. The underlying assumption is that a passive stance on the part of the practitioner is always bad—an active stance is the only stance. It is a dichotomy well-known in Japanese *sumō* as *ukemi ni naru* 受け身になる ("end up on the defensive/lose the initiative") versus *mae ni deru* 前に出る ("charge straight ahead/take the initiative").

LJL 3: "Spoken [by Linji] at a Dharma-Hall Convocation: 'Beyond the red-meatball [*chi routuan* 赤肉團] there is the one *true person* [*zhenren* 真人] who can't be ranked.'"

- Kassan, 456, Eishu, 340, Dōchū, 1270, Dōkū, 999, Kōunshi, 1117, and Anonymous, 218, all comment that the "red-meatball" (*chi routuan* 赤肉團) is traceable to Zongmi's *Chan Prolegomenon*. For instance, Kassan, 456: "The *Prolegomenon to the Expressions of the Chan Source* says: '[The first type of mind is Sanskrit] *hṛdaya*. This means the *meatball mind*. This is the mind [that is the first] of the five viscera in the physical body.'"[41]

- Kassan, 456: "'True person' means the 'real mind.' The *Expressions of the Chan Source* says: '[The fourth type of mind is also Sanskrit] *hṛdaya*. This means the *real mind* or *true mind*. This is the *true mind*.'"[42] (According to Zongmi, the true mind is the *tathāgatagarbha* or one mind.[43])

3. Equivalencies between Everyday Words and Zen Terms

LJL **13**.2: "The vishayas are of myriad types, but the *person* [ren 人] remains the same."

- Eishu, 370: "'Person' is *that one person* [*na yi ren* 那一人], just the one person in the universe. He is the companion [of Śākyamuni], who said, 'Above heaven and below heaven I am the solitary honored one.'"
- Kōunshi, 1163: "'Person' is *that one person* in the house of Linji."

Though the term *zhenren* 真人 ("true person") is used only a few times in the LJL, many of the occurrences of the ordinary word *ren* 人 ("person"/"persons") may well simultaneously imply a parallel Chan meaning of *zhenren* 真人.[44] The Zen commentators indicate this by sometimes glossing *ren* 人 with *na yi ren* 那一人 ("that one person"), that is, the true person or true mind. The LJL makes use of this double reading as an ingenious, built-in way of expressing one of its central motifs: that every person is the *person*, the *true person/true mind*. To use the classical Buddhist term, every person has the *tathāgatagarbha* or "buddha-in-embryo." This translation has made use of italics for *person* to highlight the possibility of this double reading.

> LJL **13**.5: "[Linji said,] 'It's none other than *you*: right now, the *person, in that way* listening to the dharma. [So] how do you intend to "cultivate" him [*ta* 他], "realize" him [*ta* 他], "adorn" him [*ta* 他]? He [*qu* 渠] is not a being that can be "cultivated," not a being that can be "adorned." But if you make him [*ta* 他] do the adorning, all things would be adorned.'"

- Dōkū, 1032: "'Him' in the end means '*that one person* without characteristics and without form.'"

- Eishu, 373: "'Him' refers to the person listening to dharma. . . . 'He' is *that one person*, your very own self. 'Adorn' is to use written words and verbal phrases to comment on the meaning of the Way principle."
- Dōchū, 1313: "'Him' refers to '*that one person* listening to dharma' mentioned above. 'Adorn' means 'the adornment of the [thirty-two major] characteristics and [eighty minor] marks [of a buddha].'"
- Eishu, 373: "This 'he' is the *person* listening to dharma."
- Kōunshi, 1168: "'He' refers to *that one person*."

LJL **44**.1: "Huangbo said, 'Come over here—let's hash out *this matter* [箇事] together.'"

- Eishu, 426: "He says *this matter*, but it is the *one person*."
- Dōkū, 1081: "This is the matter of the *original portion*."

As with many other Chan texts of the Song period and later, in the LJL a number of everyday pronouns bear Chan weight: *zhe ge* ("this"; 這箇); *ge shi* ("this matter"; 箇事); *ci shi* ("this matter"; 此事); *ge ren* ("this person"; 箇人); *ci ren* ("this person"; 此人); *zhe han* ("this Han/this fellow"; 這漢); *ni* ("you"; 你); *ta* ("he"; 他); *qu* ("he"; 渠); *zhe li* ("in this/here"; 這裏); *ci jian* ("within this/here"; 此間); *ashei* ("who"; 阿誰); and *shenme chu* ("what place"; 什麼處). In general, these have been italicized in the translation to indicate that they simultaneously carry parallel Chan meanings, such as "mind of the buddhas and patriarchs," "the matter of the original portion" (*benfen shi* 本分事), "original mind," "non-dependent Way-person," "person without form and characteristics," "place of not a single thing," and so on. Perhaps Linji in the LJL could even be referring to these parallel meanings when he says in section **13**.24: "All day long I'm calling a spade a spade for 'em [i.e., talking without holding anything back], but no student pays any heed!" [山僧竟日與他說破學者總不在意]

4. Establishment of Linkages Between Themes in the LJL and Sutra Teachings

LJL **12**.5: "[Linji said,] 'Stream-enterers! The one who is a Superman should know by now that from the outset there is *nothing-to-do*. Because you don't have enough confidence, *from moment to moment you rush about seeking* [*niannian chiqiu* 念念馳求]. *You lose track of your head and go looking for it* [*shetou mitou* 捨頭覓頭]—you can't stop yourself.'"

- Kōunshi, 1153: "'Rush around seeking on the outside' is like Yajñadatta's craziness that did not stop. This is the story of Yajñadatta's looking for his head [in the *Śuraṃgama Sūtra*]."[45]

  LJL **13**.20: "[Linji said,] 'If you *bring* [*mind*] *to a stop* [*xiede* 歇得], right away it is the realm of the pure *dharmakāya*.'"

- Kassan, 535: "The place where thoughts stop is the buddha realm of the pure *dharmakāya*. Therefore, the *Śuraṃgama Sūtra* in its Yajñadatta story[46] says: 'Stopping is *bodhi*. The enlightened mind of superior purity pervades the *dharmadhātu*. It is not obtained from anyone else.'"
- Dōkū, 1044, is very similar.
- Kōunshi, 1186: "When false thoughts come to a stop, it is the buddha body or buddha realm. The *Vimalakīrti Sūtra's* line[47] to the effect that 'when mind is pure, then the buddha-lands are pure' and the *Śuraṃgama Sūtra's* line 'stopping is *bodhi*'[48] are both this idea."

5. Contradictory Interpretations in Two or More Commentaries

LJL **12**.1: "[Linji said,] 'Such a crew [of current practitioners] has entered the Way wrong-mindedly and is quick to enter into *noisy and bustling places* [*naochu* 閙處]. They cannot be called true leavers of home. They are really householders.'"

- Eishu, 359: "'Noisy and bustling places' has the meaning 'noisy markets.'"
- Kassan, 490: "'Noisy and bustling' is not city markets, and 'quiet' is not the mountains. In the end it is your own mind and that is all."
- Dōchū, 1298: "As to 'entering into noisy and bustling places,' having already [left home] for the sake of food and clothing, they do not select out the good and bad in masters, but, upon just seeing a bustling place [i.e., a thriving monastery], enter and hang [their robe, bowl, and] tin staff [on the wall of the Sangha Hall]."
- Chitetsu, 710: "'Noisy and bustling places' means 'the pondering-of-objective-supports of the human mind.'"
- Dōkū, 1020: "The crowd that 'enters the Way wrong-mindedly' takes places of leisure as peaceful and joyful places of entering the Way, and, therefore, they love quiet and loathe noise. They frequently do lengthy [cross-legged] sitting beneath trees or on top of stones. This is completely

the occupation of those in the demon cave [i.e., the heretical Chan of silence-and-illumination]."

- Kōunshi, 1150: "'Entering into noisy and bustling places' means they do not select out the good and bad in masters. If the monastery is bustling with crowds, if there is food and clothing and they can do as they wish, then they enter."

6. Two Interpretations in One Commentary

LJL 15: "The Master [Linji] asked a monk, 'What *place* do you come from?' The monk instantly gave a shout. The Master instantly *did obeisance and [indicated for him] to take the seat [yizuo 揖坐]*."

- Kassan, 566–567, and Dōkū, 1067: "An old commentary has two interpretations: The first is that the Great Master did obeisance to the monk and himself took the seat at the top rank [on the platform]. The second is that the Great Master did obeisance to the monk and ordered him to take the seat at the [position of the] Advanced Seat. The latter interpretation is better."

7. Highly Metaphorical Glosses

LJL 21: "The Master pointed to the open-air pillar [in the center of the courtyard] and asked, 'Is it a worldling or is it an *ārya?*' The *guard officer was silent [yuanliao wuyu 員僚無語]*."

- Kōunshi, 1219: "An Indian doesn't understand Chinese."

LJL 43.1: "Seeing the Head Seat doing cross-legged sitting, [Huangbo] said, 'The youngster [Linji] down there in the lower [southern] part of the Hall is indeed doing *cross-legged sitting [zuo-chan 坐禪]!*'"

- Kassan, 587: "Out in a boat taking a nap and forgetting cognizables—indeed this is the true cross-legged sitting!"

LJL 58: "When the Master was on the verge of transmigrating, he righted his sitting posture and said, 'After I die, you mustn't let my "*saddharma* vision" die out.' Sansheng advanced and said, 'How could we dare to let the Preceptor's "*saddharma* vision" die out?' The Master said, 'If later there is a *person* who asks you about it, what will you say to him?' Sansheng instantly *gave a shout* [*he* 喝]. The Master said, 'Who could have guessed that my "*saddharma* vision" would die out thanks to this dumb-ass!'"

- Kōunshi, 1242: "A true lion cub can give a lion's roar" [i.e., a buddha's speaking dharma is like the roar of a lion].

8. Glosses Consisting of a Line or Couplet of Chinese Poetry

LJL 12.1: "[Linji said,] 'When *vishayas* [*jing* 境] come, they will not be able to turn you.'"

- Shukitsu, 916: "Question: 'What vishayas are these?' Answer: 'Shrieking monkeys all night long circle around the frosted branches.'"

LJL 47.1: "The Master [Linji] one day took his leave of Huangbo. Huangbo asked, 'What *place* are you going to?' The Master said, "If it's not Henan, then right away I will go back to Hebei.' Huangbo instantly [went to] slap him. The Master caught the hand doing the *slapping* [*yizhang* 一掌] and stopped it."

- Kassan, 589, and Kōunshi, 1236: "Let us have another cup of sake—West of the Yang Pass there are no old friends"[49] [i.e., the slap is the last cup of sake before Linji goes out into the world].

9. References to Secular Works Such as the Chinese Classics

LJL 1.1: "The Master [Linji], at that [Dharma] Hall Convocation, said, 'This mountain monk today finds no alternative but to bow to customary etiquette and get up onto *this* seat. If I keep to the Chan gate's [non-verbal approach to] presenting the *great matter*, I simply won't be able to open my mouth, and then *you'd have no place to put your feet* [*wu ni cuozu chu* 無你措足處].'"

- Dōchū, 1265, cites *Analects*, "Zilu 子路": "When ritual and music do not flourish, punishments do not hit the mark; when punishments do not hit the mark, the people have no place to put their hands and feet."

10. Asides on the Part of the Commentator

LJL **13**.18: "[Linji said,] 'I have no "dharma" [of the sort that can be] given to them. Curing the illness [of no confidence] and releasing bonds are all it is.'"

• Anonymous, 270: "Lower your voice, lower your voice—the walls have ears!"

11. Rhetorical Questions Posed by the Commentator

LJL **31**: "Advanced Seat Ding arrived for an audience and asked, 'What is the great meaning of the buddhadharma?' The Master [Linji] got down from the Chan chair, grabbed him and gave him a slap, and instantly shoved him aside. Ding *stood there blankly* [zhuli 佇立]."

• Kassan, 576: "Tell me—what time is this time [of 'standing there blankly]?'"

12. Explanations of the Functions, Daily life, Conventions, Material Culture, and Personnel of Chan/Zen Monastic Life

LJL **2**: "When the time [for the convocation came, the monk] Mayu emerged to ask, 'Of the eyes in each palm of the Thousand-hand Avalokiteśvara, which is the main eye?' The Master [Linji] said, '"Of the eyes in each palm of the Thousand-hand Avalokiteśvara, which is the main eye!?" C'mon! C'mon!' Mayu dragged the Master down from the seat. Mayu substituted himself in the seat. The Master approached the front, saying, '*bu shen* 不審.' Mayu dithered. The Master dragged Mayu down from the seat and substituted himself in the seat. Mayu instantly went out. The Master instantly got down from the seat."

• Dōchū, 1269: "When monks see each other, they bend the body [in a bow], put the palms together [in salutation], and say 'I don't know [*bu shen* 不審].' These are the three karmans [i.e., ritual actions] of respect."

• Anonymous, 217: "*bu shen* 不審 is a ritual formula. Here it has the meaning of 'How are you?'"

- Dōkū, 999: "*bu shen* 不審 [is a polite formula: 'I hope you are unburdened by] illness or worries and in a spry state of health.'"

LJL **14.1**: "Once, when Huangbo entered the storehouse pantry, he asked the *Chief of Provisions* [*fantou* 飯頭], 'What are you doing?' The *Chief of Provisions* [*fantou*] said, 'I'm sorting out [the impurities in] the rice for the monks of the sangha.'"

- Dōchū, 1361, and Kōunshi, 1214: "The *Regulations of Purity of Illusion-Abiding [Hermitage]* . . . glosses *fantou* 飯頭 as: 'He watches over the time schedule from morning to evening; deliberates over the number [of monks] who will be eating [for the day]; gathers the rice and grains and sees if they are of good or poor quality; differentiates the purity levels of the water and starch; practices economy in the amount of vegetables; attends to whether there is firewood or not, etc.'"[50]
- Chitetsu, 849: "*fantou* 飯頭 is a job [in a Zen monastery]. He is the person who works with foodstuffs, but he is not the 'Head Cook.'"
- Eishu, 409, and Anonymous, 302: "*fantou* 飯頭 is the same as 'Head Cook.'"
- Dōkū, 1066: "*fantou* 飯頭 is the Head Cook."

LJL **43.1**: "The Master [Linji] was dozing off [at his seat on the sitting platform] in the [Sangha] Hall. When Huangbo came down and saw this, with his staff he gave a whack to the *bantou* [板頭]. The Master lifted his head, saw that it was Huangbo, but went back to his nap."

- Kassan, 586–587: "*bantou* 板頭 is the plank of the long platform in the lower part [of the Hall]."
- Dōkū, 1081, Anonymous, 318, and Kōunshi, 1234, are similiar.
- Dōchū, 1379: "The *tan* plank ['single plank'] at the front [edge] of the platform is called the *bantou* 板頭."

13. Paraphrases in Japanese

LJL **13.42**: "[Linji said,] 'Venerables! Make no mistake! No matter how much you are conversant with the sutras and treatises, I won't have any of it.'"

- Eishu, 405: "Even if he understands the entire canon of scriptures, Linji doesn't give it the least thought."

14. Japanese Parallels

LJL 1.1: "[Linji said,] 'So—is there a masterful, battle-hardened general who will *right on this spot* deploy to battle stations and open up his banners? [I.e., who will pose a hard question to present an all-out manifestation of the capability of his whole character/give me everything he's got?] Let him prove his skill before the sangha.'"

- Kassan, 448: "*Shōgun* Linji to his *bakufu* [military government] subordinates: 'Is there such a person?'"[51]

15. Editorial Emendations

LJL 39.2: "*predicts Preceptor Fengxue* [讖風穴和尚也]." (not included in this translation)

- Dōchū, 1378: "This must be a comment added by a later person—it should be excised."
- The text as found in Kōunshi, 1231, lacks this line and Kōunshi comments: "A variant edition below this in fine print has the comment: 'predicts Preceptor Fengxue.'"

The following topics addressed by the ten commentaries have not been much used in this translation:

1. Tracing of intertextualities with other Chan texts;
2. Division of the text into manageable sections (most modern translators seem to more or less follow Edo-period guidelines);
3. Tracing of the lineages of Chan figures mentioned in the text;
4. Historical information on Linji and others;
5. Geographical information on Linji's activities.

As stated at the outset, these topics have been comprehensively addressed by previous translations, and there is no need to duplicate that work here.[52]

Postwar Japanese "Commentators" on the LJL

The LJL turned out to be the catalyst for English-language scholarship on Chan as we now know it. It is ultimately traceable to a small group of Japanese and American scholars who gathered at the Zen monastery

Daitoku-ji in Kyoto beginning in 1956.[53] Their main purpose was to produce a first definitive English translation of the LJL. The core of this group consisted of Iriya Yoshitaka (入矢義高; 1910–1999), Yanagida Seizan (柳田聖山; 1922–2006), Philip B. Yampolsky (1920–1996), Burton Watson (b. 1925), and others. The work of Iriya and Yanagida to a tremendous extent has molded the field of postwar Chan studies (*Zengaku kenkyū*) in Japan down to the present day. Thanks to the collaboration on the LJL, their influence extended to the West when Yampolsky in the 1960s introduced their work to America.[54]

Iriya Yoshitaka, a specialist in *baihua* Chinese literature (literature in vernacular-based literary language), forged a new axis in the study of Chan records such as the LJL—an axis oriented to the words themselves, as opposed to the Zen received meaning of the texts.[55] He began with the assumption that much of what had been taken as a specialized Chan vocabulary and rhetoric, unique to a book like the LJL, was *ordinary colloquial Chinese to begin with*. In order to construct a mental lexicon, he collected examples of vocabulary and grammatical constructions from all sorts of *baihua* (written vernacular Chinese) texts—Yuan dynasty plays, Ming dynasty novels, Dunhuang popular literature, and so on. (One of our ten Edo-period commentators, Mujaku Dōchū, partially anticipated this strategy.) Iriya concluded that most of the mistakes made in reading Chan records in the Zen monasteries of Japan and in pre-war scholarship, which he typically refers to as "the usual or conventional reading" (*jūrai no yomi* 従来の読み) or "the old understanding" (*kyūkai* 旧解), had been the result of not distinguishing between *baihua* and *wenyan* (literary Chinese).[56] Though Iriya sometimes bluntly criticized the conventional Rinzai Zen readings of Chan records and went to lengths to lay out what he saw as the correct readings, he himself remained personally sympathetic to Chan.[57] Whenever possible, this translation has used Iriya's method as a corrective in instances where the ten commentaries provide inaccurate philology.

Yanagida Seizan, born the son of a Rinzai Zen priest, after the war formulated a life mission to read "untouched" Chan texts that were outside the Rinzai reading list, such as the Dunhuang Chan manuscripts and a few Chan texts preserved in Korea.[58] He also found himself drawn back to well-known Rinzai texts like the seminal LJL. Though he deliberately set out to read them in a manner untrammeled by the interpretations of Rinzai Zen insiders over the centuries, at a deep level he remained informed by Rinzai Zen. Throughout his life he returned again and again to the LJL. As he said late in life: "Through my continuous involvement in this [Daitoku-ji] project, this text was to become an imperative to me."[59]

Iriya's translation of the LJL, Iriya's Zen dictionary (Zengo), and Yanagida's notes to his translation have constituted modern "commentaries" for
this translation. On occasion, when glosses of an LJL word or phrase in
the ten commentaries are plainly mistaken, the following translation has
used corrections and supplements found in their work and in recent dictionaries that contain *baihua* words and phrases.[60] These dictionaries are
based on such sources as Dunhuang popular literature and the classic
novels.

In Conclusion

The most poetic of the Japanese Zen commentators, Kōunshi, describes
Linji's "house tune" as "*that one tune* of our [Zen] personal-realization-of-
the-meaning-beyond-words"[61]—it is a tune that cannot be heard with the
ears.[62] To take liberties with this musical metaphor, the LJL in its themes
constitutes a kind of polyphony, formed around *that single source melody*
(the *cantus firmus*), numbered "zero," that cannot itself ever be heard, or
voiced, or put into words: but its central presence is integral to the har-
monies formed by the strands of counterpoint it has informed, such as
numbers one through five below. These are essentially restatements of
each other, and allude always to *that one tune* numbered "zero":

1. To hesitate is to lose—dithering (*niyi* 擬議) or mental reflection is bad.
2. A realized true person (*zhenren* 真人) brings to bear everything he's
   got; that is, exhibits the non-verbal, unconstrained embodiment of the
   spontaneity of the buddha nature (*quanti zuoyong* 全體作用).
3. Vishayas (*jing* 境) are just terms (i.e., the sense objects have nominal
   existence only and hence are unreal), so the realized true person actively rides vishayas and is never rotated passively by vishayas.
4. Every person (*ren* 人) is a true person (*zhenren* 真人).
5. In one's current venue of activities (*ni jin yongchu* 你今用處), nothing
   is lacking.

Though this translation has faithfully sought to play up the frequent
use of *baihua* elements throughout the LJL, the reader should not assume
that the LJL was a sort of "popular music" accessible to a mass Chinese
audience. This was probably not the case. As Christoph Anderl states:
"[A]lthough some passages of the *Recorded Sayings* texts might have been
understandable for a more general audience when read aloud (e.g., some

sections of the dialogues), the text as a whole is by no means easily accessible. Indeed, quite the contrary seems to be the case."[63] Despite its appealing down-to-earth charm, the LJL was not the "demotic" text it might seem—by Song times its *baihua* had fossilized into a sacerdotal genre within literary Chinese, formally parsed and intoned by Chan and Zen masters in "acoustic events" known as "expositions" (*tichang/teishō* 提唱).

Another discrepancy between semblance and reality is the LJL's infamous claim that "the three vehicles and twelve divisions of the teachings *all* are obsolete papers now useful only for the toilet to wipe away feces" (section 13.9). The reality is that the LJL exhibits a striking erudition in "toilet-paper" sutras, an erudition duly noted by two of our ten Zen commentators. Kōunshi in his 1698 commentary says: "I have researched this record, and, even though not a word or half a line falls into the theories of the scholiasts, nevertheless, the deep purport of all the Mahāyāna sutras can be seen clearly therein. The Master Linji indeed broadly cultivated the three baskets of the Buddhist canon."[64] Mujaku Dōchū in his 1726 commentary concurs: "As to [Linji's statement that he had in past days] 'inquired into the sutras and treatises,' when one reads the *Instructions to the Sangha* section of this record, its broad erudition is evident."[65]

The LJL at heart is not anti-sutra—in fact, it is grounded in the sutras: quoting without citation, paraphrasing, and alluding to a wide range of Mahāyāna sutras (and even treatises). Of all those sutras, the *Śūraṃgama Sūtra* stands out as particularly important. The LJL is quite indebted to teachings of the *Śūraṃgama*: all sentient beings lose their original mind (*benxin* 本心) and are spun around by things (*wei wu suozhuan* 為物所轉); the one spirit-brightness (*yi jingming* 一精明) or solitary brightness (*guming* 孤明) pervades the ten directions; and "stopping" the movement of mind is *bodhi* (*xie ji puti* 歇即菩提). Ironically, it turns out that those toilet-paper sutras are indispensable to the LJL.

As the Zen commentators tell us, the LJL, despite its bold rhetoric of "the separate transmission outside the teachings," is actually an erudite distillation of classical Buddhism, replete with sutra teachings and technical terminology. However, it is classical Buddhism exquisitely costumed, to calculated effect, in earthy *baihua* language—an unexpected but addictive juxtaposition that is zestful and galvanic: much like eating Korean chilled noodles in iced broth, *naengmyeon*.

Record of the Sayings of Chan Master Linji Huizhao of Zhenzhou

*Collected by the Disciple [Sansheng] Huiran in Residence at
Sansheng [Monastery] and Successor to [Linji's] Dharma[1]*

[Part I]

[Dharma-Hall Convocations][2]

I.I

The Commandery Governor,[3] [Cavalier] Attendant-in-ordinary Wang,[4] along with civilian officials [in his retinue], had requested the Master to ascend the [high] seat [in the Dharma Hall to hold a formal convocation]. The Master, at that [Dharma] Hall Convocation,[5] said, "This mountain monk[6] today finds no alternative but to bow to customary etiquette and get up onto *this* seat.[7] If I keep to the Chan gate's[8] [non-verbal approach to] presenting the *great matter* [the original mind possessed by everyone/the matter right under our feet/awakening to the knowing-seeing of the buddhas],[9] I simply won't be able to open my mouth, and then you'd have no place to put your [hands and] feet.[10] But, just for today, given the adamant request of the Attendant-in-ordinary, why should this mountain monk keep a lid on [Chan's] 'headrope'—the personal-realization-of-the-meaning-beyond-words?[11] So—is there a masterful, battle-hardened general[12] who will *right on this spot* deploy to battle stations and open up his banners? [I.e., who will pose a hard question to present an all-out manifestation of the capability of his whole character/give me everything he's got?][13] Let him prove his skill before the sangha."

I.2

A monk asked, "What is the great meaning of the buddhadharma?" The Master instantly shouted [severing the samsaric world of defiled "red dust"].[14] The monk bowed.[15] The Master said, "Isn't *this* monk a splendid debate opponent!"[16]

1.3

Question: "Whose house tune [not a worldly tune, but *that one tune* of the Chan personal-realization-of-the-meaning-beyond-words] does the Master sing? Whose Chan style does his succeed?"[17] The Master said, "I was at Huangbo's *place*—three times I raised a question, and three times I got whacked." The monk dithered [i.e., compared several options for a response and consequently was too slow].[18] The Master gave a shout and immediately followed it with a hit: "Don't go around driving nails into the sky!"

1.4

There was a Master of the [Lecture] Seat [with the low understanding level typical of a scholar of the teachings][19] who [poked his head out of the kudzu-cave of verbal entanglement and] asked, "The three vehicles and twelve divisions of the teachings—how could it be that they don't elucidate the buddha nature?"[20] The Master said, "A wasteland overgrown with weeds [of *avidyā* (ignorance)/of canonical abstractions][21] was never tilled with a hoe like yours." The Seat Master said, "But surely the Buddha wouldn't have misled people!" The Master said, "In what *place* is that buddha?" The Seat Master was silent. The Master said, "[*Here I am,*] *right in front of* the Attendant-in-ordinary; *you're* trying to hoodwink *this old monk*! Step back at once! Step back at once! You're blocking other people/*persons* from asking questions."

1.5

He continued, "This day's dharma assembly is for the sake of the one *great matter* [the original mind possessed by everyone/the matter right under our feet]. Are there any more questioners? Quickly come out [of the standing group] and ask.[22] But just as you are in the act of opening your mouth, you will already be at a remove [from the *certain matter*].[23] Why so? It's no wonder[24] that 'Śākyamuni' said that dharma [the *certain matter*] is independent of the written word, given that [dharma] has nothing to do with causes and conditions.[25] Today's kudzu [of written characters and spoken phrases] has been brought to you by your own insufficient confidence.[26] I'm afraid that we are holding up the Attendant-in-ordinary and the officials [of his staff] and making the buddha nature even more impenetrable. Perhaps it's best to withdraw." He gave a single shout and said, "For people/*persons* endowed with little confidence, [the one *great matter* of the original mind, possessed by each *person*,] will always remain unsettled. [Thank you for your patience—I have troubled you to] stand for a long time [during this convocation]. Take care of yourselves."[27]

2

The Master on a certain day went to the Hebei prefectural office. The Commandery Governor, [Cavalier] Attendant-in-ordinary Wang, requested the Master to "ascend the seat." When the time came, [the monk] Mayu emerged to ask, "Of the eyes in each palm of the Thousand-hand Avalokiteśvara [the lord of the six rebirth paths], which is the main eye?" The Master said, "'Of the eyes in each palm of the Thousand-hand Avalokiteśvara, which is the main eye!?'[28] C'mon! C'mon!" Mayu dragged the Master down from the seat. Mayu substituted himself in the seat. The Master approached the front [of the chair and performed the three ritual actions of respect: bending his body in a bow, placing his palms together in the gesture of respect, and giving the customary greeting between monks], saying, "How are you?" [I.e., literally, "I don't know (whether or not you have experienced illness or worries lately, but I hope you are doing well)."][29] Mayu dithered.[30] The Master dragged Mayu down from the seat and substituted himself in the seat. Mayu instantly went out. The Master instantly got down from the seat.

3

Spoken at a Dharma-Hall Convocation: "Beyond the red-meatball [mind][31] there is the one true *person* [true mind or buddha nature][32] who can't be ranked. [I.e., who does not belong to the 'buddha' ranking and does not belong to the 'sentient-being' ranking.][33] [That true *person*/true mind] is constantly exiting and entering from the face-gates of all of you people/*persons* [like the dazzling rays of light emitted from the face-gate of a buddha].[34] Those who have not seen with their own eyes—look! Look!" At one point there was a monk who emerged to ask: "What is the true person who can't be ranked?" The Master got down from the [curved-wood] Chan chair,[35] and grabbed him by the collar, saying, "C'mon! C'mon!"[36] The monk dithered.[37] The Master, thrusting him back, said, "[This] 'true *person* who can't be ranked'—what a magnificent piece of dried shit!"[38] And he at once returned to the *fangzhang*.[39]

4.1

Spoken at a Dharma-Hall Convocation: [Even before the Master had uttered the preliminary "fishing words," after which Chan guests emerge from the standing group to ask questions,] there was a monk who emerged and bowed.[40] The Master gave a shout. The monk said, "Elder Preceptor, don't [even bother] to calibrate [my level of understanding]—case closed."[41] The Master said, "So—to what *place* do you think [the shout] subsided?" The monk shouted. There was another monk who asked, "What is the great meaning of the buddhadharma?" The Master gave a shout. The monk bowed. The Master [taking poison to attack poison,][42] said, "Would you say that was a good shout?" The monk said, "[Your] army of traitors [waving the flag of revolt][43] has suffered a great defeat." The Master said, "At what *place* did [my traitors] make a mistake?"[44] The monk said, "A second sortie will not be tolerated." The Master gave a shout.

4.2

One day the Advanced Seats of the two halls [front and back] encountered each other and let out a shout.[45] A monk asked the Master, "Was there a guest and a host?" The Master said, "'Guest' and 'host' are clearly demarcated." The Master said, "Great sangha! If you want to understand Linji's topics, 'guest' and 'host,' go and ask the two Advanced Seats of the halls." He then got down from the seat.

5.1

Spoken at a Dharma-Hall Convocation: A monk asked, "What is the great meaning of the buddhadharma?" The Master raised his flywhisk [i.e., demonstrated the buddhadharma/*original portion*].[46] The monk instantly gave a shout. The Master instantly whacked him. Another monk asked, "What is the great meaning of the buddhadharma?" The Master raised his flywhisk again. The monk instantly gave a shout. The Master also shouted again. The monk dithered.[47] The Master instantly whacked him.

5.2

The Master then said, "Great sangha! One who practices the dharma must not begrudge even the loss of one's own life. Twenty years [ago][48] I was at my Master Huangbo's *place*. Three times I asked about the very topic of the great meaning of the buddhadharma, and three times I was on the receiving end of his staff.[49] It was just like being brushed by a [fragile and delicate] frond of mugwort [that is placed on the head of a child at the coming-of-age ceremony].[50] I've gotten nostalgic for one more blow from that kind of stick. Is there anyone who could do that for me?" At that time a monk emerged from the sangha and said, "Yours truly can do it!" The Master picked up the stick and held it out to him.[51] When the monk was just about to take it from him [i.e., much too slowly], the Master instantly whacked him.

6.1

Spoken at a Dharma-Hall Convocation: A monk asked, "What is it—the matter of the sword blade [that cuts off all knowing and understanding; i.e., the matter of the *original portion*]?"[52] The Master said, "A debacle! A debacle!" The monk dithered.[53] The Master instantly whacked him.

6.2

Question: "Take, for example, the postulant Shishi—while pedaling the mortar, he forgot his moving feet [in utter no-mind]. To what *place* did he go?" The Master said, "Plumb sunk into a deep pool [of the state of the *original portion* and no-mind/mired (hopelessly) in a deep pit]."[54]

6.3

At that point the Master said, "Whoever comes to me [i.e., the student who comes to ask a question],[55] I do not let him down. I always know the *place* he is coming from [i.e., his level of understanding].[56] If someone comes *in that way* [i.e., with a good level of understanding, certain about *this matter*], it is only natural that he should lose [his footing before me].[57] If someone comes not *in that way* [i.e., with a bad level of understanding, uncertain and doubtful about *this matter*], he will have tied himself up without a rope.[58] Don't get into the three-ring circus of mental reflection and calcula-tion [i.e., selecting and conjecturing].[59] 'Understanding' and 'not under-standing'[60]—the entire package is a mistake! [I.e., 'delusion' and 'awakening' are both to be extinguished.][61] I have clearly spoken *in that way*. I entrust all questions [of whether I am 'right' or 'wrong'] to the judgment of the people

of all-under-heaven. [I.e., if the world is of the opinion that I do not understand and judges me as such, why should that bother me? Let it!][62] [Thank
you for your patience—I have troubled you to] stand for a long time. Take
care of yourselves."

7

Spoken at a Dharma-Hall Convocation: "[Here's one:] 'One *person* is at the
top of a lonely peak [i.e., the place of the *original portion*] with no way
down.[63] One *person* is at a crossroads [i.e., the gate of *upāyas* issuing from
worldly truth][64] and neither accomodates [beings] nor abandons them.
[I.e., approaches beings according to their mental dispositions.][65] Which is
ahead, and which is behind?'[66] Don't pull a Vimalakīrti [silence], and don't
pull a Great Master Fu [speech]. [I.e., in the end, both having no words and
having words are to be stripped away.][67] Take care of yourselves."

8

Spoken at a Dharma-Hall Convocation: "[Here's one:] 'One *person* is on
the road [of worldly truth and cultivation][68] for immeasurable kalpas,[69]
and is not away from the family homestead [i.e., the *original portion*].[70]
One *person* is away from the family homestead [the *original portion*], and
is not [to be found] on the road. [I.e., he is the leisurely Way-person of
non-action who is beyond the course of training.][71] Which one should
be reverenced by humans and *devas*?'"[72] He then got down from his
seat.

9.1

Spoken at a Dharma-Hall Convocation: A monk said, "What is the first
couplet [of the eight-line poem]?" The Master said, "The seal of the three
essentials[73] being lifted, the red markings [appear] at the side [of the docu-
ment].[74] There is no dithering permitted [i.e., there is only one try for a seal
imprint, and so there is no dithering permitted]—'host' and 'guest' are
clearly demarcated."[75] Question: "What is the second couplet?" The Master said, "How [could it be that] Miaojie [the bodhisattva Mañjuśrī/'wonderful
understanding of mind'] allowed the questions of Wuzhuo [the Chan
monk Wuzhuo who met Mañjuśrī on Mt. Wutai and had a dialogue/'non-
attachment']? [In other words,] how could such an *upāya* [compassionate

expedient] be at odds with knowing reality as it truly is?"[76] Question: "What is the third couplet?" The Master said, "Observe the puppets on the stage. There is a *person* backstage moving them."

9.2

The Master also said, "[Here's one:] 'The language of each couplet cannot help but contain the gates of the three mysteries. Each one of the mystery gates cannot help but contain the three essentials.[77] [This is why] there are *upāyas* [i.e., the methods of the scholars of the teachings] and "function-ings" [i.e., a Chan master's wielding the stick, letting out the shout, picking up the stick, holding the flywhisk upright, and so forth].'[78] What do all of you people/*persons* make of this?" He got down from his seat.

[Part II]

[Sangha Instruction]

10.1

At the evening assembly the Master instructed the sangha, "[When a student comes to me,] sometimes I rip away 'the [true] *person*' [i.e., the mental construct of 'the true mind' or 'the *original portion*' brought by the student] but don't rip away the vishayas [i.e., all the ready-made characteristics of forms in the questions which the student brings].[1] Sometimes I rip away the vishayas but don't rip away 'the [true] *person*.' Sometimes I rip away both 'the [true] *person*' and the vishayas. Sometimes I rip away neither 'the [true] *person*' nor the vishayas."

10.2

At the time there was a monk who asked, "What about ripping away the [true] *person* but not ripping away the vishayas?" The Master said, "The shining sun emerges, arraying the earth with brocade;[2] a child's hanging hair, white like silk."[3] The monk said, "What about ripping away the vishayas but not ripping away the [true] *person*?" The Master said, "The king's writ has already taken hold throughout the empire;[4] the general beyond the passes has been cut off [stranded] by the smoke [of alarm signals in the borderlands] and the dust [kicked up by the cavalry horses]."[5] The monk said, "What about ripping away both the [true] *person* and the vishayas?" The Master said, "News from Bing prefecture and Fen prefecture is cut off; they have become an independent place."[6] A monk said, "What about ripping away neither the [true] *person* nor the vishayas?" The Master said, "The king ascends the jeweled hall; the old farmers [i.e., those who are finished with *the matter*] are singing in the fields. [I.e., there is great peace with *nothing-to-do*.]"[7]

10.3

The Master thereupon said, "For today's practitioners of the buddhadharma, first of all, the important thing is to seek to behold reality as it truly is.[8] If they were to attain a beholding of reality as it truly is, then samsara would not stain them [i.e., they would not accumulate habit energy from past lives due to the karman of samsara],[9] and they would be able to go [as they pleased through stone walls without obstruction] or stay freely.[10] There is no need to seek 'excellence'; 'excellence'[11] will arrive spontaneously. Stream-enterers![12] Take, for example, the worthies who are our predecessors from ancient times onward—they all had *upāyas* [like mine] for liberating people.[13] What I want to impress upon you is that only this is important: Don't get discombobulated by [other] people/[other] *persons*/'the *person.*'[14] If you want to use [this teaching], then use it.[15] Never hesitate![16] Today's practitioners are hopeless.[17] From what does the disease [of hesitation] come? The disease lies in your not having confidence in yourself [i.e., being unaware that all sentient beings are endowed with *tathāgata* wisdom].[18] You: if you don't have enough confidence in yourself, right away in a fluster[19] you will submit to being spun around by 'all the vishayas.' You will get turned around by 'the myriad vishayas,' and you will not be able to be free."[20]

10.4

"You: if you are able to stop the mind that rushes around and around seeking from moment to moment, right away you will be no different from the buddhas who are our patriarchs.[21] Are you thinking you want to know 'the buddhas who are our patriarchs?' They are none other than *you* yourselves [living buddhas] standing right in front of me listening to the dharma![22] You students don't have enough confidence and right away rush around seeking on the outside [in the manner of the madman Yajñadatta in the *Śūraṃgama Sūtra*, who ran around searching for his own head].[23] Even if you were successful in seeking out something [on the outside], it all would be excellent characteristics [but only] of the written word.[24] You would never get the intention of *living* patriarchs.[25] Make no mistake, Chan worthies! If you do not have an encounter [with the buddhadharma] at this time [i.e., in your present birth],[26] then for tens of thousands of kalpas and thousands of births, the samsaric wheel will keep revolving through the three realms [of desire, form, and formlessness]. Submitting to vishayas you like,[27] and picking them up,[28] you will be reborn into the womb of a donkey or a cow [i.e., fall into the animal rebirth path].[29] Stream-enterers! According to my vision,[30] we ourselves are no different from 'the buddha Śākyamuni.' This very day—the venue of all your varied daily activities—what could possibly be lacking?[31] The divine light of the six paths[32] has never been interrupted. If you can see *in that way*, throughout your whole life you will be the *person* who has *nothing-to-do*."[33]

10.5

"Venerables![34] In the three realms there is no peace—like a burning house.[35] This [i.e., the three realms] is not a place you should loiter for long.[36] The killer-demon of impermanence at [any given] single moment doesn't make any distinctions between 'high-born' and 'low-born,' 'old' and 'young.' If you want to be no different from the 'buddhas who are our patriarchs,' never seek on the outside. You, in [the same] single moment, are pure light [the wisdom light of the one mind]—are the '*dharmakāya* buddha in your own house [the human body].'[37] You, in [the same] single moment, are non-discriminative light—are the '*saṃbhogakāya* buddha in your own house.'[38] You, in [the same] single moment, are non-distinction-making light—are the '*nirmāṇakāya* buddha in your own house.'[39] These three types of [buddha-] bodies are none other than *you*, the *person* [*that one person* or true *person*] right now in front of me listening to the dharma.[40] Precisely because you are not rushing around seeking on the outside,[41] do you have *this* effectiveness [in your venue of activities].[42] According to sutra and treatise scholars, these three types of [buddha-]bodies are to be taken as the ultimate standard. But in my vision, this is incorrect. These three types of [buddha-]bodies are just terms,[43] [and as such] they are merely three types of dependent [sleights-of-hand of the magical arts used by the sutra and treatise scholars].[44] [Scholars of the sutras and treatises come up with such convoluted claptrap as:] 'An ancient said, "The postulation of [buddha-]bodies is grounded in doctrinal points; the discussion of [buddha-]lands is based in substance."'[45] [But according to my vision,] we patently know that the 'dharma-nature bodies' and the 'dharma-nature lands' are both [nothing but unreal] reflected images."[46]

10.6

"Venerables! *You* must come to know the *person* who plays with these [un-real] reflected images [i.e., the one who is formless, clear, solitary bright-ness].[47] He is the original source of all the buddhas. Every place[48] is the home-*place* [the original source] to which [*you*] the stream-enterer returns [i.e., the place of smooth-and-steady cross-legged sitting and great rest].⁴⁹ For sure, your form-body of the four elements⁵⁰ does not have the ability to speak dharma or listen to it. Your spleen, stomach, liver, and gallbladder⁵¹ don't have the ability to speak dharma or listen to it. The sky doesn't have the ability to speak dharma or listen to it. Then just what is it that has the ability to speak dharma or listen to it? It's none other than *you*, a solitary brightness [the original nature/one mind/true mind]⁵² clearly standing right in front of me, devoid of even a single describable attribute—it's none other than *this* that has the ability to speak dharma and listen to it. If you see *in that way*, right away you are no different from the buddhas who are our patriarchs. Just let there never be a break. Everything that meets the eye is [the real].⁵³ [Scholars of the sutras and treatises come up with such convoluted claptrap as:] 'Just as [an ancient says:] "Emotions arise, and *prajñā* is cut off; characteristics undergo transformation, and the substance evolves." Therefore, you are turned on the [samsaric] wheel in the three realms and undergo various sufferings.'⁵⁴ [However,] according to my vision, there is nothing that is not very deep [i.e., inconceivable]; and nothing that is not liberation."⁵⁵

10.7

"Stream-enterers! Mind dharma [true mind/buddha mind/one mind] is formless⁵⁶ and pervades the ten directions. In the eye it is called seeing; in the ear it is called hearing; in the nose, smelling; in the mouth, speaking; in the hands, grasping; and in the feet, walking or running. At the outset this one spirit-brightness [the one buddha nature/one mind, in the manner of a sleight-of-hand seems to] divide into the six [causal] combinations [i.e, the six sense organs that come into being due to the coming together of causes and conditions].⁵⁷ This one mind is no [mind].⁵⁸ Every *place* is liberation.⁵⁹ What is my intention in speaking *in that way*? It's simply because you stream-enterers cannot stop your seeking mind from rushing about everywhere,⁶⁰ and you clamber up on top of those good-for-nothing gimmick vishayas [provisionally established as *upāyas*] by the ancients [i.e., the canonical sutras and treastises as well as the Chan records].⁶¹ Stream-enterers! Run with my vision: [With one stroke of the sword instantly] sever the heads of the *sambhoga* and *nirmāṇa* buddhas.⁶² [The 'bodhisattva] who has completed the ten stages' is like a day laborer;⁶³ [a '*tathāgata*] who has ascended to the stages of perfect and wonderful awakening' is a Han in a cangue with a lock;[64] 'arhats' and 'independent buddhas' are like toilet excrement; '*bodhi*' and 'nirvana' are like posts to which you hitch a donkey.[65] Why hasn't this [sunk in with you]? It's simply because you stream-enterers don't comprehend that the 'three immeasurable kalpas' [you supposedly spend traversing all of these 'stages'] are empty; that's why you have these [karmic] blockages [such as 'locked cangues,' 'toilet excrement,' and 'donkey posts'].[66] If you are a Way-*person* who [beholds] reality as it truly is, it's not like this at all. All you're doing is being capable of dissolving your old karman [from previous births], no matter what karmic situation comes along—giving free rein to luck, and putting on your clothes. If you want to walk, you walk; if you want to sit, you sit [i.e., you wade through the day in a bold and unconstrained manner].[67] There is not a single moment of hoping for the fruit of buddhahood. Why is it *this way*? An ancient said, 'If you are about to seek a buddha through taking action [i.e., creating karman], that very buddha would only be a great harbinger of samsara.'"[68]

10.8

"Venerables! Your days are precious. In spite of that, you're determined to bustle along, go astray onto byways [i.e., digressions],[69] studying 'Chan,' studying 'the Way,' using terminological items and phrasings of doctrinal points [as guides], seeking 'buddhas' and 'patriarchs,' seeking out 'good teachers.' This is mental reflection and conjecture—make no mistake about it.[70] Stream-enterers! You already have a father and mother [i.e., the original source].[71] Who else are you seeking? Try re-training the light [of the true mind] back upon yourself [to become aware of your original awakening].[72] An ancient says: 'Yajñadatta [thought he had] lost his head. But, if his seeking mind had stopped, [even] he would have had *nothing-to-do*.'[73] Venerables! You definitely must be just your usual self [i.e., must discard the creation of karman—the rush to seek out something].[74] Don't concoct special effects [i.e., don't have preferences and engage in mental reflection, calculation, and conjecture].[75] There is a certain type of bald-headed hack [i.e., bad teacher][76] around, who doesn't know good from bad.[77] At the drop of a hat he 'sees spirits' and 'sees ogres' [i.e., engages in crazy and false talk about the strange and unusual];[78] he points towards the east and gesticulates towards the west [i.e., without rhyme or reason he uses his hands to concoct special effects];[79] and he [crazily runs around repeating such fatuous gabble as:] When the weather is clear, 'Great weather!' and when it's rainy, 'Fine moisture!'[80] There will come a day when the whole lot of them [i.e., bald-headed hacks/bad teachers][81] will be forced to repay their debt before Yama, the Old One [Judge of the Hells], by swallowing red-hot iron balls. Children of good family [i.e., practitioners]![82] You are [allowing yourself] to be attached to this type of wild-fox demon,[83] and you immediately come to adore strangeness and to toy with it.[84] Blind imbeciles![85] There will come a day when [Yama] will exact your 'food money' [i.e., you will have to pay the tab for your food]."

II.I

The Master instructed the sangha: "Stream-enterers! You really have got to attain a beholding of reality as it truly is[86] and march out across the world [freely and autonomously].[87] [It is imperative] that you avoid being confused by that pack of wild-fox demons [bad teachers].[88] To have *nothing-to-do* is to be a highborn *person* [already].[89] Just don't engage in [karmic] performance [such as calculating, running around seeking, and so forth]— just be your usual self.[90] But you're trying to proceed outside yourself, down byways, running around seeking,[91] looking for your own feet and hands [i.e., searching by the road of rational principle, searching for terms and phrases].[92] That's a big mistake! You want to seek out a buddha, but 'buddha' is just a term. Do you even know the one who is rushing about seeking [i.e., do you even know *this*, the *original portion*]?[93] Even 'the buddhas of the three times and ten directions' and 'the patriarchs' cropped up just to seek dharma. Even you practicing stream-enterers today [are the same]—you are just seeking dharma. Attain the dharma: that's it! Don't attain it: the wheel turns through the five rebirth paths, the same as always! Just what is dharma? Dharma is the [true-]mind dharma. The [true-]mind dharma is formless and penetrates the ten directions. Before your very eyes [this true-mind dharma] is active.[94] [However, because a] *person's* confidence in this [true-mind dharma] is insufficient, he right away sets up terms and phrases [as guides], and, from within the written word, he makes conjectures[95] about the buddhadharma. [He and the buddhadharma are] as far apart as heaven and earth!"[96]

II.2

"Stream-enterers! In my dharma talk, just what dharma is it that I am talking about? I am talking about the mind-ground dharma[97] that can enter instantaneously into both 'worldling' and '*ārya*,'[98] enter into both 'pure' and 'defiled,'[99] enter into both 'real' and 'conventional.'[100] When all is said and done, what you [call] 'real' and 'conventional' and 'worldling' and '*ārya*'[101] can't even stick names on [i.e., assign rank to, or prioritize][102] each and every 'real' and 'conventional' and 'worldling' and '*ārya.*' [So how could] 'real' and 'conventional' and 'worldling' and '*ārya*' ever be capable of sticking a name on *this person* [i.e., *that one person* or true *person*]![103] Stream-enterers! If you have caught on [to this stuff], then right away make practical application of it, and you won't be hung up on names anymore—this one we'll name 'the mysterious purport.'"

II.3

"My dharma talk is different from that of the world at large. For example, supposing there is a Mañjuśrī and a Samantabhadra who crop up before my eyes, each manifesting a body, to ask about dharma. As soon as they inquire 'Preceptor . . . ,' I have already seen through them.[104] [Or] I am doing smooth-and-steady [cross-legged] sitting[105] and, when once again[106] along comes a stream-enterer to see me, [in this instance too] I have utterly seen through him. How is it that [I can do] this? It's exactly because my vision is different [from the people of all-under-heaven][107]—externally, I don't seize on 'worldling' and '*ārya*'; internally, I am not permanently fixed in 'nirvana' [i.e., not detained even in the *original portion*];[108] and my vision is penetrating,[109] untrammeled by doubt or error."[110]

I2.I

The Master instructed the sangha: "Stream-enterers! The buddhadharma is not a matter of putting in [special/unusual/exceptional] work [i.e., there is no 'karmic performance' at all].[111] It is just a matter of the usual *nothing-to-do*—shitting, pissing, putting on clothes/costumes, eating meals; and when tired, lying down. Idiots will laugh at me, but the wise are in the know. An ancient said, 'One who makes [special/unusual/exceptional] effort at [*dhyāna*] practice directed outside [the usual *nothing-to-do*] is, in the final analysis, a dullard.'[112] Whatever *place* you are, you play the master [i.e., enjoy the use of each and every thing];[113] every *place* you stand is reality.[114] When vishayas come, they will not be able to turn you [i.e., you will remain unbound by them].[115] Even if there were to be habit energy from previous lives,[116] and even if there were the five karmans that bring on immediate retribution,[117] leading to rebirth in the Avīci hot hell, these themselves would constitute the great sea of liberation. Current practitioners, the whole lot of them, do not have a [personal experience of] coming to know dharma.[118] They are just like goats that butt their noses up against things.[119] No matter what they come across, they pop it into their mouths. They can't distinguish between 'slave' and 'master' and can't differentiate 'guest' from 'host.' Such a crew has entered the Way wrongmindedly [for the sake of food and clothing][120] and is quick to enter into noisy and bustling places [noisy markets/one's own mind/bustling monasteries].[121] They cannot be called true leavers of home. They are really [still] householders."

12.2

"Those who have left home must [have the keen eyesight to] discern, [within their] daily activities, reality as it truly is; to discern 'buddha and Māra,' to discern 'real and false,' to discern 'worldling and *ārya*' [for the categories that they are]. Only if they [have the keen eyesight to] discern *in that way* can they be said truly to have left home. If they can't discern 'Māra and buddha,' it's the same as leaving one home only to enter another. We dub them 'karman-creating sentient beings.' There is no way we can call them true leavers of home. For example, suppose there were to emerge right now a [combined] 'buddha-Māra,' blended together in a single body, like a mixture of water and milk. The king of geese would drink only the milk.[122] [But] if you are a stream-enterer with a clear eye, you strike out both [categories] 'Māra' and 'buddha.'[123] You: if you love '*ārya*' and hate 'worldling,' you'll be bobbing up and down in the samsaric sea."

12.3

Question: "What is 'buddha' and what is 'Māra?'"[124] The Master says, "A single moment of being perplexed is 'Māra.' You: if you come to know that the myriad dharmas are non-arising [and non-extinguishing], like a *māyā*, that there is not a single vishaya or a single dharma, that every place is purity—this is 'buddha.' But 'buddha' and 'Māra' are [only] two vishayas, 'purity' and 'impurity.' According to my vision there is neither 'buddha' nor 'sentient being,' neither 'ancient times' nor 'present.' To attain [awakening][125] is to attain it immediately,[126] without going through the time sequence [i.e., not passing through the fifty-two stages, which takes immeasurable kalpas].[127] There is no 'practicing' and no 'realization,' no 'attaining' and no 'losing.' At no time are there any distinct dharmas beyond this.[128] Suppose there were a single thing that surpassed this [i.e., nirvana], I say it would be like an [illusory, unreal] dream or a magical transformation.[129] Everything I have said is. . . ."[130]

12.4

"Stream-enterers! The one who is listening [to dharma], a solitary brightness [of the one mind/true mind/mind ground] clearly standing in front of me right now,[131] this [true] *person* is nowhere detained and pervades the ten directions, with freedom throughout the three realms.[132] He goes into all manner of vishayas,[133] but they cannot turn him around. In a single moment[134] he traverses the *dharmadhātu*. If [the true *person*] meets a buddha, he speaks [dharma] as a buddha. If he meets a patriarch, he speaks [dharma] as a patriarch. If he meets an arhat, he speaks [dharma] as an arhat. If he meets a *preta*, he speaks [dharma] as a *preta*.[135] Throughout all locations he playfully strolls through the lands [of the ten realms—the hell realm, *preta* realm, animal realm, *asura* realm, human realm, *deva* realm, *śrāvaka* realm, *pratyeka-buddha* realm, bodhisattva realm, and buddha realm], teaching and transforming sentient beings; but, [though he goes through many lifetimes,] he never leaves the single moment [just as the youth Sudhana in the *Huayan Sutra* never leaves the single location but passes through one hundred and ten cities and their fifty-three good teachers].[136] Everywhere his light of purity [of the true mind] penetrates the ten directions;[137] the myriad dharmas are the one *tathatā* [i.e., the single moment]."[138]

12.5

"Stream-enterers! The one who is a Superman[139] should know by now that from the outset there is *nothing-to-do*. Because you don't have enough confidence, from moment to moment you rush about seeking. You lose track of your head and go looking for it—you can't stop yourself [like Yajñadatta, whose craziness did not stop, in the *Śūraṃgama Sūtra*].[140] Even the Bodhisattva Perfect-and-Sudden, though he was able to manifest himself throughout the *dharmadhātu*,[141] [when he yearned for rebirth] into the pure land, was disgusted with 'worldling' and rejoiced in 'ārya.'[142] This type has yet to forget 'seizing and discarding'; and 'impurity and purity' remain in their minds.[143] According to the Chan personal-realization-of-the-meaning-beyond-words, beholding [reality as it truly is] is a bit different. In a word, it is right now: and there is no more [passing through a] time sequence [of the bodhisattva's three immeasurable kalpas going through the stages].[144] Everything I have said is a one-off medicine [*upāya*] to cure [a particular case of] illness.[145] There is no such thing as a 'real' teaching [i.e., a single panacea that works for every malady of delusion].[146] If you can see *in that way*, then you are a true leaver of home indeed. Daily you'll enjoy ten thousand gold coins at your disposal."

12.6

"Stream-enterers! Don't haphazardly allow any old master from who-knows-where [i.e., a bad teacher][147] to tattoo the seal onto your face [as if you were a prisoner or exiled person];[148] and then go around mouthing that 'I understand Chan!' or 'I understand the Way!' That kind of glibness, though it may flow like a waterfall,[149] is all karman that will send you to a hell. If you are a student of the Way who [beholds] reality as it truly is, you do not [waste your time] seeking after the worldly mistake [i.e., terms and language/glibness].[150] You urgently want to seek to behold reality as it truly is. If you can reach a beholding of reality as it truly is—the complete brightness [of enlightenment][151]—then you are, for the first time, done."

12.7

Question: "What is beholding reality as it truly is?"[152] The Master said, "At all [times and locations][153] it's simply a matter of your entering both 'worldling' and '*ārya*' [realms, i.e., the six rebirth realms from hells to *deva* heavens, and the four realms of *śrāvaka*, *pratyeka-buddha*, bodhisattva, and buddha], entering both 'impure' and 'pure' [realms, i.e., the same six and four realms],[154] entering 'lands of all the buddhas' [of the three times and ten directions],[155] entering 'the tower of Maitreya' [as the youth Sudhana does in the *Huayan Sutra* at the end of his visits to good teachers],[156] entering 'the *dharmadhātu* of Vairocana.'[157] [*That one person*, the true *person* who is constantly exiting and entering from the face-gate of all you, can] display any 'land' anywhere [as an *upāya*];[158] he [can] bring them into 'existence,' make them 'abide,' make them 'disintegrate,' and have them 'enter the void.'[159] [In the same way] buddhas 'appear in the world,' 'turn the great dharma wheel,' and thereafter 'enter nirvana': but there is no trace of their coming or going. You seek their 'birth-and-death,' which is ungrasp-able mentally. They [can] at once 'enter into the non-arising *dharmadhātu,*' 'playfully stroll throughout all the lands,' 'enter the lotus-womb world [of the *Huayan* assembly]':[160] exhaustively seeing that all dharmas are empty and unreal. All along there has only ever been the non-dependent Way-person[161] who is listening to this dharma talk—who is the mother of the buddhas. Therefore, the buddhas are born of non-dependence. If you awaken to non-dependence, then even 'buddhahood' becomes ungrasp-able mentally. Seeing *in that way* is [what I mean by] *beholding reality as it truly is.*"[162]

12.8

"Students are unable to apprehend this because they grasp terms and phrases, becoming hung up on such terms as 'worldling' and *'ārya'*; and, therefore, with their dharma eye beclouded, they can't see clearly.[163] For example, the 'twelve divisions of the teachings'[164] are all merely expres-sive explanations [logical principles designed to reveal the real/the 'fin-ger pointing at the moon'].[165] Students, not aware of this, right away erect their understanding on top of the terms and phrases of these expressive explanations. This is all the dependence [of samsaric wheel-turning],[166] falling into [the fallacy of gradual practice being the] 'cause' and [realiza-tion being the] 'effect.'[167] They will not avoid birth and death in the three realms.[168] You: if you're hankering after '[the supernormal power to freely] go or stay in samsara' or 'release from attachment, and freedom,'[169] then right now recognize the [true] *person* [the non-dependent Way-person*] listening to my dharma talk.[170] He has neither form nor character-istics, neither root nor source. He is not fixed anywhere—he is lively, like a fish waving its tail.[171] [In carrying out] all sorts of myriad *upāyas,* his venue of activities is simply *no place.*[172] This is why 'chasing after makes for further away, and seeking after makes for further astray.' This one we'll name the 'secret.'"

12.9

"Stream-enterers! This [human-body] companion of yours that is like a dream or a *māyā*—don't assume [that it is real].[173] In your sunset years or in your robust years things will go impermanent on you.[174] What on earth are you looking for to liberate yourself? Having secured a mouthful of rice, rather than whiling away the rest of your time mending your *kāṣāya* [monk's robe],[175] better that you seek out a teacher. Don't follow the same old routine, [aimlessly] chasing after pleasure.[176] You should regret the passing of time. Moment after moment [you are confronted by] impermanence: in gross terms by [the four elements of] 'earth,' 'water,' 'fire,' and 'wind'; [but] in subtle terms by [the four conditioned characteristics of] 'arising,' 'abiding,' 'changing,' and 'disintegrating'—by these four [conditioned] characteristics you are being driven. Stream-enterers! Right now you must recognize that these four [conditioned characterstics] are non-characteristics: [they are unreal] vishayas. You must leave off being smacked about by [unreal] vishayas [i.e., being turned upside down]!"[177]

12.10

Question: "What are the four types of [unreal] vishayas that have no characteristics?" The Master said, "You, in a single moment of 'being perplexed,' are being obstructed by 'the earth element.'[178] You, in a single moment of 'love,' are being drowned by 'the water element.'[179] You, in a single moment of 'anger,' are being burned by 'the fire element.'[180] You, in a single moment of 'joy,' are being blown about by 'the wind element.'[181] If you can [have the keen eyesight to] discern *in that way*, you will not be turned by vishayas. *Place* after *place* [you find yourself] you will use the vishayas. [When you discern *in that way*, throughout the worlds there will occur the six types of shaking:] the east will surge and the west will disappear; the south will surge and the north will disappear; the center will surge and the perimeter will disappear; the perimeter will surge and the center will disappear.[182] You will [be free to work miracles such as] walking on 'water' as if it were 'land,' and walking on 'land' as if it were 'water.'[183] Why is it like this? Because you have come to know that the 'four elements' are like a dream, like a *māyā*."

12.11

"Stream-enterers! You: the listening-to-the-dharma-right-now-*you* is not the-four-elements-you [the 'skin bag']. [It is *that one person* who] is capable of using the-four-elements-you.[184] If you can see *in that way*, right away [you can] go or stay [anywhere without obstruction in complete] freedom [like the lion at play].[185] According to my vision, there *is* no 'dharma' to dislike.[186] You: if you like '*ārya*,' '*ārya*' is just a [provisional] name for '*ārya*.'[187] There is a clique of students, [unaware of their very own living Mañjuśrī,] who look for Mañjuśrī on Mt. Wutai.[188] Already mistaken! 'Mt. Wutai' has no 'Mañjuśrī.' So you want to come to know Mañjuśrī? He's just *you*—in the venue of your [daily] activities at this very moment, never separate, with no room whatsoever for doubt— *this* is the living Mañjuśrī.[189] Your single moment of undifferentiated light itself is at all times and places the true Samantabhadra. Your single moment free of bondage, everywhere liberated, this is the dharma of the *Avalokiteśvara-samādhi*. [These three personages— 'Mañjuśrī,' 'Samantabhadra,' and 'Avalokiteśvara'—and their referents are] interchangeable, whether as master or as attendants. Once one is manifest, they are all manifest.[190] The one is the three; the three are one.[191] If you understand it *in that way*, then, for the first time, you may read the teachings [of the buddhas and bodhisattvas]."[192]

13.1

The Master instructed the sangha, "You students of the Way right now must have self-confidence. Don't search on the outside, invariably clambering up on top of those good-for-nothing [gimmick] vishayas [provisionally established as *upāyas* by teachers, i.e., the sutras and the old cases of Chan,] and not distinguishing at all between the wrong and the correct.[193] For example, 'there are patriarchs,' 'there are buddhas,' but these are all issues [only] within the leftovers [that we call] 'the teachings' [i.e., the buddha teachings and Chan records, such as this very one].[194] Say there were a person [a teaching master][195] who plucks out a single line [from those sutras and treatises], and says that he infers from it half-closed and half-open [meanings]:[196] all of sudden [you the student] are thrown into perplexity![197] You flail about in a panic, sniffing around in the byways, in a terrible bustle. A Superman[198] simply doesn't pass his days discussing [such silly topics as] 'kings and bandits,' 'right and wrong,' 'sex and worldly goods.'[199] *Here* [in my monastery/in beholding reality as it truly is], I do not discuss [such silly topics as] 'monk' or 'layman.' Whoever comes, I recognize him [the student/the true *person*] utterly.[200] Regardless of what position he's cropping up from,[201] all of the sounds, names, and written phrases [he chants] are [vishayas to me, unreal like] a dream, a *māyā*."[202]

I3.2

"Conversely, [instead of his sounds, names, and phrases] what I do see is the [true] *person* who 'rides' [makes use of, or 'turns'] the [unreal] vishayas;²⁰³ this is 'the mysterious purport of all the "buddhas."' [But even] a 'buddha' vishaya can't tell you: 'I am a "buddha" vishaya.' In any case,²⁰⁴ this non-dependent Way-*person* crops up riding [even such] vishayas. If there is a *person* who crops up and demands a 'buddha' of me, in response I manifest a vishaya of 'purity.'²⁰⁵ If there is a *person* who demands a 'bodhisattva' of me, in response I manifest a vishaya of 'compassion.'²⁰⁶ If there is a *person* who demands '*bodhi*' of me, in response I manifest a vishaya of the 'miraculous.' If there is a *person* who demands 'nirvana' of me, in response I manifest a vishaya of 'peaceful quiet.' The vishayas are of myriad types, but the [true] *person* [i.e., *that one person*] remains the same.²⁰⁷ Therefore, 'in response to beings [the *dharmakāya*] manifests forms [vishayas]: but they are like the moon's reflections on the water.'²⁰⁸

I3.3

"Stream-enterers! You: if you're thinking you want to attain [an under-standing] in accord with dharma [i.e., behold reality as it truly is],²⁰⁹ in the end you have to be an [iron-Han] Superman.²¹⁰ A wishy-washy weakling [who shifts in accordance with worldly convention] won't do.²¹¹ Keeping your clarified butter in a cracked pottery vessel—it's the same thing.²¹² The great vessel [the one of extra-superior sense faculties]²¹³ must not get discombobulated by [other] people/[other] *persons*/'the *person*' [by intellec-tual understanding, emotional assessments, calculations, and plans].²¹⁴ Whatever *place* you are, play the master; every *place* you stand is reality.²¹⁵ Whatever [vishayas invasively] come at you, don't [take a] passive [stance].²¹⁶ If you [experience even] a single moment of being perplexed, Māra will enter your mind.²¹⁷ Even [in the case of] a bodhisattva, if he were to fall prey to perplexity, Māra, who *is* samsara,²¹⁸ will run into a suitable oppor-tunity. Above all, stop thoughts [through Chan sitting]²¹⁹ and don't seek on the outside. When things come [at you, retrain] the light [of the true mind back upon yourself].²²⁰ Just have confidence in your immediate venue of activities. There is *not a single thing to do* [i.e., not a single thought arises].²²¹ For you—with a single thought—the [one] mind [of solitary brightness] produces the three realms [the three poisons of greed, anger, and stupidity]; with [this production] as a condition, it [the one

mind of solitary brightness] undergoes fragmentation into the six 'dusts.'²²²
In your current venue of activities [the venue of walking, standing, sitting,
lying down, putting on your clothes, and eating meals], what exactly could
be lacking?²²³ In a moment, though you 'enter pure [lands],' 'enter defiled
[lands],' 'enter the tower of Maitreya,' 'enter the Land of Three Eyes' [where
the monk Sudarśana dwelled in the *Huayan Sutra*]:²²⁴ playfully strolling
everywhere, all you see are only empty names."²²⁵

13.4

Question: "What sort of thing is the Land of Three Eyes?"²²⁶ The Master
says, "I, the same as you, when 'entering the land of purity,' don the costume [i.e., manifest a vishaya] of 'purity' and speak as 'the *dharmakāya*
buddha';²²⁷ or when 'entering the land of non-differentiation,' don the costume of 'non-differentiation' and speak as 'the *sambhogakāya* buddha';²²⁸
or when 'entering the land of liberation,' don the costume of 'radiance' and
speak as 'the *nirmāṇakāya* buddha.'²²⁹ These 'Lands of Three Eyes' are all
dependent [illusory] magical transformations.²³⁰ According to the sutra
and treatise scholars, the *dharmakāya* is the fundamental [substance], and
the *sambhogakāya* and *nirmāṇakaya* are merely functions of it.²³¹ In my vision, [that sort of] *'dharmakāya'* does not have the ability to speak dharma.²³²
[Scholars of the sutras and treatises come up with such convoluted claptrap as:] 'Therefore, an ancient said, "The postulation of [buddha-] bodies
is grounded in doctrinal points; the discussion of [buddha-] lands is based
in substance."' [But according to my vision,] we patently know that the
'dharma-nature bodies' and 'dharma-nature lands' are both [nothing but
unreal] provisionally erected dharmas,²³³ 'lands' of supernormal powers
dependent [upon alchemical recipes, charms, mantras, etc.].²³⁴ These are
like an empty fist or yellow leaves, [games] used to distract a [crying]
child.²³⁵ The spikes of the puncture-vine [i.e., furze] or the water chestnut,
a dried bone—what juice is in there to search for? [I.e., there is no juice in
there to be gotten at.]²³⁶ Outside mind there are no dharmas; inside [mind]
is also mentally ungraspable. What thing are you seeking?"

13.5

"You: you say all over the place: '[The path] is [a matter of] cultivation [fol-
lowed by] realization.'²³⁷ Big mistake! Even if you got something through
'cultivation,' that itself would all be karman [by which the wheel] of samsara

[turns].²³⁸ You say [such things as]: 'The myriad practices of the six *pāramitās* are all to be cultivated.' In my vision, this is all the generation of karman. 'Pursuing buddhahood' and 'pursuing dharma' is karman generation [that will drop you into] a hell. 'Seeking to become a bodhisattva' is also the generation of karman. 'Reading the sutras and reading the teachings' is also the generation of karman.²³⁹ 'Buddhas' and 'patriarchal masters' are *persons* with *nothing-to-do*. Therefore, [for them,] 'with outflows,' 'conditioned,' 'without outflows,' 'unconditioned'—these are [just] pure karman.²⁴⁰ There is a certain type of bald-headed hack [i.e., bad teacher],²⁴¹ who, having scarfed up a belly full of food, hops off to engage in cross-legged Chan sitting practice. [While doing sitting] he suppresses thought-outflows [the *kleśas* of greed, hostility, and stupidity],²⁴² not allowing them to arise; he dislikes noise and seeks quiet. This is a non-Buddhist method. The Patriarchal Master said, 'You: if you "fix mind and gaze at quiet," "raise mind and illuminate the external," "gather in mind and clarify the internal," "coagulate mind and enter *samādhi*," those kinds [of methods] are all [karmic] performance.'²⁴³ It's none other than *you*: right now, the [true] *person, in that way* listening to the dharma. [So] how do you intend to 'cultivate' him [i.e., *that one person*/the true *person*], 'realize' him, 'adorn' him [with the thirty-two major characteristics and eighty minor marks of a buddha]?²⁴⁴ He [i.e., *that one person*/the true *person*] is not a being that can be 'cultivated,' not a being that can be 'adorned.'²⁴⁵ But if you make him [i.e., *that one person*/the true *person*] do the adorning, all [sentient and insentient] things²⁴⁶ would be adorned.²⁴⁷ You must not make a mistake here."

13.6

"Stream-enterers! You buy into the words of old [heterodox] masters of this sort and consider them to be the true Way.²⁴⁸ [You think:] 'The teacher is incredible! With my mind of a worldling, I don't have the confidence to fathom this elder monk.'²⁴⁹ Blind imbeciles! All your life you are stuck at this level of beholding, wasting your own [perfectly good] pair of eyes [the true eyes that your father and mother gave you at birth].²⁵⁰ Just like donkeys atop ice [who appear anxious and fearful, unable to proceed],²⁵¹ you are so cold, you're mute,²⁵² [thinking:] 'I don't have the confidence to disparage the teacher, for fear of producing [bad] oral karman.' Stream-enterers! A great teacher has the confidence to disparage the buddhas and patriarchs, pronounce on the falseness or correctness of the world's [teachers],²⁵³ discard the teachings of the canon, curse small children [students of small karmic roots and bad teachers][254]; and, in the midst of [both vishayas that] go against him and [vishayas that] go in his direction, he is on the lookout for the [true] *person*.[255] Therefore [as in the *Huayan Sutra*, when the youth Sudhana journeys for twelve years to get to the country of Vanavāsin, where he searches everywhere for the good teacher Vimuktika]: 'I, for twelve years, have been looking for a single karman, but not even a mustard-seed's worth of it is mentally graspable!'[256] [But] if you've got a Chan master who is [timid] like a new wife,[257] afraid of ejection from the cloister and the ending of his meal ticket—there's no peace or happiness. From of old our predecessors, wherever they went, no one had confidence in them; and they were driven out. Only after [such trials] can one's worth be known. If everyone affirms you wherever you go, what use would you be? Therefore, the single roar of the lion [the true Chan master] splits the brains of the jackals."[258]

13.7

"Stream-enterers! All over the place it is said [by bad teachers], 'There is a Way that should be cultivated and a dharma that should be realized,' and you reply: 'What dharma [must I] realize, and what Way [must I] cultivate?'[259] In your current venue of activities, what exactly is lacking? What needs to be mended by 'cultivation?'[260] Freshly minted pint-sized monks, not understanding, right away put their confidence in these wild-fox demons [heterodox masters][261] and comply with [the confused Way] they preach.[262] [These heterodox masters] bind them [the students],[263] saying: 'Only when principle [internal realization-awakening] and practice [directed toward external characteristics] are in correspondence,[264] and you protect against the three karmans [of body, speech, and mind; i.e., guard against committing the ten evil actions proscribed by the precepts],[265] will you for the first time be capable of becoming a buddha.' People who speak like this are as [numerous as] the fine rains of spring.[266] An ancient has said, 'If on the road you meet a *person* who has comprehended the Way, you absolutely must not [concern yourself] with the Way [i.e, must not address the topic of the Way].'[267] Therefore, it is said, 'If a *person* cultivates the Way, the Way does not "work," and the myriad types of false vishayas vie to take the lead [i.e., the 84,000 *kleśas* vie to arise].[268] But once the sword of *prajñā* crops up [and eradicates the *kleśa* bandits], there is not a single thing.[269] When "brightness" is not yet revealed, "darkness" is bright.'[270] Therefore, an ancient has said, 'The mind of your usual self [as in your daily activities] is itself the Way.'"[271]

13.8

"Venerables! What are you seeking? The Way-*person* of non-dependence right now in front of me, listening to the dharma [the true *person*], clear as clear, has never lacked for anything.[272] You: if you're thinking you want to be no different from the buddhas who are our patriarchs, just see *in that way*. There is no need for you to be indecisive. If, for you, [the *tathatā* gate of the one] mind and [the arising-disappearing gate of the one] mind are not [in a state of] of differentiation, we call it the living patriarch.[273] If the [one] mind [is in a state of] differentiation [into the two gates of *tathatā* and arising-disappearing], then '*svabhāva*' and 'characteristics' [for you] will be separate.[274] When the [one] mind is not [in a state of] differentiation, then [for you] '*svabhāva*' and 'characteristics' will not be separate."[275]

13.9

Question: "The place where [the *tathatā* gate of the one] mind and [the arising-disappearing gate of the one] mind are not [in a state of] differentiation—what sort of place is that?" The Master says: "Just as you are about to ask [that question], already they are [in a state of] differentiation, and [for you] '*svabhāva*' and 'characteristics' are split up [i.e., set your tongue in motion, and you have already gone astray].[276] Stream-enterers! Make no mistake. Mundane and supramundane dharmas[277] all lack *svabhāva*, and they are non-arising.[278] They exist in name only—even the names are empty. It's just that you think those meaningless [empty] names actually exist.[279] Big mistake! Even if they existed, they would all be vishayas that are but dependent [illusory] magical transformations.[280] There would be a dependent [illusory magical-transformation] '*bodhi*,' a dependent [illusory magical-transformation] 'nirvana,' a dependent [illusory magical-transformation] 'liberation,' a dependent [illusory magical-transformation] 'three buddha-bodies,' a dependent [illusory magical-transformation] 'cognizable-and-cognition,' a dependent [illusory magical-transformation] 'bodhisattva,' and a dependent [illusory magical-transformation] 'buddha.'[281] In a dependent-magical-transformation '[buddha] land,' what thing would you be looking for? Right down to and including the 'three vehicles' and 'twelve divisions of the teachings': they *all* are obsolete papers [now useful only for the toilet] to wipe away feces [the foulness of the *kleśas* and thought of the unreal].[282] 'Buddhas' are *māyā* bodies [without any reality at all], and 'patriarchs' are nothing more than [decrepit] old *bhikṣus*.[283] You, in any case, are born [ready-made]—aren't you!?[284] You: if you seek a buddha, you will be in the clutches of a Māra [named] 'the buddha.' You: if you seek a patriarch, you will be bound by a Māra [named] 'patriarch.' You: if you have *any* seeking, it will all be suffering. It's best if you have *not a thing to do*."[285]

13.10

"There is a type of bald *bhikṣu* who says to students, 'A buddha is the ultimate. Only after he has practiced for three incalculable kalpas, and the effects have come to fulfillment, does he at last attain the Way.' Stream-enterers! You: if you say 'a buddha' is the ultimate, then why, after eighty years, at the town of Kuśinagara, between two *śāla* trees, did [the Buddha Śākyamuni] lie down on his side and die? Where is this 'buddha' now? Patently this is no different from our own 'living' and 'dying.'[286] You say 'the one who has the thirty-two major characteristics and eighty minor marks is a buddha.' [If that is so,] then the wheel-turning noble king [who also is endowed with the major and minor marks] would undoubtedly be a *tathāgata*![287] Patently, [the wheel-turning king, the major and minor marks, and a buddha] are *māyās*.[288] An ancient[289] said, 'The marks on the whole body of the *tathāgata* were for the sake of according with worldly expectations [i.e., an *upāya*, just for according with the mental dispositions of the world's mass of beings].[290] Fearing that people might produce annihilationist views [that deny cause and effect], as an *upāya* he erected empty words.[291] Provisionally, we speak of the "thirty-two" and the "eighty," but they are just empty sounds. A body of existence [that can be characterized by major characteristics and minor marks] is not the *bodhi* body; no-characteristics is the true form [of a buddha].'"

13.11

"You say: 'A buddha has the six supernormal powers—it is incredible!'[292] All the *devas*, divine immortals, *asuras*, and demons of great strength[293] also have supernormal powers—are they to be regarded as buddhas? Stream-enterers! Make no mistake. For example, when the [king of the] *asuras* fought a battle with the *deva* Indra and lost, he led his 84,000 troops into hiding inside a single pore of a fiber of a lotus root.[294] Doesn't that [illustrate the same supernormal powers as] an *ārya*? [The examples] I have raised are no more than supernormal powers [attained as a fruit] of karman [i.e., as a result of the power of actions committed in past births] and supernormal powers of dependence [i.e., the illusory, 'dependent-on-something-else' sleights-of-hand of mundane conjurers].²⁹⁵ They are not like the six supernormal powers of a buddha: entering the realm of forms but not being discombobulated by 'forms'; entering the realm of sounds but not being discombobulated by 'sounds'; entering the realm of smellables but not being discombobulated by 'smellables'; entering the realm of tastables but not being discombobulated by 'tastables'; entering the realm of touchables but not being discombobulated by 'touchables'; and entering the *dharmadhātu* but not being being discombobulated by 'dharmas.'²⁹⁶ Therefore, the six vishayas—'forms,' 'sounds,' 'smellables,' 'tastables,' 'touchables,' and 'dharmas'—once they have been understood to be empty, they cannot bind *this* non-dependent Way-*person* [the true *person*]. Even though he has a five-*skandhas* [human] body with outflows,²⁹⁷ he's precisely [an immortal] with the supernormal power of earth-walking [i.e., literally, an 'earth-walking immortal' who has attained long life]."²⁹⁸

13.12

"Stream-enterers! The true 'buddha' is formless; the true 'dharma' is without characteristics. All you are doing is 'concocting special effects' [and layering them] on top of *māyās* [i.e., creating calculations and conjectures on top of *māyās*].²⁹⁹ Even supposing you did attain [something], it would all be [like the illusory magical-transformations] of a wild-fox demon [a bad teacher]—certainly not a true 'buddha.' It would be [the inferior level of] beholding of a follower of an outside Way.³⁰⁰ To begin with, the true student of the Way never acknowledges 'buddha,' never acknowledges 'bodhisattva' and 'arhat,' never acknowledges 'excellent [karmic recompense] in the three realms.'³⁰¹ Vast [as the great sky and walking in] solitariness,³⁰² he is not arrested by things. Heaven and earth could be overturned, [and he would still say,] 'I have no uncertainty.'³⁰³ Should 'the buddhas of the ten directions' appear before him, he would not have a single moment of delight. Should 'the three [bad rebirth] paths'—hells, [*pretas*, and animals]—suddenly appear, he would not have a single moment of terror.³⁰⁴ Why is this so? In my vision, all dharmas are empty. When [the one mind] transforms, there is [seeming] existence; when [the one mind] does not transform, there is none.³⁰⁵ The 'three realms' are mind-only; the 'myriad dharmas' are consciousness-only.³⁰⁶ Therefore, [all dharmas are like] dreams, *māyās*, 'flowers' in the sky—why put yourself to the trouble of catching hold of them?"³⁰⁷

13.13

"There's just you, the stream-enterer—the very *person* listening to the dharma right now in front of me [the true *person*]—who enters 'fire' but does not burn, enters 'water' but does not drown, enters 'the hells of the three bad rebirth paths' as though enjoying a garden viewing, enters 'the *preta* and animal rebirth paths' but accrues none of the effects of karman.[308] Why is this so? There is no 'dharma' to be abhorred [and no 'dharma' to be liked].[309] You: if you [as it says in Baozhi's *Praises of the Mahāyāna*] 'love "*ārya*" and hate "worldling," you will bob up and down in the sea of samsara. The *kleśas* [arise] from "mind"; and so, when there is "no mind," how can the *kleśas* arrest you? Not troubling yourself with discrimination and the seizing of characteristics, spontaneously you will attain the Way in a second.'[310] But if you are about to bustle along down byways in your practice, then, even after three incalculable kalpas, you will still be returning to samsara. It is not as good as *nothing-to-do*: cross-legged sitting on the sitting platform [in the Sangha Hall] within the 'Chan grove.'"[311]

13.14

"Stream-enterers! For example, students come from all over the place, and when [the rituals of courtesy involved in] the meeting of guest and host have been completed,[312] right away [a student throws out] a phrase [or two],[313] and there is a face-off with the teacher.[314] A [tortuous question laden with] *upāya*-phraseology pinched up by the student[315] is flung in the teacher's face [to test him; and the student thinks:] 'Let's see whether you recognize this![316] If you[317] recognize that this is an [unreal] vishaya,[318] you'll grab it and immediately throw it down a hole [i.e., won't fall into the trap].'[319] The student then is back to normal [i.e., he doesn't take any action whatsoever],[320] and only then does he demand a word of instruction from the teacher [i.e., this Han (the student) takes his time and slowly makes one more presentation].[321] As usual, [the teacher] rips it away [under the rubric 'one more shout'].[322] The student says: 'Superior insight! What a great teacher!'[323] Then [the teacher] says: 'You, [the student][324] haven't a clue about good and bad.' Or, for example, the teacher seizes a wad of vishayas [*upāya* words and phrases], and plays with it right in front of the student's face [to test the student].[325] The [student] in front of him[326] [has the keen eyesight to] discern [what is going on] and time after time plays the host, not getting discombobulated by the vishayas. The teacher [in the manner of one of Maudgalyāyana's miracles] instantly 'manifests a half-body,'[327] and the student instantly gives a shout. The teacher again enters into all manner of verbal expressions in order to topple the student [into confusion].[328] The student says: 'Doesn't know good from bad, the old bald-headed hack!' And the teacher sighs: 'A stream-enterer who [beholds] reality as it truly is!'"

13.15

"Or, for example, there are teachers all over the place who have no ability to distinguish the heterodox from the correct. A student comes and asks about *'bodhi,'* 'nirvana,' 'the three buddha-bodies,' 'cognizable-and-cognition,' and the blind master [with the level of understanding of a Seat Master] then gives him explanations [of doctrinal points].[329] When he is rebuked by the student, he instantly takes the stick and whacks him: 'Such talk is rude!' [The student says:] 'Of course—you, teacher, lack the eye. You're in no position to be angry with anyone else.' There is a type of bald-headed hack who doesn't know good from bad. He [is quick to] point toward the east and gesticulate toward the west [i.e., without rhyme or reason he uses his hands to concoct special effects]; he [runs around repeating such fatuous gabble as:] When the weather is clear, 'Great weather!' and when it's rainy, 'Fine moisture!'; [he engages in such 'Chan talk' as:] 'Lanterns and open-air pillars are fine.'[330] You'd best see how many hairs [they have left] in their eyebrows [i.e., because eyebrows fall out as a result of false speech].[331] . . . [332] Students don't understand [that they are disseminating false teachings] and immediately come to adore them.[333] The whole lot of them [the bad teachers][334] are wild-fox demons and [water] spirits.[335] They are given a smirk and a titter by the good students, who say: 'These blind old bald-headed [hacks] are discombobulating the whole world.'"

13.16

"Stream-enterers! One who leaves home must train in the Way. For example, I myself in past days took great pains over the *vinaya*. I also inquired into the sutras and treatises.[336] [But] later I came to realize that these, being [one-off] medicines to save the world, were [just] expressive verbal formulations.[337] Thereupon I all-at-once dropped [the sutras, vinaya, and treatises].[338] Searching for the Way, I came to practice Chan. Later I encountered great teachers,[339] and my eye of the Way became clear. For the first time I could recognize the old preceptors of the world, and know which were heterodox and which correct. It is not that I could immediately understand, based merely on the fact that I was born ready-made.[340] In any case, it was after personal investigation [of *this matter*] and refining [my mind], that I [all-at-once] awoke one dawn [as the *tathāgata* himself did when the bright star came out]."[341]

13.17

"Stream-enterers! If you're thinking you want to attain a beholding [of reality] according to dharma [that is, a beholding of reality as it truly is],[342] you must not get discombobulated by *persons* [i.e., by heterodox masters]/by [other] *persons*/by 'the *person*.']"[343] On the inside [within the mind] or on the outside [external vishayas], whatever you meet, instantly kill it [i.e., cut off the notion of something upon the moment of meeting it].[344] Meeting 'a buddha,' kill 'a buddha' [i.e., do not maintain the notion of 'a view unique to a buddha']. Meeting 'a patriarch,' kill 'a patriarch' [i.e., do not maintain the notion of 'a Chan-patriarch level of understanding']. Meeting 'an arhat,' kill 'an arhat' [i.e., do not maintain the notion of 'an arhat level of understanding']. Meeting 'your mother and father,' kill 'your mother and father' [i.e., do not maintain the notion of 'ignorance' and 'passion']. Meeting 'your relatives,' kill 'your relatives' [i.e., do not maintain the notion of 'the *kleśas*']. [In this manner] for the first time you will attain liberation.[345] You will not be arrested by things [such as terms like 'buddha' and 'patriarch'], and you will pass through in freedom.[346] Of those who are training in the Way all over, there has never been one who cropped up not relying on things [i.e., not relying on knowledge/not getting hung up on those good-for-nothing gimmick vishayas].[347] *Here* [in my monastery/in beholding reality as it truly is] I whack them head to toe.[348] If they crop up [doing some sort of performance] with their hands [such as clapping, holding up fingers, lifting up the sitting mat, picking up the stick, etc.], I whack [the clapping, holding up of the fingers, lifting up of the sitting mat, picking up of the stick, etc., of] the hands.[349] If they crop up [with words and phrases, making a hissing sound, clenching the teeth, etc.,] in their mouths, then I whack [the words and phrases, hissing sound, clenching of the teeth, etc.,] in their mouths.[350] If they crop up [with opening and closing, staring, winking, raising the eyebrows, etc.] of the eyes, then I whack [the opening and closing, staring, winking, rasing the eyebrows, etc.] of the eyes.[351] There has never been a single one who cropped up in solitary liberation [i.e., not depending on anything—the non-dependent Way-*person*].[352] They all crop up [riding in] on their good-for-nothing gimmick vishayas [provisionally established as *upāyas*] by the ancients [i.e., bringing the oral teachings of the buddhas and patriarchs and the old cases of Chan]."[353]

13.18

"I have no 'dharma' [of the sort that can be] given to them.[354] Curing the illness [of no confidence] and releasing bonds are all it is.[355] You stream-enterers from all over, try it out—crop up without relying on anything. I'd sure like to haggle with you![356] Ten years, five years, [however long it has been,][357] and there has not been a single [true] *person*. They have all been dependent upon blades of grass and attached to leaves [i.e., lacking a solitary liberation proceeding from their own hearts and minds]— bamboo-and-tree spirits and wild-fox demons [i.e., students dependent upon the ancients' schemes and models—akin to *pretas* or spirits in the intermediate state between death and rebirth].[358] In confusion they chew on every sort of clod of dung [i.e., the good-for-nothing terms and words of the buddhas and patriarchs].[359] Blind [low-down] Hans![360] Wastefully they use up what the lay donors from all over [have given them], saying: 'I am a leaver of home who beholds reality *in that way*.' To you I say: There is neither 'buddha' nor 'dharma,' neither 'practice' nor 'realization.' Just what are you trying to seek for down these sorts of byways? Blind [low-down] Hans! You are placing a head on top of your head [just like Yajña-datta does in the *Śūraṃgama Sūtra*]![361] It's none other than *you*: what's lacking?"[362]

13.19

"Stream-enterers! It's none other than *you*: in your venue of activities, right in front of you, no different from that of the buddhas who are our patriarchs. You just don't have confidence in this, and right away proceed to external seeking. Make no mistake! Externally there is no dharma; even the internal is ungraspable mentally.[363] Rather than appropriating the words from my mouth, it would be better for you to give it a rest and have *nothing-to-do*.[364] [Thoughts that] have already arisen—do not continue them.[365] [Thoughts that] have not yet arisen—you must not let them get loose.³⁶⁶ It would do you more good than ten-years' traveling on foot [throughout the world trying to locate a teacher in order to seek the dharma and realization].³⁶⁷ According to my vision, there's no "yadda, yadda, yadda" to it [i.e., it's not tedious, verbose, or redundant].³⁶⁸ It's just a matter of being your usual self [as in your daily activities]. Put on your clothes, eat your food, and pass your time—*not-a-thing-to-do*.³⁶⁹ You who come from all over the place are all *with-mind* [a mind of mental work, as opposed to *no-mind*], seeking 'the Buddha' and seeking 'the dharma,' seeking 'libera-tion,' seeking to 'escape the three realms.'³⁷⁰ Idiots! You want to 'escape the three realms,' but exactly what *place* do you think you're going to?³⁷¹ The 'buddhas' and 'patriarchs' [that you are seeking] are [only] terms that bestow bondage.³⁷² Do you want to know 'the three realms?' They are not apart from the mind ground of you who are listening to the dharma right now [i.e., the true *person*]. Your single moment of greed is the desire realm. Your single moment of anger is the form realm. Your single moment of stupidity is the formless realm. They are the funishings that come with your house. 'The three realms' won't say to you: 'We are "the three realms."' In any case, it's you, the stream-enterer, right now before me, clearly casting your light on all things and sizing up the world [i.e., *that one per-son*/the true *person*], who does the attaching of names to the three realms."

13.20

"Venerables! The form-body of the four elements is impermanent, right down to the spleen, stomach, liver, gallbladder, hair, nails, teeth—you are seeing nothing more than emptiness of all dharmas.³⁷³ Your stopping [movement of] mind for a single moment, let's call that 'the *bodhi* tree.'³⁷⁴ Your inability to stop [movement of] mind for a single moment, let's call that 'the *avidyā* tree.'³⁷⁵ '*Avidyā*' is not fixed anywhere; '*avidyā*' has no be-ginning and has no end.³⁷⁶ You: if moment after moment you cannot bring [mind] to a stop, right away you're up the *avidyā* tree! Right away you've entered the four forms of birth in the six rebirth paths, [being reborn as an animal that] wears fur and sports horns.³⁷⁷ You: if you bring [mind] to a stop, right away it is the [buddha] realm of the pure *[dharma]kāya*.³⁷⁸ Your single moment of non-arising *is* being up in the *bodhi* tree,³⁷⁹ *is* having the supernormal powers of magical transformation throughout the three realms, *is* [the supernormal power to] magically transform your body through thought,³⁸⁰ *is* dharma joy [wisdom] and *dhyāna* delight [*samādhi*],³⁸¹ *is* [having the ability] to radiate light from your body.³⁸² Thinking of clothes, a thousand brocades [appear]; thinking of food, you will be replete with a hundred flavorful [dishes].³⁸³ You will never again face the possibility of an unnatural affliction [or an unnatural death].³⁸⁴ [However,] '*bodhi*' [like '*avidyā*'] is not fixed anywhere;³⁸⁵ therefore, it [too] is mentally ungraspable."³⁸⁶

13.21

"Stream-enterers! The Superman Han [true *person*]—just *what* in the hell could he ever have doubts about? [In your] venue of activities right now [your very own *original portion*]—just *who* in the hell is it?³⁸⁷ If you can catch on, then just make practical application, and don't get hung up on names anymore.³⁸⁸ This one we'll name 'the mysterious purport.' If you can see *in that way*, then there is no 'dharma' [i.e., no 'vishaya'] to be abhorred. An ancient said, 'Mind is spun around by the myriad vishayas. This spinning really works in mysterious ways. If you track the [four] flows [of the *kleśas*-and-desire, views, love, and *avidyā*], you will come to recognize the [mind] nature, and be free of [the categories of] "joy and sorrow.""³⁸⁹

13.22

"Stream-enterers! As for coming to understand the Chan personal-realization-of-the-meaning-beyond-words—it is a series of death-defying efforts.³⁹⁰ The *person* who trains [in Chan] absolutely must be on high alert. When a host and a guest see each other, right away there is a back-and-forth exchange [of question and answer].³⁹¹ Sometimes in response to the other, one manifests [unreal] forms [vishayas, like the moon's reflections on water].³⁹² Sometimes [a teacher deploys] an unreserved functioning [of the buddha nature—i.e., the occasions on which the teacher rights his sitting posture or remains silent for a long time or bows his head or returns to the *fangzhang*].³⁹³ Sometimes, using an *upāya*, [a teacher] makes as if to be 'happy' or 'angry.'³⁹⁴ Sometimes [a teacher] 'manifests a half-body' [like the Buddha's disciple Maudgalyāyana, the first in supernormal powers].³⁹⁵ Sometimes [a teacher] 'rides a lion' [using the great wisdom of the bodhisattva Mañjuśrī to approach beings].³⁹⁶ Sometimes [a teacher] 'rides the king of elephants' [using the great practice of bodhisattva Samantabhadra to approach beings].³⁹⁷ A student of reality as it truly is instantly gives a shout and starts off with 'holding out a [painter's] saucer of hide glue' [to test the teacher].³⁹⁸ The teacher does not recognize that this is a vishaya [an *upāya*]. He instantly mounts the vishaya and concocts special effects.[399] The student instantly gives a shout, but the former [the teacher] makes no attempt to let go of [the vishaya].[400] This is a *gao-huang* disease, which is untreatable [and fatal].[401] This is called 'the guest's gazing at the host.' Sometimes the teacher doesn't hold up anything [i.e., utters not a word, remaining singlemindedly silent],[402] and every time the student asks a question, [the teacher] rips it away [i.e., shows no involvement with intellectual knowledge].[403] Though the student has been ripped, to the death he will not let go.[404] This is 'the host's gazing at the guest.'"

13.23

"Sometimes there is a student who, corresponding to a vishaya of 'purity' [i.e., not relying on a single thing, coming in the non-dependence of solitary liberation, not asking about the buddhadharma or the intention of the Chan patriarchal masters], comes before the teacher.[405] The teacher, [having the keen eyesight to] discern that it is a vishaya, takes it and throws it down a hole. The student says: 'Such a splendid teacher!' [The teacher scolds]: 'Tsk![406] You don't know good from bad.'[407] The student instantly bows.[408] This is called 'the host's gazing at the host.' Sometimes there is a student in a cangue with a lock who comes before the teacher [i.e., a student who is bound by the buddha teachings and the words of the Chan patriarchs comes to present his level of understanding].[409] The teacher puts another cangue with a lock on top of that one [i.e., adds another layer of thought of the unreal to the heaps of thought of the unreal brought in by the student].[410] The student is ecstatic. Neither one can evaluate the other. This is called 'the guest's gazing at the guest.'[411] Venerables! This [fourfold guest-and-host theme] I've raised here is for distinguishing Māras [i.e., seeing through demonic bad teachers] and selecting out what differs [from the Chan personal-realization-of-the-meaning-beyond-words, teaching the students of the world] to know the wrong and the correct."[412]

13.24

"Stream-enterers! Reality [free of] unreal consciousness [produced by false discrimination] is very difficult [to actuate], the buddhadharma being subtle and not obvious.[413] But you've pretty much got the ability to attain it.[414]—All day long I'm calling a spade a spade for 'em, but no student pays any heed!⁴¹⁵ Again and again and again, you tramp your feet all over the place⁴¹⁶ in pitch-black darkness with the lantern flame out [i.e., lacking understanding].⁴¹⁷ [But you, the one doing the tramping, are] the clear, solitary brightness devoid of even a single describable attribute [the true *person*].⁴¹⁸ You students' confidence is insufficient and right away on top of names and phrases you raise up understanding. Even when you are approaching fifty, you are [still] intently schlepping corpses [the 'dead words' of heterodox masters/your physical body] down byways, running around all-under-heaven [in search of a teacher and realization], shouldering your baggage [the written word, the injunctions of the ancients/ understanding based on the written word/perplexity arising from terms and phrases/ordinary traveling baggage].⁴¹⁹ There will come a day [when Yama] will exact 'straw-sandal money!'"⁴²⁰

13.25

"Venerables! I preach that there are no dharmas on the outside [external vishayas], but then students misunderstand and immediately [proceed to] construct an understanding on the inside [within the mind]: right away doing '[cross-legged] sitting facing a wall, tongue pressing against the roof of the mouth, absorbed and still.'⁴²¹ They take this to be the buddhadharma of the [Chan] patriarchal gate. Big mistake! You: if you were to take the vishaya of 'stillness' and 'purity' [wall contemplation and silent sitting] as [the ultimate],⁴²² then you would be [making the mistake of] recognizing *avidyā* as your master.⁴²³ An ancient said, 'The deep pit of darkness [into which those who excessively love Chan sitting fall] is truly to be feared.' [He meant] precisely this.⁴²⁴ [On the other hand,] you: if you [start] thinking that 'movement' is the [ultimate], why then the grasses and trees all have the ability to move—wouldn't they be the Way as well?⁴²⁵ Therefore, [in these examples of moving grasses and trees, and unmoving cross-legged sitting], 'movement' is [nothing but] the 'wind element'; 'stillness' is [nothing but] the 'earth element': 'Movement' and 'stillness' both lack *svabhāva* [and exist in name only]. You: if you [set out to] pin him [the true *person/that one person*] down in the *place* of 'movement,' then he takes a stand in the *place* of 'stillness.'⁴²⁶ You: if you [set out to] pin him down in the *place* of 'stillness,' then he takes a stand in the *place* of 'movement.'⁴²⁷ [He is] like a fish that is [usually] submerged in a spring; it stirs up waves [on the surface] in a spontaneous leap [and thus is not fixed in vishayas of 'movement' or 'stillness'].⁴²⁸ Venerables! 'Movement' and 'stillness' are two sorts of vishayas. In any case, once a non-dependent Way-*person*, one uses 'movement' and uses 'stillness.'"

13.26

"Students come from all over the place, and *here* [in my monastery/in beholding reality as it truly is] I sort them according to three types of con-figurations of sense faculties.[429] If [a student of] B-minus [middle-low] configuration of sense faculties comes, I instantly rip away his vishayas [i.e., all the ready-made characteristics of forms in the questions which the student brings], but don't eliminate his 'dharma' [i.e., the mental con-struct of 'the true *person*' or 'the *original portion*' brought by the student].[430] Or if [a student of] B-plus [middle-high] configuration of sense faculties comes, I instantly rip away both his vishayas and his 'dharma.' If [a stu-dent of] A-plus [high-high] configuration of sense faculties comes, I don't rip away either the vishayas, or 'the dharma,' or 'the [true] *person*.'[431] If a *person* comes with a level of beholding [reality as it truly is] that is off the charts,[432] *here* [in my monastery/in beholding reality as it truly is] I in-stantly [employ] unreserved functioning [of the buddha nature—such as wordlessly bowing the head, returning to the *fangzhang*, turning to take a look, correcting sitting posture, etc.], and do not put him through [any ranking according to] configuration of sense faculties.[433] Venerables! Having arrived *here* [in my monastery/in beholding reality as it truly is/at the *place* of the unreserved functioning of the buddha nature], the stu-dent's dynamism is impervious to [any blowing] wind[434] and [is like] a spark from a stone or a lightning bolt that passes [in the blink of an eye].[435] [But] if the pupils of the student's eyes show a [fleeting] movement, then he already will lack any relationship [to the unreserved functioning of the buddha nature].[436] [An ancient said,] 'Make the mind turn in a certain di-rection, and you are already in error; set in motion [a single] thought, and you have already gone astray.'[437] [However,] the one who has an under-standing [of reality as it truly is] is never separate from what is right before his eyes [the great Way].[438] Venerables! You shoulder [such trav-eling gear as] your bowl bag and sack of shit [physical body], running around byways seeking 'the buddha' and seeking 'the dharma.'[439] The one [*that one person*/the true *person*] rushing around right now *in that way*—just who do you think *he* is?[440] [*That one person*] is lively like a fish waving its tail—[*he*] has no base [i.e., *he* is not fixed anywhere].[441] Try to round [*him*] up—[*he*] doesn't coalesce; prod [*him*]—[*he*] doesn't disperse.[442]

Seek [him]—the further away [he is]; don't seek [him]—[he's] right in front of you. The divine sound [of *that one person*] is fillling your ears.[443] If you don't have confidence [in *that one person*], then even a lifetime's toil is futile."[444]

13.27

"Stream-enterers! [Like the youth Sudhana, *that one person*/the true *person*] in a single moment enters 'the lotus-treasury world,' enters 'the land of Vairocana,'[445] enters 'the land of liberation,' enters 'the land of supernormal powers,' enters 'the land of purity,'[446] enters 'the *dharmadhātu*,' enters 'defiled [lands]' and 'pure [lands],' enters 'worldling' and '*ārya*,' enters '[the rebirth paths of] *pretas* and animals':[447] anywhere he [*that one person*/the true *person*] searches, he sees no samsaric [characteristics] at all—only empty names.[448] *Māyās*, 'flowers' in the sky—don't make work for yourself clutching at them. 'Getting' and 'losing,' 'right' and 'wrong'—all-at-once jettison them."[449]

13.28

"Stream-enterers! My buddhadharma is the pivotal transmission that has come down from Preceptor Mayu, Preceptor Danxia, Preceptor Daoyi, [Preceptor] Lushan, and Preceptor Shigong.[450] One road—on it they walked all across all-under-heaven.[451] [But] people/*persons* do not have confidence [in the buddhadharma of Mayu and the others], and everyone slanders it.[452] As for Preceptor Daoyi, his venue of activities was a pure oneness without adulteration [i.e., unreserved functioning of the buddha nature].[453] Out of three hundred students, five hundred students, not a one could discern his intention. As for Preceptor Lushan, he was free and [beheld] reality as it truly is. In his venue of activities, whether [vishayas] were going in his direction or against him, students couldn't plumb his limits— they were all completely in the dark [i.e., lost any sense of a standard by which to judge].[454] As for Preceptor Danxia, he played with the *maṇi* [wishing] jewel, making it invisible and then visible.[455] The students who came were all abused by him. As for Mayu, his venue of activities was spicy-hot like the [medicinal bark of the] *huangbo* [cork] tree. None could come near him.[456] As for Shigong, his venue of activities was to seek out the [true] *person* by [saying, 'Look at the arrow,' nocking] an arrow [onto his bow, and aiming it at the student].[457] All who came were terrified."

13.29

"As for *this* mountain monk's venue of activities today, [it is beholding] reality as it truly is.[458] [As the world] comes into being, [abides,] is destroyed, [and enters the void in a beginningless and endless cycle,] I play with magical transformations [i.e., reveal magical transformations performed through supernormal powers] to enter into each and every vishaya.[459] Everywhere—*nothing-to-do*.[460] And the vishayas cannot turn me around.[461] Anyone who comes to me seeking, instantly I [*that one person*/the true *person*] crop up and see right through him, but he can't read me [i.e., *that one person*].[462] I [the true *person*] immediately put on various sorts of clothes/'costumes' [i.e., strike various poses, such as harsh preaching, firm preaching, etc.].[463] The student draws some conclusion from them, and earnestly enters into my words [of instruction; i.e., into my 'costumes'].[464] Dear me! The blind, bald-headed hack, a person without the eye,[465] grabs hold of the 'costume' I [the true *person*] am wearing, and infers that it is blue or yellow or red or white [i.e., conjectures or makes assumptions]![466] When I [the true *person*] shed [those 'costumes'], and enter into a vishaya of 'purity' [i.e., return to the *fangzhang* or get down from the Dharma Seat],[467] the student, having gotten an eyeful, right away produces the joy [of admiration].[468] Furthermore, when I [the true *person*] take [the 'costume of purity'] off,[469] the student loses his mind, and, at a loss, runs wildly about, saying that I [the true *person*] have no 'costume' [i.e., he falls into the category of Yajñadatta's losing his head].[470] I say to him: 'Do you know me, the *person* [the true *person*/*that one person*] who is wearing the "costumes?"'[471] Suddenly [the student] does a doubletake—he's acknowledged *me* [the true *person* wearing the 'costumes' of external characteristics]."[472]

13.30

"Venerables! You mustn't grant recognition to the clothes/'costumes' [clothing the true *person*]. Clothes/'Costumes' cannot take action of themselves[473]; it's the person/the [true] *person* who puts on those clothes/'costumes.'[474] There is a 'costume of purity,' there is a 'costume of nonarisingness,' a 'costume of *bodhi*,' a 'costume of nirvana,' a 'costume of the patriarchs,' a 'costume of the buddhas.'[475] Worthies! All spoken and written words are costume-transformations/dependent-transformations [illusory dependent-on-something-else transformations.][476] [An ancient said,] 'From the lower abdomen, agitating the sea of breath, clamping your teeth together, phrases and meanings come into being.'⁴⁷⁷ [From this ancient's words] it's obvious that [all spoken and written words] are *māyās*.⁴⁷⁸ Venerables! [An ancient also said,] 'Speech actions are expressed on the outside, revealing the dharmas associated with mind on the inside.'⁴⁷⁹ Because of mental reflection, [mind congeals into *avidyā*] thoughts; but all [such thoughts] are costumes/dependent [illusory dependent-on-something-else transformations].⁴⁸⁰ [Nevertheless,] you only pay attention to the costumes that *he* [the true *person*] is wearing, and you think *that* is understanding reality as it truly is.⁴⁸¹ [At that rate,] even if you passed through kalpas [as numerous] as specks [of sand or powdered ink], it would only be proficiency in costumes/costume transformations/supernormal powers of dependence!⁴⁸² You would [still continue to make] the rounds of the three realms and revolve in samsara. Better than that is to have *nothing-to-do*. [An ancient said,] 'Even if you have an encounter [with the true *person*], you won't know him; even if you speak to him, you won't find out his name.'"⁴⁸³

13.31

"Students today fall short [in their understanding] because they consider names to be understanding.⁴⁸⁴ In great big books they transcribe the sayings of some old dead geezer [i.e., some master without the eye], [stacking them] three layers deep, five layers deep, into their [monk's traveling] bags and not letting anyone else see them.⁴⁸⁵ They say, 'This is the mysterious principle,' and guard it as a [secret] treasure. Big mistake! Blind idiots! Just what kind of juice do you hope [to extract] from such dried-up bones [as these words of instruction from dead geezers, recorded in your great big books]?⁴⁸⁶ There is a type of [bad teacher] who doesn't know good from bad. They conjecture and haggle over the teachings [i.e., haggle over exegeses of the sutras and treatises], fabricating interpretations of the phrasing.⁴⁸⁷ It is as if they hold clods of [dried] shit in their mouths and spit them back out for other people.⁴⁸⁸ It's like commoners' transmitting secret passwords [and counter-passwords for identifying friend from foe]—a whole life frittered away.⁴⁸⁹ Even though [bad teachers] say [the secret password], 'I have left home,'⁴⁹⁰ the moment they are asked about the 'buddhadharma' [which is not the expected counter-password], they right away clam up and have nothing whatsoever to say. Their eyes are like the blackened vent [of a *kamado* stove],⁴⁹¹ and their [silent] mouths are like a shoulder pole [sagging under a heavy load].⁴⁹² [Beings] like this, even if they were to encounter [the next buddha] Maitreya as he emerges into this world, [would fall into an Avīci Hell. Even after kalpas in this world's Avīci Hell the destruction of the sinful karman would not yet be finished, and they] would shift to [the Avīci] Hell in another world. [In that other world they would again go through kalpas, but the destruction of the sinful karman would not yet be concluded. They would again shift to another world. In this way they would make the rounds of tens upon tens of worlds, in each going through kalpas. Eventually they would return to be reborn in the Avīci Hell of this world, all the while] undergoing suffering."⁴⁹³

13.32

"Venerables! You bustle along going to various regions—what are you looking for? The soles of your feet have gotten as wide as planks from tramping about [traveling on foot far and wide in search of a teacher and realization].⁴⁹⁴ There is no 'buddha' that ought to be sought, no 'Way' that ought to be completed, no 'dharma' that ought to be attained [i.e., *nothing-to-do*].⁴⁹⁵ Externally seeking for a 'buddha' with characteristics [i.e., a *nirmāṇakāya* buddha adorned with the thirty-two characteristics/a buddha image made of clay or wood]—he will not resemble *you* [the true buddha of your own mind/*that one person*].⁴⁹⁶ If you want to know your original mind [the true *person*], it's not something [outside of you that you can] join up with; nor is it something [you can ever] be apart from.⁴⁹⁷ Stream-enterers! The true buddha [everyone's *dharmakāya* buddha] has no form,⁴⁹⁸ the true Way has no substance, the true dharma has no characteristics. These three dharmas [the above three] come fused together as *the single, [seamless] place* [the single non-dependent true *person*].⁴⁹⁹ Those who haven't been able to perceive [*the single, seamless place*]⁵⁰⁰ we call '[transmigrating] sentient beings of confused karman-consciousness.'"⁵⁰¹

13.33

Question: "What are the true buddha, the true dharma, and the true Way like? Please give us instruction." The Master said, "A 'buddha' is mind-purity itself. The 'dharma' is mind-radiance itself. The 'Way' in every place is unobstructed radiance itself. The three are one [i.e., three words for the same thing], and they are all empty terms, without real existence.⁵⁰² For the practitioner of [beholding] reality as it truly is, moment after moment [at all times] the mind never breaks off [from beholding reality as it truly is—twenty-four hours a day peacefully dwelling in the state of the *original portion*].[503] When the Great Master Bodhidharma came from the western lands, he was only in search of a person/[true] *person* who was not discombulated by [other] people/*persons*/'the *person.*' Later he met the second patriarch [Huike]. At [Bodhidharma's] single utterance [i.e., 'My quieting mind for you is over'], [for Huike] at once everything was settled,[504] and for the first time [Huike] understood that his practice up until then had been useless effort. As for this mountain monk's vision today, it's no different from that of the buddhas who are our ancestors. If you catch on [to an eight-line poem] by its first couplet, you are a teacher of the buddhas who are our ancestors.[505] If you catch on to it by the second couplet, you are a teacher of humans and *devas*.[506] If you [only] catch on to it by the third couplet, you won't be able to save even yourself!"[507]

13.34

Question: "What was the meaning of [Bodhidharma's] coming from the west?" The Master said, "If there were a meaning to it, then you couldn't save even yourself." Question: "Since [Bodhidharma's coming from the west] had no meaning, how did the second patriarch catch on to the dharma?" The Master said, "'Catching on' is 'not catching on.'"[508] Question: "If it's 'not catching on,' what is the meaning of 'not catching on?'" The Master said, "Because you are unable to stop the mind that rushes around everywhere seeking, the Ancestral Master [Bodhidharma] said, 'Tsk! Supermen! [Like Yajñadatta] you already have a head, but [in your delusion] you are looking for another one.'[509] Immediately upon hearing these words, if you retrain the light [of the true mind] back upon yourself, if you don't seek anymore, if you come to know that your very selves [as you are] are no different from the buddhas who are our ancestors,[510] if you immediately have *nothing-to-do*, then it's called 'catching on to the dharma.'"

13.35

"Venerables! Today I haven't been able to avoid[511] talking a whole lot of trash and crap [kudzu words].[512] But you must not make a mistake! As to my vision, in fact, there is not a whole lot of [ambiguous] rationalizing in it at all.[513] If you want to use it, then use it. If you're not going to use it, just give it a rest. For example, all over the place there are those who who talk about the myriad practices of the six *pāramitās* and consider them to be the buddhadharma. But I say such things are the gate of adornment, the gate of buddha-matters [i.e., methods of teaching the dharma]—they are not the buddhadharma itself.[514] For instance, even if a person observes the rule of one meal before noon and maintains the precepts, or [possesses sufficient power of single-minded zeal] to carry [a bowl of] oil [through a crowd of people] without spilling [a drop],[515] if his eye of the Way is not bright,[516] then, without fail, he will have to pay off the debt, and there will come a day when [Yama] will exact the 'food money' [i.e., the tab for his food]. Why is it like this? '[A bhikṣu left home to] enter the [Buddha] Way but did not penetrate the principle [of the buddhadharma]; by being reborn [as a tree mushroom after his death], he repaid the donations [he had received] from the believing [father and son] donors,[517] until the wealthy householder turned eighty-one; and, [the debt the bhikṣu owed for thirty years of residence in the wealthy man's home being repaid,] the tree produced no more mushrooms.'"[518]

13.36

"Again, for instance, even [*pratyeka-buddhas*] who dwell alone on solitary peaks,[519] or those who eat but one meal in the early morning,[520] or those who do long periods of [cross-legged] sitting without lying down,[521] or those who carry out practices [such as reciting the name of Amitābha Buddha] at the six times [of the day]—all of them are people who are creating karman.[522] Again, for instance, those who give away everything—their own heads, eyes, marrow, brains; states, walled cities; wives, children; elephants, horses; the seven precious gems—an attitude like this always causes suffering to oneself and [in the future] incurs a karmic recompense of further suffering.[523] It's best to have *nothing-to-do*, a pure oneness without adulteration.[524] Again, for example, even bodhisattvas who have completed the ten stages, if they were to seek the footprints of even a stream-enterer [who is in the midst of *nothing-to-do*], they would never be able to get ahold of them [i.e., the stream-enterer in *nothing-to-do* is mentally ungraspable]. Therefore, all the *devas* welcome him, [this stream-enterer of pure oneness without adulteration, into the world] with joy,[525] the local spirits [with their right knees touching the ground] hold his feet [in both hands in worship],[526] and, of the buddhas of the ten directions, there is none who does not praise him.[527] What is the reason for this? It is because the Way-*person* [i.e, the true *person*] right now listening to the dharma, in his venue of activities, leaves no footprints."

13.37

Question: "The [buddha of the past] Great Superknowledge Wisdom-Victory Buddha sat on the terrace of enlightenment for ten kalpas, but the buddhadharma did not appear to him, and he did not complete the buddha path. I don't exactly understand the meaning behind this. Would the Master please instruct me?"[528] The Master said, "'Great Superknowledge' means that you yourself everywhere comprehend that the myriad dharmas lack *svabhāva* and lack characteristics. This is called 'Great Superknowledge.' 'Wisdom-Victory' means no uncertainty anywhere—not even one dharma is mentally graspable. This is called 'Wisdom-Victory.' 'Buddha' means mind purity, the radiant light penetrating the *dharmadhātu*. This is called 'buddha.' 'Sitting on the terrace of enlightenment for ten kalpas' means the ten *pāramitās*.[529] As for 'the buddhadharma did not appear to him,' given that a 'buddha' from the outset is non-arising [and non-extinguishing] and the 'dharma' from the outset is [non-arising and] non-extinguishing, why should there be any need for 'appearing to him'? 'Did not complete the buddha path' means [everyone is already] a buddha [to start with] and doesn't need to become a buddha all over again.[530] An ancient [Mañjusrī Bodhisattva] said, 'The buddha is always in the world but is not stained by worldly dharmas.'"[531]

13.38

"Stream-enterers! If you're thinking you want to become a buddha, you mustn't follow after the myriad things [i.e., mustn't lose your original mind and be spun around by things].[532] When thought arises, the various dharmas arise; when thought extinguishes, the various dharmas extinguish.[533] [But] when not one thought arises, the ten-thousand dharmas are without error [i.e., the error or 'disease' of the arising of thoughts].[534] In the world and beyond the world, there is neither 'buddha' nor 'dharma.' [Accordingly,] there is no instance of 'appearing' and none of 'having been lost.' Supposing there were [a 'buddha' and there were a 'dharma'], they would all be [no more than] terms and phrases[535] for enticing small children [i.e., sentient beings]; provisionally established medicines for disease, expressive terminologies [i.e., *upāyas*].[536] On top of this, names and phrases are not names and phrases of their own accord. In any case, it's *you* [*that one person*/the true *person*], right now, the one of brightness, brilliance, mirror awareness, hearing-knowing, and illumination, who does the attaching of all names and phrases [to the myriad dharmas].[537] Venerables! When you 'create the karman of the five [crimes of] uninterrupted [punishment in the Avīci Hell],' then and only then do you achieve 'liberation.'"[538]

13.39

Question: "What is the karman of the five [crimes of] uninterrupted [punishment in the Avīci Hell]?"[539] The Master said, "Killing the father, harming the mother, spilling the blood of a buddha's body, destroying the concord of the sangha, and burning sutras and images, and so on—these are the karman of the five [crimes of] uninterrupted [punishment]."[540] "What is meant by 'father'?" The Master said, "*Avidyā* is the father.[541] When you seek for the *place* where a single thought-moment [of *avidyā*] arises and extinguishes, it is ungraspable mentally,[542] like echoes reverberating through space [leaving no trace].[543] [Once you know this,] wherever you are there is *nothing-to-do*. This is called 'killing the father.'" [Question]: "What is the mother?" The Master says, "Craving is the mother. When you for a single thought-moment enter into the desire realm to seek for this craving, you only discover the empty characteristics of all dharmas, and everywhere [there is] non-attachment—this is called 'harming the mother.'" [Question]: "What is spilling the blood of a buddha's body?" The Master said, "When you, in the midst of the *dharmadhātu* of purity, produce not a single thought-moment's worth of the understanding [of awakening],[544] and everywhere [there is] non-discrimination[545]—this is 'spilling the blood of a buddha's body.'" [Question]: "What is destroying the concord of the sangha?" The Master said, "When you, for a single thought-moment, correctly comprehend that the *kleśas* and [eighty-eight latent] tendencies [from past lives] are like space with nothing to depend upon [i.e., you overturn or sweep away all the *kleśas* and latent tendencies]—this is 'destroying the concord of the sangha.'"[546] [Question]: "What is burning sutras and images?" The Master said, "You see that 'origination by dependence' is emptiness,[547] that 'mind' is empty, that 'dharmas' are empty: and in a single instant you are utterly certain. Incomparable—having *nothing-to-do*. This is 'burning the sutras and images.'"

13.40

"Venerables! If you know *in that way*, you will avoid being obstructed by 'worldling' and '*ārya*' terminology.[548] In a single thought-moment your mind [mistakes] the empty fist [of a game used to distract a crying child] or the finger [pointing at the moon] for an understanding of the real [i.e., mistakes *upāyas* for reality].[549] In the midst of the sense organs, vishayas, and dharmas [i.e., the eighteen *dhātus* consisting of the six sense organs, six vishayas, and six corresponding sense consciousnesses], you vainly come to adore strangeness and to toy with it.[550] You flinch, saying: 'I am a worldling, but *that* is an *ārya*.' Bald-headed hacks! Why, when you show such extreme urgency to deck yourself out in a lion skin, do you then make the sound of a [mere] jackal?[551] Supermen who don't show the spirit of Supermen! You don't even try to have confidence in the *thing* [i.e., the true buddha/true *person*] inside your own house [i.e., in the house of the gate of personal-realization-of-the-meaning-beyond-words].[552] You just seek on the outside, clambering up onto the good-for-nothing terms and phrases of the ancients, making [various conjectures based upon the computations of] *yin-yang* divination, unable to attain a particular comprehension [of your own].[553] Upon encountering vishayas, you right away grab on to them; upon encountering 'dusts' [i.e., vishayas], you right away grasp them; whatever place you are the *kleśas* arise: you have no standard or norm of your own [as would the true *person*].[554] Stream-enterers! [But] don't take what I am saying [as a standard or norm either].[555] Why? Talk is nothing to rely upon. It is like one-off pictures drawn in the sky, like images in colored paintings."[556]

13.41

"Stream-enterers! Don't take 'a buddha' as the ultimate. In my vision he is like a latrine hole. 'Bodhisattvas' and 'arhats' are, all of them, cangues with locks, beings that bind a *person* [the true *person*].[557] Therefore, Mañjuśrī [was induced to try to] kill Gautama with a sword;[558] and Aṅgulimāla held his sword [in an attempt] to murder Śākyamuni.[559] Stream-enterers! There is no 'buddha' that is graspable mentally, up to and including such 'traces' as 'the three vehicles,' 'the five natures,'[560] and 'the perfect and sudden teaching'—they are all one-off medicines to cure disease.[561] They are not 'real dharmas' at all! Even if they were, they would still all be nothing more than simulacra, roadside announcements that merely express [edicts, i.e., signs consisting of kudzu words and phrases],[562] written directives explained in a [plausible] fashion.[563] Stream-enterers! There is a type of bald-headed fellow who right away expends a lot of effort on [what is] inside [those written words], trying to seek out a method of escaping this world.[564] What a mistake! If a *person* seeks a 'buddha,' the *person* loses a buddha. If a *person* seeks the 'Way,' the *person* loses the Way. If a *person* seeks a 'patriarch,' the *person* loses a patriarch."

13.42

"Venerables! Make no mistake! No matter how much you are conversant with the sutras and treatises, I won't have any of it.[565] Even if you are a king or a high minister, I won't have any of it. Even if your glibness flows like a waterfall, I won't have any of it. Even if you are smart and have wisdom, I won't have any of it.[566] All I want is for you to have a beholding of reality as it truly is.[567] Stream-enterers! Suppose you were conversant with a hundred sutras and treatises,[568] it wouldn't be as good as a monk with *nothing-to-do*.[569] So you are conversant with [a hundred sutras and treatises]:[570] you go around insulting other people, you [obsess over] winning and losing like a [ferociously angry] *asura*, you [are under the sway of] *avidyā* [that divides everything into] self and other, and you increase your karman [leading to one of] the hells.[571] It's like [the case of] Sunakṣātra Bhikṣu, who was conversant with all twelve divisions of the teachings but while alive fell into [the Avīci] hell. The great earth had no place for him.[572] So it's not as good as *nothing-to-do* and taking a rest; when hungry, eating a meal; when tired, closing the eyes. Idiots will laugh at me, but the wise are in the know. Stream-enterers! Don't seek inside of the words [in those hundred sutras and treatises].[573] Your mind will fluctuate, and you will become tired out. Inhaling cold air [i.e., out of greed, clinging to written interpretations/seeking out and clinging to external things/while chanting the written word] is no good for you.[574] Best of all is, in a single moment, [to realize that] origination by dependence is non-arising [and non-extinguishing] and to leapfrog those bodhisattvas of *upāya*-type learning in the three vehicles [i.e., those whose understanding is based on the hundred sutras and treatises]."[575]

13.43

"Venerables! Don't spend your days following the same old routine [i.e., blending in with things and not standing out/being weak-kneed].[576] As for myself, in the past, when I had not an instance of seeing [reality as it truly is],[577] I was in limitless darkness.[578] [When I would think] that time must not be wasted, then my belly would get hot and my mind would be oppressed [by my seething desire for awakening], and I would run around inquiring about the Way.[579] Later, having been favored by the assistance [of teachers],[580] I was able for the first time to haggle like this, [as I am doing] with you stream-enterers today.[581] I warn all of you stream-enterers: don't [be industrious and hardworking in seeking] for clothing and food [when you have the priceless pearl of the mind sewn into the lining of your clothes]![582] Behold! Life will easily pass you by, and encountering a good teacher is a rare occurrence—an *udumbara* tree blooms but once [in three thousand years] and that's it.[583] All over the place you've heard that there is an old Han Linji, and so you crop up and right away are about to pose difficult questions, looking to stump me.[584] Upon being subjected to my unreserved functioning [of the buddha nature], you students just goggle empty-eyed and can't get your mouths to move at all. Clueless, [your mind in confusion,][585] you don't know how to answer me. I tell you: being trampled by a dragon-elephant is not something donkeys can bear.[586] Wherever you go you just point to your chest and pat your ribs [in a tribute to yourself],[587] saying: 'I understand Chan! I understand the Way!' Two or three of you arrive here [where you encounter my strategem of the unreserved functioning of the buddha nature], and you're totally helpless [i.e., you are shocked and can do nothing at all].[588] Tsk! You lug about this [five-*skandhas*] body-mind of yours[589]; wherever you go, you jabber away with your two flapping lips,[590] deceiving common people[591] [who are your donors]. There will be a day when you will be in for the iron cudgel [of Yama].[592] You are not leavers of home—you will all be admitted [as guests] into the [rebirth] realm of the [angry] *asuras*."[593]

13.44

"For example, the Way of ultimate principle is not argumentation that seeks to wash away [the impurity of others] while upholding ['my' purity]; nor is it the refutation of outside Ways in a shrill voice.[594] When it comes to the transmission from the buddhas and patriarchs, there *is* no 'other idea' [to argue about].[595] Supposing there were [such a thing as] 'oral teachings' [i.e., 'other ideas'], they would [only] fall into [such empty categories as 'the four] teaching styles,'[596] 'the three vehicles,' 'the five natures,' and 'the cause-and-effect teaching of being reborn as a human or *deva*.' Furthermore, [even] 'the perfect and all-at-once teaching' [of the *Huayan Sutra*] is not [the purport of Chan's separate transmission outside the teachings]:[597] [in the *Huayan Sutra*] the youth Sudhana in his going around was not seeking any of them [i.e., he was not seeking any three vehicles, five natures, perfect and all-at-once teaching, etc./from the outset, he never sought any dharma from the fifty-three teachers and never went through the one-hundred and ten cities].[598] Venerables! Make no mistake—be attentive! For example, the great sea does not hold onto dead bodies; but you just shoulder [the dead bodies of the oral teachings] and try to run around all-under-heaven [i.e., the Chan personal-realization-of-the-meaning-beyond-words does not retain the rights and wrongs of the oral teachings].[599] You yourself are instigating the hindrance-due-to-views that obstructs your [original] mind.[600] If there are no clouds [of thought of the unreal] crossing the sun [of the original mind], then it shines everywhere.[601] If in the eye [of the original mind] there is no cataract [of discrimination], in the sky there are no illusory 'flowers.'[602] Stream-enterers! If you're thinking you want to attain [a beholding] according to dharma [i.e., a beholding of reality as it truly is], just don't produce uncertainty.[603] Unfurled, [the clear, solitary brightness] fills up the *dharmadhātu;* rolled up, [the clear, solitary brightness occupies a space that is] not enough in which to stand up a single strand of hair. The clear, solitary brightness has never lacked anything.[604] The eye cannot see it, the ear cannot hear it—what shall we call it? An ancient said, 'Once you've [tried to] pin it down with words, you've missed the mark.'[605] Just look with your own [eyes—outside of the true *person*] what more could there be?[606] Speaking [dharma] has no end to it.[607] Each of you must exert effort on your own. Take care of yourselves."[608]

[Part III]

Calibrating and Adjudicating
[Appraising the Level of
Understanding and Rendering a
Judgment][1]

Once, when Huangbo entered the storehouse pantry,[2] he asked the Chief of Provisions,[3] "What are you doing?" The Chief of Provisions said, "I'm sorting out [the impurities from] the rice for the monks of the sangha."[4] Huangbo said, "In one day, how much [i.e, literally, "much or little"] do [the monks] eat?"[5] The Chief of Provisions said, "Two *shi* and five [250 liters]."[6] Huangbo said, "Isn't that 'too much?'"[7] The Chief of Provisions [not understanding and hence still falling into "much" or "little"] said, "No, in fact, I'm afraid it might be too little."[8] Huangbo instantly whacked him. The Chief of Provisions, not accepting this, brought the matter up with the Master [Linji].[9] The Master said, "For your sake, I'll have a go at the old man [Huangbo]." Huangbo raised the previous story as soon as [the Master Linji] arrived in attendance. The Master said, "The Chief of Provisions doesn't understand. Would the Preceptor please say a phrase as a stand-in [for the Chief of Provisions]?"[10] The Master instantly [as a stand-in for the Preceptor Huangbo] asked, "Isn't that 'too much?'" Huangbo said, "Why not say: In future days they will be eating further bowls [of rice]/eating further blows [of the stick]?"[11] The Master said, "Never mind 'future days'—eat [the bowls of rice/the blows of the stick] right now!" Having said this, he [struck Huangbo] with his palm. Huangbo said, "*This* wacko Han has come over *here* again to yank on the tiger's whiskers."[12] The Master instantly gave a shout and went out.

14.2

Later, Guishan asked Yangshan, "These two respected monks [Huangbo and Linji]—what is your take on them?"[13] Yangshan said, "What is your take, Preceptor?" Guishan said, "Once you've had a child, that's when you first understand your father's benevolent love."[14] Yangshan said, "That's not right." Guishan said, "Well then, what is your take on it?" Yangshan said, "It's a lot like bringing a thief [into your house who steals your family's wealth and] wrecks your home."[15]

15

The Master asked a monk, "What *place* do you come from?"[16] The monk instantly gave a shout. The Master instantly did obeisance [by cupping one hand in the other on his chest] and [indicated for him] to take the seat [at the advanced-seat rank on the platform].[17] The monk dithered [i.e., was about to respond but not quite capable of doing so]. The Master instantly whacked [him].[18] The Master saw a monk coming and instantly raised up his flywhisk. The monk bowed. The Master instantly whacked [him]. Seeing another monk coming, the Master also raised up his flywhisk. The monk ignored [the fact that he was in peril].[19] The Master whacked [him] too.

16.1

One day, when the Master went with Puhua to a dinner at a generous donor's house, the Master asked, "[It is said that] 'a hair swallows the great sea, and a mustard seed contains Mt. Sumeru.'[20] Is this the wonderful activity of supernormal powers or the original substance *just as it is?*" Puhua [suddenly] kicked over his dining table. The Master said, "Such crude [behavior]!"[21] Puhua said, "Just what *place* do you think *this* is that you speak of 'crude' and 'fine'? [I.e., *here* from the outset there is not a single thing—this is the original substance *just as it is.*]"[22]

16.2

The day after that, the Master along with Puhua went to another dinner. The Master asked, "Today's lay offering—how does it compare to yesterday's?"[23] Puhua as before kicked over his dining table. The Master said,

"That's all very well and good, but it's still too crude."[24] Puhua said, "Blind [low-down] Han! How could there be 'crude' or 'fine' in the buddha-dharma?" The Master lolled out his tongue [in amazement].[25]

17

The Master, one day, when he was sitting around the [open-air] brick hearth [outside] the Sangha Hall[26] together with the old worthies Heyang and Muta, said, "Puhua, every day, is in the middle of town going around acting in a [childish] frenetic manner.[27] Who knows whether he is a world-ling or an *ārya*!" [The Master] had not yet finished speaking when Puhua entered. The Master instantly asked, "Are you a worldling or an *ārya*?" Puhua said, "You tell me—am I a worldling or an *ārya*?" The Master in-stantly gave a shout [cutting off the duality 'worldling and *ārya*'].[28] Puhua, pointing his finger [at each of them in succession],[29] said, "Heyang is a new-wife Chanist [of a timid and weak level of understanding],[30] and Muta is an old-woman Chanist [of kind, loving words with no bite]."[31] [In a back-handed compliment Puhua finally said,] "Linji is a [cagey] little gofer, but he's [only] got the one eye."[32] The Master said, "*This* son of a bitch!"[33] Puhua said, "Son of a bitch, son of a bitch!" and instantly went away.[34]

18

One day Puhua was in front of the Sangha Hall eating vegetables raw. The Master saw him and said, "Just like a donkey!" Puhua immedately brayed like a donkey. The Master said, "*This* son of a bitch!" Puhua said, "Son of a bitch, son of a bitch!" and instantly went away.[35]

19

Puhua always was going around the streets shaking the "rattle" [of metal rings at the top of his tin staff],[36] and saying, "Come with 'brightness'—whack 'brightness.' Come with 'darkness'—whack 'darkness.' Come from 'four quadrants, eight directions'—whack like a whirlwind. Come from 'sky'—whack non-stop with a thresher!"[37] The Master ordered his atten-dant to go out [into the streets of town]. [The attendant] took aside [Puhua] as he was saying these things and demanded of him, "When one does not come in any of those ways [i.e., when one comes who is single-minded and off-the-charts], then what?"[38] Puhua shoved him away and said,

"There will be a [generous donor's] dinner tomorrow at the Dabei Temple."[39] The attendant came back and reported this to the Master. The Master said, "I've had my doubts about *this* Han all along, [but henceforth I have no doubts]."[40]

20.1

An old monk came to visit the Master. Without even going through the usual polite formalities [of a first meeting],[41] he right away asked, "Is it better to bow or not to bow?"[42] The Master instantly gave a shout. The old monk instantly bowed. The Master said, "What a fine army of traitors [waving the flag of revolt]!"[43] The old monk said, "Traitor, traitor!" and instantly went out. The Master said, "Don't be thinking, '[Squeaked by] without incident/*nothing-to-do* is all there is to it!"[44]

20.2

At that time the Head Seat was standing in attendance nearby, and the Master said to him, "Is there still a flaw?" The Head Seat said, "There is."[45] The Master said, "Is the flaw with the guest [the old monk] or with the host [me]?"[46] The Head Seat said, "The pair [the two extremes of 'is' and 'is not'/guest-and-host] are flawed/are flaws."[47] The Master, [chasing a dog up against a wall,] said, "So in what *place*, exactly, are these flaws?"[48] The Head Seat instantly went out. The Master said, "Don't be thinking, '[Squeaked by] without incident/*nothing-to-do* is all there is to it!"[49] Later there was a monk who raised this exchange with Nanquan. Nanquan said, "Government-supplied [purebred] horses in a kicking match."[50]

21

When the Master was invited to a dinner at the army camp [the residence of Attendant-in-ordinary Wang],[51] he encountered a guard officer at the gate entrance.[52] The Master pointed to the open-air pillar [in the center of the courtyard] and asked, "Is it a worldling or is it an *ārya*?"[53] The guard officer was silent.[54] The Master whacked the pillar and said [to both the pillar and the guard officer], "Even if you could speak, you'd still only be a log of wood." He instantly went in.[55]

22.1

The Master asked the temple Custodian, "What *place* do you come from?"[56] The Custodian said, "I've just come back from going to the provincial center to sell husked sorghum."[57] The Master said, "Were you able to sell all of it?"[58] The Custodian said, "It all sold." The Master with his staff slashed a line [on the ground] right in front of him, saying, "By the way, could you have sold *this*?"[59] The Custodian [springing free of the *vajra* cage] instantly gave a shout,[60] and the Master instantly whacked him.

22.2

The Head Cook arrived.[61] When the Master mentioned this exchange to him, the Head Cook said, "The temple Custodian hasn't understood the Preceptor's meaning." The Master said, "Well, how about yourself?" The Head Cook instantly bowed. The Master whacked him, too.[62]

23.1

When a Seat Master [a scholar of the teachings of the sutras and treatises] came to see [the Master], the Master asked, "Seat Master, what sutras and treatises do you lecture on?"[63] The Seat Master said, "Yours truly [has a head that is] barren [of learning] and has made but a crude study of the *Hundred Dharmas Treatise*."[64] The Master said, "One *person* has awakened to the three vehicles and twelve divisions of the teachings. One *person* has not awakened to the three vehicles and twelve divisions of the teachings. Are [these] the same or different?"[65] The Seat Master said, "If there's awakening, then they're the same. If there isn't yet awakening, then they're different."[66]

23.2

Lepu, who had been standing behind the Master as his attendant, said, "Seat Master, just what place do you think this is, that you speak of 'same' and 'different?'"[67] The Master turned his head around and asked the attendant [Lepu], "Well, how about yourself?"[68] The attendant instantly gave a shout.[69] The Master escorted the Seat Master out and, upon returning, asked the attendant, "Just now was that shout of yours for me?" The attendant said, "Yes." The Master instantly whacked him.

24

The Master heard that Deshan the Second passed down the following instruction: "If you nail it in words, again thirty blows with the stick; if you can't nail it in words, again thirty blows with the stick." The Master ordered Lepu to go and make an inquiry: "[Ask him,] 'If you nail it in words, why is it again thirty blows?' Wait for him to strike you, and then grab his stick and push. Keep an eye on how he does."[70] Lepu went to him [Deshan] and asked as instructed.[71] Deshan instantly whacked him. Lepu grabbed his stick and pushed back.[72] Deshan instantly returned to the *fangzhang* [i.e., did an unreserved functioning of the buddha nature].[73] Lepu came back and reported this to the Master. The Master said, "I've had my doubts about *this* Han all along.[74] All the same, *did you see* Deshan?"[75] Lepu dithered [i.e., was about to answer but not quite capable of doing so]. The Master instantly whacked him.

25

Attendant-in-ordinary Wang one day visited the Master. Upon meeting up with the Master in front of the Sangha Hall, he asked, "Do the monks inside this hall read sutras?" The Master said, "They read no [such thing as the] sutras." The Attendant-in-ordinary asked, "So then, do they train in [cross-legged sitting] Chan?" The Master said, "They don't do [cross-legged sitting] Chan either." The Attendant-in-ordinary said, "So if they don't read the sutras, and they don't practice [sitting] Chan, then, when all is said and done, what on earth goes on here?" The Master said, "The production of 'buddhas' and 'patriarchs.'"[76] The Attendant-in-ordinary said, "'Even though gold dust is precious, if it gets in your eye, it becomes an injury.'[77] What about that?" The Master said, "[Till now I've always] thought you were just an unsophisticated Han. [I.e., in the beginning I took you for a run-of-the-mill layman, but you're a damn smart cookie!]"[78]

26

The Master asked Xingshan, "[The *Lotus Sutra* in the parable of the burning house speaks of the sons sitting on the] open ground [at the crossroads] and the white-ox [cart of the Mahāyāna]—how do you regard this?"[79] Xingshan recited: *"hūṃ hūṃ,"* [the mantra/the sound of an ox lowing].[80]

The Master said, "Gone mute, have we?"[81] Xingshan said, "How about you, elder [brother, have you gone mute]?"[82] The Master, [not really scolding him,] said, "*This* one's been reborn as an animal!"[83]

27

The Master asked Lepu, "As in the past one *person* employs the stick, and one *person* employs the shout. Which one of these is spot on? [I.e., which is closer to the matter of the *original portion*?]"[84] Lepu said, "Neither one is spot on. [I.e., the stick and the shout are matters within the gate of establishing teachings for sentient beings—the gate of *upāyas*—they are not at all close to the state of the *original portion*.]"[85] The Master said, "What would be spot on?" Lepu instantly gave a shout. The Master whacked [him].

28

The Master saw a monk coming and opened his arms wide.[86] The monk was silent. The Master said, "Do you get it?" [The monk] said, "No, I don't get it." The Master said, "You're hopelessly mixed up and haven't got a clue [i.e., literally, the "Kunlun Mountains cannot be split open"]. I'll give you money [for straw sandals so you can leave here on foot in search of a teacher and realization]."[87]

29

Dajue arrived for an audience [with the Master]. The Master raised his fly-whisk. Dajue, [quickly understanding the Master's unreserved functioning of the buddha nature, silently] set up his sitting mat [i.e, a mat or rug on which to make a formal prostration, do cross-legged sitting, lie down, etc.].[88] The Master threw his flywhisk down. Dajue put away his sitting mat and went into the Sangha Hall.[89] [Some of the] monks in the sangha said, "That monk—could he be an old friend of the Preceptor?[90] He didn't bow, and he didn't even eat the stick."[91] The Master caught wind of this and had Dajue called out. Dajue emerged, and the Master said, "[Monks in the] great sangha are saying that you haven't yet had a formal audience with [me,] your elder."[92] Dajue said, "How are you?"[93] He instantly returned to the [ranks of the] sangha [as there was no further conversational give-and-take possible].

30

When Zhaozhou was traveling on foot [far and wide in search of a teacher and realization], he came for an audience with the Master. He found the Master just when he was washing his feet. Zhaozhou right away asked, "What is the meaning of the Ancestral Master [Bodhidharma's] coming from the west?"[94] The Master said, "It just so happens the old monk [I/Bodhidharma] is washing the feet [i.e., doing the unreserved functioning of the buddha nature]."[95] Zhaozhou went up to him and assumed the stance of listening. The Master said, "Still need to slosh a second ladle of sewage!"[96] Zhaozhou instantly left.[97]

31

Advanced Seat Ding arrived for an audience and asked, "What is the great meaning of the buddhadharma?" The Master got down from the Chan chair,[98] grabbed him [by the collar] and gave him a slap, and instantly shoved him aside. Ding [forgot both "before" and "after" and] stood there blankly.[99] A nearby monk said, "Advanced Seat Ding, why is it you do not bow?" Just at that moment Ding bowed [i.e., an unreserved functioning of the buddha nature], and he suddenly had a great awakening.[100]

32

Mayu arrived for an audience, set up his sitting mat, and asked, "On the twelve-faced Avalokiteśvara, which face is the main one?"[101] The Master got down from the Chan chair, with one hand retrieved the sitting mat, and with one hand grabbed Mayu, saying, "The twelve-faced Avalokiteśvara— to what *place* has it gone?"[102] Mayu flipped himself around and tried to sit on the [Master's] Chan chair. The Master picked up his staff and whacked him. Mayu had latched on, and entangled together they entered the *fang- zhang* [the unreserved functioning of the buddha nature].[103]

33

The Master asked a monk, "At a certain time a shout is like the precious sword of a Vajrapāṇi [a ferocious dharma-guardian].[104] At a certain time a shout is like a golden lion crouching on the ground. At a certain time a shout has the function of an *upāya*.[105] At a certain time a shout doesn't even have the function of a shout [i.e., the place of the *original portion*].[106] How do you understand this?" The monk dithered [i.e., was about to answer but not quite capable of doing so]. The Master instantly gave a shout.

34

The Master asked a nun, "Well come or ill come?"[107] The nun instantly gave a shout. The Master took up his stick and said, "Out with it! Out with it!"[108] The nun gave another shout. The Master instantly gave her a whack.

35

Longya asked: "What is the meaning of the Ancestral Master [Bodhidharma's] coming from the west?" The Master said, "Hand me the Chan block."[109] Longya instantly handed the Chan block to the Master. The moment the Master got it, he whacked him with it. Longya said, "Whack as you like, when all is said and done, that's not the meaning in the Ancestral Master's coming/there still won't be any meaning in the Ancestral Master's coming."[110] Longya later went to Cuiwei and asked, "What is the meaning of the Ancestral Master's coming from the west?" Cuiwei said, "Hand me the *futon* [Chan sitting cushion]." Longya instantly handed the *futon* to Cuiwei. The moment Cuiwei got it, he whacked him with it. Longya said, "Whack as you like, when all is said and done, that's not the meaning in the Ancestral Master's coming/there still won't be any meaning in the Ancestral Master's coming."[111] After Longya had become a temple head, a monk entered his room to request further instruction,[112] saying, "Preceptor, [I've heard] the story that when you were traveling on foot [far and wide in search of a teacher and realization] you had audiences with two honored monks. Did you give the okay to them?" Longya said, "I more than gave the okay to them, but, when all is said and done, that's not the meaning in the Ancestral Master's coming/there still won't be any meaning in the Ancestral Master's coming."[113]

36

Mt. Jing [Monastery] had a sangha of five-hundred [monks], but few made a request for an audience [with the master Jingshan].[114] Huangbo ordered the Master [Linji] to go to Mt. Jing and then said to the Master, "Once you get to him how [will you calibrate and adjudicate him]?"[115] The Master said, "When yours truly gets to him, an *upāya* [a means of calibrating and adjudicating his level of understanding] will naturally turn up."[116] The Master arrived at Mt. Jing [and, still wearing the traveling] clothes [he happened to have on], went up to the Dharma Hall to meet [the master] Jingshan.[117] Just as Jingshan raised his head, the Master gave a shout. As Jingshan was about to open his mouth [i.e., in a dithering way],[118] the Master instantly left with a snap of his sleeves. Eventually a monk [from Jingshan's group who was dubious] asked Jingshan, "So, this monk just now—what words of instruction did *he* have, that ended up with his giving the Preceptor a shout?"[119] Jingshan said, "That monk came from Huangbo's circle. You want to know? Ask him yourself!"[120] Of the five-hundred monks in the sangha at Mt. Jing, the majority dispersed.[121]

37

One day Puhua was in town begging people for a "two-in-one monk's costume" [a monk's costume where the customary two garments were sewn together to make a single garment, i.e., a "non-duality costume"; Puhua, however, meant a plain wooden coffin].[122] The people [did not understand his intention, and] donated one [of the former], but Puhua turned them down.[123] The Master ordered the temple Custodian to buy a coffin. When Puhua returned [from town to Linji's temple],[124] the Master said, "I've had a 'two-in-one monk's costume' made for you."[125] Puhua instantly shouldered it himself and made the rounds of the town, shouting, "Linji's made a 'two-in-one monk's costume' for me. I'll go die at the East Gate." The townspeople tried to outdo each in following along behind to get a look at him. Puhua said, "Forget about today, but tomorrow I'll go die at the South Gate." When this sort of thing [continued for] three days, nobody believed him anymore. And by the fourth day there was nobody who would follow along behind to get a look. Alone he went outside the town walls, got into the coffin by himself, and asked a *person* walking by to nail it up [making it into a "non-duality costume"]. Immediately [the news of this] spread.[126] The townspeople tried to outdo each other in rushing [to the spot]. When they opened the coffin, they saw total *mokṣa* [i.e., complete liberation—there was not even a corpse in the coffin].[127] They heard only the *yin-yin* jingle of the rattle [i.e., the metal rings at the top of his staff] receding into the sky/*śūnyatā*.[128]

Part IV

Record of the Karman
[of the Master's Career]¹

38.1

When the Master was starting out in Huangbo's circle, his karman [intentional action] was sincere and focused [i.e., in his practice he was careful and thorough, never lax].² The Head Seat praised him, saying, "Although he is of the younger generation, he's an extraordinary one in the sangha." Then [the Head Seat] asked, "Advanced Seat [Linji], how long has it been since you've come here?" The Master said, "Three years." The Head Seat said, "Have you had an audience yet [with the Abbot Preceptor Huangbo]?" The Master said, "No, no audience. I wouldn't know what on earth to ask." The Head Seat said, "Why don't you go ask the Abbot Preceptor what is the real meaning of the buddhadharma?" The Master right away went to ask. Before he had even finished his question, Huangbo instantly gave him a whack.³ When the Master returned [from Huangbo's *fangzhang*],⁴ the Head Seat said, "How did your question go over?" The Master said, "Even before yours truly had finished asking my question, the Preceptor instantly gave me a whack. Yours truly doesn't understand." The Head Seat said, "Go one more time and ask him again." The Master again went to ask. Huangbo again gave him a whack.⁵ Thus he asked the question three times and three times was whacked.⁶ The Master came to the Head Seat and said, "I've received the favor of your compassion, ordering yours truly to make an inquiry of the Preceptor. Three times I posed a question, and three times I got whacked. Regrettably, [some] condition [in my past lives constitutes a karmic] block, and I am unable to understand his deep purport. At present [I would like to request] a leave."⁷ The Head Seat said, "If you go, you must [get] a leave of absence from the Preceptor." The Master bowed and retreated.

38.2

The Head Seat went ahead [of Linji] to the Preceptor and said, "That young one who has been posing the question has an unusual [level of understanding] according to dharma [i.e., a non-discriminative level of understanding].[8] When he comes to request time off,[9] please guide him with an *upāya*. From here on he will drill holes [to open up people's eyes and noses][10] and become a great tree providing cool shade for the people of all-under-heaven [just as sentient beings dwell in the cool shade of the buddha-tree]."[11] The Master came [to request] a leave. Huangbo said, "There is only one place for you to go, and that's Dayu's place at the shoals in Gao'an. He will certainly explain things for you." The Master arrived at Dayu's [place]. Dayu asked, "What *place* do you come from?"[12] The Master said, "I have come from Huangbo's place." Dayu said, "What words of instruction does Huangbo have?"[13] The Master said, "Three times yours truly asked about that very topic of the great meaning of the buddhadharma, and three times I was whacked. Yours truly doesn't know whether it was actually a failing on my part or not."[14] Dayu said, "Huangbo is such an old grandma [in his solicitude for students]! This has resulted in thorough exhaustion on his part for your sake.[15] And what is more, you come [all the way] over here [to see me] and demand [to know] whether there was any failing on *your* part or not." At his words the Master had a great awakening, saying, "So, all along Huangbo's buddhadharma was point-blank!"[16] Dayu seized him and said, "This bed-pissing *preta* [hungry ghost]![17] Just now you were whining about whether there was a failing on your part, and now you go on about Huangbo's buddhadharma being 'point-blank.' What on earth have you understood? C'mon! C'mon!"[18] The Master with his fist gave Dayu three thumps to the ribs. Dayu thrust him aside and said, "You take Huangbo as your teacher—it has nothing to do with me."

38.3

The Master took leave of Dayu and returned to Huangbo. Huangbo saw him coming and right away asked, "All this [low-down] Han ever does is go back and forth, and exactly when is he going to get [the *great matter*] over and done with?"[19] The Master said, "I'm just [indulging] your grandmotherly kindness."[20] He immediately presented [Huangbo] a gift and assumed a standing position at his side.[21] Huangbo asked, "What *place* have you been?" The Master said, "As you directed me on an earlier day,[22] I have been to visit Dayu." Huangbo said, "Did Dayu have any words of instruction?" The Master recounted the exhange [with Dayu]. Huangbo said, "I'd like nothing more than to catch *this* Han [Dayu/true *person*] and give him a good one [with the stick]!"[23] The Master said, "What's this about 'wanting to'—take one right now!" He immediately followed it with a slap. Huangbo said, "*This* wacko Han—he comes *here* and yanks on the tiger's whiskers! [I.e., certifying the Master.]"[24] The Master instantly gave a shout. Huangbo said, "Attendant! Escort *this* wacko Han to the [Sangha] Hall."[25]

38.4

Later Guishan raised this exchange with Yangshan, asking, "At that time was Linji favored by the assistance of Dayu or favored by the assistance of Huangbo?"[26] Yangshan said, "Not only did he ride the tiger's head—he could grasp the tiger's tail."[27]

39.1

When the Master was planting pine trees, Huangbo asked him, "What's [the point of] planting so many [pine trees] deep in the mountains?" The Master said, "First, to create an ornament for the main gate.[28] Second, to make known a standard for future generations."[29] Having finished speaking, he hit the ground [i.e., *here*] with the hoe three times. Huangbo said, "All the same, you have already eaten thirty blows of the stick by me." The Master again hit the ground with the hoe three times, and [feigned indifference by] emitting a sharp sound as he slowly exhaled.[30] Huangbo said, "My personal-realization-of-the-meaning-beyond-words [i.e., my Chan] has reached you—it will flourish greatly in the world."

39.2

Later Guishan raised this exchange with Yangshan, asking, "At the time Huangbo handed over [his buddhadharma] just to Linji alone/Linji the one *person*. Will there be other *persons* [to continue the succession down to later times]?"[31] Yangshan said, "There will be. But it's down to generations so far in the future that I don't want to mention it, Preceptor." Guishan said, "All the same, I want to know. Just try me." Yangshan said, "'The one *person*' points to the south/Nan[yuan Huiyong]. The statutes of Wu-Yue [the native place of Nanyuan's successor, Fengxue Yanzhao] will be implemented. Upon the encounter with 'Great Wind' [Fengxue], [Linji's dharma] will perch."[32]

40

When the Master was standing in attendance on Deshan, Deshan said, "Boy am I having a hard time today!"[33] The Master said, "This old geezer—what is he saying in his sleep?"[34] Deshan instantly whacked him. The Master overturned [Deshan's] Chan chair.[35] Deshan gave it a rest.[36]

41.1

When the Master was tilling the ground for communal work, he saw Huangbo coming, and stood still leaning on his hoe.[37] Huangbo said, "*This* Han—is he having a hard time?" The Master said, "I haven't even raised the hoe yet—what on earth is there to have a hard time over?" Huangbo instantly whacked him. The Master took hold of [Huangbo's] stick, and, with a single jolt, knocked him down.[38] Huangbo called the Duty Master[39]: "Duty Master! Give me a hand up!" The Duty Master approached and helped him up, saying, "Preceptor! Are you going to let this wacko Han get away with this rudeness?" The moment Huangbo had straightened up, he whacked the Duty Master. The Master was hoeing the ground and said, "Cremation is on all sides [i.e., the 'dead-Han' mind is everywhere], but *here* on *my* patch [i.e., the 'live-Han' patch] it's live burial in one go [i.e., knocking down Huangbo with a single jolt is 'live burial']."[40]

41.2

Later Guishan asked Yangshan, "Huangbo whacked the Duty Master—what is your take on it?" Yangshan said, "It was the real thief [Linji, the one who stole Huangbo's buddhadharma,] who made a clean getaway, and it was the beat constable [the Duty Master who pursued Linji and certainly did not steal Huangbo's buddhadharma] who ate the [punishment of the] stick."[41]

42

One day the Master was [doing cross-legged] sitting in front of the Sangha Hall. Seeing Huangbo coming, he instantly shut tight his eyes [to make as if he were ignoring Huangbo/to make as if he were sitting inside "the ghost cave of Black Mountain"].[42] Huangbo gave an alarmed appearance and instantly returned to the *fangzhang*. The Master followed him to the *fangzhang* and made a formal apology.[43] The Head Seat was standing in attendance upon Huangbo.[44] Huangbo said, "Even though this monk is a youngster, he knows of these matters [between master and student]/ knows of *this matter* [i.e., thus certifying Linji]."[45] The Head Seat said, "Old Preceptor, your heels aren't even touching the *ground* [of the truly real], but you're going to authenticate *this* youngster?"[46] Huangbo [expressing mock regret at his own verbal slip] whacked himself with a smack on the mouth.[47] The Head Seat said, "If you know [the mistake], then fine/if he knows [*this matter*], then fine."[48]

43.1

The Master was dozing off [at his seat on the sitting platform] in the [Sangha] Hall.[49] When Huangbo came down [i.e., came down from his sitting position in the Sangha Hall/came down from the *fangzhang* to enter the Sangha Hall][50] and saw this, with his staff he gave a whack to the [single] wooden plank [running along the front edge of the sitting platform].[51] The Master lifted his head, saw that it was Huangbo, but went back to his nap. Huangbo, after whacking the wooden plank once more, went toward the upper [northern] part of the Hall.[52] Seeing the Head Seat doing cross-legged sitting [at his number-one position in the upper part of the Hall], he said, "The youngster down there in the lower [southern] part of the Hall is indeed doing cross-legged sitting![53] So how come you [all the way up] here [in the upper Hall are trying to stabilize your mind to tame it but instead are just increasing] thought of the unreal?"[54] The Head Seat retorted, "*This* old Han [has gone insane]—what are we going to do with him!"[55] Huangbo whacked the wooden plank [along the edge of the sitting platform] again and went out.

43.2

Later Guishan asked Yangshan, "Huangbo's entering the Sangha Hall— what is your take on it?" Yangshan said, "Two numbers, one die [i.e., the numbers on the two dice are identical, and so it counts as just one die— the Head Seat and Linji are the same]."[56]

44.1

One day during the communal work period Linji was lagging along at the rear.[57] Huangbo [at the front of the line] turned around, saw that the Master was empty-handed, and asked, "In what *place* is your hoe?" The Master [seeing Huangbo carrying the hoe in question] said, "*A person* [some guy/*that one person*/Huangbo] made off with it."[58] Huangbo said, "Come over here—let's hash out *this matter* [of the hoe/of the *original portion*] together."[59] The Master instantly came over. Huangbo held out the hoe and said, "*This* [this hoe/*this matter*] is something that no *person* under heaven can lift clear." The Master snatched the hoe from his hands and stabbed it into the air, saying, "Then what's it doing in yours truly's hands [i.e., each and every person is endowed with *this*—each and every *this* is perfect]?"[60] Huangbo said, "We've got quite the communal worker among us today [i.e., certifying the Master]." He right away returned to the temple.[61]

44.2

Later Guishan asked Yangshan, "The hoe was in Huangbo's hand. How come it was ripped away by Linji?" Yangshan [in praise of Linji] said, "The thief [Linji] is an ordinary *person* whose wisdom surpasses that of the noble man [Huangbo]."[62]

45.1

The Master, bearing a letter from Huangbo, hastened to Guishan's. At the time Yangshan was serving as the Guest Receptionist.[63] When [Yangshan] had received the letter, he right away asked, "So *this one* [this letter/this expression of the *original portion*/Linji][64] is Huangbo's. Which one is the special envoy's [i.e., where is your letter/your expression of the *original portion*]?"[65] The Master instantly [went to] slap him.[66] Yangshan [caught the hand doing the slapping and] stopped it,[67] saying, "Senior brother, if you've understood *this matter*, then I'll give it a rest [i.e., I have nothing more to add]."[68] Together they went to see Guishan. Guishan right away asked, "How many [i.e., literally, "many or few"] in the sangha of Master elder brother Huangbo?"[69] The Master said, "A sangha of seven-hundred." Guishan said, "Who is their 'leader'?"[70] The Master [speaking of himself] said, "Just now he has delivered the letter."[71] Later the Master asked Guishan, "Preceptor, *here* [in your monastery/in beholding reality as it truly is] how many [i.e., "do you have 'many or few' monks/true *persons*"] in the sangha?" Guishan said, "A sangha of fifteen hundred." The Master said, "Wow, that many!" Guishan said, "Master elder brother Huangbo also has not a few [monks/true *persons*—i.e., his sangha has you]."

45.2

The Master took leave of Guishan. Yangshan saw him off and said, "Hence-forth [you should] proceed north—[I guarantee] there will be a [good] spot for you to live."[72] The Master [modestly] said, "How could there be such a thing?"[73] Yangshan said, "Well, just go [and see]. Later there will be a *person* [the true *person*] there to help you, senior elder brother.[74] This *person* [the true *person*] will just have a head but no tail, a beginning but no end."[75] The Master later arrived in Zhenzhou, and Puhua was already there. When the Master emerged in the world [i.e., became abbot of a temple], Puhua helped him.[76] However, shortly after the Master became abbot [of his own temple], Puhua achieved total *mokṣa* [liberation].[77]

46

The Master, at the halfway point in the summer [retreat], ascended Mt. Huangbo; and he saw the Preceptor [Huangbo] reading sutras.[78] The Master said, "[Here] I was thinking you were *this person* [the true *person*], and [it turns out] all along you were an old preceptor [greedily] eating black beans [written words]!"[79] [Linji] was there for several days and then took his leave. Huangbo said, "[So not only have] you broken the rules by coming [into the summer retreat at midterm], now you're going to leave without finishing out [the term]." The Master said, "Yours truly just dropped in for a bit to pay my respects to the Preceptor." Huangbo then whacked him and booted him out. After the Master had gone a mile or so, he came to entertain doubts about *this matter* [Huangbo's intention in reading the sutras/finishing out the summer term/the *great matter* or *original portion*] and turned back, finishing the summer retreat.[80]

47.1

The Master one day took his leave of Huangbo. Huangbo asked, "What *place* are you going?" The Master said, "If it's not Henan, then right away I will go back to Hebei [i.e., the whole earth is home]."[81] Huangbo instantly [went to] slap him.[82] The Master caught the hand doing the slapping and stopped it. Huangbo gave a great laugh [i.e., the laugh of certification] and then called his attendant: "Bring me my late Master Baizhang's Chan-sitting armrest and backrest."[83] The Master said, "Attendant, bring some fire [too, to incinerate such supports]."[84] Huangbo said, "All the same, do take them with you. In the future, you will plunk down in [cross-legged] sitting posture [with a thud] right on the tongues of the people of all-under-heaven [i.e., with these items you will be able to prove to them that you are my successor]."[85]

47.2

Later Guishan asked Yangshan, "Did Linji [by callling for fire to burn the transmission regalia] violate Huangbo's expectation [i.e., disobey Huangbo]?"[86] Yangshan said, "No such thing." Guishan said, "Well then, what is your take on it?" Yangshan said, "Precisely because [Linji] knew the [great] kindness [he had received from Huangbo], he could [truly] repay that kindness [by burning the transmission regalia]."[87] Guishan said, "Among the people of high antiquity, was there ever anything like [Linji's recognizing the kindness and repaying it]?"[88] Yangshan said, "There was. But the age is so far back, and so I don't want to tell you about it, Preceptor." Guishan said, "All the same, I want to know. Just try me." Yangshan then said, "For example, at the Śūraṃgama assembly, Ānanda praised the Buddha, saying, 'I will dedicate this deep mind [of great compassion] to [all the beings] in the buddha-lands [as numberless as] dust particles.[89] This is called repaying the Buddha's kindness.' Is this not a matter of repaying kindness?"[90] Guishan said, "Indeed, it is so. If the view [of the disciple] is equal to that of the teacher, it will reduce the teacher's virtue by half. Only when the view [of the disciple] surpasses that of the teacher is there the qualification for receiving the transmission [i.e., only when Linji's vision surpasses that of Huangbo can Huangbo transmit to Linji]."[91]

48

Linji arrived at Bodhidharma's stupa [at the Dinglin Monastery].[92] The Stupa Steward said, "Will the Venerable be bowing first to the Buddha or bowing first to the patriarch?"[93] The Master said, "'Buddha' or 'patriarch'— I won't be bowing to either of them."[94] The Stupa Steward [with his eyes wide open, talking dream-nonsense] said, "Venerable, what do you have against the Buddha and the patriarch?"[95] The Master, [truly repaying the kindness of the buddhas and patriarchs,] instantly left with a snap of his sleeves.[96]

49

When the Master was traveling on foot [i.e., after his great awakening, he traveled on foot all over, calibrating and adjudicating], he arrived at Longguang's place.[97] Longguang held a [Dharma-]Hall Convocation at which the Master came forward and asked, "Without flashing the edge of the sword blade, how can victory be achieved?" Longguang righted his sitting posture [on the Dharma Seat].[98] The Master [playing with him] said, "Great teacher, are you all out of *upāyas* [i.e., is that the best expedient you can muster]?"[99] Longguang [angrily] glared at him, [emitting a hoarse] "Aagh!"[100] The Master pointed at him and said, "You old geezer—this day you have lost!"

50.1

[The Master] arrived at [Mt.] Sanfeng.[101] Preceptor Ping asked, "What *place* do you come from?"[102] The Master said, "I've come from Huangbo's." Ping said, "What words of instruction does Huangbo have?"[103] The Master said, "Ever since the ox [cast] of gold [Huangbo's teaching, got stuck in] mud and fell into the charcoal [fire] the other day, there's not been a trace of it left behind [i.e., Huangbo's buddhadharma does not leave any trace of words and phrases]."[104] Ping said, "The golden [autumn] wind [of the west/ of Huangbo's teaching] may blow [a new Linji tune on] the jade flute,[105] but who will be able to recognize its music [i.e., who will hit it off perfectly with the traceless teaching and get its purport]?"[106] The Master said, "[The one who recognizes its music] goes right through the ten-thousand-layer barrier, but isn't fixed to the clear sky [i.e., isn't fixed to the unconditioned]."[107] Ping, [curbing Linji,] said, "In this dialogue you have [pitched yourself] too high [i.e., you are being lofty and excessive]."[108] The Master said, "The dragon [Huangbo] gives birth to a golden phoenix son [Linji], who cracks open the blue lapis-lazuli [phoenix egg]."[109] Ping said, "Well, sit down and have some tea [i.e., mundane chatter over tea/reality as it truly is]."[110]

50.2

[Ping] also asked, "By the way, what *place* have you been visiting recently?"[111] The Master said, "Longguang's." Ping said, "What's up with Longguang these days [i.e., what words of instruction does Longguang have these days]?"[112] [Without answering] the Master instantly went out.[113]

51

[The Master] arrived at Daci's place. Daci was doing [cross-legged] sitting inside the *fangzhang*. The Master asked, "What's it like, living a peaceful life[114] [in retreat] in your *fangzhang* [i.e., have you attained realization while living a quiet life in your *fangzhang*]?"[115] Daci said, "[I am like] the mid-winter pine that retains its characteristic green even for a thousand years,[116] but when spring comes to the ten-thousand countries, the locals [like you are joyful], picking flowers [and getting drunk looking at the moon]."[117] The Master said, "The perfect [mirror-]wisdom's substance eternally transcends past and present;[118] and [speaking of which] there is a ten-thousand-layer barrier blocking the way to the three mountains [the three mythical islands of Penglai, Fangzhang, and Yingzhou; i.e., blocking the way to your *fangzhang*/blocking the way to the home mountains of the *original portion*]."[119] Daci instantly gave a shout [and the lock on the ten-thousand-layer barrier all-at-once opened up].[120] The Master also gave a shout.[121] Daci said, "So what about it?"[122] The Master instantly left with a snap of his sleeves [a thousand-foot whale, spouting amidst the vast waves, taking flight].[123]

52

[The Master] arrived at Huayan's [place] in Xiangzhou. Huayan [knowing that Linji was coming] leaned on his staff with the air of [someone] asleep.[124] The Master said, "Preceptor, you're nodding off—what's up?"[125] Huayan said, "This Chan adept is evidently different [from the run-of-the-mill—he has a level of understanding that is off-the-charts]."[126] The Master said, "Attendant, go make some tea for the Preceptor [since he has been talking in his sleep and is not yet awake—the tea will wake him]."[127] Huayan then called, "Duty Master! Find a place for this Advanced Seat at the third position [on the sitting platform in the lower hall, i.e., Head Seat of the rear hall]."[128]

53

[The Master] arrived at Cuifeng's [place]. Cuifeng asked, "What *place* did you come from?" The Master said, "I've come from Huangbo's." Cuifeng said, "Does Huangbo have any words of instruction for people?"[129] The Master said, "Huangbo has no words of instruction."[130] Cuifeng said,

"Why 'no' [i.e., why the extreme of annihilationism]?"[131] The Master said, "Suppose he had [words of instruction], there would be no way to voice it [i.e., suppose the extreme of eternalism, that would entail the extreme of annihilationism]."[132] Cuifeng said, "Just try to voice it."[133] The Master said, "The single arrow has already gone over [your head] to India [and its whereabouts are unknown/it's too late to do anything]."[134]

54

[The Master] arrived at Xiangtian's [place]. The Master asked, "Neither 'worldling' nor '*ārya*'—please, Master, speak!"[135] Xiangtian [giving a scattered and untidy answer] said, "I'm just *in that way*."[136] The Master instantly gave a shout and said, "That bunch of bald-headed ones [in your assembly]—just what kind of grub are they angling for here?"[137]

55

[The Master] arrived at Minghua's [place]. Minghua asked, "Coming and going—what are you doing?" The Master said, "It's just a scheme for wearing out straw sandals."[138] Minghua said, "In the final analysis, what's it all for?" The Master said, "You old Han—you don't even know what we're talking about!"

56.1

[The Master, while] proceeding to Fenglin's, met an old woman on the road. The old woman asked, "To what *place* are [you] going/to what *place* has [Fenglin] gone?" The Master said, "I'm going to Fenglin's." The old woman said, "It just so happens Fenglin isn't there."[139] The Master said, "To what *place* has he gone?" The old woman instantly whacked him.[140] The Master called out, "Grandma!" The old woman turned her head, and the Master instantly whacked her.

56.2

The Master arrived at Fenglin's. Fenglin asked, "May I ask you a hypothetical question—is that okay?"[141] The Master said, "[When there is originally no problem,] why would you intentionally create an issue [i.e., *nothing-to-do* is fine—why have something to ask about]?"[142] Fenglin said, "The [reflection of the] moon on the placid sea [of the innately pure mind, i.e., Fenglin,] is not [fragmented into multiple] reflections; the frolicking fish [i.e., Linji] of his own accord has lost his way."[143] The Master said, "The moon on the sea has never been [fragmented into multiple] reflections [that could mislead the fish]—how could the frolicking fish lose its way?"[144] Fenglin said, "In contemplating the wind [of *avidyā*], one comes to know that waves arise; a humble sailboat floating on the water will flutter."[145] The Master said, "The solitary wheel [of the moon] alone illuminates [all over], and the rivers and mountains are quiet; one spontaneous laugh, and heaven and earth are startled."[146] Fenglin said, "Never mind taking your three-inch [tongue] to illuminate heaven and earth,[147] just try to say a single line right to my face in the here and now [i.e., say a line that is free of words]."[148] The Master [curbed Fenglin by] saying, "If on the road you meet a swordsman, [of course] you must make a presentation of your sword; but if he's not a poet, don't make a presentation of a poem."[149] Fenglin gave it a rest. The Master then had a verse [i.e., the single line that Fenglin had demanded]:[150] "The Great Way has nothing to do with 'sameness' [and 'difference'];[151] no matter whether you are facing east or west [i.e., everywhere is the *samadhi* of freedom],[152] [even] the spark from a stone is not [instantaneous enough to] qualify as [the realm of the *original portion*, the place wherein the Great Way cuts off sameness,] nor is a lightning bolt [instantaneous enough to] penetrate [the realm of the *original portion*, the place wherein the Great Way cuts off 'sameness' and 'difference']."[153]

56.3

Guishan asked Yangshan, "[Since] 'the spark from a stone cannot qualify, and a lightning bolt cannot penetrate,' [how much more so is it the case with words, and so] what did the *āryas* of ancient times [i.e., the buddhas and patriarchs] use to instruct people?"[154] Yangshan said, "Preceptor, what is your take on it?" Guishan said, "All words [used to teach people, such as 'the spark from a stone cannot qualify,' and so forth,] completely lack any real meaning."[155] Yangshan said, "No, not so." Guishan said, "Well then, what is your take on it?"[156] Yangshan said, "The [checkpoint] officials don't allow even a needle through [i.e., lines like 'the spark from a stone cannot qualify,'], but privately [entire] carts and horses can slip through [i.e., Chan followers, in giving instruction, smuggle through provisional methods that sometimes do involve speech and sometimes involve silence]."[157]

57.1

[The Master] arrived at Jinniu's [place]. Jinniu saw the Master coming, held his staff sideways, and squatted [on the ground inside] the [Mountain] Gate, [setting up a barrier blocking the Master's way].[158] The Master struck the staff three times with his hand [showing that he wanted to make this an occasion for dharma combat],[159] and was off to the [Sangha] Hall, where he assumed the sitting posture at the first position [on the sitting platform, the position of Head Seat].[160] Jinniu came down [from the *fangzhang*], saw him [doing cross-legged sitting at the first position], and asked:[161] "In an encounter between guest and host, each is bound by rules of courtesy. Where do you come from, Advanced Seat, that you are so lacking in ritual etiquette?"[162] The Master said, "What did you say/[beyond this,] what [more] do you have to say, Old Preceptor?"[163] Jiniu was about to open his mouth when the Master instantly whacked him.[164] Jinniu looked like he was about to collapse. The Master whacked him again. Jinniu [slacking off and falling into accomodation] said, "I'm not having good luck today."[165]

57.2

Guishan asked Yangshan, "[In the exchange between] these two honored monks, was there a winner and a loser?" Yangshan said, "[If there were such a thing as 'a] winner,' both [would have been] 'winners.' [If there were such a thing as 'a] loser,' both [would have been] 'losers,' [but in the end, because these are just terms, there was neither 'winner' nor 'loser']."[166]

58

When the Master was on the verge of transmigrating [to his next birth], he righted his sitting posture [in the Dharma Hall] and said,[167] "After I die, you mustn't let my '*saddharma* vision' [i.e., 'true-dharma vision' or wonderful mind of nirvana] die out."[168] Sansheng advanced and said, "How could we dare to let the Preceptor's '*saddharma* vision' die out?"[169] The Master said, "If later there is a *person* who asks you about it, what will you say to *him*?" Sansheng instantly gave a shout.[170] The Master said, "Who could have guessed that my '*saddharma* vision' would die out thanks to *this* dumb-ass! [I.e., thereby sealing Sansheng.]"[171] Having finished speaking, in correct sitting posture [with correct mind, without even a change in expression], he showed "quiescence" [complete nirvana].[172]

[Part V]

[Stupa Record of Chan Master Linji Huizhao]

59.1

The Master's [Dharma or] taboo name was Yixuan.[1] He was a man of Nanhua in Caozhou [in Shandong]. His family name was Xing. From his childhood, he surpassed others in intelligence.[2] Later as an adult he was known for his filial devotion. When he had his head shaven and received the full [two-hundred fifty] precepts,[3] he enrolled in a [tuition-charging monastery] school that specialized in lectures [on the sutras and treatises].[4] He was researching the *vinaya* in detail and making a broad study of the sutras and treatises,[5] when suddenly he sighed, "These [sutras, *vinaya*, and treatises are just] medical prescriptions [*upāyas*] for helping [the people of] the world—this is not the [Chan] purport of the *separate transmission outside the teachings*."[6] He then changed [from the costume of a Vinaya monk/teachings monk] into the costume [of a Chan monk] and wandered in the [various] regions [seeking out teachers].[7] First of all he trained with Huangbo, and next he visited Dayu. The encounters and verbal exhanges of that [time] are contained in the [preceding] *Record of the Karman [of the Master's Career]*.[8] Having been certified by Huangbo, he proceeded to Hebei and became the abbot of a small temple facing the vicinity of the Hutuo River in the southeast corner of Zhenzhou city. This [temple] was called Linji ["facing the river crossing"] because [that was the original name] of the place.[9] Puhua was there before [Linji arrived].[10] Feigning craziness, [Puhua] mingled with the sangha.[11] It was impossible to distinguish whether he was a worldling or an *ārya*. After the Master arrived, [Puhua] assisted him [in temple rituals].[12] Just when the Master's teaching activities were flourishing, Puhua achieved total *mokṣa* [i.e., complete liberation—there was not even a corpse in Puhua's coffin]. This tallied with the prediction [mentioned above] of Yangshan,[13] [who was called] "the little Śākya."[14]

59.2

It happened that a military disturbance broke out, and the Master evacuated [Linji Temple].[15] But the Defender-in-chief Mo Junhe donated his house within the city walls [of Zhenzhou] as a temple.[16] He hung out a plaque [inscribed] "Linji Temple" and welcomed the Master to take up residence. Later [the Master] swept up his robe, [left this place also], and proceeded southward. When he arrived at the He[bei] prefectural seat [i.e., Chengde],[17] the Commandery Governor, [Cavalier] Attendant-in-ordinary Wang,[18] invited him as a master. Before any time had elapsed, he went to Xinghua Monastery in Daming superior prefecture [i.e., Weizhou],[19] where he dwelled in the East Hall. On a certain day, suddenly, showing no illness, he put in order his [Dharma] costume and righted his sitting posture. When the dialogue with Sansheng was finished [i.e., the dialogue culminating in Linji's saying, "Who could have guessed that my '*saddharma* vision' would die out thanks to *this* dumb-ass!"],[20] he peacefully departed. The time was the tenth day of the first month of Xiantong 8 [February 18, 867].[21] His disciples erected a stupa in the northwest corner of Daming superior prefecture [and placed] the Master's intact body inside [i.e., an "earth interment," not cremation].[22] By imperial proclamation he was awarded the posthumous title "Chan Master Huizhao" ["Wisdom Illumination"] and a stupa named "Chengling" ["Clear Spirit"]. Placing my palms together in *añjali* [in a state of mental concentration and respect], bowing my head, I have recorded a summary [biography] of the Master.[23]

Respectfully copied out by the humble Dharma successor
Yanzhao, in residence at Baoshou [Monastery] in Zhenzhou.[24]

Here ends The Record of the Sayings of Chan Master Linji Huizhao of Zhenzhou

Collated by the humble Dharma successor
Cunjiang in residence at Xinghua [Monastery]
in Daming superior prefecture[25]

[Printing blocks reopened by Bhikṣu Yuanjue
Zongyan in residence at Mt. Gu in Fuzhou][26]

Yuanjue Zongyan's 圓覺宗演 *Xuanhe* 宣和 *2 (1120)* Linjilu *Edition (LJL)*

(section numbers based on Yanagida Seizan's *Butten koza* 30 translation)

鎮州臨濟慧照禪師語錄
住三聖嗣法小師慧然集

[上堂]

I.1　府主王常侍。與諸官請師升座。師上堂云。山僧今日事不獲已。曲順人情方登此座。若約祖宗門下。稱揚大事。直是開口不得。無你措足處。山僧此日以常侍堅請。那隱綱宗。還有作家戰將直下展陣開旗麼。對衆證據看。

I.2　僧問。如何是佛法大意。師便喝。僧禮拜。師云。這箇師僧。却堪持論。

I.3　問師唱誰家曲。宗風嗣阿誰。師云。我在黃蘗處。三度發問三度被打。僧擬議。師便喝。隨後打云。不可向虛空裏釘橛去也。

I.4　有座主問。三乘十二分教。豈不是明佛性。師云。荒草不曾鋤。主云。佛豈賺人也。師云。佛在什麼處。主無語。師云。對常侍前擬瞞老僧。速退速退。妨他別人請問。

I.5　復云。此日法筵爲一大事故。更有問話者麼。速致問來。你纔開口。早勿交涉也。何以如此。不見釋尊云。法離文字。不屬因不在緣故。爲你信不及。所以今日葛藤。恐滯常侍與諸官員。昧他佛性。不如且退。喝一喝云。少信根人終無了日。久立珍重。

2　師因一日到河府。府主王常侍請師升座。時麻谷出問。大悲千手眼。那箇是正眼。師云。大悲千手眼。那箇是正眼。速道速道。麻谷拽師下座。麻谷却坐。師近前云。不審。麻谷擬議。師亦拽麻谷下座。師却坐。麻谷便出去。師便下座。

3　上堂云。赤肉團上有一無位真人。常從汝等諸人面門出入。未證據者看看。時有僧出問。如何是無位真人。師下禪床把住云。道道。其僧擬議。師托開云。無位真人是什麼乾屎橛。便歸方丈。

4.1　上堂。有僧出禮拜。師便喝。僧云。老和尚莫探頭好。師云。伱道落在什麼處。僧便喝。又有僧問。如何是佛法大意。師便喝。僧禮拜。師云。伱道好喝也無。僧云。草賊大敗。師云。過在什麼處。僧云。再犯不容。師便喝。

4.2　是日兩堂首座相見。同時下喝。僧問師。還有賓主也無。師云。賓主歷然。師云。大眾要會臨濟賓主句。問取堂中二首座。便下座。

5.1　上堂。僧問。如何是佛法大意。師竪起拂子。僧便喝。師便打。又僧問。如何是佛法大意。師亦竪起拂子。僧便喝。師亦喝。僧擬議。師便打。

5.2　師乃云。大眾。夫爲法者不避喪身失命。我二十年在黃蘗先師處。三度問佛法的的大意。三度蒙他賜杖。如蒿枝拂著相似。如今更思得一頓棒喫。誰人爲我行得。時有僧出眾云。某甲行得。師拈棒與他。其僧擬接。師便打。

6.1　上堂。僧問。如何是劍刃上事。師云。禍事禍事。僧擬議。師便打。

6.2　問祇如石室行者踏碓忘却移脚。向什麼處去。師云。沒溺深泉。

6.3　師乃云。但有來者不虧欠伊。總識伊來處。若與麼來。恰似失却。不與麼來。無繩自縛。一切時中莫亂斟酌。會與不會都來是錯。分明與麼道。一任天下人貶剝。久立珍重。

7　　上堂云。一人在孤峯頂上。無出身之路。一人在十字街頭。亦無向背。那箇在前那箇在後。不作維摩詰。不作傅大士。珍重。

8　　上堂云。有一人論劫。在途中不離家舍。有一人離家舍不在途中。那箇合受人天供養。便下座。

9.1　上堂。僧問。如何是第一句。師云。三要印開朱點側。未容擬議主賓分。問如何是第二句。師云。妙解豈容無著問。漚和爭負截流機。問如何是第三句。師云。看取棚頭弄傀儡。抽牽都來裏有人。

9.2　師又云。一句語須具三玄門。一玄門須具三要。有權有用。汝等諸人。作麼生會。下座。

[示眾]

10.1　師晚參示眾云。有時奪人不奪境。有時奪境不奪人。有時人境俱奪。有時人境俱不奪。

10.2　時有僧問。如何是奪人不奪境。師云。煦日發生鋪地錦。瓔孩垂髮白如絲。僧云。如何是奪境不奪人。師云。王令已行天下徧。將軍塞外絕烟塵。僧云。如何是人境兩俱奪。師云。并汾絕信獨處一方。僧云。如何是人境俱不奪。師云。王登寶殿野老謳歌。

10.3　師乃云。今時學佛法者。且要求真正見解。若得真正見解。生死不染去住自由。不要求殊勝。殊勝自至。道流。祇如自古先德。皆有出人底路。如山僧指示人處。祇要伱不受人惑。要用便用。更莫遲疑。如今學者不得。病在甚處。病在不自信處。伱若自信不及。即便忙忙地。徇一切境轉。被他萬境回換。不得自由。

10.4 你若能歇得念念馳求心。便與祖佛不別。你欲得識祖佛麼。祇你面前聽法底是。學人信不及。便向外馳求。設求得者皆是文字勝相。終不得他活祖意。莫錯諸禪德。此時不遇。萬劫千生輪回三界。徇好境掇去。驢牛肚裏生。道流。約山僧見處。與釋迦不別。今日多般用處。欠少什麼。六道神光未曾間歇。若能如是見得。祇是一生無事人。

10.5 大德。三界無安猶如火宅。此不是你久停住處。無常殺鬼一刹那間不揀貴賤老少。你要與祖佛不別。但莫外求。你一念心上清淨光。是你屋裏法身佛。你一念心上無分別光。是你屋裏報身佛。你一念心上無差別光。是你屋裏化身佛。此三種身是你即今目前聽法底人。祇爲不向外馳求。有此功用。據經論家。取三種身爲極則。約山僧見處不然。此三種身是名言。亦是三種依。古人云。身依義立。土據體論。法性身法性土明知是光影。

10.6 大德。你且識取弄光影底人。是諸佛之本源。一切處是道流歸舍處。是你四大色身不解說法聽法。脾胃肝膽不解說法聽法。虛空不解說法聽法。是什麼解說法聽法。是你目前歷歷底。勿一箇形段孤明。是這箇解說法聽法。若如是見得。便與祖佛不別。但一切時中更莫間斷。觸目皆是。祇爲情生智隔想變體殊。所以輪回三界受種種苦。若約山僧見處。無不甚深無不解脫。

10.7 道流。心法無形通貫十方。在眼曰見。在耳曰聞。在鼻嗅香。在口談論。在手執捉。在足運奔。本是一精明。分爲六和合。一心既無。隨處解脫。山僧與麼說。意在什麼處。祇爲道流一切馳求心不能歇。上他古人閑機境。道流取山僧見處。坐斷報化佛頭。十地滿心猶如客作兒。等妙二覺擔枷鎖漢。羅漢辟支猶如廁穢。菩提涅槃如繫驢橛。何以如此。祇爲道流不達三祇劫空。所以有此障礙。若是真正道人。終不如是。但能隨緣消舊業。任運著衣裳。要行即行。要坐即坐。無一念心希求佛果。緣何如此。古人云。若欲作業求佛。佛是生死大兆。

10.8 大德。時光可惜。祇擬傍家波波地學禪學道。認名認句。求佛求祖求善知識意度。莫錯。道流。你祇有一箇父母。更求何物。你自返照看。古人云。演若達多失却頭。求心歇處即無事。大德。且要平常莫作模樣。有一般不識好惡禿奴。便即見神見鬼指東劃西好晴好雨。如是之流。盡須抵債。向閻老前吞熱鐵丸有日。好人家男女。被這一般野狐精魅所著。便即捏怪。瞎屢生。索飯錢有日在。

11.1 師示衆云。道流。切要求取真正見解。向天下橫行。免被這一般精魅惑亂。無事是貴人。但莫造作。祇是平常。你擬向外傍家求過覓脚手錯了也。祇擬求佛。佛是名句。你還識馳求底麼。三世十方佛祖出來。也祇爲求法。如今參學道流。也祇爲求法。得法始了。未得依前輪回五道。云何是法。法者是心法。心法無形通貫十方。目前現用。人信不及。便乃認名認句。向文字中求意度佛法。天地懸殊。

11.2 道流。山僧說法說什麼法。說心地法。便能入凡入聖。入淨入穢。入真入俗。要且不是你真俗凡聖。能與一切真俗凡聖安著名字。真俗凡聖與此人安著名字不得。道流。把得便用更不著名字。號之爲玄旨。

11.3 山僧說法與天下人別。祇如有箇文殊普賢出來目前。各現一身問法。纔道咨和尚。我早辨了也。老僧穩坐。更有道流來相見時。我盡辨了也。何以如此。祇爲我見處別。外不取凡聖。內不住根本。見徹更不疑謬。

12.1 師示眾云。道流。佛法無用功處。祇是平常無事。屙屎送尿著衣喫飯。困來即臥。愚人笑我。智乃知焉。古人云。向外作功夫。總是癡頑漢。你且隨處作主。立處皆真。境來回換不得。縱有從來習氣五無間業。自爲解脫大海。今時學者總不識法。猶如觸鼻羊逢著物安在口裏。奴郎不辨賓主不分。如是之流邪心入道。鬧處即入。不得名爲真出家人。正是真俗家人。

12.2 夫出家者。須辨得平常真正見解。辨佛辨魔辨真辨偽辨凡辨聖。若如是辨得。名真出家。若魔佛不辨。正是出一家入一家。喚作造業眾生。未得名爲真出家。祇如今有一箇佛魔同體不分。如水乳合。鵝王喫乳。如明眼道流。魔佛俱打。你若愛聖憎凡。生死海裏浮沈。

12.3 問如何是佛魔。師云。你一念心疑處是魔。你若達得萬法無生。心如幻化。更無一塵一法。處處清淨是佛。然佛與魔是染淨二境。約山僧見處。無佛無眾生。無古無今。得者便得。不歷時節。無修無證無得無失。一切時中更無別法。設有一法過此者。我說如夢如化。山僧所說皆是。

12.4 道流。即今目前孤明歷歷地聽者。此人處處不滯。通貫十方。三界自在。入一切境差別不能回換。一刹那間透入法界。逢佛說佛。逢祖說祖。逢羅漢說羅漢。逢餓鬼說餓鬼。向一切處游履國土教化眾生。未曾離一念。隨處清淨光透十方。萬法一如。

12.5 道流。大丈夫兒今日方知本來無事。祇爲你信不及。念念馳求。捨頭覓頭。自不能歇。如圓頓菩薩。入法界現身。向淨土中厭凡忻聖。如此之流。取捨未忘染淨心在。如禪宗見解。又且不然。直是現今更無時節。山僧說處皆是一期藥病相治。總無實法。若如是見得。是真出家。日消萬兩黃金。

12.6 道流。莫取次被諸方老師印破面門。道我解禪解道。辯似懸河。皆是造地獄業。若是真正學道人。不求世間過。切急要求真正見解。若達真正見解圓明方始了畢。

12.7 問如何是真正見解。師云。你但一切入凡入聖。入染入淨。入諸佛國土。入彌勒樓閣。入毘盧遮那法界。處處皆現國土成住壞空。佛出于世。轉大法輪。却入涅槃。不見有去來相貌。求其生死了不可得。便入無生法界。處處游履國土。入華藏世界。盡見諸法空相。皆無實法。唯有聽法無依道人。是諸佛之母。所以佛從無依生。若悟無依。佛亦無得。若如是見得者。是真正見解。

12.8 學人不了爲執名句。被他凡聖名礙。所以障其道眼不得分明。祇如十二分教。皆是表顯之說。學者不會。便向表顯名句上生解。皆是依倚落在因果。未免三界生死。你若欲得生死去住脫著自由。即今識取聽法底人。無形無相無根無本無住處。活撥撥地。應是萬種施設。用處祇是無處。所以覓著轉遠。求之轉乖。號之爲祕密。

12.9 道流。你莫認著箇夢幻伴子。遲晚中間便歸無常。你向此世界中。覓箇什麼物作解脫。覓取一口飯喫補毳過時。且要訪尋知識。莫因循逐樂。光陰可惜。念念無常。麁則被地水火風。細則被生住異滅四相所逼。道流。今時且要識取四種無相境。免被境擺撲。

12.10 問如何是四種無相境。師云。你一念心疑被地來礙。你一念心愛被水來溺。
你一念心瞋被火來燒。你一念心喜被風來飄。若能如是辨得。不被境轉。
處處用境。東涌西沒。南涌北沒。中涌邊沒。邊涌中沒。履水如地。履地如水。
緣何如此。爲達四大如夢如幻故。

12.11 道流。你祇今聽法者。不是你四大能用你四大。若能如是見得。便乃去住
自由。約山僧見處。勿嫌底法。你若愛聖。聖者聖之名。有一般學人。向五臺山
裏求文殊。早錯了也。五臺山無文殊。你欲識文殊麼。祇你目前用處。始終不異。
處處不疑。此箇是活文殊。你一念心無差別光。處處總是真普賢。你一念心自能
解縛。隨處解脫。此是觀音。三昧法。互爲主伴。出則一時出。一即三三
即一。如是解得始好看教。

13.1 師示衆云。如今學道人且要自信。莫向外覓。總上他閑塵境。都不辨邪正。
祇如有祖有佛。皆是教迹中事。有人拈起一句子語。或隱顯中出。便即疑生。
照天照地。傍家尋問。也大忙然。大丈夫兒。莫祇麼論主論賊。論是論非。論色
論財。論說閑話過日。山僧此間不論僧俗。但有來者盡識得伊。任伊向甚處出來。
但有聲名文句。皆是夢幻。

13.2 却見乘境底人。是諸佛之玄旨。佛境不能自稱我是佛境。遷是這箇無依道人。
乘境出來。若有人出來問我求佛。我即應清淨境出。有人問我菩薩。我即應慈悲
境出。有人問我菩提。我即應淨妙境出。有人問我涅槃。我即應寂靜境出。境即
萬般差別。人即不別。所以應物現形。如水中月。

13.3 道流。你若欲得如法。直須是大丈夫兒始得。若萎萎隨隨地。則不得也。
夫如[斯/瓦]嗄(上音西下所嫁切)之器。不堪貯醍醐。如大器者。直要不受人惑。
隨處作主立處皆真。但有來者皆不得受。你一念疑。即魔入心。如菩薩疑時。
生死魔得便。但能息念。更莫外求。物來則照。你但信現今用底。一箇事也無。
你一念心生三界。隨緣被境分爲六塵。你如今應用處。欠少什麼。一刹那間便入
淨入穢。入彌勒樓閣。入三眼國土。處處遊履。唯見空名。

13.4 問如何是三眼國土。師云。我共你入淨妙國土中。著清淨衣。說法身佛。
又入無差別國土中。著無差別衣。說報身佛。又入解脫國土中。著光明衣。說化
身佛。此三眼國土皆是依變。約經論家。取法身爲根本。報化二身爲用。山僧見
處法身即不解說法。所以古人云。身依義立。土據體論。法性身法性土。明知是
建立之法。依通國土。空拳黃葉用誑小兒。蒺藜菱刺枯骨上覓什麼汁。心外無法。
內亦不可得。求什麼物。

13.5 你諸方言道。有修有證。莫錯。設有修得者。皆是生死業。你言六度萬行
齊修。我見皆是造業。求佛求法。即是造地獄業。求菩薩亦是造業。看經看教亦
是造業。佛與祖師是無事人。所以有漏有爲。無漏無爲。爲清淨業。
有一般瞎禿子。飽喫飯了。便坐禪觀行。把捉念漏不令放起。厭喧求靜。
是外道法。祖師云。你若住心看靜。舉心外照。攝心內澄。凝心入定。如是之流
皆是造作。是你如今與麼聽法底人。作麼生擬修他證他莊嚴他。渠且不是修底物。
不是莊嚴得底物。若教他莊嚴。一切物即莊嚴得。你且莫錯。

13.6 道流。你取這一般老師口裏語。爲是真道。是善知識不思議。我是凡夫心。
不敢測度他老宿。瞎屢生。你一生祇作這箇見解。辜負這一雙眼。冷噤噤地。如凍

凌上驢駒相似。我不敢毀善知識。怕生口業。道流。夫大善知識。始敢毀佛毀祖。是非天下。排斥三藏教。罵辱諸小兒。向逆順中覓人。所以我於十二年中。求一箇業性。如芥子許不可得。若似新婦子禪師。便即怕趂出院。不與飯喫。不安不樂。自古先輩。到處人不信。被遞出始知是貴。若到處人盡肯。堪作什麼。所以師子一吼野干腦裂。

13.7 道流。諸方說有道可修。有法可證。你說證何法修何道。你今用處欠少什麼物。修補何處。後生小阿師不會。便即信這般野狐精魅。許他說事。繫縛他人。言道理行相應護惜三業始得成佛。如此說者如春細雨。古人云。路逢達道人。第一莫向道。所以言。若人修道道不行。萬般邪境競頭生。智劍出來無一物。明頭未顯暗頭明。所以古人云。平常心是道。

13.8 大德。覓什麼物。現今目前聽法無依道人。歷歷地分明。未曾欠少。你若欲得與祖佛不別。但如是見。不用疑誤。你心心不異。名之活祖。心若有異。則性相別。心不異故。即性與相不別。

13.9 問如何是心心不異處。師云。你擬問早異了也。性相各分。道流莫錯。世出世諸法。皆無自性。亦無生性。但有空名。名字亦空。你秖麼認他閑名爲實。大錯了也。設有皆是依變之境。有箇菩提依涅槃依解脫依三身依境智依菩薩依佛依。你向依變國土中。覓什麼物。乃至三乘十二分教。皆是拭不淨故紙。佛是幻化身。祖是老比丘。你還是娘生已否。你若求佛。即被佛魔攝。你若求祖。即被祖魔縛。你若有求皆苦。不如無事。

13.10 有一般禿比丘。向學人道。佛是究竟。於三大阿僧祇劫。修行果滿方始成道。道流。你若道佛是究竟。緣什麼八十年後向拘尸羅城雙林樹間側臥而死去。佛今何在。明知與我生死不別。你言三十二相八十種好是佛。轉輪聖王應是如來。明知是幻化。古人云。如來舉身相爲順世間情恐人生斷見。權且立虛言。假言三十二八十也空聲。有身非覺體。無相乃真形。

13.11 你道佛有六通。是不可思議。一切諸天神仙阿修羅大力鬼亦有神通。應是佛否。道流。莫錯。秖如阿修羅與天帝釋戰。戰敗領八萬四千眷屬。入藕絲孔中藏。莫是聖否。如山僧所舉。皆是業通依通。夫如佛六通者不然。入色界不被色惑。入聲界不被聲惑。入香界不被香惑。入味界不被味惑。入觸界不被觸惑。入法界不被法惑。所以達六種色聲香味觸法皆是空相。不能繫縛此無依道人。雖是五蘊漏質。便是地行神通。

13.12 道流。真佛無形真法無相。你秖麼幻化上頭作模作樣。設求得者。皆是野狐精魅。並不是真佛。是外道見解。夫如真學道人。並不取佛。不取菩薩羅漢。不取三界殊勝。迥然獨脫不與物拘。乾坤倒覆我更不疑。十方諸佛現前。無一念心喜。三塗地獄頓現。無一念心怖。緣何如此。我見諸法空相。變即有。不變即無。三界唯心萬法唯識。所以夢幻空花何勞把捉。

13.13 唯有道流目前現今聽法底人。入火不燒入水不溺。入三塗地獄。如遊園觀。入餓鬼畜生而不受報。緣何如此。無嫌底法。你若愛聖憎凡。生死海裏沈浮。煩惱由心故有。無心煩惱何拘。不勞分別取相。自然得道須臾。你擬傍家波波地學得。於三祇劫中終歸生死。不如無事向叢林中牀角頭交脚坐。

13.14 道流。如諸方有學人來。主客相見了。便有一句子語。辨前頭善知識。被學人拈出箇機權語路。向善知識口角頭擺過。看儞識不識。儞若識得是境。把得便拋向坑子裏。學人便即尋常。然後便索善知識語。依前奪之。學人云。上智哉是大善知識。即云。儞大不識好惡。如善知識。把出箇境塊子。向學人面前弄。前人辨得下下作主。不受境惑。善知識便即現半身。學人便喝。善知識又入一切差別語路中擺撲。學人云。不識好惡老禿奴。善知識歎曰。真正道流。

13.15 如諸方善知識。不辨邪正。學人來問菩提涅槃三身境智。瞎老師便與他解說。被他學人罵著。便把棒打他言無禮度。自是儞善知識無眼。不得嗔他。有一般不識好惡禿奴。即指東劃西。好晴好雨。好燈籠露柱。儞看眉毛有幾莖。這箇具機緣。學人不會。便即心狂。如是之流。總是野狐精魅魍魎。被他好學人嗌嗌微笑。言瞎老禿惑亂他天下人。

13.16 道流。出家兒且要學道。祇如山僧。往日曾向毘尼中留心。亦曾於經論尋討。後方知是濟世藥表顯之說。遂乃一時拋却即訪道參禪。後遇大善知識。方乃道眼分明。始識得天下老和尚。知其邪正。不是娘生下便會。還是體究練磨一朝自省。

13.17 道流。儞欲得如法見解。但莫受人惑。向裏向外逢著便殺。逢佛殺佛。逢祖殺祖。逢羅漢殺羅漢。逢父母殺父母。逢親眷殺親眷。始得解脫。不與物拘。透脫自在。如諸方學道流。未有不依物出來底。山僧向此間從頭打。手上出來手上打。口裏出來口裏打。眼裏出來眼裏打。未有一箇獨脫出來底。皆是上他古人閑機境。

13.18 山僧。無一法與人。祇是治病解縛。儞諸方道流。試不依物出來。我要共儞商量。十年五歲並無一人。皆是依草附葉竹木精靈野狐精魅。向一切糞塊上亂咬。瞎漢枉消他十方信施。道我是出家兒。作如是見解。向儞道。無佛無法無修無證。祇與麼傍家擬求什麼物。瞎漢頭上安頭。是儞欠少什麼。

13.19 道流。是儞目前用底。與祖佛不別。祇麼不信便向外求。莫錯向外無法。內亦不可得。儞取山僧口裏語。不如休歇無事去。已起者莫續。未起者不要放起。便勝儞十年行腳。約山僧見處。無如許多般。祇是平常著衣喫飯無事過時。儞諸方來者。皆是有心。求佛求法。求解脫出離三界。癡人。儞要出三界什麼處去。佛祖是賞繫底名句。儞欲識三界麼。不離儞今聽法底心地。儞一念心貪是欲界。儞一念心嗔是色界。儞一念心癡是無色界。是儞屋裏家具子。三界不自道我是三界。還是道流目前靈靈地照燭萬般酌度世界底人。與三界安名。

13.20 大德。四大色身是無常。乃至脾胃肝膽髮毛爪齒。唯見諸法空相。儞一念心歇得處。喚作菩提樹。儞一念心不能歇得處。喚作無明樹。無明無住處。無明無始終。儞若念念心歇不得。便上他無明樹。便入六道四生披毛戴角。儞若歇得。便是清淨身界。儞一念不生。便是上菩提樹。三界神通變化意生化身。法喜禪悅身光自照。思衣羅綺千重。思食百味具足。更無橫病。菩提無住處。是故無得者。

13.21 道流。大丈夫漢更疑箇什麼。目前用處更是阿誰。把得便用。莫著名字。號爲玄旨。與麼見得。勿嫌底法。古人云。心隨萬境轉。轉處實能幽。隨流認得性。無喜亦無憂。

13.22 道流。如禪宗見解。死活循然。參學之人大須子細。如主客相見。便有言論往來。或應物現形。或全體作用。或把機權喜怒。或現半身。或乘師子。或乘象王。如有真正學人。便喝先拈出一箇膠盆子。善知識不辨是境。便上他境上作模作樣。學人便喝。前人不肯放。此是膏肓之病不堪醫。喚作客看主。或是善知識不拈出物。隨學人問處即奪。學人被奪抵死不放。此是主看客。

13.23 或有學人。應一箇清淨境出善知識前。善知識辨得是境。把得拋向坑裏。學人言。大好善知識。即云。咄哉不識好惡。學人便禮拜。此喚作主看主。或有學人。披枷帶鎖出善知識前。善知識更與安一重枷鎖。學人歡喜。彼此不辨。呼爲客看客。大德。山僧如是所舉。皆是辨魔揀異。知其邪正。

13.24 道流。寔情大難。佛法幽玄。解得可可地。山僧竟日與他說破。學者總不在意。千徧萬徧腳底踏過。黑沒焌地。無一箇形段。歷歷孤明。學人信不及。便向名句上生解。年登半百。祇管傍家負死屍行。檐却檐子天下走。索草鞋錢有日在。

13.25 大德。山僧說向外無法。學人不會。便即向裏作解。便即倚壁坐。舌拄上齶。湛然不動。取此爲是祖門佛法也。大錯。是你若取不動清淨境爲是。你即認他無明爲郎主。古人云。湛湛黑暗深坑。實可怖畏。此之是也。你若認他動者是。一切草木皆解動。應可是道也。所以動者是風大。不動者是地大。動與不動俱無自性。你若向動處捉他。他向不動處立。你若向不動處捉他。他向動處立。譬如潛泉魚鼓波而自躍。大德。動與不動是二種境。還是無依道人用動用不動。

13.26 如諸方學人來。山僧此間作三種根器斷。如中下根器來。我便奪其境。而不除其法。或中上根器來。我便境法俱奪。如上上根器來。我便境法人俱不奪。如有出格見解人來。山僧此間便全體作用不歷根器。大德。到這裏學人著力處不通風。石火電光即過了也。學人若眼定動。即沒交涉。擬心即差。動念即乖。有人解者不離目前。大德。你擔鉢囊屎擔子。傍家走求佛求法。即今與麼馳求底。你還識渠麼。活撥撥地。祇是勿根株。擁不聚撥不散。求著即轉遠。不求還在目前。靈音屬耳。若人不信。徒勞百年。

13.27 道流。一刹那間便入華藏世界。入毘盧遮那國土。入解脫國土。入神通國土。入清淨國土。入法界。入穢入淨。入凡入聖。入餓鬼畜生。處處討覓尋。皆不見有生有死。唯有空名。幻化空花不勞把捉。得失是非一時放却。

13.28 道流。山僧佛法的的相承。從麻谷和尚丹霞和尚道一和尚廬山與石鞏和尚。一路行徧天下。無人信得。盡皆起謗。如道一和尚用處。純一無雜。學人三百五百。盡皆不見他意。如廬山和尚。自在真正順逆用處。學人不測涯際。悉皆忙然。如丹霞和尚。翫珠隱顯。學人來者皆悉被罵。如麻谷用處。苦如黃蘗近皆不得。如石鞏用處。向箭頭上覓人。來者皆懼。

13.29 如山僧今日用處。真正。 成壞。翫弄神變。入一切境。隨處無事。境不能換。但有來求者。我即便出看渠。渠不識我。我便著數般衣。學人生解一向入我言句。苦哉瞎禿子無眼人把我著底衣。認青黃赤白。我脫却入清淨境中。學人一見便生忻欲。我又脫却。學人失心忙然狂走。言我無衣。我即向渠道你識我著衣底人否。忽爾回頭。認我了也。

13.30 大德。你莫認衣。衣不能動。人能著衣。有箇清淨衣。有箇無生衣。菩提衣。
涅槃衣。有祖衣。有佛衣。大德。但有聲名文句。皆悉是衣變。從臍輪氣海中
鼓激。牙齒敲磕成其句義。明知是幻化。大德。外發聲語業。內表心所法。
以思有念。皆悉是衣。你祇麼認他著底衣爲實解。縱經塵劫祇是衣通。三界循
還輪迴生死。不如無事。相逢不相識。共語不知名。

13.31 今時學人不得。蓋爲認名字爲解。大策子上抄死老漢語。三重五重複子裹。
不教人見。道是玄旨。以爲保重。大錯。瞎屢生。你向枯骨上覓什麼汁。
有一般不識好惡。向教中取意度商量成於句義。如把屎塊子向口裏含了吐過與
別人。猶如俗人打傳口令相似。一生虛過。也道我出家被他問著佛法。便即杜口
無詞。眼似漆突。口如榀擔。如此之類。逢彌勒出世。移置他方世界。寄地獄受苦。

13.32 大德。你波波地往諸方覓什麼物。踏你脚板。闊無佛可求。無道可成。
無法可得。外求有相佛。與汝不相似。欲識汝本心。非合亦非離。道流。真佛無形。
真道無體。真法無相。三法混融和合一處。既辨不得。喚作忙忙業識衆生。

13.33 問如何是真佛真法真道。乞垂開示。師云。佛者心清淨是。法者心光明是。
道者處處無礙淨光是。三即一皆是空名。而無寔有。如真正學道人。念念心不間斷。
自達磨大師從西土來。祇是覓箇不受人惑底人。後遇二祖。一言便了。始知從前虛
用功夫。山僧今日見處與祖佛不別。若第一句中得。與祖佛爲師。
若第二句中得。與人天爲師。若第三句中得。自救不了。

13.34 問如何是西來意。師云。若有意。自救不了。云既無意。云何二祖得法。
師云。得者是不得。云既若不得。云何是不得底意。師云。爲你向一切處馳求心
不能歇。所以祖師言。咄哉丈夫。將頭覓頭。你言下便自回光返照。更不別求。
知身心與祖佛不別。當下無事。方名得法。

13.35 大德。山僧今時事不獲已。話度說出許多不才淨。你且莫錯。據我見處。
實無許多般道理。要用便用。不用便休。祇如諸方說六度萬行以爲佛法。我道是
莊嚴門佛事門。非是佛法。乃至持齋持戒。擎油不[水+音符閃]。道眼不明。
盡須抵債。索飯錢有日在。何故如此。入道不通理。復身還信施。長者八十一。
其樹不生耳。

13.36 乃至孤峯獨宿。一食卯齋。長坐不臥。六時行道。皆是造業底人。乃至頭
目髓腦國城妻子象馬七珍盡皆捨施。如是等見。皆是苦身心故。還招苦果。不如
無事純一無雜。乃至十地滿心菩薩。皆求此道流蹤跡。了不可得。所以諸天歡喜。
地神捧足。十方諸佛無不稱歎。緣何如此。爲今聽法道人用處無蹤跡。

13.37 問大通智勝佛。十劫坐道場。佛法不現前。不得成佛道。未審此意如何。
乞師指示。師云。大通者。是自己。於處處達其萬法無性無相。名爲大通。
智勝者。於一切處不疑不得一法。名爲智勝。佛者。心清淨光明透徹法界。
得名爲佛。十劫坐道場者。十波羅蜜是。佛法不現前者。佛本不生。法本不滅云何
更有現前。不得成佛道者。佛不應更作佛。古人云。佛常在世間。而不染世間法。

13.38 道流。你欲得作佛。莫隨萬物。心生種種法生。心滅種種法滅。一心不生
萬法無咎。世與出世。無佛無法。亦不現前。亦不曾失。設有者。皆是名言章句。

接引小兒施設藥病。表顯名句。且名句不自名句。還是你目前昭昭靈靈鑑覺聞知照燭底。安一切名句。大德。造五無間業。方得解脫。

13.39 問如何是五無間業。師云。殺父害母。出佛身血。破和合僧。焚燒經像等。此是五無間業。云如何是父。師云。無明是父。你一念心求起滅處不得。如響應空。隨處無事。名爲殺父。云如何是母。師云。貪愛爲母。你一念心入欲界中。求其貪愛。唯見諸法空相。處處無著。名爲害母。云如何是出佛身血。師云。你向清淨法界中。無一念心生解。便處處黑暗。是出佛身血。云如何是破和合僧。師云。你一念心正達煩惱結使如空無所依。是破和合僧。云如何是焚燒經像。師云。見因緣空。心空法空。一念決定斷。迥然無事。便是焚燒經像。

13.40 大德。若如是達得。免被他凡聖名礙。你一念心祇向空拳指上生實解。根境法中虛揑怪。自輕而退屈。言我是凡夫他是聖人。禿屢生。有甚死急。披他師子皮。却作野干鳴。大丈夫漢。不作丈夫氣息。自家屋裏物不肯信。祇麼向外覓。上他古人閑名句。倚陰博陽。不能特達。逢境便緣。逢塵便執。觸處惑起。自無准定。道流。莫取山僧說處。何故。說無憑據。一期間圖畫虛空。如彩畫像等喻。

13.41 道流。莫將佛爲究竟。我見猶如廁孔。菩薩羅漢盡是枷鎖縛人底物。所以文殊仗劍殺於瞿曇。鴦掘持刀害於釋氏。道流。無佛可得。乃至三乘五性圓頓教迹。皆是一期藥病相治。並無實法。設有皆是相似。表顯路布。文字差排。且如是說。道流。有一般禿子。便向裏許著功。擬求出世之法。錯了也。若人求佛。是人失佛。若人求道。是人失道。若人求祖。是人失祖。

13.42 大德。莫錯。我且不取你解經論。我亦不取你國王大臣。我亦不取你辯似懸河。我亦不取你聰明智慧。唯要你真正見解。道流。設解得百本經論。不如一箇無事底阿師。你解得。即輕蔑他人。勝負修羅。人我無明。長地獄業。如善星比丘。解十二分教。生身陷地獄。大地不容。不如無事休歇去。飢來喫飯。睡來合眼。愚人笑我。智乃知焉。道流。莫向文字中求。心動疲勞。吸冷氣無益。不如一念緣起無生。超出三乘權學菩薩。

13.43 大德。莫因循過日。山僧往日未有見處時。黑漫漫地。光陰不可空過。腹熱心忙。奔波訪道。後還得力。始到今日。共道流如是話度。勸諸道流。莫爲衣食。看世界易過。善知識難遇。如優曇華時一現耳。你諸方聞道有箇臨濟老漢出來。便擬問難教語不得。被山僧全體作用。學人空開得眼。口總動不得。懵然不知以何答我。我向伊道。龍象蹴踏非驢所堪。你諸處祇指胸點肋。道我解禪解道。三箇兩箇到這裏不奈何。咄哉。你將這箇身心。到處簸兩片皮。誑諕閭閻。喫鐵棒有日在。非出家兒。盡向阿修羅界攝。

13.44 夫如至理之道。非静論而求激揚。鏗鏘以摧外道。至於佛祖相承。更無別意。設有言教。落在化儀三乘五性人天因果。如圓頓之教。又且不然。童子善財皆不求過。大德。莫錯用心。如大海不停死屍。祇麼擔却擬天下走。自起見障以礙於心。日上無雲。麗天普照。眼中無翳。空裏無花。道流。你欲得如法。但莫生疑。展則彌綸法界。收則絲髮不立。歷歷孤明未曾欠少。眼不見耳不聞。喚作什麼物。古人云。說似一物則不中。你但自家看。更有什麼。說亦無盡。各自著力。珍重。

勘辨

14.1　黃檗因入厨次。問飯頭。作什麼。飯頭云。揀衆僧米。黃檗云。一日喫多少。飯頭云。二石五。黃檗云。莫太多麼。飯頭云。猶恐少在。黃檗便打。飯頭却舉似師。師云。我爲汝勘這老漢。纔到侍立次。黃檗舉前話。師云。飯頭不會。請和尚代一轉語。師便問。莫太多麼。黃檗云。何不道來日更喫一頓。師云。說什麼來日。即今便喫。道了便掌。黃檗云。這風顛漢。又來這裏捋虎鬚。師便喝出去。

14.2　後潙山問仰山。此二尊宿意作麼生。仰山云。和尚作麼生。潙山云。養子方知父慈。仰山云不然。潙山云。子又作麼生。仰山云。大似勾賊破家。

15　師問僧。什麼處來。僧便喝。師便揖坐。僧擬議。師便打。師見僧來便竪起拂子。僧禮拜。師便打。又見僧來亦竪起拂子。僧不顧。師亦打。

16.1　師一日同普化赴施主家齋次。師問。毛吞巨海芥納須彌。爲是神通妙用本體如然。普化踏倒飯牀。師云。太麄生。普化云。這裏是什麼所在。說麄說細。

16.2　師來日又同普化赴齋。問今日供養何似昨日。普化依前踏倒飯牀。師云。得即得。太麄生。普化云。瞎漢。佛法說什麼麄細。師乃吐舌。

17　師一日與河陽木塔長老。同在僧堂地爐内坐。因說。普化每日在街市掣風掣顛。知他是凡是聖。言猶未了。普化入來。師便問。汝是凡是聖。普化云。汝且道。我是凡是聖。師便喝。普化以手指云。河陽新婦子。木塔老婆禪。臨濟小廝兒。却具一隻眼。師云這賊。普化云賊賊。便出去。

18　一日普化在僧堂前喫生菜。師見云。大似一頭驢。普化便作驢鳴。師云這賊。普化云賊賊。便出去。

19　因普化常於街市搖鈴云。明頭來明頭打。暗頭來暗頭打。四方八面來旋風打。虛空來連架打。師令侍者去纔見如是道便把住云。總不與麼來時如何。普化托開云。來日大悲院裏有齋。侍者回舉似師。師云。我從來疑著這漢。

20.1　有一老宿參師。未曾人事便問。禮拜即是。不禮拜即是。師便喝。老宿便禮拜。師云。好箇草賊。老宿云賊賊。便出去。師云。莫道無事好。

20.2　首座侍立次。師云。還有過也無。首座云有。師云。賓家有過。主家有過。首座云。二俱有過。師云。過在什麼處。首座便出去。師云。莫道無事好。後有僧舉似南泉。南泉云。官馬相踏。

21　師因入軍營赴齋。門首見員僚。師指露柱問。是凡是聖。員僚無語。師打露柱云。直饒道得。也祇是箇木橛。便入去。

22.1　師問院主。什麼處來。主云。州中糶黃米去來。師云。糶得盡麼。主云。糶得盡。師以杖面前畫一畫云。還糶得這箇麼。主便喝。師便打。

22.2　典座至。師舉前語。典座云。院主不會和尚意。師云。伱作麼生。典座便禮拜。師亦打。

23.1 有座主來相看次。師問座主。講何經論。主云。某甲荒虛粗習百法論。
師云。有一人於三乘十二分教明得。有一人於三乘十二分教明不得。是同是別。
主云。明得即同。明不得即別。

23.2 樂普爲侍者。在師後立云。座主這裏是什麼所在。說同說別。師回首問侍者。
汝又作麼生。侍者便喝。師送座主。回來遂問侍者。適來是汝喝老僧。侍者云是。
師便打。

24 師聞第二代德山垂示云。道得也三十棒。道不得也三十棒。師令樂普去問。
道得爲什麼也三十棒。待伊打汝接住棒送一送。看他作麼生。普到彼如教而問。
德山便打。普接住送一送。德山便歸方丈。普回舉似師。師云。我從來疑著這漢。
雖然如是。汝還見德山麼。普擬議。師便打。

25 王常侍一日訪師。同師於僧堂前看。乃問。這一堂僧還看經麼。師云。
不看經。侍云。還學禪麼。師云。不學禪。侍云。經又不看禪又不學。畢竟作箇
什麼。師云。總教伊成佛作祖去。侍云。金屑雖貴落眼成翳。又作麼生。師云。
將爲你是箇俗漢。

26 師問杏山。如何是露地白牛。山云。吽吽。師云。啞那。山云。長老作麼生。
師云。這畜生。

27 師問樂普云。從上來一人行棒一人行喝。阿那箇親。普云。總不親。師云。
親處作麼生。普便喝。師乃打。

28 師見僧來。展開兩手。僧無語。師云會麼。云不會。師云。渾崙擘不開。
與汝兩文錢。

29 大覺到參。師舉起拂子。大覺敷坐具。師擲下拂子。大覺收坐具入僧堂。
衆僧云。這僧莫是和尚親故。不禮拜又不喫棒。師聞令喚覺。覺出。師云。
大衆道。汝未參長老。覺云不審。便自歸衆。

30 趙州行腳時參師。遇師洗腳次。州便問。如何是祖師西來意。師云。恰值
老僧洗腳。州近前作聽勢。師云。更要第二杓惡水潑在。州便下去。

31 有定上座到參。問如何是佛法大意。師下繩床。擒住與一掌。便托開。
定佇立。傍僧云。定上座何不禮拜。定方禮拜。忽然大悟。

32 麻谷到參。敷坐具問。十二面觀音。阿那面正。師下繩床。一手收坐具。
一手搊麻谷云。十二面觀音。向什麼處去也。麻谷轉身擬坐繩床。師拈拄杖打。
麻谷接却相捉入方丈。

33 師問僧。有時一喝如金剛王寶劍。有時一喝如踞地金毛獅子。有時一喝如
探竿影草。有時一喝不作一喝用。汝作麼生會。僧擬議。師便喝。

34 師問一尼。善來惡來。尼便喝。師拈棒云。更道更道。尼又喝。師便打。

35 龍牙問。如何是祖師西來意。師云。與我過禪版來。牙便過禪版與師。
師接得便打。牙云。打即任打。要且無祖師意。牙後到翠微問。如何是祖師西來意。
微云。與我過蒲團來。牙便過蒲團與翠微。翠微接得便打。牙云。打即任打。要且

無祖師意。牙住院後有僧入室請益云。和尚行腳時參二尊宿因緣。還肯他也無。
牙云。肯即深肯。要且無祖師意。

36 徑山有五百眾。少人參請。黃檗令師到徑山。乃謂師曰。汝到彼作麼生。
師云。某甲到彼自有方便。師到徑山。裝腰上法堂見徑山。徑山方舉頭。師便喝。
徑山擬開口。師拂袖便行。尋有僧問徑山。這僧適來有什麼言句。便喝和尚。
徑山云。這僧從黃檗會裏來。你要知麼。自問取他。徑山五百眾太半分散。

37 普化一日於街市中。就人乞直裰。人皆與之。普化俱不要。師令院主買棺一具。
普化歸來。師云。我與汝做得箇直裰了也。普化便自擔去。繞街市叫云。臨濟與我做
直裰了也。我往東門遷化去。市人競隨看之。普化云。我今日未。來日往南門遷
化去。如是三日。人皆不信。至第四日無人隨看。獨出城外自入棺內。倩路行人
釘之。即時傳布。市人競往。開棺乃見全身脫去。祇聞空中鈴響隱隱而去。

行錄

38.1 師初在黃檗會下。行業純一。首座乃歎曰。雖是後生與眾有異。遂問。
上座在此多少時。師云。三年。首座云。曾參問也無。師云。不曾參問。不知問
箇什麼首座云。汝何不去問堂頭和尚如何是佛法的的大意。師便去問。聲未絕黃
檗便打。師下來。首座云。問話作麼生。師云。某甲問聲未絕。和尚便打。某甲
不會。首座云。但更去問。師又去問。黃檗又打。如是三度發問三度被打。師來
白首座云。幸蒙慈悲。令某甲問訊和尚。三度發問三度被打。自恨障緣不領深旨。
今且辭去。首座云。汝若去時。須辭和尚去。師禮拜退。

38.2 首座先到和尚處。問話底後生。甚是如法。若來辭時。方便接他。向後
穿鑿成一株大樹。與天下人作陰涼去在。師去辭。黃檗云。不得往別處去。汝向
高安灘頭大愚處去。必為汝說。師到大愚。大愚問。什麼處來。師云。黃檗處來。
大愚云。黃檗有何言句。師云。某甲三度問佛法的的大意。三度被打。不知某甲有
過無過。大愚云。黃檗與麼老婆為汝得徹困。更來這裏問有過無過。師於言下大
悟云。元來黃檗佛法無多子。大愚搊住云。這尿牀鬼子。適來道有過無過。如今
却道黃檗佛法無多子。你見箇什麼道理。速道速道。師於大愚脅下築三拳。大愚
托開云。汝師黃檗。非干我事。

38.3 師辭大愚。却回黃檗。黃檗見來便問。這漢來來去去。有什麼了期。
師云。祇為老婆心切。便人事了侍立。黃檗問。什麼處去來。師云。昨奉慈旨。
令參大愚去來。黃檗云。大愚有何言句。師遂舉前話。黃檗云。作麼生得這漢來。
待痛與一頓。師云。說什麼待來。即今便喫。隨後便掌。黃檗云。這風顛漢。
却來這裏捋虎鬚。師便喝。黃檗云。侍者引這風顛漢參堂去。

38.4 後溈山舉此話問仰山。臨濟當時得大愚力。得黃檗力。仰山云。非但騎虎頭。
亦解把虎尾。

39.1 師栽松次。黃檗問。深山裏栽許多作什麼。師云。一與山門作境致。
二與後人作標榜。道了將钁頭打地三下。黃檗云。雖然如是。子已喫吾三十棒了也。
師又以钁頭打地三下。作噓噓聲。黃檗云。吾宗到汝大興於世。

39.2 後溈山舉此語問仰山。黃蘗當時祇囑臨濟一人。更有人在。仰山云有。祇是年代深遠。不欲舉似和尚。溈山云。雖然如是。吾亦要知。汝但舉看。仰山云。一人指南吳越令行。遇大風即止。(讖風穴和尚也。)

40 師侍立德山次。山云。今日困。師云。這老漢寐語作什麼。山便打。師掀倒繩床。山便休。

41.1 師普請鋤地次。見黃蘗來。拄钁而立。黃蘗云。這漢困耶。師云。钁也未舉。困箇什麼。黃蘗便打。師接住棒。一送送倒。黃蘗喚維那。維那扶起我。維那近前扶云。和尚爭容得這風顛漢無禮。黃蘗纔起便打維那。師钁地云。諸方火葬。我這裏一時活埋。

41.2 後溈山問仰山。黃蘗打維那意作麼生。仰山云。正賊走却。邏蹤人喫棒。

42 師一日在僧堂前坐。見黃蘗來。便閉却目。黃蘗乃作怖勢。便歸方丈。師隨至方丈禮謝。首座在黃蘗處侍立。黃蘗云。此僧雖是後生。却知有此事。首座云。老和尚脚跟不點地。却證據箇後生。黃蘗自於口上打一摑。首座云。知即得。

43.1 師在堂中睡。黃蘗下來見。以拄杖打板頭一下。師舉頭見是黃蘗却睡。黃蘗又打板頭一下。却往上間。見首座坐禪乃云。下間後生却坐禪。汝這裏妄想作什麼。首座云。這老漢作什麼。黃蘗打板頭一下。便出去。

43.2 後溈山問仰山。黃蘗入僧堂意作麼生。仰山云。兩彩一賽。

44.1 一日普請次。師在後行。黃蘗回頭見師空手乃問。钁頭在什麼處。師云。有一人將去了也。黃蘗云。近前來。共汝商量箇事。師便近前。黃蘗竪起钁頭云。祇這箇。天下人拈掇不起。師就手掣得竪起云。爲什麼却在某甲手裏。黃蘗云。今日大有人普請。便歸院。

44.2 後溈山問仰山。钁頭在黃蘗手裏。爲什麼却被臨濟奪却。仰山云。賊是小人智過君子。

45.1 師爲黃蘗馳書去溈山。時仰山作知客。接得書便問。這箇是黃蘗底。那箇是專使底。師便掌。仰山約住云。老兄知是般事便休。同去見溈山。溈山便問。黃蘗師兄多少衆。師云。七百衆。溈山云。什麼人爲導首。師云。適來已達書了也。師却問溈山。和尚此間多少衆。溈山云。一千五百衆。師云。太多生。溈山云。黃蘗師兄亦不少。

45.2 師辭溈山。仰山送出云。汝向後北去有箇住處。師云。豈有與麼事。仰山云。但去已後有一人佐輔老兄在。此人祇是有頭無尾。有始無終。師後到鎮州。普化已在彼中。師出世。普化佐贊於師。師住未久。普化全身脫去。

46 師因半夏上黃蘗。見和尚看經。師云。我將謂是箇人。元來是揞黑豆老和尚。住數日乃辭去。黃蘗云。汝破夏來。不終夏去。師云。某甲暫來禮拜和尚。黃蘗遂打趁令去。師行數里。疑此事。却回終夏。

47.1 師一日辭黃蘗。蘗問。什麼處去。師云。不是河南便歸河北。黃蘗便打。師約住與一掌。黃蘗大笑。乃喚侍者。將百丈先師禪板机案來。師云。侍者將火來。黃蘗云。雖然如是。汝但將去。已後坐却天下人舌頭去在。

47.2 後潙山問仰山。臨濟莫辜負他黃檗也無。仰山云不然。潙山云。
子又作麼生。仰山云。知恩方解報恩。潙山云。從上古人還有相似底也無。
仰山云有。祇是年代深遠。不欲舉似和尚。潙山云。雖然如是。吾亦要知。
子但舉看。仰山云。祇如楞嚴會上阿難讚佛云。將此深心奉塵刹。
是則名爲報佛恩。豈不是報恩之事。潙山云。如是如是。見與師齊減師半德。
見過於師方堪傳授。

48 師到達磨塔頭。塔主云。長老先禮佛先禮祖。師云。佛祖俱不禮。塔主云。
佛祖與長老是什麼冤家。師便拂袖而出。

49 師行脚時到龍光。光上堂。師出問。不展鋒鋩。如何得勝。光據坐。師云。
大善知識豈無方便。光瞪目云嘎。師以手指云。這老漢今日敗闕也。

50.1 到三峯。平和尚問。什麼處來。師云。黃檗來。平云。黃檗有何言句。
師云。金牛昨夜遭塗炭。直至如今不見蹤。平云。金風吹玉管。那箇是知音。
師云。直透萬重關。不住清霄內。平云。子這一問太高生。師云。龍生金鳳子。
衝破碧瑠璃。平云。且坐喫茶。

50.2 又問。近離甚處。師云。龍光。平云。龍光近日如何。師便出去。

51 到大慈。慈在方丈內坐。師問。端居丈室時如何。慈云。寒松一色千年別。
野老拈花萬國春。師云。今古永超圓智體。三山鎖斷萬重關。慈便喝。師亦喝。
慈云。作麼。師拂袖便出。

52 到襄州華嚴。嚴倚拄杖作睡勢。師云。老和尚瞌睡作麼。嚴云。作家禪客
宛爾不同。師云。侍者點茶來與和尚喫。嚴乃喚維那。第三位安排這上座。

53 到翠峯。峯問。甚處來。師云。黃檗來。峯云。黃檗有何言句指示於人。
師云。黃檗無言句。峯云。爲什麼無。師云。設有亦無舉處。峯云。但舉看。
師云。一箭過西天。

54 到象田。師問。不凡不聖。請師速道。田云。老僧祇與麼。師便喝云。
許多禿子。在這裏覓什麼椀。

55 到明化。化問。來來去去作什麼。師云。祇徒踏破草鞋。化云。畢竟作麼生。
師云。老漢話頭也不識。

56.1 往鳳林。路逢一婆。婆問。甚處去。師云。鳳林去。婆云。恰值鳳林不在。
師云。甚處去。婆便打。師乃喚婆。婆回頭。師便打。

56.2 到鳳林。林問。有事相借問。得麼。師云。何得剜肉作瘡。林云。海月澄
無影。游魚獨自迷。師云。海月既無影。游魚何得迷。鳳林云。觀風知浪起。
翫水野帆飄。師云。孤輪獨照江山靜。自笑一聲天地驚。林云。任將三寸輝天地。
一句臨機試道看。師云。路逢劍客須呈劍。不是詩人莫獻詩。鳳林便休。師乃
有頌。大道絕同。任向西東。石火莫及。電光罔通。

56.3 潙山問仰山。石火莫及電光罔通。從上諸聖將什麼爲人。仰山云。和尚意
作麼生。潙山云。但有言說都無實義。仰山云。不然。潙山云。子又作麼生。
仰山云。官不容針私通車馬。

57.1　到金牛。牛見師來。橫按拄杖當門踞坐。師以手敲拄杖三下。却歸堂中第一位坐。牛下來見乃問。夫賓主相見各具威儀。上座從何而來。太無禮生。師云。老和尚道什麼。牛擬開口。師便打。牛作倒勢。師又打。牛云。今日不著便。

57.2　潙山問仰山。此二尊宿還有勝負也無。仰山云。勝即總勝。負即總負。

58　師臨遷化時據坐云。吾滅後不得滅却吾正法眼藏。三聖出云。爭敢滅却和尚正法眼藏。師云。已後有人問你。向他道什麼。三聖便喝。師云。誰知吾正法眼藏。向這瞎驢邊滅却。言訖端然示寂。

[臨濟慧照禪師塔記]

59.1　師諱義玄。曹州南華人也。俗姓邢氏。幼而穎異。長以孝聞。及落髮受具。居於講肆。精究毗尼。博賾經論。俄而歎曰。此濟世之醫方也。非教外別傳之旨。即更衣遊方。首參黃檗。次謁大愚。其機緣語句載于行錄。既受黃檗印可。尋抵河北鎮州城東南隅。臨滹沱河側。小院住持。其臨濟因地得名。時普化先在彼。佯狂混眾。聖凡莫測。師至即佐之。師正旺化。普化全身脫去。乃符仰山小釋迦之懸記也。

59.2　適丁兵革。師即棄去。太尉默君和於城中捨宅爲寺。亦以臨濟爲額。迎師居焉。後拂衣南邁至河府。府主王常侍。延以師禮。住未幾即來大名府興化寺居于東堂。師無疾忽一日攝衣據坐。與三聖問答畢。寂然而逝。時唐咸通八年丁亥孟陬月十日也。門人以師全身。建塔于大名府西北隅。勅謚慧照禪師。塔號澄靈。合掌稽首。記師大略。

住鎮州保壽嗣法小師延沼謹書
鎮州臨濟慧照禪師語錄終
住大名府興化嗣法小師存獎校勘
[住福州鼓山圓覺苾蒭宗演重開]

Pre-Song Linji and Puhua Sayings and Episodes Preserved in the Collection of the Patriarchal Hall (Zutangji 祖堂集)

The *Zutangji* (952) antedates by seventy-seven years the earliest complete *Linjilu* edition, which is embedded as a Linji entry in the *Extended Lamp Record of the Tiansheng Era* (*Tiansheng guangdenglu* 天聖廣燈錄; compiled in 1029 and issued in 1036). The *Zutangji*, a Chan transmission record in twenty fascicles, consists of entries for successive generations of Chan masters related by lineage. It was compiled by two Chan worthies, Jing 靜 and Jun 筠, in 952 (Baoda 保大 10) of the Southern Tang kingdom at Zhaoqing Temple 招慶院 in Quanzhou 泉州 (southeast coast of Fujian). Jing and Jun were in the Xuefeng line. The lineage runs: Xuefeng Yicun (雪峰義存; 822–908) → Baofu Congzhan (保福從展; 867–928) → Fuxian Wendeng (福先文僜) → Jing and Jun. Beyond that nothing is known about them.

It is likely that the *Zutangji* was still in circulation in China one hundred years after its compilation, as it is cited in a number of works written during the eleventh century. After the eleventh century it was superseded, and Chinese sources make no further mention of it. As Christoph Anderl states: "After the ZTJ [*Zutangji*] had been lost in China, more than 800 years passed until it was discovered in the Korean Haein Monastery [Haein-sa 海印寺]. In 1912 two Japanese scholars by the names of Sekino Tadashi 關野貞 and Ono Gemmyō 小野玄妙 traveled to Korea in order to inspect the *Korean Tripiṭaka* stored at the monastery mentioned above. By chance they discovered the woodblocks of ZTJ which were stored apart from the main *Tripiṭaka* (since it was only carved as an appendix)."[1] The *Tripiṭaka Koreana* (*Goryeo Daejanggyeong* 高麗大藏經), which is also known as the *Eighty-Thousand Woodblocks Tripiṭaka* (*Palman Daejanggyeong* 八萬大藏經), was carved between 1236 and 1251; the woodblocks for the *Zutangji* itself were carved in 1245.

The *Zutangji* maintains separate entries for Linji and for Puhua, as befits their status as individual masters in the Hongzhou 洪州 house/lineage, but through different successors of the fountainhead Mazu Daoyi 馬祖道一. For Linji, the succession runs: Mazu 馬祖 → Baizhang 百丈→ Huangbo 黃檗 → Linji 臨濟; for Puhua: Mazu 馬祖 → Panshan Baoji 盤山寶積→ Puhua 普化. It is worth noting that Puhua does not appear at all in the six narrative episodes of the Linji entry, while Linji does appear in four out of the six narrative episodes of the Puhua entry. Moreover, the Puhua entry gives Puhua his full due as "the Master" in his own right, a protagonist worthy of his own story. As such, Puhua predominates in episodes where Linji appears with him, and he is not merely a subsidiary character as he is portrayed in the LJL. The Yuanjue Zongyan standard edition (the LJL) shows some overlap with the sayings and episodes of the *Zutangji* entries. Below, in those *Zutangji* passages that do correspond with LJL passages, significant divergences have been underlined. (For convenience, a side-by-side comparison of these lines has been provided in the notes.)

Section numbers below, where used, indicate parallel LJL sections according to the numbering system used in the preceding LJL translation (which is based on the system in Yanagida Seizan, trans., *Rinzairoku, Butten kōza* 30 [Tokyo: Daizō shuppan, 1972]). Sections that have no preceding number are not found in the LJL.

The transcriptions of the *Zutangji*'s Linji and Puhua entries below are from a facsimile of the woodblock print kept at Haein-sa: Yoshizawa Masahiro and Onishi Shirō, eds., *Sodōshū* (Kyoto: Zen bunka kenkyūjo, 1994), 717–721 and 635–637. Another facsimile of the woodblock print kept at Haein-sa is: Yanagida Seizan, ed., *Sodōshū* (Kyoto: Chūbun shuppansha, 1974), 362–364 and 321–322. Both of these facsimiles are based on a copy stored in the Hanazono University Library in Kyoto. Where the printing in the Hanazono copy is indistinct, the former has included supplements at the top of the page based on the copy of the Tōyō bunka kenkyūjo of Tokyo University. There is an electronic version of the *Zutangji* at the *Tripiṭaka Koreana* website. It is K.1503 in the Supplementary Part. The Linji entry is K1503V45P0353b25L-K1503V45P0354a21L and the Puhua entry K1503V45P0339c07L-K1503V45P0340a01L. There is a Japanese translation with a few notes: Koga Hidehiko et al., eds., *Kunchū Sodōshū, Kenkyū hōkoku* 8 (Kyoto: Hanazono daigaku kokusai zengaku kenkyūjo, 2003), 792–797 and 694–696.

[Linji Entry]

59.1 臨濟和尚嗣黃蘗在鎮州師諱義玄姓邢曹南人也自契黃蘗鋒機乃闡化扵河北提綱峻速示教幽深其扵樞祕難陳示誨略申少分

Preceptor Linji succeeded to Huangbo's [dharma]; and he was [active] in Zhenzhou. His taboo name was Yixuan and his family name Xing. He was a man of Caonan [i.e., Nanhua in Caozhou in Shandong]. He was naturally receptive to the engraving of the sharp point of Huangbo's mental disposition, and in time started up his teaching activity in Hebei. His raising of the headrope [i.e., Chan's personal-realization-of-the-meaning-beyond-words] was stern and swift; his mode of instruction was profound. It is difficult to lay out the crux of his teaching, but I will now in brief state a few parts of it.

3 師有時謂衆云山僧今明向你道五陰身田內有無位真人堂堂露現無毫髮許間[間]隔何不識取時有僧問如何是無位真人師便打之云無位真人是什摩不淨之物雪峯聞舉云林際太似好手

The Master one time said to the sangha: "At present I clearly say to you that within the five-*skandhas* body-field[2] there is the true *person* who can't be ranked, imposing and revealed, not a hair's-breadth of a break [between the body-field and the true *person*]. Why don't you recognize him?" At that point there was a monk who asked, "What is the true person who can't be ranked?" The Master instantly whacked him; and said, "'The true *person* who can't be ranked'—what a magnificent thing of impurity[3] [i.e., euphemism for "feces"]!"

[Later] Xuefeng heard this and raised it, saying: "Linji seems to be an extremely skillful one."[4]

27 師問落浦從上有一人行棒有一人行喝還有親疎也無落浦云如某甲所見兩个惣不親師云親處作摩生落浦遂喝師便打之

The Master asked Lepu, "As in the past there is one *person* who employs the stick, and there is one *person* who employs the shout. Is one of them spot on?" Lepu said, "In yours truly's view, neither one of them is spot on." The Master said, "What would be spot on?" Lepu thereupon gave a shout. The Master whacked him.

24 因德山見僧參愛趂打師委得令侍者到德山打汝汝便接取柱杖以柱杖打一下侍者遂到德山皆依師指德山便歸丈室侍者却歸舉似師云從来疑這个老漢

When Deshan saw a monk [coming to] consult, he liked to chase him for a whack. The Master knew this and ordered an attendant to go to Deshan: "If he whacks you, you instantly grab his staff and give him a whack with it." The attendant then went to Deshan and acted according to the Master's instructions. Deshan instantly returned to the *fangzhang*. The attendant returned and reported this. The Master said, "I've had my doubts about *this* old Han all along."

15 因僧侍立次師竪起拂子僧便礼拜師便打之後因僧侍立次師竪起拂子其僧並不顧師亦打之雲門代云只宜專甲

When a monk was standing in attendance, the Master raised up his flywhisk. The monk instantly bowed. The Master instantly whacked him. Later, when a monk was standing in attendance, the Master raised up his flywhisk. This monk utterly ignored it. The Master whacked him too.

Yunmen, as a stand-in for [the second monk], said: "Just concentrate on being number one/being *someone*."

38.2–38.3 黃蘗和尚告衆曰余昔時同參大寂道友名曰大愚此人諸方行脚法眼明徹今在高安顧[顧?]不好群居獨栖[栖]山舍与余相別時叮囑云他後或逢靈利者指一人来相訪于時師在衆聞已便往造謁既到其所具陳上說<u>至夜間扵大愚前說瑜伽論譚唯識復申問難大愚畢夕峭[悄]然不對</u>及至旦来謂師曰老僧獨居山舍念子遠来且延一宿何故夜間扵吾前無羞慙放不淨言訖訖杖之數下推出闗却門師廻黃蘗復陳上說黃蘗聞已稽首曰作者如猛火燃喜子遇人何乃虛往師又去復見大愚大愚曰前時無慙愧今日何故又来言訖便棒推出門師復送黃蘗啟聞和尚此廻再返不是空歸黃蘗曰何故如此師曰扵一棒下入佛境界假使百劫粉骨碎身頂擎遶須弥山經無量帀報此深恩莫-可酬得黃蘗聞已喜之異常曰子且解歇更自出身師過旬日又辝[辭]黃蘗至大愚所大愚見便擬棒師師接得棒子則便掀倒大愚乃就其背毆[毆]之數拳大愚遂連點頭曰吾獨居山舍將謂空過一生不期今日却得一子先招慶和尚舉終乃問師演侍者曰既因他得悟何以却將拳打他侍者曰當時教化全因佛今日威拳惣属君師因此侍奉大愚經十餘年大愚臨遷化時囑師云子自不負平生又乃終吾一世已後出世傳心第一莫忘黃蘗自後師扵鎮府匡化雖承黃蘗常讚大愚至扵化門多行喝棒

Preceptor Huangbo told the sangha: "In the past I had a friend in the Way—we both studied with Daji [Mazu Daoyi]. His name was Dayu. This *person* traveled on foot all over [in search of a teacher and realization], and his dharma-eye was bright through and through. At present he is at Gao'an [in the northern part of Jiangxi]. However, he doesn't like to live in a group, and he roosts alone in a mountain hut. When we were parting, he exhorted me two or three times: "In the distant future, if you should meet a gifted one, have him come alone to visit me." At that time the Master was in the sangha. Having heard this, he instantly went to pay a visit. Having arrived at his [Dayu's] place, he related what [Huangbo] had said. <u>When it became nighttime, in front of Dayu he lectured on the *Yoga Treatise [Yogacārabhūmi-śāstra]* and discussed consciousness-only *[vijñāna-mātra]*—on top of that, he urged debate.</u>[5] Dayu all night long was quiet and did not reply. When it became daybreak, he said to the Master, "I dwell alone in a mountain hut. Considering that you have come from afar, well, I let you stay one night. Why, during the night—right in front of me—did you shamelessly expel feces?" When he finished speaking, he hit [the Master] with the staff several times, pushed him out, and shut the gate latch. The Master returned to Huangbo and related what [Dayu] had said. Huangbo, having heard it, bowed his head and said, "[Dayu is] an experienced Chan adept and burns like a fierce fire. I was happy to have you encounter [this] *person*, but why did you go in vain?" The Master went and again saw Dayu. Dayu said, "The last time you had no shame. Why did you come again today?" Having finished speaking, he instantly hit him with the stick and pushed him out the gate. The Master again returned to Huangbo and stated to the Preceptor, "This time I haven't come back empty-handed." Huangbo said, "How so?" The Master said, "Beneath a single hit of the stick I entered the buddha realm. Supposing for one-hundred kalpas I were to powder my bones and smash my body [i.e., sacrifice my life] and make an offering of doing immeasurable circuits around Mt. Sumeru to repay this deep kindness: it could not be requited." Huangbo, having heard this, was joyful about it; and, unusual for him, said, "Well, you've been able to *stop* [the mind that rushes around and around searching from moment to moment]—but you [must go on and] escape bondage!" The Master spent ten days, and then again took his leave of Huangbo, arriving at Dayu's place. As soon as Dayu saw the Master, he instantly was about to hit the Master with the stick. The Master took hold of the stick and instantly took Dayu into his arms, thumping him several times on the back with his fist. Dayu, continuously nodding his head, said, "I dwell alone in a mountain hut and mistakenly thought that I had spent my whole life in vain. But today unexpectedly I have obtained a son."

> The previous Preceptor Zhaoqing[6] raised this story with his Attendant Shi-yan, asking him, "Having previously attained awakening due to him, why did he nevertheless whack him with his fist?" The Attendant said, "The instruction at that time was completely dependent upon the Buddha, but today's mighty fist completely belongs to [the Master]."

The Master because of this served Dayu for more than ten years.[7] When Dayu was about to transmigrate, he enjoined the Master, "Even though you have not disobeyed [the wish of] my whole life and have kept me company for many years, when you go out into the world to transmit mind, you absolutely must not forget Huangbo." After that, the Master gave instruction in Zhen[zhou] superior prefecture. Even though he received Huangbo's [dharma], he always praised Dayu. In his instructional gate, [the Master] made much use of the shout and the stick.

10.6–10.8 有時謂衆云但一切時中更莫間斷觸目皆是因何不會只為情生智隔想[相]變體殊所以三界輪廻受種種苦大德心法無形通貫十方在眼曰見在耳曰聞在手執捉在脚雲[運]奔本是一精明分成六和合心若不生隨處解脫大德欲得山僧見處坐斷報化佛頭十地滿心猶如客作兒何以如此盖為不達三祇劫空所以有此障若是真正道流盡不如此大德山僧略為諸人大約話破綱宗切須自看可惜時光各自努力

One time [the Master] said to the sangha, "Just let there never be a break. Everything that meets the eye is [the real]. Why do you not understand? Just as [an ancient says,] 'Emotions arise, and *prajñā* is cut off; characteristics undergo transformation, and the substance evolves. Therefore, you are turned on the samsaric wheel in the three realms and undergo various sufferings.' Venerables! Mind dharma is formless and pervades the ten directions. In the eye it is called seeing; in the ear it is called hearing; in the hands, grasping; and in the feet, walking or running. At the outset this one spirit-brightness [in the manner of a sleight-of-hand seems to] divide into the six [causal] combinations [i.e., the six sense organs that come into being due to the coming together of causes and conditions]. If mind does not arise [i.e., no mind], every *place* is liberation. Venerables! If you want to attain my vision, [with one stroke of the sword] sever the heads of the *saṃbhogakāya* and *nirmāṇakāya* buddhas. The 'bodhisattva who has completed the ten stages' is like a day laborer.[8] Why hasn't this [sunk in with you]? It's simply because you don't comprehend that the 'three immeasurable kalpas' [you supposedly spend traversing all of these 'stages'] are empty;

that's why you have these [karmic] blockages. If you are a stream-enterer who [beholds] reality as it truly is, it's not like this at all. Venerables! I have tried for the sake of you people/*persons* to expose a brief encapsulation of [Chan's] "headrope"— personal-realization-of-the-meaning-beyond-words. You *must* be vigilant. Your days are precious. Each of you—make effort!"

Separate Record: 自餘應機對答廣彰別錄矣咸通七年丙戌歲四月十日示化諡号 慧照大師澄虛之塔

The remainder of [Linji's] answers in response to the mental dispositions [of students] are extensively laid out in the *Separate Record*. On the tenth day of the fourth month of Xiantong 7 [May 27, 866], he died.[9] By imperial proclamation he was awarded the posthumous title "Great Master Huizhao" and a stupa named "Clear Void."

[Puhua Entry]

普化和尚嗣盤山在鎮州未覩行錄不決化緣始終

Preceptor Puhua succeeded Panshan.[10] He was [active] in Zhenzhou. Having not yet seen a karman record for him I cannot judge the entirety of his teaching career.

師在市裏遇見馬步使便相撲勢馬步使便打五棒師云似則似是則不是

The Master was in the town and encountered an Army Commissioner. [The Master] instantly assumed a *sumō* stance, and the Army Commissioner instantly gave him five whacks with his stick. The Master said, "[If you say it's a reasonable] facsimile, then [it's a reasonable] facsimile; [but, if you say *it*] is so, then [it's] not so."[11]

19 師尋常暮宿塚間朝遊城市把鈴云明頭來也打暗頭來也打林際和尚聞此消息 教侍者探師侍者來問師不明不暗時事作摩生師曰明日大悲院有齋侍者帰來舉似 林際便歡喜云作摩生得見他

The Master usually spent the night among the [graveyard] tombs, and during the day played in the town.[12] Holding [his tin staff with its] "rattle" [of metal rings at the top], he said, "Come with 'brightness'—whack! Come with 'darkness'—whack!" Preceptor Linji heard the news of this and had his attendant [go to] calibrate the Master. The attendant came and asked the Master, "When [one comes] in neither 'brightness' nor 'darkness', then what?" The Master said, "There will be a [generous donor's] dinner tomorrow at the Dabei Temple." The attendant came back and reported this to Linji. [Linji] was immediately delighted,[13] saying, "So how did *he* look to you?"

16.1;18;and17 非久之間普化自上來林際林際便歡喜排批餘食對坐喫師凡是下底 物惣與[= 喫]却林際云普化喫食似一頭驢師便下座兩手托地便造驢聲林際無語師 云林際厮兒只具一隻眼後有人舉似長慶長慶代林際進語云也旦從更作摩生又代普 化云被長老申此一問直得酩酩酊酊林際又問大悲菩薩分身千百億便請現師便擲地 卓子便作舞勢云吽吽便去

It was not long before Puhua himself came up to Linji.[14] Linji was delighted, and arranged a meal. They sat across from each other and ate. The Master ate every last bit, [licking each dish clean to] the very bottom. Linji said, "Puhua eats like a donkey!"

The Master immediately got off his seat and set both his hands on the ground, making the sound of a donkey. Linji was silent.[15] The Master said, "Linji is a [cagey] gofer, but he's only got the one eye."[16]

Later someone reported this to Changqing.[17] Changqing, as a stand-in for [the silent] Linji, advanced the following words: "Well, let's leave that as it is—how about what comes after [the sound of a donkey]?" This time as a stand-in for Puhua, he said, "Elder, having been asked this one question of yours, I've ended up totally blotto [i.e., awakened]!"

Linji also asked: "The Great-Compassion [Dabei] Bodhisattva has divided his body into hundreds of millions of pieces, and I now request that he make a manifestation."[18] The Master immediately flung the table to the ground, assumed a dance pose, chanted *"hūṃ hūṃ"* [the mantra/the sound of an ox lowing],[19] and left.

又林際上堂師侍立次有一僧在面前立師驀推倒林際前林際便把杖子打三下師云林際廝兒只具一隻眼

Also, when Linji was holding a Dharma-Hall Convocation and the Master was standing in attendance, there was one *monk* [i.e., the true *person*] who was standing right in front [of Linji listening to the dharma]. The Master suddenly knocked down [that monk/that true *person*] in front of Linji. Linji instantly grabbed his staff and gave [Puhua] three whacks. The Master said,: "Linji is a [cagey] gofer, but he's only got the one eye."[20]

又林際与師看聖僧次林際云是凡是聖師云是聖林際便喝咄師便撫掌大[口+笑=笑]

Also, when Linji and the Master were looking at the *"āryā* monk" [the statue of Mañjuśrī riding a lion in the Sangha Hall], Linji said, "Is this a worldling or is this an *ārya*?"[21] The Master said, "An *ārya*." Linji instantly gave a shout to berate him.[22] The Master clapped his hands and gave a great laugh [certifying Linji].[23]

37 師得一日手擎函板遶郭辞人云我遷化去衆人雲集相隨東門而出云今日不好二日南門三日西門人衆漸小不信第四日北門而出更無一人隨之自覔甏[土+遂=隧]門而卒矣

The Master on the first day, his arms loaded with planks for a casket,[24] circumambulated the outer wall of town and bid adieu to people: "I'm going to pass on in transmigration." A crowd of people gathered like clouds to follow after him. He went through the East Gate, saying: "Today's no good." On the second day [he went through] the South Gate and on the third day the West Gate. The crowd of people dwindled—nobody believed him any longer. When on the fourth day he went through the North Gate, not a single person was following him. By himself he bricked up the door to the tomb passageway and passed on in transmigration.[25]

Pre-Song Linji Sayings Preserved in the Mind-Mirror Record (Zongjinglu 宗鏡錄/Xinjinglu 心鏡錄)

The *Zongjinglu* (traditional issue date 961) antedates by sixty-eight years the earliest complete *Linjilu* version, which is embedded as a Linji entry in the *Extended Lamp Record of the Tiansheng Era* (*Tiansheng guangdenglu* 天聖廣燈錄; compiled in 1029 and issued in 1036). The *Zongjinglu*, an enormous treatise (one hundred fascicles) filled with scriptural quotations and Chan sayings, was compiled by the Chan master Yongming Yanshou (永明延壽; 904–976) in the kingdom of Wu-Yue 吳越 (Jiangsu-Zhejiang). Yanshou's compendium advocates the orientation of Guifeng Zongmi's *Chan Prolegomenon* (assuming that Chan and the teachings are identical; championing Bodhidharma Chan as a whole; paring down voluminous sources to their essence, and so forth). The *Zongjinglu* had a great impact on Song Buddhism and even on Song learning outside Buddhism. The Chan materials embedded in it were neglected by modern scholarship until recently.

The *Zongjinglu* preserves a small cluster of Linji sayings , and these sayings overlap with the LJL (also with the *Zutangji* Linji entry in Appendix 1). Section numbers below indicate parallel LJL sections according to the numbering system used in the preceding LJL translation (which is based on the system in Yanagida Seizan, trans., *Rinzairoku, Butten kōza* 30 [Tokyo: Daizō shuppan, 1972]). The transcription of these Linji sayings is from the *Taishō* edition of the *Zongjinglu* (T2016.48.943c8-22).

10.4 臨濟和尚云如今諸人與古聖何別爾且欠少什麼六道神光未曾間歇若能如是秖是箇一生無事人

Preceptor Linji said, "How are you people/*persons* right now any different from the ancient *āryas*? What could you possibly be lacking? The divine light of the six paths has never been interrupted. If you can [see] *in that way*, throughout your whole life you will be the *person* who has *nothing-to-do*."

10.5 欲得與祖佛不別但莫向外馳求爾一念清淨光是爾屋裏法身佛爾一念無分別光是爾屋裏報身佛爾一念差別光是爾屋裏化身佛此三種身即是今日目前聽法底人此三種是名言明知是光影

"If you desire to be no different from the 'buddhas who are our patriarchs,' never seek on the outside. You, in [the same] single moment, are pure light—are the '*dharmakāya* buddha in your house.' You, in [the same] single moment, are non-discriminative light—are the '*saṃbhogakāya* buddha within your house.' You, in [the same] single moment, are non-distinction-making light—are the '*nirmāṇakāya* buddha in your house.' These three types of bodies are none other than the [true] *person* right now in front of me listening to the dharma. These three types of bodies are just terms. Know that they are [nothing but unreal] reflected images."

10.6 大德且要識取弄光影底人是諸佛本源是一切道流歸舍處爾四大六根及虛空不解聽法說法是箇什麼物歷歷地孤明勿箇形段是這箇解說法聽法

"Venerables! You [must] come to know the *person* who plays with these [unreal] reflected images. He is the original source of all the buddhas. Every *place* is the home-*place* to which the stream-enterer returns. Your four elements and six sense organs—and even the sky—don't have the ability to speak dharma or listen to it. Then what on earth is it that does? A solitary brightness clearly [standing right in front of me] devoid of even a single describable attribute—it's none other than *this* that has the ability to speak dharma and listen to it."

3 所以向爾道向五陰身田內有無位真人堂堂顯露無絲髮許間隔何不識取

"Therefore, I say to you: Within the five-*skandhas* body-field there is the true *person* who can't be ranked, imposing and revealed, not a hairsbreadth of a break [between the body-field and the true *person*]. Why don't you recognize him?"

10.7 大德心法無形通貫十方在眼曰見在耳曰聞本是一精明分成六和合心若不生隨處解脫

"Venerables! Mind dharma is formless and pervades the ten directions. In the eye it is called seeing; in the ear it is called hearing. At the outset this one spirit-brightness [in the manner of a sleight-of-hand seems to] divide into the six [causal] combinations [i.e., the six sense organs that come into being due to the coming together of causes and conditions]. If mind [i.e., discrimination] does not arise, every *place* is liberation."

Notes

INTRODUCTION

1. Kōunshi, 1229; found in section 38.1 of Part IV.

2. Perhaps the best translation so far is the fluid modern Japanese rendering *(gendaigo yaku)* in: Iriya Yoshitaka, trans., *Rinzairoku* (Tokyo: Iwanami shoten, 1989). Yanagida Seizan, trans., *Kunchū Rinzairoku* (Kyoto: Kichūdō, 1961) is a *kakikudashibun* treatment (Chinese rewritten in Chinese characters and Japanese syllabary following Japanese word order) with notes. Yanagida Seizan, trans., *Rinzairoku, Butten kōza* 30 (Tokyo: Daizō shuppan, 1972), a *kakikudashibun* treatment, has excellent notes. Akizuki Ryōmin, trans., *Rinzairoku, Zen no goroku* 10 (Tokyo: Chikuma shobō, 1972) is a modern Japanese translation. Nakamura Bunbō, *Gendaigo yaku* Rinzairoku (Tokyo: Daitō shuppan, 1990) is a modern Japanese translation by a chief administrator of the Nanzen-ji wing of Rinzai Zen and is useful for its "contemporary Sangha-Hall" perspective. As for translations not based on the standard edition, Yanagida did an annotated modern Japanese translation of the edition contained in fascicle 6 of the *Sijia yulu*: Yanagida Seizan, trans., *Zen goroku, Sekai no meicho* 18 (Tokyo: Chūōkōronsha, 1978), 181–288. Irmgard Schloegl, trans., *The Zen Teaching of Rinzai [The Record of Rinzai]* (Berkeley: Shambala, 1976) is an English translation by a Rinzai Zen practitioner that gives "precedence to the living teaching and the traditional way." For a scholarly English translation, see Thomas Yūhō Kirchner, ed., *The Record of Linji* (Honolulu: University of Hawai'i Press, 2009). This translation is the fruit of the work carried out during the 1950s and 1960s by a legendary group of Japanese and American scholars at Daitoku-ji in Kyoto under Ruth Fuller Sasaki. With a final revision for style, it was initially published without the extensive notes and Yanagida's historical introduction as: Ruth F. Sasaki, *The Record of Lin-chi* (Kyoto: The Institute for Zen Studies, 1975). Kirchner states (p. xxiv) only that he executed "some further stylistic polishings and the

correction of several errors of interpretation." Although the core of the translation in the Kirchner volume remains pioneering work, it is the pioneering work of half a century ago. The voluminous notes are excellent, but the introduction is now out of date. For a translation aimed at the general reader, see Burton Watson, trans., *The Zen Teachings of Master Lin-chi* (New York: Columbia University Press, 1999). Paul Demiéville, trans., *Entretiens de Lin-tsi* (Paris: Fayard, 1972) has very useful notes. Two German translations are: Pierre Brun, *Meister Linji. Begegnungen* (Zürich: Ammann, 1986) and Robert C. Mörth, *Das Lin-chi Lu des Ch'an Meisters Lin-Chi Yi-Hsüan* (Hamburg: MOAG Mittelungen, 1987). Both reorganize the section order of the standard edition into an entirely new sequence. Yang Cengwen, ed., *Linjilu* (Zhengzhou: Zhongzhou guji chubanshe, 2001) is a Chinese edition with notes (no modern Chinese translation). The above list, of course, is hardly exhaustive.

3. These ten commentaries (plus a Taishō-era [1925] commentary) are reproduced in Yanagida Seizan, ed., Rinzairoku *shōsho shūsei*, 2 vols. (Kyoto: Chūbun shuppansha, 1980). Citations of individual commentaries use the form found in "Abbreviations" in this volume, followed by the page number of Yanagida's collection of facsimiles. For example: Kōunshi, 1229. In sequence the ten correspond to nos. 3; 21; 18; 19; 24; 27; 28; 29; 30; and 37 in Komazawa, 520–521, which gives publication and storage data. The Taishō-period commentary was not consulted for this translation.

4. For excellent information on these topics, see the notes to both Kirchner's *The Record of Linji* and Yanagida's *Rinzairoku* (*Butten kōza* 30).

5. After providing a substantial fragment, the *Zutangji* Linji entry ends with the line: "The remainder of [Linji's] answers in response to the mental dispositions [of students] are extensively laid out in the *Separate Record*. On the tenth day of the fourth month of Xiantong 7 [May 27, 866], he died. By imperial proclamation he was awarded the posthumous title 'Great Master Huizhao' and a stupa named 'Clear Void'" [自餘應機對答廣彰別錄矣咸通七年丙戌歲四月十日示化謚号慧照大師澄虛之塔]. This material totals 946 characters (a complete LJL is approximately 14,500). See Appendix 1 for a complete translation. The *Zutangji* seems to have circulated in China until the end of the eleventh century, but its transmission after that is unclear. It was rediscovered in Korea at the beginning of the twentieth century. For the *Zutangji* and the Goryeo (Koryŏ) edition of the Buddhist canon, the structure and contents of the *Zutangji*, the Chinese and Korean prefaces, the problem of authenticity, the modification of Chinese graphs, and so forth, see Christoph Anderl, *Studies in the Language of Zu-tang ji* (Oslo: Unipub AS, 2004), 2–108.

6. After the *Zutangji* Linji material, the next Linji source is a fragment of 244 characters preserved in Yongming Yanshou's 永明延壽 great compendium entitled *Zongjinglu/Xinjinglu* 宗鏡錄/心鏡錄 (*Mind-Mirror Record*) of 961: T2016.48.943c8–22. See Appendix 2 for a translation. For a book-length treatment of the *Zongjinglu*, see Albert

Welter, *Yongming Yanshou's Conception of Chan in the* Zongjing lu: *A Special Transmission Within the Scriptures* (Oxford and New York: Oxford University Press, 2011).

7. At the very end it states: "*Printing blocks reopened* by Bhikṣu Yuanjue Zongyan in residence at Mt. Gu in Fuzhou" [住福州鼓山圓覺苾蒭宗演重開]. Iriya, *Rinzairoku*, 227, remarks: "Even though [Yuanjue Zongyan's 1120 edition] says it is a 'reprint,' it is not a facsimile edition of the original text. There are places where it has been supplemented with material drawn from other texts published prior to that time [1120]—such as the *Jingde chuandenglu, Sijia yulu, Tiansheng guangdenglu*, and so forth. In such supplementary parts we can even discern things that have taken for their raw material the newly produced legend within the history of Linji Chan development in the Song period." [重刊とはいっても、 原本そのままの 覆刻ではなく、それまでに出版された『景德傳燈錄』『四家語錄』『天聖廣燈錄』 などから材料を採って補ったところがある。 それらの増補部分には、 宋代における 臨濟禪展開の歷史のなかで新たに生まれた伝承を素材としたものも認められる。] The earliest complete version of the *Linjilu* is found as the Linji entry in the *Tiansheng guangdenglu* 天聖廣燈錄 *(Extended Lamp Record of the Tiansheng Era* [hereafter Tiansheng *Linjilu*]; CBETA, X78, no. 1553, p. 464, b24-p. 474, c21). The *Tiansheng guangdeng lu* was compiled by Li Zunxu 李遵勗 in 1029 and was issued in 1036. Yuanjue Zongyan's LJL is T1985.47.496b12–506c28. The Tiansheng *Linjilu* and the LJL are virtually identical except for the order of the contents. The *Supplement to Continued Biographies of Eminent Monks (Bu xu gaoseng chuan* 補續高僧傳; CBETA, X77, no. 1524, p. 522, a14–16 //Z 2B:7, p. 176, b5–7 //R134, p. 351, b5–7), which has prefaces dating to the Chongzheng era (1628–1644) of the Ming, says of Zongyan, the editor of the LJL: "Zongyan was a man of Enzhou in Hebei. His family name was Cui. He was a disciple of Chan Master Yuanfeng Man and led the chorus singing the Way of Yunmen [i.e., he was in the Yunmen line]. His dharma appearance was one of restraint; he maintained the achievements of his predecessors with precision. During the Xuanhe era [1119–1125] Emperor Huizong invited him into the palace to discourse on the dharma and granted him the purple robe." [宗演河北恩州人姓崔氏元豐滿禪師 弟子唱雲門之道者也法貌脩整持守嚴密宣和中徽宗詔入內庭說法賜紫方袍] Around the time that Zongyan produced his LJL edition, he also produced an edition of the Yunmen record (T1988). The *Record of the Comprehensive Lamp of the Jiatai Era* of 1204 *(Jiatai pudeng lu* 嘉泰普燈錄; CBETA, X79, no. 1559, p. 343, b18–c6 //Z 2B:10, p. 75, a9–b3 //R137, p. 149, a9–b3) and the *Five Lamps Converge at the Source* of 1252 *(Wu deng huiyuan* 五燈會元; CBETA, X80, no. 1565, p. 349, a21–b4 //Z 2B:11, p. 323, a7–14 //R138, p. 645, a7–14) have some Zongyan sayings. Two other Chan sources on Linji are found in the *Record of the Transmission of the Lamp of the Jingde Era (Jingde chuandenglu* 景德傳燈錄) and *Sayings Records of the Four Houses (Sijia yulu* 四家語錄). The former was originally compiled by Daoyuan 道原 in 1004 but survives only through a version edited under the supervision of Yang Yi 楊億, which was issued in 1009. It has a Linji

biographical entry in fascicle 12 (T2076.51.290a15–291a19) and in fascicle 28 a fragment of teachings in a special section appended to the main body of the work (T2076.446c10–447a10). The *Sijia yulu* has a *Linjilu* edition in fascicle 6 with the same contents as the Tiansheng *Linjilu*. The *Sijia yulu* is a Ming edition of 1607 reprinted in a Japanese edition of 1648, but it was originally issued around the time of the *Tiansheng guangdenglu*. See Yanagida Seizan, ed., *Shike goroku goke goroku* (Kyoto: Chūbun shuppansha, 1974), 53–70. For a discussion, see Albert Welter, *The* Linji lu *and the Creation of Chan Orthodoxy* (Oxford and New York: Oxford University Press, 2008), 81–130. Welter states (p. 107): "The Linji faction master Shoushan Shengnian [首山省念] (925–992) and his disciples were highly influential at the Song court. Yang Yi, the editor of the *Chuandeng lu*, was a close associate of Shengnian's disciple, Guanghui Yuanlin (951–1036). Li Zunxu, as well as Yang Yi, was closely associated with Guyin Yuncong (965–1032), another of Shengnian's disciples. Li Zunxu compiled the *Guangdeng lu* specifically to document the achievements of Shengnian and his disciples. *The links formed by Shengnian, his disciples, and members of the secular literati were instrumental in the promotion of Linji faction interpretation as Chan orthodoxy* [italics added]."

8. The phrase *jiaowai biechuan* appears in section 59.1, the *Stupa Inscription*, of the LJL but is missing in the Tiansheng *Linjilu*. However, the two, beyond the *Stupa Inscription*, are otherwise virtually identical (except for the order of contents) and therefore share the same anti-scholastic tone.

9. See Appendix 1, n. 5. The *Yogacārabhūmi-śāstra* is T1579. Xuanzang's translation is one-hundred fascicles in length and attributes authorship to Maitreya. In elaborately covering the seventeen stages, it discusses the *ālaya-vijñāna* (store-house consciousness), the three *svabhāva* (three natures), *bīja* (karmic seeds), *vāsanā* (habit-energy from past births), and so forth.

10. For instance, the opening sentence in Nakamura, *Gendaigo yaku Rinzairoku*, 1, runs: "In the *Record of Linji* disciples recorded the words and actions of the ninth-century Chan monk Linji Yixuan of China's Tang period." [『臨済録』 は中国唐時代、九世紀の禅僧、 臨済義玄の言行を弟子たちが記録したものである。]

11. See the notes to Appendix 1.

12. However, this shaping process may also have involved outright appropriation. Two texts, Dahui Zonggao's 大慧宗杲 *gong'an* collection *Saddharma Vision* (*Zhengfa yanzang* 正法眼藏; dated to after 1141) and Wenhui Wuming's 晦翁悟明 Chan transmission record *Outline of the Linked Lamps* (*Liandeng huiyao* 聯燈會要; 1183), contain the same sermon material by Deshan Xuanjian (德山宣鑑; 780/782–865). (The former is CBETA, X67, no. 1309, p. 574, a12-p. 576, a5 //Z 2:23, p. 19, a3-p. 20, d14 //R118, p. 37, a3-p. 40, b14; the latter is CBETA, X79, no. 1557, p. 171, c17-p. 174, c14 //Z 2B:9, p. 378, b1-p. 381, a16 //R136, p. 755, b1-p. 761, a16.) Some sayings in this Deshan material are

very similar to Linji sayings in the LJL. Compare the following example from the *Liandeng huiyao* (p. 173, a11–15) to lines in LJL **10.7** and **13.9**: "Old Han Deshan's [i.e., my] vision is not so. Here there are no buddhas and no patriarchs. Bodhidharma is an old barbarian who has the stench of a pig. A 'tenth-stage bodhisattva' is a Han with a carrying pole of shit. [A *'tathāgata*] who has ascended to the stages of perfect and wonderful awakening' is a common person who breaks the precepts. '*Bodhi*' and 'nirvana' are like posts to which you hitch a donkey. The 'twelve divisions of the teachings' are demon registers, paper to wipe tumors [on the surface of the body]. The 'four fruits,' the 'three worthies,' the 'first thought of awakening,' and the 'ten stages' are demons who guard over ancient tombs. You can't save even yourselves. A buddha is an old barbarian piece of shit." [德山老漢見處即不然這裏佛也無祖 [*Zhengfa yanzang:* 法]也無達磨是老臊胡十地菩薩是擔屎[*Zhengfa yanzang:* 糞]漢等妙二覺是破戒凡夫菩提涅槃是繫驢橛十二分教是鬼神簿拭瘡疣[*Zheng-fa yanzang:* 膿]紙四果三賢初心十地是守古塚鬼自救得也無佛是老胡屎橛] It is worth noting that this Deshan is the same personage who appears as a minor character in sections **24** and **40** of the LJL. In **24** Linji quotes a Deshan saying and sends someone to test Deshan, and in **40** a young Linji is Deshan's attendant. Presumably the Deshan material and the LJL are related in some way.

13. Bruce Redford, "James Boswell. *The Life of Johnson*," in *A Companion to Literature from Milton to Blake*, edited by David Womersley (Oxford: Blackwell Publishers, 2000), 399.

14. Kageki Hideo, trans., *Kunchū Kūge nichiyō kufū ryakushū: chūsei zensō no seikatsu to bungaku* (Kyoto: Shibunkaku, 1982), 4: 一日、家蔵の雑書の中に臨済録 一冊を探し得、喜び之を読む。宛も宿習の如し。父母之を怪しみ以て天授と為す。

15. See the index to book titles cited in Gidō's autobiography: Kageki, *Kunchū Kūge nichiyō kufū ryakushū*, 497.

16. Komazawa, 519.

17. Peter Kornicki, *The Book in Japan: A Cultural History from the Beginnings to the Nineteenth Century* (Honolulu: University of Hawai'i Press, 2001), 289.

18. Kornicki, *The Book in Japan: A Cultural History from the Beginnings to the Nineteenth Century*, 5 and 175, says: "A strong argument could be made for resorting to 1600 as a boundary marker. Before 1600 there was no publishing industry to speak of and quantities of books printed were small. After the imposition of the Pax Tokugawa and the sponsorship of printing by Tokugawa Ieyasu, however, a commercial publishing industry grew to maturity in Kyoto in a remarkably short space of time and transformed the production and consumption of books. . . . the net result of the printing boom of the period from 1597 to the middle of the seventeenth century was the appearance of at least 500 newly printed titles, a total which is greater than that of all the books printed during the previous

two centuries. It is at this point, then, that commercial printing and publishing come into their own, and the pace quickens over the succeeding decades."

19. Komazawa, 519–520.

20. Michel Mohr, "Zen Buddhism during the Tokugawa Period: The Challenge to Go beyond Sectarian Consciousness," *Japanese Journal of Religious Studies* 21, no.4 (1994): 348: " . . . seventeenth-century Zen Buddhism in Japan cannot be fully discussed without taking into account Ming Chinese Buddhism and its Qing-dynasty successor. The coming of Yinyuan had a significance for modern Japanese religion that added up to far more than the deeds of a single individual. In a sense it can be said that with Yinyuan's disembarkation on Japanese soil Ming Buddhism as a whole set foot on the islands."

21. Japanese authorities at first suspected Yishan Yining/Issan Ichinei of being a spy for the Mongols and confined him to Shūzen-ji in Izu (Shizuoka). However, Hōjō Sadatoki and others of the elite warrior class came to have deep confidence in him. Eventually this Chinese master headed a number of famous Zen establishments in Kamakura and Kyoto and came to be considered the grandfather of Five-Mountains Zen literature.

22. For instance, see Eishu, 395; Kassan, 548; Anonymous, 286; and Dōkū, 1053.

23. Komazawa, 520.

24. Komazawa, 520.

25. Komazawa, 520–521.

26. See n. 3.

27. Ulrich Timme Kragh, "Classicism in Commentarial Writing: Exegetical Parallels in the Indian *Mūlamadhyamakakārikā* Commentaries," in the online *Journal of the International Association of Tibetan Studies* no. 5 (December 2009). http://www.thlib.org/collections/texts/jiats. The ten Japanese commentaries frequently introduce a gloss or comment with: "a commentary says" [抄云]; "someone says" [或云]; "an intelligent commentary says" [聡抄云]; "an intelligent book says" [聡書云]; "an old commentary says" [舊抄云]; "a good commentary says" [良抄云]; "a certain commentary" [或抄]; and so forth. A recycling process is at work here, and so I have often deleted this introductory phrase. It is possible that some of these unnamed works were by Chinese authors.

28. Shūshin was a master at the Rinzai monastery Engaku-ji in Kamakura. He was in the Genjū 幻住 line (the line descending from Zhongfeng Mingben 中峰明本; 1263–1323), a Rinzai *missan* (密參) lineage prominent in the sixteenth century. For a genealogical table including Shūshin, see the following work on the history of Engaku-ji: Tamamura Takeji and Inoue Zenjō, *Engaku-ji shi* (Tokyo: Shunjūsha, 1964), 864.

29. Myōō was an important Rinzai master in the Five-Mountains milieu, belonging to the Musō Soseki (1275–1351) faction. Over time Myōō was associated with a number of Gozan monasteries in Kyoto, studying the Buddhist canon, Zen works, and secular literature under well-known monks, including the famous

poet-monk Chūgan Engetsu (中巌圓月; 1300–1375). Myōō and Zekkai Chūshin (絕海中津; 1336–1405), the most accomplished of all the Gozan poet-monks, were known as the "two sweet-dew gates" (*ni kanro mon* 二甘露門). During his career, Myōō published Li Tongxuan's 李通玄 *Huayan helun* (華嚴合論) and lectured on Yongming Yanshou's 永明延壽 *Zongjinglu* (宗鏡錄). His sayings record, the *Jōkō kokushi goroku* (常光國師語錄), is T2562. For a biography, see Tamamura Takeji, *Gozan zensō denki shūsei* (Tokyo: Kōdansha, 1983), 138–140.

30. Eishu was a Sōtō master. He revived the Kōshō-ji 興聖寺, which was associated with Dōgen, and relocated it to Uji. Among Eishu's works is the *Commentary on the Sayings Record of Zen Master Eihei Dōgen* (Eihei Gen zenji goroku *shō* 永平元禪師語錄抄). He was caught up in the "heresy incidents" (*zatsugaku jiken* 雜學事件) of 1649 and 1653. These involved the study of heretical teachings outside the Sōtō fold. Eishu's study of Rinzai works led to his expulsion for undermining Sōtō doctrine. See Yokoi Kakudō, "Edo shoki ni okeru Sōtōshu shūgaku fukkō katei no ichi kōsatsu: Bannan Eishu no zatsugaku jiken o megute," *Indogaku bukkyōgaku kenkyū* 24, no. 3 (March 1964): 265–268.

31. Zuigan Monastery was in Tanba in the Kyoto area. The Rinzai master Chitetsu compiled the *Oral Decisions on the Butsugoshin ron* (Butsugoshin ron *kuketsu* 佛語心論口訣; 1676), a commentary on Kokan Shiren's (虎關師鍊; 1278–1346) commentary on the *Laṅkāvatāra Sūtra* entitled *Treatise on the Mind Behind the Words of All the Buddhas* (*Butsugoshin ron*; 1324). Both works are found in *Nihon daizōkyō*, 5.

32. Shukitsu was a Rinzai master of the Myōshin-ji branch. At the time of this commentary, he resided on Mt. Gekkō (月江山) in Sesshū (攝州 = Settsu 攝津 = Ōsaka-Hyōgo area).

33. Dōkū was an Ōbaku master. In 1654 he heard of the arrival of Yinyuan Longqi (Ingen Ryūki 隱元隆琦; 1592–1673) in Nagasaki, and the next year he went with six others to visit the Chinese master. Dōkū subsequently visited Ingen's disciple Muan Xingtao (Mokuan Shōtō 木庵性瑫; 1611–1684) and became an assistant to him, receiving the name Tetsugai. Eventually he was sealed by Mokuan, the second-generation head of Ōbaku. For a biography, see Hayashi Yukimitsu, Otsuki Mikio, Katō Shōshun, eds., *Ōbaku bunka jinmei jiten* (Kyoto: Shibunkaku, 1988), 243–244.

34. Kōunshi's preface to his commentary (Kōunshi, 1092) explains his title: "Furthermore, if one is a real Zen adept, one does not grab onto the 'branches' and 'leaves' of commentarial exegeses but directly severs the root and brings into play the 'upwards.' . . . And so, for the sake of those in the Zen monasteries who have not yet arrived [at at the point of severing the root, that is, awakening], I will 'pluck leaves' and 'seek branches,' explaining the *Record* [*of Linji*] through endless chatter [且如真正衲子則不攀鈔解枝葉直截本源發揮向上.... 故諸方叢林爲其未至者摘葉尋枝講錄喋喋]."

35. The title involves an allusion to a line in the *Zhuangzi* chapter entitled "Knowledge Rambling in the North" [知北游]. Confucius asks Lao Dan 老聃 about the perfect Dao [*zhidao*至道], and Lao Dan replies: "By fasting and discipline, you wash the mind, cleanse the spirit until it is as pure as snow, and smash knowing" [汝齊戒疏瀹而心澡雪而精神掊擊而知].

36. The Rinzai master Dōchū, who was head priest of Myōshin-ji from 1707–1714, is the putative founder of modern Zen studies. Clearly his scholarship should be ranked alongside that of the stellar trio of Confucian and Nativist philologists of the Edo period: Itō Jinsai, Ogyū Sorai, and Motoori Norinaga. Urs App, "Chan/Zen's Greatest Encyclopaedist: Mujaku Dōchū (1653–1744), *Cahiers d'Extrême-Asie* 3 (1987): 162–163 and 166–167, says: "Mujaku's method aimed primarily at making texts speak for themselves. After a good text was established, he sought to elucidate the meaning of terms by a thorough examination of as many examples of usage as possible. The best examples found their way into commentaries [such as his LJL commentary and his commentary on *Dahui's Letters* entitled Daie Fukaku zenji sho *kōrōju* 大慧普覺禪師書栲栳珠] and dictionaries [such as his *Kattōgo sen* 葛藤語箋, a dictionary of 1,064 words and expressions in Chan texts, and his *Zenrin shōki sen* 禪林象器箋, an encyclopedia of terms related to the Chan temple (architecture, organizational structure, utensils, and so forth) and Chan monastic life (functions, rules, daily life, ceremonies, calendar, monastic conventions, and so forth)]; there he generally traces a given expression to a variety of sources, provides some good examples of usage, mentions or cites commentaries and relevant primary source materials, refutes or corroborates earlier work by textual evidence, and if necessary provides his own comment or conclusion. . . . Thus he decided for instance to draw on a wide knowledge of Chinese religious and secular literature, including Ming novels, rather than on interpretations produced by enlightened Japanese Zen masters. . . . Of a total of 374 works in 911 fascicles (卷), only one was published in Mujaku's lifetime. Even today, most of Mujaku's writings exist only in manuscript form. Almost all of Mujaku's books are written in classical Chinese." App gives a biography, a discussion of Dōchū's spheres of interest and research methodology, information about and access to his works, and an annotated list of selected works (a total of fifteen). The astonishingly prolific Mujaku Dōchū also did an edition of the LJL dated 1727, which is found in: Hirano Sōjō, ed., *Teihon Rinzai zenji goroku* (Tokyo: Shunjūsha, 1971). His manuscript commentary on *Dahui's Letters*, which is an invaluable resource for researching the numerous *kanhua*-Chan texts of the Song, Yuan, and Ming periods, has been published as: Zen bunka kenkyūjo henshūbu, ed., Daie Fukaku zenji sho *kōrōju* (Kyoto: Zen bunka kenkyūjo, 1997). See also John Jorgenson, "Zen Scholarship: Mujaku Dōchū and His Contemporaries," *Zen bunka kenkyūjo kiyō* 27 (2006): 1–60; and John Jorgenson, "Mujaku Dōchū (1653–1744) and Seventeenth-Century Chinese Buddhist Scholarship," *East Asian History* 32/33 (2008): 25–56.

37. From an anonymous reader's report on the manuscript for this book.

38. In the notes, the translation of a commentarial excerpt is followed by the Chinese or Japanese. The commentaries in Chinese *(kanbun)* have *kunten*, that is, *okurigana* (*katakana* syllabary at the lower right corner of a Chinese character to indicate the particles and suffixes that are not expressed in the Chinese characters) and *kaeri-ten* ("return markers" at the lower left of a character to show the Japanese word order). These, of course, are not replicated in the notes.

39. See Jeffrey Lyle Broughton, *Zongmi on Chan* (New York: Columbia University Press, 2009), 85–86 and 184–185.

40. Christoph Anderl, "Informal Notes on the Term *jing* 境 in the *Linji lu* 临济录," in *Wenxue yu zongjiao: Sun Changwu jiaoshou qishi huadan jinian wenji*, eds. Zhang Peifeng, Zhanru, and Puhui (Beijing: Zongjiao wenhua chubanshe, 2007), 393, argues that *jing* 境 has a "special usage" in the LJL: "The overall usage of the term did not completely match any connotations from reading other Buddhist texts and often did not quite conform to the definitions provided in reference materials. Linji (or rather: the compilers of the LJL) seems to use the term in a much broader sense, especially in some passages in which he illustrates the core tenets of his teaching. . . . I will try to show that the term—although based on a number of meanings common in traditional Buddhist literature—is used by Linji in a very particular way when embedded in the vernacular language of the text." The Japanese Zen commentators *in most LJL contexts* identify *jing* 境 as the six vishayas—for instance, Kassan, 469 and 507; Kōunshi, 1134 and 1206; Myōō, 68; Dōkū, 1009; Anonymous, 225; and Dōchū, 1310 and 1353. However, in section 13.26 (and by extrapolation 10.1), which does in fact cover what Anderl calls "core tenets," one commentary (Kōunshi, 1191) provides a special gloss of *jing*: "all the ready-made characteristics of forms [*rūpa-lakṣaṇa*] in the questions which the student brings 學人所問將來之一切現成色相." Nevertheless, even that gloss can legitimately be filed under the rubric *vishayas*.

41. *Chan Prolegomenon*, T2015.48.401c18–19.

42. *Chan Prolegomenon*, T2015.48.401c24–25.

43. Broughton, *Zongmi on Chan*, 117.

44. Yanagida, 317–318, discusses what he calls the *"ren* 人 thought of Linji" [臨済の「人」思想]: "The assertion of *ren* 人 certainly runs through all of the *Record of Linji*. The problem of identity in Buddhism—what traditional Buddhist scholars before the time of Linji called *dharmatā* or *tathatā*, buddha nature or *tathāgatagarbha*, mind nature or true nature—certainly Linji is the first to dispense with such an institution and directly capture it within actual, concrete humans[ただちに現実の具体的な人間において把えたのは], and at the same time he may have been the last." Yanagida highlights the LJL's unique emphasis on an actual, flesh-and-blood human being and describes (314) Linji's religion as a "human religion" (*ningen no shūkyō* 人間の宗教).

45. T945.19.121b25–26.

46. T945.19.121b25–26.

47. T475.14.538c5.

48. T945.19.121b25.

49. Wang Wei's 王維 "Sending Off Someone on a Mission to Anxi" [送人使安西].

50. CBETA, X63, no. 1248, p. 583, a16–18 //Z 2:16, p. 498, b4–6 //R111, p. 995, b4–6.

51. Note the following slogan, a description of the so-called five houses of Chan that has circulated widely in Japan: "Yunmen is the emperor; Linji is the *shōgun*; Gui-Yang is the foreign envoy; Fayan is the high-ranking official; and Caodong is the local people." Mujaku Dōchū cites this slogan in his commentary on *Da-hui's Letters:* 忠曰雲門天子臨濟將軍潙仰賓客法眼公卿曹洞土民. Zen bunka kenkyūjo henshūbu, ed., *Daie Fukaku zenji sho kōrōju*, 403.

52. See n. 4.

53. For a treatment of this collaborative effort under Ruth Fuller Sasaki, see Kirchner, ed., *The Record of Linji*, xiii–xxx.

54. The vehicle was Yampolsky's Ph.D. dissertation that was published as: Philip B. Yampolsky, *The Platform Sutra of the Sixth Patriarch* (New York: Columbia University Press, 1967). In 2012 Columbia published a new edition with a foreword by Morten Schlütter and an updated glossary.

55. For Iriya's general attitude toward scholarship, see Urs App, ed. and trans., "Catching the Rhythm of Ch'an: An Interview with Prof. Iriya Yoshitaka by Kenji Kinugawa," *Cahiers d'Extrême-Asie* 7 (1993): 31–43. Iriya's assumptions are laid out in: Iriya Yoshitaka, "Goroku no kotoba to buntai," *Zengaku kenkyū* 68 (1990): 1–19. For an example of his method, see Iriya Yoshitaka, *"Ma sangin,"* *Zengaku kenkyū* 62 (1983): 1–8.

56. Iriya, *Rinzairoku*, 228, remarks: "From the outset doing a *kundoku* treatment [reading Chinese characters in their Japanese readings] in literary format of a text filled with colloquialisms makes no sense whatsoever; most of the mistakes in reading in the past have been the result of not precisely distinguishing the difference between the colloquial and the literary language of the text itself." [もともと口語体の多い原文を文語体で訓読すること自体に無理があつたが、旧来の誤読の大部分は、主として原文そのものの口語と文語との違いをきちんと読み分けていないことの結果であつた。]

57. App, "Catching the Rhythm of Ch'an," 42, quotes Iriya: "I don't have many more years to live, and if I ask myself how I would like to round this life off, the attitude of the Chan monks quite naturally comes to my mind. Not that I'd try to imitate them—but I do have an expectation to detect some hint there, or a kind of strength."

58. For Yanagida's reflections on his lifework, see Urs App, trans., "Passion for Zen: Two Talks by Yanagida Seizan," *Cahiers d'Extrême-Asie* 7 (1993): 1–29. These lectures were published in book form in Yanagida Seizan, *Mirai kara no Zen* (Kyoto: Jinbun shoin, 1990), 53–99.

59. App, "Passion for Zen," 12. Yanagida, *Mirai kara no Zen*, 69–70: はからずもこの仕事を通じて、『臨済録』という本が、私にとつてのつびきならぬものとなる。

60. These dictionaries are:

- Luo Zhufeng 罗竹风 and others, eds., *Hanyu da cidian* 漢語大词典. 12 vols. Shanghai: Hanyu da cidian chubanshe, 1995. An enormous word dictionary of about 370,000 entries that includes both literary usages and *baihua* expressions.

- Jiang Lansheng 江蓝生 and Cao Anshun 曹广顺, eds., *Tang Wudai yuyan cidian* 唐五代语言词典. Shanghai: Shanghai jiaoyu chubanshe, 1997. A dictionary of the language of the Tang and Five Dynasties consisting of about 5,000 entries; mainly based on materials culled from Dunhuang transformation texts, Chan records, poetry, notes/short sketches, and so forth.

- Xu Shaofeng 许少峰, ed., *Jindai Hanyu cidian* 近代汉语词典. Beijing: Tuanjie chubanshe, 1997. An earlier, smaller version of the next dictionary.

- Xu Shaofeng 许少峰, ed., *Jindai Hanyu da cidian* 近代汉语大词典. 2 vols. Beijing: Zhonghua shuju, 2008. A dictionary of *baihua* words and phrases in books from the Tang to the Qing; contains over 50,000 entries; sources are mainly drama, novels, Chan and Neo-Confucian records, Dunhuang transformation texts, and poetry.

- Aichi daigaku Chū-Nichi daijiten hensansho 愛知大学中日大辞典編纂処, ed., *Chū-Nichi daijiten* 中日大辭典. 2nd ed. Tokyo: Taishūkan, 1999. A modern Chinese-Japanese dictionary that contains some "old *baihua*" (*ko hakuwa* 古白話).

61. LJL, **1**.3: "Question: 'Whose house tune does the Master sing?'" Kōunshi, 1113, glosses this line as: "'Tune' is not what the world calls a tune—it is *that one tune* of our [Zen] personal-realization-of-the meaning-beyond-words." [曲者非世上所謂曲調即我宗那一曲也]

62. Anonymous, 323: "In your venue of activities right now, if you listen with your ears, then you are not 'one who recognizes the music.'" [今用處若以耳聽非知音也] Dōkū, 1084: "*That one tune* of Huangbo—I fear no one can hear it." [黃蘗那一曲恐怕無人聽得徹]

63. Anderl, *Studies in the Language of Zu-tang ji*, xxvi.

64. Kōunshi, 1182: 余考此録雖一言半句不落教家說然諸大乘經深旨粲然可見師博頤三藏誠矣.

65. Dōchū, 1325: 忠曰於經論尋討者讀此錄示衆可知其博綜也.

PART I

1. For what little is known about Sansheng Huiran, see Daitoku-ji, 100–101, n. 36. Roughly four prefaces to the LJL were composed during the Song and Yuan dynasties, and almost all popular Japanese editions include the oldest of these, the one by Ma Fang 馬防. Ma Fang's preface consists of fifty-eight four-syllable lines, many taken from the text itself. It is no more than a verse

summary. The manuscript commentary of the Five Mountains Zen monk Kūkoku Myōō (空谷明應; 1328–1407), the oldest Japanese commentary used here, does not include any of the prefaces (Myōō, 1). This translation has followed that precedent.

2. This translation has arranged the LJL into five parts, with headings following Iriya, 15, 31, 149, 179, and 213. However, Yuanjue Zongyan's 1120 edition has only the headings for Parts III and IV, that is, "Calibrating and Adjudicating" (*kanbian* 勘辨) and "Record of the Karman [of the Master's Career]" (*xinglu* 行錄). See Mujaku Dōchū's 1727 edition of the Yuanjue Zongyan LJL in Hirano, *Teihon Rinzai zenji goroku*, 47 and 58. No headings are found in the Tiansheng *Linjilu* of 1029. Zongyan also did an edition of the *Extended Record of Chan Master Yunmen Kuangzhen* (*Yunmen Kuangzhen chanshi guanglu* 雲門匡真禪師廣錄). His Yunmen record, like his LJL edition, has sections labeled "Calibrating and Adjudicating" (*kanbian* 勘辨; T1988.47.567b15) and "Record of the Karman [of the Master's Career]" (*xinglu* 行錄; T1988.47.575c3). Both headings, in both instances, are Zongyan's additions.

3. Kassan, 447, makes a Japanese analogy: "*fuzhu* 府主 means '*shugo* of Zhenzhou Henan-fu.'" [府主者謂鎮州河南府之守護也] The term *shugo* (military constable) was an official title in the Kamakura-Muromachi period *bakufu* (military government) for a combination military commander and civil governor of a provincial jurisdiction. Charles O. Hucker, *A Dictionary of Official Titles in Imperial China* (1985; repr., Beijing: Beijing daxue chubanshe, 2008), 217 (no. 2047), gives *fuzhu* as an unofficial reference to a Commandery Governor or to a Prefect.

4. Kōunshi, 1111: "*changshi* 常侍 is the title of an official, that is, 'Cavalier Attendant-in-ordinary.'" [常侍者官名即散騎常侍也] Hucker, *A Dictionary of Official Titles in Imperial China*, 305 (no. 4834), describes *sanji changshi* 散騎常侍 as an honorific title. For details on Wang, see Daitoku-ji, 96–97, n. 20–22.

5. Kōunshi, 1111: "*shangtang* 上堂 is going up to the Dharma Hall and bequeathing instruction by speaking dharma. . . . The *Precious Instructions of the Chan Gate* [T2022.48.1033b13–14] . . . says: 'Wan'an said, "The ancients at a [Dharma] Hall Convocation first raised the headrope of the great dharma, questioning in detail the great sangha. Students emerged and requested [the master] to explain something again. Question and answers ensued one after another, etc."'" [上堂者上法堂垂示說法也. . . . 禪林寶訓 . . . 曰萬庵曰古人上堂先提大法綱要審問大衆學者出來請益遂問答云云] The *Chanlin baoxun* 禪林寶訓 was completed by the Eastern Wu monk Jingshan 淨善 during the period 1174–1189; Wan'an is Wan'an Daoyan 萬[卍]庵道顏/ Donglin Daoyan 東林道顏 (1094–1164). Kassan, 447–448: "The *Glossary of the Patriarchal Courtyard* for its *shangtang* 上堂 entry says: 'Question: The four groups [i.e., monks, nuns, laymen, and laywomen] when assembled for questions on the buddha sutras always sit. At the present time in a [Dharma-]Hall

Convocation of the Chan gate they must stand and listen to the dharma. Why is that? Answer: This is the deep intention of Chan Master Baizhang. Now, in the dharma talk of a buddha assembly the four groups gather like clouds, and the dharma meanings spoken of are not limited to nature and marks. It is not yet known whether they will be assembled for a long time or for a short time. As for the Chan gate of the present, six hundred years after the teaching of the buddhas flowed to the east, the patriarchal master Bodhidharma arrived in the land of Han: *No involvement with the written word; solely transmission of the mind seal; direct pointing to the human mind; see the nature and become a buddha.* This is so that the students being led will all-at-once realize non-arising. For the groups collected it is not a long time but a short time. Therefore, there is no waiting around to stand up from a sitting position." [上堂者祖庭事苑云或問每質諸佛經所集四衆未嘗不坐今禪門上堂必立而聽法何謂也曰此百丈禪師之深意也且佛會說法四衆雲萃所說法義不局性相所會時節未知久暫今禪門自佛教東流後六百年達磨祖師方至漢地不立文字單傳心印直指人心見性成佛所接學者俾於一言下頓證無生所聚之衆非久而暫故不待坐而立也] CBETA, X64, no. 1261, p. 430, c21–p. 431, a3 //Z 2:18, p. 118, c3–9 //R113, p. 236, a3–9.

6. Anonymous, 215, Dōkū, 995, and Kōunshi, 1111: "a country monk, a humble expression." [山野之僧也卑下之詞]

7. Kassan, 448: "Our [Zen] personal-realization-of-the-meaning-beyond-words is non-verbal and has never had even a single dharma that could be verbally expressed; nevertheless, because of this sort of mandate from the Commandery Governor, I have no alternative. An old monk of ancient times said, 'From its origin the arrow was *bent* [i.e., Linji's *bending* himself to accommodate customary etiquette (曲順人情)], but it scored a hit on the monkey.'" [我宗無語句元來不有一法可說雖然如斯府主之命故不獲已也古宿云由基箭曲中猿] Dōkū, 995, is similar: "Our [Zen] personal-realization-of-the-meaning-beyond-words has never had even a single dharma that could be verbally expressed; nevertheless, because of this sort of insistent request from the Commandery Governor, I cannot contravene his mandate, and, therefore, I have no alternative." [我宗元來無一法可說雖然如斯府主堅請不獲違命故不獲已也] For Chan, the *locus classicus* of the dichotomy between *zong* 宗 (= *xin* 心 ["mind"] = personal-realization-of-the-meaning-beyond-words = Chan) and *jiao* 教 ("the canonical teachings") is Zongmi's *Chan Prolegomenon.* Yanshou's *Zongjinglu* 宗鏡錄 (T2016.48.428b3–4) provides the following interpretation of *zong* 宗: "Question: 'We take mind as *zong* 宗. What are the characteristics of *zong*-comprehension?' Answer: 'Internal realization of one's own mind is the first principle. It is abiding in the stage of awakening on one's own.'" [問以心為宗如何是宗通之相答內證自心第一義理住自覺地] Yanshou then quotes the *Laṅkāvatāra Sūtra* (T670.16.499b28–c3) on the difference between *zongtong* 宗通 (*sidddhānta-naya*) and *shuotong* 說通 (*deśanā-naya*).

8. Dōkū, 996: "*zuzongmen* 祖宗門 means 'Chan gate.'" [祖宗門者謂禪門]

9. See n. 22. Kassan, 448: "for the purpose of the one *great matter*." [一大事因緣也] The *Lotus Sutra* (T262.9.7a21–22) says: "All the buddhas appear in the world just for the purpose of the one *great matter* [*ekakṛtyena*]." [諸佛世尊唯以一大事因緣故出現於世] According to the *Lotus*, the buddhas want to enable sentient beings to open up buddha knowing-seeing, and to attain purity; they want to show sentient beings the knowing-seeing of the buddhas; they want to enable sentient beings to awaken to buddha knowing-seeing; and they want to enable sentient beings to enter the path of buddha knowing-seeing.

10. Dōchū, 1265, cites *Analects*, "Zilu 子路": "When ritual and music do not flourish, punishments do not hit the mark; when punishments do not hit the mark, the people have no place to put their hands and feet." [禮樂不興則刑罰不中刑罰不中則民無所措手足]

11. Anonymous, 215, and Dōkū, 996: "In [Yanshou's] *Zongjinglu* [T2016.48.683a4] an ancient worthy [Zongmi's *Chan Prolegomenon*, T2015.48.412c2–3] says: 'The intention behind raising the headrope [of a fishing net] lies in spreading out the net. One should not discard the net and save the headrope.'" [宗鏡錄古德云提綱意在張網不可去網存綱]

12. Eishu, 338: "*zhanjiang* 戰將 is *shōgun* ." [戰將ハ將軍也]

13. Kōunshi, 1112: "'Unroll his battle line and open up his banners' means 'pose a hard question to present an all-out manifestation of the capability of his whole personality.'" [展陣開旗者設問難呈機用之義也] (The term *jiyong* 機用 is a contraction of *daji dayong* 大機大用, which Zengo, 292, glosses as: "an all-out manifestation of the capability of one's whole personality." [全人格の力量の全面的な顕現]) Kassan, 448, gives a Japanese parallel: "*Shōgun* Linji to his *bakufu* subordinates: 'Is there such a person?'" [林際將軍幕下還更有如是之人麼也]

14. Kōunshi, 1112, Dōkū, 996, Eishu, 338, and Dōchū, 1265: "An ancient worthy's brief comment: 'Severs the [samsaric world of] red dust [i.e., defiled vishayas]; [the shout is like] a single stream of [flowing] water—[its sound is unending].'" [古德著語截斷紅塵水一溪] The full line of the last portion appears in a couplet in Huiyan Zhizhao's 晦巖智昭 Chan compendium *An Eye [Guide] for Humans and Devas*, T2006.48.313a21 (*Rentian yanmu* 人天眼目, 1188): "The cold pines for miles roar in the cool and refreshing wind; a single stream of flowing water—its sound is unending." [寒松十里吼清風流水一溪聲未已] Zengo, 61, glosses *he* 喝 as: "Shout/give somebody a sharp scolding in a loud voice; it is not the vocalizing of [the word] '*kātsu*.'" [大声でどなること。「カーツ」と発声することではない。] Exactly what sound or sounds were typically shouted we do not know, but perhaps there was a great variety. Mujaku Dōchū's *Notes on Kudzu Words* (*Kattōgo sen* 葛藤語箋; Mujaku Dictionaries, 2.887) perhaps catches it best by simply leaving an empty space for the entry *he* 喝! The *Blue Cliff Record* (*Biyanlu* 碧巖錄; T2003.48.195b23–24) says: "The stick is like the sprinkling of rain, and the shout is like rolling thunder." [棒如雨點喝似雷奔] The thunder simile is also

found in non-Chan sources. For instance, the *Romance of the Three Kingdoms* (*Sanguo yanyi* 三國演義, 43): "Fei in a severe voice gave a great shout: 'I am the man of Yan named Zhang Yide. Who dares to resolve things in a fight to the death with me?' The sound was like a tremendous thunder." [飛乃厲聲大喝曰。我乃燕人張翼德也。誰敢與我決一死戰。聲如巨雷。]

15. Kōunshi, 1112, and Kassan, 449: "[The monk] gives his okay beneath the shout." [又是喝下承當]

16. Kōunshi, 1112: "An ancient worthy's brief comment: 'One hand raises; one hand grasps.'" [古德著語一手擡一手搦]

17. Kōunshi, 1113: "'Tune' is not what the world calls a tune—it is *that one tune* of our [Zen] personal-realization-of-the-meaning-beyond-words." [曲者非世上所謂曲調即我宗那一曲也] *na yi qu* 那一曲 ("that one tune") is analogous to the term *na yi ren* 那一人 ("that one person"), which is frequently used by Kōunshi, Eishu, and Dōchū. "That one person" refers to that one person of no-dependence, that one person who has no characteristics or form, and so forth.

18. The key term *niyi* 擬議 ("dither") appears nine times in LJL and shows the text's strong preference for an instantaneous reaction time over premeditation of any sort. The following is a list of glosses on this key term: Dōchū, 1269: "*niyi* 擬議 is a word from the *Changes* much used in Zen records. It has the meaning 'was about to answer but not yet capable of doing so.'" [擬議易文字而禪錄多用爲欲答未得答之義] Kassan, 457, Chitetsu, 623, and Kōunshi, 1118: "[*niyi* 擬議] is like comparing several [options for a response]." [猶較些子] Kassan, 449: "[The response on the part of the monk was] insipid and did not arrive at the deep pool/wellspring." [索短不至深泉] Anonymous, 215: "This monk has lost the rut of the wheel in the road." [此僧失途轍也] Chitetsu, 615: "It's just that this monk comes up one phrase short." [秖是此僧欠一句矣] Myōō, 5: "[This monk] gulped down his breath-energy, swallowed any audible, and was confused." [氣ヲ吞声ヲ飲迷惑スル也] Shūshin, 128: "[*niyi* 擬議 means the response was] too slow." [太遲] Kōunshi, 1113: "*niyi* 擬議 is the same as 'sunk in thought.'" [擬議與佇思同] Dōkū, 996: "*niyi* 擬議 has the meaning 'about to speak' or 'about to move.'" [擬議者取欲言欲動之義也] Mujaku Dōchū's *Notes on Kudzu Words* (*Kattōgo sen* 葛藤語箋; Mujaku Dictionaries, 2.953): "*niyi* 擬議 is 'about to speak but not yet speaking.'" [擬議者欲言而未言也] Iriya, 16.5: "means 'tries to apply reflection to it and undertakes to speak a word.'" [思案を加えようとする。 ひとこと言おうとしかける。] Zengo, 81, glosses *niyi* 擬議 as: "hesitates/wavers/hangs back/vacillates/falters/shilly-shallies; stammers/falters/is stuck for a word." [ためらう、口ごもる] The *Sayings Record of Chan Master Dahui Pujue* (*Dahui Pujue chanshi yulu* 大慧普覺禪師語錄; T1998.47.882a 1–3) says: "The Master said, 'If you call this a bamboo clapper [*zhubi/shippei*], it's an offense. If you don't call this a bamboo clapper, it's a violation. You must not make a comment. You must not remain silent. You must not engage in mental reflection. You must not dither.'"

[乃云喚作竹篦則觸不喚作竹篦則背不得下語不得無語不得思量不得擬議] For Dahui *niyi* clearly is a synonym of "mental reflection" or "mental activities" (*siliang* 思量 = *manasi-kāra*). Even in a Neo-Confucian context *niyi* and *siliang* are interchangeable; for example, the *Classified Conversations of Zhu Xi* (*Zhuzi yulei* 朱子語類), 59: "Right now—at this very moment—is the venue of putting in effort. Why wait around to dither, mentally reflect, debate right and wrong, and do research into differences in principles?" [只今眼下便是用功處何待擬議思量與辨論是非講究道理不同]

19. Kassan, 449: "Lecture Master." [講主也] Dōchū, 1266: "Zen followers call a scholar of the teachings by the general term 'master of the [lecture] seat,' speaking [disparagingly] of 'the type of understanding level of a Seat Master.'" [禪家呼教家泛稱座主云座主見解之類也]

20. Shūshin, 119: "pokes his head out of the kudzu-cave [of verbal entanglement]." [葛藤窟裏出頭來]

21. Kassan, 453: "'Wasteland overgrown with weeds' means *avidyā*.'" [荒草者無明謂也] Kōunshi, 1114: "'Wasteland overgrown with weeds' refers to the canonical abstractions [the Seat Master] asked about." [荒草者指所問教說]

22. Kōunshi, 1114: "'The one *great matter*' is the original mind possessed by everyone, the matter right under our feet. . . . The *Lotus Sutra* [T262.9.7a21–22] . . . says: 'All the buddhas appear in the world just for the purpose of the one *great matter*.'" [一大事者人人自己本心腳跟下之事也. . . . 法華 . . . 曰諸佛世尊唯以一大事因緣故出現於世]

23. Dōchū, 1267: "[Your speaking] will not involve or reach to the *certain matter*." [於某事不相涉不相及也]

24. Xu Shaofeng, ed., *Jindai Hanyu da cidian* [*Great Word Dictionary of Recent Sinitic*] (Beijing: Zhonghua shuju, 2008), 1.143b, glosses *bu jian* 不見 as: *bu guai* 不怪; *bu ze* 不责 ("it's no wonder that") and cites a Dunhuang transformation text (*bianwen* 變文) *Story of Yuan Gong of Mt. Lu* (*Lushan Yuan Gong hua* 廬山遠公話).

25. Kōunshi, 1115: "These are lines taken from the *Laṅkāvatāra* and *Vimalakīrti Sūtras*." [是楞伽維摩等撮取之文也] T670.16.506c6 and T475.14.540a11.

26. Kassan, 454, Dōkū, 998, and Kōunshi, 1115: "'Kudzu' means 'written characters and spoken phrases.'" [葛藤言文字言句也]

27. Kassan, 445, Chitetsu, 618, Dōkū, 998, and Kōunshi, 1116: "words expressing thanks." [言謝語也] Dōchū, 1268: "It is polite speech: 'I have troubled the great sangha by making it stand for a long time. Now that I am leaving, take care of your bodily self.'" [禮話也勞大眾久立且去珍重身體也] At a *shangtang* 上堂 Chan monks stood rather than sat—see n. 5.

28. Anonymous, 217: "The Thousand-hand Avalokiteśvara is one of the six Avalokiteśvaras: 1. Horse-head Avalokiteśvara; 2. Noble Avalokiteśvara; 3. Thousand-hand Avalokiteśvara; 4. Eleven-Faced Avalokiteśvara; 5. Wishing-wheel Avalokiteśvara; and 6. Cuṇḍī Avalokiteśvara. The Thousand-hand

Avalokiteśvara is the lord of the rebirth path of the hells and also the lord of the six rebirth paths." [千手觀音者六觀音之一也一馬頭觀音二聖觀音三千手觀音四十一面觀音五如意輪觀音六準胝觀音也千手觀音地獄道化主也又六道化主也]

29. Dōchū, 1269: "When monks see each other, they bend the body [in a bow], put the palms together [in salutation], and say 'I don't know [*bu shen* 不審].' These are the three actions of respect." [如比丘相見曲躬合掌口曰不審者何此三業歸仰也] Anonymous, 217: "*bu shen* 不審 is a ritual formula. Here it has the meaning of 'How are you?'" [不審禮義也此間如何義也] Dōkū, 999: "*bu shen* 不審 [is a polite formula: 'I hope you are unburdened by] illness or worries and in a spry state of health.'" [不審以病以惱起居輕利否] Xu Shaofeng, ed., *Jindai Hanyu da cidian* [*Great Word Dictionary of Recent Sinitic*], 1.149b, has a quotation from the Dunhuang transformation text *Story of Yuan Gong of Mt. Lu* (*Lushan Yuan Gong hua* 廬山遠公話) that shows a typical response to this phrase of salutation: "[An old man] arrived in front of the hut and in a loud voice said, '*bu shen*, Preceptor!' Yuan Gong said, 'Ten-thousand good fortunes to you!'" [(老人)直至庵前高聲不審和尚遠公曰萬福]

30. For *niyi* 擬議, see n.18.

31. Kassan, 456, Eishu, 340, Dōchū, 1270, Dōkū, 999, Kōunshi, 1117, and Anonymous, 218, all comment that the "red-meatball" (*chi routuan* 赤肉團) is traceable to first of the four types of mind in Zongmi's *Chan Prolegomenon*: "The *Prolegomenon to the Expressions of the Chan Source* [T2015.48.401c18–19] says: '*Hṛdaya* means *meatball mind*. This is the mind [that is the first] of the five viscera in the physical body.'" [禪源諸詮都序云紇利陀耶此云肉團心此是身中五藏心也] The *Hekiganroku Funi shō* 碧巖錄不二鈔 of the Five-Mountains Zen figure Kiyō Hōshū (岐陽方秀; 1361–1424), a commentary on the *Blue Cliff Record* (case no. 32 of the *Blue Cliff Record* is based on section 31 of the LJL), glosses the "red-meatball" of the LJL with Zongmi's four types of mind as quoted in Yanshou's *Zongjinglu* (T2016.48.434c7–17). See Zen bunka kenkyūjo, ed., *Zengo jisho ruiju 3: Hekiganroku Funi shō* (Kyoto: Zen bunka kenkyūjo, 1993), 156. By extension, "red-meatball" indicates the human body as a whole. This is confirmed by fragments of LJL material preserved in the *Zutangji* (952) and the *Zongjinglu* (961), both of which have "body of the five *skandhas*" (*wuyin shentian* 五陰身田) rather than "red-meatball." See Appendix I, n.2, and Appendix II.

32. Kassan, 456: "'True person' means the 'real mind' [i.e., the fourth type of mind in the *Chan Prolegomenon*]." [真人者謂堅實心也] Chitetsu, 623: "In the teachings it is said that all sentient beings have the buddha nature. Now in this [dharma talk in the] Dharma Hall [it is said that] beyond the red-meatball there is the one true person who can't be ranked. These statements are identical in meaning. [Though] the red-meatball is present in [all] sentient beings, [also present is] the true person who can't be ranked, i.e., the buddha nature." [教中道一切眾生悉有佛性今是上堂赤肉團上有一無位真人文

義相同赤肉團者在衆生也無位真人即佛性也] Dōkū, 999: "'True person' is an epithet of the Daoist school. . . . In the Zen house it is called *that one person*." [真人者道家之美稱 . . . 禪家所謂那一人也] Zongmi's *Chan Prolegomenon* (T2015.48.401c17–402a7) describes the four types of mind as follows: "Generally speaking, mind can be reduced to four types. The Sanskrit is different in each case, and hence the [Chinese] translations [and transliterations] also differ. The first is *hṛdaya*. This means the 'meatball mind' [*routuan xin* 肉團心]. This is the mind that is [the first of] the five viscera in the body. . . . The second is the 'pondering-of-objective-supports mind' [*yuanlü xin* 緣慮心]. This is the eight consciousnesses, because all [eight] are capable of pondering as objective supports their own objects. . . . This third is *citta*. This means 'the mind that accumulates and produces' [*jiqi xin* 集起心], because only the eighth consciousness accumulates [karmic] seeds and produces the [seven] active [consciousnesses]. . . . The fourth [type of mind is also Sanskrit] *hṛdaya*. This means the 'real mind' [*jianshi xin* 堅實心] or 'true mind' [*zhenshi xin* 真實心]. . . . The first three [types of mind] are characteristics; the last one is the nature." [汎言心者略有四種梵語各別翻譯亦殊一紇利陀耶此云肉團心此是身中五藏心也(具如黃庭經五藏論說也)二緣慮心此是八識俱能緣慮自分境故(色是眼識境乃至根身種子器世界是阿賴耶識之境各緣一分故云自分)此八各有心所善惡之殊諸經之中目諸心所總名心也謂善心惡心等三質多耶此云集起心唯第八識積集種子生起現行故(黃庭經五藏論目之爲神西國外道計之爲我皆是此識)四乾栗陀耶此云堅實心亦云貞(=真)實心此是真心也然第八識無別自體但是真心以不覺故與諸妄想有和合不和合義和合者能含染淨目爲藏識不和合者體常不變目爲真如都是如來藏故楞伽云寂滅者名爲一心一心者即如來藏如來藏亦是在纏法身如勝鬘經說故知四種心本同一體故密嚴經云佛說如來藏(法身在纏之名)以爲阿賴耶(藏識)惡慧不能知藏即賴耶識(有執真如與賴耶體別者是惡慧)如來清淨藏世間阿賴耶如金與指鐶展轉無差別(指鐶等喻賴耶金喻真如都名如來藏)然雖同體真妄義別本末亦殊前三是相後一是性]

33. Eishu, 340, Kassan, 456, Dōkū, 999, and Anonymous, 218: "'Can't be ranked' means 'does not belong to the buddha ranking and does not belong to the sentient-being ranking.'" [無位不屬佛位不屬衆生位] Kōunshi, 1117: "'Can't be ranked' means that this true person never falls into the *ārya* ranking or the worldling ranking. . . . 'True person' refers to the self, *that one person*, and originally comes from the 'Dazong Chapter' of the *Zhuangzi*." [無位者這箇真人終不墮聖凡位. . . . 真人者指自己那一人本出于莊子大宗]

34. Eishu, 340: "'Face-gate' is the mouth. It also means the gates of the six sense organs. It also means the hair tuft between the eyebrows [of a buddha]." [面門口也亦云六根門也亦云眉間也] Dōchū, 1270: "here a general term for the eyes, ears, nose, and so forth, not necessarily limited to the mouthgate." [今泛稱眼耳鼻等不必局口門也] Dōkū, 1000: "The *Śūraṃgama Sūtra* [T945.19.108b23–24] . . . says: 'At that time the World-honored-one from his

face-gate emitted various rays of light. These light rays were dazzling like a hundred-thousand suns.'" [首楞嚴 . . . 云爾時世尊從其面門放種種光其光晃耀如百千日]

35. The *Glossary of the Patriarchal Courtyard* (*Zuting shi yuan* 祖庭事苑) has the following entry: "*Occupying the rank of the curved-wood chair:* The Great Master Yunmen of Shaoyang said, 'Old bald-headed hacks from all over sit on the curved-wood Chan chair and seek fame and profit, asking, "Buddhas?" and answering, "Buddhas!"; asking, "Patriarchs?" and answering, "Patriarchs!"; and shitting and pissing.'" [曲木據位: 韶陽雲門大師云諸方老禿奴曲木禪牀上坐求名求利問佛答佛問祖答祖痾屎送尿也] CBETA, X64, no. 1261, p. 346, a22–24 //Z 2:18, p. 33, d16–18 //R113, p. 66, b16–18.

36. Anonymous, 218: "*chuanti zuoyong* [i.e., all doing and all acting are the unreserved functioning of the buddha nature]." [全躰作用] Anonymous is quoting LJL itself; this phrase occurs in 13.22, 13.26, and 13.43.

37. For *niyi* 擬議, see n. 18.

38. Eishu, 341, and Anonymous 218: "The meaning is 'dried shit resembling a stub/peg/cylinder.'" [乾屎似橛義也] Kōunshi, 118: "*ganshijue* 乾屎橛 is dried shit like a stub/peg/cylinder." [乾屎橛者乾屎如橛者] Iriya, 21.5–6: "'What' [*shenme* 什麼] is here not a question word, but an [exclamatory] word expressing wonder."

39. Kōunshi, 118: "For the entry *fangzhang* the *Glossary of the Patriarchal Courtyard* (*Zuting shi yuan* 祖庭事苑) says: 'At present the main bedroom in a Chan monastery is the *fangzhang* ["ten-foot square"]. It comes from the room of Vimalakīrti in the city of Vaiśālī. It is a room of only one *zhang* [about ten feet along one side] but can hold 32,000 lion seats, because it has inconceivable wonders. Wang Xuance of the Tang Dynasty went on a mission to the Western Regions and passed by this dwelling. With his official tablet he measured its length and width, and they came to ten tablets each. That is how it got its name.'" [方丈者事苑曰今以禪林正寢爲方丈盍取則毗耶離城維摩室以一丈之室能容三萬二千師子之座有不可思議之妙事故也唐王玄策爲使西域過其居以手版縱橫量之得十笏因以爲名] CBETA, X64, no. 1261, p. 401, b19–22 //Z 2:18, p. 89, a17–b2 //R113, p. 177, a17–b2.

40. Kōunshi, 118: "Whenever [a master] goes up to the Dharma Hall for a dharma talk, there is the [the preliminary of the] 'fishing words,' and afterwards Zen guests emerge to ask questions. However, in the case of this monk, before the Master has even raised the fishing words [i.e., thrown down a fishing hook and reeled in answers from the students in order to test their levels of understanding, the monk] emerges and bows. An all-out manifestation of the capability of his whole personality will become evident." [凡上堂法有索話(=釣語)而後禪客出請問然此僧師未舉索話先出禮拜其機用可知]

41. Kōunshi, 118: "*tantou* 探頭 ['fish around/probe/reconnoiter'] is 'calibrate/examine; hold an inquest.'" [探頭者勘驗也]

42. Shūshin, 123: "taking poison to attack poison." [以毒攻毒]

43. Zengo, 268, glosses *caozei* 草賊 as: "an army of traitors flying the banner of revolt." [叛旗をひるがえした賊軍。]

44. Dōchū, 1272: "At what place did my traitors make a mistake?" [我賊過在何處]

45. Anonymous, 219, and Dōku, 1001: "The *Glossary of the Patriarchal Courtyard* says: "'Head Seat' is the 'Advanced Seat' of ancient times. The Sanskrit is *vṛddhānta*, which means 'Advanced [i.e., Upper] Seat.' 1. He is advanced in years; 2. he is noble in bearing; and 3. he received the precepts and realized the fruit of the Way earlier than others." [祖庭事苑云首座即古之上座梵語悉替那此云上座一耆年二貴族三先受戒及證道果] CBETA, X64, no. 1261, p. 431, a22–24 //Z 2:18, p. 118, d10–12 //R113, p. 236, b10–12.

46. Myōō, 7: "'Flywhisk' is the *original portion*." [拂子ハ本分也]

47. For *niyi* 擬議, see n. 18.

48. Eishu, 343, Kassan, 460, Dōchū, 1273, and Dōku, 1002: "['Twenty years' means] 'twenty years ago.'" [二十年前卜云也]

49. *zhang/zhuzhang* 杖/拄杖 ("staff") and *bang* 棒 ("stick") appear numerous times in the LJL and seem to be used interchangeably as synonyms. The former appears in Chinese Buddhist literature as a translation equivalent of Sanskrit *daṇḍa*, a staff or scepter as a symbol of authority and punishment. *An Eye [Guide] for Humans and Devas* (*Rentian yanmu* 人天眼目, T2006.48.311c5–6) makes Huangbo's staff a "black rattan" (*wuteng* 烏藤), that is, a staff made of rattan or cane: "When [Linji] asked Huangbo about the [meaning of Bodhidharma's] coming from the west, he conferred the pain of three hits with the black rattan." [因問黃蘗西來痛與烏藤三頓] Also, see the twelfth-century quatrain used as the epigraph to this book.

50. Eishu, 343: "'Frond of mugwort' has two meanings: Even after sixty blows with it, it still seems fragile and delicate; and a frond of mugwort flexes when blown by the wind. Also, in the Daoist school they placed a frond of mugwort on the head of a child at the coming-of-age ceremony. Huangbo was an anxious old grandma." [蒿枝者二義六十棒尚輕柔而似蒿枝被風吹著動又道家如以蒿枝祝小兒撫頂黃蘗爲个底老婆心切也] Kassan, 460: "Even after being granted sixty blows with the stick, its lightness is like that of being stroked with a frond of mugwort." [雖賜六十棒其輕如蒿枝拂] Dōchū, 1273: "Though it was a painful stick, in my mind it was still not enough. It was light, like being stroked with a frond of mugwort, and so now I am thinking of again eating the stick to supplement that insufficiency." [雖是痛棒於我心猶未足輕如蒿枝之拂今更思喫棒補不足也]

51. Shūshin, 128: "The letting go of it is comparatively dangerous, and the taking in of it much too slow." [放出較危收來太遲]

52. Kassan, 460, and Dōku, 1002: "the sword that cuts off all knowing and understanding." [截斷一切知見解會劍] Myōō, 8: "'Matter of the sword blade' means matter of the *original portion*." [劍刃上事卜ハ本分事ヲ云也]

53. For *niyi* 擬議, see n. 18.

54. "Plumb sunk into a deep pool/wellspring" could be the Master's comment on the questioner as well as on the postulant Shishi. Kōunshi, 1121–1122: "Postulant Shishi is Chan Master Shishi Shandao of Tanzhou in the fifth generation from the sixth patriarch [Huineng]. . . . As to 'forgot his moving feet,' it means the thoroughgoing no-mind of Postulant. . . . 'Deep pool/wellspring' means 'state of the *original portion* and no-mind.' The *Blue Cliff Record* [T2003.48.173b14] and the *Storehouse of Radiant Light* make it 'deep pit.'" [石室行者六祖下第五世潭州石室善道禪師也. . . . 忘移腳者行者徹底無心之謂也. . . . 深泉者本分無心田地也碧巖並光明藏作深坑] The *Great Storehouse of Radiant Light* (大光明藏) by Baotan 寶曇, a transmission record of the buddhas and Chan patriarchs dated 1216, reads: 後有僧問臨濟云石室行者踏碓為什麼忘移却脚臨濟曰沒溺深阬. CBETA, X79, no. 1563, p. 675, c7–8 //Z 2B:10, p. 403, c1–2 //R137, p. 806, a1–2. "Deep pit" makes the line sound pejorative. Dōchū, 1275: "In the *Transmission of the Lamp* [T2076.51.316 a7–b18] . . . [there is] the section 'Chan Master Changzi Kuang's Dharma Successor Preceptor Shishi Shandao of Tanzhou.' . . . Shishi is sunk into a deep pit and, in later generations, only Linji knew this." [傳燈 . . . 長髭曠禪師法嗣潭州石室善道和尚章. . . . 石沒溺深坑後世唯臨濟知之]

55. Eishu, 344: "'Whoever comes' means 'the person who comes to ask a question.'" [來者ハ來問ノ者也] Kōunshi, 1122: "'One who comes' is the student who comes to ask a question." [來者來問之學者也]

56. Eishu, 344: "'Place he is coming from' is 'the place he is coming from in the six vishayas.'" [伊來處卜ハ六塵來處也] Kassan, 460: "'Place he is coming from'" is 'his level of understanding.'" [來處者謂見解] Dōchū, 1275: "Whoever advances to come before me, I know his level of understanding." [凡進前來識得其見解也] Kōunshi, 1122: "'Place he comes from' is the intention behind the level of understanding that he presents. An old commentary makes it 'the place he is coming from in the six vishayas,' but that is wrong." [來處者伊所呈來見解之底意處也古鈔爲六塵來處者非也]

57. The vernacular *yumo* 與麼 ("in that way") = *ru* 如/*zhenru* 真如/*ruru*如如 = *tathatā* ("thusness"); *yumo lai* 與麼來 ("comes in that way") = Sanskrit *tathāgata* ("thus come or gone," an epithet of a buddha). Modern translations have not granted this sort of buddhological weight to *yumo* 與麼 in the LJL, but the Zen commentators do seem aware of it: Kassan, 460: "means: 'If someone comes holding a good level of understanding, he's already lost [his footing before me].'" [言若持好見解來則早失却了] Dōchū, 1275: "*yumo lai* 與麼來 is like 'well come.'" [與麼來若善來也] (In the sutras it is the first element of *ehibhikṣuka*, the act or formula of ordination as a monk by pronouncing the words beginning *ehi bhikṣu*.) Kōunshi, 1122: "*yumo lai* 與麼來 is a coming in which the one who comes is certain about *this matter*." [與麼來者來者的當此事來底也]

58. Kassan, 460: "If someone comes holding a bad level of understanding, then he has established his own bondage." [若持惡見解來則自設纏縛] Dōchū, 1275: "badly come." [惡來] Kōunshi, 1122: "*bu yumo lai* 不與麼來 means a Han who has not yet understood, is not yet certain, embraces a level of understanding involving perplexity, and comes bringing it." [不與麼來者未了漢未的當抱疑解拈將來]

59. Eishu, 344, and Anonymous, 220: "Don't get involved in mental reflection and calculation." [莫思量計較也] Kassan, 461: "Don't get involved in the muddle of mental reflection and conjecture." [莫亂思量卜度] Dōkū, 1003: "*zhenzhuo* 斟酌 means 'calculation and conjecture.'" [斟酌者計較卜度之義] Kōunshi, 1122: "*zhenzhuo* 斟酌 is 'selecting out and conjecturing.'" [斟酌者揀擇卜度也]

60. Kassan, 461, and Dōkū, 1003: "'Delusion' and 'awakening' are both to be eliminated." [迷悟二俱遣] Kōunshi, 1122: "'Understanding' and 'not understanding' continue the above-mentioned *in that way* and *not in that way*." [會不會承上與麼不與麼]

61. Eishu, 344: "*doulai shi cuo* 都來是錯 is 'in their totality they are a mistake.'" [都來是錯總是錯也] Dōchū, 1275: "An ancient worthy said, '"Understanding" is *in that way* (well come); "not understanding" is *not in that way* (badly come).' *doulai shi cuo* 都來是錯 means that they are [both] to be extinguished." [古德曰會者與麼善來也不會者不與麼惡來也都來是錯者勦絕也]

62. Anonymous, 221: "means 'I entrust it to the people of all-under-heaven to judge right and wrong.' . . . 'Right' is *in that way* and 'wrong' is also *in that way*." [言任天下人是非也.... 是亦恁麼非亦恁麼] Kōunshi, 1122: "If 'understanding' and 'not understanding' in their totality are a mistake, then 'gain' and 'loss,' 'right' and 'wrong,' are irrelevant. Thus, if the world is of the opinion that I do not understand and judges me as such, why should that bother me? Let it!" [會不會總是錯則得失是非無所相干然則舉世說我不會貶剝我我何管肆任彼而已]

63. Myōō, 9: "'At the top of a lonely peak' is 'the place of the *original portion* facing upwards.'" [孤峰頂上トハ本分向上ノ処也] Chitetsu, 635: "'At the top of a lonely peak with no way out' is the one gate of mind *tathatā*." [言在孤峰頂上無出身路者心真如一門] Kōunshi, 1123: "'At the top of a lonely peak' is 'the realm wherein a wall stands ten-thousand *ren* [i.e., over 20,000 meters] high without a single dharma in evidence'; 'with no way out' is 'constantly sitting facing upwards, never downwards, not a single route open.'" [孤峰頂上者壁立萬仞一法不立之境界也無出身路者常坐在向上終不向下不通一線道]

64. Eishu, 344: "'Crossroads' is a place like that of a town center." [十字街頭ハ市中ノ様ナル処也] Kōunshi, 1123: "'Crossroads' is the gate of *upāyas* issuing from worldly truth." [十字街頭者世諦流布方便門也] Myōō, 9: "'Crossroads' is a place where people come and go; the students of the ten schools assemble and haggle over the buddhadharma." [十字街頭トハ諸人ノ往來スル処也十家方ノ学者ヲ集テ佛法ヲ商量スル] Chitetsu, 635: "'Crossroads' is the dependently

originated dharmas of the arising-disappearing of sentient-being mind." [十字街頭是衆生心生滅因緣之法者也]

65. Kōunshi, 1123: "'Neither accomodates [people] nor abandons them' is entering the commoner's house and teaching beings, approaching them according to their mental dispositions." [無向背者入廛乖手應機接物也]

66. Eishu, 344: "Don't get arrested by ideas of good and bad—it's just two persons without difference, and therefore there is no ahead and behind." [莫拘好惡之意也只二人共無異故無前後] Kassan, 461: "Don't formulate views of ahead and behind." [莫作前後見] Dōchū, 1276: "'Ahead and behind' are like saying 'superior and inferior.' Advancing to be ahead is superior, and retreating to being behind inferior." [前後猶言勝劣也前進者勝也退後者劣也] Dōkū, 1003: "In the end, one must make students realize that there is no way out, no such thing as accommodating or abandoning." [畢竟要令學人知無出身之路亦無向背之處耳]

67. Eishu, 344: "'Vimalakīrti' is silence, and 'Great Master Fu' is speech. In the end, having words and having no words are both to be stripped away." [維摩詰ハ默也傅大士ハ語也畢竟有語無語共ニ削テノケメ也] Kassan, 461: "The meaning is 'don't hold that wordlessness is correct and don't hold that having words is correct.'" [言不作無語是不作有語是之義] Dōchū, 1276: "means 'you yourself are it!'" [言自己即是也]

68. Eishu, 345, and Anonymous, 221: "'On the road' means 'issuing from worldly truth [saṃvṛti-satya/loka-vyavahāra], that is, mundane dharmas.'" [途中世諦流布也世間法也] Chitetsu, 636: "From first aspiring to awakening until arrival at the *tathāgata* stage—we call that 'on the road.'" [自初發心到如來地謂之途中] Kōunshi, 1124: "'On the road' is all the rebirth paths of the worlds of the ten directions. It is also the ready-made worldly-truth gates of the present day." [途中者十方世界一切諸趣又今日現成底世諦門也] Myōō, 10: "'Being on the road' means 'engaging in cultivation.'" [在途中トハ修行スルヲ云也]

69. Dōchū, 1276: "*lunjie* 論劫 means 'extremely long time, time duration eternal.'" [論劫者言極久也謂其時節長遠]

70. Eishu, 345, and Anonymous, 221: "'Family homestead' is the buddhadharma, the supramundane dharma." [家舍佛法也出世間法也] Myōō, 10: "'Not away from the family homestead' means 'not away from the cave of the *original portion*.' This is the person who is in the uninterrupted, constantly abiding *buddhadharma samādhi*." [不離家舍トハ本分窠窟ヲ不離ヲ云也是ハ不斷常住佛法三昧ニツラヲツキコウテイル者ヲ云也]

71. Myōō, 10: "This means 'the leisurely Way-person of non-action who is beyond the course of training' [i.e., an arhat]." [是ハ絕学無爲閑道人ヲ云也] Kōunshi, 1124: "'Family homestead' is the stage of the buddhas and bodhisattvas. It is also the family homestead of the self; the *original portion*; the protagonist." [家舍者諸佛菩薩之地位又自己本分主人公之家舍也]

72. Eishu, 345: "Both are abhorrent people." [兩方共ニキライノ者也] In other words, these are two extremes to be rejected.

73. Kassan, 463: "in the end, nature, wisdom, and practice." [畢竟性智行也] Dōchū, 1277: "An ancient worthy said, 'As to "the seal [imprint] of the three essentials," the seal [imprint] of emptiness is superior faculties; the seal [imprint] of water is medium faculties; and the seal [imprint] of mud is inferior faculties.'" [古德曰三要印者印空是上根印水是中根印泥是下根] Kōunshi, 1125: "'Seal' does not have the meaning of 'mind seal' or 'ocean seal,' etc., as spoken of in old commentaries—it is merely making a comparison to a worldly seal [on a document]." [印者非古鈔所謂心印海印等之義唯世印相以譬比之]

74. Kōunshi, 1125: "'Side' means that, when one affixes a seal [to a document], the seal's pattern appears on the side [of the document]." [側者謂搭(=打)印開揚時印文側見]

75. For *niyi* 擬議, see n. 18. Because the seal is applied to a finished document, an imperfect imprint cannot be redone. Dōchū, 1277: "As to 'no permitting dithering,' calligraphy and painting come into being in a series of steps, but with the [application of the] seal this is not so. There is only one try for an imprint, and so there is no permitting dithering." [未容擬議者凡書字畫畫次第成如印不然其字一時成故不容擬議也] Myōō, 10: "'No permitting dithering' means that, in pressing down on the seal there should be no [karmic] performance [i.e., intentional action] at all." [未不容擬議トハ印ヲ押スニハ何ノ造作モナイヲ云也] See 13.33, in which the Master presents a calibrating system for a monk's "catching on" to a poem by its first three couplets.

76. Literally: "How could such an *upāya* [compassionate expedient] be at odds with the mental disposition that cuts the stream [of *kleśas*]?" The translation follows the interpretation of Kassan, 463: "mental disposition that cuts the stream" = "wisdom substance of reality." [真實智体] Kassan, 463: "As to the meaning of these couplets, former wise ones have had many sorts of different theories. I will compromise by raising two of them. The first is: 'Miaojie' refers to Mañjuśrī's fundamental wisdom, because 'Mañjuśrī' is translated as 'Wonderful Virtue.' 'Wuzhuo' is the Chan monk Wuzhuo who during the Yuanhe era of the Tang Dynasty [806–820] entered Mt. Wutai and saw Mañjuśrī. . . . '*Upāya*' is the Sanskrit word for 'expedient.' 'Mental disposition that cuts the stream' means 'the wisdom substance of reality.' Generally speaking, Mañjuśrī's fundamental wisdom or 'wonderful understanding' is not something people can fathom. However, out of a compassionate expedient, Mañjuśrī permits Wuzhuo's questions when they meet. Such is the gate of expedients. . . . Another [theory] is: 'Miaojie' means 'the wonderful substance and understanding of one's own mind'; 'Wuzhuo' means 'non-attachment to the myriad dharmas'; 'the mental disposition that cuts the stream' means 'the all-at-once gate of the Zen masters' or 'the Zen of *tathāgata* purity' or 'the highest Zen.'" [此句義先哲異論多分也私折衷舉其二一妙解者指文殊之根本智也文殊翻云妙德故無著者唐元和中入五臺山見文殊禪者無著也. . . .漚和者方便

之梵語也截流機者謂真實智体也摠言文殊根本智妙解故非所諸人可及測然
文殊慈悲方便故且許容無著之相見問話如此之方便門.... 又一妙解者己心妙
体解得之謂也無著者無著万法之謂也截流機者宗師家頓門之謂也或謂之如
來清淨禪或謂之最上上禪] Myōō, 10: "'Miaojie' is Mañjuśrī." [妙解ハ文殊也]
Dōchū, 1278: "An ancient worthy takes 'Miaojie' as Mañjuśrī and 'Wuzhuo' as
Chan Master Wenxi. . . . This theory is insufficient for acceptance. . . . Dōchū
says: "'Miaojie' is "wondrous awakening." Truly, this is the first couplet. As to
Wuzhuo's questions, *wuzhuo* 無著 is "non-attachment" [*asaṅga*]. . . . This is the
second couplet.'" [古德以妙解爲文殊無著者爲文喜禪師.... 其說不足取之....
忠曰妙解者玄妙解悟正是第一句也無著問者無著者無繋著也....乃第二句也]
Koōunshi, 1125: "'Mental disposition that cuts the stream' is the upwards mental
disposition that does not set up even a single vishaya or a single dharma—the
first couplet." [截流機者不立一塵一法向上機第一句之處也]

77. Eishu, 346, gives variant interpretations: "The first couplet is superior-faculties
vessels. . . . The second couplet medium-faculties vessels. . . . The third couplet inferior-faculties vessels. . . . The first couplet is principle, the second couplet wisdom, and the third couplet *upāyas*." [第一句ハ上根器也.... 第二句ハ
中根器也.... 第三句ハ下根器也.... 第一句ハ理第二句ハ智第三句ハ方便也]

78. Kōunshi, 1129: "*Upāyas* are provisionally established gimmicks, methods that
accord with the mental dispositions of beings in order to approach them.
Scholars of the teachings call them *upāyas*, and Zen masters call them tactics
or gimmicks. 'Functionings' refers to [a Zen master's] wielding the stick, letting out the shout, picking up the stick, holding the flywhisk upright, and so
forth." [權者假設機關隨機接物手段也教家謂之方便宗師家謂之機權機關用
者行棒下喝拈槌豎拂等也]

PART II

1. The schema of *ren* 人 and *jing* 境 in this section parallels the schema of *fa* 法 and
jing 境 in 13.26, which deals with sorting students according to three types of con-
figurations of sense faculties. In 13.26 (n. 430) Kōunshi, 1191, gives the following
exegesis of *jing* 境 and *fa* 法: "'Vishayas' means 'one extreme—all the ready-made
characteristics of forms in the questions which the student brings.' 'Dharma'
is 'one extreme—the principle of the *original portion* brought by the student.'"
[境者學人所問將來之一切現成色相邊之事也法者學人所拈來之本分底理體
邊之事也] The translation here assumes that 10.1 *ren* 人 = Kōunshi's understanding of 13.26 *fa* 法 (the mental construct of the *original portion* brought
by the student) and 10.1 *jing* 境 = Kōunshi's understanding of 13.26 *jing* 境 (all
the ready-made forms and characteristics in the questions which the student
brings). Also informative is Kōunshi's comment (1129) for 10.1, where for each
of these four alternatives he cites a specific passage from the LJL itself: 1. "Rip
away the person but do not rip away the vishayas" is section 1.3, where a monk

asks about the Master's house tune; the Master responds with the story of his three hits from Huangbo; the monk dithers; and the Master gives a shout and hit, warning about hammering in a nail where none is needed. 2. "Rip away the vishayas but don't rip away the person" is section 1.2, where a monk asks about the great meaning of the buddhadharma; the Master shouts and the monk bows; and the Master exclaims that *this* is a splendid debate opponent. 3. "Rip away both the person and the vishayas" is section 3, where the Master exhorts the assembly to awaken to the true *person* who can't be ranked, who is always entering and exiting the face-gate of everyone present; a monk asks what is the true person who can't be ranked; the Master grabs him and exhorts him to speak, but the monk dithers, and the Master, thrusting him back, says: "The true *person* who can't be ranked—what a magnificent piece of dried shit!" 4. "Rip away neither the person nor the vishayas" is the "old farmers singing in the fields" of the following section (10.2). This exegesis gives us concrete examples of these enigmatic four alternatives. Alternative exegeses are as follows. Dōchū, 1282: "The feelings of the worldling are 'the person,' and the understanding of the *āryas* is 'the vishayas.'" [凡情人也聖解境也] Chitetsu, 658, makes the above four correspond, rather implausibly, to the four practices (*si xing* 四行) of Bodhidharma: the practice of repaying grudges; the practice of following conditions; the practice of nothing to seek; and the practice of according with dharma (報冤行; 隨緣行; 無所求行; and 称法行). Dōkū, 1007: "'Person' means 'mind-nature, feelings, and so forth'; 'vishayas' means 'mountains, rivers, the great earth, written and spoken language, and so forth'; 'snatch away' means 'not to set up.'" [人者謂心性及識情等境者謂山河大地文字言句等奪者謂不立也]

2. The Zen commentators again differ widely. Dōchū, 1283: "[The shining sun arraying the earth is] not ripping away the vishayas . . . The shadows of the bamboo and trees are like brocade." [不奪境也. . . . 竹木影似錦也] Eishu, 346, and Kōunshi, 1130: "'Shining sun' is 'warm sun.'" [煦日暖日也] Kassan, 467, and Dōkū, 1008: "'Shining sun' means 'spring sun.'" [煦日者謂春日也]

3. Dōchū, 1283: "In the world there is no such thing as a white-haired child—this is ripping away the person." [世無白髮之嬰兒是奪人也] Kassan, 467: "How could [a small child] have white hair like silk, but he has it!" [豈有白髮如絲乎然有之]

4. Dōchū, 1283: "The empire has only the writ of one king, and there is no other in addition to it. This is preserving the person [i.e., not ripping away the person] and having no vishayas [i.e., ripping away the vishayas]." [天下唯一王令而無餘是存人無境]

5. Dōchū, 1283: "'General' is preserving the person [i.e., not ripping away the person]; 'being cut off by the smoke and the dust'—this is ripping away the vishayas. . . .'Smoke and dust' is wolf smoke and horse dust [i.e., the smoke of burning wolf feces was used in the borderlands to transmit alarm signals, and dust was kicked up by the calvary horses]." [將軍存人絕烟塵奪境也. . . .

煙塵者狼煙馬塵] Eishu, 347: "'Beyond the passes' is the regions of other lands, foreign countries." [塞外他邦異國境也] Kōunshi, 1131: "'Beyond the passes' is the border regions." [塞外者邊境也] Eishu, 347: "'Dust' is the dust of the horses; it means that during times of great peace there is no such smoke and dust." [塵馬塵也言太平時節無如此烟塵] Kōunshi, 1131: "'Smoke and dust' is the wolf smoke and horse dust of the battle front." [煙塵者陣場之狼煙馬塵也]

6. Dōchū, 1283–1284: "'News from Bing prefecture and Fen prefecture is cut off' is ripping away the vishayas, and 'have become a single place of independence' is ripping away the person. . . . Both are in the extreme north, and contact with China has been cut off." [并汾絕信奪境也獨處一方奪人也. . . . 同在極北而與中國絕信也] Kassan, 467: "The two prefectures of Bing and Fen do not follow the court's orders and have become an independent place. If in one locale the court's orders are not in effect, that is ripping away the person. When two prefectures do not follow it, because the two prefectures no longer exist, that is ripping away the vishayas. This is ripping away both the person and the vishayas." [并汾二州不順朝命而獨處一方朝命不立是奪人也二州不順則無二州故是奪境也此人境兩俱奪也] Kōunshi, 1131: "'Bing and Fen' are the vishayas; 'have become a single place of independence' is the person." [并汾境也獨處一方者人也]

7. Kōunshi, 1129 and 1131: "Zen monks who are finished with *the matter* are their usual selves with *nothing-to-do*. Upon seeing each other, it is the state of old farmers singing in the fields. . . . These two lines are a portrait of great peace with *nothing-to-do*." [了事衲僧平常無事相見野老謳歌之境界也. . . . 此二句其太平無事之象也]

8. The term *zhenzheng jianjie* 真正見解 ("beholding reality as it truly is") is central to LJL. It appears nine times, and the first element (*zhenzheng* 真正) appears six times with the second element (*jianjie* 見解) omitted but understood. We also find synonyms such as *rushi jiande* 如是見得 ("see in that way"), the vernacular *yumo jiande* 與麼見得 ("see in that way"), *rushi jiede* 如是解得 ("understand in that way"), and *rufa jianjie* 如法見解 ("behold in accordance with dharma"). Translators have taken this key term as "true insight" (Daitoku-ji), "true and proper understanding" (Watson), "la vue juste" (Demiéville), *tadashii kokorogamae* 正しい心構え ("correct mental attitude"; Yanagida), *tadashii kenchi* 正しい見地 ("correct point of view"; Iriya), etc. Actually, it renders one of the oldest and most fundamental ideas of Buddhism: *yathābhūtam prajānāti* or *yathābhūtam paśyati* ("knowing or seeing reality as it truly is"). Both Hirakawa Akira, ed., *Buddhist Chinese-Sanskrit Dictionary Bukkyō Kan-Bon daijiten* (Tokyo: The Reiyukai, 1997), 876, and Ogihara Unrai, ed., *Kanyaku taishō Bon-Wa daijiten* (Tokyo: Kōdansha, 1986), 1078, which cites a large number of words from Chinese translations of Indic Buddhist texts, give 真正 = *yathā-bhūta* ("as it really is"), though *rushi* 如實 = *yathā-bhūta* is much more common in Chinese Buddhist texts (and more accurate). In the *Nikāyas/Āgamas* of Mainstream Buddhism, knowing or seeing things as they truly are is a necessary condition

for liberation. The monk knows or sees as it truly is "the cause and extinction of the five grasping *skandhas*," "origination by dependence and dependently originated dharmas," etc. In the Mahāyāna sutras the practitioner knows or sees as it truly is the inconceivability, *śūnyatā*, and illusion-like quality of all dharmas. Eishu, 347, and Anonymous, 224: "'Beholding reality as it truly is' . . . is the state of the *original portion*, the place of *tattva*." [真正見解 . . . 本分田地真實處也] Dōchū, 1285: "Sansheng's [prominent]] placement of this section [on beholding reality as it truly is] at the beginning of [Linji's] dharma talks is of deep significance." [三聖以此章安法說之首有深意] (Sansheng is Huiran, the monk credited with the compilation of this text in its title.) Shukitsu, 899: "All the beholding in the whole of the provisional teachings spoken by the buddhas and patriarchs is *upāyas*—not the real, not the buddhadharma—and only what one person alone in his solitary beholding beholds is called 'beholding reality as it truly is.'" [佛祖所說一切權教皆見是方便非真實又非佛法而唯獨見其所見謂之真正見解] Chitetsu, 668 and 670, comments (echoing the *Āgamas*) that seeing origination by dependence is "beholding reality as it truly is": "The continuum of arising-disappearing is dependently originated dharmas. Not discerning it is the eyeless one. Who is it that obtains the eye that discerns the arising-disappearing continuum? It is the one who beholds reality as it truly is. . . . 'Beholding reality as it truly is' is the highest meaning [*paramārtha*]. . . . 'Beholding reality as it truly is' is the personal-realization-of-the-meaning-beyond-words of the buddhas, the noble wisdom of awakening on one's own, and therefore Zen monks twenty-four hours a day work at such internal realization." [流注生滅是因緣法不照觀之為無眼子誰是得者照觀流注生滅眼目即是真正見解. . . . 真正見解即第一義. . . . 真正見解是佛宗通自覺聖智所以諸禪和子二六時中工夫内證]

9. Myōō, 13: "'Samsara would not stain them' means that people who possess a beholding of reality as it truly is do not accumulate *vāsanā* [perfuming impressions or habit energy from past lives] due to the karman of samsara." [生死不染トハ真正見解ヲ具スル人ハ生死ノ業ヲノツカラ熏習セサル也]

10. Eishu, 347: "Those who go as they please through stone walls without obstruction belong to this type." [如意去石壁無碍之者乎此類也]

11. Eishu, 347: "'Excellent' is things like [*devas*'] raining down flowers and the earth's shaking." [殊勝ハ雨花動地ノ類也] Chitetsu, 670: "If you obtain a beholding of reality as it truly is, the ten types of excellent things will arrive spontaneously [若得真正見解殊勝十種自至]. The *Tathāgatagarbha Qualities Sutra* speaks of the ten excellent things: 1. possess the ten powers; 2. possess the four fearlessnesses; 3. possses the eighteen special characteristics possessed only by a buddha; 4. possess the thirty-seven parts of the Way; 5. possess the supernormal powers of a hundred-thousand sorts of magical transformations; 6. possess the eighty-eight divine voices; 7. possess the thirty-two marks of the Superman; 8. whatever region you are born into, you increase the good roots of merit; 9. you

are the only honored one in all the three realms; and 10. the hall where you dwell is adorned with the ninety-eight thousand wondrous perfections."

12. The term *daoliu* 道流, here rendered as "stream-enterers," is one Chinese translation equivalent for Sanskrit *srotāpanna*, the first of the four stages of development: *srotāpanna* (has seven more rebirths before liberation from samsara); once-returner (one more rebirth); non-returner (no rebirths); and arhat. The stream-enterer is one who has for the first time entered the noble path and turned his back on the stream of samsara. That Chinese *daoliu* 道流 = Sanskrit *srotāpanna* is confirmed by a passage in the *Abhidharma Explanations Treatise* (*Abhidharmavibhāṣā-śāstra* 阿毘曇毘婆沙論; T1546.28.185c2–4): "Question: For what reason is he named *srotāpanna*? Answer: *srota* means *sheng daoliu* 聖道流 ['noble path stream'], and *āpanna* means 'entering.' Because he 'enters the noble path stream,' he is named *srotāpanna*." [問曰何故名須陀洹答曰須陀名聖道流洹名爲入入聖道流故名須陀洹] Kassan, 468: "'Stream-enterer' is a general term for students." [道流學者揔名也] Kōunshi, 1132: "'Stream' refers to the Zen stream." [流即指禪流]

13. Eishu, 348, and Kassan, 468: "has the meaning 'making people escape from the cave of *avidyā* and become liberated from bondage in the three realms.'" [教人脫出無明窠窟出離三界盖纏儀(=義)] Dōchū, 1286: "Ancient worthies had various *upāyas* for saving people—'liberating' is saving people." [先德救拔人有種種方便也出者救人]

14. *bu shou renhuo* 不受人惑 is a passive construction. See Anderl, *Studies in the Language of Zu-tang ji*, 291. The Zen commentators take the *ren* 人 as "other persons," rather than "*the person*" or "true *person*" as mentioned in **10.1** and **10.2**. Eishu, 348: "'Discombobulated by persons' means the heterodox understanding of bad knowledge. This is because, when there is a lack of right knowing and right seeing, everywhere there is the sluggishness of perplexity and a lack of freedom." [人惑ハ惡知識ノ邪解也無正知正見則触処皆疑滯不自由故也] Dōchū, 1286: "'Don't get discombobulated by persons' means, because you are not dependent upon someone else's awakening, not only are you are not discombobulated by heterodox preceptors and heterodox teachings, you are not discombobulated even by the buddhas and the patriarchs. This is called 'not getting discombobulated by persons.'" [不受人惑者不由他悟故不但邪師邪教所惑佛惑祖惑也不受此名不受人惑] Kōunshi, 1132: "'Discombobulated by persons' means the mistaken teachings of heterodox teachers and bad friends." [人惑者邪師惡友之教壞也]

15. Dōchū, 1286: "You need to heed Linji's teaching of not being discombobulated by persons." [你要用臨濟不受人惑之說]

16. Eishu, 348: "'Hesitation' is solitary perplexity, mental reflection, and conjecture." [遲疑ハ孤疑也思量卜度也]

17. The Zen commentaries and modern scholarship understand this line in drastically different ways. The former, which is clearly mistaken, interprets the

negative phrase *bu de* 不得 to mean "not obtain," and the latter interprets it as a vernacular expression meaning "no good; useless; hopeless." Yanagida, 72–73: "*de* 得 is a colloquialism, meaning 'all right; good.' Accordingly, [the negative] *bu de* 不得 is something that is 'no good; useless; hopeless.'" Eishu, 348, Kassan, 468, Anonymous, 224, Chitetsu, 672, and Dōkū, 1009, all interpret *bu de* 不得 as "not obtaining a beholding of reality as it truly is." Dōchū, 1286, interprets it as the Buddhist technical term "having nothing to be apprehended" or "not mentally graspable" *(anupalabdhi)*.

18. Dōkū, 1009: "'Not having confidence in yourself' is being unaware that all sentient beings are endowed with the virtues of *tathāgata* wisdom, not having confidence in intrinsic, original purity." [不自信者不知一切衆生具有如來知慧德相不信自性本清淨] Kōunshi, 1132: "'Not having confidence in yourself' is being unwilling to admit that you yourself have *this matter*." [不自信者不肯自己有此事也]

19. Kassan, 468: "giving the appearance of losing your self-possession." [失據貌]

20. Chitetsu, 673: "*yiqie jing* 一切境 means the eye, ear, nose, tongue, body, and mind plus forms, audibles, smellables, tastables, touchables, and dharmas, as well as the fifty-one mentals [*caitasa*]." [一切境者眼耳鼻舌身意之與色聲香味觸法及五十一心所] Anonymous, 225: "*huihuan* 回換 has the meaning of 'being revolved.'" [回換被轉義] Kōunshi, 1133: "*huihuan* 回換 has the meaning of 'changed' or 'transformed.'" [回換者換易也轉變之義] Dōkū, 1009, cites the *Śūraṃgama Sūtra* (T945.19.111c25–28): "[All sentient beings from without beginning have been deluded about self and acted upon by things. They lose their original mind and are spun around by things. Therefore, within this they view distinctions such as big and little.] If they can spin things around, then they will be the same as the *tathāgatas*. [With body-and-mind perfectly bright, they will be immovable at the site of the awakening. In one single hair end they will be able to contain the buddha-lands of the ten directions]." [一切衆生從無始來迷己為物失於本心為物所轉故於是中觀大觀小若能轉物則同如來身心圓明不動道場於一毛端遍能含受十方國土] This LJL theme is also found in other sutras. The *Dharmasamuccaya Sūtra* (*Zhufa jiyao jing* 諸法集要經; T728.17.515a10-12) says: "Good at subduing the sense organs; not bewitched by the vishayas; those who possess wisdom in their minds are not spun around by vishayas." [善降伏諸根不為境所嬈諸有智人心不隨境轉] The *Suvarṇaprabhāsa Sūtra* (*Jin guangming zuisheng wang jing* 金光明最勝王經; T665.16.424b8) says: "Mind everywhere rushes about chasing after things, and, wherever it is, it is is spun around. Relying on the sense organs, it grabs onto vishayas and perceives various events." [心遍馳求隨處轉託根緣境了諸事] The underlying assumption in LJL is that a passive stance on the part of the practitioner is bad—only an active stance garners approval. In fact, this passive/active dichotomy is built into LJL's grammar and phrasing.

21. LJL's central theme of "stopping the mind that rushes around and around searching from moment to moment" (*xiede niannian chiqiu xin* 歇得念念馳求心) finds its source in the *Śūraṃgama Sūtra's* "stopping the craziness of the [madman] Yajñadatta in your own mind (汝心中演若達多狂性自歇)." See the extended quotation from that sutra in the commentary to **10.8.** Iriya, 34.2: "the buddhas who are our fathers and grandfathers, a favorite technical expression at the time." [われわれの父祖である仏。このころ愛用された術語。]

22. Kōunshi, 1133: "Each of you standing before me listening to the dharma is a living buddha, a living patriarch." [各自目前聽法底是活佛活祖也]

23. See the *Śūraṃgama Sūtra* quotation in **10.8.**

24. Dōchū, 1287: "the excellent dharma characteristics of the written form of what the buddhas and patriarchs have preached." [佛祖所說文字殊勝法相也] Anonymous, 225: "'Excellent characteristics of the written word' is worldly knowledge and discriminative intelligence." [文字勝相世智辨聰也] Chitetsu, 675: "Liking poetry and linked verse and taking pains with essays is *prapañca*.'" [好詩聯句作意文章亦是戲論] Kōunshi, 1133: "the verbal characteristics of the unusual sayings and marvelous phrases of the buddhas and patriarchs in the sutras and [Zen] records." [經錄中佛祖奇言妙句之說相也]

25. Dōchū, 1287: "The written word is the dead word. How could it get the intention of living patriarchs?" [文字是死語何得活祖意哉]

26. Eishu, 348, Anonymous, 225, Shukitsu, 901, and Kōunshi, 1133: "'This time' is your present birth." [此時今生也] Dōchū, 1287: "[It means] 'if you are not able to encounter the buddhadharma.'" [若不得遇佛法也] Chitetsu, 676: "If you do not encounter awakening on your own to *tathatā*, later you will once again be extorted by the conditions of your previous births." [不遇自覺真如後更從前因緣所索] Shukitsu, 901: "'Not encounter' means 'not having an encounter your very own patriarch/buddha.'" [不遇者謂不遇自己之祖佛也] Kōunshi, 1133: "If at present you do not clarify the *great matter*, then for eternal kalpas you will endlessly revolve on the samsaric wheel." [今不明大事則永劫輪回無窮也]

27. Kassan, 469, Kōunshi, 1134, and Dōkū, 1009: "'Vishayas you like' are your beloved six vishayas." [好境者所好愛之六塵境也]

28. Eishu, 348: "*duoqu* 掇去 is grasping." [掇去執著也]

29. Eishu, 348: "'Be reborn into the womb of a donkey or cow' means 'fall into the animal rebirth path.'" [驢牛肚裏生ハ墮畜生道之義也]

30. The consensus of the commentors is that *jianchu* 見處 ("my vision") is a synonym of *zhenzheng jianjie* 真正見解 ("beholding reality as it truly is"). See n.8, **10.3,** Part II. Eishu, 349, Anonymous, 225, Kōunshi, 1134, and Dōkū, 1009: "'My vision' is 'beholding reality as it truly is.'" [山僧ガ見處ハ真正見解也]

31. Eishu, 349: "'This very day' is 'every day.'… 'venue of all your varied daily activities' means, in the case of each and every thing you find yourself in, whether walking, standing, sitting, or lying down, whether putting on your clothes or eating your

food, it is the venue in which not a single thing is lacking." [今日ハ毎日也. . . . 多般用处ハ頭頭物物ノ上ニヲィテ也行住坐臥著衣喫飯一無欠処也] The term *yongchu* 用處 ("venue of activities") appear twelve times in the LJL. The *Letters of Chan Master Dahui Pujue* (大慧普覺禪師書; T1998A.47.938a15–16) supplies a gloss: "In the venue of your daily activities, dealing with conditions, are you being snatched away by external vishayas [i.e., are you passive]? Or, when you see your desktop piled with papers, are you able to dispatch them [i.e., are you active]? When you encounter things, are you capable of operating on them?" [日用應緣處不被外境所奪否視堆案之文能撥置否與物相遇時能動轉否]

32. Anonymous, 225: "'Six paths' are the 'gates of the six sense organs.' In buddhas they are the six supernormal powers, and in sentient beings they are the six sense organs and six vishayas." [六道六根門頭也在佛六神通也在衆生六根六塵也] Kōunshi, 1134: "'Divine light of the six paths.' . . . means 'your venue of activities right now.'" [六道神光者. . . . 謂現今用處]

33. Eishu, 349: "Reaching the state of the real is *nothing-to-do*." [真實ノ田地ニ至リ得レハ無叓也] Chitetsu, 678: "*Nothing-to-do* is *bodhi*, and therefore it is not the [same as the] worthless [nonexistence in the two extremes] existence and nonexistence." [無事即菩提故非有無閑事]

34. Dōkū, 1010: "[For the Chinese term] '*dade* 大德' the *Perfection of Wisdom Treatise* gives the Sanskrit equivalent *bhadanta*. This means 'great worthy.' In the *Vinaya* the Buddha is often called *bhadanta*. At present members of the great sangha are so called." [大德智度論梵云婆相陀此云大德律中多呼佛爲大德今呼大衆爲大德] Kōunshi, 1134, and Anonymous, 225, have the same Chinese-Sanskrit equivalency.

35. Kōunshi, 1134: "The *Lotus Sutra* [T262.9.14c22–24] . . . says: 'In the three realms there is no peace—like a burning house. It is filled with sufferings that should be greatly feared. There are always the calamities of growing old, sickness, and death. These are like a fire, blazing ceaselessly.'" [法華 . . . 曰三界無安猶如火宅衆苦充滿甚可怖畏常有生老病死憂患如是等火熾然不息]

36. Kassan, 470: "'This' means 'the three realms.'" [此者言三界也] Kōunshi, 1135: "'You' refers to all people." [儞者指諸人]

37. Dōchū, 1288: "The *Mind-Mirror Record* [*Zongjinglu*; T2016.48.551c28] . . . says: 'As to emitting light, it is the wisdom light of the one mind.'" [宗鏡錄 . . . 曰夫放光者即是一心智慧之光] Eishu, 349: "'In your own house' . . . is the human body." [屋裏 . . . 人身也] Kassan, 471: "'In your own house' is called 'form mountain' [i.e., the human body]. Sometimes it is called the 'beautiful Buddha Hall,' and so forth." [屋裡者謂形山也或謂之好箇佛殿等也] Anonymous, 227: "'In your own house' refers to the human body. What a fine Buddha Hall!" [屋裏指人身也又好个佛殿] Kōunshi, 1135: "As to 'the light of purity,' you yourself from the outset have possessed a spiritual light. The scholars of the

teachings call it the great mirror wisdom [*ādarśa-jñāna*]. . . . 'In your own house' refers to inside the *svabhāva* of the form body. . . . as to the '*dharmakāya* buddha,' it is a solitary brightness from without beginning, the originally existent substance." [清淨光者自己本具靈光也教家謂之大圓鏡智. . . . 屋裏者指色身自性中. . . . 法身佛者無始已來孤明靈靈本有之體性也]

38. Kōunshi, 1135: "As to 'the light of non-discrimination,' for a single moment mind does not fall into comparing and becomes capable of awakening to the wisdom light of intrinsic sameness. . . . Scholars of the teachings call it the wisdom of non-discrimination [*nirvikalpa-jñāna*], and they also call it the sameness wisdom [*samatā-jñāna*] or contemplation wisdom [*pratyavekṣaṇā-jñāna*]. . . . 'The *saṃbhogakāya* buddha' is the wisdom of intrinsic perfection, and it is called the enjoyment body." [無分別光者一念心不墮情量而能照覺自性平等之智光也. . . . 教家謂之無分別智又謂之平等性智妙觀察智. . . . 報身佛者自性圓滿智相也謂之受用身]

39. Kōunshi, 1136: "As to 'the non-distinction-making light,' today's manifest activities of seeing, hearing, being aware, knowing, grasping, clutching, moving, and running are unlimited. . . . The *nirmāṇakāya* buddha is these intrinsic activities. According to the interpretation of the scholars of the teachings, this buddha responds to the swarm of mental dispositions [of beings], taking on millions upon millions of magical-transformation bodies in order to speak dharma and convey beings [to the other shore of nirvana]. Therefore, we speak of millions upon millions of *nirmāṇakāya* buddhas. It is also dubbed the response body." [無差別光者今日現成見聞覺知執捉運奔應用無邊. . . . 化身佛者自性應用也據教家判釋則此佛應羣機變化身於百億說法度生故曰千百億化身佛又號應身]

40. Eishu, 350: "The person listening to the dharma is *that one person*." [聽法底ノ人那一人也] Dōkū, 1012: "shows that everyone, on the basis of the one mind, is endowed with the buddhas of the three bodies." [提示人人一心上具足三身佛也]

41. This is probably another allusion to the madman Yajñadatta of the *Śuraṃgama Sūtra*. See the *Śuraṃgama Sūtra* quotation in n. 73 for **10.8**.

42. Anonymous, 227: "In their venues of activity right now every single person has the *dharmakāya*, *saṃbhogakāya*, and *nirmāṇakāya*." [今用處人人箇箇有法報化三身] Kōunshi, 1136: "'Effectiveness' is the efficacy and wonderful functioning of the three bodies." [功用者三身功力妙用也] Kassan, 474, and Dōkū, 1012, are similar.

43. Eishu, 350: "An example of 'terms' would be [mantras such as] *Namu Yakushi*, *Namu Kannon*, and so forth. . . . It means 'unreal.'" [名言トハ譬バ南無藥師南無観音ナドト云タ者ゾ. . . . 又云不實義也] Dōchū, 1289: "'Terms' are just sounds that express doctrinal points." [名言但是詮義音聲也]

44. The *yi* 依 of *san zhong yi* 三種依 (literally "three types of dependence") could be interpreted as *yitong* 依通 ("dependent on *shentong* 神通"). In section **13.11** this term *yitong* 依通 appears to refer to supernormal powers of dependence,

that is, the illlusory, "dependent" sleights-of-hand of the magical arts. However, the Zen commentators take this phrase as "dharmas grounded in the true nature or one mind." Dōchū, 1289: "'Three types of bodies' are reflected images that undergo transformation in dependence upon that true nature." [言三種身者依倚那真性而變起底光影也] Kōunshi, 1137: "means that the three [buddha-] bodies are erected in dependence on the one mind." [謂三身就一心上所依上立焉] Eishu, 350: "'Dependent' is 'dependent dharmas.' They are *tatami* mats, paper sliding doors, and so forth—things that have no [independent] reality. The three [buddha] bodies of the sutras and treatises are completely lacking in reality [in the same way]. Folding screens, *tatami* mats, and so forth, being dependent upon our homes, lack any status as stand-alone items." [依依法也畳子障子等也実モ無キ物也經論三身ハ尽ク實モ無イフ也屏風畳子等是吾家タヨツテ不独立物也]

45. The Zen commentators and modern translators (Yanagida, 75–76; Iriya, 38–39; Nakamura, 60; Daitoku-ji, 162; Watson, 24–25; and Demiéville, 59) all assume that LJL is taking this quotation at face value. The translation here assumes that LJL is poking fun at such obscure (Yogācāra) scholasticism. Kōunshi, 1137: "Dharmapāla's *Consciousness-Only Treatise* [*Cheng weishi lun* 成唯識論; T1585.31.58b26–29] . . . says: 'The self-nature bodies are dependent upon the dharma-nature lands. Even though these bodies and lands are, in their substance, without difference, in the buddhadharma they are different as characteristics and nature. Neither these buddha-bodies nor buddha-lands are captured by forms [i.e., they do not have shape and color]. Even though we cannot speak of the extent of their shape or quantity, nevertheless, in terms of phenomenal characteristics, their quantity is limitless. They are like space that pervades everywhere.'" [護法唯識論 . . . 曰又自性身依法性土雖此身土體無差別而屬佛法相性異故此佛身土俱非色攝雖不可說形量小大然隨事相其量無邊譬如虛空遍一切處] Dōchū, 1289: "Both Dharmapāla Bodhisattva's *Consciousness Only Treatise* and Dharma Master Cien Kuiji's *Grove of Meanings in the Dharma Garden* have this doctrinal point." [護法菩薩唯識論及慈恩窺基法師法苑義林章有此義]

46. Eishu, 350: "'Reflected images' are not real—the many *māyās*, bubbles, and reflections are unreal." [光影ハ未真實也多幻泡影非實也] Kassan, 476: "'Reflected images' means 'not of real substance.' This small segment criticizes the grasping of the three-body reflected images by the scholars of the teachings." [光影者言非實體也此一小節斥教家三身光影之執也]. Kōunshi, 1137, is similar to the first sentence. Dōku, 1013, is similar to Eishu and Kassan. Dōchū, 1290: "like the moon or sun reflected in water, which is a transformation of the real sun or moon." [如日月影在水中者是真月之所變起也]

47. Anonymous, 228, and Eishu, 350: "This section refers to the one who is formless, clear, solitary brightness." [此段指無形段歷歷孤明者]

48. Dōku, 1013: "'Every place' in a subtle sense refers to forms, etc., and in a coarse sense refers to mountains, rivers, etc. 'Every place' is the place wherein

the stream-enterer is unrestricted." [一切處者細指色相等麤指山河等一切處
是道流放身命之處也] Kōunshi, 1138: "As for 'every place,' the reflected images are the myriad objective supports and myriad vishayas."
[一切處者光影底即萬緣萬境也]

49. Eishu, 350: "'Home-place you return to' is the time of smooth-and-steady [cross-
legged] sitting." [歸舍処ハ穩坐底時節ヲ云也] Kassan, 476: "'Home-place you
return to' means 'the grounded place to which you yourself return.'" [歸舍處
者言自歸依處也] Dōchū, 1290: "If you know the original source of all the buddhas, then, walking, standing, sitting, or lying down, every place is the home
to which persons return, the place of smooth-and-steady sitting and great
rest." [識取諸佛本源則行住坐臥一切處處都是諸人歸家穩坐大休歇之處也]
Anonymous, 228: "'The home you return to' is the one of smooth-and-steady
sitting. All the mountains, rivers, and great earth of the three times are the
single eye of the *śramaṇa*." [歸家穩坐底也三世一切山河大地是沙門一隻眼也]
Chitetsu, 681: "'The original source of all the buddhas' is ultimate awakening. 'The home-place you return to' is *tathatā*, the *dharmadhātu*."
[諸佛本源是究竟覚歸舍處者真如法界] Kōunshi, 1138: "'The home-place you
return to' is the home you return to for smooth-and-steady sitting, great awakening, and rest. It is every place, and every place is real. Later [in this section] it
is said that 'everything that meets the eye is [the real].'" [歸舍處者歸家穩坐大
悟休歇之處也是處處真處處真後所謂觸目皆是者也]

50. Kōunshi, 1138: "The four elements are earth, water, fire, and air." [四大者地水火
風也]

51. Kassan, 476, and Kōunshi, 1138: "the five *zang* and six *fu*." [五臟六腑] This is
the terminology of Chinese medicine. The five *zang* are: heart, liver, spleen,
lungs, and kidneys; the six *fu* or hollow organs are: gallbladder, stomach, large
intestine, small intestine, bladder, and *san jiao* (三焦), that is, the three visceral
cavities containing the above internal organs.

52. Kassan, 477: "'Solitary brightness' refers to mind." [孤明者此指心謂也]
Chitetsu, 681: "'Solitary brightness' is the original nature. . . . everyone possesses this natural face." [孤明本性. . . . 人人具此自然面目] Shukitsu,
906: "'Clear, solitary brightness' is the 'original source of all the buddhas.'"
[歷歷孤明者所謂是諸佛之本源也] Dōkū, 1014: "This refers to everyone's original nature." [此指人人本性也] The one mind/mind ground/original mind/true
mind is formless, pervades the ten directions, and is the one spirit-brightness
(*yi jingming*—一精明) or solitary brightness (*guming* 孤明) or light of purity (*qingjing guang[ming]* 清淨光[明]). This is a central LJL theme.

53. Eishu, 351: "Whether it contradicts you or accomodates you—you don't turn
your back on it." [逆順皆背マイ也] Kassan, 477, and Dōkū, 1014: "every place
real, every place real." [處處真處處真] Anonymous, 228: "'Everything that
meets the eye' means 'fusing into oneness.'" [觸目皆是打成一片之義也]
Kōunshi, 1138: "If twenty-four hours a day you fuse everything into oneness,

then seeing, hearing, moving, and stopping are all *these nostrils* [i.e., your *original face*]." [謂十二時中打成一片則見聞動止皆是這箇鼻孔] Chitetsu, 682: "'Everything that meets the eye' is the sameness knowledge [*samatā-jñāna*]." [觸目皆是者平等性智]

54. The Zen commentators (with one exception) and modern translators (Yanagida, 77; Iriya, 39; Nakamura, 63; Daitoku-ji, 163; Watson, 25; and Demiéville, 62) all assume that LJL is taking the treatise quotation at face value. However, the translation here follows the commenator Shukitsu, 907, whose comment on the last lines of this section run: "This [i.e., Linji's statement below that there is nothing that is not liberation] refutes the provisional idea of the treatise quoted above. . . . However, here it says that *prajñā* is cut off, the substance differentiates, and it says that you are turned on the samsaric wheel in the three realms and undergo various sufferings. But this is nothing more than scholars of the teachings toiling over crooked talk and [unreal] terminology." [此破上所引之論文權意也. . . . 然今說智隔體異說三界輪回說種種苦却教學者勞曲談名相而已] For Shukitsu the LJL provides this example of scholasticism only in order to refute it. Also, whereas Shukitsu appears to regard the part about "turning on the samsaric wheel" as part of the "crooked talk" of the exegetes, the modern translators take it as Linji's comment on the treatise quotation. The whole unit appears to be a parody of the kinds of convoluted arguments presented by treatise masters. Kōunshi, 1139, finds a source for the treatise quotation portion in a commentary by Chengguan: "The *Profound Talks on the Huayan Sutra* . . . says: 'Certainly, sentient beings contain the nature qualities as their substance and are grounded in the wisdom sea as their source. It is just that characteristics undergo transformation, and the substance evolves; emotions arise, and *prajñā* is cut off.'" [華嚴[經疏鈔]玄談 . . . 曰良以衆生包性德而爲體依智海以爲源但相變體殊情生智隔] CBETA, X05, no. 232, p. 712, b24–c1 //Z 1:8, p. 199, d2–3 //R8, p. 398, b2–3. Kassan, 477: "'Emotions' means *vikalpa* ['false discrimination']." [情者言妄情也] Eishu, 351: "The *Glossary of the Patriarchal Courtyard* . . . for its entry *xiang bian ti shu* 想變體殊: *xiang* 想 ['thoughts'] should be [emended to] *xiang* 相 ['characteristics']." [祖庭事苑 . . . 想變體殊想當作相] CBETA, X64, no. 1261, p. 380, b9 //Z 2:18, p. 68, a6 //R113, p. 135, a6. Kassan, 477, and Dōkū, 1014, also make this emendation.

55. Shukitsu, 907: "This refutes the provisional idea of the treatise quoted above. It means, if you discuss on the basis of the real, what emotions could possibly arise and what thoughts [characteristics] undergo transformation? Why? The arising of emotions is the original root of all the buddhas; the transformation of thoughts is the original source of all the buddhas. However, here it says that *prajñā* is cut off, the substance differentiates, and it says that you are turned on the samsaric wheel in the three realms and undergo various sufferings. But this is nothing more than scholars of the teachings toiling over crooked talk and [unreal] terminology." [此破上所引之論文權意也言若

依實而論說甚麼情生想變何故情生是諸佛之本根底想變是諸佛之本源底
也然今說智隔體異說三界輪回說種種苦却教學者勞曲談名相而已] Chitetsu,
683: "'Deep' refers to *prajñāpāramitā*. . . . 'Liberation' is . . . the three gates of liberation [i.e., emptiness; marklessness; and wishlessness]." [甚深者般若波羅密. . . .
解脫者. . . . 三解脫門] Kōunshi, 1139: "'Deep' has the meaning of 'profound' or
'inconceivable.'" [甚深者玄妙不可思議之義也]

56. Kassan, 477, and Dōkū, 1014: "[In Zongmi's *Chan Prolegomenon*, T2015.48.401c17–
402a7] mind is altogether of four types: the mind [that is the first] of the five
visceras; the pondering-of-objective-supports mind; the mind that accumulates
[karmic seeds] and produces [the seven active consciousnesses], and the real
mind [i.e., true mind]. The first three are characteristics and the last one the
nature. The last one is the basis of the first three. . . . The 'mind dharma' here
is this [fourth mind,] real mind. This is the mind that pervades both nature and
characteristics. Mind is dharma, and, therefore, [the text] says 'mind dharma.'"
[心者凡有四種言五藏心緣慮心集起心堅實心是也前三是相後一是性後一為
前三所依也. . . . 茲今此心法者此堅實心此通性相之心也心即法故云心法]
Chitetsu, 684: "'Mind' is the buddha mind, not the pondering-of-objective-
supports mind. 'Dharma' is *dharmadhātu*." [心者佛心非緣慮心法者法界] Shukitsu, 907: "The 'formless mind dharma' is just the one mind that is bright and
clear." [無形心法唯是一心而明歷歷]

57. Kōunshi, 1139–1140: "The *Śūraṃgama Sūtra* [T945.19.131a26–b2] . . . says:
'It is like a mundane, skillful conjurer who by sleight-of-hand creates [illu-
sionary] boys and girls. Even though [the audience] sees their bodies move,
there must be an artifice to it. Shut down the artifice, and quiescence returns. Sleights of hand come into being lacking any *svabhāva*. The six organs
are also so. From the outset they are grounded in the one spirit-brightness,
which [seems to] divide into the six combinations. When the one place
[i.e., the one spirit-brightness] is at rest, none of these six functions comes into
being.' [首楞嚴 . . . 曰如世巧幻師幻作諸男女雖見諸根動要以一機抽息機歸
寂然諸幻成無性六根亦如是元依一精明分成六和合一處成休復六用皆不成]
The *Essential Explanations* [*of the Śūraṃgama Sūtra*] . . . says: 'As to the six
combinations, causes and conditions combine to bring into existence the six
sense organs.'" [(楞嚴經義疏)釋要(鈔) . . . 曰六和合者因緣和合乃成六根也]
CBETA, X11, no. 267, p. 150, c24 //Z 1:16, p. 488, d5 //R16, p. 976, b5.
Kassan, 478, and Dōkū, 1014, also cite this passage from the *Śūraṃgama*.
Myōō, 17: "The one spirit-brightness' is the one buddha nature." [一精明
トハ一佛性也] Chitetsu, 684: "The 'one spirit-brightness' is grounded in
the *tathāgatagarbha* and is the place from which the illumination of original brightness arises." [一精明者依如來藏元明照生所] Eishu, 351: "Also,
the 'one spirit-brightness' is the one mind, and the six combinations
are the six sense organs; they are also the divine light of the six paths."
[又一精明一心也六和合六根也又六道神光也]

58. Anonymous, 229: "The six combinations and the myriad dharmas from the outset are nonexistent. They are just the creation of the one mind. If you are of *no mind*, then ultimately you are a single ball of cast iron." [六和合万法本來無也只一心之所造也無心則畢竟一團生鉄也] Shukitsu, 908: "This one mind has many names, and, wherever you are, you will play the master." [是一心多名而隨處作主]

59. Chitetsu, 685, links the previous two lines with a passage from the *Vajracchedikā Sūtra* [T235.8.749c22–23]: "You should produce a thought that is not fixed anywhere." [應無所住而生其心] He equates "the one mind is no [mind]" with "that is not fixed anywhere," and "every place is liberation" with "should produce a thought." [一心無者應無所住隨處脱者而生其心]

60. This is probably another allusion to the madman Yajñadatta of the *Śūraṃgama Sūtra*. See the *Śūraṃgama Sūtra* quotation in n. 73 for **10.8**.

61. Many of the Zen commentators agree that this refers to the whole of canonical Buddhist literature and Zen literature. Eishu, 352: "*xian* 閑 ['good-for-nothing'] means 'in vain/useless/for nothing.'" [閑イタヅラ也] Chitetsu, 685: "*xian jijing* 閑機境 ['good-for-nothing gimmick vishayas'] means the sutra, treatise, and *vinaya* sections [of the canon] as well as the Zen records." [閑機境謂經論律部及禪録等] Shukitsu, 908: "'Gimmick vishayas' refers to the crooked talks and terms spoken of in the teachings and treatises. Because students do not understand the one mind, they clamber up on top of the gimmick vishayas of the ancients' crooked talks and terms and rush about seeking." [機境指諸教論之曲談名相而道言學者不會一心故上古人曲談名相之機境馳求] Dōkū, 1015: "'Good-for-nothing gimmick vishayas' refers to the wonderful meanings of the Mahāyāna sutras and the ancient [Zen] *kōans*." [閑機境者指大乘經妙義及古則公案等] Kōunshi, 1140: "'Good-for-nothing gimmick vishayas' refers to the talks in the buddha sutras and [Zen] patriarchal records." [閑機境者指佛經祖録等語話] Dōchū, 1292: "*ji* 機 ['gimmicks'] means, when approaching students, [a master employs] tactical speech, *samādhi*, the raising of his eyebrows, winking, and so forth; *jing* 境 ['vishayas'] means raising the mallet, standing the flywhisk upright, and so forth. They are all provisionally established, unreal dharmas, and, therefore, we say 'good-for-nothing.'" [機者接學者時作略語言三昧揚眉瞬目等境者拈槌竪拂等皆是權施設無實法故云閑]

62. The translation is informed by a line in the *Sayings Record of Chan Master Dahui Pujue* (*Dahui Pujue chanshi yulu* 大慧普覺禪師語録; T1998A.47.909a24–25): "Even though you have not yet attained the ability, with one stroke of the sword, instantly to cut off the heads of the *saṃbhogakāya* and *nirmāṇakāya* buddhas, nevertheless, you do have deep confidence." [雖未得一刀兩段直下坐斷報化佛頭然却自有簡信入處] Eishu, 352: "*zuoduan* 坐斷 has the same meaning as 'sever/cut off.'" [坐斷ハ截斷ト同義也] Kassan, 479: "*zuoduan* 坐斷 means 'a fighter who seizes his opponent

and applies a knee hold.' Ultimately has the meaning of 'sever/cut off.'"
[坐斷者有力者把捉人安在膝下之謂也畢竟截斷之義也]   Dōkū, 1015, and
Kōunshi, 1140, also have the erroneous interpretation of the verb as a wrestling
hold. Zengo, 153: "*zuo* 坐 ['sit'], in our opinion, is probably an othographical
mistake for *cuo* 挫 ['snap off; break off']. In the Tang period, examples where
it is written *cuoduan* 挫斷 are seen here and there, but from the Song onward
it is uniformly *zuoduan* 坐斷. The idea is to 'completely deny something.'"
Yanagida, 80: "*zuoduan* 坐斷 is 'to sit down with a thud right on top of something, not moving at all.' *duan* 斷 is an auxiliary word showing the decisive-
ness of the matter." Nakamura, 66, translates as: "The *saṃbhogakāya* buddha
and *nirmāṇakāya* buddha are both beneath notice." Daitoku-ji, 166, translates
as: "cut off the heads of the *saṃbhogakāya* and *nirmāṇakāya* buddhas" and remarks: "Nevertheless, over time the Japanese Rinzai tradition came to interpret
it as 'to sit firmly upon.' This interpretation continues till this day, although
there is no basis for it linguistically or otherwise."

63. Eishu, 353: "Some say it is a person you hire to do work for you; some say it is
a tramp." [或云雇令作事者也或云流浪人] Anonymous, 231: "*kezuo'er* 客作兒
is a beggar. Some say it is a person you hire to do work for you. The *Miscellany Storehouse Sutra* [*Zazang jing* 雜藏經; T745.17.558c13–14] says: 'Śāriputra
during the height of the summer heat was strolling [in Āmra Grove]. There
was a *kezuoren* 客作人 who was drawing water from a well to water the
trees.'"   [客作兒乞食也或云雇令作事者也雜藏經云舍利弗夏熱時遊行[至菴
羅園中]有一客作人汲井水灌樹] Kōunshi, 1141: "*kezuo'er* is a designation for a
very poor, low-status person. It also means someone you hire or a vagrant."
[客作兒者貧窮下賤稱又謂僱作濟世者]

64. Of the fifty-two stages of the bodhisattva, "perfect awakening" is the fifty-first,
and "wonderful awakening" the fifty-second. Eishu, 353: "A cangue with a lock
is an instrument of punishment [that is, a large wooden yoke fastened about the
neck of the prisoner]." [枷鎖八刑具也] Kōunshi, 1141: "'Perfect awakening' is a
stage beyond the ten stages. One enters various *samādhis*, realizes that the one
characteristic is no-characteristic, and attains the Way of quiescence and non-
action. However, there is still a subtle *avidyā* (the eleventh-class *avidyā*), and
therefore one looks from afar at 'wonderful awakening.' . . . 'Wonderful awakening' is the stage in which the effects of great awakening are full. . . . 'Cangue
with a lock' has the meaning of 'lack of freedom'; the cangue is a small instrument for shackling prisoners." [等覺者出十地位入諸三昧了一相無相得寂
滅無爲道然更有一品微細無明(十一品無明)故望妙覺猶有一等故名等覺. . . .
妙覺者大覺果滿之位也. . . . 檐枷鎖者不自在之義也枷小補囚械也]

65. Dōchū, 1293: "'Posts to which you hitch a donkey' keep the donkey all day long
going around and around, bereft of freedom. They are analogous to the verbal gimmick vishayas [i.e., teaching devices] that bog down [students] in the
mud." [繫驢之橛令驢終日順遶逆遶不得自在以比泥滯言句機境]   Kōunshi,

1142: "'Posts to which you hitch a donkey' are wooden posts for hitching donkeys and horses. The donkey on the course is analogous to the Hīnayānist." [繫驢橛者繫驢馬之木橛驢經中比小乘者]

66. Shukitsu, 911: "'These blockages' means 'locked cangues, toilet excrement, and donkey posts.'" [此障礙者謂柳鎖厠穢驢橛]

67. Eishu, 354: "Encountering tea, you drink tea, and, encountering rice, you eat rice. You do not select out good and bad. It is the realm of utilizing both good conditions and bad conditions. The meaning is to turn vishayas [i.e, be active] and not be turned by them [i.e., be passive]." [逢茶喫茶逢飯喫飯也善惡ヲ揀マイ也善緣モ惡緣モ用得タ境界ゾ轉境不轉ラレ境ニ義也] Kassan, 483: "As to 'old karman,' this is just following old karman to act and that is all. It means 'ordinary activities.'" [舊業者此但從舊之業作耳也言平常之作用也] Dōchū, 1293: "The person who has brought a stop [to the movement of mind] does not create new karman. He just complies with whatever accomodating or adverse conditions he encounters to dissolve the karmic effects carried over from past lives. He wades through the day in a bold and unconstrained manner and that is all." [歇得底人不作新業但隨所遇順逆之緣消遣宿業所感之果報而放曠涉日而已] Myōō, 18: "'Old karman' is karman from previous lives." [旧業トハ前世ノ業也] Eishu, 354: "'Give free rein to luck' is the principle of self-so-ness, being contented and unhurried." [任運自然之理自得從容] Kassan, 483: "'Give free rein to luck' has the meaning 'contentedness, non-action, the heavenly real, and freedom.'" [任運者自得無爲天真自在之義也] Dōchū, 1293: "It does not rely on [karmic] performance, and so we call it 'giving free rein to luck.'" [不假造作故曰任運] Kōunshi, 1143: "'Giving free rein to luck' is the appearance of naturalness." [任運者自然貌]

68. Kōunshi, 1143, identifies the source of this quotation as *Mahāyāna Praises* (*Dasheng zan* 大乘讚) by the Liang Dynasty monk Baozhi 寶誌 (*Jingde chuandeng lu* 景德傳燈錄; T2076.51.449b). Eishu, 354: "*zhao* 兆 is 'show signs or symptoms/give indications of.'" [兆キザス也] Kassan, 484: "*zhao* 兆 is 'divination through heating tortoise shells.'" [兆灼龜拆也] Dōchū, 1293: "*zhao* 兆 is 'omen.'" [兆朕兆也]

69. For *pangjia* 傍家, the Zen commentators give such mistaken interpretations as: "heterodox roads" (Eishu, 354: 傍家ハ邪路也); "one who is near to other family gates loses his own family's treasure" (Kassan, 484: 傍他門戸者失却自家珍); "like saying 'other families'" (Kōunshi, 1143: 傍家者猶言他家也), etc. They are unaware that this is a vernacular phrase. Iriya, 43.1: "[傍家 is] an adverb, meaning 'straying off onto a byway' or 'digression.'" [副詞で、わき道にそれるさまをいう。] Zengo, 427: "The '*jia* 家' is an adverbial inflection without meaning. It is going astray on a side street, divorced from the correct route." [「家」は意味のない副詞語尾。横道にそれて、本筋からはなれて。]

70. Eishu, 354: "*yidu* 意度 is mental reflection and conjecture." [意度者思量卜度也] Chitetsu, 691, associates *yidu* 意度 with the sixth consciousness, the

mano-vijñāna. The *mano-vijñāna* makes discriminations or judgments after the sense perceptions of the five sense consciousnesses.

71. Eishu, 354: "Students lose their own father and mother and in delusion seek out a father and mother elsewhere." [学者失自己父母向他求父母迷] Myōō, 19: "'Father and mother' is the original source." [父母卜ハ本源也] Anonymous, 232: "'The single father and mother' is the Buddha." [一箇父母者佛也] Dōkū, 1017: "'The single father and mother' is the father and mother in the intimate home, the so-called 'mother of all the buddhas.'" [一箇父母者一箇親切底屋裡之父母所謂諸佛之母也]

72. Kōunshi, 1144, and Dōchū, 1294, cite one of Zongmi's sutra commentaries: "In his *Abbreviated Commentary on the Perfect Awakening Sutra* . . . Zongmi says: 'The Chan house's re-training the light is to take the other initial awakening to become aware of 'my' original awakening, and so it is called 're-training.'" [圓覺畧鈔 . . . 宗密云禪家返照者即是以他始覺照我本覺故云返也] 圓覺經略疏鈔: CBETA, X09, no. 248, p. 882, c1–2 //Z 1:15, p. 151, a13–14 //R15, p. 301, a13–14. Chitetsu, 691: "'Re-training the light' means 'seeing-the-nature.'" [返照者謂見性]

73. Dōkū, 1017: "This passage abbreviates the words of the *Śūraṃgama Sūtra*. The ancient who is mentioned refers to the Buddha." [此處略首楞嚴語舉古人者指佛云也] Kōunshi, 1144, is similar. The passage [T945.19.121b4–27] runs as follows: "Pūrṇa says: "I and the *tathāgata* [possess] the perfect enlightenment of awakening, the true and wonderful mind of purity, the non-dual perfection, but in the past I met beginningless false thought and have long revolved on the wheel of samsara. Now I have obtained the noble [Mahāyāna] vehicle, but still have not achieved the ultimate. The World-honored-one has extinguished all false [thought] and is a solitary, true eternality. Dare I ask the *tathāgata*: Why do all sentient beings have false [thought], covering over their wonderful brightness and [leading them to] undergo sinking [in samsara]?' The Buddha told Pūrṇa: 'Even though you have eliminated doubt, residual confusions have not yet been exhausted. I will now question you about events as they appear in the world. How could you not have heard of them? In the city of Śrāvastī Yajñadatta one morning abruptly looked at his face in a mirror. He [was used to] adoring the look of his eyebrows and eyes visible in the mirror, but [this morning] became infuriated that his own head didn't manifest a face. He held that it was because of demons that there was no image and crazily ran about [looking for his head]. . . . It is like the Yajñadatta in that city. Without cause he feared that his head had run off. If suddenly his craziness stopped, his head would not be obtainable from without, and, even if he didn't stop his craziness, his head would not be lost. Pūrṇa! Since this is the nature of the false, where is its cause? If you will just cease discriminating the threefold continuum of world, karmic fruits, and sentient beings, the three conditions will be severed, and so, the three causes will no longer arise. The craziness of the Yajñadatta in your mind will stop, and that stopping is

bodhi. Your mind of purity and brightness pervades the *dharmadhātu* and is not obtainable from someone else. Why would you toil over cultivation and realization [of that mind] as if it were the crux of the matter?'" [富樓那言我與如來寶覺圓明真妙淨心無二圓滿而我昔遭無始妄想久在輪迴今得聖乘猶未究竟世尊諸妄一切圓滅獨妙真常敢問如來一切衆生何因有妄自蔽妙明受此淪溺佛告富樓那汝雖除疑餘惑未盡吾以世間現前諸事今復問汝汝豈不聞室羅城中演若達多忽於晨朝以鏡照面愛鏡中頭眉目可見瞋責己頭不見面目以爲魑魅無狀狂走.... 如彼城中演若達多豈有因緣自怖頭走忽然狂歇頭非外得縱未 歇 狂 亦 何 遺 失 富 樓 那 妄 性 如 是 因 何 爲 在 汝 但 不 隨 分 別 世 間 業 果 衆生三種相續三緣斷故三因不生則汝心中演若達多狂性自歇歇即菩提勝淨明心本周法界不從人得何藉劬勞肯綮修證]

74. Dōkū, 1017: "'Be your usual self' is discarding the creation of karman—the rush to seek out something." [平常者免作業馳求也] Kōunshi, 1114: "'Be your usual self' is like saying *nothing-to-do*." [平常者猶言無事也] Myōō, 19: "daily activities, just the usual." [日用只常ノ如ク] Chitetsu, 691: "'Be your usual self' is *tathatā*." [平常是真如]

75. The line is *mo zuo moyang* 莫作模樣. Eishu, 355: "*moyang* 模樣 sometimes has the meaning 'preferences,' sometimes 'mental reflection,' and sometimes 'calculation and conjecture.'" [模樣ハ或趣向或思量之義也或計較卜度也] Kōunshi, 1144: "*moyang* 模樣 refers to the 'seeing spirits and ogres' mentioned below." [模樣者指下見神見鬼等]

76. Eishu, 355, and Anonymous, 232: "'Bald-headed hacks' are the bad teachers of the present time." [禿奴今時惡知識] Kassan, 485: "'Bald-headed hack' was a term of abuse in the speech of the Tang Dynasty epoch, meaning 'bad teacher.'" [禿奴者唐世話罵人語也此云惡知識] Kōunshi, 1144, is very similar. Dōkū, 1017: "'Bald-headed hacks' refers to bad teachers. Their external appearance is not that of a layman, but their mind range is not that of a monk. They are called 'bald-headed hacks.'" [禿奴者指惡知識也外相非俗心行非僧謂之禿奴]

77. Shukitsu, 912: "At the time of awakening he cherishes his awakening." [悟時存悟者也]

78. The Zen commentators focus on the sensationalism involved. Eishu, 355, and Anonymous, 233: "refers to shamans and so forth who seek the strange and unusual." [奇特ヲ求ルミコ子ギ等ヲ云ナリ] Kassan, 485: "the type who engages in crazy and false talk about the strange and unusual." [誑妄言奇特邊類也]

79. The Chan transmission record *Outline of the Linked Lamps* (*Liandeng huiyao* 聯燈會要) has this idiom: "Don't just on this side and that side pick up a few words and phrases and insert them everywhere, pointing towards the east and gesticulating towards the west, raising ancient [examples] and raising current [examples]." [莫只這邊那邊迍得些言句到處插語指東劃西舉古舉今] CBETA, X79, no. 1557, p. 201, b8–9 //Z 2B:9, p. 408, c1–2 //R136, p. 816, a1–2. Kōunshi, 1144: "*zhi dong hua xi* 指東劃西 merely refers to the idea of pointing to the east and pointing to the west." [指東劃西者唯指東指西之意] Zen bunka

kenkyūjo henshūbu, ed., *Daie Fukaku zenji sho kōrōju*, 402, glosses *zhi dong hua xi* 指東劃西 (citing the appearance of the phrase in section 13.15) as: "without rhyme or reason to use the hands to concoct special effects." [忠曰胡亂以手作模樣也]

80. Eishu, 355: "saying various things such as 'the weather is good,' 'the weather is bad.'" [天気ガヨクテ惡クテナドト種種ノ叓ヲ云] Anonymous, 233: "one who crazily runs around and is unsettled or restless." [狂走而不安着底] Kōunshi, 1144: "He doesn't comprehend that every day is a good day. Sometimes he likes clear weather and hates rainy weather, sometimes he likes rainy weather and hates clear weather." [不達日日好日或時好晴惡雨或時好雨惡晴]

81. Eishu, 355: "the bald-headed hack type." [禿奴類也] Kassan, 485: "In the end, it means 'bad teachers.'" [畢竟言惡知識也]

82. Kassan, 485: "[*nannü* 男女] is the phrase 'good sons and good daughters' found in the sutras." [經所謂善男子善女人也] Dōchū, 1295: "They are called 'good' because they are persons who from the outset have been their usual selves with *nothing-to-do*." [好者本是平常無事底人故云好也] Iriya, 43.8: "*nannü* 男女 is a Tang colloquialism for 'children.' Here it refers to practitioners." [「男女」は唐代の俗語で子どものこと。ここでは修行者たちを指していう。]

83. The *Śūraṃgama Sūtra* (T945.19.151b1–5) portrays "evil Māra masters" (*e moshi* 惡魔師) as "demons" (*jingmei* 精魅): "Ānanda! You should know of these ten types of Māra at the time of the end of dharma. Within my dharma they leave home and cultivate the Way. Sometimes they attach themselves to a human form; sometimes they manifest their own shape. They all say that they have completed perfect awakening, but they praise lascivious desires and destroy the disciplinary rules of the Buddha. The evil Māra masters and Māra disciples are in a lasciviousness transmission. This sort of heterodox demon [*xie jingmei* 邪精魅] enters the chest and abdomen. . . . They make true practitioners all become Māra's hosts." [阿難當知是十種魔於末世時在我法中出家修道或附人體或自現形皆言已成正遍知覺讚歎婬欲破佛律儀先惡魔師與魔弟子婬婬相傳如是邪精魅其心腑. . . . 令真修行總爲魔眷] Eishu, 355: "A wild-fox demon is a goblin or apparition. This refers to the previously mentioned bald-headed hacks and means 'heterodox masters.'" [野狐精魅バケ物ゾ指前禿奴也邪師ヲ云也] Kassan, 485: "This refers to bad teachers." [此指惡知識云也] Dōchū, 1295: "This rebukes bad teachers who discombobulate persons by manifesting strange appearances as 'wild-fox demons.' They are like the [sly] fox demons that discombobulate persons." [罵惑人現異相惡知識為野狐精魅猶如狐魅惑人也] Dōkū, 1017: "refers to heterodox masters and bad teachers." [指邪師惡知識云也] Kōunshi, 1145, quotes the *Śūraṃgama Sūtra* (T945.19.145a9–10) and one of its commentaries (T1799.39.939a9–11): "The *Śūraṃgama* . . . says: 'For those people whose sin is being greedy for duping others, when their sin is finished [being expiated], upon encountering animals they take on forms called demon ogres.' The *Commentary*

on the Meanings [of the Śūraṃgama . . . says: 'The practice of duping others is
the karmic cause of their plight. Because of practicing trickery, they dupe the
upright into relying on falsehoods. Reborn as an animal, they become of an
ogre-like nature, that is, they have the various auras of a fox, wolf, pig, and
dog. They are not of just one type, and so the sutra speaks of encountering
animals and taking on their forms.] The demons manifest beautiful forms in
order to discombobulate people.'" [楞嚴 . . . 曰貪惑爲罪是人罪畢遇畜成形名爲
魅鬼義疏 . . . (曰詐習爲因也因成詐僞惑正憑虛託附畜生便成鬼質即狐狸猪犬
有異靈者其類非一故云遇畜成形)魅即現美形以惑人也]

84. Luo Zhufeng and others, eds., *Hanyu da cidian [Great Word Dictionary of Sinitic]*
(Shanghai: Hanyu da cidian chubanshe, 1995), 6.609b, glosses the term *nieguai*
捏怪 as: "making up stories or tales; portraying bizarre imagery." [編造鬼怪故事;
塑造怪相] Kassan, 485: "*nieguai* 捏怪 means, when they see bad teachers, they
vainly value their heterodox dharmas, giving them shape and considering them
as strange and unusual." [捏怪者蓋言見惡知識虛貴邪法捏聚之怪異之也]
Dōchū, 1295: "Boys and girls of good family are discombobulated and love
to fabricate strangeness." [好人家男女亦被惑好捏怪也] Also, Zen bunka
kenkyūjo henshūbu, ed., Daie Fukaku zenji sho *kōrōju*, 189: "*nieguai* 捏怪
means 'to adore the odd and toy with strangeness.' . . . Whoever adores the
odd and considers inconceivable things to be special is called *nieguai*."
[忠曰今捏怪者好奇弄怪之義. . . . 凡好奇特不思議事曰捏怪也]

85. Eishu, 356: "'Blind imbeciles' is the language of abuse. It means that the
good children are deceived by heterodox masters and made into blind Hans."
[瞎屢生罵人語也言善男女被邪師誑作瞎漢] Kassan, 485: "This refers to the
heterodox disciples [of bad teachers]." [此指邪弟子云也] Dōchū, 1295: "This rebukes both the bad teachers and the fabricators of bizarre features who fall prey
to the bad teachers." [都罵惡知識及隨惡知識捏怪者]

86. Eishu, 356: "Beholding reality as it truly is is the essential thing." [真正見解卜
ハ肝要也] Chitetsu, 694: "The perfectly bright beholding of reality as it truly is
awakening on one's own." [圓明真正見解即是自覺]

87. Eishu, 356: "'Marching out across the world' involves freely and autonomously
spreading out your elbows [as you march out]." [向天下橫行卜ハ自由自在ニ臂
ヲハル也] Kassan, 486: "The 'Fan Guai Biography' of the *Han History* says: 'Having
obtained 100,000 troops, he marched out into the land of the Xiongnu bar-
barians.'" [漢史樊噲傳云願得十万兵橫行匈奴中] Anonymous, 234: "with urgency." [切急也]

88. Eishu, 356: "Don't fall into the clutches of bad teachers." [惡知識ニ接せ(セ)ラル
ルナ也] Kōunshi, 1146: "'Demons' refers to the heterodox masters in the above
section." [精魅者指上段邪師]

89. Dōkū, 1018: "In the midst of confusion and hurry, at all times and in all places, he
is like a wooden person looking at the flowers and birds—this is truly the person
with *nothing-to-do*." [擾擾忽忽之中一切時一切處如木人見花鳥此真無事人也]

90. *zaozuo* 造作 ("performance; accomplishment") is a translation equivalent of *abhisaṃskāra*. The *Great Perfection of Wisdom Treatise* (*Da zhidu lun* 大智度論; T1509.25.609b26–28) says: "Subhūti reports to Śāriputra: 'Sentient beings, due to the conditioning of perverted views, perform [*zaozuo* 造作] body, speech, and mind karman. As recompense for the fundamental karman, they receive a body in one of the six paths of rebirth: hell-being, *preta*, animal, human being, *deva*, and *asura*.'" [須菩提報告舍利弗衆生顛倒因緣故造作身口意業隨欲本業報受六道身地獄餓鬼畜生人天阿修羅身] Chitetsu, 695: "Good and bad lie in intention, and by that one performs good and bad karman." [善惡在思以造作善惡業] Kōunshi, 1146: "'Performance' is calculating, running around seeking, and so forth." [造作者計校馳求等也] Myōō, 20, glosses *pingchang* 平常 ("be your usual self") as: "just daily activities." [只日用]

91. Dōkū, 1018: "A certain commentary takes the *guo* 過 of *qiuguo* 求過 as the *guo* 過 in 'mistake.' . . . In my opinion, this is not correct. The *guo* 過 character should be taken as the *guo* 過 meaning 'run to distant parts.'" [或鈔求過之過作過咎之過. . . . 恐非正義過字作走迴之過可也] Kōunshi, 1146: "*qiuguo* 求過 is 'running around seeking.'" [求過者求覓走過也]

92. Jiang Lansheng and Cao Anshun, eds., *Tang Wudai yuyan cidian* [*Word Dictionary of Tang and Five Dynasties Language*] (Shanghai: Shanghai jiaoyu chubanshe, 1997), 188a, glosses *jiaoshou* 脚手 as: "'feet and hands'; refers to 'action' or 'acts.'" [手和脚; 指行动, 行为] Dōchū, 1295: "What is *jiaoshou* 脚手 ['feet and hands']? It is searching by the road of rational principle, searching for terms and phrases—it most certainly is not *that true person*." [脚手何也求理路求名句是也全非那真人也].

93. Kassan, 486: "'Rushing about seeking' is like saying 'practicing.'" [馳求猶言修行也] Dōchū, 1295: "The above . . . criticized rushing about seeking on the outside but, because [Linji] fears that the student has stubbornly taken a rest from seeking dharma and come to consider this [rest] as *nothing-to-do*, he now shows the dharma of true seeking. And what is true seeking? Seeking the person who rushes about seeking is true seeking." [上 . . . 斥向外馳求却恐學人一向休求法以此為無事故今示真求之法真求者何也所謂求馳求底人是真求也] Dōkū, 1018: "You—the one rushing about seeking—when all is said and done, what are you?" [你馳求底畢竟是什麼物] Kōunshi, 1146: "What is the one rushing about seeking? [It is] *this*, the whole 'I,' the self. . . . A certain commentary says that 'rushing about seeking' is like saying 'practicing.' In my opinion, this interpretation is no more than a detour." [馳求底是何物這箇全我自己. . . . 或鈔馳求猶言修行也義恐迂回而已]

94. Kassan, 486: "Quiescent illumination is right before your very eyes. This is the true-mind dharma. The common people in their daily activities know nothing of it." [寂照現前此真心法也百姓日用不相知] Dōkū, 1018: "An ancient said, '[All doing and all acting are the] unreserved functioning [of the buddha nature].'" [古人云全體作用也]

95. Eishu, 357: "*yi* 意 is 'mental reflection,' and *du* 度 is 'discrimination.'" [意ハ思量度ハ分別] Kassan, 486: "*yidu* 意度 is 'dithering' and 'mental reflection.'" [意度者擬議思量也] (For *niyi* 擬議, see n. 18 for I.3.) Dōkū, 1018: "*yidu* 意度 is 'mental reflection' and 'calculation.'" [意度者思量計度也]

96. Dōchū, 1296: "The student and the buddhadharma will be very far apart!" [學者與佛法太遠矣]

97. Kōunshi, 1147: "Scholars of the teachings refer to original awakening, the substance nature, as the 'mind ground.'" [教家指本覺體性云心地]

98. Kōunshi, 1147: "'Worldlings and *āryas*' are the two vishayas of 'wisdom and stupidity,' 'tainted and pure,' etc." [凡聖者智愚染淨等二境也]

99. Kassan, 487: "'Enter into the pure' is 'pure lands.' . . . 'Enter into the defiled' is 'defiled lands.'" [入淨淨土也. . . . 入穢穢土也] Kōunshi, 1147: "'The pure and the defiled' are the two vishayas of '*bodhi* and the *kleśas*,' 'the buddhas and Māras,' etc." [淨穢者菩提煩惱佛魔等二境也]

100. Kassan, 487: "'The real and the conventional' are *paramārtha-satya* and *saṃvṛti-satya*." [真俗者真諦俗諦也] Dōkū, 1018: "'The real and the conventional' are the *paramārtha-satya* and *saṃvṛti-satya* spoken of in the teachings." [真俗者教所謂真諦俗諦也] Kōunshi, 1147: "'The real and the conventional' are the two vishayas of 'the *original portion* and the "ready-made,"' 'the world and beyond-the-world,' etc." [真俗者本分現成世出世等二境也]

101. The Zen commentaries identify this "you" (*ni* 你) as the Way-person of no-dependence, but this is not a plausible interpretation. Iriya, 49.2: "[This line refers to] the standard of value or ranking system that you yourself suppose." [お前が自ら措定する価値規範・ランク付け。]

102. Iriya, 49.4: "[This line means] 'to affix names or assign rank.' In a broad sense, 'to prioritize individual things as individual things.'" [名前を付ける。格付けする。広義には、個物をそれぞれ個物として位置付けること。]

103. Eishu, 357: "*This person* is the person of knowing." [此人トハ知有底ノ人也] Kassan, 488, and Dōkū, 1019: "*This person* refers to the non-dependent Way-person." [此人者指無依道人也] Kōunshi. 1148: "not capable of sticking a name on *that one person*." [與此那一人安名不得]

104. Eishu, 357, and Anonymous, 235: "As soon as they open their mouths, I already know them." [開口我早可知之也] Kōunshi, 1148: "clarifies that Master [Linji] can in a single glance instantly see them." [明師能一見便見也]

105. Dōchū, 1297: "*wenzuo* 穩坐 ['smooth-and-steady sitting'] has no deep meaning—it is just what is called 'the peaceful [cross-legged] sitting time of *nothing-to-do*.'" [穩坐無深意但是謂無事安坐時也] Dōkū, 1019: "'Smooth-and-steady sitting' is the state of the *original portion*." [穩坐本分田地] Kōunshi. 1148: "'Smooth-and-steady sitting' is the times when the Master has not gone up to the Dharma Hall for a dharma talk and is just being his usual self with *nothing-to-do*. An old commentary says that 'smooth-and-steady sitting' is the *original portion*—this is

a mistaken interpretation." [穩坐者師不上堂說法只平常無事之時也古鈔爲穩坐本分者取義過矣]

106. Dōchū, 1297: "Above it has said that Mañjusrī and Samantabhadra come for an audience. Now for a second time it says that stream-enterers come for an audience and, therefore, 'once again.'" [上言文殊普賢相見今復再言道流相見故云更也]

107. Kōunshi, 1148: "different from the people of all-under-heaven." [與天下人別]

108. Eishu, 357: "not detained even in the *original portion*." [本分ニモ不滯在也] Myōō, 21: "'Internally, not permanently fixed in nirvana' means 'in the mind not putting even a single tiny bit on the principle of the fundamental or ultimate.'" [内不住根本トハ胸中ニ根本至極ノ道理ヲ一点モ不置也] "Internally unfixed to the fundamental" (*nei bu zhu genben* 内不住根本) is "not permanently fixed in nirvana" (*bu zhu niepan* 不住涅槃 = *apratiṣṭhita-nirvāṇa*), a central theme of the Mahāyāna.

109. Eishu, 357: "'Vision is penetrating' is 'awakening is penetrating.'" [見徹悟徹也]

110. Eishu, 357: "mistake, cheating or feigning." [誤也詐也欺也] Dōkū, 1019: "This is Master [Linji's] speaking of himself—if it were not Linji it would be impossible to speak in this manner." [師之自道也若非臨濟不得恁麼道]

111. Eishu, 358: "'Putting in work' means 'rare/special/unusual/exceptional.'" [用功 奇特ヲ云ゾ] Kassan, 488: "The *Four-Teachings Meaning* says: 'Before the seventh stage [of the bodhisattva] it is called the path of putting in work. From the eighth stage onward it is called the path of putting in no work.'" [四教義云七地以前名有功用道八地以上名無功用道] (*Si jiaoyi jijie* 四教儀集解: 七地已前等者如華嚴云菩薩未至第八地時如人乘船欲渡大海未至大海多用功力若至八地從大方便近佛智慧無功用心不加功力; CBETA, X57, no. 976, p. 589, b17–19 //Z 2:7, p. 52, d8–10 //R102, p. 104, b8–10). Dōchū, 1297: "*gong* 功 is 'exploits, practice, karmic performance.'" [功者功勲也修行造作也] Myōō, 22: "There is no karmic performance at all." [何ノ造作モ無也] Anonymous, 235: "Grabbing on to objective supports and [engaging in] karmic performance is called 'putting in work.'" [攀縁造作是名功用] Shukitsu, 916: "'Not a matter of putting in work' means not seizing 'worldling' and '*ārya*,' and being unfixed to the fundamental [i.e., nirvana]." [無用功處者謂不取凡聖不住根本] Kōunshi, 1149: "'Not a matter of putting in work' means 'not a matter of karmic performance.' Scholars of the teachings call [the stages] up to and including the seventh 'the path of putting in work' because [the bodhisattva] applies effort in practice. From the eighth stage onward it is called 'the path of no putting in work.'" [無用功處者無造作處也教家七地已前名有用功道是用修行功力故八地已上名無用功道]

112. Kōunshi, 1149: "'An ancient' refers to Preceptor [Nanyue] Lanzan and his *Song of Lanzan*.... 'Practice' [*gongfu*] is *dhyāna*. Our [Zen] gate speaks of *dhyāna* as 'practice.'" [古人者指(南嶽)懶瓚和尚懶瓚歌.... 工夫者思惟也吾門謂禪定為工夫]

113. Kassan, 489: "You will enjoy the use of each and every thing." [於頭頭物上受用也]

114. Eishu, 358, and Anonymous, 236: "'*Place* you stand' is *pratītya-samutpāda*. The *place* of dependently originated dharmas is called 'the *place* you stand.' Each and every thing [in this *place*] is utter *tattva*." [立処者縁起也法縁起処ヲ立処ト云ナリ頭頭物物全真] Kassan, 489, is similar.

115. Eishu, 358, and Anonymous, 236: "Each time you encounter the myriad things, you will remain unbound by them." [每逢萬物不被縛彼也] Dōchū, 1297: "When you are safeguarding the *original portion*, vishayas come to force you to relax your safeguarding, and this is 'being turned.'" [守本分時境來令改其守是回換也] Shukitsu, 916: "Question: 'What vishayas are these?' Answer: 'Shrieking monkeys all night long circle around the frosted branches. The one who possesses the eye tries to do away with [monkeys/vishayas].'" [問境是什麼境答鳴猿終夜遶霜枝具眼底斷看]

116. Eishu, 358: "'*Vāsanā* from previous lives' is the *vāsanā* of *avidyā* and the *kleśas*." [從來習氣ハ無明煩惱ノ習氣也] Kassan, 489: "*Vāsanā* means 'subtle *kleśas*.'" [習氣者言微細煩惱也]

117. Eishu, 358: "The five karmans that bring on immediate retribution are the five crimes [i.e., killing the mother; killing the father; killing an arhat; shedding the blood of a buddha; and destroying the unity of the sangha]." [又五無間業ハ五逆罪也]

118. Zongmi's *Chan Prolegomenon* uses this phrase "not know dharma" (*bu shi fa* 不識法) to describe lecturers who lack a personal experience of dharma: "Today, most Chan adepts, unaware of doctrinal principles, merely shout 'mind is Chan,' and most exegetes, not [having a personal experience of] coming to know dharma, merely use terms to discourse on doctrinal principles." [講者多不識法故但約名說義; T2015.48.401c7]

119. Eishu, 359: "'Goats that butt their noses' is a phrase from the *Changes*. . . . A billy goat butts up against a hedge, [its horns get caught,] and it can neither retreat nor proceed." [觸鼻羊トハ易ヨリ出ル語也. . . . 羝羊觸藩不能退不能遂] Kassan, 489: "It means that the eyes of goats do not distinguish things [clearly]. In general, whatever they butt their noses up against, they mistakenly eat. They are like students who don't know good masters from bad, heterodox dharmas from true." [言羊者目不辨物故摠有觸鼻者即誤食之譬如學者不識師善惡法邪正] Dōchū, 1298: "An ancient worthy said, 'The eyesight of a goat is weak, and it is incapable of distinguishing things. It just eats everything that it butts its nose against.' . . . This interpretation is groundless." [古德云羊眼力鈍不能辨物但一切物觸鼻則食之. . . . 此說未得據]

120. Kassan, 489: "'Wrong-mindedly' means bad knowledge and bad beholding." [邪心者言惡知惡見也] Dōchū, 1298: "'Entering the Way wrong-mindedly' is to leave home for the sake of food and clothing. This is wrong livelihood, and so we say 'wrong-mindedly.'" [謂邪心入道者為衣食出家是邪命故云邪心] Kōunshi, 1150: "'Entering the Way wrong-mindedly' refers to the type who in the very beginning raises the aspiration for awakening for the sake of food and clothes

or leaves home for the sake of fame and profit." [邪心入道者最初發心本爲
衣食而發或爲名利而出家類也]

121. Eishu, 359: "'Noisy and bustling places' has the meaning 'noisy markets.'"
[鬧処者鬧市之義也] Kassan, 490: "'Noisy and bustling' is not city markets, and 'quiet' is not the mountains. In the end it is your own mind and
that is all." [鬧非城市靜非山畢竟自心耳] Dōchū, 1298: "As to 'enter-
ing into noisy and bustling places,' having already [left home] for the
sake of food and clothing, they do not select out the good and bad in masters, but, upon just seeing a bustling place [i.e., a thriving monastery], enter
and hang [their robe, bowl, and] tin staff [on the wall of the Sangha Hall]."
[鬧處即入者已爲衣食故不擇師家好惡只見鬧熟處即入掛錫矣] Chitetsu, 710:
"'Noisy and bustling places' means 'the pondering-of-objective-supports of
the human mind.'" [鬧處者謂人心緑慮] Dōkū, 1020: "The crowd that 'enters the Way wrong-mindedly' takes places of leisure as peaceful and joyful
places of entering the Way, and, therefore, they love quiet and loathe noise.
They frequently do lengthy [cross-legged] sitting beneath trees or on top of
stones. This is completely the occupation of those in the demon cave [i.e.,
the heretical Zen of silence-and-illlumination]." [言邪心入道底輩流者以閑處
爲入道安樂處是故愛靜厭喧往往長坐樹下石上總是鬼窟裡活計也] Kōunshi,
1150: "'Entering into noisy and bustling places' means they do not select
out the good and bad in masters. If the monastery is bustling with crowds,
if there is food and clothing and they can do as they wish, then they enter."
[鬧處即入者不擇師家好惡其門庭繁鬧有衣食穩便則即入]

122. Dōkū, 1021: "The *Glossary of the Patriarchal Courtyard* quotes the *Mindfulness
Pillars of the True Dharma Sutra*: 'It is like water and milk put into one vessel.
When the king of geese drinks it, he drinks just the milk, and the water still
remains.'" [祖庭事苑云正法念處經云譬如水乳同置一器鵝王飲之但飲其乳汁
其水猶存] CBETA, X64, no. 1261, p. 383, a10–11 //Z 2:18, p. 70, d1–2 //R113,
p. 140, b1–2.

123. Eishu, 360: "'Strike out both Māra and buddha' means 'sever both "Māra" and
"buddha." . . . 'Striking out both' means 'fusing into oneness.'" [魔佛俱打ト ハ
截斷魔佛也. . . . 謂俱打者打成一片之義也] Chitetsu, 717: "'Clear eye' means
'[beholding] reality as it truly is.' 'Māra' means 'peoples' minds.' 'Buddha'
means 'seeing one's own mind.' 'Striking out both' means '[applying an] an-
tidote/counteracting.' With counteracting, in the end, there is neither 'Māra'
nor 'buddha'—it is just the clear-eyed Way-person who [beholds] reality as it
truly is." [明眼真正魔人人心佛見自心俱打對治對治究竟無魔無佛唯是真正
明眼道人]

124. Eishu, 360: "A certain edition is missing the 'buddha' character and has only
the 'Māra' character." [或本ハ削佛字魔ノ字バカリアル也]

125. Eishu, 360, and Anonymous, 238: "[Attaining] is attaining awakening."
[得悟者ゾ]

126. Kassan, 491: "'To attain is to attain it immediately' is all-at-once leaping over and directly entering the *tathāgata* stage. How dare one wade through the three kalpas or one-hundred kalpas, step-by-step passing through the fifty-two stages!" [得者便得一超直入如來地何敢涉三祇百劫漸次歷五十二位階級乎]

127. Eishu, 360: "[The practitioner] does not pass through the fifty-two stages. When he first sends up the aspiration [for awakening], he immediately becomes perfectly awakened. . . . He does not go through immeasurable kalpas." [不歷五十二位初發心時便成正覺. . . . 阿僧祇劫ヲモ不歷也] Anonymous, 238, has the first part. Dōchū, 1299: "Because there is neither ancient times nor the present, on the ground one stands upon, one becomes a buddha—it is not a matter of passing through three immeasurable kalpas, etc." [無古無今故立地成佛非歷三祇劫等]

128. Eishu, 360: "'No distinct dharmas beyond this' is hells, heavenly palaces, mustard plants, humans, animals, mountains, rivers, the great earth—in the end it is the realm wherein everything is fused into oneness. . . . Everything is exhausted in a single iron ball." [更無別法者地獄天堂草芥人畜山河大地畢竟而打成一片境界也. . . . 都盡一團鉄] Anonymous, 238, has the first part.

129. Kassan, 491–492, Shujitsu, 918, and Dōkū, 1021, all cite the second of the three *zong* 宗 of Chan in Zongmi's *Chan Prolegomenon*. In fact, the wording here, from "According to my vision" onward (約山僧見處無佛無眾生無古無今得者便得不歷時節無修無證無得無失一切時中更無別法設有一法過此者我說如夢如化), is strikingly similar to Zongmi's formulation of the "idea" of *śūnyatā* Chan, the second Chan *zong* 宗, in the *Chan Prolegomenon* (T2015.48.402c3–7): "The second is the *zong* 宗 of cutting off and not leaning on anything. . . . There is neither 'buddha' nor 'sentient being.' Even '*dharmadhātu*' is a provisional name. Since mind is not [really] existent, who [could possibly exist to] say '*dharmadhātu*'? There is neither 'practice' nor 'non-practice,' neither 'buddha' nor 'non-buddha.' Suppose there were a single thing that surpassed nirvana, I say it would be like an [illusory] dream or a *māyā*." [二泯絕無寄宗者說凡聖等法皆如夢幻都無所有本來空寂非今始無即此達無之智亦不可得平等法界無佛無眾生法界亦是假名心既不有誰言法界無修不修無佛不佛設有一法勝過涅槃我說亦如夢幻]

130. This line (*shanseng suoshuo jie shi* 山僧所說皆是) appears to be an incomplete fragment—the remainder of the line is missing. In section 12.5 just below virtually the same sequence of characters appears as part of a complete sentence: 山僧說處皆是一期藥病相治 ("Everything I have said is a one-off medicine to cure a particular case of illness."). Eishu, 360, and Dōchū, 1300, have tried to squeeze meaning out of the fragment by glossing the *shi* 是 as *rushi* 如是 ("like this"), thus making the line: "Everything I have said is like this." Modern translators seem to be following in their footsteps. For instance, Iriya, 56, translates: "Everything I have said is exhausted in the above"; Yanagida, 100: "My thinking does not go beyond the above"; Nakamura, 82: "What I have said is like this";

Daitoku-ji, 191: "This is all I have to teach"; Watson, 33: "All I have to say to you is simply this"; and Demiéville, 74: "Voilà tout ce que j'ai à dire, moi le moine de montagne." One Zen commentator, Shukitsu, 919, does sense that something has been dropped out: "[We must] be willing to bear with the very strange break here." [下得甚奇絕] The translation has taken a cue from Shukitsu.

131. Kassan, 492, and Dōkū, 1022: "The *Śūraṃgama Sūtra* [T945.19.131b5–7] says: 'Great sangha and Ānanda! Rotate your perverted sense organ of hearing, and you will return [to the source] and hear [dharma] with the self-nature of hearing. That nature will bring to completion the un-excelled Way. Perfect comprehension is truly like this.'" [首楞嚴 . . . 云大衆及阿難旋汝倒聞機反聞聞自性性成無上道圓通實如是] In other words, now you are hearing by means of sounds, but, if you can rotate the flow of sounds and return to the source to hear dharma without falsity, then you have returned to the self-nature of hearing. Original awakening will be completed. Anonymous, 238: "[refers to] *that one person.*" [那一人] Chitetsu, 721: "The *ārya* knowledge of awakening on one's own is called 'solitary brightness.'" [自覺聖智曰孤明] Shukitsu, 919: "'The one who is listening [to dharma], a solitary brightness,' is the dharma substance of the mind ground." [孤明歷歷地聽者便是心地法體]

132. Kōunshi, 1152: "*This person* is the person listening to the dharma. Because *this person* is without form and characteristics, he gets hung up nowhere." [此人者聽法底人也此人無形無相故處處不滯]

133. Eishu, 361: "*chabie* 差別 is the myriad dharmas." [差別八万法也]

134. Eishu, 361: "One moment [*eka-kṣaṇa*] is the duration of one thought." [一刹那間一念心間也]

135. Dōkū, 1022, and Eishu, 361: "The *Dengyin Bodhisattva Sutra* says: 'If among the *devas*, manifest a *deva* body in order to speak dharma; if in the dragon palace, create a dragon body in order to speak dharma; if among *yakṣas*, manifest a *yakṣa* body in order to speak dharma; if among *pretas*, create a *preta* body to speak dharma; if among humans, create a human body to speak dharma; you should take on the magical-transformation body of a buddha to create a buddha body [and speak dharma]. . . .'" [等因菩薩經云若爲諸天現天身而爲說法若在龍宮作龍身而爲說法於夜叉中現夜叉身而-爲說法於餓鬼中作餓鬼身而爲說法若於人道作人身而爲說法應以佛身而受化者作佛身而爲說法云云] The sutra is entitled *Saṃghāṭa Sūtra* (僧伽吒經; T423.13.966b13–17.) Kassan, 492, and Dōkū, 1022: "This is identical to the thirty-two *nirmāṇakayas* of Avalokiteśvara." [此與觀音三十二應身一準也] Dōchū, 1300: "If you meet Tang and Yu [i.e., the paragon emperors Yao and Shun], then ritual and music; if you meet the [the evil Xia dynasty king] Jie and [the evil Shang dynasty king] Zhou, then shield and dagger-axe." [遇唐虞則禮樂遇桀紂則干戈]

136. Kōunshi, 1153: "This means that in a moment he playfully strolls through the lands of the ten realms, everywhere teaching and transforming sentient

beings. Sudhana [in the *Huayan Sutra*] never leaves the single location but passes through one-hundred and ten cites and their listed masters. Stroking his sword, he passes many lifetimes without ever leaving the single moment." [謂一念間游戲十界國土遍教化衆生不見善財不離一處過一百一十城列土按劍經多生未曾離一念也] Li Tongxuan's 李通玄 *Treatise on the New Huayan Sutra* (*Xin huayan jing lun* 新華嚴經論; T1739.36.731c4–6) says: "The youth Sudhana, without leaving the single moment, goes through one lifetime. Without leaving the single location, he arrives everywhere throughout the ten directions. He proceeds through fifty-three good teachers and obtains the dharma teachings of one hundred and ten cities." [善財童子不離一念而經一生不離一處遍至十方經歷五十三善知識得一百一十城之法門]

137. Eishu, 361: "['Light'] is the person of solitary brightness." [(光ト㆑)孤明歷歷地一㆑物也] Kōunshi, 1153: "The *Śūraṃgama Sūtra* [T945.19.131a23–24] . . . says: 'The light of extreme purity is permeating, its quiescent illumination enveloping the sky.'" [楞嚴 . . . 曰淨極光通達寂照含虛空]

138. Anonymous, 239: "The 'single moment' mentioned above is identical to the one *tathatā*." [上云一念此云一如同一也]

139. Eishu, 361, and Dōkū, 1022: "'Superman' [*mahāpuruṣa*] is one of the ten epithets of a buddha." [丈夫佛之十号内之一也]

140. Kōunshi, 1153: "'Rush around seeking on the outside' is like Yajñadatta's craziness that did not stop. This is the story of Yajñadatta's looking for his head [in the *Śūraṃgama Sūtra*]." [向外馳求如演若狂性不歇演若覓頭之事]

141. Dōchū, 1301: "The *Huayan Sutra* [T279.10.315c14] . . . says: 'The bodhisattva's body was limitless, manifesting itself in every location.'" [華嚴經 . . . 曰菩薩身無邊普現一切處]

142. Eishu, 361: "Perfect-and-Sudden Bodhisattva is a Mahāyāna bodhisattva. The pure land is Hīnayāna." [圓頓菩薩大乘菩薩也淨土小乘也] Kassan, 493: "'Perfect-and-Sudden Bodhisattva' refers to the Mahāyāna practitioner." [言圓頓菩薩者指大乘修行人云也]

143. Dōchū, 1301: "He seizes '*ārya*' and discards 'worldling.' [He thinks that] a buddha is 'purity,' and a worldling is 'defilement.'" [於聖取之於凡捨之佛為淨凡為染也]

144. Eishu, 362, and Anonymous, 240: "In one leap one directly enters the *tathāgata* stage—there is no time. . . . 'It is right now' shows directly that one does not wade through the realm of *pratītya-samutpāda*." [一超直入如來地時節モ無イゾ . . . . 直是現今者直指示不涉因緣之境界也] Kassan, 493: "'Time sequence' is the bodhisattva's three immeasurable kalpas going through the stages." [時節者菩薩三祇歷位階等也] Dōchū, 1301: "There is no time sequence of practice going through the three immmeasurable kalpas." [無修行時節歷三祇劫也] Dōkū, 1023: "'No time sequence' means there is no discussion of the three immeasurable kalpas, stages, and so forth." [無時節者不論三祇階級等也]

Kōunshi, 1154: "It is not the same as the long time periods such as three kalpas or one hundred kalpas of the scholars of the teachings—in a word, it is right now." [不同教家論三祇百劫長時直是現今]

145. Eishu, 362, and Anonymous, 240: "In my dharma talks on a single occasion I respond to a disease by giving a medicine." [山僧ガ説處ハ一往應病與薬也] Dōchū, 1301: "From the outset there is no 'real' dharma to be preached. Thus, why have I said anything? It's because there is no alternative to one-off *upāyas*. If there is a disease, then employ a medicine." [元無實法可說然山僧有說處何也蓋一期方便不得已矣如有病則用藥] Dōkū, 1023: "'One-off' has the meaning of 'a single time' or 'a single occasion.'" [一期者一時之義一往之義] Kōunshi, 1154: "'[One-off] medicine to cure illness' means that, when the sick person has taken the medicine and the illness has been eliminated, then the medicine is also discarded." [薬病相治者病人服藥病除則薬亦捨]

146. Kassan, 493: "Illnesses have ten thousand different medicines, and the prescriptions cannot be uniformly standardized. Therefore, a good doctor dispenses the prescription according to the disease. When the disease is eliminated, the medicine is no longer of any use." [病有万殊薬無一準是故良醫應病施方病若除薬亦無用]

147. Eishu, 362: "'Old master from who knows where' refers to a bad teacher." [諸方老師ハ惡知識ヲ指ス也]

148. Yoshizawa Masahiro, ed., *Shoroku zokugokai* [*Explanations of Colloquial Expressions in Zen Records*] (Kyoto: Zen bunka kenkyūjo, 1999), 249 (no. 1255), glosses *yinpo mianmen* 印破面門 as follows: "[The novel] *Water Margin* has a line: 'I must tear off the golden seal on Lin Chong's face and return with it as proof.' As to 'golden seal on the face,' in Song Dynasty times, prisoners/exiles were all tattooed onto the face. This was called 'doing a golden seal.' This expression 'seal the face' was borrowed [by Chan] to say 'the master presses down the seal of awakening on the student's face.'" [(水滸傳原文: 是必揭取林衝臉上金印、回來做表證)。臉上の金印とは、宋時、徒流の人には皆な臉上に刺字す。これを打金印と云う。印破面門も、此の語を借りて師家が悟りの印を學者の面に捺してやると云うことなり。] Dōchū, 1302: "This *mianmen* 面門 just means 'face.' It means 'being certified by a bad teacher.'" [此面門但言面也為惡知識所印可也] Anonymous, 240: "*yinpo* 印破 is 'certification.'" [印破印可也] Chitetsu, 726: "to be verified." [受印證也]

149. Eishu, 362: "*xuanhe* 懸河 is 'falls/cataract.'" [懸河ハ瀑布也] Kōunshi, 1154: "As to *xuanhe* 懸河, the glibness never languishes—it is an unbroken continuum, like a waterfall." [懸河者辯無凝滯連續不絕如瀑布流]

150. Kassan, 494: "*shijian guo* 世間過 means 'terms, language, etc.' It also refers to those who raise glibness like a cataract." [世間過者云名相言語等也又指振懸河辯者云也]

151. Eishu, 362: "'Complete brightness' means 'moon of the fifteenth night, the stage of the full ripening of wonderful awakening.'" [圓明十五夜月妙覺果滿位ヲ云]

152. Shūshin 138–139: "Beholding reality as it truly is . . . is truly penetrating the ten-thousand layer barrier [of characteristics] but not being fixed in the thin, floating clouds [i.e., unfixed nirvana]. . . . Beholding reality as it truly is: this is viewed as the essential thing of the Zen gate." [真正見解.... 正透萬重関不住青霄裏.... 真正見解ヽ]

153. Kassan, 494, glosses *yiqie* 一切 as: "at all times and all locations." [一切時中一切處處也] Dōkū, 1024, and Kōunshi, 1155, are similar.

154. Kōunshi, 1155: "'Worlding and *ārya*' are the six worldly [rebirth realms from hells to *deva* heavens] and the four *ārya* [realms of *śrāvaka, pratyeka-buddha, bodhisattva,* and buddha]. As to the 'impure and pure,' within the ten realms nine are taken as impure and the buddha realm as pure. Or the six worldly are taken as impure and the four *ārya* as pure." [凡聖六凡四聖也染淨十界內以九界爲染以佛界爲淨或以六凡爲染以四聖爲淨]

155. Kōunshi, 1155: "the pure lands of all the buddhas of the three times and ten directions." [三世十方諸佛淨土也]

156. Eishu, 362: "[In the *Huayan Sutra*] the youth Sudhana goes through one hundred ten cities in the South visiting fifty-three good friends, arriving in front of the tower of Maitreya." [善財童子參五十三員善知識過南方一百十城到弥勒樓閣前]

157. Eishu, 363: "'Vairocana' . . . is a name for the *dharmakāya*." [毘盧遮那 . . . 是法身之名也] Dōchū, 1302: "The land on which the *dharmakāya* buddha relies." [法身佛所依之土也] Kōunshi, 1155: "As to Vairocana, the *dharmakāya tathāgata* is the non-differentiating principle of innate purity." [毘盧遮那者法身如來即自性清淨無差別理也]

158. Dōchū, 1302: "It means that *that one person* can everywhere display the lands. He can bring them into being on down to emptying them. This is the function of that non-dependent Way-person." [言那一人能處處現國土能成之乃至能空之即是那無依道人之作用] Eishu, 363: "the lands of the ten directions." [十方國土也] Kōunshi, 1155: "a responsive functioning without limit, like a moon reflected on the waters [i.e., an *upāya*]." [應用無邊如一月現衆水]

159. Eishu, 363: "Guifeng [Zongmi's] *Treatise on the Origin of Humanity* [T1886.45.709a18–19] says: 'The body goes through birth, old age, illness, and death. Having died, it is reborn. The realms come into existence, abide, disintegrate, and enter the void. Having entered the void, they come into existence again.'" [圭峰原人論云身則生老病死而復生界則成住壞空空而復成] Kassan, 495: "The four characteristics of coming into existence, abiding, disintegrating, and entering the void go in cycles of twenty kalpas each. Eighty kalpas constitutes a great kalpa." [按成住壞空四相循環各二十劫合八十劫為一大劫]

160. Eishu, 364: "Refers to the Huayan assembly. . . . the lotus-womb world." [華嚴會上ヲ指テ云也. . . . 蓮華藏世界也] Dōchū, 1303: "the *dharmakāya* reward land." [法身報土]

161. Dōchū, 1303: "There is only the non-dependent Way-person who is standing alone, incomparable." [唯有無依道人獨立無比] Kōunshi, 1157: "The non-dependent Way-person is *that one person*." [無依道人者那一人也]

162. Kōunshi, 1157: "This is tied to the question 'What is beholding reality as it truly is?' at the start of this section [i.e., **12.7**]." [是結此段發端如何是真正見解之問]

163. Kōunshi, 1157: "It is like the 'flowers' in the sky seen when you have an eye disease." [如病眼見空華]

164. Eishu, 364: "refers to the written word." [文字ヲ指也]

165. Eishu, 364: "'Expressive' means 'taking logical principles to reveal the *svabhāva* and thereby delimiting it.'" [表顯者以道理顯自性分齊シ云欤] Kassan, 497, and Dōkū, 1025: "As to 'expressive' . . . they are, in the end, explanations that await a refutation and are thus unreal." [表顯者 . . . 畢竟是待對之說而非真實也] Dōchū, 1304: "express terms and phrases." [表顯名句也] Chitetsu, 731: "the theory or teachings [*deśanā-naya*] of all the buddhas." [諸佛說通] Kōunshi, 1157: "such things as the finger indicating the moon spoken of in the *Laṅkāvatāra* and *Perfect Awakening Sutras*." [楞伽圓覺所謂標月指之類也]

166. Eishu, 364, glosses *yiyi* 依倚 as: "Depending on things, in the end you are not independent—the [samsaric] wheel has turned." [依物終不独脱也輪廻シタ也]

167. Eishu, 365: "the twelve-fold *pratītya-samutpāda*." [十二因緣] Kōunshi, 1157: "Depending upon the expressive terms and phrases, one cultivates the cause-and-effect of the three vehicles, going and coming in the three realms and receiving a body that changes in birth-and-death." [依倚表顯名句修三乘因果往來三界受分段變易生死] Dōchū, 1304: "Depending upon [unreal] light reflections, one engages in practice, and, therefore, one falls into the gradual steps of cultivating causes and realizing effects." [依倚光影邊修行故落在修因證果之階級]

168. Eishu, 365: "The wheel turns through the six rebirth paths." [六道輪廻スル也]

169. The Zen commentators (Eishu, 365; Kassan, 497; Dōkū, 1025: Dōchū, 1304), as well as modern translators, who are probably following Dōchū (Yanagida, 106; Iriya, 62; Nakamura, 90; Daitoku-ji, 198; Watson, 36; Demiéville, 81), understand *tuozhuo* 脫著 as ""taking off and putting on clothes." However, a passage in the *Mahāprajñāpāramitā Sūtra* (大般若波羅蜜多經; T220.7.1108c24–26) understands that phrase as "release from attachment [*abhiniveśa*]": "Good Hero! 'Attachment-bondage' [*zhuofu* 著縛] means 'attachment [*abhiniveśa*] and bondage [*bandha*] to the dharma nature.' Since the dharma nature is nonexistent, we cannot say that attachment exists and bondage exists. 'Release' means 'release from attachment-bondage.' Since those two do not exist, release does not exist." [善勇猛言著縛者謂於法性執著繫縛法性既無故不可說有著有縛言解脫者謂脫著縛彼二既無故無解脫]

170. Kōunshi, 1158: "'The person listening to my dharma talk' means 'the non-dependent Way-person spoken of above.'" [聽法底人者前所謂無依道人也]

171. Eishu, 365, and Anonymous, 247: "When a fish is swimming in water, it moves its tail in freedom and self existence." [言魚游水則動尾自由自在也] Dōchū, 1304: "takes a fish's leaping as a metaphor for liveliness." [活鱍鱍以魚跳比活處] Dōkū, 1025: "The person who is released from attachment and free is like a fish swimming in water that moves its tail as it dances about in self existence." [言脫著自由之人猶如魚游水動尾踊躍自在]

172. Kassan, 498, and Dōkū, 1025, gloss *wuchu* 無處 as: "having no place or location." [無方處也] Kōunshi, 1158: "has the meaning 'no place.'" [無方之義也]

173. Eishu, 365, and Anonymous, 247: "the human body of five feet [in height]. . . . the stinky skin sack." [五尺ノ形骸也. . . . 臭皮袋也] Dōchū, 1305: "It means 'human body,' because the non-dependent Way-person is the host, and the human body is his companion." [謂形骸也蓋無依道人是主形骸其伴子也] Chitetsu, 734: "All the world's body-minds are dream-and-*māyā* companions." [世間一切身心皆是夢幻伴侶] Dōkū, 1026: "'Dream-and-*māyā* companions' refers to the four elements [earth; water; fire; and wind]." [夢幻伴子指四大也] Kōunshi, 1158: "'Dream-and-*māyā* companions' refers to the form body of the four elements." [夢幻伴子者指四大色身也]

174. Eishu, 365, and Anonymous, 247: "*chiwan* 遲晩 is 'sunset years,' and *zhongjian* 中間 is 'robust years.'" [遲晩暮年謂也中間壯年也] Kōunshi, 1158, is similar. Dōchū, 1305: "*chiwan* 遲晩 means 'old age.' . . . *zhongjian* 中間 means 'interval between the robustness of youth and the weakness of old age.'" [遲晩謂老也. . . . 中間少壯與老衰之中間也]

175. Dōchū, 1305: "*cuiyi* 毳衣 is *kāṣāya*." [毳衣袈裟也]

176. Anonymous, 247: "*yinxun* 因循 ['follow the same old routine'] has the meaning 'ordinarily/aimlessly.'" [因循等閑之義]

177. Kassan, 499: "'Four types' refers to the gross characteristics of the four elements of earth, water, fire, and wind; and concurrently to the subtle four characteristics. *baibu* 擺撲 ['smacked about'] is like saying 'turned upside down.'" [四種者舉地水火風四大種麁相兼細四相也擺撲者猶言顛倒也] Dōchū, 1305: "*baibu* 擺撲 is 'whacked into confusion.'" [擺撲者打亂也] Dōkū, 1026: "*baibu* 擺撲 means 'changed' or 'beaten into a broken state.'" [擺撲者轉換或撲碎之義]

178. Kassan, 499: "because earth has a persistent solidity." [地者�㑊持質礙故] Kōunshi, 1159: "A perplexed mind is coagulated into a lack of understanding, just as the great earth is solid." [疑心堅凝不解如大地有質礙]

179. Kassan, 499: "because water is moist and weak." [水者津潤柔弱故] Kōunshi, 1159: "People sink in loving attachment just as they drown in water." [人流沉愛著如溺水]

180. Kassan, 499: "because fire is hot and scorches." [火者暖氣炎盛故] Kōunshi, 1159: "Anger extinguishes the mind of *bodhi*, just as fire burns a forest house." [瞋恚滅㳄(亡)菩提心如火燒㳄林屋]

181. Kassan, 499: "because wind moves and is light and sharp." [風者動氣輕利故]
     Kōunshi 1159: "A joyful thought moves feeling in the mind, just as the wind
     blows about waves or dust." [喜念動心情如風飄波塵]

182. Eishu, 367: "Of the six shakings [of the earth when a buddha speaks dharma]
     here four are raised." [六種震動ノ中爰ニハ四ヲ挙タ也] Dōchū, 1306: "This
     relies on the passage about the six shakings. The *Mahāprajñāpāramitā Sūtra*
     [T220.6.642c13–15] . . . says: '[Just as he spoke *in that way* of the mark of *tathatā*,]
     throughout the three-thousand great-thousand worlds [there occurred] the six
     types of shaking: the east surged and the west disappeared; the west surged
     and the east disppeared; the south surged and the north disappeared; the north
     surged and the south disappeared; the center surged and the perimeter disap-
     peared; and the perimeter surged and the center disappeared.'" [假六震動語大
     般若經 . . . 曰[正說如是真如相時]三千大千世界六種變動東涌西沒西涌東沒
     南涌北沒北涌南沒中涌邊沒邊涌中沒] Kōunshi, 1159: "These are four shakings
     of the six shakings." [是六震動中四震動也]

183. Eishu, 367: "The capability of using the four elements like this is called 'the
     eighteen magical transformations of the bodhisattva.'" [能用四大如此謂之
     菩薩十八神變] Kassan, 499, Dōkū, 1026, and Anonymous, 249, cite the eigh-
     teen magical transformations in the *Lotus Sutra* (T262.9.59c17–60a10): "The
     mother told her sons: 'Your father believes in a non-Buddhist Way and is
     deeply attached to the dharma of the brahmins. You should go and talk to
     your father so he goes together with you [to hear the Buddha preach the *Lotus
     Sutra*].' Pure Storehouse and Pure Eye, pressing their palms together, said
     to their mother: 'We are the sons of the Dharma King, and yet we have been
     born into this family of heterodox views.' The mother said to her sons: 'You
     should be anxious about your father and manifest miracles [*shenbian* 神變
     = *prātihārya*] for him. When he sees them, his mind will certainly become
     purified, and he will allow us to go the place where the buddha [is preaching
     the *Lotus Sutra*].' Thereupon the two sons, mindful of their father, sprung
     up into the air to the height of seven *tāla* trees and manifested various mir-
     acles: walking, standing, sitting, and lying in midair; having their upper
     bodies gush forth water; having their lower bodies gush forth fire; having
     their lower bodies gush forth water; having their upper bodies gush forth fire;
     manifesting gigantic bodies that filled the sky and reverting to a manifesta-
     tion of small [bodies]; having the small ones revert to a manifestation of big
     ones; disappearing in midair and suddenly being on the ground; entering
     the earth as if it were water; and walking on water as if it were land. They
     manifested all these sorts of miracles in order to bring the mind of their fa-
     ther the king to pure belief and understanding." [母告子言汝父信受外道深著
     婆羅門法汝等應往白父與共俱去淨藏淨眼合十指爪掌白母我等是法王子而
     生此邪見家母告子言汝等當憂念汝父爲現神變若得見者心必清淨或聽我等
     往至佛所於是二子念其父故踊在虛空高七多羅樹現種種神變於虛空中行住

坐臥身上出水身下出火身下出水身上出火或現大身滿虛空中而復現小小復
現大於空中滅忽然在地入地如水履水如地現如是等種種神變令其父王心淨
信解] Kōunshi, 1159: "Within the eighteen magical transformations this raises
the ninth and the tenth." Kōunshi also cites the *Lotus*. (The numbering system
for these miracles is unclear.)

184. Anonymous, 249, and Dōkū, 1027: "The four elements are the skin bag."
[四大者皮袋也] Eishu, 367: "The one capable of using you-the-four-elements is
that one person." [你四大能用得夕者ノハ那一人也]

185. Eishu, 367: "It is like the lion at play." [如獅子遊戲] Dōkū, 1027: "From the
question [at the beginning of 12.10] to this point the section [is divided in the following manner]: In the beginning it shows the principle that the four elements
are characteristic-less; in the middle it raises the enjoyment of working miracles; and at the end it holds up *that one person* who can use the four elements."
[自問如至此一段始示四大無相之理中舉受用之神變末提用得四大那一人也]
Kassan, 500, is very similar.

186. Kassan, 500: "Because there are no characteristics and karmic action, you enjoy each and every thing—therefore, meet tea, drink tea, meet food, eat food."
[無相無作故於物物上受用故逢茶喫茶逢飯喫飯] Dōchū, 1306: "These words
must be linked up with the passage below." [此語要與下文連貫]

187. Kassan, 500: "The first two '*ārya*' characters refer to the provisional name; the last
'*ārya*' character refers to the real substance." [上聖二字指假名云下聖一字指實
体云也] Dōchū, 1306, comments that the second is a name, and the third is the
real *ārya* [聖者之聖名言也聖之之名之聖真聖也]. However, the LJL itself seems
to be saying that even the third "*ārya*" is a provisional name. Kōunshi, 1160:
"The one who dislikes 'worldling' must necessarily like '*ārya*'; the one who likes
'*ārya*' must necessarily dislike 'worldling.'" [嫌凡者必愛聖愛聖者必嫌凡]

188. Kōunshi, 1160: "Students who like provisional names do not know their very
own living Mañjuśrī and go seeking on the outside." [愛假名底學人不知
自己活文殊向外尋]

189. Eishu, 368: "'Never separate' means 'substance of the *dharmakāya*.'" [始終不異
トハ法身体也] Chitetsu, 742: "refers to the *ārya* wisdom of awakening on one's
own." [指自覺聖智]

190. Eishu, 368: "The master-and-attendants Mañjuśrī, Samantabhadra, and
Avalokiteśvara are, when all is said and done, [equally] the protagonist."
[主伴ノ文殊普賢観音モ畢竟主人公ナリ] Kōunshi, 1161: "The three great
bodhisattvas Mañjuśrī, Samantabhadra, and Avalokiteśvara are interchangeable as master and attendants. There is no higher and lower [among them].
Once one is manifest, they are all manifest. Once one enters, they all enter."
[文殊普賢観音三大士互爲主爲伴無高下出則一時出入則一時入]

191. Kōunshi, 1161: "Masters and attendants are inexhaustively fused without obstruction. One *ārya* is three *āryas*; three *āryas* are one *ārya*." [主伴無盡圓融無礙一
聖三聖三聖一聖也]

192. Kassan, 503: "the oral teachings of the buddhas and bodhisattvas." [諸佛菩薩言教] Dōchū, 1307: "'Teachings' is the buddha sutras." [教者佛經也] Dōkū, 1028: "Guifeng [Zongmi in his *Chan Prolegomenon;* T2015.48.400b10–11] says: 'The first patriarch of all the [Chan] lineages is Śākyamuni. The sutras are buddha word, while Chan is the intention of the buddhas. The mouth and mind of the buddhas cannot possibly be contradictory.'" [圭峯云諸宗始祖即是釋迦經是佛語禪是佛意諸佛心口不相違] Eishu, 368: "'Teachings' refers to this record." [教ト ハ指此録欤]

193. Kassan, 504, and Dōkū, 1028: "'Good-for-nothing [gimmick] vishayas' means 'mashed-up kudzu phrases.'" [閑塵境者言爛葛籐言句] Dōchū, 1307: "An ancient says: 'Good-for-nothing [gimmick] vishayas are verbal phrases, the entire canon of sutras [preached by the Buddha] during his lifetime and the 1700 [Zen] *kōans*.'" [古德云閑塵境 言句也一代藏經一千七百公案也] Kōunshi, 1161: "'Good-for-nothing [gimmick] vishayas' refers to the written word and verbal phrases." [閑塵境者指文字言句]

194. Eishu, 368: "'Teachings-leftovers' means 'sutra texts.'" [教迹ト ハ經文也] Dōchū, 1307: "'Teachings' are not necessarily limited to the buddha teachings. All verbal phrases are called 'teachings.' The buddha teachings and the [Zen] patriarchal records are both verbal leftovers.'" [教不必局佛教凡言句名教佛教祖録皆言言迹也]

195. Eishu, 369: "'Person' refers to a master. Here it means 'teacher.'" [人指師家爰ニ知識アリト云也]

196. Kassan, 504: "*yinxian* 隱顯 means 'half-closed and half-open.'" [隱顯者言半合半開也]

197. Anonymous, 252: "This is the student." [是学者也]

198. Anonymous, 252: "refers to the student." [指学者]

199. Chitetsu, 747: "'Discussing' is *prapañca.*" [論者戲論] Myōō, 31: "As for what is outside your own mind, going down byways, whatever strained interpretations you make are all *prapañca.*" [自心ノ外ハコトゴトク傍家ニ?何フシ穿鑿スルモ皆戲論也] The *Mahāparinirvāṇa Sūtra* (佛臨涅槃記法住經; T390.12.1113b24–c1) has a similar list: "For a thousand years after my nirvana within my noble teaching *prapañca* will be firmly [established]. Most of my disciples will diligently study all manner of *prapañca.* They will discard the true teachings of the buddhas who have transcended the world. . . . They will zealously recite worldly *prapañca,* such as discussions of kings, discussions of bandits, discussions of war, discussions of food, discussions of drink, discussions of clothes, discussions of vehicles, discussions of self, discussions of lewdness, discussions of men, discussions of women, discussions of countries, discussions of rivers and seas, and discussions of non-Buddhist Ways." [我涅槃後第十百年吾聖教中戲論堅固我諸弟子多勤習學種種戲論捨出世間諸佛正教. . . . 精勤習誦世間戲論所謂王論賊論戰論食論飲論衣論乘論我論婬論男論女論諸國土論諸河海論諸外道論]

200. Eishu, 369: "*yi* 伊 ['him'] refers to the one who comes and means 'student.'" [伊來者ヲ指口云也学者ヲ云ナリ] Dōchū, 1308: "The 'one who comes' is the

student who brings a question; *yi* 伊 refers to his question." [來者問將來底學者也伊指其一問也] (In that case, *yi* 伊 would be "it" rather than "him.") Kōunshi, 1162: "*yi* 伊 refers to the one who comes." [伊者指來者也]

201. Dōkū, 1029: "'His position' refers to the student's strange words and wonderful lines." [其處者指學人奇言妙句]

202. Eishu, 369: "He emits sounds and chants written words and verbal phrases. They are the verbal phrases of a sound *samādhi*." [出音声唱說文字言句也音声三昧言句也]

203. Eishu, 369: "It has the meaning of 'use the vishayas.' It is the *person* who 'turns the vishayas.'" [用得境義也轉境底人也] Chitetsu, 749: "'The one who rides the vishayas' has awakened on his own to *tathatā*." [乘境底者自覺真如]

204. Aichi daigaku Chū-Nichi daijiten hensansho, ed., *Chū-Nichi daijiten [Great Chinese-Japanese Dictionary]*, 2nd ed. (Tokyo, Taishūkan, 1999), 720, glosses *haishi* 還是 as: "やはり ['as well/obviously; still; after all (is said and done)/in any event/in any case/no matter what; sure enough']." *haishi* is a *baihua* word and appears in 13.2; 13.9; 13.16; 13.19; 13.25; and 13.38.

205. Anonymous, 252: "'Vishaya of purity' is the buddha land of the *dharmakāya*." [清淨境法身佛土也]

206. Dōkū, 1029: "'Vishaya of compassion' is the vishaya of uprooting suffering, giving joy, and [carrying out] *upāyas* to ferry [beings to the other shore of nirvana]." [慈悲境者拔苦與樂方便濟度之境也]

207. Eishu, 370: "'Person' is *that one person*, just the one person in the universe. He always accompanies the statement: 'Above heaven and below heaven I am the solitary honored one.'" A buddha says this at birth. [人那一人也乾坤只一人也天上天下唯我独尊ノツレ也] Dōkū, 1029: "'Person' is the non-dependent Way-person." [人者即無依道人也] Kōunshi, 1163: "'Person' is *that one person* in the house of Linji." [人者即臨濟屋裏那一人也]

208. Kōunshi, 1163, cites two sutras: "The *Golden Light Sutra* [T663.16.344b3–4] . . . says: 'The Buddha's true *dharmakāya* is like the sky. In response to beings it manifests forms, but they are like the moon's reflections on the water.' *The Mind-Ground Contemplation Sutra* [T159.3.295a7] . . . says: 'Wisdom is limitless like the sky. In response to beings it manifests forms, but they are like the moon's reflections on the water.'" [金光明經 . . . 曰佛真法身猶若虛空應物現形如水中月心地觀經 . . . 曰智慧如空無有邊應物現形如水月]

209. Kassan, 506, and Dōkū, 1029, gloss *rufa* 如法 ("in accord with dharma") as: "beholding reality as it truly is." [真正見解也] Eishu, 370: "*rufa* 如法 . . . is the dharma of *tathatā*." [如法トハ . . . 如ノ法也如如ノ法也]

210. Anonymous, 253: "means an iron Han." [言鉄漢也]

211. Eishu, 370: "giving the appearance of shifting in accordance with things. . . . appearance of a style in accordance with worldly convention, not stabilized." [隨物迁兒也 . . . . 隨世俗之風不定兒也] Dōkū, 1030, is similar. Kassan, 506:

"means 'twisting in accordance with things.'" [蓋隨物委曲之義也] Kōunshi, 1163: "appearance of being feeble and weak." [萎腇頓弱貌]

212. Eishu, 370: "'Clarified butter' means 'true dharma.'" [醍醐真法云也] Kōunshi, 1163: "'Cracked [pottery vessel]' is a metaphor for a vessel [i.e., a sentient being] of Hīnayānist sense faculties." [(斯/瓦)嘎者比小乘根器者也]

213. Kassan, 506: "'Great dharma vessel' is one of extra-superior sense faculties." [大法器即上上根也]

214. Eishu, 370: "'Discombobulated by persons' means their intellectual understanding, emotional assessments, calculations, and plans." [人惑ハ知解情量計較按排也] Kassan, 506: "'Discombobulated by persons' refers to the things and terminologies of others." [人惑者指他之事相名字也] Dōkū, 1030: "'Discombobulated by persons' refers to all the bad teachings of bad teachers." [人惑者指一切不善知識之教壞] Kōunshi, 1164: "Discombobulated by persons' refers to the bad teachings of bad companions and bad teachers. Grasping at the teachings of the sutras is getting discombobulated by the buddhas; attachment to the [Zen] sayings records is getting discombobulated by the patriarchs." [人惑者指惡件惡知識之教壞夫執經教是佛惑著語錄是祖惑]

215. Eishu, 370: "means 'place of *pratītya-samutpāda*.'" [緣起処ヲ云也] Kōunshi, 1164: "An ancient's brief comment is: 'The staff [i.e., symbol of authority] is always in your hand.'" [古德著語柱杖子常在手]

216. Eishu, 370: "'Come at you' refers to the myriad vishayas and myriad objective supports [*ālambana*]. . . . The myriad false vishayas come to invade, but you are not susceptible to them." [來者萬境萬緣也. . . . 萬般邪境來侵不受之也] Kassan, 507: "It is just that, when dependently originated vishayas strongly come at you, you are not susceptible to them at all." [但如緣起之境競來則揔不受] Dōchū, 1310, Dōkū, 1030, and Kōunshi, 1164: "One who enters from the gate is not a family treasure [one who enters from the gates of the six sense faculties is not an awakened person]." [自門入者不是家珍]

217. Kōunshi, 1164: "The *Commentary on Meanings in the Śūraṃgama Sūtra* [T1799.39.953c6] . . . says: 'If there is perplexity in the mind, then there is a disparity. In the end this will lead to getting discombobulated by Māra.' Also, the *Dahui Record* . . . 'Letter in Answer to Lü Sheren' [T1998A.47.930a16–18] says: 'If you produce perplexity over the written word, if you produce perplexity over the teachings of the sutras, if you produce perplexity over the *kōans* of the ancients, if you produce perplexity in the midst of the *kleśas* of everyday life, all of this is the coterie of the evil Māra.'" [楞嚴義疏 . . . 曰疑心即差遂招魔惑又大慧錄 . . . 答呂舍人書曰文字上起疑經教上起疑古人公案上起疑日用塵勞中起疑皆是邪魔眷屬]

218. Shukitsu, 927: "Māra is samsara." [魔是生死也]

219. Dōchū, 1310: "You should stop the thoughts that rush about seeking—this does not mean being like a withered tree or dead ashes." [可息馳求念也非謂如枯木死灰也] Shukitsu, 927: "The place wherein perplexed thoughts stop is

the site of the buddhas." [疑念息處是佛場] Dōkū, 1030: "Just try: be able to investigate through Zen sitting." [但能禪坐相究看]

220. Kassan, 507: "In all events and all places, just try to re-train the light [of the true mind] back [upon yourself]." [只於一切事一切處直回光返照看] Dōchū, 1310: "'Things' are the myriad vishayas. *zhao* 照 ['the light'] . . . is 'sever.'" [物萬境也照 . . . 截斷也] Kassan is referring to focusing *the light* inwards, and Dōchū is referring to focusing *the light* outwards to sever or cut off "things." This translation has followed Kassan.

221. Eishu, 371: "As to 'have confidence in your immediate venue of activities,' if you function as the master of the mind, then not a single thought arises, and so it is said that 'there is *not a single thing to do*.'" [信現今用底ハ作心主用得則一念不起ノ故云一个叟也無] Dōchū, 1310: "means within the dharmas of this mind of direct perception [*pratyakṣa*] 'there is *not a single thing to do*.'" [言此現量心法中一箇事亦無之也]

222. Eishu, 371: "The three realms here are the three poisons of greed, anger, and stupidity. The one mind fragments into these three poisons, becoming the six 'dusts.'" [爰ノ三界ハ貪嗔痴ノ三毒也一心ガ此三毒ニ分タレテ六塵トナル也] Kassan, 507: "A single thought is born, and in a split second the three poisons arise. In the end, with this arising as its condition, vishayas are falsely manifested. Therefore, one will be turned around by the vishayas, discombobulated by the six vishayas." [一念僅生三毒瞥起終隨其生起緣妄現境界是故被境回換受六塵惑也] Dōkū, 1030, is very similar. Dōchū, 1310: "'By the vishayas' is like the previous example [in **12.9**] 'by [the four elements of] earth, water, fire, and wind.' 'Conditioned' is 'my mind follows previous conditions.' 'By the vishayas' is 'I am turned around by the vishayas.' Mind and vishayas serve as causes and conditions for each other, creating forms, sounds, smellables, tastables, touchables, and dharmas. Mind follows forms, forms produce mind, etc." [被境者如前被地水火風之語例隨緣者我心隨前緣也被境者我為境所回換也心境相因緣造色聲香味觸法也心隨色色生心等]

223. Eishu, 371: "'Venue of activities' is the venue of walking, standing, sitting, lying, putting on your clothes, and eating meals. . . . With each and every thing it is the venue wherein the one mind is performing the action." [應用處トハ行住坐臥著衣喫飯処也. . . . 頭頭物物一心ノ爲ス処ゾ] Kassan, 507: "Everywhere ahead of you and everywhere right under your feet directly points to [*that one person/the true*] person." [頭上漫漫脚下漫漫直指為人也]

224. Dōchū, 1310: "The country of Three Eyes is the country where the *bhikṣu* named Sudarśana dwells." [三眼國名善見比丘所住之國也] Kōunshi, 1164: "The *Huayan Sutra* [T279.10.349b19–c3] . . . says: 'Good son! In the South there is a country named Three Eyes. It has a *bhikṣu* named Sudarśana. You should visit him and ask: "How does one train in the bodhisattva practice and cultivate the bodhisattva Way?". . . . He gradually wandered until he arrived at the country of Three Eyes. In the cities where people congregate, in the villages, neighborhoods,

markets, and stores, in the rivers, plains, mountains, and valleys, in every place, everywhere, he sought out the *bhikṣu* Sudarśana. He saw him in a grove walking back and forth. His appearance was that of someone in the prime of life, handsome, upright, and pleasing.'" [華嚴 ... 曰善男子於此南方有一國土名爲三眼彼有比丘名曰善見汝詣彼問.... 漸次遊行至三眼國於城邑聚落村隣市肆川原山谷一切諸處周徧求覓善見比丘見在林中經行往還壯年美貌端正可喜]

225. Kassan, 508: "This section shows the principle of working miracles." [此一節示變通(= *prātihārya*)之理也]

226. Anonymous, 253: "This Land of Three Eyes is [an aspect] of the one mind, as the section below explains." [此三眼國土在一心上故下分明說] Dōchū, 1311: "The Master takes the three bodies—*dharma*, *saṃbhoga*, and *nirmāṇa*—as the three eyes. He also divides them into lands." [師以法報應三身爲三眼又分爲三箇國土]

227. Dōchū, 1311: "the dharma eye of the three eyes." [三眼中法眼也]

228. Dōchū, 1311: "the compassion eye of the three eyes." [三眼中慈眼也]

229. Dōchū, 1311: "the wisdom eye of the three eyes." [三眼中慧眼也]

230. The term *yibian* 依變 here is probably equivalent to *yi bianhua* 依變化 ("depends on *nirmita* or *nirmāṇa*" = "depends on a magical or supernatural creation or transformation that has no material basis; a magical or supernatural 'projection'"). The *Great Prajñāpāramitā Sūtra* (T220.6.481a2-11) has an example of *yi bianhua* 依變化: "At that time the Heavenly Emperor Śakra [Indra] asked the venerable Subhūti: 'Great Worthy! How does the bodhisattva, the Great Being, practice the *prajñāpāramitā*? Even though he knows that all dharmas are like a *māyā*, like dream, like an echo, like an image, like a tongue of flame, like a reflection, like a magical-transformation event, like a city of the *gandharvas*, and yet this bodhisattva, Great Being, does not cling to [the notion that] it is a *māyā*, that it is a dream, that it is an echo, that it is an image, that it is a tongue of flame, that it is a reflection, that it is a magical-transformation event, that it is a city of the *gandharvas;* nor does he cling [to the notion that it] is due to a *māyā*, due to a dream, due to an echo, due to an image, due to a tongue of flame, due to a reflection, due to a magical-transformation event, due to a city of the *gandhavas;* nor does he cling to [that notion that it] belongs to *māyā*, belongs to a dream, belongs to an echo, belongs to an image, belongs to a tongue of flame, belongs to a reflection, belongs to a magical-transformation event, belongs to a city of the *gandharvas;* nor does he cling to [the notion that it] depends on a *māyā*, depends on a dream, depends on an echo, depends on an image, depends on a tongue of flame, depends on a reflection, *depends on a magical-transformation event*, depends on a city of the *gandharvas*." [亦不執依幻依夢依響依像依陽焰依光影依變化事依尋香城] To a certain extent modern translations skirt the pervasive illusionism in LJL. For instance, Daitoku-ji, 209, comments: "'Dependent transformations' . . . expresses the standpoint that the buddha is no more than a relative concept with

no intrinsic or inherent nature"; Watson, 42: "But these lands of the three eyes
are all just a change in the dependent condition, a change of robes"; Demiéville,
90: "Ces royaumes des Trois Yeux ne sont que des transformations de dépen-
dance"; Yanagida, 123, comments on *yibian* 依変: "A difference in standpoint;
to go on changing in response to the other party" [立場の相違。相手に応じ
て移り変ってゆくこと。]; Iriya, 73, comments: "a change of the object in response to this side's way of existing" [こちらの在り方に応じた対象の変化。];
Nakamura, 102, comments: "Even though one speaks of the Land of Three
Eyes, it is like a reflected image of the true nature, and so it is something
that changes depending on the object." [三眼国土と言っても真性の光の影の
ようなもので、対象によって変化するものである。] In general, these transla-
tors seem to be following Dōchū, 1311: "Also, *yibian* 依變 means 'light reflections that arise in dependence upon the true nature.' It is like the previously mentioned [in **10.5**] *san zhong yi* 三種依 [literally 'three types of
dependence.'" [又依變者依倚真性而變起底光影也如前云三種依] Kassan,
508, and Dōkū, 1031, are similar to Dōchū: "*yibian* 依變 means 'transforms
in dependence upon *that thing* [i.e., the true nature], completely unreal.'" [依變者依倚那物而變也總非實法也] This translation has followed
Kōunshi, 1165–1166: "These lands of the three bodies are all dependent
upon magical transformations in things and completely lacking in reality."
[此三身國土皆是依物變化都無實體] Myōō, 34, seems to agree: "The *yi* 依 ['de-
pendent'] is not the *yi* 依 of *suoyi* 所依 ['basis']; it is the *yi* 依 ['dependent'] of
yitong 依通 ['supernormal powers dependent upon alchemical recipes, charms,
mantras, etc.'" [依ハ所依ノ依ニアラズ依通ノ依也]

231. Eishu, 371: "'Fundamental' means 'substance.' Sutra and treatise scholars take
the *dharmakāya* as substance and the *saṃbhogakāya* and *nirmāṇakaya* as functions." [根本トハ体也經論家ニハ法身ヲ躰トシ報化二身用スル也] Dōchū,
1311: "'Fundamental' means 'substance.' The *saṃbhoga* and *nirmāṇa* [bodies]
are functions." [根本謂體也報化爲用]

232. Dōchū, 1311: "repudiates the dependent transformations of Three Eyes."
[斥三眼之依變]

233. This Yogācāra quotation appears in **10.5**. See n. 45. Dōchū, 1312: "Bodies and
lands that are established in dependence upon doctrinal points are called
dharmas without reality." [依義建立身土名非有實法也]

234. Kōunshi, 1166: "*yitong* 依通 means 'to know based upon the alchemical arts, to
work magical transformations that come and go based on magical charms and
alchemical recipes.'" [依通者依法術而知依符藥而往來靈變等也] Eishu 371:
"*tong* 通 is the same thing as *bian* 変." [通モ変ト同支也]

235. Eishu, 371–372, and Kōunshi, 1166: "The *Nirvāṇa Sūtra* [T374.12.485c10–13] . . .
says: 'It is like when a child is crying. The father and mother take yellow leaves
of a poplar tree and say to him: "Do not cry! Do not cry! We will give you gold!"
When the child has produced the notion of true gold, he right away stops his

crying. However, the poplar leaf is not really gold.'" [涅槃經 . . . 云如彼嬰兒啼哭之時父母即以楊樹黃葉而語之言莫啼莫啼我与汝金嬰兒見已生真金想便止不啼然此楊葉實非金也]

236. Kassan, 509: "In the end it is saying that wanting to seek out the bud-dhadharma in terms and words is like looking for juice in spikes of water chesnuts or dried bones. The meaning is 'has no good flavor.'" [畢竟言於名言上欲求佛法猶如於菱刺枯骨上 覓汁之謂也又是沒滋味義也] Kōunshi, 1166: "The puncture-vine and a dried bone lack wetness. Seeking juice from them—how could you possibly get it? It is a sim-ile for wanting to seek out the buddhadharma in terms and words." [蒺藜枯骨其無潤濕者向之求汁豈可得比是向名言上欲求佛法]

237. Dōkū, 1031: "The Great Way from the outset lacks nothing. Why on earth would you [try to] further cultivate *this matter?*" [大道本來無有欠缺更修這什麼事]

238. Dōchū, 1312: "Cultivation wades through [karmic] performance. Because one has taken [karmic] performance as the cause, the result that is obtained also corresponds to [karmic] performance or samsaric karman. The reason is that cause-and-effect is a *niṣyanda* ['outcome/natural result/cause-correspondence'] method." [修涉造作已以造作因故其所得果亦當造作生死業也因果等流法故] Kassan, 509, and Dōkū, 1031: "Even if you got something through cul-tivation and realization, none of it would be the original dharma, and so it would end in becoming karman by which the wheel of samsara turns." [設修證得底者亦皆是非本法故終成生死輪回業也]

239. Kassan, 509: "completely annihilates the grasping mind of terms, words, and seeking." [揔破名言求覓之執心也]

240. Dōchū, 1313: "'With outflows,' 'without outflows,' 'conditioned,' 'unconditioned'—when all creation of karman is completely exhausted, it is pure karman. . . . Scholars of the teachings talk about 'with outflows-conditioned' (the worldling's creation of karman), 'with outflows-unconditioned' (the four *dhyānas*, eight *samādhis*, and the fruit of non-thought [concentration], etc., of the non-Buddhist Ways), 'without outflows-conditioned' (the myr-iad practices of the six *pāramitās*), and 'without outflows-unconditioned' (*dharmakāya* and *tathatā*). This meaning is also present." [言有漏無漏有爲無爲一切作業無不盡是清淨業也. . . . 教家談有漏有爲(凡夫作業)有漏無漏(外道四禪八定無想果等)無漏有爲(六度萬行)無漏無爲(法身真如)此亦義通] Dōkū, 1032: "Buddhas and patriarchal masters are people with *nothing-to-do*. They don't wade through cultivation and realization, and they don't en-gage in selecting out. Therefore, [for them] 'conditioned,' 'with outflows,' 'without outflows,' 'unconditioned' taken together are pure karman." [佛與祖師是無事人不涉修證不作揀擇所以有爲有漏無漏無爲共爲清淨業] Kōunshi, 1167: "The *Mahāprajñāpāramitā Sūtra* says: 'The meaning of the words "all with-outflows and without-outflows dharmas, conditioned and uncondi-tioned dharmas, mundane and supramundane dharmas are empty and pure"'

is the meaning of the word "bodhisattva".'" [大般若 . . . 曰有漏無漏法有爲無爲法世間出世間(法)空寂清淨句義是菩薩句義]

241. Eishu, 372: "This also means 'bad teacher.'" [是モ惡知識ヲ云也]

242. Eishu, 372: "'Suppresses' means 'quelling thought-outflows.' . . . 'Thought-outflows' are the *kleśas*." [把捉ハ念漏ヲ取リシヅメテ也. . . .念漏ハ煩惱也]

243. In works associated with Heze Shenhui, which were discovered among the Dunhuang manuscripts in the early twentieth century, these four aphorisms are said to be the (inferior) teaching of the "Northern" masters Puji 普寂 and Xiangmo Zang 降魔藏. The Zen commentators of Muromachi and Edo period Japan, of course, were unaware of these Dunhuang-manuscript texts and followed the traditional attribution of the four aphorisms to Bodhidharma and the sixth patriarch Huineng. Eishu, 372: "This is a saying from Bodhidharma's *Treatise on Eradicating Characteristics*." [是達磨破相論之語也] Kassan, 510, and Dōkū, 1032, place the four aphorisms within the context of Zongmi's three *zong* 宗 of Chan in his *Chan Prolegomenon* (T2015.48.402b15–403a15): "Even though the above practice of counteracting [i.e., the teaching embodied in the aphorisms] is meticulous and thorough, it is all [karmic] performance. It has not yet arrived at the *zong* 宗 of directly revealing the mind nature [i.e., Dharma-nature Chan]—it is just the benefit from the [first] *zong* 宗 of stopping [thought of] the unreal and cultvating mind only [i.e., merely Yogācāra Chan]." [言上來對治修行雖似綿密皆是造作未至直顯真性宗只是息妄修心宗受用也] Kōunshi, 1168: "Patriarchal Master"—how could it not refer to the two great masters Bodhidharma and the sixth patriarch [Huineng]?" [祖師者盍指達磨六祖二大師] Dōchū, 1313: "Fixing it, raising it, gathering it in, coagulating it—how are these not [karmic] performance?" [住之舉之攝之凝之豈非造作耶]

244. Chitetsu, 763: "*Citta, manas,* and *mano-vijñāna* are called 'him.'" [心意意識曰佗曰渠] Dōkū, 1032: "'Him' in the end means '*that one person* without characteristics and without form.'" [佗者畢竟無相無形之那一人也] Eishu, 373: "'Him' refers to the person listening to dharma. . . . 'He' is *that one person,* your very own self. 'Adorn' is to use written words and verbal phrases to comment on the meaning of the Way principle." [他トハ聽法底人指云也. . . . 他那一人自己本身也莊嚴以文字言句著道理義也] Myōō, 37: "'Adorn' means 'the four [bodhisattva] necklace adornments [*alaṃkāra*]: *śīla* adornment, *samādhi* adornment, *prajñā* adornment, and *dhāraṇī* adornment.'" [莊嚴トハ四種瓔珞莊嚴ト云フ事アリ戒莊嚴三昧莊嚴智慧莊嚴陀羅尼莊嚴ナリ] (From the *Mahāvaipulyamahāsaṃnipāta Sūtra* (大方等大集經; T397.13.5c28–6a1.) Dōchū, 1313: "'Him' refers to '*that one person* listening to dharma' mentioned above. 'Adorn' means 'the adornment of the [thirty-two major] characteristics and [eighty minor] marks.'" [他者即上所謂聽法底那一人. . . . 莊嚴者相好莊嚴也]

245. Eishu, 373: "This 'he' is the person listening to dharma." [此渠トハ聽法底人也] Kōunshi, 1168: "'He' refers to *that one person.*" [佗指那一人]

246. Kassan, 511, glosses "all" [一切] as: "all sentient and insentient things." [一切有情無情]

247. Kōunshi, 1168: "The 'adornment' spoken of here is not an adornment with characteristics—it is a non-adornment adornment. Therefore, the *Vajracchedikā Sūtra* [T235.8.751b10–11] says: 'In the *tathāgata*'s speaking of adorning buddha-lands a non-adornment is called an adornment.'" [今言莊嚴者不是有相莊嚴非莊嚴之莊嚴也故金剛曰如來說莊嚴佛土者即非莊嚴是名莊嚴]

248. Eishu, 373: "'Old masters like this' are heterodox masters." [一般老師邪師也]

249. Eishu, 373: "'Old monk' refers to the 'old masters' spoken of above." [老宿ハ上云老師ヲ指ス也] Kōunshi, 1169: "'This' refers to the heterodox masters of silence-and-illumination in the above section." [這者指上段默照邪師]

250. Eishu, 373: "What is 'a pair of eyes?' Everyone possesses them, and each and every one is perfect. . . . The eyes your father and mother gave you at birth are true eyes." [一双眼是什广人人具足个个圓成. . . . 父母所生眼便是正眼] Dōkū, 1032, is the same as the first portion. Kassan, 511: "The [*Lotus*] *Sutra* [T262.9.47c17] says: 'The eyes your father and mother gave you at birth see throughout the three thousand worlds.'" [經云父母所生眼徹見三千界]

251. Eishu, 373: "the appearance of being fearful and lacking autonomy." [恐怖而不自在兒也] Chitetsu, 764: "the appearance of being unable to proceed." [行不得貌] Dōchū, 1314: "the appearance of being anxious and fearful." [比危懼貌]

252. Eishu, 373: "the appearance of being killed by the cold, [to the point of] not speaking." [被寒殺不言兒也] Kassan, 511, and Dōkū, 1032: "mouth closed." [口閉也] Dōchū, 1314: "unable to open the mouth." [不得開口也] Kōunshi, 1169, is very similar.

253. Eishu, 373: "'Falseness or correctness of the world' means 'pronounce on the falseness or correctness of teachers, of [any old master from] who knows where.'" [是非天下トハ善知識或諸方是非ナリ] Kōunshi, 1169: "distinguish whether teachers of the world are heterodox or true." [辨天下知識邪正] Dōchū, 1314: "pronounce on whether old preceptors are heterodox or true." [是非於天下老和尚邪正也]

254. Dōchū, 1315: "[refers] not merely to students of small [karmic] roots but [also] to bad teachers without the eye [who are found] all over the place." [不但小根學者諸方無眼惡知識] Eishu, 373: "[refers to] heterodox masters as well as those belonging to the two vehicles of *śrāvaka* and *pratyeka-buddha*." [邪師也又声聞緣觉二乘屬也] Kassan, 511, and Dōkū, 1033: "refers to students." [指學者云也] Chitetsu, 766: "Those of small good [karmic] roots who [pursue] the two vehicles are 'children.'" [二乘小善根為兒] Shukitsu, 931: "'Small children' means 'students.'" [諸小兒者謂學人也] Kōunshi, 1169: "'Small children.' . . . here means 'students of [karmic] roots of small confidence.'" [小兒者. . . . 今謂小信根學者]

255. The Zen commentators seem unsure of the meaning of *nishun* 逆順 and provide a number of exegeses. Eishu, 373: "Vishayas that go against you and vishayas that go in your direction are the two vishayas of joy and anger." [逆
境界順境界喜怒二境] Chitetsu, 766: "'Go against' and 'go in the same direction' refer to contemplating [backward and forward] the twelve-fold *pratītya-
samutpāda*." [順逆觀察十二緣起] Dōkū, 1033: "Masterful Chan artisans in
approaching people do not [use] just one model. Sometimes it is *upāyas* of
compassion; sometimes it is bitter scolding. [The point is to] make students
decisively become buddhas and patriarchs." [夫作家宗匠接人非一模或時方便
慈悲或時辛辣罵辱但教學人直下成佛作祖也] Dōchū, 1315: "Sometimes going
in the same direction and praising a teacher, sometimes going against and cen-
suring a teacher, but the idea [always] lies in seeking out the [true] *person* and
that is all." [或順褒善知識或逆貶善知識但意在求人而已]

256. Both the Zen commentators and modern translators have taken this line as
Linji's speaking of his own experience, which makes this line a *non sequitur*.
There is no completely convincing way to read this quotation, but, given the
context of "twelve years" and "good teachers," this translation has made the
tentative assumption that it is an allusion to the "Entering the *Dharmadhātu*"
chapter of the *Huayan Sutra* (even though the exact quotation does not appear
there). The youth Sudhana travels all over the South of India, visiting fifty-three
teachers *(kalyāṇa-mitra)* in succession. The fifth of these is the master merchant
(śreṣṭhin) Vimuktika (T278.9.694a1): "Having thought thusly, [Sudhana] went on
a gradual journey, going through twelve years, until he arrived at the country of
Vanavāsin, where he searched everywhere for the master merchant Vimuktika."
[如是念已漸漸遊行經十二年至住林國周遍推求解脫長者] The Zen commenta-
tors offer a wide range of exegeses of "twelve years" [*shi'er nian* 十二年]. Eishu, 373,
glosses it as: the twelve *āyatanas* [*shi'er ru ye* 十二入也]; the twelve links of *pratītya-
samutpāda* [*shi'er yinyuan* 十二因緣]; the twelve years since Linji's great awakening
[臨濟大悟以來十二年也]; and the speech of the goddess in the *Vimalakīrti Sūtra*
(T475.14.548a27–b3): "Śāriputra! Indra, Brahma, the four Heavenly Kings, *devas*,
nāgas, demonic spirits, etc., have entered this house and heard this superior person [Vimalakīrti] expound the true dharma—all of them have taken joy in the scent
of buddha merit, sent up the aspiration [for awakening] and departed. Śāriputra! I
have stopped in this room for twelve years. From the beginning I never heard him
speak of *śrāvaka* and *pratyeka-buddha* dharmas. All I heard was the great friendliness
and great compassion of the bodhisattva, the inconceivable dharma of the all the
buddhas." [舍利弗其有釋梵四天王諸天龍鬼神等入此室者聞斯上人講說正法
皆樂佛功德之香發心而出舍利弗吾止此室十有二年初不聞說聲聞辟支佛法但
聞菩薩大慈大悲不可思議諸佛之法] Kassan, 511: "For 'twelve years' there are two
theories: the first is twelve years since the Master took over his temple. Because the
'twelve branches' revolve in twelve-year cycles, he raises the large number twelve....
The second is the twelve *āyatanas*." [十二年者有二說一師出世以來十二年間也

蓋十二支以十二年運轉了是故舉年大數謂十二年. . . . 二十二入也] Dōkū, 1033, is similar. Dōchū, 1315, comments: "The *Vimalakīrti Sūtra* [T475.14.548b22–23] says: 'The goddess said, "For twelve years I have sought a female form but have not been able to obtain it."'" [天曰我從十二年來求女人相了不可得] Kōunshi, 1169, also cites this passage in the *Vimalakīrti*. Chitetsu, 766, refers to the twelve limbs of *pratītya-samutpāda* as the "new theory" (*xinshuo* 新說). Shukitsu, 931: "'Twelve years' means the 'twelve *āyatanas*.'" [十二年者謂十二入也]

257. Kassan, 512, and Dōkū, 1033: "She fears going against her husband's will and being ejected." [恐違夫意被趁出也] Dōchū, 1315, glosses: "When a Zen master is weak and delicate, he resembles a new wife, and so he is called 'a new-wife Zen master.'" [禪師輕弱似新婦故名新婦子禪師也] Eishu, 373, Kassan, 512, and Dōkū, 1033: "refers to a bad teacher." [指惡知識也]

258. The *Glossary of the Patriarchal Courtyard* (*Zuting shi yuan* 祖庭事苑) says: "The *Nirvāṇa Sūtra* [T374.12.522c7–9] says: 'It is like the jackal. Even if it studies the lion for three thousand years, it can never make the roar of the lion. In the case of a lion cub, in three years it can emit a roar.' *yegan* [野干]: The Sanskrit is *śṛgāla*. This means 'jackal.' It is also called the 'night jackal' or 'emitting jackal.' Its color is a greenish yellow, and it roams in packs like dogs. At night the sounds it makes are like that of a wolf. Also, jackals are of small size with a big tail. They can clamber up trees, but, if they think a branch is dead, they won't go up." [涅槃云猶如野干雖學師子至百千年終不能作師子之吼若師子子三歲則能哮吼野干梵云悉迦羅此言野干亦名夜干或射干色青黃如狗群行夜鳴其聲如狼又野干形小尾大能上樹疑枯枝不登] CBETA, X64, no. 1261, p. 423, b18–22 //Z 2:18, p. 111, a14–18 //R113, p. 221, a14–18.

259. Eishu, 374: "This section is a discussion of the fact that bad teachers should not be believed." [此段惡知識不可信ト云フヲ說也]

260. Eishu, 374: "Since in your current venue of activities each and every thing, the whole of the great earth, is all the Zen Way or buddhadharma, not the least thing could be lacking, and there is nothing that should be mended through cultivation." [你今用処頭頭物物都盧大地皆悉禪道佛法ナレバ欠少スベキ物モナク修補スベキ処モ無イゾ] Kassan, 512: "The Way from the outset is uncultivatable, but great worthies exhort cultivation." [道本無修大德強修]

261. Eishu, 374: "'Pint-sized monks' refers to students; 'wild-fox demons' refers to heterodox masters." [小阿師ハ學者也野狐精魅ハ邪師也]

262. Eishu, 374, glosses *ta shuo shi* 他說事 as: "They have faith in and consent to the random talk and confused Way of these heterodox masters." [他說事トハ邪師ノ口任乱道スルヲ信仰メユルシウケガウ也] Dōchū, 1316: "*xu* 許 means that the pint-sized monks comply with the orders of the bad teachers; *ta* 他 is the bad teachers." [許者小阿師許惡知識令言也他者惡知識也]

263. Eishu, 374: "The first *ta* 他 is the heterodox masters; the second *ta* 他 is the students." [上ノ陀ハ邪師下ノ他ハ学者也] Dōchū, 1316: "This *ta ren* 他人 refers in general to students." [此他人泛指學者]

264. Eishu, 374: "Internal realization is called 'principle'; cultivation is called 'practice.'" [内證云理修行云行也] Kassan, 512, glosses *li xing* 理行 as: "Taking the inner nature as principle is realization-awakening; practice [directed toward] external characteristics is cultivation." [理行者理内性即證悟也行外相即修行也]

265. Kassan, 512: "The 'three karmans' are the three karmans of body, speech, and mind—in general, the ten evil actions [proscribed by the precepts]." [三業者身口意三業摠十惡也]

266. Eishu, 374: "This is a metaphor for things of which there are many. A large number of bad teachers are said to be like the spring rains—one does not know their number." [物多フニ喻也喻惡知識其數多フ如細雨サゥ云者不知數ト云心也] Kassan, 512, and Dōkū, 1033: "Like the above *shuo shi* 說事, their numbers are as troublesome as the fine rains of spring." [如上來說事者其數多煩如春細雨之謂也] Dōchū, 1316: "means 'so many they cannot be numbered.'" [言多而不可數也] Kōunshi, 1170: "'People who speak like this' are scholars of the teachings and Seat Masters. Their usual talk is as plentiful as the spring rains." [如上說是教家座主尋常說其多如細雨]

267. Eishu, 374: "*mo xiang dao* 莫向道 has the meaning 'should not concern oneself with/should not have to do with the Way.'" [莫向道トハ道ニカカワルベカラズト云義] Dōchū, 1316: "As you are just about to face the Way, you have already turned your back on the Way." [擬向道早與道背矣]

268. Eishu, 374: "For one who is about to cultivate the Way, the Way doesn't come into being, and the 84,000 *kleśas* vie to arise." [欲修道者却道不成而八萬四千煩惱競頭出生也] Dōchū, 1317: "A single thought of cultivation is [karmic] performance; if a single thought is produced, from this the myriad heterodox [views] arise in a cluster." [修一念是造作苟一念生自此萬邪群起]

269. Kōunshi, 1171: "The *Vimalakīrti Sūtra* [T475.14.554b21–22] . . . says: 'Take the sword of *prajñā* to eradicate the *kleśa* bandits.'" [維摩 . . . 曰以智慧劒破煩惱賊]

270. Eishu, 375: "In brightness there is darkness; in darkness there is brightness. Neither brightness nor darkness is erected." [明中有暗暗中有明明暗不立云也] Kassan, 513: "This is the nonduality of brightness and darkness." [是即明暗不二]

271. Eishu, 375: "Raising your feet and putting them down is the Way." [舉足下足是道也]

272. Eishu, 375: "'Has never lacked for anything' means 'right in front of you a single filament of silk, continuous and unbroken.'" [未曾欠少トハ面前一絲長時無間也]

273. Kassan, 513, and Dōkū, 1034: "As to *xin xin* 心心, the *tathatā* of the one mind is the substance, and the arising-disappearing of the one mind is characteristics and functions. Guifeng [Zongmi in his *Chan Prolegomenon;* T2015.48.401c2–3] says: 'Aśvaghoṣa [in his *Awakening of Faith;* T1666.32.576a5–6] considers the one mind to be dharma and the two gates, *tathatā* and arising-extinguishing, to be principles.'" [心心者一心真如即躰性也一心生滅即相用也圭峰云馬鳴以一

心為法以真如生滅二門為義] Shukitsu, 933: "As to 'mind and mind not differ-
entiated,' Aśvaghoṣa considers the one mind to be dharma and the two gates,
tathatā and arising-extinguishing, to be principles." [心心不異者馬鳴以一心爲
法以真如生滅二門為義] The relevant passage of the *Awakening of Faith*
(*Dasheng qixin lun* 大乘起心論; T1666.32.576a4–7) states: "Revelation of the
true principle is grounded in the one-mind dharma and has two gates. What
are the two? The first is the gate of mind *tathatā*, and the second is the gate
of mind arising-disappearing. These two gates both include all dharmas.
Why is this? Because these two gates are never divorced from each other."
[顯示正義者依一心法有二種門云何爲二一者心真如門二者心生滅門是二種
門皆各總攝一切法此義云何以是二門不相離故]

274. Chitetsu, 770: "The place wherein *svabhāva* and characteristics are separate is
sentient-being mind." [性相別處是衆生心]

275. Kassan, 514, and Dōkū, 1034: "The sum total of reflections *is* the mirror; the
sum total of waves *is* the water." [全像是鏡全波是水] Kōunshi, 1171: "xing 性
is the *svabhāva* of all dharmas internal and external. *xiang* 相 is the terminological characteristics, the provisional names, of all dharmas internal and
external. Being divorced from these two terms [*svabhāva* and characteristics]
means '*svabhāva* is empty' and 'characteristics are empty.' This is '*svabhāva*
and characteristics are not separate.' [This formulation] is grounded in the
Awakening of Faith's [T1666.32.575c25–28] 'three greats': Taking the substance
'great' as *svabhāva*, and taking characteristics and functions, the two 'greats,',
[both] as characteristics." [性者內外諸法自性也相者內外諸法名相假名也
離此二名謂性空相空是即性與相不別依起心三大則以體大爲性相用二大
爲相]

276. Eishu, 375, and Anonymous, 259: "Know nothing, understand nothing, and
fuse into oneness." [一切不知不會打成一片也] Kōunshi, 1171: "Set your tongue
in motion, and you have already gone astray." [動舌即乖]

277. Dōchū, 1318: "all dharmas with outflows and without outflows."
[有漏無漏一切法也]

278. Kassan, 514: "means that mundane and supramundane dharmas all are
dependently originated and so have no *svabhāva*." [言世間出世間諸法皆因緣生
故無自性] Dōchū, 1318, cites the three no-natures (*san zhong wuxing*三種無性
= *trividha niḥsvabhāvatā*) of the *Consciousness-Only Treatise* (*Weishi lun* 唯識論;
T1587.31.61a22–27): no-nature of characteristics, no-nature of arising, and no-
nature of the highest meaning (*xiang sheng shengyi wuxing* 相生勝義無性).
Kōunshi, 1171: "'Lack *svabhāva*' means 'empty of *svabhāva*.'" [無自性者性空也]

279. Anonymous, 259: "those empty names." [佗空名也]

280. See 13.4 for the term *yibian* 依變. The translation here takes *bian* 變 as *nirmita*/
prātihārya ("a magical or supernatural creation; miracle"), but most of the Zen
commentators take it as something like *pariṇāma* ("change" or "transform"
without the implication of magical creation.) Modern translations in general are

also devoid of the implication of magical creation. One Zen commentary, however, does at least suggest the magical element by invoking fictional creation (i.e,
"magical" creation) in the most famous work of classical Japanese literature, the
Genji Monogatari. Myōō, 41: "For example, 'Hikaru Genji' is a person who never
existed. It is like Murasaki Shikibu's sixty-book tale, which depends upon the
Minamoto family for the production of transformation tableaux [i.e., pictures
of fictional scenes] under such rubrics as 'Paulownia Pavilion,' 'Broom Tree,'
etc. These are all human creations and are called 'vishayas that are dependent
[magical] transformations.'" [タトヘ八光源氏ト云ハ元來ナイ人也紫式部ガ六十帖
ノ物語ハ源氏ニ依テ変現メ相(桐)壷掃木等ハ種種ノ名目ノ生スルガ如シ是皆人作
也是ヲ依変ノ境ト云也] Eishu, 375: "The [*Complete*] *Treatise* [*on the Huayan Sutra*
by Li Tongxuan; 華嚴經合論] says: 'As for *yibian* 依變, waves take water as
their basis.'" [論云依変者波浪以水爲依] CBETA, X04, no. 223, p. 13, c5 //Z
1:5, p. 334, a14 //R5, p. 667, a14. Kōunshi, 1172: "It refers to the above [state-
ment] that all mundane and supramundane dharmas are empty names without reality." [佗指上世出世諸法皆是空名無實有] Dōchū, 1318: "As transformed
vishayas that depend upon the original substance, they are without reality."
[依倚本體所變起之境而無實也]

281. Eishu, 375, and Anonymous, 259, clearly understand *bian* 變 as *pariṇāma*
    ("transformation of consciousness"), not *nirmita/prātihārya* ("magical transfor-
    mation; miracle"). Their comment runs: "These are the seven *yibian* 依變. The
    myriad dharmas are transformations of mind." [此七依變也萬法心所變也]

282. Jiang and Cao, eds., *Tang Wudai yuyan cidian* [*Word Dictionary of Tang and
    Five Dynasties Language*], 33, glosses *bu jing* 不淨 (literally "impurity") as
    fenbian 糞便 ("feces; excrement") and cites the Dunhuang transforma-
    tion text entitled *Mahamaudgalyāyana Rescues His Mother from the Nether-
    world* (大目乾連冥間救母変文): "[Maudgalyāyana's mother in the form of a
    black dog says:] 'When I'm hungry, in the latrines I eat human feces; when
    I'm thirsty, I drink the water flowing from the eaves to relieve my thirst.'"
    [飢即于坑中食人不淨渴飲长流以济虚] Kōunshi, 1173: "'*bu jing* 不淨' refers
    to the foulness of the *kleśas* and thought of the unreal. The *tathāgata* spoke
    the eighty-four thousand dharma gates in order to get rid of sentient be-
    ings' eighty-four thousand *kleśa*-feces. 'Obsolete papers' is an expression of
    condemnation."[不淨者指煩惱妄想之汗穢如來說八萬四千法門仚(去)衆生之
    八萬四千煩惱不淨故紙者罵奪之語也]

283. Eishu, 376: "Buddhas are *māyā* bodies without any reality at all, and the patri-
    archs are collapsed old *bhikṣus*." [佛是幻化身真實デハ無イ也祖是老倒比丘也]

284. Eishu, 376: "has the meaning of 'already prepared/finished/ready-made/on
    hand/to be used at any time.'" [現成底ト云義也]

285. Kōunshi, 1173: "This is what is born of a mother." [是娘生已底也]

286. Dōkū, 1035: "This small section eliminates grasping at a *nirmāṇakaya* buddha's
    three kalpa's worth of filling up [karmic] effects." [此一小節遣化佛三祇果滿之執]

287. Kōunshi, 1174: "The *Vajracchedikā Sūtra* [T235.8.752a13–14] says: 'If you take the thirty-two characteristics to view a *tathāgata*, then the wheel-turning noble king is a *tathāgata*.'" [金剛經曰若以三十二相觀如來者轉輪聖王即是如來]

288. Eishu, 377: "The wheel-turning noble king is also a *māyā*." [轉輪聖王モ幻化也] Kassan, 518, and Dōku, 1036: "The thirty-two major characteristics and the eighty minor marks are all *māyās*, unreal characteristics." [三十二相八十種好揔是幻化而非真實相也] Dōchū 1319: "connects with the above [line in 13.9 to effect that] 'buddhas are *māyā* bodies.'" [結上佛是幻化身]

289. Kōunshi, 1175, cites *Liang Dynasty Great Master Fu's Verses on the Vajracchedikā Sūtra* (*Liangchao Fu Dashi song Jingang jing* 梁朝傳大士頌金剛經; T2732.85.2b23–26).

290. Kōunshi, 1175: "The *tathāgata's* form body possessed of the major characteristics and minor marks is not the true form of a buddha. It is just for according with the mental dispositions of the world's mass of beings; the provisional characteristics of *upāyas* for approaching beings." [如來相好具足色身非佛真形唯一應順世界群生機接物方便之假相也]

291. Kōunshi, 1175: "'Annihilationist views' [*uccheda-dṛṣṭi*] are views that deny cause and effect. The Buddha had compassion for people who follow this view and as an *upāya* displayed the thirty-two characteristics and eighty minor marks. They were empty names, mere one-off [unreal] concepts." [斷見者因果撥無之見也佛愍人隨此見權現三十二相八十種好虛名唯一期施設也]

292. Kōunshi, 1176: "The six supernormal powers: [Zongmi's] *Commentary on the Ullambana Sūtra* [T1792.39.507c29–508a5] says: 'The first is the supernormal power over vishayas, because it is supernatural knowledge of vishayas. It is also called the as-one-wishes power, because, as soon as the mind desires to go somewhere, the body arrives. The second is the power of the heavenly eye and the third the power of the heavenly ear, meaning one can see forms or hear sounds, whether near or far, whether inside obstructions or outside obstructions. The fourth is the power of past lives, because one has the capability of knowing events of past births. The fifth is the power of other minds. It means knowing everything about stabilized and dispersed minds, minds with outflows and minds without outflows. The sixth is the power of the exhaustion of the outflows [*āsrava*]. This means that one can know that the outflows have been exhausted in oneself.'" [六通者盂蘭盆疏曰一神境通智證神境故亦名如意通身如其意欲往即到故二天眼通三天耳通謂能見能聞若近若遠障內障外色聲等故四宿命通能知宿世本生本事故五佗心通謂於定散漏無漏心一切能知故六漏盡通謂身中漏盡而能知故]

293. Kōunshi, 1176: "*da li gui* 大力鬼 ['demons of great strength']: "The *Commentary on the Golden Light Sutra* [T1785.39.79b22] says: 'Those of great strength can move mountains and stop up seas; those of small strength can work miracles such as disappearing and appearing.'" [大力鬼者光明疏曰大力者能移山填海小力者能隱顯變化]

294. Kōunshi, 1177, cites the story of the *asuras* and Indra as given in the *Pearl Grove of the Dharma Garden* (*Fayuan zhulin* 法苑珠林; T2122.53.310a29–b8): "[Indra took as a wife a daughter of the king of the *asuras* but in time neglected her. Her father became very angry. With his four great armies he attacked Indra, shaking Indra's castle Sudarśana and Mt. Sumeru. Indra became terrified.] At that time in the palace there was a spirit who said to the heavenly king [Indra]: 'Do not be terrified. In the past the Buddha spoke the *Prajñāpāramitā* [*Sūtra*]. The king should chant it, and the demon soldiers will be smashed.' At that time Indra sat in the Good Dharma Hall, burned bundles of renowned incense, and made a great vow, [reciting the *Heart Sutra*]: 'The *prajñāpāramitā* is the incantation of great enlightenment, is the unexcelled incantation, is the equal-to-the-unequaled incantation, true and not false. I will hold this dharma and complete the Buddha Way, making the *asuras* spontaneously retreat and disperse.' As he spoke these words, there was in the sky a great sword wheel. Because of Indra's merit, it spontaneously descended upon the *asuras*. At that time the *asura* ears, noses, hands, and feet were simultanously lopped off, making the great sea as red as a clam's pearl. At that time the *asuras* were terrified. Having no place to run to, they entered into a single pore of a fiber of a lotus root." [. . . . 時宮有神白天王言莫大驚怖過去佛說般若波羅蜜王當誦持鬼兵自碎是時帝釋坐善法堂燒衆名香發大誓願般若波羅蜜是大明呪是無上呪是無等等呪審實不虛我持此法當成佛道令阿修羅自然退散作是語時於虛空中有刀輪帝釋功德故自然而下當阿修羅上時阿修羅耳鼻手足一時盡落令大海水赤如蟀珠時阿修羅即便驚怖遁走無處入藕絲孔]

295. See **10.5**. Kassan, 521: "*yetong* 業通 [*karma-ṛddhi*] is to obtain supernormal powers through the perfomance of karman and ripening of [karmic] fruits. This is called 'supernormal powers of karman.' [An example is] the story of the young girl whose spirit and body became separated, [the spirit marrying and the real one lying on her sick bed]. [Other examples include]: Think of Avalokiteśvara and your mind arrives at Poṭalaka; think of Maitreya and you are sitting up in the Tuṣita Heaven. These are all due to karman-power thought—one provisionally sees the existence of characteristics. *yitong* 依通 [*ṛddhi-prātihārya*] is the supernormal power of transformation grounded in that thing. [As the *Śūraṃgama Sūtra* (T945.19.131a26–28) says:] 'It is like a mundane, skillful conjurer who by sleight-of-hand creates [illusionary] boys and girls. Even though [the audience] sees their bodies move, there must be an artifice to it.' In the end, [such things] are not independent, real supernormal power. This small section eliminates grasping at the six supernormal powers of a *nirmāṇakāya* buddha." [業通者由行業純熟果得通力謂之業通亦是倩女離魂等或念觀音則心到補陀思彌勒則坐上兜率此皆由業力思念假見有相也依通者体倚那物而變通也譬如世巧幻師幻作諸男女雖見諸根動要以一機抽也畢竟非獨脫真箇神通也此一小節遣化佛六通之執也] Dōchū, 1320: "The *Commentary on the Abhidharma-kośa Verses* [T1823.41.869b9–10] says: '. . . .

Supernormal powers obtained through karman are called *yetong* 業通.'" [俱舍頌疏曰. . . . 通由業得名爲業通] On *yitong* 依通 Dōchū, 1320, quotes the *Treasure Storehouse Treatise* [*Baozang lun* 寶藏論; T1857.45.147b5–7], which describes five supernormal powers (the third being *yitong* 依通): "What is *yitong* 依通? [It includes such things as:] knowledge of the [magical] arts; uses of the physical body; going and coming by the use of magical drawings/charms; and magical transformations through alchemical recipes—these are *yitong*依通." [何謂依通約法而知緣身而用乘符往來藥餌靈變此爲依通] Kōunshi, 1177: "*yetong* 業通 is the supernormal power of karmic reward obtained through the power of actions 'I' have performed. . . . *yitong* 依通 is the supernormal power to make things manifest themselves as in the art of a conjurer." [業通者依我行業力所得業報之通也. . . . 依通者依物而現通如幻術]

296. Kōunshi, 1177: "It is like entering the forest without making the foliage move, entering the water without stirring up waves." [如入林不動艸入水不立波]

297. Kōunshi, 1178: "refers to the form body as a collection of the five *skandhas*." [指五蘊積聚色身]

298. Eishu, 380, and Anonymous, 264: "The *Zongjinglu* says: 'Lifting the feet and putting down the feet in all cases are a supernormal power, etc.'" [宗鏡録云舉足下足皆是神通云云] Actuallly, the *Zongjinglu* (T2016.48.956c17–18) says: "Lifting the feet and putting down the feet in all cases are not apart from the one mind, *tathatā*, and the range of the buddhas." [舉足下足皆不離一心真如諸佛行處矣] Anonymous, 264: "As to the supernormal power of earth-walking, every person is endowed with it." [地行神通人人具足] Kōunshi, 1178: "Earth-walkers are not yet capable of flying. The *Śūraṃgama Sūtra* [T945.19.145c1–4] . . . has an earth-walking immortal." [地行者未能飛行也楞嚴 . . . 有地行仙] Dōchū, 1320: "Although it does not involve flying in the sky, it can be called a supernormal power. The phrase *dixing* 地行 ['earth-walking'] comes from the *Śūraṃgama Sūtra*, but here does not necessarily assume the sutra's meaning." [雖不虛空飛行而可稱神通也地行字出于楞嚴而不必取經義] The *Śūraṃgama Sūtra* passage to which the Zen commentators are referring (T945.19.145c1–15) runs: "Ānanda! There are also those who cultivate *samādhi* without being grounded in correct awakening. Separately they cultivate false thoughts. They preserve their thoughts and make firm their bodies, roaming in the mountains and forests. There are ten types of immortals in places where people do not go. Ānanda! [The first of the ten is] those sentient beings who are firmly [committed to] ingesting cinnabar without taking any breaks. When their 'Way of Eating' is perfected, they are called 'earth-walking immortals.' . . . Ānanda! These [ten types] among men refine their minds but do not follow correct awakening. Separately they may obtain a lifespan of a thousand or ten-thousand years. They hole up in deep mountains or on islands in the great seas, cut off from the realm of men. But for them the wheel [of samsara] still turns, and false thought flows onward—they do not cultivate *samādhi*. When their karmic reward is

exhausted, they will come back to reenter the various rebirth paths." [阿難復
有從人不依正覺修三摩地別修妄念存想固形遊於山林人不及處有十仙種阿
難彼諸衆生堅固服餌而不休息食道圓成名地行仙. . . . 阿難是等皆於人中鍊
心不循正覺別得生理壽千萬歲休止深山或大海島絕於人境斯亦輪迴妄想
流轉不修三昧報盡還來散入諸趣]

299. See 10.8. Kōunshi, 1178: "Since the true buddha is formless and the true
dharma without characteristics, why would you create calculations and
conjectures on top of *māyās* made up of forms and characteristics?"
[真佛無形真法無相何向有形有相幻化上作計較卜度]

300. Kōunshi, 1178: "taking a fish eye as a bright pearl or recognizing a tangerine
skin as a fierce fire." [將魚目作明珠認橘皮作猛火]

301. Kassan, 523: "refers to conditioned good fortune, etc." [指有爲之福相等也]
Dōchū, 1321: "excellent karmic recompense in the [realms of] desire, form, and
formlessness." [欲色無色殊勝之果報也]

302. Eishu, 380: "vast as the great sky . . . walking in solitariness." [迥然太虛廓然也 . . .
独脱独歩也] Anonymous, 264, has the first part.

303. Kōunshi, 1178: "Sengzhao's *Things Do Not Change* [T1858.45.151c26–27] says:
'Heaven and earth could be overturned, and there would be no saying that there
is unquiet; floods could gush over heaven, and there would be no saying that
there is movement.'" [肇公物不遷論曰乾坤倒覆無謂不靜洪流滔天無謂其動]

304. Kassan, 523: "In the end, the one who has no perplexity, delight, or terror
will not get discombobulated." [畢竟無疑喜怖者不受惑也] Kōunshi, 1178:
"He enters the hells as if strolling through a garden. As to 'three paths,'
the [*Collection of Translation*] *Terms and Meanings* [T2131.54.1092a23–24] . . .
quotes the *Four Liberations Sutra:* 'The hell [path] is called the fire path. The
preta [path] is called the sword path. The animal [path] is called the blood path.'"
[入地獄如遊園觀三塗者(翻譯)名義(集) . . . 曰按四解脱經云地獄名火塗道
餓鬼名刀塗道畜生名血塗道]

305. Eishu, 380–381: "When the one mind transforms, it becomes the conditioned dharmas. When the one mind does not transform, it is an unconditioned dharma. When the one mind transforms, the various dharmas arise.
When the one mind does not transform, not even one single vishaya or one
single dharma exists." [一心ガ変バ有爲法トナリ一心ガ不変無爲法也一心
ガ変バ種種法生也一心ガ不変一塵一法モ無イ也] Kōunshi,1179:"According to
the scholars of the teachings, 'transforming' is the gate of arising-disappearing,
and 'no transforming' is the gate of *tathatā*. This is extensively [explained in]
the *Awakening of Faith* [T1666.32.576a5–6ff.]." [據教家則變即生滅門不變即真
如門廣如起信論] Dōkū, 1038: "'When [the one mind] transforms, there is
[seeming] existence' is like 'the advancing [*pravṛtti*] of the conditioned [aspect]
of *tathatā*'; 'when [the one mind] does not transform' means 'no advancing.'
This conforms to scholastic categories." [變即有者譬如真如之隨緣者流轉不
變者不流轉是準教相也] Myōō, 44: "When 'my' mind transforms, then things

exist; when mind does not transform, then things do not exist." [我心ガ変ズレ
ハ即物アリ心ガ変セザレハ即物ナシ] Dōchū, 1321: "When causes and con-
ditions come together, dharmas arise. When causes and conditions join, in
the midst of no-characteristics 'transforming' arises as a 'seeming existence.'
When there is no coming together of causes and conditions, the no-characteristics original substance 'does not transform,' and, therefore, 'there is none.'"
[諸法因緣會遇而生苟因緣合時無相中變起似有也若無因緣會時無相本體不
變起故無也]

306. Dōkū, 1038: "'Mind-only' means 'the eighth consciousness'; 'consciousness'
refers to all eight consciousnesses concurrently." [唯心者言第八識也識
者總兼八識云也]

307. Eishu, 381: "Both the three realms and the myriad dharmas are all *māyās*, 'flowers'
in the sky. They all arise from the one mind." [三界モ万法モ尽多幻空花也尽一
心カラ起也]

308. Kōunshi, 1180, cites the italicized portion of this *Śūraṃgama Sūtra* passage
(T945.19.137a16–19): "Ānanda! I will now for you again speak this mantra. It
protects the world and obtains the great fearlessness. It brings to completion
the supramundane wisdom of sentient beings. If, after I extinguish, sentient
beings of the end time have the capability of reciting it, and teach others to
recite it, you should know that reciting in that way will uphold those sentient
beings—*fire will not be able to burn them, and water will not be able to drown
them*. Neither great poison nor small poison will be able to harm them."
[阿難我今爲汝更説此呪救護世間得大無畏成就衆生出世間智若我滅後末世
衆生有能自誦若教他誦當知如是誦持衆生火不能燒水不能溺大毒小毒
所不能害] Dōkū, 1039, gives citations for three sutras: "The *Śūraṃgama Sūtra*
[T945.19.137a18–19] . . . : 'Fire will not be able to burn them, and water will
not be able to drown them.' Also, the *Lotus Sutra* [T262.9.54c10–11] . . . : 'Fire
will not be able to burn, and water will not be able to wash away.' *Lotus Sutra* [T262.9.15c29–16a1] . . . : 'Constantly abide in the hells as though enjoying
a garden viewing; exist in the other bad rebirth paths as though in your own
home.'" [楞嚴 . . . 火不能燒水不能溺又法華 . . . 火不能燒水不能漂法華 . . .
常處地獄如遊園觀在餘惡道如己舍宅] Kōunshi, 1180, also gives three sutra cita-
tions: "The *Lotus Sutra* [T262.9.15c29–16a1] . . . says: 'Constantly abide in the hells as
though enjoying a garden viewing.' The *Vimalakīrti Sūtra* [T475.14.554b14–15] . . .
says: 'Be in the various *dhyānas* as though in thoughts of the hells; in the
midst of samsara as though in thoughts of garden viewing.' The *Huayan Sutra*
[T279.10.296c10–11] . . . says: 'Coming and going in samsara as though enjoying
a garden viewing, never even briefly producing a mind of weariness.'" [法華 . . .
曰常處地獄如遊園觀維摩 . . . 曰在諸禪定如地獄想於生死中如園觀想華嚴 . . .
曰往來生死如遊園觀未曾暫起疲獸之心]

309. Kassan, 528: "Because there is no dharma to be abhorred, there is also no
dharma to be liked." [無嫌底法故亦無好底法也] Kōunshi, 1180, is very similar.

310. Found in the *Record of the Transmission of the Lamp of the Jingde Era* (*Jingde chuandeng lu* 景德傳燈錄, T2076.51.449b11–13. Eishu, 381: "From false mind the *kleśas* arise. False mind is the mind of thought of the unreal [*abhūta-vikalpa*]." [妄心カラ煩惱ハ起也妄心妄想心也] Kōunshi, 1180, cites two sutras: "The *Huayan Sutra* [T279.10.66a21] . . . says: 'Discrimination and the seizing of characteristics is not seeing the Buddha. To be free of attachment is to be able to see.' The *Vimalakīrti Sūtra* [T476.14.557b2–3] . . . says: 'Even though understanding the deep dharma, nevertheless to seize characteristics and [engage in] discrimination is a dualistic teaching.'" [華嚴 . . . 曰分別取相不見佛離著乃能見維摩 . . . 曰雖解深法而取相分別是爲二法]

311. Eishu, 382: "*conglin* 叢林 ['grove of trees'] in Sanskrit is *vana*. . . . A place where monks collect has gotten the name 'grove of trees.' . . . In the *Glossary of the Patriarchal Courtyard* (*Zuting shi yuan* 祖庭事苑) *chuangjiaotou* 牀角頭 means 'platform in the Sangha Hall.' . . . *jiaojiao zuo* 交脚坐 is full cross-legged sitting or half cross-legged sitting." [叢林梵語貧婆那. . . . 僧聚処得名叢林云云. . . . 事苑牀角頭ト ハ僧堂床也. . . . 交脚坐者結跏趺坐或半跏趺坐也] The *Glossary of the Patriarchal Courtyard* does state: "In the [Sangha] Hall there is an array of long '*chuang* 牀' [堂布長牀] CBETA, X64, no. 1261, p. 430, b2 //Z 2:18, p. 117, d14 //R113, p. 234, b14. Kōunshi, 1180: "*conglin* 叢林 designates a great monastery." [叢林者巨刹稱也]

312. Eishu, 382, and Anonymous, 267: "The meaning is 'when the rituals of courtesy of the meeting of guest and host have been completed.'" [賓主相見之礼了義]

313. Eishu, 382, and Anonymous, 267: "words of the student." [學人語也]

314. Eishu, 382, and Anonymous, 267: "*qiantou* 前頭 means 'general discussion.'" [前頭ハ總論也] Dōchū, 1323: "*qiantou* 前頭 means 'in front of the face of the student." [前頭者學人之面前義]

315. Eishu, 382: "*jiquan yulu* 机權語路 means 'a slightly difficult, troublesome, or tortuous question, a question with all sorts of differentiations.'" [机權語路ト ハ コムツカシイ問也種種差別問也]

316. Eishu, 382: "*xiang koujiaotou* 向口角頭 means 'face to face.' . . . *cuanguo* 攛過. . . . means 'flung to test a person.'" [向口角頭者對面之義也. . . . 攛過. . . . 放出驗人也] Anonymous, 267, and Dōkū, 1040, are very similar. Dōchū, 1323: "'You' refers to the teacher." [你指善知識也] This line expresses the student's mental calculation. Most modern translations end the student's quotation at this point.

317. Eishu, 382: "'You' refers to the master." [你師家ヲ指也] Kassan, 528, glosses *ni* 你 as: "the host." [主也] Most modern translations take this "you" as Linji's addressing his sangha as an aside. However, as this entire sentence expresses strategy and calculation (*niyi* 擬議), it is unlikely to be anything the LJL would endorse. So, this translation has followed Eishu and Kassan in taking this "you" as the master/host in this dialogue; and therefore has treated this line as a continuation of the student's thoughts to himself, with the "you" constituting a rather impertinent form of address toward the master.

318. Kassan, 528: "'Vishaya' is 'unreal.'" [境者不真實也] Dōkū, 1040: "'Vishaya' is 'terms and verbal phrases, etc.'" [境者名相言句等]

319. Kōunshi, 1181: "The host, knowing that it is a good-for-nothing gimmick vishaya, will snatch it away and throw it into the land of non-arising—he won't fall into 'his trap.'" [主家識得是閑機境奪卻抛向無生國裏不落他圈繢] This translation ends the student's quotation here.

320. Kassan, 528: "His spirit has no fluctuation, and he doesn't take any action whatsoever." [氣概平穩少無動轉也] Dōkū, 1040, is very similar. Eishu, 382, and Anonymous, 267: "*xunchang* 尋常 means that the student takes no action." [尋常學人不動轉義也]

321. Dōkū, 1040: "This Han takes his time and slowly presents one more inquiry." [這漢不忙緩緩地再呈問話] "Slowly" [*huanhuan* 緩緩] implies "dithering" [*niyi* 擬議]. Dōchū, 1324: "An ancient says: 'one more inquiry.'" [古德曰再問也]

322. See section **10.1**. Eishu, 382: "The master, as before, instantly rips it away." [師家也如前ヤガテ奪也] Dōchū, 1324: "An ancient says: 'It is classified under the rubric "one more shout."'" [古德曰再喝之類]

323. Kōunshi, 1181: "The *Vimalakīrti Sūtra* [T475.14.541b29–c1] . . . says: 'Superior insight! This is something [the Buddha's disciple] Upāli did not reach to.'" [維摩 . . . 曰上智哉是優波離所不及]

324. Eishu, 382, adds *shijia* 師家 ("the master") and *xueren ye* 学人也 ("the student") in small characters connected by lines to the root text—the former to *ji* 即 and the latter to *ni* 你.

325. Eishu, 382: "a testing of the student by the master." [師家ヨリ学者ヲ験也] Kassan, 529, and Dōkū, 1040: "'Wad of vishayas' means '*upāya* words and phrases.'" [境塊子者機權等言句] Myōō, 46: "In 'wad of vishayas' [the term] 'vishayas' means 'verbal phrases.'" [境塊子トハ境トハ言句也] Kōunshi, 1181: "'Wad of vishayas' is 'the language-road of *upāyas*.'" [境塊子者機權之語路也]

326. Eishu, 382, Anonymous, 268, and Kōunshi, 1181: "*qianren* 前人 is 'student.'" [前人學者也] Kassan, 529: "*qianren* 前人 is 'the student who comes before him.'" [前人者前來學人也] Dōkū, 1040, is very similar.

327. The *Mahīśāsaka-vinaya* (彌沙塞部和醯五分律; T1421.22.22a2–8) says: "Thereupon Maudgalyāyana displayed magical transformations. He divided his body into a hundred thousand pieces and united it back into one. He went completely through stone walls and walked on water as if on land. He sat and lay in the sky like a soaring bird. His body arrived at the Brahma Heaven, and his hands touched the sun and moon. His upper body emitted fire, and his lower body emitted water. His upper body emitted water, and his lower body emitted fire. Sometimes he displayed a half-body, and sometimes he displayed a whole body. The east surged, and the west disappeared. The west surged, and the east disappeared. The south surged, and the north disappeared. The north surged, and the south disappeared. The center surged, and the perimeter disappeared. The perimeter surged, and

the center disappeared. Having displayed these magical transformations, he again sat down at his original spot." [於是目連爲現神變分身百千還合爲一石壁皆過履水如地坐臥空中如鳥飛翔身至梵天手捫日月身上出火身下出水身上出水身下出火或現半身或現全身東踊西沒西踊東沒南踊北沒北踊南沒中踊邊沒邊踊中沒現神變已還坐本處]

328. Dōchū, 1324: "topple into confusion." [打亂也] Dōkū, 1041: "'All manner of verbal expresssions' means 'all the language and phrases of the buddhas and patriarchs.'" [差別語路者一切佛祖語句等也]

329. Kassan, 530: "Bad teachers are not able to handle their bandit questions and give verbal explanations of doctrinal points—the understanding of a Seat Master." [惡知識不辨他賊問而隨語說義成座主解會也] Kōunshi, 1182: "They fall into the level of understanding of a Seat Master, [engaging in] the kudzu of the sutras and treatises and talking rubbish." [落在座主見解上經論葛藤上胡説亂説]

330. Iriya, 94.6: "*luzhu* 露柱 is probably the pillar standing in the front garden of a Sangha Hall or Dharma Hall. Because there is a line in the *Record of the Transmission of the Lamp* that runs "hanging a lamp on the open-air [*Jingde chuandeng lu* 景德傳燈錄: 露柱掛燈籠; T2076.51.396a27]," it seems to have been a pillar providing illumination at night." Zengo, 484: "*luzhu* 露柱 appears often in the Chan sayings records, but we don't really know exactly what it was. Surmising from the Chinese characters, it seems to have been a stone or wooden pillar in the open air outside a building. In our opinion, it probably stood in the front garden or at the foot of the steps of a Dharma Hall or Sangha Hall and bore some sort of carved inscription. In the sayings records there are a lot of instances in which it is referred to as a symbol of 'non-sentient thing,' 'the cutting off of knowledge and feelings,' and 'the apperception of reality without obscuration.'" Kassan, 530: "It is merely that ignorant Chanists fervently like to use such phrases as 'lantern,' 'open-air,' 'tortoise hair,' 'rabbit horn,' 'stone woman,' etc., as Chan talk, but without understanding Chan principle." [但痴禪者一向好用燈籠露柱龜毛兔角石女兒等言説為之禪話而不會禪理]

331. Eishu, 383: "Eyebrow hairs fall out for the crime of false speech." [眉鬚墮落八妄語ノ罪也] Kassan, 530: "It is just because of thought of the unreal and careless talk about the buddhadharma that eyebrow hairs must fall out." [只以妄想心胡亂説話佛法必須眉鬚墮落也] Dōkū, 1041, and Kōunshi, 1182, are similar.

332. These ellipsis points represent the line *zhe ge ju jiyuan* 這箇具機緣 ("these possess karmic connection") for which the Zen commentators (Eishu, 383; Kassan, 530; Myōō, 46; and Dōkū, 1041) have produced something like: "These [bad teachers] possess an old karmic connection [with the students from a previous birth, and so today there is a rapport between them]." Dōchū, 1325: "This old interpretation [i.e., the above interpretation] is completely wrong. *zhe ge* 這箇 ['this'] is the *great matter* of this section." [忠曰古解大非也. . . . 這箇者此一段大事也] None of the commentators is satisfactory. The line is

almost certainly a later comment that has come to be embedded in the text—hence the ellipsis points. Iriya, 94.8 glosses *zhe ge ju jiyuan* 這箇具機緣 as: "This line makes no sense in this context. It can be regarded as a comment written in by a later person that was mistakenly mingled with the text itself." Yanagida, 138: "This line is extremely difficult to understand. Various exegeses were carried out in the past, but we can consent to none of them. . . . or is it the mixing in of a later person's comment?"

333. Eishu, 383, and Anonymous, 268: "Heterodox masters disseminate heterodox theories, and so students, not understanding, come to adore them." [邪師演邪説故学人不會却心狂也]

334. Eishu, 383: "refers to the bad teachers mentioned above." [上云惡知識ヲ指口云也] Dōkū, 1041, and Kōunshi, 1182, are similar.

335. Eishu, 383, and Anonymous, 269: "*jingmei* 精魅 are mountain spirits, and *wangliang* 魍魎 are water spirits." [精魅山神也魍魎水神也] Dōkū, 1041, and Kōunshi, 1182, are similar. Dōchū, 1325: "*wangliang* 魍魎 are mountain and river spirits." [魍魎山川精物] Kōunshi, 1182, glosses *wangliang* 魍魎 as: "[Zhiyǐ's] *Cessation and Discernment* [T1911.46.66c24] . . . says: 'The *Lotus Sutra* [T262.9.14a3] says: *chimei* 魑魅 and *wangliang* 魍魎 are everywhere.'" [法華云魑魅魍魎處處皆有]

336. Two of the Zen commentators are struck by the canonical erudition evinced in LJL: Kōunshi, 1182: "I have researched this record, and, even though not a word or half a line falls into the theories of the scholiasts, nevertheless, the deep purport of all the Mahāyāna sutras can be seen clearly therein. The Master Linji indeed broadly cultivated the three baskets of the Buddhist canon." [余考此錄雖一言半句不落教家說然諸大乘經深旨粲然可見師博頤三藏誠矣] Dōchū, 1325: "As to [Linji's statement that he had in past days] 'inquired into the sutras and treatises,' when one reads the *Sangha Instructions* section of this record, its broad erudition is evident." [於經論尋討者讀此錄示衆可知其博綜也] For a pre-Song Linji episode that connects Linji to scholasticism—in particular, the *Yoga Treatise* (*Yogacārabhūmi-śāstra*; T1579)—see Appendix 1, n. 5.

337. Dōchū, 1325: "medical prescriptions in response to the diseases of the *kleśas*." [應煩惱病之方藥也]

338. Eishu, 384, and Dōkū, 1042: "dropped the sutras, *vinaya*, and treatises." [放却經律論也]

339. Dōchū, 1326: "a concealed reference to Huangbo and Dayu." [暗謂黃檗大愚等也]

340. Dōchū, 1326: "means 'innate knowledge that does not rely upon practice.'" [謂生知而不假修行也]

341. Kōunshi, 1183: "*tijiu* 體究 means 'personal investigation of *this matter*'; *lianmo* 練磨 means 'smelting and cultivating the mind.'" [體究者體明究竟此事之義也練磨者鍛煉燒磨修練其心之義也] Eishu, 384, and Dōkū, 1042, are similar. Kassan, 531: "'One morning' refers to coinciding with the Way all at once." [一朝者指投機一時也] Chitetsu, 783: "'Awoke one

dawn' is the World-honored-one's awakening to the Way when the bright star came out." [一朝自省世尊悟道明星出時]

342. Eishu, 384, Anonymous, 270, and Kōunshi, 1183: "'Beholding according to dharma' is 'beholding of reality as it truly is.'" [如法見解真正見解也] Chitetsu, 783, is similar.

343. Dōkū, 1042: "'Discombobulated by persons' refers to the bad teachings of heterodox masters." [人惑者邪師之教壞也]

344. Eishu, 384: "'Inside' means 'inside the mind'; 'outside' means 'vishayas on the outside.' These are the internal Māras and external Māras. 'Meet' means 'giving rise to thoughts.' 'Kill' means 'sever the thoughts that have arisen.'" [裏心中外境外也内魔外魔也逢著ト ハ生念ヲ云殺ト ハ所生之念ヲ截レ也] Kassan, 531: "Inside, outside, and in between [you must] not set up a single thing—this is the meaning of 'kill.'" [内外中間不立一物此即殺之義也] Dōchū, 1326: "With internal mind and external vishayas not to continue thoughts is called 'killing.' 'Killing a buddha' is not to continue [the notion of] a buddha view. 'Killing the patriarchs' is not to continue the [notion of a] Zen-adept level of understanding. 'Killing an arhat' is not to continue the [notion of a] *śrāvaka* level of understanding. 'Killing the mother' is not to continue *avidyā* and passion. 'Killing relatives' is to discontinue all of the *kleśas*." [於内心外境不續念是名殺也殺佛不續佛見也殺祖不續禪子見解也殺羅漢不續聲聞見解也殺父母不續無明貪愛也殺親屬不續一切煩惱也] Anonymous, 270: "towards the internal, the external, and the in between not to preserve a single thing." [向内外中間不存一物也] Kōunshi, 1183: "'Inside' means 'in one thought-moment.' 'Outside' means 'all external vishayas, terms, written phrases, etc.' 'Kill' means 'cut off the thought [of something] at the moment of encountering it.'" [裏者一念心上也外者一切外境名相文句等也殺者截斷逢著之當念也] LJL did not invent this antinomian-sounding theme—it is common in the Mahāyāna sutras. The *Mahāprajñāpāramitā Sūtra* [T220.7.987c23–28] says: "If you are able to hear the very deep principle of this *prajñāpāramitā*, have confidence in it, hold it, intone it, and practice it, even if you killed all of the sentient beings gathered into the three realms, you would not fall again into the hells, or the animal and *preta* rebirth paths. Thereby you could subdue all the *kleśas* and minor *kleśas*, bad karman, etc., and you would be constantly reborn into good rebirths and receive surpassing, wonderful joy. Practicing the bodhisattva-great being practice, you would quickly realize unexcelled, perfect awakening." [大般若波羅密多經: 若有得聞如是般若波羅蜜多甚深理趣信解受持讀誦修習假使殺害三界所攝一切有情而不由斯復墮於地獄傍生鬼界以能調伏一切煩惱及隨煩惱惡業等故常生善趣受勝妙樂修諸菩薩摩訶薩行疾證無上正等菩提] More common in the sutras is glossing "killling" as "killing the notion of" (as our Zen commentaries on LJL do): The *Treasure-Heap Sutra* [T310.11.588b19–26] says: "Mañjuśrī says: 'Devaputra! Therefore, I say you right now should kill any notion of a self, kill any notion of people, kill any notion of sentient beings, kill

any notion of life duration, up to and including extinguishing any notion of names, etc. . . . This is called the true killing of all sentient beings.'" [大寶積經: 文殊師利言天子是故我言汝今當須殺害我想殺害人想殺衆生想殺壽命想乃至滅除名字等想. . . . 是名真殺一切衆生] The *Questions of Susthitamati Sūtra* [T341.12.130c7–10]: "Mañjuśrī said, 'It is thus, Devaputra. Kill the notion of a self, kill the notion of living, kill the notion of a hero.' Devaputra asks: 'Sir, with what do I kill the notion of living?' Mañjuśrī answers: 'Devaputra, kill with the weapon of wisdom.'" [聖善住意天子所問經: 文殊師利言如是天子殺取我想殺取命想取丈夫想天子問言仁以何物殺取命想文殊師利答言天子以慧鐵殺]

345. Dōkū, 1042: "Buddhas, patriarchs, and arhats are the most honored of the supramundane. The one who 'kills' them abstains from grasping at them. Fathers, mothers, and relatives are the most honored of the mundane. One who 'kills' them abstains from loving attachment to them." [佛祖羅漢者出世間最尊貴之者殺之者忌其執著父母親眷者世間最尊貴之者殺之者忌其愛著大凡真正道流脫情捐累] Kōunshi, 1183: "As for 'attaining liberation,' the *Vimalakīrti Sūtra* [T475.14.540b25] . . . says: 'Take the five crimes to attain liberation.'" [得解脫者維摩 . . . 以五逆相而得解脫方是也]

346. Kōunshi, 1183: "'Things' refers to terms and words like 'buddha,' 'patriarch,' etc., and beyond that to each and every thing." [物者上佛祖等名相言句其外一切頭頭物物也]

347. Eishu, 384, and Anonymous, 270: "'Things' means 'knowledge.'" [物ト ハ知解ヲ云也] Myōō, 47: "'Relying on things' means 'harden/tighten/congeal into thingness.'" [依物ト ハ事ニ固ムヲ云也] Dōkū, 1042: "In general, it is getting hung up on those good-for-nothing gimmick vishayas." [總是滯在他閑機境者也]

348. Eishu, 384, and Anonymous, 270: "Whack both 'self' and 'other'; ['whack'] is 'rip away' or 'sever.'" [自他共打也奪義也截斷也]

349. Eishu, 384, and Anonymous, 270: "*shoushang* 手上 ['with their hands'] means 'a performance done with the hands, perhaps lifting up the sitting mat or standing erect the tin staff, etc.'" [手上ハ手デスルワザ也或提起坐具或卓錫等也] Kassan, 531, and Dōkū, 1042: "perhaps lifting up the sitting mat or giving a shake to the tin staff, etc." [或提起坐具或振錫一下等] Kōunshi, 1183: "perhaps clapping the hands or holding the fingers vertically; perhaps lifting up the sitting mat, picking up the stick, holding the flywhisk upright, etc."' [或拍手竪指或提起坐具拈搥竪拂等]

350. Eishu, 384, and Anonymous, 270: "*kouli* 口裡 ['in their mouths'] means 'verbal phrases.'" [口裡言句也] Kassan, 532: "As for the one who crops up with verbal phrases, the teacher brings him under control vis-à-vis his verbal phrases." [以言句為是出來底者師亦於言句上調伏之] Dōkū, 1042: "crops up playing with strange words and wonderful phrases." [弄奇言妙句出來等]

351. Eishu, 384, and Anonymous, 270: "raising the eyebrows and winking the eyes." [揚眉瞬目] Kassan, 532, and Dōkū, 1042: "perhaps recognizing

raising the eyebrows and winking the eyes as correct." [或認揚眉瞬目爲是] Kōunshi, 1183, is similar. Dōchū, 1327: "*shoushang* 手上 means 'opening up the two hands, holding the fingers vertically, clapping the hands, lifting up the sitting implement, etc.' *kouli* 口裏 means 'words and phrases, making a hissing sound, clenching the teeth, knocking the teeth together, etc.' *yan-li* 眼裏 means 'opening and closing the eyes, staring, winking, or watching from top to bottom, etc.' They are all coming in dependence on something." [手上者展兩手豎指拍手提起坐具等口裏者言句噓噓聲咬齒扣齒等眼裏者以目開合瞠目瞬目或直上直下覰等皆依倚物來也]

352. Eishu, 385, and Anonymous, 270: "'Solitary liberation' is 'not depending on anything.' It is the non-dependent Way-person." [独脱不依倚也無依道人也]

353. Dōkū, 1042, and Kōunshi, 1183: "They come bringing the oral teachings of the buddhas and patriarchs, the old [Zen] *kōans*." [將佛祖言教古則公案來底也]

354. Anonymous, 270: "Lower your voice, lower your voice—the walls have ears!" [低聲低聲墻壁有耳]

355. Kōunshi, 1183–1184: "'Curing illness' is 'curing the illness of no confidence.'" [治病者治不信病也] He cites the *Huayan*, *Lotus*, and *Vimalakīrti Sūtras*.

356. The *Glossary of the Patriarchal Courtyard* (*Zuting shi yuan* 祖庭事苑) for its *shangliang* 商量 entry says: "The term *shangliang* 商量 is like the bargaining or haggling of merchants." [商量如商賈之量度] CBETA, X64, no. 1261, p. 318, c5 //Z 2:18, p. 6, b18 //R113, p. 11, b18.

357. Kōunshi, 1184: "'Ten years, five years' means 'unrestricted number.'" [十年五歲者非限數]

358. Eishu, 385: "*pretas* in the vast wilds." [曠野餓鬼等也] Kassan, 532: "The fine energy of the minute outpouring of *avidyā* and the *kleśas* comes to take form as dependent beings—it is a type of spirit." [無明煩惱微細流注精氣依物成形魍魎類也] Dōchū, 1327: "Students come who are dependent upon the ancients' schemes and models. Theirs is not a solitary liberation proceeding from their own hearts and minds, and so they are like the demons who attach to grasses and trees." [依古人作略模樣學來非從自己胷襟獨脱來故如精魅附託草木者也] Myōō, 48: "refers to intermediate-state [*antarā-bhava*] spirits." [中有ノ精靈ヲ云也]

359. Eishu, 385, and Anonymous, 271: "refers to the fact that the verbal phrases of the buddhas and patriarchs are called 'clods of dung.'" [指佛祖言句曰糞塊也] Dōkū, 1042: "All the time they are chewing on the good-for-nothing terms and words of the buddhas and patriarchs." [只管咬嚼佛祖閑名言等]

360. Non-Chan materials cast some light on this term, which is often derogatory. Luo and others, eds., *Hanyu da cidian* [*Great Word Dictionary of Sinitic*], 6.48b, cites the *Notes of the Hermitage of the Old Scholar Full of Learning* (*Laoxue an biji* 老学庵筆記, 3) by the Song Dynasty figure Lu You 陆游: "Today's people call a guy of low status a 'Han.'" [今人謂賤丈夫曰漢子] Also, Xu Shaofeng, ed., *Jian-ming Hanyu suyu cidian* [*Concise Dictionary of Sinitic Common Sayings*] (Beijing: Zhonghua shuju, 2007), 532, has the following saying: "When a blind Han

leaps a ditch, he just looks in front." [瞎漢跳渠只看前面] The pun is *qianmian* 前面 ("in front") = *qianmian* 錢面 ("money aspect"). It appears in the *Qujiang Pond* (*Qujiang chi* 曲江池) by Shi Junbao 石君宝 of the Yuan Dynasty.

361. This is another allusion to the story of Yajñadatta in the *Śuraṃgama Sūtra*.

362. Eishu, 385: "The meaning is 'each and every thing is the true buddha.'" [頭頭物物真佛ゾト云義也] Dōkū, 1042: "Each person is complete; each one is perfect." [人人具足箇箇圓成]

363. Dōkū, 1042: "The Master fears that students, upon hearing criticism of external seeking, will come to acknowledge the internal. Therefore, he says 'even the internal is ungraspable mentally.'" [師恐學者聞斥外求而又認内故云内亦不可得] Kōunshi, 1184: "The *Vimalakīrti Sūtra* [T475.14.541b19–20] . . . says: 'Mind is not in the internal, not in the external, and not in the middle.'" [心亦不在内不在外不在中間]

364. Dōkū, 1043: "The Master makes this statement because he also fears that students will be fixated by the [above] statement that the internal and external are not mentally graspable." [師又恐學者認取内外不可得之話而亦有此話]

365. Eishu, 385: "The arising of thoughts—do not continue it." [念起者相續サスルナ也] Kassan, 532: "False thoughts [*vikalpa*] that have already arisen—do not continue them. When you do not continue what has already arisen, it extinguishes." [已起妄念者莫相續不相續已起即滅] Dōkū, 1043, is similar.

366. Eishu, 386: "as in *zazen*." [坐禅ノヤウ也] Dōchū, 1328: "Also, the not-yet-arisen state of thoughts—nurture it. Don't allow them to arise again. 'You must not let them loose' does not mean 'restrain thoughts so that they do not arise.' It merely has the meaning 'nurture.' Also, the 'suppressing thought-outflows and not allowing them to arise' mentioned previously [in 13.5] means 'forcibly restraining.' The 'must not let them get loose' here, [however,] means 'nurturing no mind.'" [又念之未起者長養之莫令更起也不要放起者非按捺念不起之義但是長養義也又前把捉念漏不令放起者謂強按捺也今之不要放起者謂長養無心也] Kōunshi, 1184: "The *Pared-Down Notes on the Awakening of Faith* [T1848.44.388b11–12] . . . says: 'Evils that have already arisen—cut them off and do not allow them to continue. Evils that have not yet arisen—cut them off and do not allow them to arise.' Dharma Master Kumārajīva [in Sengzhao's *Commentary on the Vimalakīrti Sūtra*; T1775.38.386b1–2] says: 'When bad dharmas arise, extinguish them. [In the case of those that] have not yet arisen, do not allow them to arise.'" [起信筆削 . . . 曰已起之惡斷令不續未起之惡斷令不起什法師曰惡法生則滅之未起不令生(注維摩)]

367. Kōunshi, 1184: "In the *Glossary of the Patriarchal Courtyard* . . . : "*xingjiao* 行脚 means to leave your home village and travel by foot throughout all-under-heaven. Sloughing off feelings and abandoning tiredness, [the Chan trainee] tries to locate a teacher-friend in order to seek the dharma and realization. . . . Searching for a master to consult with about the Way is 'making an on-the-spot investigation of Chan.'" [事苑 . . . 行脚者謂遠離鄉曲行脚天下

脱情捐累尋訪師友求法證悟也.... 尋師訪道爲参禪] CBETA, X64, no. 1261, p. 432, c19–22 //Z 2:18, p. 120, c1–4 //R113, p. 240, a1–4.

368. Kassan, 533, and Dōkū, 1043, gloss *wu ru xuduo ban* 無如許多般 with a line from 38.2: "[So, all along Huangbo's] buddhadharma was point-blank." [佛法無多子] Yanagida, 143, glosses *wu ru xuduo ban* 無如許多般 as: "There is nothing at all that is troublesome." [しち面倒なものは何もない。] Zengo, 362, glosses *ru xuduo ban* 如許多般 as: "this, that, and the other; tedious, verbose, redundant." [あれやこれや、くだくだしいこと。]

369. Kassan, 533: "just the right *pūjā* [act of worship]!" [正好供養]

370. Eishu, 386: "*youxin* 有心 ['with mind'] is an unusually bad intention." [有心ハ尤ワルキ也] Kōunshi, 1185: "*youxin* 有心 ['with mind'] is most poisonous." [有心最毒] Kassan, 533, and Dōkū, 1043: "The *Perfect Awakening Sutra* [T842.17.915c23–25] says: 'Taking a mind of mental work to fathom the realm of perfect awakening of the *tathāgata* is like taking a firefly to incinerate Mt. Sumeru. You will never be able to do it.'" [圓覺云能以有思惟心測度如來圓覺境界如取螢火燒須彌山終不能著]

371. Dōchū, 1328: "This scolds [those with] thoughts [based in] having characteristics." [呵責有相念也] Dōkū, 1043: "Your greed, anger, and stupidity *are* the three realms. If you were to separate from greed, anger, and stupidity, you would not be separated from the *place* you're in right now.' Decisively departing from the three realms—how could that not be enjoying ordinary life to the full?" [你貪瞋痴是三界若離貪瞋痴不離當處直下出離三界豈不暢快平生耶]

372. Some of the Zen commentators and modern translators state that this term *shangji* 賞繫 is obscure. Those Zen commenators who attempt an exegesis generally come up with something like "esteeming the buddhas and patriarchs brings on a type of bondage." Dōchū, 1328: "The two characters *shangji* 賞繫 are certainly nouns, but I have not yet found them in my investigations." [賞繫二字必名目未考得之] Anonymous, 272: "The two characters *shangji* 賞繫 have been unknown since ancient times." [賞繫二字古來不審] Kassan, 533: "If a person, having a mind [of deliberation as opposed to no mind], esteems the merit of the buddhas and patriarchs, then, from the increase in the mind of grasping, the buddhas and patriarchs, on the contrary, become terms of bondage." [若人有心尚佛祖功德則由增執著之心而佛祖却是成繫縛底名句也] Shukitsu, 943: "*shang* 賞 means 'esteem/value.'" [賞者尚貴之義] Dōkū, 1043: "The word *shang* 賞 means 'esteem; to esteem their merit.' The one who praises the buddhas and patriarchs takes their merit as something to esteem, but it is a term of bondage." [賞之言尚也尚其功也稱佛祖者以功德賞而繫縛之名也] Kōunshi, 1185: "*fozu shangji* 佛祖賞繫 means 'to delight in the buddhas and patriarchs and be bound by them.'" [佛祖賞繫者賞玩佛祖被繫縛之義也] Iriya, 102.1, glosses *shangji* 賞繫 as: "The meaning is unclear. Heretofore, it has been understood as 'to give praise to and bind (or be bound),' but that is quite unreasonable. There are no other examples—it is a strange expression."

373. Kōunshi, 1185: "The *Perfect Awakening Sutra* [T842.17.914b22–26] ... says: 'This body of mine right now is the coming together of the four elements. The defiled forms hair, nails, teeth, skin, flesh, muscle, bone, marrow, and brain all revert to the earth element. ... When the four elements have each separated out, where would that present unreal body be located? Thus, we know that this body is ultimately without substance.'" [圓覺經 ... 曰我今此身四大和合所謂髮毛爪齒皮肉筋骨髓腦垢色皆歸於地.... 四大各離今妄身當在何處即知此身畢竟無體]

374. The *Śūraṃgama Sūtra* [T945.19.121b25] says: "Stopping is *bodhi*." [歇即菩提] Eishu, 386: "The *great matter* finished, it is the *place* of rest." [大事了畢也休歇処也] Chitetsu, 788: "'Stopped and not stopped' mean 'awakened and not yet awakened.'" [歇與不歇謂悟未悟] Shukitsu, 944: "The *place* where you [utterly] stop movement of mind for a single moment is called 'great awakening.'" [一念心歇得處者云大悟矣]

375. Eishu, 386, Anonymous, 273, Dōkū, 1043, and Kōunshi, 1186: "The *Awakening of Faith* [T1666.32.577c6–7] says: 'Suddenly [out of the blue] thoughts arise, and this is called *avidyā*.'" [起信論云忽然念起名無明]

376. Kōunshi, 1186: "The *Commentary on the Vimalakīrti Sūtra* [T1778.38.676c3–5] ... says: 'Topsy-turvy thought—who [*sic*] is the root? [Next Vimalakīrti answered:] 'Take the unfixed [*apratiṣṭhita*] as the root. The unfixed is beginingless *avidyā* [*sic*].'" [淨名疏 ... 曰顛倒想復誰爲本以無住爲本無住即是無始無明]

377. Kōunshi, 1186: "The *Commentary on the Abhidharma-kośa Verses* [T1823.41.866a25–26] ... says: 'The various sentient-being types have four kinds of birth: egg-born, womb-born, wetness-born, and spontaneous generation.' ... In the *Pearl Grove of the Dharma Garden* [T2122.53.317a15–18] ... : '[Now we will discuss rebirth as an animal. Most cases of this type are set in motion as karmic recompense for delusion. ... Some] wear fur and sport horns.'" [俱舍頌疏 ... 曰諸有情類有四種生卵生胎生濕生化生.... 法苑 ... (夫論畜生癡報所感種類既多.... 或復)被毛戴角]

378. Kassan, 535: "The *place* where thoughts stop is the buddha realm of the pure *dharmakāya*. Therefore, the *Śūraṃgama Sūtra* [T945.19.121b25–26] in its Yajñadatta story says: 'Stopping is *bodhi*. The enlightened mind of superior purity pervades the *dharmadhātu*. It is not obtained from anyone else.'" [思念歇處即是清淨法身之佛界也故楞嚴演若達多事迹云歇即菩提勝淨明心本周法界不從人得] Dōkū, 1044, is very similar. Myōō, 49: "If you bring [mind] to a stop, right away you reach the realm of the pure *dharmakāya*." [你ガ心若歇得スレハ便ヲノツカラ清淨法身ノ境ニイタル也] Kōunshi, 1186: "When false thoughts come to a stop, it is the buddha body or buddha realm. The *Vimalakīrti Sūtra's* line [T475.14.538c5] to the effect that 'when mind is pure, then the buddha-lands are pure' and the *Śūraṃgama Sūtra's* line 'stopping is *bodhi*' [T945.19.121b25] are both this idea." [妄念歇得則佛身佛界也維摩心淨佛土淨楞嚴歇則菩提皆此意也] However, Dōchū, 1329, takes *shenjie* 身界 as *kāya-dhātu*. [十八界時有身界目即身根名身界], one of the eighteen *dhātus* (= the six senses plus the corresponding

six vishayas plus the corresponding six sensory perceptions). In other words, he takes *shenjie* 身界 as the body (sense-organ) *dhātu* that corresponds to the touchables *dhātu* and the body-consciousness *dhātu*.

379. Kōunshi, 1186: "The *Talk of Huayan Mysteries* [Fazang's *Huayan jing tanxuan ji* 華嚴經探玄記: T1733.35.115c12–13] says: 'As for the all-at-once teaching, just a single moment of non-arising is called "buddha."'" [華嚴玄談 . . . 曰頓教者但一念不生即名爲佛]

380. Myōō, 50: "'Magical transformation of the body through thought' means that a tenth-stage bodhisattva, upon attaining the like-a-*māyā* *samādhi*, displays innumerable supernormal powers . . . and is free and unobstructed in entering into all the buddha-lands everywhere." [意生化身トハ十地ノ菩薩如幻三昧ヲ得レハ無量ノ神通ヲ現 . . . 普ク一切ノ佛刹ニ入ルニ自在無碍ニ] Eishu, 387: "'Supernormal powers of magical transformation throughout the three realms' is taking the place of one thing after another because you want to use them. . . . 'Magical transformation of the body through thought' is assuming transformation bodies at will. . . . It is receiving rebirth as you please. . . . Buddhas and bodhisattvas have various sorts of magical transformations of the body through thought. If in their minds they desire to go somewhere, their transformation bodies go." [三界神通変化トハ其其ニ成代テ用イタイ樣ニアル也. . . .意生化身トハ意ノママニ化身シタイ樣ニスル也. . . .隨意欲処受生也. . . . 佛菩薩亦有種種意生身意欲行処化身行也] Kōunshi, 1186: "'Magical transformation of the body through thought' means that anything that my mind desires has nothing to block it." [意生化身者生我心念所欲無物有障礙] He cites three types in the *Laṅkāvatāra Sūtra*.

381. Kōunshi, 1187: "'Dharma joy and *dhyāna* delight' are the two meals of *samādhi* and *prajñā*. Dharma joy is *prajñā*; *dhyāna* delight is *samādhi*. Sometimes it is opened up into three meals. The *Lotus Sutra* [T262.9.27c29] says: 'The first is the dharma joy meal, and the second the *dhyāna* delight meal.'" [法喜禪悦者定慧二食也法喜慧也禪悦定或開爲三食法華 . . . 曰一者法喜食二者禪悦食]

382. Kōunshi, 1187: "As to 'radiating light from your body,' it is like the *devas* of the form realm—their own wisdom light is like this. It does not rely on the external light rays of illumination by the sun or moon. Their brightness is self-illuminating." [身光自照者如色界天人自己智光亦然不假外日月燈燭之光光明自照]

383. Eishu, 387: "If you are thinking you want clothes, brocades appear." [衣ガホシイト思ヘバ羅綺モ現也] Kōunshi, 1187, cites a passage in the *Amitāyus Sūtra* that describes the buddha land named Sukhāvatī (*Wuliang shou jing* 無量壽經: T360.12.271b25–c2).

384. Eishu, 387, and Anonymous, 276: "means 'an affliction you are unaware of because it has no symptoms.'" [中夭病無之義也] Dōchū, 1330: "[It means] 'dying an unnatural death.' There are various theories in the sutras about the nine unnatural deaths." [橫死之病也九橫死諸經異説] They include untimely

death from lack of medical attention, execution by the state, burning to death, drowning, falling off a cliff, etc. Kōunshi, 1187: "'Unnatural afflictions' means 'afflictions such as being troubled by curses or poisonous drugs, having one's vital energy snatched by non-humans, or being eaten by evil beasts.'" [橫病者爲咒詛毒藥所惱或爲非人奪精氣爲惡獸所噉蒙□病惱等也]

385. Kassan, 536, Anonymous, 276, and Dōkū, 1044: "The *Vajracchedikā Sūtra* [T235.8.749c22–23] says: 'You should produce a thought that is nowhere fixed.'" [金剛經云應無所住而生其心]

386. Kōunshi, 1187: "The *Vimalakīrti Sūtra* [T475.14.548c17] . . . says: '*Bodhi* is nowhere fixed; therefore, it is mentally ungraspable.'" [維摩 . . . 曰菩提無住處是故無有得者]

387. Dōkū, 1044: "'Venue of activities right in front of you' is *bodhi* [in the face of] everything that meets your eye." [目前用處即是觸目菩提也] Kōunshi, 1187: "The great Way is right in front of you. When all is said and done, it is hard to see—don't make a mistake!" [大道在目前要且難覷勿蹉過] Anonymous, 276: "'Venue of activities right in front of you' means 'your very own *original portion*.'" [目前用處自己本分云也] Zengo, 133, glosses *gengshi* 更是 as: "いったい [just how/what/why/who on earth/the hell/in heaven's name]." It strengthens the tone of a question or negation.

388. Kōunshi, 1187: "'Names' are the four elements, three realms, *bodhi*, *avidyā*, etc." [名字四大三界菩提無明等也]

389. Kōunshi, 1187, identifies this saying as the transmission-of-the-dharma verse of the twenty-second patriarch Venerable Manorhita [第二十二祖摩拏羅尊者付法偈] and cites the *Outline of the Linked Lamps* (*Liandeng huiyao* 聯燈會要: CBETA, X79, no. 1557, p. 20, c15–16 // Z 2B:9, p. 227, d1–2 // R136, p. 454, b1–2). Kōunshi, 1187: "'Flow' is another name for the *kleśas*. It means 'unbroken continuation or continuity [*prabandha* = unbroken continuation or continuity of the *kleśas* and *abhūta-vikalpa*].' There are four 'flows': *kleśas*-and-desires flow; views flow; love flow; and *avidyā* flow." [流煩惱異名云流注有四流煩惱欲流見流愛流無明流]

390. The line *sihuo xunran* 死活循然, as Iriya, 107.1, notes, is "difficult to understand. . . . a strange line." The Zen commentators are of little help. For instance, Eishu, 388, and Anonymous, 277: "The one phrase of the Chan adept must be concurrently equipped with both the dead phrase [i.e., the words] and the live phrase [i.e., the meaning]." [作家一句死句活句可相兼備也] Other examples are: Kōunshi, 1188, who says that the great death [*dasi* 大死, wherein all views of self and discrimination have stopped] and the great aliveness [*dahuo* 大活, i.e., the new life born from this great death] are in an orderly sequence; Dōkū, 1045: "means the person of the great death returns to aliveness" [大死底人還活之義也]; and Dōchū, 1132: "*xunran* 循然 is 'one after the other'; in [Zen] dialogue [sessions] there is rising and being toppled." [循然次第也問答有起倒也] Xu Shaofeng, ed., *Jindai Hanyu cidian* [*Word Dictionary of Recent Sinitic*] (Beijing: Tuanjie chubanshe, 1997), 1067, gives as one

of its definitions of *sihuo* 死活 the phrase *panming* 拚命 ("risk one's life; make a death-defying effort; go all out; exert one's strength to the utmost") and cites an example from the novel *Dream of the Red Chamber* (*Honglou meng* 紅樓夢, 63): "Xiren also made a death-defying effort to haul Xiangling there. They set up another table on the *kang* [a brick bed warmed by fire underneath] and took their seats." [襲人又死活拉了香菱來、炕上又開了一張桌子方坐開了。] The translation has followed this definition and example.

391. Kōunshi, 1188: "'Host' is the master; 'guest' is the student. 'Back and forth exchange' is one question and one answer." [主師家客學人言論往來一問一答也] Eishu, 388, Kassan, 536, and Dōchū, 1332, are similar to the second half of this comment.

392. Anonymous, 277, and Kōunshi, 1188: "like a moon's reflections on water." [如水中月] Chitetsu, 791: "'In response to the being manifesting forms' is the teachings principle, instruction, guidance." [應物現形即是說通教授教]

393. *quanti zuoyong* 全體作用 also appears in 13.26 and 13.43. Zongmi in his *Chan Letter* describes the Hongzhou teaching with a very similar phrase: "The idea of the Hongzhou is: The raising of mind, the moving of thoughts, the snapping of the fingers, the shifting of the eyes, all do-ing and all acting, are the unreserved functioning of the buddha nature [佛性全體之用]. There is no functioning separate [from the buddha nature]." [洪州意者起心動念彈指動目所作所為皆是佛性全體之用更無別用 (CBETA, X63, no. 1225, p. 33, a22–23 //Z 2:15, p. 435, d4–5 //R110, p. 870, b4–5)] The same phrasing appears in his encapsulation of the Hongzhou house of Chan in his *Chan Notes* (CBETA, X09, no. 245, p. 534, b1–24 //Z 1:14, p. 279, a2–b7 //R14, p. 557, a2–b7). Chitetsu, 791: "*quanti zuoyong* 全體作用 is the *siddhānta-naya* [of the *Laṅkāvatāra Sūtra*]." [全體作用即是宗通] Kōunshi, 1188: "It is like [occasions on which the Master] rights his sitting posture or remains silent for a long time or bows his head or returns to the *fangzhang*." [據坐良久無語底頭歸方丈之類也] Anonymous, 277: "It is like Linji's approach to Advanced Seat Ding [in section 31]." [若臨濟接定上座之類也] Dōkū, 1045: "*quanti zuoyong* 全體作用 is like the method [employed by] the Master to ap-proach Advanced Seat Ding." [全體作用者如師接 定上座手段] The story of Ding in section 31 runs as follows: "Advanced Seat Ding arrived for an audi-ence and asked, 'What is the big idea of the buddhadharma?' The Master got down from the Chan chair, grabbed him [by the collar] and gave him a slap, and instantly shoved him aside. As Ding [lost his train of thought and] stood there blankly, a nearby monk said, 'Advanced Seat Ding, why is it you do not bow?' Just at the moment Ding bowed, he suddenly had a great awakening."

394. Anonymous, 277: "one whack with the stick and one shout as an approach to people. . . . *jiquan* 機權 is *upāya*." [一棒一喝接人也. . . . 機權方便也] Dōkū, 1045, is similar. Kōunshi, 1188: "The host from the outset is without happi-ness or anger. Provisionally, in order to approach them, he establishes *upāyas*." [主家本無喜怒假爲接彼設機關方便]

395. This is one of the powers of magical transformation displayed by the Buddha's disciple Maudgalyāyana, "the first in supernormal powers." See **13.14**

396. Anonymous, 277: "taking wisdom to approach people." [以智接人也] Dōchū, 1332: "shows the realm of Mañjuśrī, the great person." [示文殊大人境界]

397. Anonymous, 277: "taking the realm of principle to approach [beings]. . . . The buddhadharma takes Mañjuśrī of great wisdom as the emptiness axiom of the buddha . . . and takes Samantabhadra of great practice as the wonderful function of the buddha." [以理境接也. . . . 佛法以大智文殊為佛之空宗. . . . 以大行普賢為佛之妙用] Dōchū, 1332: "shows the realm of Samantabhadra, the great person." [示普賢大人境界]

398. Eishu, 388, and Anonymous, 278: "because the present student desires to test the teacher." [蓋今學者欲試知識也] Dōku, 1045: "This just refers to 'kudzu talk.'" [此只指葛藤話頭也] Kōunshi, 1188, is similar. Zengo, 139, glosses *jiao penzi* 膠盆子 as: "when painting, a dish of reconstituted glue used [as a medium] to affix the pigments." [絵を画くとき、絵具を定着させるための膠を溶いた容器。] The *Mahāprajñāpāramitā Treatise* (*Da zhidu lun* 大智度論; T1509.25.164b10) says: "It is like the pigments in painting—once you have the glue, they are firmly affixed." [譬如畫彩得膠則堅著] Another example from the same treatise (T1509.25.314b2): "It is like the various pigments in painting. If you have no glue, they are of no use." [如種種畫彩若無膠者亦不中用]

399. Eishu, 388: "'Vishaya' is 'provisional *upāya*.' Coming to ask questions—in all cases they are vishayas." [境ハ權方便也來問ハ皆境也] Kassan, 537, and Dōku, 1045: "calculations and planning concerning a platter of glue." [向膠盆子上計較按排也] Kōunshi, 1188: "clambering up onto a platter of glue to do 'work.'" [上膠盆子上作活計]

400. Dōku, 1046: "'Former person' refers to the master." [前人者指師家也] Eishu, 388, and Kōunshi, 1188, are similar.

401. In Chinese medicine the fat at the tip of the heart is called the *gao* 膏, the section between the heart and the diaphragm is called the *huang* 肓, and the place between the *gao* and the *huang* is considered untreatable. Eishu, 388: "When disease enters the *gao-huang*, it will necessarily result in death." [病入膏肓必死也] Dōku, 1046: "In cases of illness in the *gao-huang*, drugs can do nothing." [疾在膏肓藥不可爲] Kōunshi, 1188: "refers to bad teachers and the disease of ignorant Zen." [指是惡知識癡禪病也]

402. Anonymous, 278: "uttering not a word or a half of a phrase." [一言半句不吐也] Dōchū, 1333: "singlemindedly silent, gazing at the student, [as if to ask:] how?" [一向默然看學者如何也]

403. Dōku, 1046: "'Doesn't hold up' means 'not a single dharma is verbally expressible'; 'asks a question and [the teacher] rips it away' means 'no involvement with intellectual knowledge.'" [不拈出者無一法可說問處即奪者不立知解也] See section **10.1**.

404. Dōchū, 1333: "*disi* 抵死 means 'resist unto death.'" [抵死者敵當于死也]
Kōunshi, 1189: "Kudzu binds and kills." [葛藤縛殺]

405. Dōkū, 1046: "'Vishaya of purity' means 'not relying on a single thing, coming in the non-dependence of solitary liberation, not asking about the buddhadharma, not asking about the intention of the [Chan] patriarchal masters.'"
[清淨境者不依倚一物獨脱無依來不問佛法不問祖師意] Kōunshi, 1189: "'Vishaya of purity' means 'not caught up in the buddha teachings or the words of the patriarchs.'" [清淨境者不拘佛教祖語底也] Eishu, 389, and Anonymous, 278: "The meaning is 'not involved with a single vishaya, a single dharma.'" [不立一塵一法義也] Kassan, 538: "'Vishaya of purity' means 'the appearance of being uncontaminated by the buddha teachings and the words of the patriarchs.'" [清淨境者無佛教祖語之染著底樣子也]

406. Dōchū, 1333: "a scolding/admonishing." [咄叱警戒]

407. Eishu, 389: "These are the words of the teacher." [是知識語也] Anonymous, 279, is similar.

408. Eishu, 389: "a fine bow." [好礼拜也] Kōunshi, 1189: "sophisticated, lovely." [風流可愛]

409. A cangue is a large wooden yoke fastened about the neck as a punishment for crimes. Eishu, 389: "He comes bound by a lot of things. He comes bringing a lot of thought of the unreal. . . . He comes bringing buddha word and the words of the [Zen] patriarchs." [許多ノ物ニ縛せ(セ)ラレテ來也妄想ヲタント持來也. . . . 佛語祖語ヲモチ來ヲ云也] Kassan, 538: "A student, bound by the buddha teachings and the words of the [Zen] patriarchs, comes to present his level of knowing-seeing and understanding." [學者被佛教祖語繫縛來而呈其知見解會也] Kōunshi, 1189, is very similar. Dōchū, 1333: "'Cangue with a lock' is 'knowing-seeing.' He is bound by the good-for-nothing gimmick vishayas of the buddhas and [Zen] patriarchs." [枷鎖者知見也為佛祖閑機境所繫縛也] Dōkū, 1046: "Carrying on his shoulders the ancient *kōans* of the buddhas and [Zen] patriarchs, he comes to present his level of knowing-seeing and understanding." [擔佛祖古則公案來而逞知見解會底]

410. Eishu, 389: "The teacher adds a layer of bondage. To the heaps of thought of the unreal brought in [by the student] he adds more thought of the unreal." [師家ガ一重縛也妄想ヲタント持來タニ又妄想ヲ添テトラせ(セ)タ也] Kassan, 538: "The bad teacher adds even more understanding on top of the understanding. Truly it is another layer of cangue-with-a-lock." [惡知識更又解會之上加解會實是一重枷鎖也] Kōunshi, 1189, is similar.

411. Eishu, 389: "*bi* 彼 ['that'] is the master; *ci* 此 ['this'] is the student." [彼師也此学也] Dōchū, 1333: "also, the *bici* 彼此 of master and student." [又師學之彼此也]

412. Eishu, 389 (as well as Kassan, 538, and Dōkū, 1046), gloss *rushi suoju* 如是所舉 as: "the above fourfold guest-and-host theme." [如是所举ハ上四賓主也] Kassan, 538: "The Great Master raises the four guest-host rules and distinguishes their realms [of application]. This will necessarily teach the students of

the world to know the wrong and the correct." [大師舉四賓主則而辨其境界此要教天下學者知其邪正也] Chitetsu, 794: "'Selecting out what differs' means 'different from the headrope of the [Zen] personal-realization-of-the-meaning-beyond-words.'" [揀異謂異宗綱] Dōchū, 1334: "'Differs' means 'different from [beholding] reality as it truly is,' that is, a heterodox understanding." [異者異于真正乃邪見解也] Kōunshi, 1189: "*rushi* 如是 refers to the fourfold guest-and-host theme. 'Distinguishing Māras' refers to seeing through the bad teachers who are wild-fox demons. As to 'selecting out what differs,' 'differs' is 'heterodox,' meaning the non-Buddhist heterodox views of annihilationism and eternalism. Here it is selecting out the bad teachings of heterodox masters." [如是者指上四賓主話辨魔者識破野狐精魅惡知識也揀異者異異端謂外道斷常異見今揀邪師教壞也]

413. Kassan, 538: "*shi* 寔 is the same as *shi* 實 ['reality']. When *qingshi* 情識 [i.e., unreal consciousness produced by false discrimination] is cut off, we call it *shiqing* 寔情. *shiqing* 寔情 is not easy to actualize, and therefore it says 'very difficult.' The person of *shiqing* 寔情 is called 'one who beholds reality as it truly is.'" [寔實同字情識泯絕謂之寔情寔情不易成故云大難也寔情之人謂之真正見解也] Eishu, 389: "The two characters *shiqing* 寔情 together mean 'real.'" [寔情二字共マコト也]

414. Iriya, 110.2, glosses *keke de* 可可地 as: "In the colloquial language of the Tang period it has the meaning 'pretty; fairly; tolerably' or 'appropriate; adequate; reasonable.'" [唐代の俗語で「かなりに」「相当のところ」の意]

415. Kōunshi, 1189: "Their hearing is like that of a deaf person." [耳聞如聾] Kassan, 539, Dōkū, 1047, and Anonymous, 279: "They don't confidently take it in." [不信受也] Eishu, 389: "No students understand." [共學者ガ不心得也] Jiang and Cao, eds., *Tang Wudai yuyan cidian* [*Word Dictionary of Tang and Five Dynasties Language*], 426, glosses *zaiyi* 在意 as *liuxin* 留心 ("take care")" or *zhuyi* 注意 ("pay attention to") and cites the *Subduing Māra Transformation Text* (*Jiangmo bianwen* 降魔變文): "He then sent down an order to the mass of officials: 'Each of you must pay heed. The Buddha house is on the east side; the six commanders-in-chief are on the west side." [即敕群僚各須在意佛家东边六帅西畔]

416. Eishu, 389: "treading around and around everywhere." [ドコニモカシコニモ蹈ツケマワル也]

417. Eishu 389, and Anonymous, 279: "no understanding." [無分曉也] Kassan, 539: "This means that students are in the midst of darkness and do not understand." [此學者暗昧而不分曉之謂也]

418. Eishu, 390: "The one who, a thousand times, ten thousand times, is trampling about, the one who is turning around and around, is the clear, solitary brightness devoid of even a single describable attribute." [千徧萬徧蹈者マワル者ハ無一个形段歷歷孤明也] Kassan, 539, and Dōkū, 1047: "This points out the being doing the trampling. Now, tell me, what is [that being]?" [指出脚底蹈過底物且道是什麼]

419. Eishu, 390: "'Corpses' are the dead words of heterodox masters. . . . 'Baggage' refers to the written word, the injunctions of the ancients." [死屍邪師死句也. . . . 擔子指文字古訓也] Kassan, 539: "'Baggage' refers to understanding [based on] *avidyā*, the *kleśas*, the written word, verbal phrases, etc." [擔子者指無明煩惱文字言句等解會也] Dōkū, 1047: "'Corpses' refers to the physical body of five feet." [死屍者指五尺形骸] Kōunshi, 1190: "'Corpses' refers to terms and phrases—it is like saying 'the dead phrase.' 'Baggage' refers to perplexity arising from terms and phrases." [死屍者指名句猶言死句也擔子者指名句上疑解也] Dōchū, 1335: "It is just [ordinary] traveling baggage." [直是行脚擔子]

420. Modern translators in the case of *caoxie qian* 草鞋錢 ("straw-sandal money") appear to be following Dōchū, 1335, who gives the following interpretation: "Today, 'straw-sandal money' refers to the donated [straw sandals] of a faithful lay donor . . . since [the student] travels on foot [far and wide in search of a teacher and realization], they are worn out and become a debt. On a later day King Yama will ask for [repayment of] this debt." [今日草鞋錢亦是信施之物? 其趣向行脚則盡成債後日閻羅王當徵求其債也] However, Luo and others, eds., *Hanyu da cidian* [*Great Word Dictionary of Sinitic*], 9.375, glosses *caoxie qian* 草鞋錢 as: "In old times money or goods which a bailiff in a government office extorts [*lesuo* 勒索] from a convicted criminal or litigant. 'Straw-sandal money' is popular slang. A Yuan Dynasty work, *Iron-Cane Li* [*Tieguai Li* 铁拐李; one of the eight immortals] by Yue Bochuan 岳伯川, says: 'He is a banker in a gambling den. I urged elder brother to spare your life—what straw-sandal money are you going to give me?'" [正是簡莊家老子我勸哥哥饒了你性命有甚麼草鞋錢與我些] This would expand the scope of meaning of the passage to: "There will come a day [when you will be in the clutches of Yama, who as a matter of course] will extort straw-sandal money [from you]."

421. Myōō, 55: "*yibi zuo* 倚壁坐 means 'quiet sitting facing a wall.'" [倚壁坐卜ハ面壁靜坐也] Eishu, 390: "doing *zazen* facing a wall." [倚壁坐禪スル也] Anonymous, 280: "the heterodox Zen of silence-and-illlumination, like the ghost cave of Black Mountain." [默照邪禪如黑山鬼窟] Kassan, 539: "*zazen* contemplation practice." [坐禪觀行] Dōchū, 1335: "means *zazen*." [謂坐禪也]

422. Eishu, 390: "as the ultimate." [為究竟也] Kōunshi, 1190: "seize the vishayas of wall contemplation and silent sitting as correct." [取壁觀默坐境爲是]

423. Shukitsu, 947: "Whoever loves Zen sitting falls into quiescence and sinks into *śūnyatā*, [mistakenly] taking this stillness and making it into a vishaya of purity. Maintaining [this quietist view] and not giving it up is a great disease that blocks the Way. If you want to attain a beholding of reality as it truly is and be able to declaim it, you must eliminate this disease." [凡愛禪坐者墜寂沉空即以此不動而為清淨境認持不捨是障道之大病也若欲得真正見解誦之須除此病矣] Kōunshi, 1190: "The *Nirvāṇa Later Part Sūtra* [T377.12.901b20–21] . . . says: '*Avidyā* the master does harm moment after moment; sentient beings

are unaware of it, and the wheel of samsara turns.'" [涅槃後分經 . . . 曰無明郎主念念傷害衆生不覺輪轉生死]

424. Eishu, 390: "the ghost cave of Black Mountain. . . . the appearance of coagulating thoughts and [remaining in] stillness." [黑山鬼窟也. . . . 凝念不動兒] Anonymous, 280, is very similar. Kōunshi, 1190: "This refers to Tiantai Zhiyi. His [*Great*] *Stopping and Discerning* [T1911.46.38c24–26] . . . says: 'You should know that the heterodox [teaching of] emptying mind is to be feared. If you fall into this view, you will be sinking for eternity. You will not even be able to attain the nirvana of humans and *devas*, much less the great nirvana.'" [指天台智者大師歇止觀 . . . 曰當知邪僻空心甚可怖畏若墮此見長淪永沒尚不能得人天涅槃何況大涅槃耶]

425. Dōkū, 1047: "Because the Master fears that students will grasp onto the place of movement, he makes this statement." [師爲恐學者認執動處故有此語也]

426. Dōchū, 1336, and Anonymous, 280: "'Him' is the *original portion, that one person.*" [他者本分那一人也]

427. Kōunshi, 1190: "'He' refers to *that one person* of non-dependence." [佗指無依那一人]

428. Kassan, 540, and Dōkū, 1048: "In the end it [the fish] is not fixed in vishayas of movement or stillness." [畢竟他是不住動不動境也] Dōchū, 1336: "not fixed anywhere, lively like a fish waving its tail." [無住處活鱍鱍地] Kōunshi, 1191: "Vasubandhu Bodhisattva's *Treatise on the Establishment of Karman in the Mahāyāna . . .* verse says: 'Body and speech [karmans] arise on the outside, revealing the dharmas associated with mind on the inside. It is like a fish submerged in the depths, stirring up waves revealing its presence.'" [世親菩薩大乘成業論 . . . 頌曰由外發身語表内心所思譬彼潛淵魚鼓波而自表]

429. Kassan, 541: "As to the 'three types of sense faculties,' comprehensively speaking, they are the three sense faculties of high, middle, and low. These are subdivided into nine grades, running from high-high, high-middle, and high-low down to low-low." [三種根器者遍言上中下之三根也別言上上上中上下乃至下下之九等也] Dōkū, 1048: "'Three types of sense faculties' means the three sense faculties of high, middle, and low. An old commentary says that there are nine grades, running from high-high, high-middle, and high-low down to low-low. This is incorrect. The Great Master speaks only of middle-low sense faculties, middle-high sense faculties, and the highest sense faculties. 'High-high' means 'highest.' It is not necessary to speak of nine grades of sense faculties." [三種根器者言上中下之三根也古鈔言上之上上之中上之下乃至下之下九等不然如大師之意只言自中下之根器自中上之根器又最上之根器耳言上上者最上之義也不必言九等之根器] Kōunshi, 1191: "'Three types of sense faculties' refers to the three sense faculties of middle-low, middle-high, and high-high, the usual three sense faculties of high, middle, and low." [三種根器者指中下中上上上三根尋常上中下三根也] Dōchū, 1336: "The 'three sense faculties' are middle-low, middle-high, and high-high. . . . The Zen

personal-realization-of-the-meaning-beyond-words is not for those of low sense faculties." [三根中下中上上上也. . . . 忠曰禪宗不接下根]

430. The Zen commentators vary in their exegeses, and the translation follows Kōunshi, 1191: "'Vishayas' means 'one extreme—all the ready-made forms and characteristics in the questions which the student brings.' 'Dharma' is 'one extreme—the principle of the *original portion* brought by the student.'" [境者學人所問將來之一切現成色相邊之事也法者學人所拈來之本分底理體邊之事也] Myōō, 56: "'Dharma' means 'mentals [i.e., *caitta*].'" [法卜ハ心法也] Dōkū, 1048: "'Vishayas' means 'the four elements, mountains and rivers, terms and words, etc.' 'Dharma' means 'the principle relied upon by the student.' If it is [a student of] middle-low faculties, [the Master] just sweeps away the myriad vishayas, making the student abide in the *place* wherein not a single vishaya or dharma is erected. Therefore, it says 'not eliminate his dharma.' The meaning is 'provisionally setting up a single dharma.'" [境者四大或山河或名言等也法者學人所依理也若中下根器只拂萬境令學者住不立一塵一法-處故云不除其法權立一法之義]

431. Dōchū, 1336, has a diagram showing that "vishayas [*jing* 境] = characteristics/forms empty [*xiang* 相/*sekong* 色空]"; "dharma [*fa* 法] = principle/*ārya* understanding [*li* 理/*shengjie* 聖解]"; and "person [*ren* 人] = knowledge/worldling-feelings [*zhi* 智/*fanqing* 凡情]."

432. Dōkū, 1048: "A person who has a strategy of surpassing the buddhas and patriarchs is called 'off the charts.'" [有超佛越祖之作略人謂之出格]

433. Myōō, 56: "*quanti zuoyong* 全體作用 means that Linji's whole body directly is the buddha nature." [全體作用卜ハ林際ノ全身直ニ是佛性也] Eishu, 391: "*quanti zuoyong* 全體作用 means that there is nothing left behind/kept back." [全體作用卜ハノコス処モ無ゾ Kassan 541 glosses: "*quanti zuoyong* 全體作用 is the type in which [the Master] wordlessly bows his head and returns to the *fangzhang*. Or it is Vimalakīrti's single silence, etc. The student just looks on." [全體作用者無語低頭歸方丈之類也或維摩一默等也學者自看] Dōkū, 1048: "*quanti zuoyong* 全體作用 is the type in which [the Master] wordlessly bows his head and returns to the *fangzhang*. It is the approach used with Advanced Seat Ding [in section **31**]." [全體作用者無語低頭歸方丈之類也又云接定上座的] Kōunshi, 1191: "'Level of beholding that is off the charts' is vision that surpasses the buddhas and patriarchs. *quanti zuoyong* 全體作用 is wordlessly bowing the head, returning to the fangzhang, turning to take a look, correcting one's sitting posture, etc. It is a strategy of not falling into words and phrases." [出格見解者超佛越祖之見處也全體作用者無語低頭歸方丈顧視據坐等不落言句作略也]

434. Kassan, 541: "'*zhe li* 這裡' ["here"] refers to the *place* of unreserved functioning [of the buddha nature]. The realm of the unreserved functioning [of the buddha nature]—this is the *place* wherein the student on his own is exerting his energy. It is not obtained from any other person." [這裡者指全体作用處也全体作用底境界此是學人自著力處非從人得]   Anonymous,

281, Dōkū, 1048, and Kōunshi, 1191, are similar. Eishu, 391: "Having arrived *here*, the blowing wind cannot enter." [到這裏風吹不入]

435. The Yuan Dynasty work *Certain Questions on the Pure Land* (*Jingtu huo wen* 淨土或問; T1972.47.300c2) says: "A spark from a stone and a lightning bolt in the blink of an eye pass by." [石火電光眨眼便過] Kassan, 541: "Unreserved functioning [of the buddha nature]—truly its quickness is impossible to clarify in words. Suppose there is a spark from a stone or a lightning bolt—it's already passed by." [全體作用端的其疾難以言彰假令石火電光他即早過了也] Dōkū, 1048, and Kōunshi, 1191, are similar.

436. Zengo, 317, glosses *dingdong* 定動 as: "a fleeting movement of the pupils of the eyes." [瞳がちらりと動くこと。]

437. Kōunshi, 1191–1192: "The *Songs of the Twelve Hours of Baozhi* [found in the *Verses of the Patriarchal Masters of the Chan Gate* (*Chanmen zhu zushi jisong* 禪門諸祖師偈頌; CBETA, X66, no. 1298, p. 726, a16–b1 //Z 2:21, p. 460, c8–17 //R116, p. 920, a8–17)] says: 'If you are about to make the mind turn in a certain direction in your search to become a buddha, you are questioning the sky, and it will produce [only] dust [i.e., vishayas].' . . . Making the mind turn in a certain direction and setting in motion thoughts are dithering and reflection. . . . A fleeting movement of the eyes is precisely this. [Zongmi's] *Huayan Dharmadhātu Discernment* [T1884.45.687a2] says: 'Producing mind and moving thoughts perverts the dharma substance and loses correct thought.'" [寶誌十二時歌若欲擬心求作佛問虛空始出塵. . . . 擬心動念是擬議思惟. . . . 眼目定動是也華嚴法界觀曰以生心動念即乖法體失正念故]

438. Eishu, 391: "Right in front of you there is the great Way!" [目前大道アルゾ] Dōkū, 1048: "An ancient said, 'The great Way is just right in front of you. When all is said and done, though it is right in front of you, it is difficult to see.'" [古人云大道只在目前要且在目前難見] Kōunshi, 1192: "Zhigong says: 'The great Way is just right in front of them, but the deluded idiots don't understand.'" [誌公曰大道祇在目前迷倒愚人不了]

439. Eishu, 391: "means 'gear for traveling on foot [far and wide in search of a teacher and realization].'" [行脚道具底ヲ云也] Kassan, 542: "This refers to the five-foot physical body." [此指五尺形骸也] "Kōunshi, 1192: "'Sack of shit' is just a sack." [屎擔子者唯擔子也] Dōchū, 1337: "'Sack of shit' is the sack overflowing with shit and piss that is the five-foot physical body." [屎擔子五尺形骸盛屎尿擔子也]

440. Eishu, 391, and Anonymous, 281: "*qu* 渠 is *that one person*." [渠那一人也] Dōkū, 1049: "*That one right now*—who is it? The person you are deluded about is the protagonist in the house." [即今渠是阿誰汝迷倒底物即屋裡主人公也] Kōunshi, 192: "*He*—what person?" [渠甚麼人]

441. Eishu, 391: "'Has no base' means 'not fixed anywhere' [i.e., *apratiṣṭhita*]." [勿根株者無住處義也] Kōunshi, 1192: "Having neither a base nor a root is 'not fixed anwhere.'" [無根無本無住處]

442. Kassan, 542: "Knead—doesn't become a ball; chop—doesn't split into vishayas." [捏不成團劈不開境界也] Kōunshi, 1192: "neither coming nor going—always peaceful." [不來不去常湛然]

443. *lingyin* 靈音 ("divine sound") means both "the music of the immortals" and *brahma-svara* ("brahma voice"), that is, the sound of sutra chanting. Eishu, 392: "This is also *he*. It is the divine sound of *that one person*." [是又渠也那一人ガ靈音也] Kōunshi, 1192: "[Chengguan's] *Elaboration of the Meanings of the Huayan* [*Da fangguan fo huayan jing shu* 大方廣佛華嚴經疏; T1735.35.610a4–5] . . . says: 'Because you seek awakening, your mind is concentrated, and the voice fills your ears.'" [華嚴演義 . . . 曰求悟解故專一趣心聆音屬耳]

444. Eishu, 392: "If persons don't have confidence in *this one*, then even a hundred years' toil is futile. 'Hundred years' refers to one lifetime." [諸人若此渠ヲ信ぜ(セ)ズンバイタヅラニ空辛勞ヲ百年せ(セ)ウズルゾ百年指一生也] Kassan, 542: "'Hundred years' is like saying 'one lifetime.'" [百年猶如言一生] Dōkū, 1049, Kōunshi, 1192, and Dōchū, 1338, are similar.

445. See 12.7. In the *Huayan Sutra* the youth Sudhana goes through one hundred ten cities in the south visiting fifty-three teachers.

446. Eishu, 392: "the freedom *samādhi*, simply referring to the Huayan assembly. . . . the land of *that one person*." [自由三昧也只華嚴會上指云也. . . .那一人國土也]

447. Eishu, 392: "The enterer is *that one person*. It is also called 'the student.'" [入那一人也又云学人也]

448. Eishu, 392: "He doesn't see the existence of samsara anywhere." [ドコニモ有生死フヲ見ザル也] Dōchū, 1338: "In that way he enters all places, and, as a matter of course, there is birth and death [i.e., samsara]. However, everywhere he searches there is nothing to be characterized as 'samsara.'" [言如是入一切處固當有生有死然處處尋覓都無生死之相也]

449. Kassan, 543: "This section . . . at the end shows that the non-dependent Way-person enters all but is liberated from all." [此一段 . . . 末示無依道人入得一切而解脱一切也]

450. Kōunshi, 1193: "[This section] clarifies the venue of activities of [Linji's] predecessors." [明先輩用處也]

451. Eishu, 392: "As for these persons, their practice is one. It is practice in a single rut. 'The one road' is one thorough penetration." [此人タチハ行ガ一也一轍行也一路一徹也]

452. Dōchū, 1338: "'One road' means 'my buddhadharma and the buddhadharma of Mayu and the others are identical.' It is like persons who walk along the same road. However, because this dharma is deep, persons do not have confidence in it, and, on the contrary, produce criticism." [一路者言我佛法與麻谷等佛法同如人同一路行也然其法深大故人不信却生誹也]

453. Myōō, 58: "means that Mazu did unreserved functioning [of the buddha nature]." [馬祖全体作用スル云也] Kōunshi, 1193: "The *Lotus Sutra* [T262.9.3c21–22]

says: 'A pure oneness without adulteration, complete and unsullied—the characteristics of *brahma* practice.'" [法華 . . . 曰純一無雜具足清白梵行之相]

454. Eishu, 392: "*zhenzheng* 真正 is 'beholding reality as it truly is.'" [真正真正見解也] Kōunshi, 1194: "*mangran* 茫然 is 'limitless breadth and the appearance of losing [all sense] of standards/criteria.'" [茫然者廣大無窮失情量貌也] Dōchū, 1338: "His beholding of reality was as it truly is, and he was able to enter into the midst of both vishayas that went in his direction and vishayas that went against him in order to look for the [true] person. Therefore, he was 'free.'" [見解真正而能入順逆境中覓人故曰自在]

455. Eishu, 392: "As for the jewel, when it is turned over, it is invisible, and, when rubbed, it becomes visible." [珠者覆則隱磨則顯]

456. Eishu, 393: "'*ku* 苦 like the huangbo tree' means 'spicy/peppery/hot.'" [苦如黃蘗者辛辣義] Yanagida, 155, glosses *jin jie bu de* 近皆不得 as: "This line as it is is difficult to read. It is probably a mistake for *jie jin bu de* 皆近不得."

457. Eishu, 393: "[Shigong would say:] 'Look at the arrow!'" [看箭]

458. Eishu, 393: "*zhenzheng* 真正 is 'beholding reality as it truly is.'" [真正ハ真正見解也]

459. Myōō, 59: "'Play with magical transformations' means 'always revealing magical transformations performed through supernormal powers [*shengtong bianhua* 神通変化 = ṛddhi-vikurvita].' Using the six supernormal powers in a variety of ways one makes things follow one's will." [翫弄神變トハ常ニ神通変化ヲ顯ス也 六種ノ神通ヲ以テ種種ニ大自在ヲ働クヲ云也] Eishu, 393, and Anonymous, 283: "'Play with magical transformations' is the *samādhi* of self-enjoyment. Magical transformations are inconceivable." [翫弄神變自受用三昧神變不思議也] Kōunshi, 1195: "[Zhanran's *Explanatory Oracle of the Lotus Sutra's*] *Profound Meaning* [*Fahua xuanyi shiqian* 法華玄義釋籤; T1717.33.878a11] . . . says: "*shenbian* 神變 means 'nonexistent and suddenly existent; existent and suddenly nonexistent.'" [玄義 . . . 曰言神變者無而欻 (= 欻 = 忽然) 有有而欻無]

460. Kōunshi, 1195: "enters the forest without making the foliage move; enters the water without stirring up waves." [入林不動艸入水不立波]

461. Kōunshi, 1195: "The bamboo is dense but doesn't obstruct the flowing river passing by; the mountains are high, but how could they block the white clouds flying by?" [竹密不妨流水過山高豈礙白雲飛]

462. Eishu, 393: "'See right through him' means 'see right through the student.' 'He can't read me' means: 'Even if you encounter him [that is, *that one person*], you won't know him; even if you speak to him, you won't find out his name.'" [看渠者看破學人也渠不識我者相逢不相知共語不知名] Kassan, 545: "He illumines the student's heart like the medicine-king tree [i.e., possessing this tree, one can see into others—what is in their belly is visible from the outside]." [照見學者心肝如藥王樹] Dōku, 1051: "He sees through to the student's heart—as in a mirror, beauty and ugliness are illumined." [見徹學者心肝如鏡當臺妍媸即照] Kōunshi, 1195: "With one glance [the Master]

instantly sees." [一見便見] Kassan, 545, glosses "he can't read me" as: "Because a wall of ten thousand *ren* [i.e., over 20,000 meters] is erected." [壁立万仞故也] Dōchū, 1339: "'Him' is the student who comes." [渠者來底學人也]

463. Eishu, 393: "'Put on various sorts of costumes' refers to words and phrases." [著數般衣者指言句也] Kassan, 545: "Harsh preaching, firm preaching, discussion, and spoken phrases, etc., are all external directives, but they are not internal reality. They are the so-called 'various sorts of costumes.'" [橫說堅說言論語句等皆是外飾而非裡箇真實是所謂數般衣也] Anonymous, 283: "'Put on various sorts of costumes' means 'making various grand designs for the student.'" [着數般衣者為學人作種種摸樣] Dōkū, 1051: "'Various sorts of costumes' means 'one after the other to let drop all sorts of words and phrases in order to respond to mental dispositions and lead beings, revealing a system.' That is called 'various sorts of costumes.'" [數般衣一一下說一切言句等應機接物表顯之體裁謂之數般衣也]

464. Anonymous, 284, glosses *wo yanyu* 我言語 ("my words") as: "costumes, vishayas." [衣也境也] Kōunshi, 1195: "[The student] enters into the ghost cave [of Black Mountain] to make a livelihood [i.e., engages in conjecturing]." [入鬼窟裏作活計]

465. Anonymous, 284: "a student who does not possess the eye." [不具眼學者也]

466. Eishu, 393: "[engages in] inference and planning." [計推按排也] Kassan, 546: "in accordance with [the Master's] words of instruction [engages in] inference and planning." [隨言句上計校按排] Dōkū, 1051, is very similar.

467. Eishu, 393: "'Vishaya of purity' is 'not setting up even a single dharma.'" [清淨境不立一法也] Kassan, 546: "These are vishayas such as returning to the *fangzhang* or getting down from the [Dharma] Seat. Now tell me: What are these vishayas? They are inconceivable, supernormal power! They are inconceivable, miraculous function!" [或歸方丈或下座底境界也且道是什麼境界不可思議神通不可思議妙用也] Chitetsu, 801: "'When I shed [those costumes] and enter into a vishaya of purity' . . . means 'speak concerning the buddha nature.'" [我脫却入清淨境中者 . . . 說似佛性]

468. Kassan, 546: "'*xinyu* 忻欲' is 'the joy of admiration.'" [忻欲者顧樂也]

469. Eishu, 393, and Anonymous, 284: "when I take off the costume of purity." [又清淨衣ヲモ脫却スレバ也] Dōchū, 1339: "The one who takes off the costume of purity—now tell me: what is his bearing?" [脫却清淨衣底且道是什麼風致] Dōkū, 1052: "Having taken off the costume of purity and not set up a single vishaya or dharma, the student has nothing to depend upon." [脫清淨衣不立一塵一法學人無所依憑]

470. Eishu, 393, and Anonymous, 284: "[falls into] the category of Yajñadatta's losing his head." [演若達多失却頭類也] Dōkū, 1052, and Kōunshi, 1195: "The student runs wildly about, saying that Linji has no human bodily appearance." [言學者狂走言臨濟無爲人體裁] Dōchū, 1339: "'I' is Linji himself speaking.

The student runs wildly about, saying that Linji has no buddhadharma. Because the student's eyesight power halts at the costumes, if there are no costumes, he sees nothing at all." [我者臨濟自言學人狂走言臨濟無佛法也蓋學人眼力但止于衣若無衣則都無所見也]

471. Eishu, 393, and Anonymous, 284: "Who is 'the one who is wearing the costumes?' He is the protagonist, the *true person* who can't be ranked." [著衣底人是什广人主人公也又無位真人也] Dōkū, 1052: "Listen to the Great Master: 'Do you recognize me, *that one person* who is wearing the costumes?'" [聽大師識我著衣底那一人否] Dōchū, 1339: "'I' is Linji himself speaking. 'The person' is the *original portion, that one person*." [我臨濟自言也人本分那一人]

472. Eishu, 393, and Anonymous, 284: "means suddenly acknowledges my costume of external forms.'" [我外相衣忽認卜云也] Dōchū, 1339: "This student . . . has erroneously acknowledged the old Han Linji of forms and characteristics." [言此學人 . . . 謬認色相臨濟老漢了也]

473. Anonymous, 284: "'Costumes' are vishayas—they are 'no mind.'" [衣者境也無心]

474. Eishu, 393, and Anonymous, 284: "They are called 'clothes/costumes' because they 'cover up.' They are just decorations on top [of people/persons/*the true person*]." [衣者蓋覆爲義也只上飾也] Kōunshi, 1195: "'Costumes' are empty names without real substance." [衣空名無實體]

475. Dōchū, 1339: "*yi* 依 ['dependent-on-something-else'] and *yi* 衣 ['clothes/costume'] in meaning amount to much the same thing." [依衣義之所歸大同]

476. Eishu, 394, Anonymous, 284, and Dōkū, 1052: "*yibian* 衣變 ['costume transformation'] is *yibian* 依變 ['illusory dependent-on-something-else transformation']." [衣変依變也]

477. Kōunshi, 1195: "The *Great Treatise* [*Mahāprajñāpāramitā Treatise*; T1509.25.103a15–20] . . . says: 'When a person is about to speak, the wind in the mouth is called *udāna* ["utterance"]. It returns to enter the lower abdomen, makes contact with the lower abdomen, and sound is emitted. When sound is emitted, it makes contact with seven loci and ebbs. This is called "speech." Verse: Wind is called *udāna*. It makes contact with the lower abdomen and ascends. This wind makes contact with seven loci: the nape of the neck, gums, teeth, lips, tongue, throat, and chest. Therein speech arises.'" [大論 . . . 曰如人欲語時口中風名憂陀那遷走入至臍觸臍響出時觸七處退是名語言如偈說風名憂陀檀觸臍而上去是風七處觸項及斷齒唇舌咽及以胸是中語言生]

478. Kassan, 546: "One should know that it is all the work of 'wind.' In this way even speech is something turned by 'wind power,' and so it is *māyā*." [當知皆是依風之所作也如是言語亦是風力所轉故是幻化也]

479. In **13.25** (n. 428) Kōunshi, 1191, cites a verse from Vasubandhu Bodhisattva's *Treatise on the Establishment of Karman in the Mahāyāna*: "Body and speech [karmans] arise on the outside, revealing the dharmas associated with mind on the inside. It is like a fish submerged in the depths, stirring up waves

that reveal its presence." [世親菩薩大乘成業論 . . . 頌曰由外發身語表內心 所思譬彼潛淵魚鼓波而自表] Eishu, 394: "Also, *xinsuo* 心所 is *xinshu* 心數 [both = *caitta/caitasika*]." [又心所者心數也] Kassan, 547: "Mentals [*caitta*] mark the eight consciousnesses. [Zongmi's] *Chan Prolegomenon* in its explanation of the eight consciousnesses says: '[Each of these eight consciousnesses has mentals. Within these, some are just neutral, while] some are distinguished as either good or stained. Sutras and treatises view mind to be a collective term for all these mentals. [They speak of the good mind, the bad mind, etc.]' I say: This includes everything from the eye [sense organ] to the storehouse consciousness." [心所者標八識云也禪詮八識釋云或通善染經論之中目爲心所摠名心也 私云此兼眼乃至賴耶云也; the *Chan Prolegomenon* [T2015.48.401c19–22] actually says: 二緣慮心此是八識俱能緣慮自分境故(色是眼識境乃至根身種子器 世界是阿賴耶識之境各緣一分故云自分也)此八各有心所於中或唯無記或通 善染之殊諸經之中目諸心所總名心也謂善心惡心等] For a translation in context, see Broughton, *Zongmi on Chan*, 117.

480. Kōunshi, 1196: "*yi si you nian* 以思有念 means 'because of mental reflection, mind congeals into [*avidyā*] thoughts.'" [以思有念者以思慮凝心念之義也] Eishu, 394: "They have no reality. They are all provisional costumes. . . . *yi* 衣 ['costumes'] is the same as *yi* 依 ['dependent-on-something-else'], that is, illusory dependent-on-something-else transformations." [*yibian* 依変; 實処ナイゾ皆 悉カリノ衣也. . . . 衣為依同依変也] Kassan, 547: "exterior ornament and not internal substance." [表餝(= 飾)而非裡体也] Dōchū, 1341: "not real substance." [非真體也]

481. Eishu, 394: "*shijie* 寔解 means 'beholding reality as it truly is.'" [寔解實見解也] Kōunshi, 1196: "not understanding that the above-mentioned 'constumes'— sounds, terms, written phrases, mentals, etc.—are all empty names and perceiving them as real dharmas." [不了如上聲名文句心所等衣皆是空名認以爲 實法]

482. Eishu, 394: "*yitong* 衣通 ['proficiency in costumes'] is *yibian* 衣変 ['costume transformations']." [衣通衣変也] Dōkū, 1052, and Kōunshi, 1196: "*yitong* 衣通 ['proficiency in constumes'] is the same as *yitong* 依通 ['dependent *shentong* 神通']." [衣通與依通同] In section 13.11 this term *yitong* 依通 appears to refer to supernormal powers of dependence, that is, the illlusory, dependent-on-something-else sleights-of-hand of mundane conjurers. Kōunshi, 1196: "*chenjie* 塵劫 is 'kalpas as numerous as specks of sand or specks of ink.' The *Lotus Sutra* [T262.9.22b7–13] . . . says: 'I am thinking of a past era, immeasurable, limitless kalpas ago, when there was a buddha, the most honored of bipeds. He was named Great Penetrating Wisdom Excellence. [Imagine that] a person uses his strength to grind up the three-thousand great-thousand lands, exhausting all the earth particles of these lands and making them all into powdered ink. As he passes by a thousand lands, he drops one speck of ink on each. In this way he goes around and around with the specks of ink until he

has exhausted all of these specks of ink. If in this way all of the lands, those he had dropped a speck on and those he had not, were again ground into specks, and if one speck were counted as one kalpa, the number of kalpas [ago that this buddha lived] would surpass the number of these minute specks.'" [塵劫者塵沙塵點劫也法華 . . . 曰如人以力磨三千大千土盡此諸地種皆悉以爲墨過於千國土乃下一塵點如是展轉點盡此諸塵墨如是諸國土點與不點等復盡抹爲塵一塵爲一劫此諸微塵數其劫復過是] Dōchū, 1341: "[Section 13.4 speaks of] *yitong guotu* 依通國土 ['lands of supernormal powers dependent (upon alchemical recipes, charms, mantras, etc.)]. The meaning is much the same as the present *yitong* 衣通 ['fluency in costumes']." [前十四張(右)云依通國土今衣通義大同]

483. Eishu, 394, and Anonymous, 285: "Even if you encounter him, you won't know him" refers to *that one person*." [相逢不相識者那一人上也] Dōchū, 1342: "I have not yet verified [the source of] this ancient saying. It refers to meeting the *original-portion* person." [古語未考本分人相見]

484. Eishu, 394, and Anonymous, 285: "*bu de* 不得 is 'not understand.'" [不得不會也]

485. The phrase *san zhong wu zhong fuzi li* 三重五重複子裏 is difficult to understand. Kassan, 547: "*fuzi* 複子 is a big bundle in olden times. Some say it is a waist bag or a three-cloth bag. It is a piece of equipment of travelers." [複子者古之打 (= 大)包或云腰囊也三衣等袋也此游方之人道具也] Modern translators give such renderings as: "carefully wrap in four or five layers of silk gauze" (Iriya, 122); "wrap in a three or five-layered *furoshiki*" (Yanagida, 158); "wrap it up in four or five squares of cloth" (Daitoku-ji, 260); "wrapping it up in three layers, five layers of carrying cloth" (Watson, 61), etc. Eishu, 395: "'Old dead geezer' is 'heterodox master.'" [死老漢邪師ゾ] Kōunshi, 1196: "'Old dead geezer' refers to a master without the eye." [死老漢者指無眼師家也]

486. Eishu, 395: "refers to the words of instruction [of old dead geezers]." [言句指云也] Kōunshi, 1197: "They seek to extract understanding from great big books—even in kalpas they won't get any." [向大策子上覓解會論劫不可得] Dōchū, 1342: "'Dried-up bones' is being compared to 'words of old dead geezers.' It means that in the words of instruction of old dead geezers there is none of the tastiness of the buddhadharma." [枯骨比死老漢語謂死老漢言句上無佛法之汁味也]

487. Eishu, 395: "'Those who don't know good from bad' are always the bad teachers." [不識好惡ハイツモノ惡知識也] Myōō, 61: "That sort haggles over exegeses of the sutras and treatises." [ソノヤウノ者ガ經論ノ中ニ向テ意解ヲ以テ商量]

488. Eishu, 395: "The scent of the teachings stinks." [教香クサキ也]

489. Luo and others, eds., *Hanyu da cidian* [*Great Word Dictionary of Sinitic*], 3.3b, glosses the term *kouling* 口令 as: "a type of oral secret password, always used to identify friend and foe" [一种口头暗号。常用来识别敌我] and cites Xu Huaizhong's 徐懷中 *Anecdotes of the West Line* (*Xixian yishi* 西線軼事, 4): "Tonight's password is 'mountain tea,' and the counter-password is 'crabapple.' Execute!" [今晚的口令是山茶、回令是海棠、执行吧] Eishu, 395, and Anonymous, 285:

"*chuan kouling* 傳口令 means 'one person speaks an untruth and gradually it revolves around and around.' . . . One dog barks, and ten dogs make the barking sound." [傳口令ハ一人實モ無フヲ云ハ次第展轉云ヲ傳口令ト云也. . . . 一犬吠形十犬吠聲] Dōkū, 1053: "*chuan kouling* 傳口令 refers to terms and phrases of bad teachings. An ancient [i.e., the *Sayings Record of Chan Master Dahui Pujue*; T1998.47.876c4–5] said, 'One person transmits a lie, and ten-thousand people transmit it as truth.'" [傳口令者指名句教壞也古人云一人傳虛萬人傳實] Kōunshi, 1197: "'Clods of shit' refers to the phrases and doctrinal points in the teachings; *chuan kouling* 傳口令 refers to spreading rumors in a village." [屎塊子者指教中句義也傳口令者村里言觸也] Dōchū, 1342: "It is like the transmission belt of an order in a village—there is no distinct person in charge." [如村裏令事展轉相傳無別掌者] Yoshizawa, ed., *Shoroku zokugokai* [*Explanations of Colloquial Expressions in Zen Records*], 250 (no.1258), glosses *chuan kouling* 傳口令 as follows: "a drinkers' forfeit game." [酒令] Modern translators seem to be working from this sort of gloss.

490. Dōchū, 1343: "This is the bad teacher." [此惡知識云也]

491. A zao 竈 (Chinese *zao*; Japanese *kamado*) is a stove made of earth, stone, brick, etc. The hole on the top accomodates a pot or cauldron. In addition to ordinary home cooking purposes, *zao* were used for preparation of elixirs by alchemists in the mountains. Dōchū, 1343: "The *tu* 突 is the window of a *kamado* stove. *qi* 漆 means 'black.' The so-called black window must not be allowed to become black, etc." [突竈囪也漆謂黑所謂黑突不得黔此此] Anonymous, 286, and Dōkū, 1053, are similar.

492. Eishu, 395: "Issan [i.e., the Chinese Chan master Yishan Yining/Issan Ichinei 一山一寧, who arrived in Japan in 1299,] said, 'When the pole is on the shoulders, its two ends curl downwards. Its appearance is like that of lips that are not speaking.'" [一山云擔子在肩時兩頭下褁凸也其兒如不言脣也] Kassan, 548, Anonymous, 286, and Dōkū, 1053, quote the same Yishan Yining comment. Dōchū, 1343: "*dan* 擔 is a wooden pole for carrying things." [擔荷物木]

493. Dōchū, 1343: "[Chengguan's] *Profound Talks on the Huayan Sutra* . . . says: 'In the *Mahāprajñāpāramitā Sūtra* the sin of slandering the dharma is widely discussed. It says that in this land they would fall into an Avīci Hell. Even after kalpas in this land's [Avīci Hell] the destruction of the sinful [karman] would not yet be finished, and they would shift to the Avīci Hell in another land. In that other land they would again go through kalpas, but the destruction of the sinful [karman] would not yet be concluded. They would again shift to another land. In this way they would make the rounds of tens upons tens of lands, in each going through kalpas. Eventually they would return to be reborn in the Avīci Hell of this land. Even if a thousand buddhas emerged in this world, saving them would still be difficult.'" [華嚴玄談 . . . 曰大般若中廣說謗法之罪謂此方墮阿鼻地獄此土劫壞罪猶未畢移置他方阿鼻地獄中他方復經劫壞罪亦未盡復移他方如是巡歷十方十方各經劫盡還生此土阿鼻地獄中千佛出世救

之猶難] CBETA, X05, no. 232, p. 800, b7–11 //Z 1:8, p. 288, a17–b3 //R8, p. 575, a17–b3.

494. Eishu, 395, glosses *jiaoban* 脚板 as: "the bottoms of the feet. . . . Because of traveling on foot [far and wide in search of a teacher and realization] the feet become bigger, and the lower legs thicken." [脚ウラ也. . . . 行脚故ニ足大成テハバキモヒロクナル也] Kassan, 548: "As for *jiaoban* 脚板, some say it is the feet stumbling; some say it is the underside of the feet. I do not know which is correct." [脚板者或云脚絆也或云脚之裡也不知孰是] Dōkū, 1053, has the first interpretation. Anonymous, 286: "It means that traveling on foot [looking] for the buddhadharma is useless." [言行脚於佛法無用也] Kōunshi, 1198: "*jiaoban* 脚版 means 'bottom of the feet.' The bottoms of the feet stamp down so much they become like woodblocks." [脚版者謂脚底脚底蹈多如版也] Dōchū, 1343: "In rushing about in a search all over their stamping footsteps are many, and so the bottoms of their feet become as wide as planks." [馳求諸方蹈步多故脚底如板濶]

495. Dōkū, 1053: "An ancient said, 'It is naturally generated, without reliance on carving/chiseling.'" [古人云元自天然不假彫琢]

496. Kassan, 548: "the *nirmāṇakāya* [buddha] or an image made of clay, wood, etc." [應身或泥木等像也] Eishu, 395: "'A buddha with characteristics' is the *nirmāṇakāya* buddha of thirty-two characteristics." [有相佛三十二相化身佛也] Myōō, 62: "'Not resemble you' means 'is not the true buddha in your house.'" [与你不相似トハ你ガ屋裡ノ真佛ニアラズト也] Dōkū, 1053–1054: "means the thirty-two marks [of the *nirmāṇakāya* buddha] and buddhas of clay and wood, etc., do not resemble your true buddha." [言三十二相及泥木等佛不似汝真佛] Kōunshi, 1198: "Externally seeking for the *nirmāṇakāya* of thirty-two marks and buddhas of clay and wood, etc., they will not be the same as the true buddha of your own mind." [向外求應化三十二相及泥木等佛與己心真佛不同] Dōchū, 1343: "'You' is *that one person.*" [汝者那一人也]

497. Dōchū, 1344: "It is neither joined with characteristics nor apart from characteristics." [非與相合又非與相離也] Dōkū, 1054: "means your original mind is neither joined with the true buddha nor apart from it." [言者汝本心與真佛非合亦非離] Kōunshi, 1198: "Mind and buddha are neither identical nor different." [心與佛非同非異] Anonymous, 286: "[neither] joined with the four elements [nor] apart from the four elements." [四大之合四大之離也]

498. Myōō, 62: "'True buddha' is every person's *dharmakāya* buddha." [真佛トハ人人ノ法身佛也]

499. Eishu, 396: "'Three dharmas' means the above 'true buddha, true Way, and true dharma.'" [三法トハ上真佛真道真法ヲ云也] Dōkū, 1054: "As to the 'three dharmas of buddha, Way, and dharma fused together,' if we are forced to give this a name, it is the 'single non-dependent true person' or the 'non-dependent Way-person.' The so-called single place is, when all is said and done, *that place.*" [佛道法之三法和合強名之云一無位真人或云無依道人也所謂一處者畢竟那處]

500. Yanagida, 160, based on *Outline of the Linked Lamps* (*Liandeng huiyao* 聯燈會要), makes the following emendation: 辨既不得 → 既辨不得. (聯燈會要: 道流真佛無形真道無體真法無相三法混融和合一處既辨不得喚作忙忙 業識眾生; CBETA, X79, no. 1557, p. 88, a2–4 //Z 2B:9, p. 294, c9–11 //R136, p. 588, a9–11)

501. Dōchū, 1344: "If he doesn't perceive it, we call him a transmigrating, confused common person of karman-pursuing consciousness.... The *Awakening of Faith* [T1666.32.577b6–7] ... says: 'The first is called karman consciousness. This means, due to the power of *avidyā*, unawakened mind is in movement.'" [若辨不得則喚作遷流忽忙逐業識凡夫也....起信論...曰一者名爲 業識謂無明力不覺心動故] Dōkū, 1054: "The person who has not perceived the principle of the single place of the three dharmas we call a sentient being." [不得辨三法一處道理者喚作眾生也]

502. Myōō, 62: "'Buddha' is just the one mind. Within the one mind it is divided into three grades: buddha, dharma, and Way. Within the three grades, we call the innately pure substance 'buddha.'" [佛トハ只是一心也一心ノ中ニ三種ノ 品アルヲ分テ佛ト云イ法ト云イ道ト云也三品ノ内本然清淨ノ体ヲ佛ト云也]

503. Eishu, 396: "'Moment after moment mind does not break off' means 'the Way twenty-four hours a day.'" [念念心不間斷者十二時中道也] Anonymous, 287: "towards beholding reality as it truly is twenty-four hours a day, no breaking off." [於真正見解十二時中無間斷也] Dōkū, 1054: "*zhenzheng zuo daoren* 真正作道人 is the Zen monk who beholds reality as it truly is and tramps about on the ground of reality [*tattva*]. 'Moment after moment mind does not break off' means 'twenty-four hours a day peacefully dwelling in the state of the *original portion* with unmixed diligence.'" [真正作道人者真正見解腳蹋實地底 祠子也念念心不間斷者十二時中安住本分田地無雜用心之義也] Kōunshi, 1198: "'Not breaking off' means 'at all times fusing into oneness.'" [不間斷者一 切時中打成一片之義也] Dōchū, 1344: "*zuo dao* 作道 is like saying 'practicing the Way for the sake of the Way.'" [作道者猶言爲道行道也]

504. Dōchū, 1344: "'Single word' is Bodhidharma's single word, that is, 'my quieting mind for you is over' [found in the Bodhidharma section of the *Transmission of the Lamp*]." [一言者達磨之一言所謂與汝安心竟 (傳燈達磨章)也] The *Record of the Tranmission of the Lamp of the Jingde Era* (*Jingde chuandeng lu* 景德傳燈錄; T2076.51.219b21–23) says: "Guang [i.e., Huike] said, 'My mind is not yet at peace. Please, Master, quiet it for me.' The Master [Bodhidharma] said, 'Bring mind here, and I will quiet it for you.' [Huike] said, 'I search for mind but cannot apprehend it.' The Master said, 'My quieting mind for you is over.'" [光 曰我心未寧乞師與安師曰將心來與汝安曰覓心了不可得師曰我與汝安心竟] Myōō, 63, Dōkū, 1054, and Kōunshi, 1199, are similar.

505. See 9.1, in which the Master presents three couplets. Here the Master may be referring to those three couplets or he may be talking in general terms of poetic practice.

Note that in regulated verse (*lǘshi* 律詩) there is the optional observance of a four-stage progression of the four couplets: the first couplet "begins" (*qi* 起); the second couplet "carries on" or "continues" (*cheng* 承); the third couplet "turns" (*zhuan* 轉); and the final couplet "brings closure" or "completes" (*he* 合). Kassan, 549, and Dōkū, 1054, gloss the "first topic" [*di-yi ju*第一句] as: "principle." [*ji li* 即理]

506. Kassan, 549, and Dōkū, 1054, gloss the "second topic" [*di-er ju* 第二句] as: "wisdom." [*ji zhi* 即智]

507. Kassan, 549, and Dōkū, 1054, gloss the "third topic" [*di-san ju* 第三句] as: "practice." [*ji xing* 即行]

508. Dōkū, 1055, and Kōunshi, 1199: "The *Vajracchedikā Sūtra* [T235.8.749c17–18] says: 'No dharma at all was in reality gotten by the *tathāgata* in the presence of Dīpaṅkara Buddha.'" [金剛經云如來在然燈佛所於法實無所得]

509. Eishu, 397: "*jiang tou mi tou* 將頭覓頭 means 'delusion.' It refers to the story of Yajñadatta." [將頭覓頭 ト ハ 迷 タ 事也演若達多 ガ 故事也] (See the *Śūraṃgama* quotation in **10.8**.) Kōunshi, 1199: "This adopts the phrasing of the *Śūraṃgama* and *Dharma Words Sutras*. The *Śūraṃgama* [T945.19.108c18–21] . . . says: 'The Buddha said: "Tsk! Ānanda! This is not your mind." [Ānanda, startled, stood up from his seat and said to the Buddha: "If this is not my mind, what name should I give it?" The Buddha told Ānanda: "This is the vishayas in front of you; thought of the unreal is deluding your true nature. Because from without beginning until the present birth you have recognized a bandit as a son and lost your source, you have been turning on the samsaric wheel]."' The *Śūraṃgama* also has the metaphor of Yajñadatta's looking for his head [see **10.8**]. Also, the *Dharma Words Sutra* [T2902.85.1435a23] says: 'All appearances in the universe are sealed by the one dharma [i.e., one mind].' Outside of this [one] mind there is no other mind. If you say that there is another [mind], you are Yajñadatta looking for another head." [按盃是楞嚴法句等取意文歟楞嚴 . . . 曰佛言咄阿難此非汝心(阿難靉然避座合掌起立白佛此非我心當名何等佛告阿難此是前塵虛妄相想惑汝真性由汝無始至于今生認賊爲子失汝元常故受輪轉)又同 . . . 有演若將頭覓頭之喩又法句經曰森羅及萬像一法之所印初此心外更無別心若言別更有者汝即是演若達多將頭覓頭]

510. Kōunshi, 1200: "This is the *Huayan Sutra's* [T278.9.465c29] idea that 'mind, buddha, and sentient beings are three undifferentiated things.'" [華嚴所謂心佛及衆生是三無差別之意也]

511. Dōchū, 1346: "This means that the fundamental is inexpressible. But, because persons lack the mind of the Way, one must not cease—one must speak by means of a detour." [言根本上無可說事但爲諸人無道心故不得休爲繞路之說也]

512. Eishu, 398: "*bu caijing* 不才淨 ['trash and crap'] is a companion of kudzu. . . . The *General Talks of Dahui* [T1998.47.863b9–10] says. . . . '[Masters] accumulate this sort of trash and crap in their bosoms, insult good people, and create hell karman.'" [不才淨葛藤ノツレ也. . . . 大惠普說曰. . . .

將這般不村(=才)不淨蘊在胸襟輕薄好人作地獄業云云] Dōkū, 1055, and Kōunshi, 1200, are very similar; Anonymous, 288, and Dōchū, 1346, have the Dahui quotation. Kassan, 550: "As for 'trash and crap,' the *General Talks of Dahui* has the phrase *bu cai bu jing* 不才不淨. This means 'defiled.'" [不才淨者大慧普說有不才不淨之語是污穢之義也]

513. Eishu, 398: "the mind of 'do not acknowledge my words!'" [我語認ルナト云心也] Kassan, 550: "because it does not involve an interest in reason." [不涉理致故也] Kōunshi, 1200: "This is 'Huangbo's buddhadharma was point-blank.'" [a line in **38.2**; 是黃蘗佛法無多子底]

514. Eishu, 398: "'Gate of adornment' is 'methods of teaching instruction.' . . . 'Gate of buddha matters' is 'methods of teaching the dharma.'" [莊嚴門化義門也. . . . 佛事門化法門也] Kassan, 550, and Dōkū, 1055, are very similar. Kōunshi, 1200, glosses *fo shi* 佛事 ("buddha matters") with a Kumārajīva comment in *Commentary on the Vimalakīrti Sūtra* [*Zhu Weimojie jing* 注維摩詰經: T1775.38.400b9]: "'Buddha matters' means 'transforming sentient beings.'" [什曰佛事謂化衆生]

515. Chitetsu, 811: "The *Mahāprajñāpāramitā Treatise* [T1509.25.173c15–18] . . . says: '[Furthermore, if the bodhisattva wishes release from birth, old age, sickness, and death, and also wishes to release sentient beings, he should always be zealous, of one mind, never scattered,] like someone carrying oil in a bowl and walking midst a great crowd. Because he is right now of one mind with no scattering, he obtains great fame and benefit.'" [大論 . . . 曰(復次菩薩欲脫生老病死亦欲度脫衆生常應精進一心不放逸)如人擎油鉢行大衆中現前一心不放逸故大得名利] Dōkū, 1056, and Kōunshi, 1201: "The *Nirvāṇa Sūtra* [T375.12.740a8–16] . . . says: 'It is as if in the world a great crowd fills up twenty-five neighborhoods, and the king orders an official to carry a bowl of oil through the neighborhoods without tipping it. "If you spill one drop I will end your life." He also dispatches a person wielding a sword to follow behind and frighten him. The official accepts the king's order and tries mightily to persist, going through the midst of the great crowd. . . . Finally [he arrives] without spilling a single drop of oil. The bodhisattva is also like this. In the midst of samsara he never loses mindfulness and wisdom.'" [涅槃經 . . . 曰譬如世間有諸大衆滿二十五里王勅一臣持一油鉢經里中過莫令傾覆若棄一滴當斷汝命復遣一人拔刀在後隨而怖之臣受王勅盡心堅持經歷爾所大衆之中. . . . 乃至不棄一滴之油菩薩亦復如是於生死中不失念慧以不失故雖見五欲心不貪著]

516. Chitetsu, 811: "'Eye of the Way' means 'awakened to the one vehicle.' It is the '*saddharma* vision' or 'wonderful mind of nirvana.'" [道眼者謂一乘道覚是則正法眼藏涅槃妙心]

517. Dōchū, 1347: "'Enter the Way' is 'leave home to enter the Buddha Way.' 'Not penetrate the principle' is 'lazy and slack and so not comprehending the principle of the buddhadharma.' As to 'by being reborn repay the donations received from the believing donors,' the body dies and is reborn. This is called

'returning.' Those who have left home do not engage in worldly work, and so clothing, food, dwelling, and medicine . . . are all donations from believing donors. Therefore, they return to repay the debt." [入道者出家入佛道也不通理者懶惰懈怠不通達佛法之理也復身還信施者身死再生此云復也出家不營世業故衣食住藥 . . . 無非信施故再來償其債也]

518. Dōkū, 1056, and Kōunshi, 1201: "The *Comprehensive Record of the Buddhas and Patriarchs* [T2036.49.504a6–23] . . . says: 'The fifteenth patriarch Kāṇadeva was a South Indian. . . . After obtaining [the fourteenth patriarch Nāgārjuna's] dharma, he arrived in the country of Kapila. There was a wealthy man named Brahma Pure Virtue. One day a tree in his garden produced a large fungus, which had an excellent taste. Only the wealthy man and his second son Rāhulata picked and ate it. Having been picked, it grew again; exhausted, it reproduced. None of the other family members were capable of seeing it. At the time the honored one [Kāṇadeva] knew the karmic cause in a past life for this, and he subsequently arrived at this home. The wealthy man asked the reason [for the mushroom]. The honored one said, "You in the past made offerings to a *bhikṣu*. However, this *bhikṣu's* eye of the Way was not yet bright. Because he falsely profited from a believing donor, he repaid with the original fungus. Only you and your son out of true sincerity made offerings to him. You provided for him—the others did not." [Kāṇadeva] also asked, "Householder, how old are you?" He replied: "Seventy-nine." The honored one then spoke a verse: "He entered the Way but did not penetrate the principle; by being reborn, he repaid the donations he had received from the believing donors; when your age is eighty-one; this tree will no longer produce the mushrooms." The wealthy man, upon hearing the verse, gave out an extreme sigh and did a prostration.'" [佛祖通載 . . . 云第十五祖迦那提婆南天竺國人也. . . . 師得法後至毘羅國彼有長者曰梵摩淨德一日園樹生大耳如菌味甚美唯長者與第二子羅睺羅多取而食之取已隨長盡而復生自餘親屬皆不能見時尊者知其宿因遂至其家長者問其故尊者曰汝家昔曾供養一比丘然此比丘道眼未明以虛露信施故報爲本菌唯汝與子精誠供養得以享之餘即否矣又問長者年多少曰七十有九尊者乃說偈曰入道不通理復身還信施汝年八十一此樹不生耳長者聞偈彌加歎伏] Kōunshi, 1201, cites same passage.

519. Dōchū, 1348: "In the *Tiantai Four-Teachings Model* [of the Goryeo monk] Jegwan [T1931.46.777a27–28] it says: '*Pratyeka-buddha* is one who emerges when there is no buddha and dwells alone on a solitary peak. Contemplating change in things, he awakens on his own to non-arising.'" [諦觀四教儀中曰言獨覺者出無佛世獨宿孤峯觀物變易自覺無生] Kōunshi, 1201: "'Dwelling alone on a solitary peak' is the *pratyeka-buddha* practice of the Hīnayāna." [孤峰獨宿者是即小乘獨覺之修行也] Kōunshi also cites the same passage from Jegwan's (?–970) treatise.

520. Kōunshi, 1201: "The *Mahāsāṃghika-vinaya* [T1425.22.359b11–13] says: 'Because the *tathāgata* took one meal, his body was spry and light, and he was able to

dwell in peace and joy. You *bhikṣus* should also take one meal.'" [(摩訶)僧祇律曰如來以一食故身體輕便得安樂住汝等比丘亦應一食] Iriya, 129.5: "*mao* 卯 means 'early morning.' [「卯」は早朝をいう。]

521. Eishu, 399: "'Long periods of [cross-legged] sitting without lying down' is *zazen*." [長坐不臥坐禪也] Kōunshi, 1201: "'Constant [cross-legged] sitting without lying down' is one of the twelve ascetic practices [*dhūta*]." [常坐不臥者十二頭陀之一也]

522. Eishu, 399: "'Carrying out practices at the six times' is the practice of *nenbutsu* [i.e., recitation of the name of Amitābha Buddha]." [六時行道念佛修行也] Dōchū, 1348: "According to Shandao's *Verses of Praise on Rebirth* [*in Amitābha's Pure Land;* T1980.47.446a25], sunset, first night, middle night, late night, dawn, and noon are the 'six times.'" [忠按善導往生禮讃偈記以日沒時初夜時中夜時後夜時晨朝時午時爲六時] Anonymous, 290: "the *nenbutsu sāmadhi*." [念佛三昧也]

523. Kōunshi, 1202: "The *Nirvāṇa Sūtra* [T374.12.403a6–7] . . . says: 'In the past he practiced austerities and gave away all sorts of things—his own head, eyes, marrow, brains, states, walled cities, wives, and children. Therefore, now he is able to complete the buddha path.' The *Lotus Sutra* [T262.9.34b27–29] . . . says: 'Because I desired to completely fill the six *pāramitās*, I diligently practiced giving. My mind was never stingy [in giving] elephants, horses, the seven precious gems, countries, walled cities, wives, children, female servants, male servants, my own head, eyes, marrow, brains, body, flesh, hands, and feet. I did not begrudge my own life.'" [涅槃 . . . 曰往昔苦行種種布施頭目髓腦國城妻子是故今者得成佛道法華 . . . 曰爲欲滿足六波羅蜜勤行布施心無慳惜象馬七珍國城妻子奴婢僕從頭目髓腦身肉手足不惜軀命] Dōkū, 1057: "The gate of practice which extends from the six *pāramitās* to this is all conditioned dharmas. Therefore, it will 'incur a karmic recompense of further suffering.'" [自六度至此之行門盡皆有爲法故還是招苦果也]

524. Eishu, 399: "'Pure oneness without adulteration' means 'fusing into oneness.'" [純一無雜ハ打成一片之義也]

525. Kōunshi, 1202: "All the *devas* welcome into the world with joy this stream-enterer of pure oneness without adulteration." [諸天歡喜者諸天歡喜此純一無雜道流在世也]

526. The *Good Reverence Sutra* (*Shan gongjin jing* 善恭敬經; T1495.24.1101b12–14) says: "At that time, the student, having received the dharma, with his right knee touching the ground, holds the feet [of the master] in both hands in worship. With singleness of mind he does a full prostration in the presence of his master." [是時學者既受法已右膝著地兩手捧足一心頂禮師所住處] Kōunshi, 1202: "'Holding the feet' means that the local spirits reverence this stream-enterer." [捧足者地神恭敬此道流也]

527. Dōkū, 1057: "In the sutras this is where [the Buddha] says: 'Good! Good!'" [經中云善哉善哉是也]

528. Dōkū, 1058, and Kōunshi, 1203: "The *Lotus Sutra* [T262.9.22a19–20] . . . says: 'The seventh buddha tells the *bhikṣus:* "In the past—immeasurable, limitless, inconceivable *asaṃkhyeyas* of kalpas ago—at that time there was a buddha named Great Superknowledge Wisdom-Victory *Tathāgata*."'" [法華 . . . 第七佛告諸比丘乃往過去無量無邊不可思議阿僧祇劫爾時有佛名大通智勝如來云云] Chitetsu, 813: "Linji is outside the teachings. [The monk] wants to know [whether or not Linji] can explicate sutra texts. This is the reason why the monk asks about the text of the *Lotus Sutra*." [臨濟教外欲知可解釋經文否所以僧問法華經文]

529. Kōunshi, 1203: "The verse of the [*Lotus*] *Sutra* [T262.9.26b3] says: 'Having passed ten small kalpas, he completed the Buddha Way.' The 'ten kalpas' are the ten *pāramitās*. . . . The ten *pāramitās* are the six *pāramitās* plus the four *pāramitās* of *upāyas*, vowing, wisdom, and power." [故經偈曰過十小劫已乃得成佛道十劫即十波羅蜜. . . . 十波羅蜜者六波羅蜜加方便願智力之四波羅蜜也] Dōchū, 1350: "To the six *pāramitās* [four] are added: *upāyas*, vowing, power, and wisdom." [六度加方便願力智]

530. Eishu, 400, and Anonymous, 293: "Every person is originally a buddha. How can one say 'should become a buddha?'" [人人本來佛也如何可成佛卜云也] Dōchū, 1350: "From the outset [everyone] is a buddha. There is no logic to becoming a buddha all over again." [元來是佛無更作佛道理也]

531. Kōunshi, 1204: "The *Mañjusrī Dharmakāya Rites* [文殊法身禮; T2844.85.1296b18] says: 'The Buddha is always in the world but is not stained by worldly dharmas.' . . . The *Nirvāṇa Sūtra* [T374.12.372c20] . . . says: 'The Buddha is not stained by worldly dharmas, like a lotus in [muddy] water.'" [文殊法身禮曰佛常在世間而不染世法. . . . 涅槃 . . . 曰佛不染世法如蓮華處水]

532. Eishu, 400, and Dōkū, 1059: "'Myriad things' is the 'myriad vishayas.' Do not be spun around by the myriad vishayas." [萬物萬境也莫被轉萬境也 (mistake for: 莫被萬境轉也)] Anonymous, 293, has the second part. Dōchū, 1350: "The *Śūraṃgama Sūtra* [T945.19.111c25–26] . . . says: 'All sentient beings from without beginning have been deluded about self and [acted upon] by things. They lose their original mind and are spun around by things.'" [楞嚴經 . . . 曰一切眾生從無始來迷己爲物失於本心爲物所轉] Kōunshi, 1204, cites the same *Śūraṃgama* passage and comments: "'Myriad things' means 'myriad objective supports [*ālambana*], myriad vishayas.'" [萬物者萬緣萬境也]

533. Dōchū, 1350, and Kōunshi, 1204: "The *Awakening of Faith* [T1666.32.577b22–23] . . . says: 'Because, when thought arises, the various dharmas arise; when thought extinguishes, the various dharmas extinguish.'" [起心論 . . . 以心生則種種法生心滅則種種法滅故]

534. Eishu, 400: "The arising of thoughts is the disease." [念起病也]

535. Dōchū, 1350: "means 'supposing there were a buddha and there were a dharma.'" [言設有佛有法也] Eishu, 400: "They would all be just terms." [皆是名バカリナリ]

536. Kassan, 556: "When you carefully look at the sayings of the buddhas and patriarchs down through the ages, they are all expressive *upāyas* for enticing small children." [歷代佛祖言說子細看來揔是接引小兒表顯方便也] Anonymous, 293: "The teachings of [the Buddha's] whole lifetime are books of medical prescriptions." [一代時教方書也] Dōkū, 1059: "The sayings of the buddhas and patriarchs down through the ages are all in accordance with mental dispositions of sentient beings, givng medicine in response to illness. They are expressive *upāyas*, like taking yellow leaves to entice small children." [歷代佛祖言說總是隨眾生機應病與藥表顯方便譬如以黃葉接引小兒也] Kōunshi, 1204: "The *Laṅkāvatāra Sūtra* [T670.16.485a2–7] . . . says: '. . . . For people with this and that illness, the good doctor prescribes according to the case. The *tathāgata* for the sake of sentient beings speaks in response to their [particular] minds.'" [楞伽 . . . 曰 . . . . 彼彼諸病人良醫隨處方如來爲眾生隨心應量說]

537. Eishu, 400–401, and Anonymous, 293: "The names of the myriad dharmas are not self-revealing. *That one person* is capable of revealing the names of the myriad dharmas. He is *that one person* of 'brightness and brilliance.'" [万法名字不自顯那一人能顯万法名字也昭昭靈靈那一人] Dōkū, 1059: "As to this 'brightness and brilliance,' every person is endowed with the single ray of light." [此所謂昭昭靈靈者人人具足一段光明也] Kōunshi, 1204: "'Mirror awareness, hearing, and knowing' is like saying 'seeing, hearing, awareness, and knowing.' It is the 'divine light of the six paths.'" [found in 10.4; 鑑覺聞知猶言見聞覺知前所謂六道神光也]

538. Eishu, 401, and Anonymous, 293: "The five transgressions are called the 'five uninterrupted' because those who [commit] the five crimes fall into uninterruped [punishment in the Avīci Hell]." [五逆謂五無間也五逆罪者墮無間故也] Kōunshi, 1204: "These words are completely rooted in the *Vimalakīrti* and *Laṅkāvatāra Sūtras*. The *Commentary to the Vimalakīrti Sūtra* [T1775.38.350b8–11] . . . says: '[Sutra:] By the five transgressions one obtains liberation. Sengzhao comments: The five transgressive sins are the superior points of the liberation path. If one can obtain liberation by the five transgressions, one will be able to seize the food of men.' The *Laṅkāvatāra Sūtra* [T670.16.498a13–15] . . . says: 'Mahāmati Bodhisattva, the great being, said to the Buddha: "World-honored-one! As the World-honored-one has said, if men and women create the karman of the five uninterrupted, they will not enter the Avīci Hell."'" [此語全本于維摩楞伽注維摩 . . . 曰以五逆相而得解脫(注肇曰五逆罪尤者解脫道之勝者若能即五逆相而得解脫者可取人之食也楞伽 . . . 曰爾時大慧菩薩摩訶薩白佛言世尊如世尊說若男子女人行五無間業不入無擇地獄] Dōchū, 1351: "The liberation of the five uninterrupted is based on teachings in the *Laṅkāvatāra Sūtra*." [includes the same citation as above; 五無間解脫依楞伽說相]

539. Myōō, 67: "'Karman of the five uninterrupted' means 'five transgressions.' Those who commit these crimes necessarily fall into the Avīci Hell." [五無間業トハ五逆罪ヲ云也此罪ヲ造レハ必阿鼻地獄ニ落也]

540. Eishu, 401: "In the [*Laṅkāvatāra*] *Sūtra* [T670.16.498a19] 'burning sutras and images' is replaced by 'killing an arhat.'" [經中除焚燒經像加殺羅漢也] Actually, it is replaced by "harming an arhat." [害羅漢] Kassan, 557, Dōkū, 1060, and Dōchū, 1351, are similar.

541. Kōunshi, 1205: "In the *Laṅkāvatāra Sūtra* [T670.16.498b11–13] . . . a verse says: 'Craving is called the "mother." *Avidyā* is the "father." The consciousness that is aware of vishayas is the "Buddha." The [latent] tendencies are the "arhat." The collection of *skandhas* is called the "sangha."'" [楞伽 . . . 偈曰貪愛名爲母無明則爲父覺境識爲佛諸使爲羅漢陰集名爲僧]

542. Kōunshi, 1205: "'Arises and extinguishes' is 'thoughts arising and thoughts extinguishing.'" [起滅念起念滅也] Dōchū, 1353: "The *Awakening of Faith* [T1666.32.576b24–25] says: '[In a moment of conjunction,] one is aware of the first arising of mind, but mind has no characteristic first.'" [起心論 . . . 曰[一念相應]覺心初起心無初相]

543. Eishu, 401: "*xiang ying kong* 響應空 means 'not getting hung up on.'" [響應空トハ不滞在也] Dōchū, 1353: "There is no trace." [沒蹤迹]

544. Dōchū, 1353: "You do not produce the understanding of awakening." [不生覺明之解會也]

545. Emendation based upon the Tiansheng *Linjilu*, which reads: 便處處不分別 ("everywhere non-discrimination"). CBETA, X78, no. 1553, p. 473, c1 //Z 2B:8, p. 351, b3 //R135, p. 701, b3. The standard Yuanjue Zongyan edition, the LJL (Yanagida, 168), reads: 便處處黑暗 ("everywhere darkness").

546. Eishu, 401: "'Comprehend that the *kleśas* and latent tendencies' means 'overturn the *kleśas* and latent tendencies.' . . . 'sweep away the *kleśas*.'" [達煩惱結使トハ轉煩惱結使也. . . . 掃除煩惱也]

547. Kōunshi, 1206, and Dōchū, 1353: "[Nāgārjuna's] *Middle Treatise* [T1564.30.33b11–12] says: 'Origination by dependence—we say that is *śūnyatā*. [That is a provisional name (*prajñaptir upādāya*) and the meaning of the middle path.]'" [中論曰因緣所生法我說即是空(亦爲是假名亦是中道義)]

548. Kōunshi, 1206: "'Worldling and *ārya* terminology' refers to the 'father, mother, buddha, sangha, etc.,' in the above section." [結上凡聖名者指上父母佛僧等]

549. Anonymous, 295: "*kongju* 空拳 and *zhi* 指 are two metaphors. The first [involves] taking an empty fist or yellow leaves to stop a small child's crying—to entice children. In the case of the second, the *Perfect Awakening Sutra* [T842.17.917a27–28] says: 'The sutra teachings are like a finger indicating the moon.' . . . The one who [mistakenly] recognizes the finger as the moon is an idiot." [空拳指有二喻一將空拳黃葉止小兒啼誘孫兒也二圓覚經云修多羅教如標月指. . . . 認指為月愚也]

550. The term *nieguai* 捏怪 refers to the imaginary depiction, both literary and visual, of bizarre and strange imagery. See n. 84. The commentators have

different interpretations. Kōunshi, 1206: "'Sense organs, vishayas, and dharmas' are the eighteen *dhātus* of sense organs, vishayas, and sense consciousnesses. *nieguai* 捏怪 has the meaning 'inference and planning.'" [根境法者根境識之十八界也捏怪者計較按排之義也] Myōō, 68: "'Sense organs and vishayas' are the six sense organs and six vishayas. When you by means of the six sense organs grab on to the six vishayas, mind produces the various dharmas." [根境トハ六根六境也你六根ヲ以テ六境ニ着スル時心生シ種種ノ法生] Dōkū, 1061: "*nieguai* 捏怪 is 'karma-formations.' It also means 'inference and planning.'" [捏怪者造作也又云計較安排也] Dōchū, 1353: "'Sense organs and vishayas' are the six sense organs and six vishayas. 'Dharmas' are the myriad dharmas." [根境六根六境法即萬法]

551. Dōchū, 1353: "As for *si* 死 ['death'], when anyone desires to say 'extreme,' he often uses the word 'death.'" [又曰死凡欲言極甚多用死字] Anonymous, 295: "This means that every person's shape is like that of a living lion, but their minds are like that of jackals. [言人人其形雖如生師子其心却如野干] Dōkū, 1061: "This metaphor refers to the line above: 'I am a worldling, but that is an *ārya*.'" [此譬指上我是凡夫他是聖人語] Kōunshi, 1207: "'Lion skin' means 'dharma clothes of the Mahāyāna.' The *Kṣitigarbha Ten Wheels Sutra* [T411.13.757b22] . . . says: 'To pretend to call yourself the Mahāyāna for the sake of fame and profit is like a broken-down donkey decking itself out in a lion skin.' 'Sound of a jackal' means 'teachings of the Hīnayāna.'" [師子皮者謂大乘之法服地藏十論經 . . . 曰詐號大乘爲名利如弊驢披師子皮野干鳴者謂小乘之所說]

552. Eishu, 403, and Anonymous, 295: "your own true buddha." [自己真佛也] Dōkū, 1061: "You do not have confidence in the formless, markless true buddha in your own house." [不信自己屋裡無形無相之真佛也] Chitetsu, 833: "This 'in your own house' means 'in the house of the gate of personal-realization-of-the-meaning-beyond-words'; 'thing' means 'noble wisdom of awakening on one's own.'" [此自家謂宗門屋裡物謂自覺聖智]

553. Eishu, 403: "the procedure for doing *yin-yang* divination, etc." [又陰陽占ナドヲスル程フ也] Myōō, 68: "By investigating the *yin-yang* computational teachings, one makes various calculations and conjectures." [陰陽ノ算教ヲ考テ種種ニ計較卜度スル也] Dōkū, 1061, and Kōunshi, 1207: "means '*yin-yang* adept.'" [謂陰陽家]

554. Myōō, 68: "'*zhunding*' 准定 is 'established rule/set pattern.'" [准定ハ定規也] Dōkū, 1061: "means 'having no standard/norm.'" [無準則之義] Kōunshi, 1207: "[having no] definite standard or norm by which to decide." [準定準則決定也]

555. Myōō, 68: "You: don't take what I am saying right now as an established rule." [你等我ガ只今說処ヲ取テ准定トナ] Chitetsu, 834: "[Zen] patriarchal masters of '[a separate transmission] outside the teachings' do maintain the teachings principle. This is 'speaking Zen,' and so it says: 'Don't take what I am saying [as an established rule].'" [教外祖師護持說通此是說禪故云莫取山僧說處]

556. Kōunshi, 1207: "*pingju* 憑據 means 'to rely on a basis.' The *Śūraṃgama Sūtra* [T945.19.120c28] . . . says: 'In the false there is no basis to be relied upon.' *yiqi* 一期 means 'a one-off response to the mass of mental dispositions [of beings].' For the simile of 'images in colored paintings,' commentaries quote the painter simile of the *Huayan Sutra*, but this is not the source. . . . The actual source is the *Laṅkāvatāra Sūtra*. The *Laṅkāvatāra* [T670.16.484c24–26] . . . says: 'It is like the master painter and his painting disciples, who spread colors to depict various forms. I say it is like this: the colors don't produce the pattern, neither does the brush, nor does the blank silk.'" [憑據依憑本據也楞嚴 . . . 虛妄無可憑據一期一往應群機之間也彩畫像喻諸鈔引華嚴工畫師喻者非本據. . . . 當據楞伽楞伽 . . . 曰譬如工畫師及與畫弟子布彩圖衆形我說亦如是彩色本無文非筆亦非素]

557. Kōunshi, 1207: "This criticizes those who grasp on to the three vehicles. Bodhisattvas take the six *pāramitās* to bind people; arhats take the practice of the four noble truths to bind persons." [斥是執三乘者菩薩以六度縛人羅漢以四真道行縛人]

558. Kōunshi, 1207–1208: "The *Ratnakūṭa Sūtra* [T310.590b11–c6] says: '. . . . At that time the World-honored-one, because he wanted to eliminate the discriminating minds of those five-hundred bodhisattvas, used his miraculous power to awaken Mañjuśrī. Mañjuśrī yielded to the Buddha's magical power and rose from his seat. He grasped a sharp sword in hand, and directly approached the World-honored-one. Just as he was about to commit murder, the Buddha promptly announced to Mañjuśrī: "Stay! You should not commit a [deadly] sin. Do not murder me. . . . Mañjuśrī! From the outset there is no self and no person. It is merely that internal mind sees the existence of a self and person. When internal mind has arisen, that is already the murdering of me—it is called murder." At the time the bodhisattvas, having heard the Buddha speak, all had this thought: "All dharmas are like illusions. . . . Therefore, within [all dharmas] there is no person to apprehend the sin, and there is no sin to be apprehended. Who is the one who kills and then undergoes the disaster?" Those bodhisattvas, having thus investigated and come to know clearly, at the time obtained the non-arising dharma patience.'" [寶積經云. . . . 爾時世尊爲欲除彼五百菩薩分別心故即以威神覺悟文殊文殊承佛神力從座而起手執利劍直趣世尊欲行逆害時佛遽告文殊汝住不應造逆勿得害我. . . . 文殊從本已來無我無人但是内心見有我人内心起時彼已害我即名爲害時諸菩薩聞佛說已咸作是念一切諸法悉如幻化. . . . 是故於中無人得罪無罪可得誰爲殺者而得受殃彼諸菩薩如是觀察明了知已即時獲得無生法忍]

559. Kōunshi, 1208: "The *Glossary of the Patriarchal Courtyard* . . . says: '*aṅguli*: the full form is *aṅguli-māla*. This is translated as "finger garland." The *Worthies and Fools Sutra* [T202.4.423b4–424a26] says: "The assistant minister of King Prasenajit had one son. He was upright and strong. He could take on one thousand men. His name was No Anger [later called Finger Garland], and he was studying under a brahmin. . . . The brahmin said, 'The assistant minister's

son—it is difficult to bring him under control. I will set up an unusual plan.'
He then said to No Anger: 'You—if within seven days you chop off one hand
from a thousand people—out of every ten of those [thousand hands], keep just
one finger. When you get to one-hundred fingers, make it into a garland.' . . .
Within the seven days he got ninety-nine fingers. He was only short one person but couldn't find one. At the time there was a mother who gave him food
she was holding, and he was about to kill that mother. Just then, the World-
honored-one happened to witness this, so he magically created [himself as] a
bhikṣu and walked along the side of that one [No Anger]. He [No Anger] discarded the mother and hastened after the *bhikṣu*. The Buddha saw him coming
and walked along slowly, rejecting him. Finger Garland [No Anger] ran with
extreme effort, but could not catch up. He then called out: 'Stop for a bit.' The
Buddha said, 'I'm always at a stop. It's only you who haven't stopped.' Finger
Garland further said, 'How is it that you are stopped, and I am not stopped?'
The Buddha said, 'My sense organs are stilled, and I have obtained freedom.
You have followed a bad master and changed your heart, so you haven't attained the stopping that is *samādhi*.' Having heard these words, [Finger Garland's] mind opened, and he obtained awakening. He committed himself to the
tathāgata, who manifested a body to speak dharma. [Finger Garland] left home
and realized the fruit.'"' [事苑 . . . 曰央掘: 具云央崛摩羅此飜云指鬘賢愚經
云波斯匿王輔相家生一男端正有力可敵千人字曰無惱從學於婆羅門. . . . 婆
羅門曰輔相之子難以治之當設異謀乃謂無惱曰汝若於七日之中斬千人手去
十取一指凡得百指以爲鬘餝. . . . 至七日中得九十九指唯少一人求覓不得時
母持食與之輒欲殺母爾時世尊遙見化作比丘行於彼邊遂捨母趣是比丘佛見
其來徐行捨去指鬘極力走不能及即便喚言小住佛云我常自住但汝不住指鬘
復曰云何汝住我不住耶佛言我諸根寂定而得自在汝從惡師變易汝心不得定
住聞是語已心開意悟歸投如來即爲現身說法出家證果] Following the CBETA
text: CBETA, X64, no. 1261, p. 397, a21–b14 //Z 2:18, p. 84, d13–p. 85, a12 //R113,
p. 168, b13–p. 169, a12.

560. Kōunshi, 1209: "The five natures are based in the sutras and treatises, which
have different [exegeses]." [五性者依經論有差別]

561. Kōunshi, 1209: "'Perfect and sudden teaching' is the teaching of the *Huayan,
Lotus, Nirvāṇa*, etc." [圓頓教者華嚴法華涅槃等之教也]

562. Eishu, 404, employs a Japanese analogy: "When the great Shōgun is notifying
troops of assignment to various countries, he first posts the orders in broad day-
light on the thoroughfares." [大將軍下知兵遣諸國時先布札昼法令立道衢也]
Kassan, 561: "The *Glossary of the Patriarchal Courtyard* [CBETA, X64,
no. 1261, p. 398, a20 //Z 2:18, p. 85, d12 //R113, p. 170, b12] says: "*lubu*
路布" should be "*lubu* 露布." An unsealed imperial edict is called a "*lubu*
露布"'. . . . Here it is a sign [consisting of] kudzu words and phrases."
[事苑云路布當作露布不封詔表曰露布. . . . 此者標葛藤言句也] Dōkū, 1063,
and Dōchū, 1356, have the same emendation.

563. Taking *wenzi chapai* 文字差排 as "written directives" is based on an example found in the *Sayings Record of Chan Master Dahui Pujue* (*Dahui Pujue chanshi yulu* 大慧普覺禪師語錄; T1998.47.920c19–20): "By all means pull yourself together, make the skin of your face thicken—you must not accept the directives of others." [須是急著手脚冷却面皮不得受人差排]

564. Dōchū, 1356: "*lixu* 裏許 means 'inside the expressive written word.'" [裏許者表顯文字之裏也] Dōkū, 1063, and Kōunshi, 1209, are similar.

565. Myōō, 70: "Even if you are conversant with a thousand sutras and ten-thousand treatises, I cast it aside and won't have any of it." [你ガ千經万論ニ通シタルモ我ハステテ不取] Eishu, 405: "Even if he understands the entire canon of scriptures, Linji doesn't give it the least thought." [一大藏教ヲ解トモ林際ハ何トモ不思ゾ]

566. Anonymous, 298: "worldly wisdom." [世智] Dōkū, 1063: "An old commentary takes *congming zhihui* 聰明智慧 as worldly wisdom. The discriminating intelligence [behind this interpretation] is inadequate. [The line] means: 'The Great Master is truly smart and has *prajñā*, and he is having nothing of it.'" [古鈔以此聰明智慧爲世智辨聰不可也言大師眞聰明眞智慧亦不取之]

567. Eishu, 405: "Only Linji loves 'beholding reality as it truly is.'" [唯林際好眞正見解也] Kassan, 561: "This is what the Great Master considers most necessary." [此箇是大師所要也] Kōunshi, 1209: "Discard the [terra-cotta] tile and seize the bright pearl [of the mind]." [捨瓦礴取明珠]

568. Chitetsu, 838: "'Being conversant with a hundred sutras and treatises' is great understanding, [but no more than] an understanding that lies in the *mano-vijñāna* [i.e., the sixth consciousness that takes dharmas as its object]." [解得百部經論大解解在意識]

569. Eishu, 405: "'*ashi* 阿師' means 'monk.'" [阿師ハ僧也]

570. Eishu, 405, and Anonymous, 299: "The meaning is 'conversant with a hundred sutras and treatises.'" [解得百本經論義也]

571. Eishu, 405, and Anonymous, 299: "*Asuras* have a great deal of anger." [脩羅瞋多也] Kōunshi, 1210: "The *Perfect Awakening Sutra* [T842.17.920a8–9] . . . says: 'Sentient beings of the final age hope to complete the Way but do not exert themselves in pursuit of awakening. They add to their learning and increase the [erroneous] self-view.'" [圓覺經 . . . 曰末世衆生希望成道無令求悟益多聞增長我見]

572. Kōunshi, 1210: "The *Nirvāṇa Sūtra* [T374.12.561c10–21] . . . says: 'Though Sunakṣātra Bhikṣu chanted the twelve sections of scripture and attained the four *dhyānas*, he did not understand the meaning of a single verse or a single word. He associated with bad friends and retreated from the four *dhyānas*. Having retreated from the four *dhyānas*, he produced evil heterodox views. He said [from an extremist, annihilationist point of view] such things as: "There is no buddha and no dharma; there is no nirvana." . . . Because of his evil mind, while alive he fell into the Avīci Hell.'" [涅槃經 . . . 曰善星比丘雖復讀誦十二部經獲得四禪乃至不解一偈一字之義親近惡友退失四禪退四禪

已生惡邪見作如是說無佛無法無有涅槃. . . . 以惡心故生身陷入阿鼻地獄]
Dōkū, 1064, also cites this *Nirvāṇa* passage and gives another quotation: "The
Śūraṃgama Sūtra [T945.19.143a23–24] . . . says: 'Sunakṣātra falsely preached
[an extremist view of] the emptiness of all dharmas and while alive fell into the
Avīci Hell.'" [楞嚴 . . . 云善星妄說一切法空生身陷入阿鼻地獄]

573. Kōunshi, 1210, and Kassan, 562: "This continues the line above: 'being conversant with a hundred sutras and treatises.'" [承上解得百本經論等之文]

574. Dōkū, 1064: "The *Śūraṃgama Sūtra* . . . says: 'The *vāsanā* of greed intersects
with mental construction [*kalpanā*] and develops into rapid breathing that
cannot be stopped. Thus, there is a feeling of being very cold inside a block
of ice. This is like someone who recoils at inhaling air through the mouth as
contact with the cold arises.'" [楞嚴 . . . 云貪習交計發於相吸吸覽(攬)不止如
是故有積寒堅氷於中凍冽如人以口吸縮風氣有冷觸生] Kōunshi, 1210: "'Inhal-
ing cold air' means 'out of greed clinging to external written interpretations.'"
[吸冷氣者貪取外文字義解之義也] He cites the same *Śūraṃgama* passage.
Anonymous, 299: "Exhaled breath is hot, and inhaled breath is cold. Lascivious
desires bring into being hot hells, and material desires bring into being cold hells.
Propulsion into the two hells of cold and hot is due to the two desires of material
things and sex. Seeking out and clinging to external things is 'cold breath.' Producing internal mind is 'hot breath.'" [呼氣熱吸氣冷婬欲成熱地獄財欲成寒
地獄感乎寒熱二地獄由於財色二欲求取外物冷氣也發起內心熱氣也] Dōchū,
1357: "[You 'inhale cold air'] because of chanting the written word." [調誦文字故]

575. Kassan, 562: "This uses the term *quanxue* 權學 ['*upāya*-type learning'] to con-
nect to [the line above:] 'conversant with the hundred sutras and treatises.'"
[此呼權學之名而結百本經論之解也] Dōkū,1064: "The bodhisattva of the *upāya*-
type teachings is not a Mahāyāna bodhisattva." [權教之菩薩非大乘菩薩也]
Kōunshi, 1210–1211: "This is a passage from [Li Tongxuan's 李通玄] *Complete
Treatise on the Huayan Sutra.* That treatise . . . says: 'In the effortless effort, the
effort is not in vain. In the effortful effort, all of the effort is impermanent—
though many kalpas accumulate, the cultivation ends up failing, and it is not
as good as, in a single moment, [realizing that] origination by dependence is
non-arising [and non-extinguishing] and leapfroging those views of *upāya*-type
learning in the three vehicles.'" [是華嚴合論文也彼論 . . . 曰無功之功功不
虛棄有功之功功皆無常多劫積修終歸敗壞不如一念緣起無生超彼三乘權學
等見] CBETA, X04, no. 223, p. 15, b21–23 //Z 1:5, p. 336, a6–8 //R5, p. 671, a6–8.

576. Eishu, 406: "*yinxun* 因循 is 'blending in with things and not standing out.'"
[因循打マキレテ也] Myōō, 70: "*yinxun* 因循 is 'weak/weak-kneed.'" [因循ハ
荏苒ノ義也] Dōchū, 1358: "without having done anything." [無所作爲也]

577. Eishu, 406: "prior to awakening." [未悟先也]

578. Eishu, 406, Anonymous, 299, Kassan, 563, and Dōkū, 1064: "without understanding." [無分曉]

579. Kassan, 563: "In his heart he was not peaceful and steady." [胸懷不平穩也] Anonymous, 299: "He had a seething desire for awakening." [又發憤而欲悟也] Dōkū, 1064, and Kōunshi, 1211, are similar to these two glosses.

580. Iriya, 254.1, glosses *de li* 得力 as: "'owe something to a person; be indebted to a person.' It is a Tang period colloquialism. During the Song period, it shifted meaning to 'store/lay in stock strength on one's own.'" [人のお蔭をこ うむる。唐代の俗語。宋代には、自らに力を蓄える意に変わる。]

581. Eishu, 406: "A commentary glosses *huadu* 話度 as: 'bargain/haggle.'" [話度鈔 云商量也]

582. Kōunshi, 1211: "The *Lotus Sutra* [T262.9.29a5–11] . . . says: '[World-honored one! It is like a person who arrives at a close friend's house, drinks wine, and lies down to sleep. At the time the close friend is going out on official busi- ness. He takes a priceless pearl, sews it into this man's clothes, and leaves him with it to depart. This man is in a drunken sleep and completely unaware. When he arises, he journeys to other countries. He is industrious and hard- working in seeking for clothing and food, meeting extreme difficulties. What little he can obtain he considers enough. Later the close friend encounters him and says the following:] "Tsk! My fellow! Why for the sake of clothing and food has it reached this point?"'" [法華 . . . 曰(世尊譬如有人至親友家 醉酒而臥是時親友官事當行以無價寶珠繋其衣裏與之而去其人醉臥都不覺 知起已遊行到於他國爲衣食故勤力求索甚大艱難若少有所得便以爲足於後 親友會遇見之而作是言咄哉丈夫何爲衣食乃至如是] The close friend then relates the story of installing the pearl and says it must still be there.

583. Kōunshi, 1211: "*The Mind-Ground Contemplation Sutra* [T159.3.305a16] . . . says: 'The miraculous fruit of *bodhi* is not difficult to complete. Encoun- tering a good teacher is truly a rare occurrence.' . . . The *Laṅkāvatāra Sūtra* [T670.16.511c10–11] . . . says: 'Encountering a buddha is a rare occurrence, like an *udumbara* tree blooming.'" [心地觀經...曰菩提妙果不難成真善知識實難遇.... 楞伽...曰佛難值遇如優曇鉢華] Kōunshi also cites this line in the *Lotus Sutra* (T262.9.60a29).

584. Eishu, 406: "People from all over hear that there is an old Han Linji, and they crop up and pose difficult questions, trying to make Linji 'dither.'" [諸方人ガ 臨済老漢ト云者ガ有ト聽テ出來テ難問ヲ置テ林際ヲ擬議させ(セ)ウトスル也] Dōchū, 1358: "They want to drive him into silence." [欲令不開口也]

585. Eishu, 406, Anonymous, 300, Dōkū, 1064, and Kōunshi, 1211, gloss *mengran* 懵然 as: "mind in confusion." [心乱也] Kassan, 563, and Dōkū, 1064: "'*meng* 懵' is 'giving the appearance of not knowing.'" [懵無知貌]

586. Anonymous, 300: "Dragon and elephant are one." [龍象一也] Kōunshi, 1212: "The *Commentary on the Vimalakīrti Sūtra* [T1775.38.383b9–16] . . . says: '[The sutra:] The bodhisattva who is fixed in inconceivable liberation has might and virtue, and so he compellingly instructs sentient beings in this sort of

difficult matter. The common person is inferior and lacks power. He cannot compel the bodhisattva in this way. Just as being trampled by a dragon-
elephant is not something donkeys can bear.' Sengzhao's commentary: . . .
'The most superior of elephants is called a "dragon-elephant."'" [注維摩 . . .
曰住不可思議解脫菩薩有威德力故行逼迫示諸衆生如是難事凡夫下劣無
有力勢不能如是逼迫菩薩譬如龍象蹴踏非驢所堪(注)肇曰 . . . 象之上者名
龍象也]

587. Anonymous, 300: "the appearance of praising oneself, a tribute to yourself."
[自讚兒自貢也]

588. Myōō, 71: "As to [the line] 'two or three of you come here,' upon encountering the strategem of the unreserved functioning [of the buddha nature], they
are shocked and can do nothing at all." [三箇兩箇這裡ニ来テハ全體作用ノ
作略ニ逢テアキレテ奈何トモ得セス也] Dōkū, 1065: "'Here' is the 'state of
the *original portion*.'" [這裡本分田地也] Kōunshi, 1212: "'Here' refers to the
Master's assembly. Some say it is the 'state of the *original portion*,' but this is
unacceptable." [這裏者指師會裡或說爲本分田地者不可也] Dōchū, 1358: "Re-
fers to 'unreserved functioning [of the buddha nature].' Some say it refers to
'[arrival] at the Master's assembly.'" [指全體作用也或謂指師之會裡]

589. Chitetsu, 842: "'This body-mind' is the 'five *skandhas*.'" [這箇身心所謂五陰]

590. Eishu, 407, and Anonymous, 300: "The meaning is 'much talk.' 'Two slices of
skin' refers to 'upper and lower lips.'" [多口之義也兩片皮者上下唇也] Dōchū,
1358: "moving the lips." [動唇也]

591. Kōunshi, 1212: "using verbal dexterity to deceive the boys and girls of the village." [以口才欺誑村家男女]

592. Anonymous, 300: "the old one Yama's iron rod." [閻老鐵棒也]

593. Eishu, 407: "'Deceiving common people' necessarily involves anger. . . . *she* 攝
means 'receive/admit [a guest].'" [誑謼閭閻之処必有嗔恚也. . . . 摄接待義也]
Anonymous, 300, has the last gloss. Dōchū, 1358: "because they just want to
query and argue, gaining victories over others and elevating self," [但欲問難勝
他自高故]

594. Myōō, 72: "*jiyang* 激揚 ['wash away and uphold'] means 'to oppose other
persons and uphold *my* principle.'" [激揚トハ人ニサカラウテ我ガ理ヲ
舉揚スル也] Kassan, 564: "according to the sutras: 'uphold the essence and
destroy the heterodox views.'" [如契經而激揚其要摧破其異乎] Dōkū, 1065:
"*jiyang* 激揚 means 'argue/debate and interrogate.'" [激揚者論難答喩之義也]
Kōunshi, 1212: "From here down . . . shows that the purport of the transmission
of the buddhas and patriarchs does not lie in arguing over teachings-traces."
[以下 . . . 說示佛祖相承意旨不在論辯教迹也]

595. For this line down to "Venerables!" the commentators' exegeses vary. Myōō,
72: "It is merely that in the one Way there is no other idea." [只一道ニテ別
ノ意子ナイ也] Eishu, 407, and Anonymous, 300: "has no idea of another
teaching." [無別教意也] Kassan, 564: "It is 'taking mind to transmit mind' and

that is all." [以心傳心耳也] Kōunshi, 1212: "[Huangbo's] buddhadharma was point-blank." [佛法無多子] (This line appears in **38**.2.) Dōchū, 1359: "This seals the fact that outside the locus wherein notions and feelings are cut off there is not another thing." [自印意解情識絕慮外無別事也]

596. Kōunshi, 1212: "*huayi* 化儀 means 'provisionally established teaching styles.' The *tathāgata* throughout his career spoke sutras of four teaching styles, including all-at-once, step-by-step, secret, and indeterminate." [化儀者施設化法之儀式也如來一代說經以四種化儀收之頓漸秘密不定也]

597. Eishu, 407, and Anonymous, 300–301, gloss *you qie bu ran* 又且不然 as: "has the meaning 'is not so.' . . . The meaning is 'furthermore, is not.' . . . The 'perfect and all-at-once teaching' is a teaching that is one level higher. Even though it is the perfect and all-at-once teaching, it is not the purport of [Zen's] separate transmission [outside the teachings]." [サウナイト云義也. . . . 又且不是ト云義也. . . . 圓頓教一重上教也縱是圓頓之教非別傳旨也] Kassan, 564: "'Perfect and all-at-once teaching' in general refers to the Mahāyāna teachings. Specifically it refers to the *Huayan Sutra*. *bu ran* 不然 means 'is not/not be .'" [圓頓教者通指諸大乘教別此指華嚴也不然者不是也] Dōkū, 1065, is similar. Shukitsu, 963: "'Perfect and all-at-once' means the Mahāyāna [sutras]. Specifically it means the *Huayan Sutra*." [圓頓謂諸大乘別謂華嚴] Kōunshi, 1213: "refers to the *Huayan Sutra*." [指華嚴經] Dōchū, 1359: "Even though the Buddha had oral teachings, they were merely discourses on the three vehicles and five natures and that is all. They were not the true perfect and all-at-once. If [we discuss] the true perfect and all-at-once, it is not something that falls into the teaching styles. Therefore, the youth Sudhana could not have sought it out. Why? Because from the outset it is not a dharma that can be sought out and obtained." [言佛雖有言教但是說三乘五性而已非真箇圓頓矣若復真箇圓頓則非落化儀底是故善財童子亦不得求之何故元來非求之而可得之法故]

598. Eishu, 407: "*jie* 皆 ['all'] refers to the [four] teaching styles, three vehicles, five natures, perfect and all-at-once, etc., that are mentioned above" [皆者指上化儀三乘五性圓頓等也] Kōunshi, 1213: "The youth Sudhana, following Mañjuśrī, sends up the aspiration [for awakening] and passes through one-hundred ten cities in the south, visiting more than fifty teachers to ask about the dharma. At the very end with Maitreya's finger-snap the gate of his tower opens, and, entering, [Sudhana] catches sight of the *dharmadhātu*, the realm of the limitless. . . . Sudhana's seeking in the past is now said to be 'non-seeking.' This is because beholding reality as it truly is 'rips away [the seeking].' *jie* 皆 refers to the sites of the fifty-three teachers; the *guo* 過 of *qiuguo* 求過 is an auxiliary word [i.e., a postpositional word functioning as an auxiliary to a main word]." [善財童子從文殊發心南邁過一百一十城參五十餘員善知識問法末後依彌勒一彈指樓閣門開即入得見法界無邊境界. . . . 往昔善財所求過今卻言不求過是約真正見解奪之皆者指五十三善知識所求過過字助字也] Kassan, 564: "The youth Sudhana depended on the ten *pāramitās* to practice. Even though

he went through one-hundred and ten cities visiting fifty-three people, never-theless, in the matter of the Way of ultimate principle, he was not yet finished in completely seeking out the dharma. He had only gotten one half. If Sudhana was like this, then how much more so is it in the case of those who [just] lecture on a couple of books?" [善財據十波羅蜜修行雖歷一百十城參五十三人然後至理之道者未全求法了畢只得一半也善財猶如此而況講得三五本者乎]   Dōkū, 1065: "Even though the youth Sudhana went through one-hundred and ten cit-ies visiting fifty-three people, nevertheless, in the matter of the Way of ultimate principle, he did not completely obtain it. The word *jie* 皆 refers to the fifty-three teachers." [善財童子雖歷一百十城參五十三人然於至理之道者未全求得皆字指五十三處] Dōchū, 1359: "*jie* 皆 relates to the fifty-three teachers. *qiu* 求 is 'seeking the dharma.' *guo* 過 is 'gradually going through one-hundred and ten cities.' Here the perfect and all-at-once does not fall into the ranks of the teaching styles. The meaning is that Sudhana from the outset never sought any dharma from the fifty-three teachers and never went through one-hundred and ten cities. Therefore, [the LJL] says: '*jie bu qiu guo* 皆不求過.'" [皆者係五十三知識也求者求法也過者次第經過於一百十城去也今約真箇圓頓不落化儀階位言善財元來未曾求法于五十三善知識未曾經過一百十城故云皆不求過也]

599. Eishu, 408: "This means that this [Zen] personal-realization-of-the-meaning-beyond-words does not retain the rights and wrongs of the oral teachings. Also, the great sea of the buddhadharma does not retain the dead bodies of the teaching styles."[言此宗不留言教是非也又佛法大海不留化儀死屍也]Dōkū,1065:"The great sea does not hold onto dead bodies' is a metaphor for not retaining a single thing inside the mind. 'Great sea' is the buddhadharma; 'dead bodies' is words and phrases." [大海不停死屍者譬胸中不畱一物大海者佛法死屍者言句也] Kōunshi, 1213: "The *Huayan Sutra* [T279.10.422a19–20] says: 'Good teachers are not affected by evils, just as the great sea gives no lodging to dead bodies.' The *Kṣitigarbha Ten Wheels Sutra* [T411.13.739b20–22] says: 'It is like the great sea's not giving lodging to dead bodies. Our *śravaka* monks and sangha of disciples are also like this. Do not dwell together with the dead bodies of *bhikṣus* who break the precepts and are of evil conduct.' . . . 'Dead bodies' refers to all external vishayas and also refers to the oral teach-ings." [華嚴 . . . 曰善知識者不受諸惡譬如大海不宿死屍地藏十輪經 . . . 曰譬如大海不宿死屍我聲聞僧諸弟子眾亦復如是不與破戒惡行苾芻死屍共住. . . . 死屍一切外境又指上言教]

600. Eishu, 408, and Anonymous, 301: "You load written words and verbal phrases on your shoulders and run around and around. . . . Your five-foot physical body loads on its shoulders *avidyā* and *kleśas*. . . . 'Hindrance of views' . . . means 'hindrances of strange and heterodox views.'" [文字言句ヲ擔イマワル也. . . . 五尺形骸又無明煩惱ヲ擔却也. . . . 見障 . . . 異見邪見障也] Myōō, 72: "'Obstruction of views' is '*kleśas* of discrimination.'" [見障トハ分別ノ煩惱也] Dōkū, 1065: "You load on your shoulders written words and verbal

phrases. Also, loading on your shoulders *avidyā* and *kleśas*, you uselessly run around all-under-heaven and are duped by heterodox masters. You yourself produce the hindrance of views. You darken your own single ray of light, obstructing your mind." [擔却文字言句也又擔却無明煩惱徒天下奔走被邪師誑惑自起見障昧沒自己一段光明以礙於心]   Kōunshi, 1213: "You load on your shoulders the dead bodies of the oral teachings and try to run all over. But your own knowledge and understanding becomes the hindrance of views, obstructing your mind. The hindrance of views is one of the four hindrances. The four hindrances are: karman; *kleśas*; karmic results; and views (from the *Huayan Sutra*)." [擔却言教死屍擬諸方走自己知見解會卻成見障礙心見障四障之一也四障者一業障二煩惱障三報障四見障(出華嚴)] Dōchū, 1359: "You yourself load on your shoulders the dead bodies of thought of the unreal and run around all-under-heaven. You are not able to stop. However, the great sea of the *original portion* has never accepted these dead bodies of thought of the unreal. . . . 'Hindrance of views' is 'buddha view and dharma view.' . . . 'Mind' is 'original mind.'" [汝自擔妄想死屍走天下不得歇得也然本分大海元來不受此妄想死屍也. . . . 見障佛見法見也. . . . 心者本來心也]

601. Dōchū, 1360: "'Sun' is compared to the 'original mind.' When there are no clouds of thought of the unreal, the mind flower shines throughout the ten directions." [日者比本心無妄想雲時心華照十方也] Kōunshi, 1213: "The *Huayan Sutra* [T279.10.100b24–26] . . . says: 'The sky is clear with no cloud covering, and the red sun shines forth. It fills the ten directions, its rays without limit.'" [華嚴 . . . 曰空淨無雲翳赫日揚光輝十方靡不充其光無限量]

602. Eishu, 408: "The original mind, which has no hindrance-due-to-views, is the body of the clear, solitary brightness." [無見障本心孤明歷歷躰也] Dōchū, 1360: "The eye is also compared to the original mind. When there is no cataract of discrimination, it is a clear sky without a jumble of 'flowers' [i.e., unreal things perceived by those with faulty eyes]." [眼亦比本心無分別翳時清空無亂華也] Kōunshi, 1213: "The *Perfect Awakening Sutra* [T842.17.913b25–26] says: 'That diseased eye sees a 'flower' and a second moon in the sky. Good sons! There is no 'flower' in the sky. The disease is grasping of the unreal.' . . . Here in this record the sun and the eye are metaphors for mind; clouds and cataracts are metaphors for hindrance-due-to-views." [圓覺經曰彼病目見空中華及第二月善男子空實無華病者妄執. . . . 今此錄日眼喻心雲翳喻見障]

603. Dōchū, 1360: "'According to dharma' means 'a beholding of reality as it truly is.'" [如法者真正見解也] Kōunshi, 1214: "'According to dharma' means 'being attentive [to things] as they really are, without the hindrance-due-to-views.' A mind of uncertainty is like clouds or cataracts—it can obstruct [beholding] 'according to dharma.' A mind of uncertainty does not produce this [beholding] according to dharma." [如法真正用心無見障底也疑心如雲翳能礙如法疑心不生是如法也]

604. Eishu, 408: "The thing 'you let loose to fill up the *dharmadhātu* and roll up so that it is not enough to stand up a single strand of hair' is the clear, solitary brightness." [展則弥綸法界收則絲髮不立底物歷歷孤明也] Kōunshi, 1214: "Every person is endowed with each and every perfection." [人人具足箇箇圓成]

605. Kōunshi, 1214: "You don't see it, and you don't hear it. If you open your mouth, you've made a mistake. . . . 'Ancient' refers to Preceptor Nanyue Huairang. The *Extended Lamp Record of the Tiansheng Era* says: 'He [Huairang] directly went to visit Caoxi and did obeisance to the sixth patriarch. The Patriarch asked, "What *place* do you come from?" The Master said, "I came from the site of Chan Master Hui'an of Mt. Song." The Patriarch said, "*Who* has come *in that way?*" The Master was silent. He passed eight years and suddenly had an awakening. He then said to the Patriarch, "I have had an understanding." The Patriarch said, "How?" The Master said, "Once you've [tried to] pin it down with words, you've missed the mark."'" [不見不聞開口即錯. . . . 古人者指南嶽懷讓和尚也廣燈錄 . . . 曰直詣曹溪禮六祖祖問什麼處來師云嵩山安禪師處來祖云什麼物與麼來師無語經于八載忽然有省乃白祖云某甲有箇會處祖云作麼生師云說似一物即不中] CBETA, X78, no. 1553, p. 447, c16–19 //Z 2B:8, p. 325, c5–8 //R135, p. 650, a5–8.

606. Dōchū, 1360: "means 'outside of your own home *who* else could there be?'" [言自家之外更有何物耶] Kōunshi, 1214: "Look carefully in your own house." [自己屋裏子細看]

607. Eishu, 409: "Speaking dharma has no end to it." [説法亦無盡也] Kōunshi, 1214: "Even supposing that from dawn to dusk, from birth till death, one does one's utmost to pin it down with words, there will still be no end to it. Therefore, the old yellow-faced one [Śākyamuni] said, 'In the time between first attaining buddhahood until the complete nirvana I didn't say a word.' This is what it means." [設從朝至暮從生至死竭力說破亦無盡期故黃面老子云從初得佛至般涅槃於其中間不說一字此之謂也]

608. Dōchū, 1360: "Each of you take care of the vessel of the Way that is your form body. When it is healthy, you can cultivate this Way." [各各珍重色身道器康健而可修此道也] Kōunshi, 1214: "words of thanks when one is about to retire." [將退時謝語也]

PART III

1. Anonymous, 302: "The meaning is 'keeping an eye on [someone's] level of understanding; appraising and deciding; discriminating; judging.' Both masters and students calibrate and adjudicate." [要看知識之淺深義也勘定也辨別也判也師學共勘辨也] Dōkū, 1066: "*kanbian* 勘辨 means that, in our patriarchal [Zen] house, with 'one stab' the master tests the student's level of proper [understanding], and the student tests the master's level of proper

[understanding]. They make distinctions concerning each other's [level of] proper [understanding]." [勘辨者祖宗家於一機一境一挨一拶處師家探試學者之深淺邪正學者探試師家之深淺邪正互辨邪正] Dōchū, 1361, glosses *kanbian* 勘辨 as: "investigating the person and distinguishing his faults." [勘撿其人而辨別体咎也]

2. Dōchū, 1361, and Kōunshi 1214: "*chu* 厨 is the storehouse office." [廚庫司也]

3. Dōchū, 1361, and Kōunshi, 1214: "The *Regulations of Purity of Illusion-Abiding [Hermitage]* . . . glosses *fantou* 飯頭 as: 'He watches over the time schedule from morning to evening; deliberates over the number [of monks] who will be eating [for the day]; gathers the rice and grains and sees if they are of good or poor quality; differentiates the purity levels of the water and starch; practices economy in the amount of vegetables; attends to whether there is firewood or not, etc.'" [幻住[庵]清規 . . . 飯頭曰觀察時分之早晚酌量食指之寡多撿看米穀之精麁分別水漿之清濁撙節菜蔬之多少顧慮柴薪之有無云云] CBETA, X63, no. 1248, p. 583, a16–18 //Z 2:16, p. 498, b4–6 //R111, p. 995, b4–6. This Chan code by the Yuan dynasty master Zhongfeng Mingben 中峰明本 was compiled in 1317. Chitetsu, 849: "*fantou* 飯頭 is a job [in a Zen monastery]. He is the person who works with foodstuffs, but he is not the 'Head Cook.'" [飯頭者職役食物人非謂典座] Eishu, 409, and Anonymous, 302: "*fantou* 飯頭 is the same as 'Head Cook.'" [飯頭典座同者也] Dōkū, 1066: "*fantou* 飯頭 is the Head Cook." [飯頭者典座也]

4. Eishu, 409: "sorting out the sand in the rice." [米中ノ砂ヲエル也] Anonymous, 302, and Dōkū, 1066, are very similar. Dōchū, 1361: "He is sorting out the good and bad in the rice, getting rid of impurities, sand, etc. It is the assignment of the Chief of Provisions." [揀米之好惡去塵濁沙等也飯頭職分]

5. Eishu, 409: "How much do all of the monks eat in one day?" [一日二僧達八皆イカホドクエルゾ] Dōchū, 1361: "calibrating and adjudicating." [勘辨]

6. Eishu, 409, and Anonymous, 302: "It is two *shi* five *dou*. . . . Ten *dou* is a *shi* [1 *shi* = 100 liters]." [二石五斗也. . . . 十斗曰石]

7. Dōchū, 1361: "calibrating once more." [再勘]

8. Eishu, 409: "The Chief of Provisions does not understand and is still falling into 'much' or 'little.'" [飯頭不會依前落多少] Kassan, 566, and Dōkū, 1066, are similar. Dōchū, 1361: "He is still not clearheaded and awake." [依然不惺惺]

9. Eishu, 409: "'Master' is Linji. . . . *que* 却 . . . means 'repulse; stop; not accept,' etc." [師林際也. . . . 却 . . . 退也止也不受也云云] Kōunshi, 1215: "A poor man mulls over an old debt." [貧兒思舊債]

10. Eishu, 410, and Anonymous, 302: "say a phrase standing in for the Chief of Provisions." [代飯頭道一句]

11. Eishu, 410, and Anonymous, 302: "One *dun* 頓 is twenty blows of the stick. . . . One bowl of rice is called 'one *dun* 頓.' . . . some say 'one meal.'" [一頓二十棒也. . . . 飯一鉢ヲ一頓ト云也. . . . 或云食之一次也] Dōkū, 1067: "One *dun* 頓 is 'one time.'" [一頓一次也]

12. Kōunshi, 1215: "Beneath the cliff the wind is stirring—the tiger plays with her cub." [巖下風生虎弄兒]

13. Eishu, 410: "The two respected monks are Huangbo and Linji." [二尊宿檗與濟也] Anonymous, 302: "Deep in the night together they gaze at the snow on a thousand crags." [夜深共看千岩雪]

14. Dōchū, 1361: "The son is Linji, and the father is Baizhang.... [But] it is not necessary to pair Linji and Baizhang. It is merely saying that Huangbo's benevolent compassion was very deep." [子者臨濟父者百丈.... 不必配當臨濟百丈但云黃檗慈悲深重也] Kassan, 566: "Once Huangbo nurtured Linji, he first understood Baizhang's benevolent love." [黃檗已養出林際方知百丈慈恩也] Xu, ed., *Jianming Hanyu suyu cidian* [*Concise Dictionary of Sinitic Common Sayings*], 571, has the following saying: "Once you've raised a child, that's when you first understand your father and mother's kindness." [養兒方曉父母恩] It appears in the novel *Record of a Journey to the West* (*Xiyou ji* 西游記), 28.

15. Eishu, 410: "He brought in a thief called Linji, who stole the family's wealth and wrecked the home." [臨濟ト云賊ヲ勾入テ家財ヲ盗取レテ破家散宅トナツタ也] Anonymous, 302: "If a thief with a stratagem wrecks your home, then all your money and grain are gone." [有謀略底賊破家則資糧悉盡] Dōkū, 1067: "It takes a thief to know a thief." [是賊知賊]

16. Eishu, 410: "calibrating and adjudicating." [勘辨也]

17. Kassan, 566–567, and Dōkū, 1067 (up to last sentence): "An old commentary has two interpretations: The first is that the Great Master did obeisance to the monk and himself took the seat at the top rank [on the platform]. The second is that the Great Master did obeisance to the monk and ordered him to take the seat at the [position of the] Advanced Seat. The latter interpretation is better." [舊抄有二義一大師揖僧自坐主位也二大師揖僧令坐上座也末義最好] Dōchū, 1362, gives two glosses of *yizuo* 揖坐: "The Master did obeisance to this monk and ordered the monk to take a seat.... The Master did obeisance to this monk, and, having finished, the Master took a seat.... The latter interpretation is incorrect. It is unacceptable." [師揖其僧令僧坐.... 師揖其僧畢師却坐.... 後義非也不可取] Kōunshi, 1215: The *Shuowen* [i.e., the first Chinese dictionary compiled in 121 CE] says: "Hands [cupped] on the chest is called *yi* 揖." [說文手著胸曰揖]

18. Dōkū, 1067: "An old worthy said, 'A sudden clap of thunder doesn't reach stopped-up ears.'" [古德云迅雷不及掩耳]

19. Eishu, 410: "It does not mean that, while leaving, he turned around and looked—it's that he didn't take into consideration that he was in peril." [出去非不面顧義不顧危亡也]

20. Dōkū, 1067, and Kōunshi, 1216: "The *Vimalakīrti Sūtra* [T475.14.546b25–27 and 546b29–c2]: 'If the bodhisattva dwells in liberation, he takes the height and breadth of Mt. Sumeru and inserts it into a mustard seed, with no increase or decrease. This is because the King of Mt. Sumeru's original mark is *just as it is*....

Also, he takes the waters of the four great seas and inserts it into the pore of a single hair, without disturbing the beings of the waters such as fishes, soft-shell turtles, and alligators, because the original mark of that great sea is *just as it is*.'" [維摩經 ... 曰若菩薩住是解脱者以須彌之高廣納芥子中無所增減須彌山王本相如故.... 又以四大海水入一毛孔不嬈魚鼈黿鼉水性之屬而彼大海本相如故]

21. Eishu, 411: "a crude lie." [アラウサウ]

22. Kassan, 567: "*Here* from the outset there is not a single thing. Where is this that you speak of 'crude and fine'? *Here* from the outset there has never been 'crude and fine,'" [者裡本無一物何之所在而説麁(= 麤)細者裡從來無麁(= 麤)細也] Kōunshi, 1216: "It is the original substance *just as it is*—why discuss 'crude and fine?'" [本體如然何論麤細]

23. Eishu, 411: "again calibrated and adjudicated." [又勘辨せ(せ)ラレタ也]

24. Kōunshi, 1216: "In so far as it's correct, it's correct, but it's slow." [是則是且緩緩]

25. Eishu, 411, and Anonymous, 303: "the appearance of being startled." [驚皃也] Kassan, 567: "shows shock." [示震驚相] Dōkū, 1068: "the appearance of being greatly surprised." [大驚貌]

26. Eishu, 411: "The hearth of the Sangha Hall is at the rear door." [僧堂ノ炉ハ後門ニアル也] Kassan, 569, Dōkū, 1068, and Kōunshi, 1217: "*dilu* 地爐 is the open-air hearth of the Sangha Hall." [地爐者僧堂露地之爐也]

27. Kassan, 569, Dōkū, 1068, and Kōunshi, 1217: "frenetic; mad." [風狂風顚] Dōchū, 1363: "frenetic like a small child who is full of surprises and quick." [風狂如小兒風驚疾也]

28. Kassan, 569: "The 'worldling/*ārya*' road is cut off." [凡聖路絶] Kōunshi, 1217: "He occupies the essential ferry crossing, and there is no passage to 'worldling/*ārya*.'" [把断要津不通凡聖]

29. Dōchū, 1363: "He points at each person with his finger." [每人以指指之也]

30. Kassan, 569, Dōkū, 1068, and Kōunshi, 1217: "[His level of] understanding is timid and weak." [見解軟弱]

31. Kassan, 569: "He has only affectionate, loving words and completely lacks any spicy/peppery/hot spirit." [只有親切之愛語全無辛辣之氣概] Dōkū, 1068: "means 'excessively affectionate.'" [言親切太過] Kōunshi, 1217, glosses: "His oversights are not few." [漏逗不少]

32. Eishu, 411, glosses *xiaosi'er* 小廝兒 as: "a clever/shrewd/cagey/cunning one." [小廝兒ハコザカシキ者也] Anonymous, 304: "an attendant/part of an entourage." [從使者] Kōunshi, 1217: "He is still a little cagey one." [猶是小機巧] Eishu, 411: "He is extolling [Linji]." [揚スル也] Kassan, 569: "I say that, when all is said and done, it is the designation of a menial. The phrase 'endowed with a single eye' is not fully complimentary." [私云畢竟奴僕之称也具一雙眼者十成不許之辞也] Kōunshi, 1217, and Dōchū, 1363, are similar. Myōō, 76: "'Endowed with the single eye' is praise." [具一隻眼ト云タハ褒美 ... 云也] Iriya, 156.7, believes the comment on Linji is not complimentary: "The oldest text, *Zutangji*, 17 [see the Puhua entry, n. 16, in Appendix 1], has 'only possesses'. . . . So the meaning

is: 'but he's only got the one eye.'" [最も古いテキスト『祖堂集』十七では「只具 ...」。すると「片目だけしかない」という意。]

33. Eishu, 412: "'*This* son of a bitch' ... means a person whose [level of understanding] is off-the-charts." [這賊 ... 格外之人ト云義也] See **13.26**.

34. Kōunshi, 1217: "It takes a son of a bitch to know a son of a bitch." [是賊識賊]

35. Kōunshi, 1217: "It takes a son of a bitch to know a son of a bitch." [是賊識賊]

36. Eishu, 412: "the 'rattle' of metal rings at the top of his tin staff [*khakkhara*]." [錫杖之輪鈴也]

37. Dōchū, 1364: "*lianjia* 連架 ... is a tool for threshing grain." [連架 ... 打穀具也]

38. Dōchū, 1364: "the coming of one who is single-minded and off-the-charts." [一向格外來也]

39. Eishu, 412: "'There will be a dinner' means 'dinner of a generous lay donor.'" [有斉施行之斉也]

40. Dōchū, 1364: "This means: 'From today I have no doubts about *this* Han.'" [言從今日不疑這漢也]

41. Eishu, 413, glosses *renshi* 人事 as: "polite formalities; not peforming the polite formalities." [礼儀也不爲礼儀也] Dōchū, 1365: "*renshi* 人事 means 'upon meeting someone carrying out the rituals." [人事者見人行禮也]

42. Eishu, 413, and Anonymous, 305: "It's a calibration and adjudication of Linji." [勘辨林際也] Kassan, 570: "The old monk is *no-minding* [the duality of] bow/not bow. In actuality, he justs wants to see whether Linji has the spirit of a son of a bitch." [老宿無心拜不拜其實唯要看林際是賊精也] Kōunshi, 1218: "This old son of a bitch sets up a two-tier checkpoint." [這老賊設兩重關]

43. Kōunshi, 1218: "The brightness of the moon reveals the person walking in the night." [月明照見夜行人] For *caozei* 草賊, see n. 43, **4.1**, Part I.

44. Eishu, 413: "You haven't eaten the stick. Don't think that with *nothing-to-do* it's finished!" [棒ヲモ不喫無事シスマイタト思ナ也] Anonymous, 305: "The meaning is: 'You haven't eaten the stick. With *nothing-to-do* it's okay/that's enough/it's done—do not think this!'" [棒不喫無事好汝莫思之義也] Dōchū, 1365: "An ancient says: '*Nothing-to-do* has produced *something-to-do*, and, for that reason, there is this line.'" [古德曰有無事生事處故有此語] Shukitsu, 967: "If you are awakened to the passages [**17** and **18**] where Puhua says 'Son of a bitch, son of a bitch' and instantly leaves, then you understand this passage." [若悟解普化賊賊出去話則會此話去] Yanagida, 205, remarks that the line *mo dao wushi hao* 莫道無事好 can be read in two ways, but the meaning remains the same: either "ended without incident" [事なく済んだ] or *nothing-to-do* [無事にして]. Iriya, 159, translates as: "Don't think that this closes the matter!" [これで事は済んだと思うまいぞ] Nakamura, 190, translates as: "Don't think that this is the whole of Zen!" [これが禅のすべてだと思うなよ]

45. Kōunshi, 1218: "The [Master's] nest comes to know [the Head Seat's] wind; the [Master's] den comes to know [the Head Seat's] rain." [巢知風穴知雨]

46. Eishu, 413, and Anonymous, 305: "'Guest' refers to the old monk." [賓家指老宿也] Kōunshi, 1218: "The 'guest' is the old monk; the 'host' is the Master." [賓老宿主師也]

47. Kōunshi, 1219: "He severs both heads." [兩頭共坐斷] This could refer to avoiding the duality of the extremes (離二邊 = *anta-dvaya-vivargita*) as well as to the Master and the old monk.

48. Kōunshi, 1219: "chasing a dog up against a wall." [趁狗逼墙]

49. Dōkū, 1069: "The Master wants to smash his burrow [i.e., place of retreat]." [師要打破他窠窟]

50. Eishu, 413, and Anonymous, 305: "Refers to the horses of officials. It is an exaggeration." [官人馬也誇義也]

51. Eishu, 413, Anonymous, 305, Kassan, 571, Dōkū, 1069, and Dōchū, 1365, make a Japanese analogy: "the residence of the *shōgun*." [將軍居処也]

52. Eishu, 413, and Anonymous, 305: "*shou* 首 means 'vicinity.' *yuanliao* 員僚 is a type of gate guard." [首ホトリ也員僚門守類也] Dōkū, 1069, is similar. Kassan, 571: "*yuanliao* 員僚 is a gate officer." [員僚者門司也] Dōchū, 1365: "*menshou* 門首 is 'gate entrance.'" [門首者門口也]

53. Eishu, 413, and Anonymous, 305: "A *luzhu* 露柱 is the central pillar [in the courtyard]." [露柱中央柱也] On these open-air pillars, see n. 330, **13**.15, Part II.

54. Kōunshi, 1219: "An Indian doesn't understand Chinese." [西天人不會唐言]

55. Kōunshi, 1219: "Does the guard officer even know the pain [i.e., does he even know that he was whacked]? A person of the east house dies, and a person of the west-house will assist in the lamentations." [員僚還知痛痒麼東家人死西家人助哀]

56. Eishu, 413: "calibrating and adjudicating." [勘辨也] Dōchū, 1365, glosses *yuanzhu* 院主 ("temple Custodian") as: "*jiansi* 監寺 ['Monastery Supervisor'] . . . The 'Monastery Supervisor' in olden times was called the *yuanzhu*." [監寺也忠曰監寺古稱院主] Eishu, 413, Anonymous, 305, Kassan, 571, Dōkū, 1069, and Kōunshi, 1219, give the same gloss.

57. Eishu, 413, Kassan, 571, Dōkū, 1070, and Kōunshi, 1219, gloss *huangmi* 黃米 as *heimi* 黑米 ['wild rice']. [黃米 . . . 黑米也] Dōchū, 1365: "*huangmi* 黃米 is a type of husked grain. In old interpretations it is 'wild rice,' etc. This is wrong." [黃米米一種舊解為古米黑米等非也] Luo and others, eds., *Hanyu da cidian* [*Great Word Dictionary of Sinitic*], 12.975a, glosses *huangmi* 黃米 as: *shumi* 秫米 ['husked sorghum'] and quotes the *New Tang History* (*Xin Tang shu* 新唐書, *Wuxing zhi* 五行志, 2 [3.922]): "Before [the rebel army of] Huang ['Yellow'] Chao entered the capital [in 881], the people of the metropolis took *huangmi* 黃米 ['husked sorghum'] and black bean shavings, steamed them, and ate it. They called it 'yellow traitor smashes black traitor.'" [黃巢未入京師時都人以黃米及黑豆屑蒸食之謂之黃賊打黑賊]

58. Eishu, 413, and Anonymous, 306: "calibrated once more." [再勘せ(セ)ラレタ]

59. Myōō, 80: "A single stroke on the ground can't be sold!" [地上ノ一畫ハ賣ラレマイン] Kōunshi, 1219: "*This*—what is it? In the world of people it is perhaps priceless." [這箇是何物人間恐無價]

60. Kōunshi, 1219: "sprang free of the *vajra* cage." [跳出金剛圈] The *vajra* cage is a cage made of diamond that is impossible to escape.

61. Mujaku Dōchū's *Notes on Images and Implements of the Zen Forest* (*Zenrin shōki sen* 禪林象器箋; Mujaku Dictionaries, 1.284) glosses *dianzuo* 典座 as: "The *Pure Regulations of the Chan Garden* says: 'The job of the *dianzuo* 典座 ['head cook'] is to be in charge of the great sangha's [regular pre-noon] meal and the [supplementary early morning meal] of porridge.'" [禪苑清規云典座之職主大衆齋粥] The *Pure Regulations of the Chan Garden* reference is CBETA, X63, no. 1245, p. 531, a1 //Z 2:16, p. 446, d2 //R111, p. 892, b2.

62. Kōunshi, 1219: "taking poison to attack poison." [以毒攻毒]

63. Eishu, 414, and Anonymous, 306: "calibrating and adjudicating." [勘辨也] Kōunshi, 1220: "Whacking kudzu—to what end?" [打葛藤爲甚麼]

64. Eishu, 414: "*huangxu* 荒虛 ['barren'] is a term of self-deprecation: 'There is really nothing at all . . . in my empty head.' . . . The meaning is 'I know nothing at all.'" [荒虛卑下之辞也何ニ虛頭ニ . . . 實モナイト云心也. . . . 何モ知ラスト云義] Anonymous, 306, Kassan, 572, Dōkū, 1070, Kōunshi, 1220, and Dōchū, 1365, are similar to the first sentence. The *Treatise of the Bright Gate of the Hundred Dharmas of the Mahāyāna* (*Mahāyānaśatadharmaprakāśamukha-śāstra/Dasheng baifa mingmen lun* 大乘百法明門論) by Vasubandhu is T1614. It is an *abhidharma* text of the Yogācāra school.

65. Kassan, 572, and Dōkū, 1070: "With the two hypothetical people, he wants to look at the Seat Master's level of understanding." [假設二人之事猶要看座主見解]

66. Eishu, 414, and Anonymous, 307: "The meaning is 'awakened, then the same; not yet awakened, then different.'" [言悟則同未悟則別云義也] Kassan, 572: "What a fine level of understanding on the part of the Seat Master." [好箇座主見解也]

67. Eishu, 414, and Anonymous, 307: "*suozai* 所在 ['place'] means 'in the mind.'" [所在心中如何義] Kassan, 572: "He directly rips away the Seat Master's understanding [based] on the discrimination of two characteristics." [直奪破座主二相分別見解也] Kōunshi, 1220: "The bystander has an official post." [傍觀者有分]

68. Kōunshi, 1220: "On the eastern extreme declining moral norms, but he still wants to pull out the roots on the western extreme." [東邊落節還要西邊拔本] Perhaps this refers to the attendant Lepu.

69. Kōunshi, 1220: "Severing both heads—the single sword that leans against heaven is cold." [兩頭共截斷一劍倚天寒]

70. Kōunshi, 1221: "Look over the precipice and keep your eye on the tiger cub." [臨崖看虎兒]

71. Eishu, 414: "*bi* 彼 is Deshan's place." [彼德山処也] Kōunshi, 1221: "The fishhook lies in the no-doubt stage." [鈎在不疑之地]

72. Eishu, 414: "This is also according to instructions." [是又如教也]

73. Kassan, 573, Dōkū, 1071, and Kōunshi 1221: "This is the realm of unreserved functioning [of the buddha nature]." [此是全体作用境界也]

74. Kassan, 573, and Dōkū, 1071: "doesn't reach to praise." [不及讚嘆] Dōchū, 1366: "This line perhaps approves of the person and perhaps disapproves of the person. In the sense of approval, it would mean: 'In the beginning I had doubts about whether this person was sound, and, seeing this tactical speech, I now know that he is sound.' In the disapproval sense, it would mean: 'In the beginning I had doubts about whether this person was sound, and, seeing his tactical speech, I now know that he is unsound.'" [此語或肯人或不肯人其肯義謂我初疑此人好惡及見此作略言語方知其為好不肯義謂我初疑此人-好惡及見作略語言方知其爲惡]

75. Kōunshi, 1221: "The stripes on a tiger are easy to see; the stripes on the *person* are difficult to see." [虎班易見人班難見]

76. Dōchū, 1366: "Kazan says: '"Becoming buddhas and patriarchs" is meaningless—it is just to calibrate and adjudicate the Attendant-in-ordinary.'" [家山曰成佛作祖無意只是勘辨常侍]

77. Eishu, 415: "When the grinding dust of gold gets in the eye, it becomes a defeat." [金スリクヅモ目ニ入テハマケトナル也] Xu, ed., *Jianming Hanyu suyu cidian* [*Concise Dictionary of Sinitic Common Sayings*], 227, has this saying and comments: "Metaphor for, if any good thing is used inappropriately, it also has detrimental aspects."

78. Dōchū, 1366–1367: "In the beginning I took you for a run-of-the-mill layman, but you're such a smart cookie!" [我始以汝爲尋常俗人然如此伶利] Eishu, 415, and Myōō, 82 are similar.

79. Dōchū, 1367, cites the *Lotus Sutra* (T262.9.12c13–13a1): "[The house of a wealthy man was in flames. He decided to set up an *upāya* to save his sons. He told them that rare playthings—goat-carts, deer-carts, and ox-carts—were outside the gate in order to lure them out at once. They came running out of the house.] At that time the wealthy man saw that his sons had gotten out to safety and were all sitting on the open ground at the crossroads. There was no further obstacle, his mind was relieved, and he danced for joy. At that time the sons said to the father: 'Father, the toys that you promised us before—goat-carts, deer-carts, and ox-carts—we wish you would give them to us.' Śāriputra! At that time the wealthy man gave to each son a single great cart. . . . drawn by a white ox. . . . At that time each of the sons mounted his great cart, obtaining something he had never expected." [是時長者見諸子等安隱得出皆於四衢道中露地而坐無復障礙其心泰然歡喜踊躍時諸子等各白父言父先所許玩好之具羊車鹿車牛車願時賜與舍利弗爾時長者各賜諸子等一大車. . . .駕以白牛. . . .是時

諸子各乘大車得未曾有非本所望] Dōchū also quotes Li Tongxuan's *Complete Treatise on the Huayan Sutra*: "'Open ground' is the buddha stage.... 'White ox' is the *dharmakāya*." [華嚴合論 ... 曰露地者即佛地也.... 白牛者即法身也] CBETA, X04, no. 223, p. 25, c14–15 //Z 1:5, p. 346, b4–5 //R5, p. 691, b4–5.

80. Anonymous, 309: "The mantra *hūṃ hūṃ* [吽吽] is flavorless, neither arising nor disappearing; calculation does not reach it; it cannot be talked about.... It is the sound made by an ox." [真言吽吽沒滋味不生不滅情量不及如何可道也.... 牛鳴也] Eishu, 415, Kassan, 574, Dōkū, 1072, Myōō, 82, Shukitsu, 970, and Kōunshi, 1122: "the sound made by an ox." [牛鳴声也, etc.] The seed syllable *hūṃ hūṃ* [吽吽] appears in the *Vajra Summit Sūtra Vairocana One-Hundred Eight Honored* [*Merits*] *Dharmakāya Mudrā* (金剛頂經毘盧遮那一百八尊法身契印; T877.18.332b23–26): "唵 跋 日囉 阿 奚 吽 吽 莎 訶 [*oṃ vajra ahi hūṃ hūṃ svāhā*]."

81. Eishu, 415: "*ya* 啞 is a dumb person—faced with '*hūṃ hūṃ*.'... He has become a dumb person." [啞ヲシ也吽吽ニ當テ也.... ヲシニナツタカト也] Anonymous, 309, Dōkū, 1072, and Kōunshi, 1222: "*ya* 啞 ... is 'muteness.'" [啞 ... 瘂也]

82. Eishu, 415: "This also implies the idea 'Gone mute?'... He is calibrating and adjudicating. [*Five*] *Transmission Lamps Converge at the Source* has 'elder brother' rather than 'elder.'" [是モ只啞那卜云心也 ... 勘辨濟也傳灯會元長老作老兄] (*Wu deng huiyuan* 五燈會元: 山曰老兄作麼生; CBETA, X80, no. 1565, p. 272, a3–4 //Z 2B:11, p. 245, b8–9 //R138, p. 489, b8–9.) Anonymous, 309, is similar.

83. Anonymous, 309: "This line is not a scolding line." [此句非罵句也]

84. Kassan, 574: "What person is the *one person*? The Great Master is asking: 'Of the stick and the shout, which is closer to the matter of the *original portion*?'... a fishing-hook gimmick." [一人者是什麼人大師謂棒喝於本分事那箇親是 ... 又是釣等機也] Kōunshi, 1222: "Of the stick and the shout, which is closer to the matter of the *original portion*? Pretty much like Yue, pretty much like Yangzhou." [棒喝於本分事那箇親依稀越國彷彿揚州]

85. Eishu, 415, and Anonymous, 309: "The stick and the shout are matters within the gate of establishing teachings [for sentient beings, that is, the gate of *upāyas*]. They are not at all close to the state of the *original portion* of the patriarchal Zen gate." [棒喝建化門中叓也於祖宗門下本分田地全不親也] Kassan, 574, and Dōkū, 1072, make the same comment and add: "Every *person*—resolve to look for yourself!" [諸人斷自看]

86. Eishu, 415, and Anonymous, 309: "calibrating and adjudicating this monk." [勘辨此僧]

87. Mujaku Dōchū's *Notes on Kudzu Words* (*Kattōgo sen* 葛藤語箋; Mujaku Dictionaries, 2.912–913) gives four meanings for the entry *kunlun* 崑崙 and its orthographic variants: "1. 'the name of the Kunlun Mountains;' 2. 'ethical relations;' 3. 'blurred/confused/mixed up and not separated out;' and 4. 'head.' However, the first three are used across the Chan records, and the orthography

is not fixed." [一崑崙山名二昆命人倫名三混淪或作渾圖鶻淪等混淆無分之義四頭曰崑崙然前三禪録交用文字不定] He indicates that he thinks the third meaning applies in this LJL passage. Luo and others, eds., *Hanyu da cidian* [*Great Word Dictionary of Sinitic*], 5.1522b, glosses 渾淪/渾命 as: "refers to the hazy state before the universe took form" [指宇宙形成前的迷蒙状态]," citing the *Liehzi, Tianduan* (列子, 天端): "*hunlun* means 'the ten-thousand things are in a muddy/turbid state and not yet separated out from each other." [渾淪者言萬物相渾淪而未相離也] Eishu, 416: "*hunlun bo bu kai* means 'stupid/dull-witted.' . . . The meaning is: 'Buy straw sandals with this and practice Zen!' Some say [it means]: 'You are stupid. The money is for buying straw sandals—go on pilgrimage [i.e., go in search of a teacher and realization]!'" [渾崙擘不開トハ鈍義也. . . . 是デ草鞋ヲ買テ参禅せ(セ)ヨト云義也或云你鈍也為兩文钱買草鞋行脚せ(セ)ヨト也] Anonymous, 309, Kassan, 574, Dōkū, 1072, and Kōunshi, 1222, are similar.

88. Eishu, 416: "'Sitting cloth' in Chinese is *zuoju* 坐具." [隨坐衣唐言坐具] Myōō, 84: "Quickly understanding Linji's unreserved functioning [of the buddha nature], Dajue doesn't utter a word." [林際ノ全躰作用スル早ク心得テ大覚モ又一言不云] Kōunshi, 1223: "With respect [Dajue] politely declines instruction." [謹謝指示] The *Notes on the Yoga Treatise* (*Yuqie lun ji* 瑜伽論記; T1828.42.437a24) says: "[Sanskrit] *niṣīdana* ['rug or mat for sitting on'] is [in Chinese] *zuoju* 坐具." [尼師壇者是坐具]

89. Kōunshi, 1223: "You could say that two mirrors facing each other have no reflected images." [可謂兩鏡相對中無影像]

90. Dōchū, 1368: "*mo shi* 莫是 indicates a question." [莫是者莫是耶也]

91. Eishu, 416: "Is this monk an understanding friend/alter ego of the Preceptor?" [此僧ハ和尚知音乎] Kōunshi, 1223: "The monks of the sangha are taking human feelings as a match for the buddhadharma." [衆僧以人情當佛法]

92. Eishu, 416: "'You' is Dajue; 'elder' is the Master." [汝大覚長老師也] Dōchū, 1368: "'Elder' is the Master speaking of himself." [長老師自言也]

93. Eishu, 416, and Anonymous, 310: "*bu shen* 不審 [literally, 'I don't know what vexations you have experienced lately'] is polite speech. The meaning is: He returns to the sangha—there is no further conversational give-and-take possible." [不審ト礼話歸衆此外更無可酌對義] Kassan, 575: "He spits out what is in his mind and guts—there is no possible conversational give-and-take beyond this." [吐露心肝五藏此外更無可酌對法也]

94. Anonymous, 310: "calibrating and adjudicating Linji." [勘辨濟也]

95. Dōkū, 1073: "An ancient says: 'unreserved functioning [of the buddha nature]." [古云全體作用] Iriya, 169.2, glosses the line *qiazhi laoseng xijiao* 恰值老僧洗脚 as: "The implication is that the Ancestral Master [Bodhidharma] has just arrived here right now and is in the middle of washing the feet [dirtied] from his long journey." [祖師は今ここに到着して長旅の足を すすいでいるところだという含み。]

96. Kōunshi, 1223: "A second offense is not permitted." [再犯不容] Iriya, 169.3, glosses the line *geng yao di-er shao eshui po zai*更要第二杓惡水潑在 as: "The old interpretation of 'Do you want to get doused with a second ladle of polluted water?' is a mistake." [「二杯目の汚れ水を ぶつかけられたいのか」 という旧解は 誤り。] Xu, ed., *Jindai Hanyu da cidian* [*Great Word Dictionary of Recent Sinitic*], 1.515b, glosses *eshui* 惡水 as *wushui; choushui* [污水; 臭水] ("sewage") and cites a Yuan dynasty play *Qiu Hu Makes Fun of His Wife* (*Qiu Hu xi qi* 秋胡戏妻) by Shi Junbao 石君宝.

97. Kōunshi, 1223: "A thief doesn't enter the gate of a careful family." [賊不入慎家之門]

98. Eishu, 416: "[*Five Lamps*] *Converge at the Source*, *Blue Cliff* [*Record*], etc., make *sheng chuang* 繩床 ['rope chair'] into *chan chuang* 禪床 ['Chan chair']." [會元碧岩等繩床作禪床] (*Foguo Yuanwu chanshi Biyanlu* 佛果圓悟禪師碧巖錄: 濟下禪床擒住與一掌便托開 [T2003.48.171b27–28]; *Chanlin leiju* 禪林類聚: 師下禪床擒住打一掌便托開 [CBETA, X67, no. 1299, p. 27, a11–12 //Z 2:22, p. 27, a3–4 //R117, p. 53, a3–4]).

99. Eishu, 417: "a time in which he forgot 'before' and lost 'after'—a fine time." [忘前失後時節也好時節也] Anonymous, 310, is similar. Kassan, 576: "Now tell me—what time is [this time of 'standing there blankly']?" [且道是什麼時節] Myōō, 88: "lost the thought he was thinking and became blocked up/went blank." [所思ノ念ヲ失テ ウツカトナツタ]

100. Anonymous, 311: "This is unreserved functioning [of the buddha nature], the method of a [Zen] adept." [此則全躰作用作家手段也] Kōunshi, 1224: "It is like acquiring a lamp in the midst of darkness or like a poor person acquiring a treasure. Knowing that you have already made a mistake you go along with the mistake and continue. Tell me—what did Advanced Seat Ding see as he bowed?" [如暗得燈如貧得寶將錯就錯且道定上座見箇什麼便禮拜]

101. Dōchū, 1369: "On the top of the head, eleven [faces] added to the original face makes twelve faces." [頂上十一加本面正為十二面] Kōunshi, 1224: "The twelve faces heretofore have lacked 'main and side.' At the place of 'no main or side' he forcibly sets up 'main and side' and asks about it. The fact is he just wants to watch Linji." [十二面從來無正傍於無正傍處強設正傍而問之其實只要看臨濟耳]

102. Eishu, 417, and Anonymous, 311: "calibrating and adjudicating Mayu." [勘辨麻谷也]

103. Kassan, 576: "This is the realm of unreserved functioning [of the buddha nature]." [此是全体作用境界也]

104. Eishu, 417: "The Sanskrit is '*vajrapāṇi*,' which means '*vajra* hand.' . . . The name derives from the fact that in his hand he holds a *vajra* club." [梵語跋闍羅波膩此云金剛手 . . . 謂手執金杵以立名云云]

105. The commentators (Eishu, 417–418, Kōunshi, 1225, and Dōchū, 1370) gloss *tan-gan yingcao* 探竿影草 as either a probe used by house thieves to find out if anyone is at home or a fisherman's tool for catching fish. The most useful comments

are: Eishu, 418, who says it refers to *upāyas* (皆是方便云也), and Kōunshi, 1225, who says it is for calibrating and adjudicating people (以此勘辨人之義者也).

106. Eishu, 418: "when all is said and done, the place of the *original portion*." [畢竟本分処也] Kōunshi, 1225: "This shout is *that one shout* upward. It does not follow from the three shouts above, but it can subsume them." [此喝向上那一喝也不隨上來三喝中而亦能收攝之]

107. Eishu, 418: "Seeing someone coming into his presence, the Buddha said, 'Well come, *bhikṣu!*' Here this line derived from this precedent." [佛処人行ヲ見テハ善來比丘ト佛云也今此云モ其ヨリ出タ也] Kassan, 578: "In this case the Great Master wants to calibrate this nun, so he provisionally sets up this greeting." [此者大師要勘過這尼假設言] Anonymous, 311: "calibrating and adjudicating." [勘辨也] Kōunshi, 1225: "In the sutras the Buddha addresses monks with 'Well come, *bhikṣu!*'" [經中佛稱僧呼善來比丘]

108. Anonymous, 312: "calibrating once more." [再勘也]

109. Eishu, 418, and Anonymous, 312: "The Chan block is a tool for relieving the fatigue [of long sitting] in the Sangha Hall [i.e, a block to rest the back during long cross-legged sitting periods]." [禅版於僧堂扶老(勞カ)具也] Dōchū, 1371, glosses *chanban* 禪版 as *yiban* 倚版 and cites his *Notes on Images and Implements of the Zen Forest (Zenrin shōki sen* 禪林象器箋; *Mujaku Dictionaries,* 1.776–777): "*yiban* 倚版: When sitting on a rope chair, one leans on it in order to ease the back of the torso' [i.e, a backrest]." [倚版坐繩床時倚之所以安背也] Kōunshi, 1226: "*A Look at the Essentials [of the Śākya Family;* T2127.54.297b10] says: 'An *yiban* 倚版 is today called a *chanban* 禪版.'" [(釋氏)要覽 ... 曰倚版今呼禪版]

110. Kōunshi, 1226: "[The *Blue Cliff Record (Biyanlu* 碧巖錄, case no. 20; T2003.48.160b1–2)] also says: 'Obviously [Longya] is making a living within the ghost cave [i.e., he is mistakenly taking delusion as the realm of awakening and living complacently]. He mistakenly thinks that he has gotten the initiative. The son of a bitch is late in drawing his bow.'" [又云灼然在鬼窟裏作活計將謂得便宜賊過後張弓] Yanagida, 226: "The line *wu zushi yi* 無祖師意 is the core of this anecdote. A problem exists in the fact that there are two meanings: 1. the move of the other party is not allowed as it does not have any relation to the meaning of the Ancestral Master's coming; and 2. the position that there is no inherent meaning in the Ancestral Master's coming." [祖師意なしは、この話の中心となる句で、相手の出方が、祖師意と関係なしとして許さぬのと、祖師意そのものに意なしとするものとの両義があるところに問題がある。] The double meaning depends upon the fact that the all-purpose negative *wu* 無 means both *meiyou* 没有(negative form of "have" or "possess"/negative form of "existence") and *fei/bu shi* 非/不是 ("x is not y"). Hence *wu zushi yi* 無祖師意 means both "there is no meaning in the Ancestral Master's coming" and "x is not the meaning of the Ancestral Master's coming."

111. Eishu, 418: "Even though Longya consulted with the two great elders Linji and Cuiwei, beneath a single blow he did not understand. His abilities were inferior."

[龍牙雖參臨濟翠微之二大老一棒下不會得也根機少劣也]   Kōunshi, 1226: "[The *Blue Cliff Record* (*Biyanlu* 碧巖錄, case no. 20; T2003.48.160a24)] also says: 'This Han has fallen into the second head' [i.e., has fallen behind/is one step behind/is starting second at a game of *weiqi/go*)." [又云這漢落在第二頭了也]

112. Dōchū, 1371: "When there is something remaining that you want to ask about, it is called *qingyi* 請益. The Zen house has borrowed a phrase found in Confucian texts as a name for entering the room and requesting the dharma." [有所已與更復請餘分言請益禪家借儒典字以命入室請法也]   Kōunshi, 1226: "*qingyi* 請益 comes from *Analects, 7*." [請益者論語七]

113. Kōunshi, 1226: "[The *Blue Cliff Record* (*Biyanlu* 碧巖錄, case no. 20; T2003.48.161a10–12)] also says: 'In the mud there is a thorn. In letting [the initiative] slip to the other person [Longya] has already fallen into second [i.e., has fallen behind/is one step behind/is starting second at a game of *weiqi/go*]. This old Han has grasped the attainment of meditative concentration [*samādhi*], but he is no more than an accomplished monk in the Caodong [Sōtō] lineage. If he were in the [Rinzai] lineage of Deshan and Linji, he would necessarily know that there is a special *life/liveliness*.'" [又同評云爛泥裏有棘放過與人已落第二這老漢把得定只做得洞下尊宿若是德山臨濟門下須知別有生涯] Kōunshi here is voicing a Rinzai school polemic against the alleged quietism of the Sōtō school. Longya Judun (龍牙居遁; 835–923) was in the Qingyuan 青原 line; he was a successor of Dongshan Liangjie (洞山良价), a fountainhead of the Caodong/Japanese Sōtō lineage. The *Record of the Transmission of the Lamp of the Jingde Era* (*Jingde chuandeng lu* 景德傳燈錄; T2076.51.337b12–14) contains the following exchange: "One day [Longya] asked: 'What is the meaning of the Ancestral Master's [coming from the west]?' Dongshan said, 'Wait for the Dong River to flow backwards, and then I will tell you.' The Master [Longya] at this point awakened for the first time to the purport." [一日問如何是祖師意洞山曰待洞水逆流即向汝道師從此始悟厥旨]

114. Eishu, 419: "The elder Jingshan did not understand the buddhadharma, and so the monks of the monastery did not come to consult." [徑山長老不會佛法故寺僧不參学也] Kōunshi, 1227: "'Few made a request for an audience' means that the five hundred monks of the great sangha just circumambulated trees as practice and did not make requests for an audience." [少人參請者五百大衆只遶樹行道不事參禪請益也]

115. Eishu, 419: "'How will you calibrate and adjudicate Preceptor Jingshan?' 'Him' refers to Jingshan." [如何勘辨徑山和尚卜ㅏ彼卜ㅏ指徑山] Kassan, 579: "What sort of skill in *upāyas* will you use in approaching the five-hundred monks of the sangha?" [可接五百衆善巧方便如何也]

116. Kōunshi, 1227: "*Upāya* is 'means of calibrating and adjudicating.'" [方便勘辨之手段也]

117. Dōchū, 1371: "*zhuangyao* 裝腰 is 'did not remove his traveling clothes.'" [裝腰者不釋旅裝也] Dōku, 1076: "As for *zhuangyao* 裝腰, a traveling monk does not possess a dignified appearance." [裝腰者行腳僧不具威儀貌]

118. Eishu, 419: "He doesn't understand the buddhadharma. Because he isn't clever, he is like this." [不會佛法不伶利故如此]

119. Eishu, 419: "The monk was a monk under Jingshan." [有僧之僧徑山下僧也] Kōunshi, 1228: "Sure enough, [the monk under Jingshan] is dubious." [果然疑著]

120. Eishu, 419: "'You' is the monk. [The meaning is:] 'You want to know why Linji shouted at Jingshan?' . . . 'Him' is Linji." [你僧也林際徑山ヲ喝スルヲ 知要广也 . . . 他林際也] Dōchū, 1371: "'Him' is Huangbo." [他者黃檗也]

121. Eishu, 419, and Anonymous, 313: "'Greater-than-half' is 'two-thirds.'" [太半三分二也] Dōchū, 1371: "*Records of the Historian* [*Shi ji*] . . . 'Xiang Yu Basic Annals' . . .: 'The sum total of two-thirds is a greater-than-half; one-third is a less-than-half.'" [史記 . . . 項羽本紀 . . . 曰凡數三分有二爲太半一爲少半]

122. Anonymous, 313: "People did not understand his intention." [人不會其意] Dōkū, 1076: "The *Regulations of Purity* [*of Baizhang*; T2025.48.1139a25–27] says: '*zhiduo* [literally "straight/direct robe"]: Tradition has it that our seniors viewed monks as having [two separate garments to their outfit]: an asymmetrical outer garment, not having a [pleated] skirt; and having an inner [pleated] skirt that did not have an asymmetrical upper portion. Finally, the two [separate] garments were combined [i.e., stitched together] into an [easier-to-wear one-piece] *zhiduo*. However, in the case of Puhua it was a *zhiduo* of unornamented white wood' [i.e., a plain wooden coffin]." [(百丈)清規. . . . 直裰相傳前輩見僧有偏衫 而無裙有裙而無偏衫遂合二衣爲直裰然普化索木直裰]

123. Dōchū, 1371: "was not comfortable with their 'straight robe.'" [不受用直裰也]

124. Eishu, 419: "returned from town to Linji's temple." [街市ヨリ歸來林際院也]

125. Anonymous, 313: "a section of calibrating and adjudicating." [勘辨之段]

126. Anonymous, 313: "Immediately the news was transmitted—everyone knew of it." [即時傳語人皆知之也]

127. Dōchū, 1372: "His whole body had slipped out of the coffin—there was no corpse in the coffin." [全身脫棺去棺中無尸也] This is reminiscent of the Bodhidharma story. When Bodhidharma's stupa is opened, there is only a single shoe in the empty coffin (唯空棺一隻革履存焉; for instance, *Jingde chuandeng lu*, T2076.51.220b9–10).

128. Dōkū, 1076: "[The sound] *yin-yin* has the meaning 'dark and distant.'" [隱隱者幽遠之義也] Kōunshi, 1228: "tallies with Yangshan's prediction that '[this person will just] have a head but no tail, a beginning but no end.'" [in **45.2**; 符合仰山有頭無尾有始無終之懸記也]

PART IV

1. Kōunshi, 1229: "*xinglu* 行錄 is a *xingzhuang* 行狀 [profile or brief biography of the deceased] or a *shilu* 實錄 ['veritable record,' i.e., an annalistic record for each emperor]; it records the 'action vestiges' of the Master's career." [行錄者行狀實錄也言記錄師一代之行迹] Eishu, 420, Anonymous, 314, and

Dōkū, 1077, are similar. Dōchū, 1372: "records the karman of the Master's life." [記錄師平生行業也] This translation has taken the "*xing* 行" in the title "*xinglu* 行錄" as an abbreviation of the "*xingye* 行業" in the first line. The term *xingye* is a translation equivalent for Sanskrit *karman*; for instance, the *Dazhidulun* (大智度論; T1509.25.238b12-14) says: "By proper karman a person is rewarded with good; by improper karman a person is rewarded with bad." [若人以正行業則與好報若以邪行業則與惡報]

2. Eishu, 420: "In his *gongfu* [practice] he was careful and thorough, in his cultivation never lax." [工夫綿密修行無懈也] Anonymous, 314: "'His karman was sincere and focused' is 'he beheld reality as it truly is.'" [行業純一真正見解也] Chitetsu, 858: "'His karman was sincere and focused' is what is called the bodhisattva practice of *prajñāpāramitā*." [行業純一所謂般若波羅密之菩薩行也] Dōkū, 1077: "'His karman was sincere and focused' is like saying 'fused into oneness.'" [行業純一者如言打成一片] Kōunshi, 1229, is similar.

3. Kōunshi, 1229: "The *person* of Silla eats the chilled noodles." [新羅人喫冷淘]

4. Eishu, 420: "came down from the *fangzhang* and returned to the reading room." [自方丈下歸來眾寮也]

5. Kōunshi, 1229: "Why whack a dead Han?" [打死漢作什麼]

6. Kōunshi, 1229: "He died three times." [三回死了]

7. Eishu, 421: "*zhangyuan* 障緣 is 'karman block.' . . . old karman, the habit energy of past lives." [障緣業障也. . . . 旧業宿習也] Dōchū, 1373: "*zhangyuan* 障緣 is 'causes and conditions that block the Way.'" [障緣者障道因緣也]

8. Kōunshi, 1229: "The *Vimalakīrti Sūtra* [T475.14.548a1–2] . . . says: 'If you leave home for the buddhadharma but have discrimination, it is "not according to dharma." If you are without discrimination, then it is "according to dharma."'" [維摩 . . . 曰若於佛法出家有所分別爲不如法若無分別則如法]

9. Eishu, 421, glosses *ruo lai ci shi* 若來辞時 as: "when he requests time off." [請暇時也]

10. Eishu, 421, glosses *chuanzao* 穿鑿 as: "open people's eyes and noses [citing the *Zhuangzi* story of drilling holes in Chaos, who dies after seven days]. . . . The *Kei Commentary* says: '*chuanzao* 穿鑿 means "in teaching to refine metal by fire to remove dross."'" [人目鼻アクル也莊子云. . . . 圭抄云穿鑿教化煆煉義也] Anonymous, 314, also quotes this commentary. The term *chuanzao* 穿鑿 also appears in the *Lotus Sutra* (T262.9.31c9–10) as "digging for water to quench thirst." [譬如有人渴乏須水於彼高原穿鑿求之猶見乾土知水尚遠]

11. Kōunshi, 1230: "The *Nirvāṇa Sūtra* [T375.12.691c13–14] says: 'These sentient beings dwell in the cool shade of this buddha-tree, and all the poisons of the *kleśas* disappear.'" [涅槃 . . . 曰是諸衆生住是佛樹陰涼中者煩惱諸毒悉得消滅]

12. Kōunshi, 1230: "[Dayu] deeply calibrates the coming wind." [深辨來風]

13. Kōunshi, 1230: "He still wants to test him." [猶要驗他]

14. Kōunshi, 1230: "comes bearing a load on both shoulders." [兩肩擔來]

15. Eishu, 421, and Anonymous, 315, gloss *chekun* 徹困 as: "*che* 徹 is 'extreme' and *kun* 困 is 'fatigue'—'extreme fatigue.'" [徹極也困勞也極勞也] Kassan, 582, and Dōkū, 1078: "*chekun* 徹困 means 'earnest/sincere.'" [徹困者丁寧之義也] Dōchū, 1374: "*chekun* 徹困 is 'compassionate kindness.'" [徹困者慈悲親切也]

16. Eishu, 422, glosses *wu duozi* 無多子 as: "not much/not a lot—not even enough to count on one hand." [無許多也 ソコバク(= 若干 = イクラカ/イクツカ) モナイト云義] Anonymous, 315, is the same as the first part. Kōunshi, 1230: "Like a dragon gaining the waters or a tiger approaching the mountains." [如龍得水似虎靠山] Iriya, 183.1, glosses *wu duozi* 無多子 as: "'no bothering about this and that; direct, point-blank, straightforward, blunt, and frank'—conventional interpretations such as 'there is not much to it' or 'nonsensical; trivial' are mistakes." [あれやこれやの面倒なことはない。端的である。従来の「大したことはない」「たわいない」と解するのは誤り。]

17. Myōō, 94: "*guizi* 鬼子 is *preta* ['hungry ghost']." [鬼子トハ餓鬼也]

18. Kōunshi, 1230: "catching a tiger cub, calibrating a dragon serpent [i.e., an outstanding person]." [捉虎兒辨龍蛇]

19. Myōō, 94: "It is saying: 'When will the *great matter* be finished?'" [何レノ時カ大事了畢センソト云也] Eishu, 422: "also, the finishing of *this matter*." [又這事了畢也]

20. Dōchū, 1375: "It is in the nature of a grandmother to love her sons and grandsons earnestly—her heart is kind." [老婆性丁寧愛子孫其心親切也]

21. Eishu, 422: "*renshi* 人事 is 'gift.'" [人事礼也]

22. Dōchū, 1375: "*zuo* 昨 is 'a past day.'" [昨往日也]

23. Kōunshi, 1230: "On the exterior he seems to be curbing Dayu, but the fact of the matter is he just wants to look at the Master's level of understanding." [外面似抑大愚其實只要看師會處] Kōunshi assumes that "*this* Han" refers to Dayu—it could also refer to the "true person." The *this* perhaps gives it away.

24. Kōunshi, 1231: "words of certification." [證明語也]

25. Dōchū, 1375: "'Hall' is 'Sangha Hall.'" [堂僧堂也]

26. See the comment of Iriya, 254.1, in n. 580, **13.43**, Part II.

27. Dōchū,1375: "By being equally favored by the assistance of the two honored monks, he for the first time got the 'great completeness.'" [齊得二尊宿力始獲大全] Kōunshi, 1231: "Praises to the Master—at the sites of both Dayu and Huangpo his venue of activities from beginning to end was true." [讚是師於大愚黃檗兩處其用處始終正也]

28. Eishu, 423, and Anonymous, 316: "*zhingzhi* 境致 is 'ornament.'" [境致飾也]

29. Dōkū, 1078: "*biaobang* 標榜 is 'making known a standard.'" [標榜者表準也] Kassan, 583, is similar. Eishu, 423: "*biaobang* 標榜 is 'symbol.' . . . 'model.'" [標榜シルシ也. . . . 手本也]

30. Kassan, 583, Dōkū, 1079, and Kōunshi, 1231, gloss *zuo xuxu sheng* 作噓噓聲 as: "Exhaling rapidly is called *chui* 吹; [exhaling] slowly is called *xu* 噓."

[出氣急曰吹緩曰噓] Myōō, 96: "*xuxu sheng* 噓噓声 is 'feigning indifference/ assuming a nonchalant air.'" [噓噓声ハソラ吹（そらふく＝そらうそぶく）也] Iriya, 186.1, glosses *zuo xuxu sheng* 作噓噓聲 as: "to emit a sharp sound while breathing out from deep down in the throat—in a word, feigning indifference/assuming a nonchalant air." [喉の奧から息を長く吐きながら鋭い音を出す。つまり長嘯すること。]

31. Eishu, 423: "It means: 'will there be persons to continue the succession down to later times?'" [亦後マデ人有テ相續可カト云也]

32. At this point there is the line *chen fengxue heshang ye* 讖風穴和尚也 ("predicts Preceptor Fengxue"), which this translation has deleted. Dōchū, 1378: "This must be a comment added by a later person—it should be excised." [此必後人加此注當削去也] The text as found in Kōunshi, 1231, lacks this line and comments: "A variant edition below this in fine print has the comment: 'predicts Preceptor Fengxue.'" [異本此下細注有讖風穴和尚也] "South" refers to Nanyuan ("South Temple") Huiyong (南院惠顒; c. 860–930). He succeeded to the dharma of Xinghua Cunjiang (興化存獎; 830–888), the successor of Linji and editor who collated (*jiaokan* 校勘) the *Linjilu* (see the very end of the text in Part V). Nanyuan dwelled at the Baoying chan yuan Nanyuan 寶應禪院 南院 (South Temple of the Baoying Chan Temple) in Ruzhou 汝州 (Henan) and transmitted his dharma to Fengxue ("Cave of Wind") Yanzhao (風穴延沼; 896– 973). Fengxue was a native of Yuhang 餘杭 (Zhejiang 浙江), and Wu-Yue 吳越 is a designation of the Zhejiang region. Thus, both "Wu-Yue" and "wind" refer to Fengxue. The prediction here is to the line Linji → Xinghua → Nanyuan → Fengxue. Shoushan Shengnian (首山省念; 925–992) inherited Fengxue's dharma. Shengnian and his disciples were highly influential at the Song court and had strong connections to both Yang Yi 楊億, the editor in 1009 of the *Record of the Transmission of the Lamp of the Jingde Era* (*Jingde chuandeng lu*), and Li Zunxu 李遵勖, the compiler of the *Extended Lamp Record of the Tiansheng Era* (*Tiansheng guangdeng lu*) of 1029. The latter contains the earliest complete version of the *Linjilu* as a Linji entry (the Tiansheng *Linjilu*). See n. 7 in the Introduction. For other readings of the prophecy, see Daitoku-ji, 318–320.

33. Kōunshi, 1232: "the mental disposition of a sleeping tiger." [睡虎機]

34. Kōunshi, 1232: "even capable of yanking on the tiger's whiskers." [也解捋虎鬚]

35. Kōunshi, 1232: "Mountain [note that the name 'Deshan' means 'Virtue Mountain'] collapses, and the stones crack open." [山崩石裂]

36. Eishu, 424: "Two dragons contend over the pearl." [二龍爭珠也] Kōunshi, 1232, Dōkū, 1080, and Dōchū, 1378: "When the waters of the Xiang and Xiao Rivers converge, they are of a single clarity [水到湘瀟一段清]." The Xiang and the Xiao meet at Lingling in Hunan province.

37. Dōchū, 1378: "The *Brief History of the Sangha* [of Great Song; T2126.54.240b2] . . . says: 'Work in common is called *puqing* 普請.'" [僧史略 . . . 云共作者謂之普請]

38. Dōkū, 1080: "An ancient said, 'Supernormal power, the *samādhi* of play.'" [古云神通遊戯三昧]

39. Kōunshi, 1233: "As for the term *weina* 維那, the *Brief History of the Sangha* [of Great Song; T2126.54.245a3–5] . . . says: 'The Chinese and Sanskrit are simultaneously raised [i.e., it is a compound consisting of both a Chinese translation and an abbreviated Chinese transliteration of the Sanskrit term *karma-dāna*]. *wei* 維 is "headrope of a fishing net/prime part"; it is a Chinese word. *na* 那 is an abbreviated [transliteration] of the Sanskrit; it shaves off the three characters *jiemo duo* 羯磨陀, [leaving only the *-na* of *dāna*].'" [僧史略 . . . 曰華梵兼舉也維是綱維華言也那是略梵語刪去羯磨陀三字也]

40. Eishu, 425: "'On all sides' means 'dead-Han mind.' . . . ['The Master took hold of the stick, and,] with a single jolt, knocked Huangbo down' has the intention of 'live burial.' . . . Linji's 'here on my patch' is the 'live Han.'" [諸方死漢ト云心也. . . . 黄檗ヲモ一送送倒スルハ活埋意也. . . . 林際我這裡活漢也]

41. Eishu, 425: "The one who pursued the thief still met punishment. . . . The real thief was Linji. He stole Huangbo's buddhadharma. . . . The beat constable was the Duty Master, who did not steal the buddhadharma." [追賊者還遭罪也. . . . 此正賊ハ林際也盗黄檗佛法. . . . 邏蹤人ハ維那也不盗佛法] Dōchū, 1379: "The real thief was Linji, and the beat constable was the Duty Master." [正賊臨濟邏蹤人維那] Kōunshi, 1233, is similar.

42. Kassan, 586: "The mental disposition of a sleeping tiger—in reality he wants to keep an eye on Huangbo. How?" [睡虎之機其實要看黄檗如何] Manuals of cross-legged Chan sitting criticize sitting with the eyes closed—for instance, the one in the *Regulations of Purity of Baizhang* (*Chixiu Baizhang qinggui*敕修百丈清規; T2025.48.1143a11–12) says: "Chan Master Fayun Yuantong scolded people who shut the eyes in cross-legged sitting and called it the ghost cave of Black Mountain." [法雲圓通禪師呵人閉目坐禪謂黑山鬼窟]

43. Kassan, 586: "This is the basic meaning of the master-student relationship." [是師資本意也]

44. Kassan, 586: "What a fine occasion! Also, he wants to see the encounter between the two persons." [好箇時節又要見二人相見之機]

45. Eishu, 425: "certifying Linji." [證明林際] Kassan, 586: "On the surface he is engaging in a ritual of ordination for Linji; inside he wants to see [the level of understanding of] the Head Seat." [外面摩頂林際裡許要見首座]

46. Eishu, 425, Kassan, 586, and Dōchū, 1379: "The meaning is 'his feet aren't stepping on ground of the truly real.'" [足不蹈實地義也] The term *shidi* 實地 is defined in the Yanshou's *Zongjinglu* (宗鏡錄; T2016.48.916b7–9): "As for 'the one-reality discernment,' it is the reality discernment of mind-only and *tathatā*. Outside of mind everything is an unreal *māyā*, and therefore it is called 'the one-reality realm.' It is also called 'the characteristic of *tattva*,' '*tattva/bhūta* ground [*shidi* 實地],' 'reality limit [*bhūta-koṭi*],' 'real dharma' . . .

'buddha knowing-seeing,' '*ārya* wisdom,' etc." [所言一實觀者即是唯心真如實觀離心之外盡成虛幻故稱一實境界亦云實相實地實際實法乃至名佛知見聖智慧等] Dōchū, 1379: "An ancient worthy says: '*zhengju* 證據 is "authenticate."'" [證據者印可也]

47. Kassan, 586: "Huangbo gives a deep okay to the Head Seat's words." [黃蘗深肯首座語] Iriya, 190.2: "Here it is an action that expresses regret at his own verbal slip." [ここでは、自らの失言を悔いた動作。]

48. Kassan, 586, and Dōkū, 1081: "means 'if you know it's wrong, then fine.'" [自知非即得之謂也] Anonymous, 318, and Kōunshi, 1234, are similar. Kassan, 586, adds: "Longbao says: 'If the Head Seat were not a clear-eyed Han, how could Huangbo on the mountaintop have responded [to a poem with a poem] in this way?'" [龍寶云首座若非明眼漢黃蘗山頭恁麼酬唱乎] Dōchū, 1379: "Both meanings relate to Linji. It is the word 'know' in the above line '*he knows of this matter.*'" [忠曰二義俱係臨濟上知有此事之知字也] Yanagida, 245, glosses *zhi ji de* 知即得 as: "If you understand the mistake, then it's all right. The line 自知罪過即得 ['If you yourself know the mistake, then it's fine'] also appears in the *Zhaozhou Sayings Record*." [間違いが判っているならよろしい。『趙州語録』にも、「自ら罪過を知らば即ち得ん」、という句がある。] For the *Zhaozhou Sayings Record*, see *Gu zunsu yulu* 古尊宿語録: CBETA, X68, no. 1315, p. 80, b22–23 //Z 2:23, p. 157, a14–15 //R118, p. 313, a14–15. Nakamura, 223: "The give-and-take of intimate comrades—Huangbo, Linji, and the Head Seat." [黃蘗・臨済・首座、知音同志のやりとり。]

49. Dōchū, 1379: "The Master was asleep at his seat [on the sitting platform] in the lower [southern] part [of the Hall]." [師在下間單睡也]

50. Eishu, 425: "Huangbo came down from his sitting position; or, he came down from the *fangzhang* to enter the Sangha Hall." [黃蘗坐処ヨリ下來也又從方丈下來入僧堂也]

51. Kassan, 586–587: "*bantou* 板頭 is the plank of the long [sitting] platform in the lower part [of the Hall]." [板頭者下間長牀板也] Dōkū, 1081, Anonymous, 318, and Kōunshi, 1234, are similiar. Dōchū, 1379: "The *tan* plank ['single plank'] at the front [edge] of the [sitting] platform is called the *bantou* 板頭." [牀前單板此謂板頭而已] Nakamura, 225, translates as: "With his staff he gave a hit to the edge of the *tan*. . . ." [柱杖で単のふちを一打してから]

52. Dōchū, 1380: "Because the Sangha Hall system is oriented to the east, north is the upper part [of the hall], and south is the lower part [of the hall]. The Head Seat's *tan* [seat] is the first in the upper part." [僧堂制東向故北為上間南為下間首座單在上間第一]

53. Kassan, 587: "Out in a boat taking a nap and forgetting cognizables [*jñeya*]—in fact, this is the true *zazen*!" [舟杭一睡忘却所知實是真箇坐禪也]

54. Kassan, 587: "Stabilizing mind to tame it but instead increasing thought of the unreal [*abhūta-vikalpa*] is not the true *zazen*!" [住心調伏却增長妄想非是真箇坐禪也]!"

55. Dōchū, 1380: "The *Transmission of the Lamp* [*Record of the Jingde Era;* T2076.51.300a1] . . . makes it 患風耶 [rather than 作什麼]. Dōchū says: *feng* 風 is *xin feng* ['confused thinking']; it means 'insanity.'" [傳燈 . . . 作患風耶忠曰風心風謂風狂疾也]

56. Dōchū 1380 glosses: "*cai* [彩] is the number shown on the dice. *sai* [賽] is the dice. As for 'two numbers one die,' if the numbers on the two dice are identical, then, even though there are two numbers, it counts as just one die." [彩是骰子所照數目也賽即骰子也兩彩一賽者兩箇骰子彩數齊則雖有兩彩同但一賽也] Eishu, 426: "The meaning is that both the Head Seat and Linji are the same." [首座林際同者卜云義也]

57. Eishu, 426: "At the time of the communal work period Huangbo went out at the front, and Linji went out at the rear." [普請時黃檗前出林際後出也]

58. Eishu, 426: "He says 'one person,' but it is *that one person* or *this matter*. Dō [?] says: '"One person" means Huangbo. It means he saw Huangbo carrying the hoe.'" [一人卜云ガ那一人也箇事也道云一人卜ハ黃檗ヲ云檗钁ヲ持ルルヲ見テ云也] Kassan, 587: "An old commentary says: '"One person" refers to Huangbo.' Not so. Now tell me: Who is it?" [舊抄云一人者指黃檗也不然且道是何人] Dōchū, 1380: "Kazan [?] says: '"One person" is not Huangbo and is not *that one person*. Now, take another look!'" [家山曰一人非黃檗又非那一人且辨別看] Dōkū, 1081: "*This one person*—when all is said and done, what *place* is he?" [這箇一人畢竟在什麼處] Kōunshi, 1234: "Now tell me: Who is the *one person*?" [且道一人是何人]

59. Eishu, 426: "He says *this matter*, but it is the *one person*." [亇事卜云ガ一人也] Dōkū, 1081: "This is the matter of the *original portion*." [是爲本分事]." Kōunshi, 1234: "*This matter* refers to the matter of the hoe." [簡事者指钁頭事]

60. Kōunshi, 1234: "This hoe—each and every person is endowed with *this*; each and every *this* is perfect." [這箇钁頭人人具足箇箇圓成] Anonymous, 319, and Dōkū, 1081, are the virtually the same.

61. Kōunshi, 1234: "This is the true communal work! It is an expression that definitely certifies the Master." [是真箇普請大證明師之語也]

62. Eishu, 426: "Yangshan is speaking in praise of Linji. The thief is Linji, and the noble man is Huangbo." [仰山林際ヲホメテ云也賊ハ林際君子ハ黃檗也] Dōkū, 1081: "An ancient said, 'The person who wields the stick must necessarily have times when he eats the stick.'" [古云行棒人必有喫棒時] Kōunshi, 1235: "The thief is compared to the Master, the noble man to Huangbo." [賊比師君子比黃檗]

63. Eishu, 426: "The Guest Receptionist is the official who receives guests." [知客接客官也] Kōunshi, 1235: "As for 'Guest Receptionist,' the *Baizhang Regulations of Purity* [T2025.48.1131b9–11] . . . says: 'The Guest Receptionist is in charge of guests. He is the one who has contact with all officials, generous donors, honorable monks, and famous and virtuous scholars from all over. He greets them with incense and tea, and, carrying out the rules correctly, notifies

[the abbot in] the *fangzhang* [of their arrival]. Afterwards, he escorts them up [to the *fangzhang*] for a visit. . . .'" [知客者百丈清規 . . . 曰知客職典賓客凡官員檀越尊宿諸方名德之士相過者香茶迎待隨令行者通報方丈然後引上相見云云]

64. Eishu, 426: "means the letter." [書ヲ云]

65. Eishu, 426: "'Special envoy' refers to Linji." [專使林際ヲ指云也]

66. Dōkū, 1082: "What letter is this?" [是什麼書]

67. Dōchū, 1381: "The idea is 'caught the slapping hand and stopped it.'" [有捉掌之手止之意]

68. The Zen commentators struggle with this line *laoxiong zhi shiban shi bian xiu* 老兄知是般事便休. Iriya, 195, translates it as: "If you've understood to this extent, then I have nothing to complain of." [そこまでお分かりなら文句はない]

69. Eishu, 426: "Even though, for Guishan, Huangbo is the 'Master younger brother,' he refers to him as 'Master elder brother.' This is a good precedent." [爲溈山黃檗師弟ナレドモ師兄ト云也好例也] Anonymous, 319: "Even though Guishan is 'Master elder brother' to Huangbo, here he refers to [Huangbo] as 'Master elder brother.' This is polite speech on the part of Guishan." [溈山雖為黃檗師兄於此云師兄是則溈山之禮話也]

70. "Leader" (*daoshou* 導首 = *parināyaka*) is an epithet of a buddha and said of a herd of deer; also said of a bodhisattva in the *Mahāprajñāpāramitā Sūtra* (大般若波羅蜜多經; T220.5.15a14–16): "If the bodhisattva, the great being, wants to be leader for all the *śrāvakas* and *pratyeka-buddhas*, he should train in the *prajñāpāramitā*." [若菩薩摩訶薩欲與一切聲聞獨覺而爲導首應學般若波羅蜜多] The Zen commentators interpret it as the "Head Seat" of a Zen monastery. Dōchū, 1381: "'Leader' means 'Head Seat.' The Head Seat has jurisdiction over the great sangha. He substitutes for the master in sharing the seat to speak dharma, and so he is called 'leader.'" [導首謂首座首座領大眾代師家分座說法故云導首] Anonymous, 319: "Who substitutes for the master in preaching dharma and leads the great sangha as its head?" [何人代長老說法導大衆為首麼云也] Kōunshi, 1235: "The 'leader' is the First Seat." [導首者第一座也]

71. Eishu, 427: "Linji is speaking of himself as 'leader.'" [臨濟自我ヲ導首ト云]

72. Dōchū, 1381: "Yangshan is in possession of the supernormal power of knowing the future, and so he makes an announcement like this." [仰山具神通知未來故告如此] Kōunshi, 1235: "This predicts Linji Temple in Hebei." [是讖河北臨濟院也]

73. Dōchū, 1381: "an expression of modesty." [謙詞也] Anonymous, 320, and Kōunshi, 1235, are similar.

74. Eishu, 427: "'One person' refers to Puhua." [一人指普化也]

75. Kōunshi, 1235: "This predicts Puhua." [是讖普化也]

76. Eishu, 427: "Linji emerged in the world, dwelling at Linji Temple [as abbot]." [林際出世住臨濟院也]

77. Anonymous, 320: "This is 'having a head but no tail.'" [是有頭無尾也] Kōunshi, 1235: "tallies with Yangshan's prediction [in **45.2** to the effect that 'this person will just have a head but no tail, a beginning but no end']." [符合仰山懸記也]

78. Eishu, 427: "first day of the sixth month." [六月一日也] Nakamura, 230, glosses *banxia* 半夏 as: "It is the day at the midpoint of the summer *ango* [retreat]. The summer retreat is also called the 'rains retreat.' It is a period of practice from the fifteenth day of the fourth month to the fifteenth day of the seventh month. 'Half summer' is the first day of the sixth month. During this period there is confinement [for Zen monks]. To break this confinement is called 'breaking summer.'" [夏安居の中半の日。夏安居は雨安居とも云い、四月十五日より七月十五日の修行の期間。半夏は六月一日、期間中は禁足、この禁を破ることを破夏という。]

79. Dōchū, 1381: "As for *an* 揞, the *Transmission of the Lamp* reading [T2076.51.290c5] is *an* 唵 ['hold in the mouth'], and this is correct. . . . Here black beans are being compared to written words. Moving the mouth to read is taken as greedily eating black beans with a big mouth, and, therefore, it is said *an heidou* 唵黑豆." [揞傳燈作唵為正. . . . 今黑豆比文字揺口看讀以爲噉黑豆也故云唵黑豆] Eishu, 427: "*an heidou* 揞黑豆 is 'lettered Zen.'" [揞黑豆ト ハ文字禪也] Kassan, 589: "All [interpretations of the character *an* 揞] refer to understanding based on the teachings." [俱作教會之謂也] Anonymous, 320: "It means 'to play with the written word of the sutra rolls.' It is like counting black beans in the hand." [言弄經卷文字之義猶手中數黑豆也] Chitetsu, 868: "'Black beans' are written words. Anyone who reads the sutras and teachings is spoken of in this way." [所謂黑豆即文字也凡看經看教謂之] Dōkū, 1082: "It means playing with the written words of the sutra rolls. It is like counting black beans. When all is said and done, it is criticizing sutra reading." [言弄經卷文字猶數黑豆畢竟斥看經]

80. Anonymous, 320: "The Master came to have doubts about [Huangbo's] intention in reading the sutras and returned." [師疑看經意又回也]

81. Kōunshi, 1236: "The whole earth is the home to which one returns, the place of smooth-and-steady sitting." [盡大地是歸家穩坐處]

82. Kassan, 589, and Kōunshi, 1236, quote a couplet from the Wang Wei 王維 poem "Sending Off Someone on a Mission to Anxi" (送人使安西): "Let us have another cup of sake/West of the Yang Pass there are no old friends." [勸君更盡一杯酒西出陽関無故人] The Yang Pass is southwest of the oasis town Dunhuang on the Silk Road. The slap is a last cup of sake before Linji goes out into the world.

83. Dōchū, 1382: "the laugh of certification." [證明之笑] Anonymous, 320: "This great laugh is the seal." [此大咲印可也] Nakamura, 230: "As to *chanban* 禅版, it is something one leans forward on when taking a rest during cross-legged sitting. *ji'an* 机案 is a desk, but, in this case, it is called a *jiban* 掎版 ['support block'], and so we can surmise that it was something placed on the rope chair during *zazen*

that one could lean back on." [禅版は坐禅中休息のとき、前に倚りかかるもの。机案はつくえであるが、ここの場合掎版というもので、坐禅中縄床の上におき、うしろによりかかるものが妥当と推測される。] Nakamura cites Mujaku Dōchū's *Notes on Images and Implements of the Zen Forest* (*Zenrin shōki sen* 禪林象器箋; Mujaku Dictionaries, 1.776–777): "An old theory says: 'The *chanban* is an instrument used to rest the hands on or lean against the body during *zazen*.' . . . Dōchū says: 'The *yiban* was used to lean against the back as a support during sitting in a rope chair.'" [舊說曰禪板者坐禪時安手或靠身器也. . . . 忠曰倚版坐繩床時倚之所以安背也.

84. Eishu, 428: "The attendant is to bring fire to burn it up." [侍者將火來燒ステン也] Dōchū, 1382: "He wants to burn up the Chan armrest and backrest." [欲燒禪版机案也]

85. Dōchū, 1383: "Later, on the day you set up your [own] dharma pennant, the people of all-under-heaven will debate, saying: 'He says he has obtained Huangbo's seal of cerification, but what is there to take as proof?' At that time you can show them these dharma vessels that you have received in transmission. Their criticism will suddenly cease.' . . . Bodhidharma told Huike: 'Perhaps you will encounter difficult karmic conditions. Just take out this robe to commend faith. Its transformative [power] will be unobstructed. . . .' That is the idea here." [言向後建法幢日天下人議云他言得黃蘗印可何以爲證那時汝示此傳來法器譏嫌嘗頓止也. . . . 達磨謂慧可曰或遇難緣但出此衣用以表信其化無礙此此今亦其意也]

86. Eishu, 428: "In Linji's saying 'Attendant, bring some fire [too to incinerate them],' did he disobey Huangbo?" [侍者將火來卜林際云ヘタハ黃蘗ニソムイテ云ヘタ乎] Kassan, 590, and Dōchū, 1383, are similar.

87. Kassan, 590: "His wanting to burn the backrest is true repayment of kindness." [要火机案是真報恩底也] Yanagida, 256: "Based on a proverb of the time, which appears in the Dunhuang manuscript *House Teachings of Taigong* [*Taigong jiajiao* 太公家教]."

88. Eishu, 428: "Among the ancients was there ever anything like Linji's skillful method of calling for fire from the attendant?" [林際ノ侍者將火來卜云作畧底相似古人在也無卜也] Dōchū, 1383: "similar to [Linji's] recognizing the kindness and repaying the kindness." [相似知恩報恩底也] Anonymous, 321: "In high antiquity was there ever such a person [as Linji]?" [上古亦有如是人否也]

89. Eishu, 429: "The Buddha's deep mind of great friendliness and great compassion." [佛大慈大悲之深心也] Dōchū, 1383: "'Deep mind' is knowing kindness [and repaying kindness]." [深心即是知恩底也].

90. Dōkū, 1083, and Kōunshi, 1237: "In the *Śūraṃgama Sūtra* [T945.19.119b12–15]: 'Deep *dhāraṇī*, immovable honored one—the *Śūraṃgama* King is rare in the world; you cancel out my topsy-turvy thought of untold kalpas; without going through incalculable [eons] I will obtain the *dharmakāya*; I now vow to get the

fruit and become a treasure-king; I will return and save beings [as numberless as] the sands of the Ganges; I will dedicate this deep mind [of great compassion] to [all the beings] in the buddha-lands [as numberless as] dust particles; this is called repaying the Buddha's kindness.'" [首楞嚴.... 妙湛總持不動尊首楞嚴王世希有銷我億劫顛倒想不歷僧祇獲法身願今得果成寶(寶)王還度如是恒沙衆將此深心奉塵刹是則名爲報佛恩]

91. Kōunshi, 1237: "Only when Linji's vision surpasses that of Huangbo can they stand to transmit and receive." [臨濟見處勝過黃蘗方堪傳受]

92. Kōunshi, 1237: "This is the Dinglin Monastery." [即定林寺也]

93. Kōunshi, 1237: "can't be loaded on his two shoulders." [兩肩擔不起]

94. Kōunshi, 1237: "[At one stroke of the sword] he severs the head of Vairocana—he saw neither buddhas nor patriarchs." [坐斷毗盧頂[寧+頁]曾不見有佛祖]

95. Kōunshi, 1237: "With his eyes wide open he is talking dream nonsense." [開眼說夢]

96. Eishu, 429: "This is truly repaying the kindness of the buddhas and patriarchs." [是寔報佛祖之恩也] Anonymous, 322, is similar.

97. Eishu, 429: "The Master, after his great awakening, traveled on foot all over calibrating and adjudicating." [師大悟後爲諸方勘辨行脚也]

98. Eishu, 430: "Longguang righted his sitting posture, leaning on the back of the Dharma Seat." [龍光居直テ法座ノ後ニヨリカカル也] Kassan, 591: "The *Dahui* [*Sayings Record;* T1998.47.831a18–19] states: 'Longguang righted his sitting posture. Although he was silent, the sound was like thunder.'" [大慧云龍光據坐雖然無語其聲如雷]

99. Eishu, 430: "With the words 'great teacher [great *kalyāṇa-mitra*]' he is playing with him." [大善知識ト弄云也] Kōunshi, 1237: "calibrating once more." [再勘]

100. Eishu, 430, Anonymous, 322, and Dōkū, 1084: "Looks straight at him with angry eyes.... *sha* 嗄 is a change of voice, with the appearance of being startled." [怒目直視也.... 嗄声變也又驚兒也] Kassan, 591, and Kōunshi, 1237, are similar. Dōchū, 1384: "*Laozi*, 55, says: 'All day long yelling without becoming hoarse, [the height of harmony].'" [老子五十五章曰終日號而嗌不嗄(和之至也)]

101. Kōunshi, 1238: "the name 'Mt. Sanfeng.'" [三峰山名]

102. Kōunshi, 1238: "wants to calibrate." [要勘過]

103. Kōunshi, 1238: "still wants to calibrate relative depth." [猶要辨淺深]

104. Eishu, 430: "The meaning is 'there is not even a single word to it; it doesn't set up even a single vishaya.' *bu jian zong* 不見蹤 is 'not leave behind a trace.'" [一句モナキ義一塵ヲモ不立也不見蹤トハ不留蹤跡也] Dōchū, 1384: "The ox cast of gold fell into the charcoal fire and got stuck in the mud." [金所鑄牛墜炭火陷塗泥] Myōō, 104: "means 'got stuck in mud and fell into fire.'" [陷泥墜火ヲ云也] Anonymous, 322: "means that right now, in [Huangbo's] venue of activities, there is not a trace—the wonderful classic of nontransmission." [今用處只無蹤跡之義不傳之妙典也] Dōkū, 1084: "This refers to the fact that Huangbo's buddhadharma did not leave behind any trace of

words and phrases." [此蓋指黃檗佛法不曾囲言句蹤跡] Kōunshi, 1238: "The meaning is that Huangbo's venue of activities was a non-venue, without a trace. As to 'mud and charcoal,' the *Book of Documents*, 'Mandate of Zhonghui,' says: 'Because of Xia's immorality, the people fell into mud and charcoal.'" [是黃檗用處無處沒蹤跡之義也塗炭者書經仲虺之誥篇曰有夏昏德民墜塗炭]

105. Eishu, 430: "It is a new tune. 'Golden wind' is the autumn wind." [新曲調也金風秋風也] Myōō, 104: "'Golden wind' is the autumn wind." [金風ハ秋風也] Kōunshi, 1238: "The direction west is gold, and, therefore, 'golden wind.'" [西方爲金故曰金風] Anonymous, 323: "The 'golden wind' is the autumn wind, the west wind." [金風秋風也西風也]

106. Kassan, 592: "An old commentary says: 'The meaning is: Who will pass on *that one tune* of Huangbo?' I say: 'The first sentence ["The golden (autumn) wind (of the west/of Huangbo's teaching) blows (a new tune on) the jade flute"] refers to the fact that at the bottom of Huangbo's words of instruction there are no traces whatsoever; the second sentence ["but who will be able to recognize its music?"] means: "Who will hit it off perfectly with his wonderful song?" The reality of it is that we must look to Linji.'" [舊抄云黃檗之那一曲誰人傳授之謂也愚謂上之句者指黃檗言句沒蹤跡之底裡下之句者謂何人契其妙唱也其實要看林際也] Dōchū, 1384: "It means: 'With that sort of wonderful song by Huangbo who will get his purport?'" [言黃檗恁麼妙唱誰得其旨耶] Anonymous, 323: "In your venue of activities right now, if you listen with your ears, then you are not 'one who recognizes the music.'" [今用處若以耳聽非知音也] Dōkū, 1084: "*That one tune* of Huangbo—I fear no one can hear it." [黃檗那一曲恐怕無人聽得徹]

107. Compare Shūshin, 138–139, in **12.7**: "Truly penetrating the ten-thousand layer barrier [of characteristics] but not being fixed in the thin, floating clouds [i.e., unfixed nirvana]." [正透萬重関不住青霄裏] Kassan, 592: "Even though Linji says of himself: 'Huangbo's song of personal-realization-of-the-meaning-beyond-words—I know all of its music,' he doesn't dwell inside his song of personal-realization-of-the-meaning-beyond-words.'" [林際自謂黃檗宗唱我能悉習知音雖然不住其宗唱内也] Dōkū, 1084: "Linji thoroughly hears *that one tune* of Huangbo. However, he doesn't dwell inside his wonderful tune." [臨濟聽徹黃檗那一曲然不住其妙曲] Dōchū, 1384: "The Master thinks highly of himself." [師自負]

108. Anonymous, 323: "The meaning is: 'You are being lofty and excessive.' [Ping] is curbing [Linji]." [言巍巍也又過分之義也抑下] Dōchū, 1384: "[Ping] is curbing [Linji]." [抑下臨濟也]."

109. Kassan, 592, and Dōkū, 1084: "'Dragon' refers to Huangbo. 'Golden phoenix son' is Linji's self-designation. A dragon should give birth to a dragon son, but it gives birth to a golden phoenix son—this is the transmission of non-transmission. 'Blue lapis-lazuli' is a phoenix egg." [龍者指黃檗也金鳳子者林際自謂也龍合生龍子却生金鳳子者是不傳之傳也碧瑠璃者鳳卵也] Dōchū, 1384:

"'Dragon' is Huangbo; 'golden phoenix' is Linji." [龍是黃檗金鳳是林際] Myōō, 105, makes the same identification and adds: "'Blue lapis-lazuli' is the blue heaven." [碧瑠璃ハ青天也] Anonymous, 323: "'Blue lapis-lazuli' is the sky, the heavens." [碧瑠璃者空也天也] Kōunshi, 1238: "'Dragon' is a metaphor for Huangbo; 'golden phoenix son' is the Master's metaphor for himself. 'Blue lapis-lazuli' means 'phoenix egg.' Or some say it means 'the deep blue of the blue heavens that is like lapis-lazuli.'" [龍比黃檗金鳳子師自比碧琉璃者謂鳳卵也或曰謂碧天蒼蒼如琉璃]

110. Kassan, 592: "This is mundane chatter with a guest. . . . This is 'twofold take-in'; it is also enjoyment of reality as it truly is." [此對客世話也. . . . 此是雙收又是真正受用也] Dōkū, 1084, is similar. A Huayan commentary (*Huayan yisheng jiaoyi fenji zhang yiyuan shu* 華嚴一乘教義分齊章義苑疏, a commentary on Fazang's 法藏 treatise by Daoting 道亭 of the Song; CBETA, X58, no. 995, p. 239, b9–10 //Z 2:8, p. 147, d12–13 //R103, p. 294, b12–13), defines "twofold take-in" (*shuangshou* 雙收) as follows: "'Twofold take-in' of the whole substance means that because of *śūnyatā*, dependently originated characteristics are taken into the nature; because of origination by dependence, *śūnyatā* is taken into the characteristics. The 'twofold fusion' of nature and characteristics is achieved—in the end, non-duality." [釋曰全體雙收者謂空故緣生相收於性也緣生故空性收於相也性相雙融成畢竟無二也] Kōunshi, 1238: "Ordinariness." [平常底]

111. Eishu, 431: "This is also a Preceptor Ping question to Linji." [是モ平和尚問林際也] Kōunshi, 1238: "For a second time he grasps the fishing pole [to reel in Linji for calibration]." [重把釣竿]

112. Eishu, 431, and Anonymous, 323: "The meaning is: 'What words of instruction does Longguang have these days?'" [龍光近日有什广言句云義] Kōunshi, 1238: "calibrating once more." [再勘]

113. Dōchū, 1384: "At the very beginning [of 50.1 Ping] asks the *place* he comes from. The dialogue [of 50.1] is thorough. [At the beginning of 50.2 Ping] asks another question about where he has been visiting recently. One could say that [in 50.1] 'the bell tolled, and the outflows [*āsrava*] were exhausted' [i.e., an arhat with destruction of the outflows achieves nirvana]. [But in 50.2 Ping] lights one more fire, and the Master therefore leaves without answering." [最初問來處問答一場周借更問近離可謂鐘鳴漏盡更舉火把師所以不答而出去也]

114. Xu, ed., *Jindai Hanyu da cidian* [*Great Word Dictionary of Recent Sinitic*], 1.490a, glosses *duanju* 端居 as: *anju; shenju* 安居; 深居 ("living a peaceful life in retreat; having no contact with the outer world"), citing a couplet from a Wang Wei 王維 poem and a passage in a Dunhuang transformation text. The former, "Ascending to the Small Terrace with Scholar Pei Leading the Way" (*Deng Pei xiucai di xiaotai* 登裴秀才迪小台), runs: "Living a peaceful life in retreat without going out the door; Filling the eyes gazing at the clouds and mountains." [端居不出戶滿目望云山] Modern translators (Yanagida, 262; Iriya,

203; Nakamura, 236; Daitoku-ji, 332; Watson, 119; and Demiéville, 230–231) all construe the term *duanju* 端居 as *duanzuo* 端坐/*zhengzuo* 正坐 ("sitting erect/straight; cross-legged sitting").

115. Anonymous, 323: "The meaning is: 'Have you obtained the purport [i.e., realization] while living [a peaceful life in retreat] in your *fangzhang*?' [The Master] is curbing [Daci]." [言得旨居在丈室也抑下] Kōunshi, 1239: "It's truly a matter of wanting to calibrate him." [正要辨的]

116. Eishu, 431: "The master [Daci] is of stern conduct. Daci is speaking of himself." [師家凜然タル操也大慈自云也] Anonymous, 323: "Daci is talking about himself." [慈自謂也]

117. Anonymous, 323: "*yelao* 野老 is 'locals.' *wanguo chun* 萬國春 ['spring in the ten-thousand countries'] is 'joyful.' It means 'sitting under the flowers and getting drunk with looking at the moon, the locals are joyful.' . . . He is curbing Linji." [野老土民萬國春樂也言坐花醉月土民樂也.... 抑下臨濟云也] Myōō, 105: "He is curbing Linji." [林際ヲ抑下スル也]

118. Eishu, 431: "The 'perfect wisdom substance' is one of the four wisdoms, the great, perfect mirror-wisdom [*ādarśa-jñāna*]." [圓智体四智一大圓鏡智也] Anonymous, 323, is similar. Dōchū, 1384: "The substance of the great, perfect mirror-wisdom eternally transcends past and present times." [大圓鏡智之體永超今古時也]

119. Eishu, 431: "The 'three mountains' are the three [mythical] islands of Penglai, Fangzhang, and Yingzhou." [三山蓬萊方丈瀛洲三嶋也] Kassan, 592: "The 'three mountains' . . . are the abodes of the roaming immortals. This is a borrowing to refer to the home mountains of the *original portion*." [三山者.... 是遊仙之居處也此借用指本分家山也] Dōchū, 1385: "The three mountains [i.e., actual mountains] are southwest of [the city of] Jinling." [三山在金陵西南] Kōunshi, 1239: "The 'three mountains' are Penglai, Fangzhang, and Yingzhou. Here they are compared to the home mountains of the *original portion*." [三山者蓬萊方丈瀛洲也今比本分家山]

120. Kōunshi, 1239: "The lock on the ten-thousand-layer barrier all-at-once opens up." [萬重關鎖一時開]

121. Kōunshi, 1239: "The higher the river, the higher the boat." [水長舩高] *Five Lamps Converge at the Source* (*Wu deng hui yuan*; 五燈會元) says: "The higher the river, the higher the boat; the more clay, the bigger the buddha image." [水長船高泥多佛大] CBETA, X80, no. 1565, p. 196, a8-9 // Z 2B:11, p. 169, a2-3 // R138, p. 337, a2-3.

122. Kōunshi, 1239: "calibrating once more." [再勘]

123. Kōunshi, 1239: "A thousand-foot whale, spouting amidst the vast waves, taking flight." [千尺鯨吐洪浪飛]

124. Eishu, 431: "Knowing that Linji was coming, he leaned on his staff with the air of someone asleep." [是モ林際來ト知テ倚主丈作睡勢也]

125. Eishu, 431: "The Master takes him to task." [師ノトガメラレタ也]

126. Eishu, 432: "The meaning is [a level of understanding] that is off the charts, beyond that of the crowd." [出格出群義也] Dōchū, 1385: "innately different from others." [天然不與諸人同也] Anonymous, 324: "not the same as the run-of-the-mill." [又與尋常不同也]

127. Dōchū, 1385: "This means 'The Preceptor has been talking in his sleep and is not yet awake. Attendant, go make some tea and present it to him to make him wake up.'" [言和尚寐語睡未醒在侍者點茶進之令睡覺也] Anonymous, 324, and Kōunshi, 1239, are similar.

128. Eishu, 432: "'Third position' is also called the 'rear hall.'" [第三位後堂トモ云] Kassan, 593, Dōchū, 1385, and Kōunshi, 1239: "'Third position' is Head Seat of the rear hall." [第三位者後堂首座也] Anonymous, 324, and Dōkū, 1085: "'Third position' is the rear hall." [第三位後堂也]

129. Kōunshi, 1239: "routine calibrating and testing." [家常勘驗]

130. Eishu, 432: "What words of instruction does the buddhadharma have?" [佛法有何言句]

131. Anonymous, 324: "This Han has stagnated in [the two extremes of] 'is' and 'is not.'" [此漢滯在有無處] Anonymous is alluding to the middle that avoids the two extremes (*li er bian* 離二邊 = *anta-dvaya-parivarjana*) of "all exists" (*you* 有 = *astitā*) and "all does not exist" (*wu* 無 = *nāstitā*). Kōunshi, 1239: "calibrating once more." [再勘]

132. Kassan, 593: "Wonderful singing has nothing to do with the tongue—do you hear it?" [妙唱不于舌又云聞麼] Kōunshi, 1239: "The good merchant deeply conceals things—it's like fakery." [良賈深藏如虛] This popular saying comes from the *Records of the Historian*, "Biography of Laozi" (*Shi ji, Laozi zhuan* 史記,老子傳): "I have heard that the good merchant deeply conceals things—it's like fakery. The noble man has overflowing virtue, but his appearance is like that of an idiot." [吾聞之良賈深藏如虛君子盛德容貌若愚]

133. Kōunshi, 1239: "persecuting the person to death." [逼殺人]

134. Kassan, 593, Dōkū, 1085, Dōchū, 1386, and Kōunshi, 1239, gloss *yi jian guo xitian* 一箭過西天 as: "topolect, meaning 'whereabouts unknown.'" [方語云不知落處]

135. Kōunshi, 1239: "Given that the tainted and pure are both to be forgotten, the roads of worldling and *ārya* both cut off—how will he speak?" [染淨雙忘凡聖路絕底作麼生道]

136. Myōō, 107, glosses *laoseng zhi yumo* 老僧祇与麼 as: "I, like you [Linji], have divorced from worldling and *ārya*." [老僧祇与麼ハ老僧モ又林際ノ如ク凡聖ヲ離タリト云也] Eishu, 432: "an answer that is scattered/not in good order/not tidy." [七零八落答話也] Anonymous, 324: "scattered, an answer on the road of principle [i.e., excessive rationality]." [七零八落又理路答也]

137. Anonymous, 324: "refers to the followers of Xiangtian's gate." [指象田門下之徒弟] Eishu, 432: "'Bunch of bald-headed ones' means 'Xiangtian's sangha.'" [許多禿子トハ象田會下衆ヲ云也] Kassan, 593: "scolding the members of the sangha for not possessing the eye." [罵門下徒衆之不具眼也] Kōunshi, 1240: "In

one theory it is scolding a bunch of sangha members for being in the assembly of this blind master just for the sake of food and clothing." [又一說許多大衆爲衣食在這瞎老師會裏罵詈之也]

138. Eishu, 432, Kassan, 593, Dōchū, 1386, and Myōō, 107, gloss *tu* 徒 as *itazura ni* 徒ニ ("vainly/uselessly/to no avail"). Iriya, 205.2, glosses *zhi tu tapo caoxie* 祇徒踏破草鞋 as: "The *tu* 図 of the original text is here *tu* 徒, but there are many examples in contemporary texts [i.e., Dunhuang transformation texts] where there is an interchange of these two characters, which are homophones. Reading it as *itazura ni* is a mistake." [「図」の原文は「徒」であるが、この二字の同音通用は当時の文献に例が多い。「徒らに」と読むのは誤り。]

139. Kōunshi, 1240: "In the words there is an echo." [言中有響]

140. Mujaku Dōchū's 1727 LJL edition in Hirano, ed., *Teihon Rinzai zenji goroku*, 69, reads: 婆便行師乃喚婆婆回頭師便行 ("The old woman instantly walked off. The Master called out: "Grandma!" The old woman turned her head, and the Master instantly walked off"). Kassan, 594: "At this Linji for the first time seems to realize that the old woman harbors a [ripened] mental disposition." [林際於此始似知婆子含機也]

141. Kassan, 594: "His tongue is pure, but the wind [of speech still] arises." [舌頭清風起] Kōunshi, 1240: "*Nothing-to-do* produces *something-to-do*." [無事生事]

142. *he de wan rou zuo chuang* 何得剜肉作瘡 is literally: "Why would you gouge out your flesh and [intentionally] create a wound?" Eishu, 433, and Anonymous, 325: "*Nothing-to-do* produces *something-to-do*." [又無事生事] Kassan, 594: "As soon as you have something to ask a question about, it is creating a wound in [perfectly] good flesh." [纔有問話之事是即好肉上作瘡也] Dōchū, 1387: "*Nothing-to-do* is fine—why have something to ask about?" [無事好何得有事問也] Dōkū, 1085: "As soon as you are involved in asking a question, *nothing-to-do* produces *something-to-do*." [纔涉問話無事生事] Kōunshi, 1240: "Just as you are about to ask a question, it is already gouging out a wound in [perfectly] good flesh." [已擬問早是好肉上剜瘡]

143. The *Awakening of Faith* (*Dasheng qixin lun* 大乘起信論; T1666.32.576c11–14) compares the great sea (*da haishui* 大海水) to the innately pure mind of sentient beings (*zhongsheng zixing qingjing xin* 衆生自性清淨心) and the wind that creates waves (*yin feng po dong* 因風波動) to *avidyā* (*wuming* 無明). Eishu, 433: "The [reflection of the] moon on a placid sea is not [fragmented into multiple] reflections' is Fenglin's referring to himself. 'The frolicking fish of his own accord has lost his way' refers to Linji." [海月澄無影鳳林自己ヲ指テ云也遊魚独自迷林際ヲ指テ云也] Kassan, 594: "The first line refers to the principle of the reality-limit [*bhūta-koṭi*]. The second line refers to Linji's mental disposition to frolic all over." [上句指實際理地下句指林際遊方機] Dōkū, 1085: "'Frolicking fish' refers to Linji." [遊魚指臨濟] Kōunshi, 1240: "The first line is a metaphor for the fact that Fenglin in his mind is settled and pure, without a

single thing. The second line is a metaphor for the fact that the Master comes frolicking." [上句比鳳林胸中澄清無一物下句比師游方來]

144. Eishu, 433: "The moon on the settled and waveless sea—what is there [to lead the fish] to lose its way?" [海月澄清無波則有什广迷] Dōchū, 1387: "If there are shadows, then the fish may recognize the shadows and lose its way. Since there are no shadows, how could it lose its way?" [言若有影則可魚認影而迷 已無影有何可迷者也]

145. Eishu, 433, and Anonymous, 325: "*yefan* 野帆 is 'shabby/humble sailboat.'" [野帆賎 帆也] Dōchū, 1387, is similar. Kassan, 594: "The first line refers to Linji's adaptabi-lity in tactics. The second line refers to Linji's possession of a mental disposition to transform humans and *devas*" [上句指林際機變下句指林際有人天化度之機]

146. Myōō, 109: "'Solitary wheel on its own illuminates' means 'I am like the single wheel of the moon that illuminates everywhere.'" [孤輪獨照卜ハ 我ハ一輪ノ月ノ普ク照ス如ク] Anonymous, 325: "solitary wheel of the moon." [孤輪月也] Kōunshi, 1240: "The first line is a metaphor for the im-pressive style of the Master's own mind ground. The second line is a meta-phor for how the Master with just a word or half a line shakes persons up." [上句比師自己本地風光下句比師一言半句驚動諸人]

147. Anonymous, 325, and Dōchū, 1387: "three-inch tongue." [三寸舌也]

148. Eishu, 433: "Try to say a line that is free of words." [言句ヲ離テ道看也] Anon-ymous, 325, is similar. Dōchū, 1387: "Try to say a single line right to my face." [且一任汝於我面前道一句看也]

149. Eishu, 433: "This is also [the Master's] curbing [Fenglin]." [是モ抑下也] Anonymous, 325, is similar. Dōchū, 1387: "[The Master] is curbing Feng-lin. Fenglin is not one who 'knows the music.'" [抑下鳳林也鳳林不是知音] Kōunshi, 1241: "The idea of this line is, if you don't meet one who 'knows the music,' it is not possible to converse. The line on the surface seems to be curbing Fenglin, but at bottom it means 'inexpressibility in words.'" [此句不逢是知音不可共語之意句面似抑鳳林底意無言無說之義也]

150. Kassan, 595: "This is that single line that Fenglin demanded." [是鳳林所索之 那一句也]

151. Eishu, 433: "The time of 'having nothing to do with sameness' ['cutting off same-ness'] means 'the single *tathatā* of the myriad dharmas.'" [絕同ノ時万法一 如之義也] Dōchū, 1387: "Because of the existence of sameness, there is non-sameness. Because of cutting off sameness now, non-sameness is also cut off." [有同故有不同今絕同故亦絕不同] Kōunshi, 1241: "not to be a companion of the myriad dharmas." [不與萬法爲侶]

152. Eishu, 433: "everywhere the body of freedom and self-existence." [剎剎塵塵自 由自在躰也] Anonymous, 325: "everywhere the *samādhi* of freedom." [剎剎塵塵自由三昧也] Dōkū, 1086: "An ancient said, 'Unreserved functioning [of the buddha nature].'" [古云全體作用] Kōunshi, 1241: "inside the great thou-sand worlds a single body of freedom." [大千沙界内一箇自由身]

153. Eishu, 433: "When all is said and done, the realm of the *original portion*, the place wherein the Great Way cuts off sameness—even a spark from a stone cannot reach this, nor can a lightning bolt penetrate it." [畢竟本分境界大道絕同処石火莫及電光罔通也] Kassan, 595: "Even the speediness of a spark from a stone or a lightning bolt cannot reach to this or penetrate to this—even they are late." [石火電光之迅速亦未得及於茲通於此猶遲了也]

154. Kassan, 595: "Since 'the spark from a stone [cannot reach this], and a lightning bolt cannot penetrate this,' how much more so is it the case with words, and so what did the buddhas and patriarchs use to instruct persons?" [既石火電光罔通於茲者況又於言説乎然者佛祖以何誨示人乎也]

155. Dōchū, 1388: "The *Śūraṃgama Sūtra* [T945.19.117c10–11] . . . says: 'It is all the discrimination and calculation of consciousness and mind. All words completely lack any real meaning.'" [楞嚴經 . . . 曰皆是識心分別計度但有言説都無實義] Kōunshi, 1241: "The words spoken by the *āryas* of ancient times to instruct persons are all provisionally established medicines to cure disease, expressive bulletins—all of them lack real meaning." [從上諸聖爲人所說言句是皆施設藥病表顯露布悉無實義] He then cites the same *Śūraṃgama Sūtra* passage above. Eishu, 433–434: "The previously [mentioned line] 'the spark from a stone cannot reach this, and a lightning bolt cannot penetrate this' is just words and completely lacks any real meaning." [前石火 . . . 罔通ト云タモ只言説也都實無義也]

156. Eishu, 434, glosses *you zuomosheng* 又作麼生 as: "If that's the case/well then—what?" [サラバ又作广生ト也]

157. Kassan, 595: "'The spark from a stone cannot reach this and a lightning bolt cannot penetrate this' is that which controls/dominates. It is 'the officials don't allow even a needle through.' However, when you carefully look, that locus of control has a big omission/oversight that very much lets things pass. This is the 'privately [entire] horses and carts can slip through.' This is the [Zen] patriarchal lineage's 'great provisional designations' [i.e., *upāyas*] to instruct people. Thus, [Zen uses] sometimes silence and sometimes speech in order to make people arrive at the stage of the non-duality of speech and silence. How could [Zen] be bound to one side?" [蓋謂石火莫及電光罔通是把住底即是官不容針處也然子細看來把住處太放行太漏逗了也是即私通車馬處也是即祖宗家為人大段也如是故或默或語而令人到語默無二之地也豈繫一偏也] Dōkū, 1086: "This means that the realm of the great teacher is not limited to speaking and not speaking. Speech and silence are according to the time; letting go and taking in are in response to the mental dispositions [of beings]." [言大善知識境界不局說不說語默隨時放收應機] Dōchū, 1388: "a mundane saying of China." [蓋唐世話]." The proverb as it appears here is found in *Words of Understanding that Warn the World* [*Jingshi tongyan* 警世通言], 36, and a variant appears in the Dunhuang transformation text *Prose Poem of the Swallow* [*Yanzi fu* 燕子賦].

158. Eishu, 434, Kassan, 595, and Dōkū, 1086: "He held a staff in his hand at the [Mountain] Gate and set up a barrier." [手裡拄杖當門設一関ヲ之義] Dōchū,

1388: "On the outside he did not allow entrance; at the bottom he wanted to lead him along to enter." [外面不容入底裡欲牽入也] Kōunshi, 1241: "Even supposing a thousand buddhas and ten-thousand patriarchs had displayed their wonderful functioning, they would not have been able to pass through this barrier!" [設雖千佛萬祖現妙用不得透過此關]

159. Eishu, 434: "The meaning is that he desires a site for dharma combat." [欲法戰一場之義也]

160. Eishu, 434, and Anonymous, 325: "'Hall' is Sangha Hall. . . . 'First position' is the position of the Head Seat." [堂僧堂也. . . . 第一位首座位也] Dōchū, 1388: "'First position' is the seat of the Head Seat in the front hall of the Sangha Hall." [第一位僧堂前堂首座板也] Kassan, 595, Dōkū, 1086, and Kōunshi, 1241: "'First position' is the position in the front hall." [一位者前堂位也]

161. Eishu, 434: "[Jinniu] went from the gate to the Sangha Hall and saw Linji sitting at the first position. Another meaning would be: Jinniu from the gate returned to the *fangzhang* and from the *fangzhang* came down to enter the Sangha Hall." [門ヨリ僧堂ヘ行テ林際第一位坐スルヲ見テ也又金牛従門歸方丈従方丈下來入僧堂ト云義モアリ]

162. Kōunshi, 1241: "calibrating once more." [再勘]

163. Anonymous, 326: "There are two [interpretations]: [The sentence] *dao shenme* 道什麼 resolves the previous question [and so = 'what did you say?'], or [the sentence] *dao shenme* 道什麼 means 'beyond this, what more do you have to say?'" [有兩点道什麼決前一問也又道什麼此外更道什麼也]

164. Kōunshi, 1241: "When you have spirit, add more spirit." [有意氣時添意氣]

165. Eishu, 435: "Jinniu slacks off, or we might say that he has a mind that has fallen into convenience/accommodation." [金牛ダルム也又云便宜ニ落タ心也] Dōkū, 1086: "An ancient said, 'The white clouds return to the summit; the echo of the [temple] bell [reaches] the palace of the *brahma* heaven.'" [古云白雲歸峰頂鐘聲響梵宮] Jiang and Cao, eds., *Tang Wudai yuyan cidian* [*Dictionary of Tang and Five Dynasties Language*], 39–40, glosses *bu zhuobian* 不著便 as: "not have good luck; not be in luck." [*bu zouyun* 不走运]

166. Eishu, 435: "The meaning is: 'Had there been "a winner," both guest and host would have been "winners"; had there been "a loser," both guest and host would have been "losers."' But, when all is said and done, there was neither 'winner' nor 'loser.'" [勝則賓主共勝負則賓主共負畢竟無勝負義也] Kassan, 596: "In the functioning of these two monks, winning is correct, and losing is correct. Therefore, on this single site of dharma combat, both escape superior/inferior." [於這二尊宿作用者勝亦是負亦是也是故這法戰一場俱是無優劣也] Dōchū, 1389: "It means: 'If you discuss "winning," then guest and host are both "winners"; if you discuss "losing," then guest and host are both "losers."'" [言若論勝則賓主俱勝若論負則賓主俱負也] Anonymous, 326: "The meaning is that there is no winner and loser." [無勝負之義也]

167. Eishu, 435, and Anonymous, 326: "At the time of transmigrating, he went up to the Dharma Hall [and ascended the high seat]." [迁化時分上堂也]

168. Kōunshi, 1242: "*zhengfa yanzang* 正法眼藏 is the dharma passed down through the buddhas and patriarchs." [正法眼藏者佛祖傳相承之法也] He cites the *Collection of Similar Items of the Chan Grove* (*Chanlin leiju* 禪林類聚): "The World-honored-one in the past at an assemby at Vulture Peak picked up a flower and showed it to the audience. At that time everyone in the audience was silent. Only Mahākāśyapa had a slight smile on his face. The World-honored-one said, 'I have the *saddharma* vision, the wonderful mind of nirvana, the reality mark that is markless, the subtle dharma gate. It is not involved with the written word; it is a separate transmission outside the [canonical] teachings.' He handed it over to Mahākāśyapa." [世尊昔在靈山會上拈華示衆是時衆皆默然唯迦葉尊者破顏微笑世尊云吾有正法眼藏涅槃妙心實相無相微妙法門不立文字教外別傳付囑摩訶大迦葉] CBETA, X67, no. 1299, p. 115, b15–18 //Z 2:22, p. 114, d14–17 //R117, p. 228, b14–17.

169. Kōunshi, 1242: "Although horns are numerous, one unicorn [i.e., one horn] is enough." [衆角雖多一麟足] A unicorn horn (*linjiao* 麟角) is said to be a rarity of rarities.

170. Kōunshi, 1242: "A true lion cub can give a lion's roar." [真師子兒能師子吼] (A buddha's speaking dharma is like the roar of a lion [*siṃha-nāda*].)

171. Myōō, 111: "With these words Linji seals Sansheng." [林際ノ如此云シタハ三聖ヘノ印可ゾ] Anonymous, 326: "'Would be extinguished by this dumb-ass is a sharp sword point that belongs to the [true] person who [beholds] reality as it truly is." [瞎驢邊滅者箇鋒鋩属箇真正人]

172. Eishu, 435: "with correct mind, without even a change in expression." [タダシイ心也色ヲモ不変也] Dōchū, 1390: "Sitting with straight posture he expired." [身體端直而坐化也] Chitetsu, 876: "*shiji* 示寂 is what is called 'entering *parinirvāṇa*.'" [示寂所謂入般涅槃]

PART V

1. Eishu, 435: "The dharma name [given to a monk] when he has left home is called the *hui* 諱. The [master's] dharma name is taboo for his disciples, and they are not to use it [whether in life or death]. Therefore, it is called the 'posthumous name.'" [諱トハ出家ナラバ法名也法名字門第子諱之不使用故イミナト云]

2. Eishu, 435, and Anonymous, 326, gloss "*yingyi* 頴異 as: "The meaning is 'of sharp faculties.'" [利根義也]

3. Kassan, 596: "The 'full precepts' are the two-hundred fifty precepts." [具戒者二百五十戒也] Eishu, 436 is similar. Anonymous, 326: "A *śramaṇa* at age twenty receives the full precepts." [沙門年二十受具足戒也]

4. Eishu, 436: "They are like *kangakuin* in our country. . . . lectures on the sutras and treatises for which one must pay tuition." [如本朝勸学院. . . . 言講説經論賣座也] Anonymous, 326, has the first part. In Japan *kangakuin* were established within monasteries for the education of priests.

5. Kōunshi, 1243: "This narrates how the Master, after leaving home, first studies the *tripiṭaka*." [此述師出家先學三藏也]

6. Eishu, 436: "'These' refers to the sutras, *vinaya*, and treatises. . . . They are no more than *upāyas* for ferrying the world [from this shore of samsara to the other shore of nirvana]." [此卜ハ經律論ヲ指云也 . . . 只世ワタリノ方便マテ]

7. Eishu, 436: "Set aside the costume of a Vinaya monk and donned the costume of a Zen monk. . . . 'Changing costume' means he left the Vinaya house and entered the Zen house." [捨律僧衣着禅僧衣也. . . . 更衣者出律家而入禅家之義也] Anonymous, 326, is the same for the last part. Kōunshi, 1243: "'Changing costume' is 'changing from the costume of a teachings monk to the costume of a Zen monk.'" [更衣者教衣改禪衣也]

8. Eishu, 436: "'Karman Record' is the karman ['action'] record within this record." [行録此録中行録也]

9. Dōchū, 1391: "The original name of the place was 'Linji,' and so the monastery that was established was also called 'Linji Temple.'" [言地本名臨濟故所建寺亦名臨濟院也]

10. Eishu, 436: "'There' is Hebei. Puhua went to Hebei before Linji." [彼卜ハ河北也普化林際ヨリ先ニ河北ヘ行也]

11. Dōchū, 1392: "It was not real craziness—he faked the appearance of craziness." [非真狂而詐為狂狀也]

12. Eishu, 436, and Anonymous, 327: "The assistant Puhua assisted Linji in his temple rituals." [佐之普化佐臨済之道儀也]

13. Kōunshi, 1244: "*xuanji* 懸記 is the prediction '[this person will just] have a head but no tail, a beginning but no end.'" [in 45.2; 懸記者有頭無尾有始無終之記也]

14. Eishu, 437, Anonymous, 327, Kassan, 597, Dōkū, 1087, and Kōunshi, 1244, cite the following story from the [*Five Lamps*] *Converge at the Source* (*Wudeng huiyuan* 五燈會元): "There was an Indian master who arrived via the sky. The Master [Yangshan] asked, 'What *place* have you come from?' He said, 'India.' The Master said, 'When did you leave there?' He said, 'This morning.' The Master said, 'Why were you so slow?' He said, 'I was roaming the mountains and playing in the rivers.' The Master said, "Of course you have supernormal powers to play with, but, Ācārya, the buddhadharma—that you must get from me!' He said, 'I came especially to this eastern land to do obeisance to Mañjuśrī—but I've encountered a little Śākya!' He subsequently took out a palm-leaf Sanskrit book and gave it to the Master. He then bowed and left riding the sky. From this time onward [Yangshan] was called 'the little Śākya.'" [有梵師從空而至師曰近離甚處曰西天師曰幾時離彼曰今早師曰何太遲生曰遊山翫水師曰神通遊戲則不無闍黎佛法須還老僧始得曰特來東土禮文殊却遇小釋迦遂出梵書貝多葉與師作禮乘空而去自此號小釋迦] CBETA, X80, no. 1565, p. 189, c2–7 //Z 2B:11, p. 162, c8–13 //R138, p. 324, a8–13.

15. Eishu, 437: "As a military disturbance arose, he evacuated Linji Temple." [兵乱ガ起タ程ニ林際院ヲ棄ラレタ也]

16. Kōunshi, 1244: "*chengzhong* 城中 is 'within the city walls of Zhenzhou.'" [城中者鎮州城中也] For details on Mo Junhe, see Daitoku-ji, 98–99, n. 25.

17. Dōchū, 1393: "Hebei superior prefecture." [河北府也] Anonymous, 327, Dōkū, 1088, and Kōunshi, 1244: "Henan superior prefecture." [河南府也] Yanagida, 277: "He *fu* 河府 is the prefectural seat of Hebei *fu* 河北府 and means Chengde *fu* 成德府."

18. For details on Wang, see Daitoku-ji, 96–97, n. 20–22.

19. Yanagida, 277: "Daming *fu* 大名府 is Weizhou 魏州, which at the time was under the jurisdiction of Military Governor Wei Bo [魏博節度使]." Yanagida gives a citation for further details.

20. Eishu, 437: "the single succession of 'who could have guessed that my "*saddharma* vision" would be extinguished by *this* dumb-ass!'" [誰知吾正法眼藏向這瞎驢边滅却之一絡索也]

21. Dōkū, 1088: "In various records the year and month for his entering extinction are not the same." [諸錄入滅年月不同] Kōunshi, 1244, is similar. For the various theories on his death date, see Yanagida, 277.

22. Eishu, 438: "'Took the Master's whole body' is 'earth interment.' . . . It means they did not cremate." [以師全身ト八土葬也. . . . 不火葬之義也] Dōchū, 1394: "The whole body was put into the stupa—they did not cremate." [全身入塔不火化也] Anonymous, 327, is similar.

23. Kōunshi, 1245, for "summary" (*dalue* 大畧) cites *Zhuangzi*, 3, and *Mencius*, 5.

24. For Baoshou Yanzhao, see Daitoku-ji, 101, n. 37.

25. For Xinghua Cunjiang (830–888), see Daitoku-ji, 101, n. 38.

26. Supplied from Mujaku Dōchū's 1727 edition in Hirano, ed, *Teihon* Rinzai zenji goroku, 72. For Yuanjue Zongyan, see Introduction, n. 7.

APPENDIX 1

1. Anderl, *Studies in the Language of Zu-tang ji*, 3–21.

2. 五陰身田内 ("within the five-*skandhas* body-field") → 赤肉團上 ("on the red-meatball [mind]")

3. 不淨之物 ("thing of impurity/feces") → 乾屎橛 ("piece of dried shit")

4. Note that the commentarial role, played by Guishan Lingyou (潙山靈祐; 771–853) and his successor Yangshan Huiji (仰山慧寂; 807–883) in the Yuanjue Zongyan standard edition, is, in the *Zutangji*'s Linji entry, played by: 1. Xuefeng Icun (雪峰義存; 822–908) and his successor Yunmen Wenyan (雲門文偃; 864–949); and 2. Preceptor Zhaoqing and his attendant. For the Yunmen comment, see section 15 below; for the comment of Preceptor Zhaoqing and his attendant, see sections 38.2–38.3.

5. The *Yogacārabhūmi-śāstra* is T1579. The fact that the Yuanjue Zongyan standard edition does not mention Linji's lecturing on Yogācāra materials is, no doubt, of

great significance in the formation of the Linji image. Overall, this account of Linji and Dayu is drastically different from the one in the LJL.

6. Preceptor Zhaoqing is either Zhaoqing Shengdeng 招慶省僜, a Chan monk in the Xuefeng line, or Zhaoqing Daokuang 招慶道匡, also in the Xuefeng line. Little is known of either of them. The former is probably the more likely candidate, since he was said to be the master of the two compilers of the *Zutangji*, the Chan worthies Jing 靜 and Jun 筠. The attendant is unknown.

7. The LJL has Linji making one visit to Dayu, not a stay of ten years. Once again the discrepancy is probably of great significance in the formation of the Linji image.

8. The Yuanjue Zongyan standard edition has additional picturesque similes: 地滿心猶如客作兒 ("The 'bodhisattva who has completed the ten stages' is like a day laborer.") → 地滿心猶如客作兒等妙二覺擔枷鎖漢羅漢辟支猶如厠穢菩提涅槃如繫驢橛 ("The 'bodhisattva who has completed the ten stages' is like a day laborer; a '*tathāgata* who has ascended to the stages of perfect and wonderful awakening' is a Han in a cangue with a lock; 'arhats' and 'independent buddhas' are like toilet excrement; '*bodhi*' and 'nirvana' are like posts to which you hitch a donkey.")

9. Note that the LJL gives his death date as the tenth day of the first month of Xiantong 8 (February 18, 867).

10. Panshan Baoji 盤山寶積, a successor of Mazu Daoyi. Nothing is known of him.

11. This episode does not appear in the LJL.

12. This line does not appear in the LJL.

13. In the LJL Linji's emotional state is never described directly in this way. Likewise the next episode has Linji "delighted." In both cases the delight relates to encountering Puhua.

14. This appears to be the first meeting between Puhua and Linji; it does not appear in the LJL.

15. In the LJL Linji is never characterized as being "silent."

16. 只具一隻眼 ("but he's only got the one eye") → 却具一隻眼 ("but he's got the one eye"). The *Zutangji* version, with the addition of *zhi* 只 ("only; merely"), clearly makes it a negative evaluation.

17. Possibly Changqing Hongbian 長慶弘辨, a Chan monk of the Five-dynasties period in the Xuefeng line. He resided at the Changqing Temple in Fuzhou (Fujian).

18. 林際又問大悲菩薩分身千百億便請現 ("Linji also asked: 'The Great-Compassion [Dabei] Bodhisattva has divided his body into hundreds of millions of pieces, and I now request that he make a manifestation'") → 師問毛吞巨海芥納須彌爲是神通妙用本體如然 ("The Master asked: '[It is said that] "a hair swallows the great sea, and a mustard seed contains Mt. Sumeru." Is this the wonderful activity of supernormal powers or the original substance just as it is?'")

19. See section **26** of Part III, where Xingshan is the monk who says "*hūṃ hūṃ*."

20. See n. 16. This episode also does not appear in the LJL.

21. The question is the same as the one in section **21**, and the episodes have structural similarities.

22. Although in the LJL Linji makes constant use of the shout, his purpose or emotional motivation in doing so is never explained in this way.

23. This episode also does not appear in the LJL. In section **47.1** of the LJL, Huangbo gives the "great laugh." There, the Japanese Zen commentators agree that this is "the laugh of certification" or "the seal." See n.83, **47.1**, Part IV. It is just possible that here Puhua is "sealing" Linji, much as Huangbo did.

24. 手擎函板 ("his arms loaded with planks for a casket") → 就人乞直裰 ("was in town begging people/*persons* for a 'two-in-one monk's costume'") Note that Linji does not appear in this scene; in the LJL he is the one who provides Puhua with a ready-made coffin.

25. 自甓瘞[土+遂=隧]門而卒矣 ("By himself he bricked up the door to the tomb passageway and passed on in transmigration") → 自入棺内倩路行人釘之 ("got into the coffin by himself, and asked a *person* walking by to nail it up")

Bibliography

Aichi daigaku Chū-Nichi daijiten hensansho 愛知大学中日大辞典編纂処, ed. *Chū-Nichi daijiten* 中日大辭典. 2nd ed. Tokyo: Taishūkan, 1999.

Akizuki Ryōmin 秋月龍珉, trans. *Rinzairoku* 臨濟録. *Zen no goroku* 禅の語録 10. Tokyo: Chikuma shobō, 1972.

Anderl, Christoph. "Informal Notes on the Term *jing* 境 in the *Linji lu* 臨济录." In *Wenxue yu zongjiao: Sun Changwu jiaoshou qishi huadan jinian wenji* 文学与宗教: 孙昌武教授七十华诞纪念文集, 391–423. Edited by Zhang Peifeng, Zhanru, and Puhui. Beijing: Zongjiao wenhua chubanshe, 2007.

Anderl, Christoph. *Studies in the Language of Zu-tang ji*. Oslo: Unipub AS, 2004.

Anonymous. *Rinzai shō* 臨濟鈔 (1630). In Yanagida, Rinzairoku *shōsho shūsei* 臨濟録抄書集成, 205–329.

App, Urs. "Chan/Zen's Greatest Encyclopaedist: Mujaku Dōchū (1653–1744)." *Cahiers d'Extrême-Asie* 3 (1987): 155–174.

App, Urs., ed. and trans. "Catching the Rhythm of Ch'an: An Interview with Prof. Iriya Yoshitaka by Kenji Kinugawa." *Cahiers d'Extrême-Asie* 7 (1993): 31–43.

App, Urs, trans. "Passion for Zen: Two Talks by Yanagida Seizan." *Cahiers d'Extrême-Asie* 7 (1993): 1–29.

Bannan Eishu 萬安英種. Rinzairoku *shō* 臨濟録鈔 or *Kana shō* カナ鈔 (1632). In Yanagida, ed., Rinzairoku *shōsho shūsei* 臨濟録抄書集成, 331–439.

Broughton, Jeffrey Lyle. *Zongmi on Chan*. New York: Columbia University Press, 2009.

Brun, Pierre. *Meister Linji. Begegnungen*. Zürich: Ammann, 1986.

CBETA (Chinese Buddhist Electronic Text Association). [http://www.cbeta.org].

Demiéville, Paul, trans. *Entretiens de Lin-tsi*. Paris: Fayard, 1972.

Hayashi Yukimitsu 林雪光, Otsuki Mikio 大槻幹郎, Katō Shōshun 加藤正俊, eds. *Obaku bunka jinmei jiten* 黃檗文化人名辞典. Kyoto: Shibunkaku, 1988.

Hirakawa Akira 平川彰, ed. *Buddhist Chinese-Sanskrit Dictionary Bukkyō Kan-Bon daijiten* 佛教漢梵大辭典. Tokyo: The Reiyukai, 1997.

Hirano Sōjō 平野宗浄, ed. *Teihon Rinzai zenji goroku* 定本臨濟禅師語録. Tokyo: Shunjūsha, 1971.

Hucker, Charles O. *A Dictionary of Official Titles in Imperial China.* 1985. Reprint, Beijing: Beijing daxue chubanshe, 2008.

Iriya Yoshitaka 入矢義高. "*Goroku no kotoba to buntai* 語録の言葉と文体." *Zengaku kenkyū* 68 (1990): 1–19.

Iriya Yoshitaka 入矢義高. "*Ma sangin* 麻三斤." *Zengaku kenkyū* 62 (1983): 1–8.

Iriya Yoshitaka 入矢義高, trans. *Rinzairoku* 臨濟録. Tokyo: Iwanami shoten, 1989.

Iriya Yoshitaka 入矢義高 and Koga Hidehiko 古賀英彦, eds. *Zengo jiten* 禅語辞典. Kyoto: Shibunkaku shuppan, 1991.

Jiang Lansheng 江藍生 and Cao Anshun 曹广顺, eds. *Tang Wudai yuyan cidian* 唐五代语言词典. Shanghai: Shanghai jiaoyu chubanshe, 1997.

Jorgenson, John. "Mujaku Dōchū (1653–1744) and Seventeenth-Century Chinese Buddhist Scholarship." *East Asian History* 32/33 (2008): 25–56.

Jorgenson, John. "Zen Scholarship: Mujaku Dōchū and His Contemporaries." *Zen bunka kenkyūjo kiyō* 27 (2006): 1–60.

Kageki Hideo 蔭木英雄, trans. *Kunchū Kūge nichiyō kufū ryakushū: Chūsei zensō no seikatsu to bungaku* 訓注空華日用工夫略集—中世禅僧の生活と文学. Kyoto: Shibunkaku, 1982.

Kassan 夾山. *Rinzairoku Kassan shō* 臨濟録夾山鈔 (1654). In Yanagida, ed., *Rinzairoku shōsho shūsei* 臨濟録抄書集成, 331–439.

Kensō Chitetsu 見叟智徹. *Rinzairoku Zuigan shō* 臨濟録瑞巌鈔 (1671). In Yanagida, ed., *Rinzairoku shōsho shūsei* 臨濟録抄書集成, 599–885.

Kirchner, Thomas Yūhō, ed. *The Record of Linji*. Honolulu: University of Hawaiʻi Press, 2009.

Koga Hidehiko 古賀英彦 et al., eds. *Kunchū Sodōshū* 訓注祖堂集. *Kenkyū hōkoku* 研究報告 8. Kyoto: Hanazono daigaku kokusai zengaku kenkyūjo, 2003.

Kohan Shūshin 古帆周信 (1570–1641). *Rinzairoku Kohan missan seieki roku* 臨濟録古帆密参請益録 (date unknown). In Yanagida, ed., *Rinzairoku shōsho shūsei* 臨濟録抄書集成, 113–203.

Komazawa daigaku toshokan 駒沢大学図書館, ed. *Shinsan zenseki mokuroku* 新纂禅籍目録. Tokyo: Komazawa daigaku toshokan, 1962.

Kornicki, Peter. *The Book in Japan: A Cultural History from the Beginnings to the Nineteenth Century.* Honolulu: University of Hawaiʻi Press, 2001.

Kōunshi 耕雲子. *Rinzai goroku tekiyō* 臨濟語録摘葉 (1698). In Yanagida, ed., *Rinzairoku shōsho shūsei* 臨濟録抄書集成, 1091–1249.

Kragh, Ulrich Timme. "Classicism in Commentarial Writing: Exegetical Parallels in the Indian *Mūlamadhyamakakārikā* Commentaries." *Journal of the International Association of Tibetan Studies* no. 5 (December 2009). [http://www.thlib.org/collections/texts/jiats].

Kūkoku Myōō 空谷明應 (1328–1407). *Rinzairoku chokki* 臨濟録直記 (date unknown). In Yanagida, ed., *Rinzairoku shōsho shūsei* 臨濟録抄書集成, 1–111.

Luo Zhufeng 罗竹风 et al., eds. *Hanyu da cidian* 漢語大詞典. 12 vols. Shanghai: Hanyu da cidian chubanshe, 1995.

Mohr, Michel. "Zen Buddhism during the Tokugawa Period: The Challenge to Go beyond Sectarian Consciousness." *Japanese Journal of Religious Studies* 21, no. 4 (1994): 341–372.

Mörth, Robert C. *Das Lin-chi Lu des Ch'an Meisters Lin-Chi Yi-Hsüan.* Hamburg: MOAG Mittelungen, 1987.

Mujaku Dōchū 無著道忠. Rinzai Eshō zenji goroku soyaku 臨濟慧照禪師語録疏瀹 (1726). In Yanagida, ed., Rinzairoku shōsho shūsei 臨濟録抄書集成, 1251–1403.

Nakamura Bunbō 中村文峰, trans. *Gendaigo yaku* Rinzairoku 現代語訳臨済録. Tokyo: Daitō shuppan, 1990.

Ogihara Unrai 荻原雲来, ed. *Kan'yaku taishō Bon-Wa daijiten* 漢訳対照梵和大辞典. Tokyo: Kōdansha, 1986.

Redford, Bruce. "James Boswell. *The Life of Johnson.*" In *A Companion to Literature from Milton to Blake.* Edited by David Womersley, 393–401. Oxford: Blackwell Publishers, 2000.

Sasaki, Ruth F. *The Record of Lin-chi.* Kyoto: The Institute for Zen Studies, 1975.

Takakusu Junjirō 高楠順次郎 and Watanabe Kaigyoku 渡邊海旭, eds. *Taishō shinshū daizōkyō* 大正新脩大藏經. 100 vols. Tokyo: Taishō issaikyō kankōkai, 1924–1934.

Takudō Shukitsu 暉同守佶. Rinzairoku *Takudō nenko* 林際録暉同拈古 (1680). In Yanagida, ed., Rinzairoku shōsho shūsei 臨濟録抄書集成, 887–982.

Tamamura Takeji 玉村竹二. *Gozan zensō denki shūsei* 五山禪僧傳記集成. Tokyo: Kōdansha, 1983.

Tamamura Takeji 玉村竹二 and Inoue Zenjō 井上禅定. *Engaku-ji shi* 圓覺寺史. Tokyo: Shunjūsha, 1964.

Tetsugai Dōkū 鉄崖道空. Rinzairoku *satsuyō* 臨濟録撮要 (1691). In Yanagida, ed., Rinzairoku shōsho shūsei 臨濟録抄書集成, 983–1090.

Tripiṭaka Koreana. [http://kb.sutra.re.kr/ritk eng/search/searchBranch.do].

Watson, Burton, trans. *The Zen Teachings of Master Lin-chi.* New York: Columbia University Press, 1999.

Welter, Albert. *The* Linji lu *and the Creation of Chan Orthodoxy.* Oxford and New York: Oxford University Press, 2008.

Welter, Albert. *Yongming Yanshou's Conception of Chan in the* Zongjing lu: *A Special Transmission Within the Scriptures.* Oxford and New York: Oxford University Press, 2011.

Xu Shaofeng 许少峰, ed. *Jianming Hanyu suyu cidian* 简明汉语俗语词典. Beijing: Zhonghua shuju, 2007.

Xu Shaofeng 许少峰, ed. *Jindai Hanyu cidian* 近代汉语词典. Beijing: Tuanjie chubanshe, 1997.

Xu Shaofeng 许少峰, ed. *Jindai Hanyu da cidian* 近代汉语大词典. 2 vols. Beijing: Zhonghua shuju, 2008.

Yampolsky, Philip B. *The Platform Sutra of the Sixth Patriarch.* New York: Columbia University Press, 1967.

Yanagida Seizan 柳田聖山. *Mirai kara no Zen* 未来からの禅. Kyoto: Jinbun shoin, 1990.

Yanagida Seizan 柳田聖山, ed. *Rinzairoku shōsho shūsei* 臨濟錄抄書集成. Kyoto: Chūbun shuppansha, 1980.

Yanagida Seizan 柳田聖山, ed. *Shike goroku goke goroku* 四家語錄五家語錄. Kyoto: Chūbun shuppansha, 1974.

Yanagida Seizan 柳田聖山, ed. *Sodōshū* 祖堂集. Kyoto: Chūbun shuppansha, 1974.

Yanagida Seizan 柳田聖山, ed. *Zenrin shōki sen Kattōgo sen Zenrin kushū benbyō* 禪林象器箋葛藤語箋禪林句集辨苗. *Zengaku sōsho* 9. 2 vols. Kyoto: Chūbun shuppansha, 1979.

Yanagida Seizan 柳田聖山, trans. *Kunchū* Rinzairoku 訓註臨濟錄 (Kyoto: Kichūdō, 1961).

Yanagida Seizan 柳田聖山, trans. *Rinzairoku* 臨濟錄. *Butten kōza* 仏典講座 30. Tokyo: Daizō shuppan, 1972.

Yanagida Seizan 柳田聖山, trans. *Zen goroku* 禅語録. *Sekai no meicho* 世界の名著 18. Tokyo: Chūōkōronsha, 1978), 181–288.

Yang Cengwen 杨曾文, ed. *Linjilu* 临济录. Zhengzhou: Zhongzhou guji chubanshe, 2001.

Yokoi Kakudō 横井覺道. "Edo shoki ni okeru Sōtōshu shūgaku fukkō katei no ichi kōsatsu: Bannan Eishu no zatsugaku jiken o megute 江戸初期における曹洞宗宗學復興過程の一考察：萬安英種の雜學事件をめぐて." *Indogaku bukkyōgaku kenkyū* 24, no. 3 (March 1964): 265–268.

Yoshizawa Masahiro 芳澤勝弘, ed. *Shoroku zokugokai* 諸録俗語解. Kyoto: Zen bunka kenkyūjo, 1999.

Yoshizawa Masahiro 芳澤勝弘 and Onishi Shirō 小西司朗, eds. *Sodōshū* 祖堂集. Kyoto: Zen bunka kenkyūjo, 1994.

Zen bunka kenkyūjo 禅文化研究所, ed. *Zengo jisho ruiju 3: Hekiganroku Funi shō* 禪語辭書類聚 三碧巖録不二鈔. Kyoto: Zen bunka kenkyūjo, 1993.

Zen bunka kenkyūjo henshūbu 禅文化研究所編集部, ed. *Daie Fukaku zenji sho kōrōju* 大慧普覚禅師書栲栳珠. Kyoto: Zen bunka kenkyūjo, 1997.

Zhu Qingzhi 朱慶之 and Mei Weiheng 梅維恒, eds. *Ogihara Unrai Kan'yaku taishō Bon-Wa daijiten Hanyici suoyin* 荻原雲来漢譯對照梵和大辭典漢譯詞索引. Chengdu: Sichuan chuban jituan, 2004.

Index

Abbreviated Commentary on the Perfect Awakening Sutra (Zongmi), 169

Abhidharma Explanations Treatise, 157

abhiniveśa (attachment), 183

active/passive dichotomy in LJL, 16, 26, 50, 157, 158, 160, 168

adornment of *that one person*, 52, 194–195

Advanced Seat, 85, 97, 100, 148, 218

ahead and behind, 151

Amitābha Buddha, 71, 238

Amitāyus Sūtra, 216

Analects, 21, 142, 264

Ānanda, 95, 171, 179, 203, 205, 235

Ancestral Master (Bodhidharma), 85–86, 263

Anderl, Christoph, 26, 119, 130, 137, 157

Anecdotes of the West Line (Xu Huaizhong), 231

Aṅgulimāla, 74

animal rebirth paths, 57, 172

annihilationism, 98, 201

answer paper (*missanroku*) in *kōan* practice, 9

anti-scholastic tone in LJL, 5, 132

arhats, 41, 45, 74, 151, 157, 241

arising-extinguishing, 198–199, 213, 241

army camp, 81

arrow, 66, 98, 141, 227, 279

āryas (noble ones), 42–47, 49, 55, 57, 74, 80–81, 98–99, 101, 154, 180, 182, 186, 241–242, 279, 282

"Ascending to the Small Terrace with Scholar Pei Leading the Way" (Wang Wei), 277

asuras (angry demons), 55, 75, 76, 202

Aśvaghoṣa, 198–199

attachment-bondage, 183

Attendant-in-ordinary Wang, 30–32, 83, 102, 259. *See also* Commandery Governor

Avalokiteśvara, 49, 85, 179, 186, 202

Thousand-hand, 22, 32, 144–145

Twelve-faced, 85, 262

Avalokiteśvara-samādhi, 49

Avīci hot hell, 43, 69, 73, 75, 232, 240–241, 245

avidyā (ignorance), 61, 62, 64, 73, 75, 99, 144, 157, 167, 175, 212, 215, 250–251

awakening, 76, 82, 85, 96, 141, 150, 158–159, 167, 169–170, 174, 215, 246–247

Awakening of Faith, 198–199, 215, 234, 239, 241, 280

baggage (*danzi*), 14–15, 64, 222

baihua (vernacular/vernacular-based literary language), 4, 6, 25, 26–27 *baihua* dictionaries, 26, 139

Baizhang, 94, 120, 254

bald-headed hack (*tunu;* bad teacher/monk), 41, 42, 52, 58, 67, 74, 147, 170, 171

bamboo-and-tree spirits, 60, 212

Bannan Eishu, 10

bantou (plank of sitting platform), 23, 270

Baofu Congzhan, 119

Baoshou Monastery, 102

Baoying Chan Temple, 268

Baozhi, 57, 168

behold(ing) reality as it truly is (*zhenzheng jianjie*), 38, 46–47, 58–60, 67, 69, 75, 155–156, 158–159, 172, 182, 210, 227, 230, 234, 284

benxin (original mind; *Śūraṃgama Sūtra* teaching in LJL), 27. *See* original mind

bhadanta (venerables), 160

bhikṣus (monks), 54–55, 71, 190–191, 200, 238–239, 244

bian (transformation of consciousness/ magical transformation), 200

Bing prefecture, 37, 155

birth-and-death of buddhas, 47

Biyanlu/Biyanji. See Blue Cliff Record (Biyanlu/Biyanji)

blackened vent of *zao/kamado* stove, 68, 232

blades of grass, 60

blind Hans (*xia han*), 60, 80, 172

blind imbeciles (*xia lüsheng*), 42, 52, 172

blind master (*xia laoshi*), 58

Blue Cliff Record (Biyanlu/Biyanji), 7, 142, 145, 149, 262–264

blue lapis-lazuli phoenix egg, 96, 276–277

bodhi (awakening), 19, 27, 41, 58, 62, 160, 170, 184, 215, 247

bodhi body, 55

bodhi tree, 61

Bodhidharma (Ancestral Master), 70, 85, 86, 234, 261, 263, 265, 274

Bodhisattva Perfect-and-Sudden, 45

bodhisattvas, 74, 194, 236

Boswell, James, 6

bowing, 81, 95, 145

bowl bag, 65

brahma, 226–227

Brief History of the Sangha of Great Song, 268–269

brightness, come with, 80, 124

bu de (no good/hopeless), 158

bu jing (impurity), 200

bu shen (I don't know/how are you), 22–23, 145, 261

bu yumo lai (comes not in that way), 150

buddha-bodies, 39, 51, 54, 58, 162

Buddha Hall, 160

buddha-lands, 39, 51, 95, 158, 162, 195, 215, 216, 275

buddha-Māra, 44, 123

buddha mind, 40, 165

buddha nature

elucidated by teachings, 31

as one spirit-brightness, 40, 165

spontaneity of, as theme of LJL, 5, 26

as true mind/true *person,* 32, 137, 145

unreserved functioning of, 15, 62, 65–66, 76, 83, 84, 85, 147, 173, 218, 224–225, 226, 248, 259, 261, 262, 281

buddha-tree, 89

buddhadharma

bad teachers and, 68

of Chan patriarchal gate, mistakenly taking stillness as, 64

crude or fine in, 80

did not appear to Great Superknowl- edge Wisdom-Victory Buddha, 72

as family homestead, 151

great meaning of, 30, 33, 34, 85, 89, 154

Huangbo on the real meaning of, 34, 88, 89

not encountering in present birth, 38, 159

principle of, 71

students' mistaken conjectures about, 42

subtle and not obvious, 63

work, not a matter of putting in, 43, 175

buddhas, 44, 95, 177, 239

Amitābha Buddha, 71, 238

with characteristics, 69

gate of buddha-matters, 71

Great Superknowledge Wisdom-
Victory Buddha, 72

independent buddhas, 41

is the ultimate, 55

knowing-seeing, 142

lands of, 46

production of, 83

seeking, 41

seeking of, 42, 55, 60–61, 75

spilling the blood of, 73

of the ten directions, 56

transmission from, 76

true buddha, 69, 74, 233

as ultimate, 74

vishaya, 50

who are our patriarchs, 38, 39, 40,
54, 60, 128. See also *dharmakāya*
buddha; *nirmāṇakāya* buddha;
pratyeka-buddhas; *saṃbhogakāya*
buddha

Buddhist Chinese-Sanskrit Dictionary
(*Bukkyō Kan-Bon daijiten*)
(Hirakawa), 155

burning house, of *Lotus Sūtra*, 39, 83,
160, 259

burning the sutras and images, 73, 241

burning transmission regalia, 94, 95,
273–274

byways (*pangjia; baihua* word), going
astray onto, 41, 168

calculation and conjecture, 9, 170, 204, 206

calibrating and adjudicating (*kanbian*),
78–87, 152, 252–265

cangues, 40–41, 63, 74, 167, 220

canonical erudition of LJL, 27, 209

Cao Anshun, 173, 200, 221, 283

Caodong (Sōtō) lineage, 264

caozei (army of traitors), 33, 148

Caozhou (in Shandong), 101

catching on to the dharma, as not
catching on, 70, 235

cause-and-effect teaching of being
reborn as a human/*deva*, 76

certain matter (*moushi*), 31, 144

Certain Questions on the Pure Land, 225

Cessation and Discernment (Zhiyi), 209

Chan block, 10, 86, 263

Chan gate, 30, 141, 142

Chan grove (*conglin*; a Chan
monastery), 57, 206

Chan Letter (Zongmi), 218

Chan Notes (Zongmi), 218

Chan Prolegomenon (Zongmi), 10, 11, 16,
127, 141, 142, 145–146, 165, 176, 178,
187, 194, 198, 230

Chan scholarship
modern, 4
postwar Japanese, 24–25

Changes, Book of (*Yijing*),143, 175

changshi (Cavalier Attendant-in-ordinary),
140

characteristics (*xiang/lakṣaṇas*), 40, 48,
52, 53, 54, 55, 69, 123, 146, 156, 162,
164, 165, 182, 184, 194, 198, 199,
201, 202, 206, 214, 227, 229, 233,
258, 276, 277

empty, 73, 199, 224

non-, 48

no/without, 9, 17, 18, 47, 48, 55, 56,
66, 69, 72, 143, 167, 179, 186, 194,
195, 204, 205, 241

ready-made, brought by students, 37,
65, 137, 153, 224

seizing on, 57

unreal, 201, 269

of the written word, 38, 159

chekun (thorough exhaustion), 89, 267

Chengde, 102

Chengguan, 164, 226, 232

Chengling ("Clear Spirit"; Linji's stupa), 102

Chief of Provisions (*fantou*), 23, 78, 253

chilled noodles, Korean (*naengmyeon*), 3, 27

Chinese commentaries on LJL, 7, 8, 12, 134

Chinese language, colloquial, 25

Chū-Nichi daijiten (Great Chinese-Japanese Dictionary) (Aichi daigaku), 188

chuangjiaotou (sitting platform in the Sangha Hall), 57, 206

chuanti zuoyong. See buddha nature, unreserved functioning of

clarified butter in a cracked pottery vessel, 50

classic novels, 25, 26, 136, 139, 181, 218, 254

Classified Conversations of Zhu Xi, 144

clothes. *See* costumes

coffin, 87, 265

cognizable-and-cognition, 58

Collection of Similar Items of the Chan Grove (Chanlin leiju), 284

Collection of Translation Terms and Meanings, 204

Commandery Governor (*fuzhu*) Wang, 30, 32, 140. *See also* Attendant-in-ordinary Wang

commentarial tradition, 3, 7, 8, 9, 12, 134

commentaries, Japanese Zen
    commentarial tradition, 9, 12
    contradictory interpretations in, 19–20
    editorial emendations, 24
    embedded in translation, 3–4, 12–13
    equivalencies between LJL and Buddhist terms, 16–18
    glosses

Chinese poetry in, 21
    highly metaphorical, 20–21
    of words and phrases, 13–15
    Japanese parallels, 24
    Japanese paraphrases, 23
    mid-Edo period, 7–8
    monastic life, explanations of, 22–23
    references to secular works, 21–22
    rhetorical questions in, 22
    sutra teachings and themes in LJL, 18–19
    ten commentaries, facsimile edition of, 3, 8–12
        material selected from, 13–24
        two interpretations in a single, 20

Commentary on the Abhidharma-kośa Verses, 202, 215

Commentary on the Golden Light Sutra, 201

Commentary on the Meanings in the Śūraṃgama Sūtra, 171, 189

Commentary on the Ullambana Sūtra (Zongmi), 201

Commentary on the Vimalakīrti Sūtra (Sengzhao), 213, 215, 236, 240, 247

comments (*agyo*), 10

companion, human-body, 47

Comprehensive Record of the Buddhas and Patriarchs (Fozu tongdai), 237

confidence
    great teachers having, 52
    having, 166, 210
    in immediate venue of activities, 50, 190
    insufficient/not enough, 31, 38, 42, 45, 64
    little, 32, 195
    no/having no/not having, 38, 52, 60, 66, 74, 158, 212, 226, 242
    self-, 49

Confucius, 136, 264

confused karman-consciousness, 69

consciousness-only, 5

Consciousness-Only Treatise
   (Dharmapāla), 162, 199

contemplation wisdom
   (*pratyavekṣaṇājnāna*), 161

corpses (*sishi*), 14–15, 64, 222, 265

costumes, 67, 68, 87, 228–230, 285
   costume-transformations, 67, 68
   of radiance, 51

couplets, poetry, 70, 153, 235

cross-legged sitting, 9, 20, 40, 43, 52,
   57, 71, 83, 91, 92, 97, 100, 163, 174,
   206, 238, 263, 269, 273, 278
   facing a wall, 64, 222
   See also smooth-and-steady sitting;
   zazen

crossroads, 150

crude behavior, 79–80, 255

Cuifeng, 97

Cuiwei, 86, 263

cultivation, 51–53, 193, 197–198

Cunjiang, 102

cuoduan (sever), 40, 167

Custodian (*yuanzhu*), 82, 87, 257

da li gui (demons of great strength), 201

Dabei (Great Compassion)
   Bodhisattva, 125
   Temple, 81, 124

Daci, 97, 278

dade. See *bhadanta*

Dahui's Letters (*Dahui shu*), 136, 138, 160

Dahui Zonggao, 7

daily activities, 39, 44, 49, 53, 61,
   159–160, 170, 173

Daitoku-ji group of scholars, 24–25,
   25–26, 129

daji dayong (all-out manifestation of the
   capability of one's whole character/
   personality), 30, 142. See also
   jiyong

Dajue, 84

Daming, 102

Danxia, 66

Daoism, 148

daoliu (*srotāpanna*; stream-enterers), 157

Daoyi, 66

darkness, 53, 76, 198
   come with, 80, 124

Dayu, 5, 89–90, 101, 209, 266–267

de li (favored by the assistance of. . .),
   76, 247

dead bodies, 77, 250, 251

deep pit, 34, 64, 149

deep pool, 34, 143, 149

defiled lands, 174

demons (*jingmei*), 55, 171–172

Dengyin Bodhisattva Sutra, 179

dependent (*yi*)
   as clothes/costumes, 43, 51, 67, 68,
      228, 229, 230, 231
   as costume-transformations, 67, 68,
   illusory magical transformations, 51,
      54, 67, 68, 161, 192, 200, 229, 230
   sleights-of-hand of the magical arts/
      of mundane conjurers, three types
      of, 39, 56, 162, 192, 230
   upon alchemical recipes, charms,
      mantras, supernormal powers, 51, 231

Deshan the Second (Deshan Xuanjian),
   83, 91, 132–133, 264, 268

destroying the concord of the sangha, 73

devas (gods), 35, 45, 46, 55, 70, 71, 76,
   142, 148, 156, 173, 179, 182, 196, 216,
   223, 238, 281

dharma
   asking about, 43
   attaining, 42, 50, 69
   of the *Avalokiteśvara-samādhi*, 49
   a beholding according to, 59, 77, 89,
      155, 210, 251, 266
   as beholding reality as it truly is, 88,
      210, 251
   can't be sought/obtained, 249

dharma (*continued*)

can't be verbally expressed, 141

catching on to, 70

combat, 100, 283

eye, 122, 191

eye, beclouded, 47

independent of the written word, 31

as mind-ground dharma, 42, 179

as mind radiance, 65

none/none to give, 60, 69, 72, 181, 235

no personal experience of, 44, 176

nothing to do with causes and conditions, 31

as one mind, 198, 199, 235

the one who is listening to, 38, 39, 45, 48, 52, 54, 57, 61, 72, 125, 128, 159, 161, 179, 184, 194

original, 193

as *original portion*, 65

practicing, 33

as principle/*ārya* understanding, 224

pursuing of, as karman generation, 52

seeking, 42, 61, 65, 66, 77, 173, 213, 250

speaking, 45, 51, 77, 140, 161, 179, 185, 244, 252, 272, 284

substance, perverting, 225

as synonym for "teaching," 42, 43, 47, 60, 69, 71, 77, 90, 102, 120, 123, 131, 140, 141, 145, 147, 149, 156, 171, 172, 174, 176, 180, 181, 184, 185, 196, 200, 202, 217, 224, 226, 232, 233, 234, 236, 237, 238, 245, 249, 264, 268, 272, 274, 284

as *tathatā*, 188, 269

as the *certain matter*, 31

that should be realized, 53, 69

true, 189, 196

as true-mind dharma, 42, 165, 173

as the true *person*, 69

true, without characteristics, 56, 69, 204

unconditioned, 204

what has the ability to speak/listen to, 40, 128

wheel, 46

Dharma Words Sutras, 235

dharmadhātu (dharma sphere), 19, 45, 56, 72, 73, 77, 163, 170, 178, 196, 215, 249

non-arising, 47

of Vairocana, 46

dharmakāya (dharma body), 19, 50, 61, 186, 260, 274

dharmakāya buddha, 39, 51, 69, 161, 182–183, 188, 233

Dharmapāla, 162, 199

dharmas

arise when causes and conditions come together, 205

associated with mind, 68, 223, 229

bad, 213

can't be expressed in words, 219

characteristics of the written word, 159, 193

conditioned, 204, 238

dependently originated, 151, 156, 162, 176, 199

emptiness of, 61

empty, 56, 73

empty and unreal, 47

empty characteristics of, 73

extremist view of the emptiness of, 246

illusory, 243

like dreams, *māyās*, flowers in the sky, 56, 191, 205

mentally ungraspable, 72

of mind of direct perception, 190

mundane/supramundane, 54, 68, 193, 200

myriad/various, 44, 45, 56, 72, 73,
  152, 166, 179, 200, 204, 205, 239,
  240, 242, 281
names/terms, 49, 200, 230, 240, 284
(non)arising/(non)extinguishing, 72, 239
none to be abhorred/disliked, 57, 178,
  205
not one exists, 204
outside mind, 51
provisionally erected, 51, 72, 166
svabhāva (own-being) of, 199
in two gates of mind *tathatā* and
  mind arising-disappearing, 199
unreal, 74, 166, 192
as vishayas, 16, 44, 45, 56, 62, 74, 153,
  158, 190, 220, 228, 242, 245
with/without outflows, 199
worldly, not stained by, 72, 239
Dharmasamuccaya Sūtra, 158
dhyāna (meditation), 43, 61, 175, 193,
  205, 245
dhyāna delight (*samādhi*), 61, 216
dice/die, 92, 271
*Dictionary of Official Titles in Imperial
  China* (Hucker), 140
differentiation of *svabhāva* (own-being)
  and characteristics, 54
Ding, Advanced Seat, 15, 22, 85, 218,
  224, 262
Dinglin Monastery, 95, 275
dining table, Puhua's kicking over, 79
Direct Account of the Record of Linji
  (Rinzairoku *chokki*) (Kūkoku
  Myōō), 10
discombobulation, 38, 50, 56, 58–59,
  157, 171–172, 189, 190, 204, 210
disparagement, 52, 144
dithering (*niyi*), 13–14, 26, 31–35, 79, 83,
  86–87, 143–144, 152, 154, 174, 207
divine sound of *that one person*, 66, 226
dixing (earth-walking) immortal, supernormal power of, 56, 203

Dongshan Liangjie, 264
donkey, 6, 39, 41, 52, 76, 80, 124, 125,
  133, 159, 167–168, 242, 248, 287
donkeys atop ice, 52
doubt, 34, 43, 49, 62, 81, 83, 94, 121,
  169, 256, 259, 273
dragon-elephant, 76, 248
dragons, 267, 268, 276–277
dream, 45, 47, 48, 49, 56, 95, 178, 184,
  191, 275
dream-and-*māyā* companions, 184
Dream of the Red Chamber, 218
dried bones, 51, 68, 193
dried shit (*ganshijue*), 6, 14, 32, 68, 147, 286
driving nails into the sky, 31
dumb-ass (*xialu*), 21, 100, 102, 284, 286
Dunhuang Chan manuscripts, 25, 194,
Duty Master (*weina*), 91, 97, 269
dynamism of students, 65

earth interment (of Linji), 286
eating bowls of rice/eating blows of the
  stick (*dun*), 78, 253
Edo period, 6–7, 194
eight consciousnesses, 146, 205, 229
eighteen *dhātus* (Psycho-physical
  constituent elements), 74, 215–216,
  242,
eighteen magical transformations, 185–186
eighty minor marks of a buddha, 18, 52,
  55, 194, 201
*Eighty-Thousand Woodblocks Tripiṭaka
  (Palman Daejanggyeong)*, 119
*Elaboration of the Meanings of the
  Huayan* (Chengguan), 226
elements, four, 40, 48, 61, 128, 163, 184,
  185, 186, 190, 215, 217, 224, 233
emotional state, Linji's, 287
empty fist, 51, 74, 241
empty names, 51, 54, 66, 199, 200, 201,
  229, 230
entering lands, 51, 66

entering the Way, 236–237

entering the Way wrong-mindedly, 176–177

Entretiens de Lin-tsi (Demiéville), 130

erudition behind LJL, 27, 209

Essential Explanations [of the Śūraṃgama Sūtra], 165

established rules, 242

eternalism, the extreme of, 98, 221

etiquette, 30, 100, 141

everyday pronouns bearing Chan weight, 18

everyday words as Chan/Zen terms, 13, 17

every *place*, 39, 40, 43, 44, 50, 123, 128, 162–163, 166, 191

excellence, no need to seek, 38

explanation-style commentaries (gloss), 9–12

Explanatory Oracle of the Lotus Sutra's Profound Meaning (Zhanran), 227

expositions (*tichang/teishō*), 8, 27

expressive explanations, 47

expressive terminologies, 72

expressive verbal formulations, 58

Extended Lamp Record of the Tiansheng Era (Tiansheng guangdeng lu) (Li Zunxu), 119, 127, 131, 132, 252, 268

Extracting the Essential Points of the Record of Linji (Rinzairoku *satsuyō*) (Tetsugai Dōkū), 11

Eye Guide for Humans and Devas, An (Rentian yanmu) (Huiyan Zhizhao), 142, 148

eye of the Way, 59, 71, 236

eyebrows, 58, 59–60, 146, 166, 169, 208, 211–212

eyes, 58, 67, 195, 255–256

face-gate(s), 32, 46, 146–147, 154

face-off with teachers, 57

family homestead, 35, 151

fangzhang (abbot's quarters), 32, 62, 65, 67, 83, 85, 88, 91–92, 97, 100, 272

Fangzhang, Mt., 97, 278

fantou. See Chief of Provisions

fathers, 41, 73, 79, 169

feces (*fenbian*), 27, 54, 121, 122, 154, 200, 286

feet, 85, 233, 238, 261

Fen prefecture, 37, 155

Fenglin, 98–99, 280–281

Fengxue, Preceptor, 268

Fengxue Yanzhao, 90, 268

fifty-three teachers (*Huayan Sutra*), 45, 77, 180, 182, 196, 226, 249, 250

Finger Garland (No Anger), 243–244

fire, 48, 57, 94–95, 163, 274

fish

frolicking, 99, 280–281

lively, waving its tail, 47, 65, 184, 223, 225

submerged, 64, 223, 229–230

fishing words, 33, 147

fist, Linji thumping Dayu with, 89, 123

five crimes of uninterrupted punishment, 73, 176, 240–241

Five Lamps Converge at the Source (Wu deng hui yuan), 131, 260, 262, 278, 285

Five-Mountains (Gozan) Zen, 4, 6–7, 134, 145

five natures, 76–77, 244

five *skandhas* (aggregates), 56, 145, 156, 203, 248

five *zang* and six *fu* (terminology of Chinese medicine), 163

flowers in the sky, 56, 66, 205, 251

flywhisk, 33, 36, 79, 84, 121, 148, 153, 166, 211

food money, 42, 71

form-body of the four elements, 40, 61

four aphorisms (of Shenhui), 194

four characteristics, 48, 182

four elements, 48, 163, 184–186, 190, 215

four flows, 62, 217

four forms of birth, 61

Four Liberations Sutra, 204

four practices of Bodhidharma, 154

four teaching styles, 76, 249

Four-Teachings Meaning, 174

four types of mind (in Zongmi's *Chan Prolegomenon*), 145–146, 165

frond of mugwort, 34, 148

Fu, Great Master, 35, 151

functionings (*yong;* gimmicks/tactics of a Chan master), 36, 153

futon (Chan sitting cushion), 10, 86

Fuxian Wendeng, 119

gandharvas (heavenly musicians), 191

gao-huang disease, 63, 219

Gao'an, Dayu's place at the shoals of, 89, 122

gate of adornment, 71, 236

gate of buddha-matters, 71

Gateless Gate (Wumenguan), 7

gates of the three mysteries, 36

Gautama, 74

Gendaigo yaku Rinzairoku (Nakamura), 129, 132

General Talks of Dahui (Dahui pushuo), 235

Genji Monogatari, 200

ghost cave of Black Mountain, 91, 222–223, 228, 269

Gidō Shūshin, 6–7

giving away everything, as creating karman, 71

glibness, 46, 75, 181

Glossary of the Patriarchal Courtyard (Zuting shiyuan), 10, 140, 147, 148, 164, 177, 197, 206, 212, 213, 243, 244

goats, 44, 176

gold dust, 83

Golden Light Sutra, 188

Good Reverence Sutra, 238

good-for-nothing gimmick vishayas (*xian jijing*), 40, 49, 59, 60, 166, 167, 187, 211, 220,

great matter, the (one), 21, 30, 31, 32, 89, 94, 142, 144, 159, 208, 215, 267

Great Stopping and Discerning (Tiantai Zhiyi), 223

Great Storehouse of Radiant Light (Da guangming zang) (Baotan), 149

Great Superknowledge Wisdom-Victory Buddha/*Tathāgata*, 72, 239

Grove of Meanings in the Dharma Garden (Cien Kuiji), 162

guard officer, 20, 81, 257

guest, 33, 35, 44, 57, 62, 63, 218, 220–221, 257, 283

Guest Receptionist Yangshan, 93, 271

Guifeng Zongmi. *See* Zongmi

Guishan, Preceptor, 79, 90–95, 99, 100, 272

guming (solitary brightness; *Śūraṃgama Sūtra* teaching in LJL), 27. *See* solitary brightness

Haein Monastery, 119–120

haishi (in any case; *baihua* word) 188

half-body, manifestation of, 58, 62, 207

Han History, 172

Hanazono University Library, Kyoto, 120

Hanyu da cidian (Great Word Dictionary of Sinitic) (Luo Zhufeng), 172, 212, 222, 231, 257, 261

Head Cook (*dianzuo*), 23, 82, 253, 258

Head Seat, 81, 88, 91, 92, 148, 256, 270, 272, 279, 283

headrope, 142, 269

Hebei, 94, 101, 272, 285

Hekiganroku Funi shō (Kiyō Hōshū), 145

hells of the three bad rebirth paths, 57

hell, what/who in the (*gengshi; baihua* word), 62, 217

Henan, 94

hesitation, 38, 157

heterodox masters, 15, 52–53, 58–59, 64, 195, 197, 209, 210, 251

Heyang, 80

Heze Shenhui, 194

hide glue, holding out a (painter's) saucer of, 62, 219

hindrance of views, 250–251

Hirakawa Akira, 155

hoe, 31, 91, 92–93, 271

Hōjō Tokiyori, 8

home-place you return to, 163

Hongzhou house of Chan, 15, 120, 218

Hongzhou lineage of Linji and Puhua, 120

host, 33, 35, 44, 57, 62, 63, 218, 220–221, 257, 283

host-and-guest discriminations, 11, 33, 35, 44, 57, 58, 59, 63, 81, 100, 206, 207, 218, 220, 221, 218, 257, 283

House Teachings of Taigong, 274

house tune, 26, 31

hṛdaya (mind/heart), 145, 146

Huang Chao, 257

Huangbo, 5, 20–21, 23, 31, 34, 78–79, 86–97, 101, 120, 148, 209, 236, 254, 265, 269–272, 274–276

huangbo tree, 66

huangmi (husked sorghum), 82, 257

Huayan, Preceptor, 97

Huayan Dharmadhātu Discernment (Zongmi), 225

Huayan Sutra, 11, 12, 45, 51, 53, 76–77, 179, 180, 182, 190, 196, 205–206, 212, 226, 235, 243, 249–251

huayi (teaching styles), 76, 249

Huike, 70, 274

Huineng, 194

Huiran, 29, 139, 156

Huiyan Zhizhao, 142, 148

hūṃ hūṃ (mantra/sound of ox lowing), 83, 125, 260, 288

human body, 39, 47, 56, 145, 160, 179, 184

Hundred Dharmas Treatise (Vasubandhu), 82, 258

hungry ghosts (*pretas*), 45, 56, 57, 60, 66, 89, 173, 179, 204, 210, 212, 267

Hutuo River, 101

idiots (*chiren*), 61

illness, 22, 23, 32, 46, 60, 102, 145, 178, 181, 182, 212, 216–217, 219, 240

immediate attainment of awakening, 40–41, 44–45, 167–168, 177–178

impermanence, 39, 48

imprint, seal, 35, 152

impurity, 6, 44, 45, 76, 121, 200, 286

in that way, 17, 34, 39, 40, 44, 46, 47, 48, 49, 52, 54, 60, 62, 65, 74, 98, 127, 149, 150, 155, 185, 205, 226, 252

in your own house (human body), 160–161

independent buddhas, 41

Indra, 55, 191, 196, 202

inhaling cold air, 75, 246

intellectual understanding, emotional assessments, calculations, and plans, 9

Iriya Yoshitaka, 25–26, 140

Iron-Cane Li (Yue Bochuan), 222

jackal(s), 53, 74, 197, 242

jade flute, 96, 276

Japanese Zen commentaries. *See* commentaries, Japanese Zen

jianchu (my vision), 39, 40, 43, 44, 49, 51, 52, 56, 61, 70, 74, 123, 133, 159, 178

Jiang Lansheng, 173, 200, 221, 283

Jianming Hanyu suyu cidian (Concise Dictionary of Sinitic Common Sayings) (Xu Shaofeng), 212, 254, 259

jiao (canonical teachings), 141

jiaoban, (feet wide like planks from tramping), 233

jiaowai biechuan (separate transmission outside the teachings), 5, 11, 27, 77, 101, 132, 242, 249, 284

Jindai Hanyu da cidian (Great Word Dictionary of Recent Sinitic), 144, 145, 217, 277

jing (vishayas), 16, 153

Jing (a compiler of the *Zutangji*), 119

jingmei (demons/spirits), 171, 209

Jingshan, Master, 86, 87, 264, 265

Jinniu, Preceptor, 100, 283

jiyong (an all-out manifestation of the capability of one's whole character/personality), 142

Johnson, Samuel, 6

joy, 48, 61, 62, 67, 71, 188, 196, 210, 216, 228, 238, 259

juice, 51, 68, 193

Jun (a compiler of the *Zutangji*), 119

kalpas, 35, 38, 41, 45, 46, 55, 57, 68, 69, 72, 122, 123, 159, 178, 180, 181, 182, 200, 230, 231, 232, 239, 246, 274

Kana Notes (Kana shō) (Bannan Eishu), 10

Kāṇadeva, 237

kangakuin (in Japan, monastery school for training priests), 284

Kanyaku taishō Bon-Wa daijiten (Ogihara Unrai), 155

karman-creating sentient beings, 44, 173

karman, 41, 51, 73, 75, 168, 173, 193, 202–203, 266
  consciousness, 234
  generation of, 52
  record of, 88–100

karmic performance, 52, 174, 193

Kassan, 11

Kassan's Notes on the Record of Linji (Rinzairoku Kassan shō), 11

Kei Commentary, 266

keke de (pretty much; *baihua* word), 63, 221

Kensō Chitetsu, 11

kezuo'er (day laborer), 40, 123, 167, 287

kicking over dining table, Puhua's, 79

killing, 59, 210–211

kindness, 89, 95, 122, 254, 267, 274, 275

king ascends the jeweled hall, 37

king of elephants, riding on, 62

king of geese, 44, 177

king's writ, 37

kleśas (depravities of passion, hostility, and stupidity), 15, 52, 53, 54, 57, 59, 62, 73, 74, 152, 174, 176, 189, 194, 198, 200, 206, 209, 210, 212, 217, 222, 241, 250, 251, 266

kōan/gong'an (cases), 9, 10, 132, 166, 187, 189, 212, 220

Kohan Shūshin, 9–10

Kohan's Record of Secret-Consultation Instructions on the Record of Linji (Rinzairoku Kohan missan seieki roku) (Kohan Shūshin), 9–10

Korea/Korean, 25, 27, 119, 130

kouling (secret password), 68, 231, 232

Kōunshi, 12, 19, 26–27

Kṣitigarbha Ten Wheels Sutra, 242, 250

kudzu (entanglement in words), 5, 31, 70, 74, 142, 143, 144, 187, 208, 219, 220, 235, 244, 258, 260

Kūkoku Myōō, 10

kundoku treatment of Chan records, 138

kunlun (mixed up), 84, 260–261

Kunlun Mountains, 84, 260

Kuśinagara, 55

land of liberation, 51, 66

land of non-differentiation, 51

Land of Three Eyes, 51, 190–192

lands of all the buddhas, 46

language of abuse, 170, 172

Laṅkāvatāra Sūtra, 11, 141, 144, 183, 216, 218, 240–241, 243, 247

lanterns and open-air pillars, 58

Lanxi Daolong/Rankei Dōryū, 8
Lao Dan, 136
leader (*daoshou*), 93, 272
leaves, attached to, 60
leaving/leaver of home, 19, 44, 46, 58,
    60, 68, 71, 76, 171, 176, 177, 236,
    237, 244, 266, 284, 285
leftovers called the teachings, 49, 187
Lepu, 82, 84, 258
Li Tongxuan, 179, 200, 246, 260
little Śākya (Yangshan), 101, 285
Li Zunxu, 119, 127, 268
*Liang Dynasty Great Master Fu's Verses
    on the Vajracchedikā Sūtra*, 201
lianjia (tool for threshing grain), 80, 256
liberation, 40, 44, 51, 54, 59, 60, 61, 63,
    68, 73, 87, 94, 101, 123, 128, 156, 157,
    164, 165, 166, 204, 211, 212, 220,
    240, 247, 254
Life of Johnson (Boswell), 6
light of purity, 163
lightning bolt, student's dynamism as,
    65, 99, 225, 282
Linji, 76, 90, 92, 93, 228–229, 254, 268
    biography, 101–102
    death of, 102, 286
    Hongzhou lineage of, 120
    literary portrait of, 4–6
    Zongjinglu entry, 127–128
    Zutangji entry, 120–124
Linji Temple, 101–102, 272, 285
Linjilu (LJL), 120, 127
    appropriation in, 132–133
    as "authentic" nonfictional transcript, 6
    evolution of, 5
    material from other texts, 131
    printed editions in Japan, 7
    translations of, 3, 24–25, 129–130
lions, 74, 85, 242, 284
    riding, 62
    roar of, 53, 197
live burial, 91, 269

living patriarch(s), 38, 54, 159
lonely peak, at the top of, 150
Longbao, 270
Longguang, 96, 275, 277
Longya Judun, 86, 263–264
*Look at the Essentials, A [of the Śākya
    Family]*, 263
lose track of your head and go looking
    for it (*shetou mitou*), 18–19
losers, 100, 283
lotus root, 55, 202
Lotus Sutra, 83, 142, 144, 160, 185, 195,
    205, 209, 212, 215, 226, 230,
    238–239, 247, 259, 266
lotus-womb world, 46
Luo Zhufeng, 172, 212, 222, 231, 257, 261
Lushan, Preceptor, 66
luzhu (open-air pillar), 10, 20, 58, 81,
    208, 257

Ma Fang, 139
mae ni deru (charge straight ahead/take
    the initiative; *sumō* term), 16
Mahākāśyapa, 284
Mahāmati Bodhisattva, 240
*Mahamaudgalyāyana Rescues His Mother
    from the Netherworld* (Dunhuang
    transformation text), 200
Mahāparinirvāṇa Sūtra, 187
Mahāprajñāpāramitā Sūtra, 183, 185, 193,
    210, 232, 272
*Mahāprajñāpāramitā Treatise (Da zhidu
    lun)*, 160, 173, 219, 229, 236
Mahāsāṃghika-vinaya, 237
Mahāyāna bodhisattva, 180
Mahāyāna Praises (Dasheng zan), 168
Mahāyāna sutras, 11, 27, 156, 166, 175, 209
Mahīśāsaka-vinaya, 207
Maitreya, 51, 69, 182, 202, 249
maṇi jewel (wishing jewel), 66, 227
Mañjusrī, 43, 49, 72, 74, 152–153, 175,
    186, 210, 219, 243, 285

Mañjusrī Dharmakāya Rites, 239
mano-vijñāna (perception by the thought-organ), 169
mantras (incantations), 51, 83, 125, 161, 192, 205, 231, 260
Māra, 44, 50, 55, 63, 171, 174, 177, 189, 210, 221
Maudgalyāyana, 58, 62, 200, 207, 219
māyā (sleight-of-hand/illusion) 44, 47, 48, 49, 54, 55, 56, 66, 68, 162, 178, 184, 191, 200, 201, 204, 205, 216, 229, 269
Mayu, 22, 32, 66, 85, 262
Mazu Daoyi, 120, 226
meatball mind (*routuan xin*), 17, 32, 145, 146, 286
meatball, red- (*chi routuan*), 6, 16, 32, 145, 286
medicine, 46, 58, 163, 181, 209, 219, 240
meeting and killing Buddha/patriarch/ arhat/father and mother/relatives, 59, 73, 176, 210–211, 241
mental disposition that cuts the stream, 152–153
mental reflection, 144, 170, 174, 230
mental reflection and calculation, 9, 34, 150
mental reflection and conjecture, 9, 41, 150, 168
Miaojie (Mañjuśrī Bodhisattva)/*miaojie* (wonderful understanding of mind), 35, 152–153
Middle Treatise (Nāgārjuna), 241
mind
    buddha mind, 40
    four types of, 145–146, 165
    meatball mind (*routuan xin*), 17, 32, 145, 146, 286
    mind dharma, 40, 165
    mind ground, 45, 61, 174
    mind-ground dharma, 42
    mind-purity, 69
    mind-radiance, 69

no mind, 34, 166
one mind, 40, 45
original, 77, 158, 163, 251
pondering-of-objective-supports mind, 146
seeking mind, 40
stopping the mind that rushes around and around searching from moment to moment, 38, 159
true mind, 40, 45, 146, 165, 173
with-mind, 61
of your usual self, 53
Mind-Ground Contemplation Sutra, 188, 247
Mindfulness Pillars of the True Dharma Sutra, 177
Ming dynasty, 7
Minghua, 98
Miscellany Storehouse Sutra, 167
missanroku (secret-consultation record), 9, 134
mistakes in reading Chan records, 25, 138, 267
Mo Junhe, Defender-in-chief, 102, 286
mokṣa (liberation), 87, 94, 101
Monastery Supervisor (*jiansi*), 257
moon on the sea, 99, 280–281
mortar, 34
mother, 41, 73, 169, 200
mountain monk, 21, 30, 67, 70
moyang (special effects), 41, 56, 58, 63, 170–171
Mt. Huangbo, 94
Mt. Jing, 86–87
Mt. Sanfeng, 96
Mt. Sumeru, 79, 214, 254
Mt. Wutai, 35, 49, 152
Mujaku Dictionaries, 142, 143, 258, 260, 263, 274
Mujaku Dōchū, 11, 12, 25, 27, 136, 138, 140, 142, 143, 258, 260, 263, 274, 280, 286

multiple meanings in a line or word in this translation of LJL, slashes or italics to indicate, 4
Murasaki Shikibu, 200
Muromachi period, 7, 194
music, 26, 96, 139, 142, 179, 226, 276, 281
mustard seed, 53, 79, 254, 287
Muta, old worthy, 80
mute/muteness, 52, 84, 260
myriad things, 72, 176, 239. *See also* vishayas
mysterious principle, 68
mysterious purport, 43, 50, 62

Nāgārjuna, 9, 241
nail it in words (*daode*), 83
Nakamura Bunbō, 273–274
names, 43, 49, 50, 51, 54, 61, 62, 64, 66, 68, 72, 73, 166, 174, 186, 199, 200, 201, 211, 217, 229, 230, 240. *See also* dharmas
Nanhua (Shandong), 101
Nanquan, 81
Nanyuan Huiyong, 90, 268
Nanyue Huairang, 252
napping, 20, 23, 92, 270
nenbutsu, 238
New Tang History (*Xin Tang shu*), 257
nirmāṇakāya buddha (body-of-magical-transformation buddha), 39–40, 51, 69, 161, 166–167, 179, 200, 202, 233
nirmita/prātihārya (magical creation/miracle), 199
nirvana, 5, 6, 41, 43, 45, 46, 50, 54, 58, 67, 100, 133, 161, 175, 178, 182, 187, 188, 223, 236, 245, 252, 276, 277, 284, 285, 287
Nirvāṇa Later Part Sūtra, 222
Nirvāṇa Sūtra, 192, 197, 238–239, 245–246, 266
niyi. *See* dithering
No Anger (Finger Garland), 243–244

no base (not fixed anywhere), 65, 225
no mind, 34, 166
no place, 47, 184
noisy and bustling places, 19–20, 44, 177
non-arising, 44, 47, 54, 61, 72, 75, 141, 207, 216, 237, 243, 246
non-dependent Way-person (*wuyi daoren*), 18, 47, 56, 60, 65, 69, 174, 182–184, 188, 212, 226, 233
non-discriminative level of understanding, 89
non-discriminative light, 39
non-distinction-making light, 39, 128, 161
non-duality costume, Puhua's, 87, 265, 277, 282
non-extinguishing, 44, 75, 246
not a single thing, 18, 53, 79, 160, 255
not a single thing to do, 50, 190
not a thing to do, 55, 61
not *in that way*, 34, 150
Notes of the Hermitage of the Old Scholar Full of Learning, 212
Notes on Images and Implements of the Zen Forest (*Zenrin shōki sen*) (Mujaku Dōchū), 136, 258, 263, 274
Notes on Kudzu Words (*Kattōgo sen*) (Mujaku Dōchū), 136, 142, 143, 260
Notes on Linji (*Rinzai shō*) (Anonymous), 10
Notes on the Record of Linji (Rinzairoku shō) (Bannan Eishu), 10
Notes on the Yoga Treatise, 261
nothing-to-do (*wushi*), 18, 37, 39, 41, 43, 45, 52, 57, 60, 67, 68, 70, 71, 73, 75, 81, 98, 127, 155, 160, 170–174, 256, 280
nun, 86, 263

Ogihara Unrai, 155
Old Commentary of [National Teacher] Daitō on the Record of Linji (Rinzairoku *Daitō koshō*) (Shūhō Myōchō), 8

old dead geezer (*silao Han*), 68, 231

old farmers singing in the fields, 37

old woman, 98, 280

on the road, 35, 53, 98, 99, 151, 279

one mind, 17, 39, 40, 45, 50, 54, 56, 160, 161, 162, 163, 165, 166, 190, 191, 198, 199, 203, 204, 205, 234, 235

one-off medicine, 46, 58, 74, 178, 181

one-off pictures drawn in the sky, 74

one-off *upāya*, 181, 243

one road (Linji's lineage), 66, 226

one spirit-brightness (*yi jingming*; *Śūraṃgama Sūtra* teaching in LJL), 27, 40, 123, 163, 165

Onishi Shirō, 120

Ono Gemmyō, 119

oral traditions on the *Linjilu*, Chinese, 7

original mind (*benxin; Śūraṃgama Sūtra* teaching in LJL), 18, 27, 30, 31, 32, 69, 72, 77, 144, 158, 163, 233, 239, 251

original nature, 40, 163

original portion (*benfen/honbun*), 9, 18, 33–35, 37, 42, 43, 62, 65, 70, 84, 86, 93, 94, 97, 99, 148, 149, 150, 151, 153, 156, 174, 175, 176, 217, 223, 224, 229, 231, 234, 248, 251, 260, 263, 271, 278, 282

original substance, 79, 200, 205, 255, 287

outflows (*āsrava*), 52, 56, 193–194, 199, 201, 213, 277

Outline of the Linked Lamps (Liandeng huiyao), 132, 170, 217, 234

Panshan Baoji, 120

paramārtha-satya (highest-meaning truth), 174

pāramitās (perfections)
  six, 52, 71, 238–239, 243
  ten, 72, 239, 249

Pared-Down Notes on the Awakening of Faith, 213

pariṇāma (transformation without implication of magical creation), 199–200

Pearl Grove of the Dharma Garden, 202, 215

Penglai, Mt., 97, 278

perfect and all-at-once teaching, 76–77, 249–250

Perfect-and-Sudden Bodhisattva, 45, 180

Perfect Awakening Sutra, 11, 12, 169, 183, 214, 215, 241, 245, 251

perplexity, 15, 49, 50, 64, 150, 157, 189, 204, 222

person (ren), italicized to indicate parallel meaning of true *person (zhenren)*, 17

personal-realization-of-the-meaning-beyond-words (*zong*), 9, 11, 26, 30, 31, 46, 62, 63, 74, 77, 90, 121, 124, 139, 141, 143, 156, 221, 224, 242, 250, 276

phoenix-egg, 96, 276–277

pine trees, 90

Ping, Preceptor, 96, 276, 277

pint-sized monks, 53, 197

piss (*sui/songsui*), 43, 89, 147, 225

place he is coming from, 149

place you stand, 176

placing a head on top of your head, like Yajñadatta, 60

Plucking Leaves from the Sayings Record of Linji (Rinzai goroku tekiyō) (Kōunshi), 12

poet, 99

point blank (*wu duozi; baihua* word), Huangbo's buddhadharma was, 89, 214, 236, 249, 267

poison(s)/poisonous, 33, 50, 148, 190, 205, 214, 217, 258, 266

pondering-of-objective-supports mind (*yuanlü xin*), 146, 165, 177

posts to which you hitch a donkey, 6, 41, 133, 167, 168, 287

Praises of the Mahāyāna (Dasheng zan)
   (Baozhi), 57
prajñā (insight), 164, 198
prajñāpāramitā (perfection of insight),
   165, 191, 202, 210, 266, 272
Prajñāpāramitā Sūtra, 183, 185, 191, 193,
   202, 210, 232, 272
prapañca (joke discourse/silly talk), 10,
   159, 187
pratītya-samutpāda (origination by
   dependence), 176, 180, 183, 189,
   196, 197
pratyakṣa (direct perception), 190
pratyeka-buddhas (independent buddhas),
   45, 46, 71, 182, 195, 196, 237, 272
precepts, 53, 71, 101, 133, 148, 198, 250, 284
pretas. See hungry ghosts
Profound Talks on the Huayan Sutra,
   (Chengguan), 164, 232
Prose Poem of the Swallow (Dunhuang
   transformation text), 282
publishing industry in Muromachi and
   Edo Japan, 7, 133–134
Puhua, 5, 79–80, 87, 94, 101, 119, 120,
   255–256, 265, 272, 285, 287, 288
   Zutangji entry, 124–125
Puji, 194
pupils of the student's eyes, 65, 225
puppets, 36
pure land(s), 45, 174, 180, 182, 225,
   238
*Pure Regulations of the Chan Garden
   (Chanyuan qinggui)*, 258
Pūrṇa, 169
putting in special work, buddhadharma
   not a matter of, 43, 174

Qiu Hu Makes Fun of His Wife (Shi
   Junbao), 262
quanti zuoyong. See unreserved
   functioning
Qujiang Pond (Shi Junbao), 213

ranking students according to sense
   faculties, 15, 65
ranked, true man/*person* who can't be
   (*wu wei zhenren*), 10, 14, 16, 32, 121,
   128, 145, 146, 154, 229
Ratnakūṭa Sūtra, 243
rattle of Puhua's staff, 80, 87, 124, 256
re-training the light of the true mind,
   41, 169
real teaching, no such thing as a, 46
rebirth paths/realms, 10, 32, 39, 42, 43,
   45, 46, 56, 57, 60, 61, 66, 76, 145,
   151, 157, 159, 173, 182, 183, 204, 205,
   210, 215, 216, 238
Record of a Journey to the West, 254
*Record of Expositions of the Record of
   Linji (Rinzairoku teishō ki)* (Lanxi
   Daolong/Rankei Dōryū), 8
Record of Linji, The (Kirchner), 129–130,
   138
*Record of the Transmission of the Lamp
   of the Jingde Era (Jingde chuandeng
   lu)*, 131, 149, 206, 208, 234, 264,
   268, 271, 273
Records of the Historian, 265, 279
red-meatball (*chi routuan*), 16, 32, 145
reflected images, unreal, 39, 128, 162,
   163, 192, 261
*Regulations of Purity of Baizhang
   (Baizhang qinggui)*, 265, 269, 271
*Regulations of Purity of Illusion-Abiding
   [Hermitage] (Huanzhu [an]
   qinggui)*, 253
repaying kindness, 95, 122, 254, 274, 275
rice, bowls of, 78, 253
Rinzairoku (Iriya), 26, 129, 131, 138, 140
Rinzairoku, *Butten kōza* 30 (Yanagida),
   103, 120, 127, 129, 130
Romance of the Three Kingdoms, 143
*Root Verses on the Middle Way
   (Mūlamadhyamakakārikā)*
   (Nāgārjuna), 9

rope chairs, 262, 263, 273, 274

rufa (in accord with dharma), 188

rufa jianjie (beholding in accordance with
dharma), 59, 77, 89, 155, 210, 251, 266

rush about seeking (*chiqiu*), 18, 45, 166, 189

rushi jiande (see *in that way*), 39, 40, 46,
48, 54, 62, 127, 155

rushi jiede (understand *in that way*), 49, 155

sack of shit (*shi danzi*; physical body),
65, 184, 225

saddharma vision (*zhengfa yanzang*), 20,
21, 100, 102, 236, 284, 286

Saddharma Vision (Dahui), 132

Śākyamuni, 17, 31, 39, 55, 74, 187, 252

śāla trees, two, 55

samādhi (concentration), 10, 49, 52, 61, 99,
151, 166, 167, 188, 193, 194, 203, 216,
226, 227, 238, 244, 264, 269, 281

Samantabhadra, 43, 49, 62, 175, 186, 219

saṃbhogakāya buddha (reward-body
buddha), 39–40, 51, 161, 166–167

sameness and difference, 82, 99, 281, 282

sameness wisdom (*samatā-jñāna*), 161

Saṃghāṭa Sūtra, 179

samsara, 38, 41, 47, 50, 57, 66, 68, 156,
157, 169, 189, 205, 226, 236, 285

samsaric characteristics, 66

samsaric karman, 193

samsaric sea, 44, 57

samsaric wheel, 38, 40, 47, 51, 123,
159, 164, 169, 183, 193, 203, 223, 235

samsaric world of defiled "red dust,"
30, 142

saṃvṛti-satya (conventional truth), 174

san zhong yi (three types of dependence), 161, 192

sangha, number of monks in
Huangbo's, 93

Sangha Hall, 19, 23, 57, 80, 83, 84, 90,
91, 92, 100, 125, 129, 177, 206, 208,
255, 263, 267, 270, 283

Sansheng (Huiran; heir of Linji, credited
with compilation of the *Linjilu*), 20,
21, 29, 100, 102, 139, 156, 284

Śāriputra, 167, 173, 196, 259

*Sayings Record of Chan Master Dahui
Pujue (Dahui Pujue chanshi yulu)*,
143, 166, 189, 232, 245, 275

sea
of breath, 68
great, 77, 79, 202, 203, 250–251, 255,
287
of liberation, 44
moon on the, 99, 280–281
of samsara, 44, 57
wisdom, 164

seal, tattooed onto student's face by bad
teacher, 46, 181

seal of the three essentials, 35, 152

seal(ing) (a master's certifying of a
student), 100, 135, 141, 273, 274,
284, 288

second patriarch, 70

seeking, 18, 19, 38, 39, 40, 41, 42, 45, 46,
47, 48, 50, 51, 52, 54, 55, 60, 61, 65,
66, 67, 69, 70, 71, 73, 74, 75, 76,
77, 101, 128, 135, 147, 154, 166, 169,
170, 173, 180, 186, 189, 193, 196, 213,
226, 231, 233, 246, 247, 249, 250

Sekino Tadashi, 119

"Sending Off Someone on a Mission to
Anxi" (Wang Wei), 273

Sengzhao, 240, 248
Commentary on the Vimalakīrti Sūtra,
213, 215, 236, 240, 247
Things Do Not Change, 204

sense faculties (of students),
configuration of, 65

Separate Record (bielu), 5

separate transmission outside the
teachings (*jiaowai biechuan*), 5, 11,
27, 77, 101, 242, 249, 284

Shandao, 238

shangtang (Dharma Hall Convocation), 140–141, 144

Shi Junbao, 213, 262

Shigong, 66

Shinsan zenseki mokuroku (Newly Edited Catalogue of Zen Books) (Komazawa), 7, 8, 130, 133, 134

Shishi, 34, 149

shit (*shi/eshi*), 43, 65, 68, 133, 147, 225, 232

shit, piece of dried (*ganshijue*), 6, 14, 32, 147, 154, 286

shōgun Linji, 24, 142

Shoroku zokugokai (Explanations of Colloquial Expressions in Zen Records) (Yoshizawa), 181, 232

shoulder pole, 69, 232

Shoushan Shengnian, 132, 268

shout (*he*), 13, 20, 21, 30, 31, 33, 36, 57, 58, 62, 63, 78, 79, 80, 81, 82, 84, 85, 86, 87, 90, 97, 98, 100, 121, 123, 125, 142, 143, 153, 154, 176, 207, 218, 260, 263, 265, 288

Shūhō Myōchō, 8

silence, 15, 35, 99, 151, 224, 247, 282

silence-and-illumination Chan, 20, 177, 195, 222

single seamless place, 69

sitting. *See* cross-legged sitting; smooth-and-steady sitting; *zazen*

six causal combinations, 40, 123, 128, 165, 166

six dusts (six vishayas), 51, 74, 190

six (or five) rebirth paths, 32, 39, 42, 56, 57, 61, 66, 127, 145, 151, 160, 165, 173, 183, 204, 205, 210, 240

six shakings, 48, 185, 207

slap (*zhang*), 85, 90, 93, 94, 218, 272, 273

slave and master, distinguishing between, 44

smooth-and-steady cross-legged sitting (*onza*), 9, 40, 43, 163, 174, 273

Sodōshū (Yoshizawa and Onishi), 120

solitary brightness (*guming; Śūraṃgama Sūtra* teaching in LJL), 27, 39, 40, 45, 50, 51, 64, 77, 128, 161, 162, 163, 179, 180, 221, 251, 252

Song of Lanzan (Lanzan ge), 174

Songs of the Twelve Hours of Baozhi (Baozhi shi'er shi ge), 225

son of a bitch (*zei*), 80, 256, 263

sorghum, 82, 257

Sōtō Zen, 11, 135, 264

Southern Tang kingdom, 4, 119

spark from a stone, student's dynamism as, 65, 99, 225, 282

speaking Chan (*setsuzen*), 11

special effects. *See moyang*

spikes of the puncture-vine/water chestnut, 51, 193

spilling the blood of a buddha's body, 73

spontaneous reaction, ideal of in LJL, 14

spun around by things/vishayas (*wei wu suozhan; Śūraṃgama Sūtra* teaching in LJL), 16, 21, 26, 27, 38, 43, 45, 48, 50, 62, 67, 72, 158, 168, 176, 188, 190, 239

śramaṇa (monk), 163

śrāvakas (hearers), 272

srotāpanna (stream-enterers), 157

staff (*zhang/zhuzhang*), 19, 23, 31, 34, 80, 82, 85, 87, 92, 97, 100, 121, 122, 124, 125, 148, 177, 189, 211, 256, 270, 278, 282

stick (*bang*), 34, 36, 58, 59, 78, 83, 84, 86, 90, 91, 121, 122, 123, 124, 142, 148, 153, 211, 218, 253, 256, 260, 269, 271

stopping (mind) is *bodhi* (*xie ji puti; Śūraṃgama Sūtra* teaching in LJL), 19, 27, 61, 159, 169–170, 215

Story of Yuan Gong of Mt. Lu (Dunhuang transformation text), 144, 145

strangeness, adoring (*nieguai*), 42, 74, 172, 241–242

straw-sandal money (*caoxie qian*), 64, 222

straw sandals, scheme for wearing out, 98

stream-enterer

who beholds reality as it truly is, 58, 124

(who is in the midst of *nothing-to-do*), 71

with a clear eye, 44

students

adoring/bound by heterodox masters, 53, 55, 58, 58, 176, 209

constructing an understanding on the inside, 64, 213

dependent upon teachings, 60, 212

don't have (enough) confidence, 38, 49, 64,

grasping terms and phrases, 47, 68, 166, 167, 186, 212

helplessness of, 76, 221

looking for Mañjuśrī on Mt. Wutai, 49, 186

losing own father and mother, 169

of small karmic roots, 52, 195

sorting of, 57, 62–63, 65, 153, 220–221, 252

Studies in the Language of Zu-tang ji (Anderl), 130, 157

Stupa Record of Chan Master Linji Huizhao (Linji Huizhao chanshi taji), 101–102

Stupa Steward (at Bodhidharma's stupa), 95

Subduing Māra Transformation Text (Dunhuang transformation text), 221

Subhūti, 173, 191

Sudarśana, 51, 190, 191, 202

Sudhana (youth in *Huayan Sutra* who visits fifty-three teachers), 45, 46, 53, 66, 77, 180, 182, 196, 226, 249–250

suffering(s), 40, 55, 69, 71, 123, 160, 164, 188, 238,

Sukhāvatī, 216

summer retreat at Mt. Huangbo, 94, 273

sumō, 16, 124

Sunakṣātra Bhikṣu, 75, 245

śūnyatā (emptiness), 87, 156, 178, 222, 241, 277

Superman (*da zhangfu*), 18, 45, 49, 50, 62, 70, 74, 156, 180

supernormal powers, 47, 51, 55, 56, 61, 62, 66, 67, 68, 79, 156, 160, 161, 192, 201, 202, 203, 216, 219, 227, 228, 230, 231, 269, 272, 285, 287

Śūraṃgama assembly, 95

Śūraṃgama Sūtra, 11, 12, 19, 27, 38, 45, 60, 146, 158–159, 161, 165–166, 169, 171, 172, 179, 180, 189, 202–203, 205, 213, 215, 235, 239, 243, 246, 274, 282

sutras in LJL, 5, 10, 11, 12, 13, 18, 19, 27, 38, 45, 46, 51, 53, 60, 76, 77, 83, 141, 142, 144, 146, 156, 158, 159, 160, 161, 164, 165, 166, 167, 169, 171, 172, 177, 179, 180, 182, 183, 185, 187, 188, 189, 190, 191, 192, 193, 194, 195, 196, 197, 198, 200, 201, 202, 203, 204, 205, 206, 207, 209, 210, 211, 212, 213, 214, 215, 216, 217, 218, 222, 226, 227, 230, 232, 235, 236, 238, 239, 240, 241, 242, 243, 245, 246, 247, 248, 249, 250, 251, 254, 259, 260, 266, 272, 274, 282

sutras/study of sutras, maligned in LJL, 5, 23, 27, 39, 40, 49, 51, 52, 58, 68, 73, 75, 82, 83, 94, 101, 166, 187, 189, 192, 208, 209, 231, 244, 245, 246, 273, 285

sutras/teachings, study of, permitted in LJL, 49, 94, 187, 273

Suvarṇaprabhāsa Sūtra, 158

svabhāva (own-being), 54, 64, 72, 132, 161, 165, 183, 199

sword blade that cuts off knowing and understanding, 34, 96, 148

sword of *prajñā* (insight), 53, 198

swordsman, 99

Takudō Shukitsu, 11

Takudō's Comments on Old Cases of the Record of Linji (Rinzairoku Takudō nenko) (Takudō Shukitsu), 11

Talk of Huayan Mysteries (Fazang), 216

Tang Wudai yuyan cidian (*Word Dictionary of Tang and Five Dynasties Language*) (Jiang and Cao), 139, 173, 200, 221, 283

tathāgata (thus-come-one), 38, 40, 55, 59, 133, 149, 151, 152, 158, 169, 178, 180, 182, 195, 200–201, 214, 235, 237, 239, 240, 244, 249, 287

tathāgatagarbha (buddha-in-embryo), 17, 137, 156, 165

Tathāgatagarbha Qualities Sutra, 156

tathatā (thusness/reality), 9, 45, 54, 137, 149, 150, 159, 163, 170, 180, 185, 188, 193, 198–199, 203, 204, 269, 281

tattva (reality), 156, 176, 234, 269

teachers
  bad, 41–42, 46, 52, 53, 58, 170–172, 181, 197, 198, 208, 231
  disparagment of, 52
  face-off with, 57
  good, 76
  styles of, 66

Teihon Rinzai zenji goroku (Mujaku Dōchū's edition of the LJL), 286

ten stages of bodhisattva practice, 40, 71, 123, 133, 167, 287

terms and phrases, 15, 42, 47, 64, 72, 74, 161, 173, 183, 222, 232

terrace of enlightenment, 72

Tetsugai Dōkū, 11

that one person (*na yi ren*), 9, 17, 18, 39, 43, 46, 48, 50, 52, 61, 64, 65, 66, 67, 69, 73, 93, 143, 146, 161, 174, 179, 182, 183, 186, 188, 190, 194, 223, 225, 226, 227, 229, 231, 233, 240, 271

that one tune (*na yi qu*), 26, 31, 139, 143, 276

thief (*zei*), 79, 91, 93, 254, 262, 269, 271

thirty-two major characteristics/marks of a buddha, 18, 52, 55, 69, 156, 194, 201, 233

this matter (*ge shi/ci shi*), 18, 34, 59, 92, 93, 94, 149, 158, 193, 209, 267, 270, 271

three karmans (body, speech, and mind actions), 22, 32, 53, 145, 198

three no-natures, 199

three realms (of desire, forms, and formlessness), 38, 39, 40, 45, 47, 50, 56, 61, 68, 123, 157, 160, 164, 183, 190, 205, 210, 214, 216, 217

three vehicles of teachings, 27, 31, 54, 74, 75, 76, 77, 82, 183, 243, 246, 249

throw it down a hole, 57, 63

Tiansheng *Linjilu*, 131, 132, 140, 241, 268

Tiantai Four-Teachings Model (Goryeo monk Jegwan), 237

tiger, 78, 90, 254, 258, 259, 267, 268, 269

time off, Linji's request for, 89, 266

toilet excrement, 6, 41, 168, 200, 287

"toilet-paper" sutras, 27, 54

Tokugawa peace, 7

tower of Maitreya (*Huayan Sutra*), 46, 51, 182, 249

traitor(s) (*zei*), 33, 81, 148, 257

transformation texts (Dunhuang *bianwen*), 139, 144, 145, 200, 221, 277, 280, 282

Transmission of the Lamp. See *Record of the Transmission of the Lamp of the Jingde Era*

trash and crap (*bu caijing*; kudzu words), 70, 235–236

Treasure-Heap Sutra, 210

Treasure Storehouse Treatise, 203

Treatise of the Bright Gate of the Hundred Dharmas of the Mahāyāna (Vasubandhu), 258

Treatise on Eradicating Characteristics, 194

Treatise on the Establishment of Karman in the Mahāyāna (Vasubandhu), 229

Treatise on the New Huayan Sutra (Li
Tongxuan), 180, 200, 246, 260
Treatise on the Origin of Humanity
(Zongmi), 182
treatises (*śāstras*), 5 , 10, 11, 12, 23, 27, 39,
40, 49, 51, 58, 68, 75, 82, 101, 122,
127, 135, 157, 160, 162, 164, 166, 173,
180, 182, 192, 194, 199, 200, 203,
208, 209, 219, 223, 229, 230, 231,
236, 237, 241, 244, 245, 246, 258,
260, 261, 277, 284, 285
tree mushroom (fungus), 71, 237
Tripiṭaka Koreana (Goryeo
Daejanggyeong), 119–120
true mind (*zhenxin*), 17, 32, 37, 40, 41,
42, 45, 50, 70, 146, 163, 165, 173, 190
true *person* (*zhenren*), 9, 14, 16, 17, 26, 32,
37, 39, 43, 45, 46, 47, 49, 50, 52, 53,
54, 56, 57, 60, 61, 62, 64, 65, 66,
67, 69, 70, 72, 73, 74, 77, 90, 93,
94, 121, 125, 128, 145, 146, 154, 157, 173,
190, 196, 227, 229, 233, 267, 284
tune, 26, 31, 96, 139, 143, 154, 276
twelve divisions of teachings, 27, 31, 47,
54, 75, 82, 133
twelve years of Linji's looking for a
karman, 53, 196–197
two-in-one monk's costume, Puhua's,
87, 288
twofold take-in (*shuangshou*), 277

udāna (utterance), 229
udumbara tree, 76
ukemi ni naru (end up on the defensive/
lose the initiative; *sumō* term), 16
uncertainty, 34, 56, 72, 77, 251
understanding
on the inside (inside mind), 64
level of, 31, 33, 34, 58, 59, 63, 80, 87,
89, 97, 144, 147, 149, 150, 208, 210,
220, 252–253, 255, 256, 258, 267,
269, 279

unreserved functioning (*quanti*
zuoyong) of the buddha nature,
15, 26, 62, 65, 76, 83–85, 147, 173,
224–225, 259, 261–262, 281
upāyas (expedients/teaching devices), 35,
36, 38, 40, 46, 47, 49, 55, 57, 60, 62,
63, 72, 74, 75, 84, 85, 87, 89, 96, 101,
150, 152, 153, 156, 157, 181, 182, 188,
196, 201, 207, 218, 219, 239, 240,
246, 259, 260, 263, 264, 282, 285
usual self, be(ing) (*pingchang*), 41, 42,
44, 53, 61, 170, 173, 174

Vairocana, 46, 66, 182, 260, 275
vajra cage (diamond cage), 82, 258
Vajra Summit Sūtra Vairocana
One-Hundred Eight Honored
[Merits] Dharmakāya Mudrā, 260
Vajracchedikā Sūtra, 166, 195, 201, 217, 235
Vajrapāni (ferocious dharma-guardian),
85, 262
Vanavāsin (country of the teacher
Vimuktika in the *Huayan Sutra*), 53
vāsanā (habit energy from past births),
10, 38, 43, 132, 156, 176, 246, 266
Venerable Manorhita, 217
venue of activities (*yongchu*), 26, 39, 47,
49, 50, 51, 53, 60, 62, 66, 67, 72,
139, 150, 160, 161, 190, 197, 217, 226
267, 275, 276
Verses of the Patriarchal Masters of the Chan
Gate (Chanmen zhu zushi jisong), 225
Verses of Praise on Rebirth [in Amitābha's
Pure Land] (Shandao), 238
vikalpa (false discrimination), 164, 206,
213, 217, 270
Vimalakīrti, 15, 35, 147, 151, 196, 215, 224
Vimalakīrti Sūtra, 12, 19, 144, 196, 197,
198, 205, 206–207, 211, 212, 213,
215, 217, 236, 240, 247, 254, 266
Vimuktika (teacher in the *Huayan*
Sutra), 53, 196

vinaya (rules of discipline), 5, 58, 101, 160, 166, 207, 209, 237, 285

vishayas (*jing*; sense objects/fields), 21, 53, 59, 66, 74, 137, 154, 155, 176, 190, 196, 201, 219, 226, 227, 228, 235, 241, 242

actively ride, 26, 50, 188

not being discombobulated by, 58, 190

not bewitched by, 158

of compassion, 188

as costumes, 228, 229

dependent (illusory magical) transformations, 54, 200

dependently originated, 189, 190

definition of, 16, 153, 154, 166, 207, 219, 224, 239

as (red) dusts, 74, 142, 225

entering each and every, 67

external, 64, 160, 210, 250

four types of, 48

good-for-nothing gimmick, 40, 49, 59, 60, 166, 167, 187, 207, 211, 220

grabbing onto/seizing, 75, 158, 222

hanging onto, 63

insight to discern, 63

manifesting, Linji's tactic of, 50, 51

as shrieking monkeys, 176

of movement and stillness, 64–65, 223

myriad types, 17, 50, 53, 163, 189, 190, 239

not a single, 44, 204, 220,

purity, 63, 64, 67, 188, 220, 222, 228

not recognizing, 62, 63

ripping away, 37, 65, 153, 154, 155, 160, 224

set up not (even) a single, 153, 224, 228, 275

six, 56, 137, 149, 159, 160, 190, 216, 242

spun around/rotated/turned by, 16, 21, 26, 38, 43, 45, 48, 62, 67, 158, 168, 188, 190, 239

stillness and purity, 64

submitting to, 38

unreal, 48, 49, 57, 62, 200, 207

as unreal terms, 26, 44, 50, 174, 207

using, 48, 188

wad of, 57, 207

wacko (*fengdian*), 78, 90, 91

Wan'an Daoyan/Donglin Daoyan, 140

Wang Wei, 273, 277

Wang Xuance, 147

washing feet, 85, 261

Washing the Mind in the Sayings Record of Chan Master Linji Huizhao (Rinzai Eshō zenji goroku *soyaku*) (Mujaku Dōchū), 12

Water Margin, 181

Watson, Burton, 25

wei wu suozhuan, (spun around by things/vishayas; Śuraṃgama Sūtra teaching in LJL), 27. See spun around by things/vishayas

weishi (consciousness-only), 5, 162, 199

Welter, Albert, 130

Wenxi, Chan Master, 153

wenyan (literary Chinese), 25, 27

whack (*da*), 3, 13, 23, 31, 33, 34, 58, 59, 78, 79, 80, 81, 82, 83, 84, 85, 86, 88, 89, 91, 92, 94, 98, 100, 121, 123, 124, 125, 184, 211, 218, 257, 258

wheel-turning noble king, 55

white-ox cart (*Lotus Sutra*), 83, 259–260

wife, new, 53, 80, 197

wild-fox demons (bad/heterodox teachers), 42, 53, 56, 58, 60, 171, 197, 221

winners, 100, 283

wishy-washy weakling, 50

with-mind (*youxin*), 61

Words of Understanding that Warn the World, 282

worldling (*fan[fu]*), 20, 42, 43, 44, 45, 46, 47, 52, 57, 66, 74, 80, 81, 98, 101, 125, 146, 154, 174, 175, 180, 186, 193, 224, 241, 242, 255, 279

Worthies and Fools Sutra, 243

written word, 15, 18, 31, 38, 42, 64, 67, 68, 75, 94, 141, 159, 183, 187, 188, 189, 194, 222, 245, 246, 250, 273, 284

Wu-Yue, 90, 127, 268

Wuzhuo (Chan monk)/*wuzhuo* (non-attachment), 35, 152–153

Xiangmo Zang, 194

Xiangtian, 98, 279

Xiangzhou, 97

xie ji puti (stopping [mind] is *bodhi*; *Śūraṃgama Sūtra* teaching in LJL), 27. *See* stopping (mind) is *bodhi*

Xing (Linji's family name), 101, 120

Xinghua Cunjiang (successor to Linji who collated LJL), 102, 268, 286

Xinghua Monastery, 102

Xingshan, 83–84, 288

Xu Huaizhong, 231

Xu Shaofeng, 212, 254, 259

Xuefeng Yicun, 119, 121, 286, 287

yadda, yadda, yadda there's no (*wu ru xuduo ban*; *baihua* phrase), 61, 214

Yajñadatta (in the *Śūraṃgama Sūtra*), 19, 38, 41, 45, 60, 67, 70, 159, 161, 166, 169, 180, 213, 215, 228, 235

Yama (Judge of the Hells), 42, 64, 71, 76, 222, 248

Yampolsky, Philip B., 25, 138

Yanagida Seizan, 8, 12, 25, 26, 103, 120, 127, 129, 130, 132, 137, 138, 139, 155, 158, 162, 164, 167, 178, 183, 192, 209, 214, 227, 231, 234, 241, 256, 263, 270, 274, 277, 286

Yang Pass, 273

Yang Yi, 268

Yangshan, 79, 90, 91, 92, 93, 94, 95, 99, 100, 101, 265, 271, 272, 273, 285, 286

yellow leaves, 51, 192, 240, 241

yi jingming (one spirit-brightness; *Śūraṃgama Sūtra* teaching in LJL), 27. *See* one spirit-brightness

yin-yang divination, 74, 242

yin-yin (onomatopoeic for sound of Puhua's rattle), 87, 265

Yingzhou, 97, 278

Yinyuan Longqi/Ingen Ryūki, 7, 134, 135

Yishan Yining/Issan Ichinei, 7, 134, 232

Yoga Treatise (Yogacārabhūmi-śāstra), 5, 209

Yogācāra, 5, 11, 162

Yongming Yanshou, 10, 127, 128, 130, 131, 135, 141, 142, 145, 203, 269

Yongming Yanshou's Conception of Chan in the Zongjing lu: *A Special Transmission Within the Scriptures* (Welter), 130

Yoshizawa Masahiro, 120, 181, 232

Yuan Gong, 145

Yuanjue Zongyan (editor of LJL), 5, 102, 103, 120, 131, 140, 241, 286, 287

Yue Bochuan, 222

yumo (in that way; *baihua* term), 149, 150, 155, 279

Yunmen of Shaoyang, 147

zao/kamado (stove), 68, 232

zazen, 9, 213, 222, 238, 270, 273, 274. *See also* cross-legged sitting; smooth-and-steady sitting

Zen themes embodied in LJL, 9

Zhanran, 227

Zhaoqing, Preceptor, 123, 286, 287

Zhaoqing Temple, 119

Zhaozhou, 85, 270

Zhaozhou Sayings Record (Zhaozhou yulu), 270

Zhenzhou, 29, 94, 101, 102, 120, 124, 140, 286

Zhigong, 225

Zhiyi, 209

Zhongfeng Mingben, 134, 253

Zhuangzi, 146, 266

Zilu, 142

Zongjinglu/Xingjinglu (Mind-Mirror Record) (Yanshou), 10, 124–125, 127, 130, 135, 141, 142, 145, 160, 203, 269

Zongmi, 10, 15, 17, 137, 145, 178, 194, 230

    Abbreviated Commentary on the Perfect Awakening Sutra, 169

    Chan Letter, 218

    Chan Notes, 218

    Chan Prolegomenon, 10, 11, 16, 127, 137, 141, 142, 145, 146, 165, 176, 178, 187, 194, 198, 230

    Commentary on the Ullambana Sūtra, 201

    Huayan Dharmadhātu Discernment, 225

Zongmi on Chan (Broughton), 137, 230

Zuigan Monastery, 11

Zuigan's Notes on the Record of Linji (Rinzairoku Zuigan shō) (Kensō Chitetsu), 11

Zutangji (Collection of the Patriarchal Hall) (compiled by Jing and Jun), 4, 5, 6, 119, 120, 127, 130, 145, 255, 286, 287